TRIQUETRA

THE UNOFFICIAL AND UNAUTHORISED GUIDE TO *CHARMED*

TRIQUETRA

THE UNOFFICIAL AND UNAUTHORISED GUIDE TO *CHARMED*

KEITH TOPPING

First published in the UK in 2005 by
Telos Publishing Ltd
17 Pendre Avenue, Prestatyn, LL19 9SH
www.telos.co.uk

Telos Publishing Ltd values feedback. Please e-mail us with any comments you may have about this book to: feedback@telos.co.uk

This Edition: 2013

Triquetra © 2005, 2013 Keith Topping

ISBN 978-1-84583-872-0

The moral right of the author has been asserted.

British Library Cataloguing in Publication Data.
A catalogue record for this book is available from the British Library.

This book is sold subject to the condition that it shall not by way of trade or otherwise, be lent, resold, hired out or otherwise circulated without the publisher's prior written consent in any form of binding or cover other than that in which it is published and without a similar condition including this condition being imposed on the subsequent purchaser.

CONTENTS

Acknowledgements	13
Introduction	15
Sisters of the 'Craft	19
Which Witch is Which	22
Three, That's the Magic Number	27
The Power Behind the Power of Three	30
A Book of Shadows (The Untransmitted Plot)	31

Charmed Season 1 (1998-99) — 33
1. Something Wicca This Way Comes — 35
2. I've got You Under My Skin — 40
3. Thank You For Not Morphing — 45
4. Dead Man Dating — 48
5. Dream Sorcerer — 51
6. The Wedding From Hell — 54
7. The Fourth Sister — 57
8. The Truth is Out There … and it Hurts — 60
9. The Witch is Back — 63
10. Wicca Envy — 66
11. Feats of Clay — 69
12. The Wendigo — 72
13. From Fear To Eternity — 75
14. Secrets & Guys — 78
15. Is There a Woogy in the House? — 81
16. Which Prue is it, Anyway? — 84
17. That 70's Episode — 87
18. When Bad Warlocks Turn Good — 91
19. Blind Sided — 93
20. The Power of Two — 96
21. Love Hurts — 100
22. Déjà vu All Over Again — 103

Charmed Season 2 (1999-2000) — 107
23. Witch Trial — 109
24. Morality Bites — 113
25. The Painted World — 117
26. The Devil's Music — 120
27. She's a Man, Baby, a Man! — 123
28. That Old Black Magic — 126

29. They're Everywhere	129
30. P³ H²O	132
31. Ms Hellfire	134
32. Heartbreak City	137
33. Reckless Abandon	140
34. Awakened	143
35. Animal Pragmatism	146
36. Pardon My Past	149
37. Give Me a Sign	152
38. Murphy's Luck	155
39. How to Make a Quilt out of Americans	158
40. Chick Flick	161
41. Ex Libris	164
42. Astral Monkey	167
43. Apocalypse, Not	170
44. Be Careful What You Witch For	173

Charmed Season 3 (2000-2001) — 177

45. The Honeymoon's Over	179
46. Magic Hour	183
47. Once Upon a Time	186
48. All Halliwell's Eve	189
49. Sigh Unseen	193
40. Primrose Empath	196
51. Power Outrage	199
52. Sleuthing With the Enemy	202
53. Coyote Piper	204
54. We All Scream for Ice Cream	207
55. Blinded by the Whitelighter	211
56. Wrestling With Demons	214
57. Bride and Gloom	217
58. The Good, The Bad and The Cursed	220
59. Just Harried	223
60. Death Takes a Halliwell	227
61. Prewitched	230
62. Sin Francisco	233
63. The Demon Who Came in from the Cold	237
64. Exit Strategy	239
65. Look Who's Barking	242
66. All Hell Breaks Loose	245

Charmed Season 4 (2001-2002) — 249

67. Charmed Again Part 1	251

68. Charmed Again Part 2	255
69. Hell Hath No Fury	258
70. Enter the Demon	261
71. Size Matters	264
72. A Knight to Remember	267
73. Brain Drain	270
74. Black as Cole	273
75. Muse to My Ears	275
76. A Paige from the Past	278
77. Trial by Magic	281
78. Lost and Bound	284
79. Charmed and Dangerous	287
80. The Three Faces of Phoebe	290
81. Marry-Go-Round	293
82. The Fifth Halliwell	295
83. Saving Private Leo	298
84. Bite Me	301
85. We're Off to See the Wizard	304
86. Long Live the Queen	307
87. Womb Raider	309
88. Witch Way Now?	312
Charmed Season 5 (2002-2003)	315
89. A Witch's Tail Part 1	317
90. A Witch's Tail Part 2	320
91. Happily Ever After	323
92. Siren Song	326
93. Witches in Tights	329
94. The Eyes Have it	333
95. Sympathy for the Demon	336
96. A Witch in Time	339
97. Sam I Am	342
98. Y Tu Mummy Tambien	345
99. The Importance of Being Phoebe	348
100. Centennial Charmed	351
101. House Call	354
102. Sand Francisco Dreamin'	356
103. The Day the Magic Died	359
104. Baby's First Demon	363
105. Lucky Charmed	366
106. Cat House	369
107. Nymphs Just Wanna Have Fun	372
108. Sense and Sense Ability	375

109. Necromancing the Stone	378
110. Oh My Goddess! Part 1	381
111. Oh My Goddess! Part 2	384

Charmed Season 6 (2003-2004) — 387

112. Valhalley of the Dolls Part 1	389
113. Valhalley of the Dolls Part 2	393
114. Forget Me … Not	396
115. The Power of Three Blondes	399
116. Love's A Witch	402
117. My Three Witches	405
118. Soul Survivor	408
119. Sword of the City	411
120. Little Monsters	414
121. Chris-Crossed	416
122. Witchstock	419
123. Prince Charmed	422
124. Used Karma	426
125. The Legend of Sleepy Halliwell	428
126. I Dream of Phoebe	431
127. The Courtship of Wyatt's Father	434
128. Hyde School Reunion	436
129. Spin City	439
130. Crimes and Witch Demeanours	442
131. A Wrong Day's Journey into Right	445
132. Witch Wars	448
133. It's A Bad Bad Bad Bad World Part 1	451
134. It's A Bad Bad Bad Bad World Part 2	454

Charmed Season 7 (2004-2005) — 457

135. A Call to Arms	459
136. The Bare Witch Project	463
137. Cheaper by the Coven	466
138. Charrrmed!	469
139. Styx Feet Under	473
140. Once Upon a Blue Moon	476
141. Someone to Witch Over Me	479
142. Charmed Noir	482
143. There's Something About Leo	485
144. Witchness Portection	487
145. Ordinary Witches	490
146. Extreme Makeover: World Edition	493
147. Charmegeddon	496

148. Carpe Demon	499
149. Show Ghouls	502
150. The Seven Year Witch	505
151. Scry Hard	508
152. Little Box of Horrors	511
153. Freaky Phoebe	515
154. Imaginary Fiends	519
155. Death Becomes Them	522
156. Something Wicca This Way Goes	526
The Seven Year Witch	529
Selected Bibliography	533
Never Mind The Warlocks	536

DEDICATED TO

David Howe, Stephen James Walker
and Roger Anderson.

Thanks, for *everything*.

ACKNOWLEDGEMENTS

The author wishes to thank the following friends and family for their support: Ian and Janet Abrahams, Holly Aird, Anna Bliss, Arnold Blumberg, Sean Brady, Suze Campagna, Martin Day, Diana Dougherty, Clay Eichelberger, Rob Francis, Robert Franks, Julia Hankin, Jamie Wilkinson, Mike Parr and all at Radio Newcastle, Jeff Hart, Tony and Jane Kenealy, Alistair Langston, Shaun Lyon, David and Lesley McIntee, Ian Mond, Melanie Pratt, Steve Purcell, Jill Sherwin, Mick Snowden, Kathy Sullivan, Jim Swallow and Mandy Mills, Susannah Tiller, Lily Topping, Bill and Jacque Watson, Deborah Williams, Michelle Wolf, Mark Wyman and Brian Young.

Also, my thanks to the contributors to the *Outpost Gallifrey Ask Keith Topping* forum and the *BuffyWatchers* mailing list.

Suggested listening: Boards of Canada, The Chemical Brothers, Anubian Lights, Jeff Buckley, Orbital, *The Wicker Man* and *Yellow Submarine* soundtracks, Be Good Tanyas, Delerium, Beth Orton, NWA, Brian Wilson, The Smiths.

Triquetra was written, on location, in Newcastle upon Tyne, Los Angeles, Madeira and Sorrento.

INTRODUCTION

'The Power of Three will set us free.'
– 'Something Wicca This Way Comes'

Readers of *Triquetra* are probably aware of this fact already but, for the uninitiated, *Charmed* has been one of television's best-kept secrets. In both America and the UK, it has found itself, for one reason or another, hidden away on what can reasonably be described as minority channels. Yet despite this apparent ghettoisation, the series has acquired, steadily over seven years and 150-odd episodes, a dedicated audience. Viewers have become hooked by the show's seductive power, attractive visuals and cunning wit.

Charmed is a drama series[1] concerning four sisters, Prudence (Shannen Doherty), Piper (Holly Marie Combs) and Phoebe (Alyssa Milano), and later Paige (Rose McGowan)[2], who live in a San Francisco home that has belonged to their family for generations. In the first episode, the sisters learn about the Halliwell family's long history of white witchcraft, via an ancient volume, *The Book of Shadows*. They also discover their own latent magical abilities: Prue has the power of telekinesis, Piper can freeze time, and Phoebe can see into the future. Together, they form

---

1 As with contemporary US telefantasy shows like Buffy the Vampire Slayer, The X-Files and Stargate SG-1 the word 'drama' doesn't even begin to describe what Charmed is all about. Although the series covers some very serious themes (quite literal representations of Heaven and Hell, for instance), it does so with a stylish, clever sense of humour. For many viewers, Charmed's charm (s'cuse the pun) lies in its scripts – full of smart-alec dialogue and knowing pop-culture references. (See, for example, the clever wordplay present in the many of Charmed's episode titles.) If, like me, you watch Charmed primarily for these reasons, then I hope you'll have a lot of fun with this book.
2 After Prue's death at the end of *Charmed*'s third season, a fourth half-sister, Paige Matthews, arrived in Piper's and Phoebe's life to restore the triumvirate to its full complement.

INTRODUCTION

the Charmed Ones, and, along with their Whitelighter, Leo,[3] are sworn by various ancient rites to protect innocent mortals from demons, warlocks and other forces of darkness.

Charmed is broadcast by the WB network in the USA. Via series like *Buffy the Vampire Slayer*, *Dawson's Creek* and *Felicity*, the WB had already captured a large proportion of the, much sought-after, teen-female demographic by the time that *Charmed* debuted in the autumn of 1998.[4] For this reason, the series is still seen in some parts of the media as little more than superior eye-candy. Nice to look at but, ultimately, rather hollow and one-dimensional. This is perhaps understandable; with beautiful stars, occasionally fluffy storylines and a lack of much moral ambiguity, *Charmed* is an easy target for ruthless parody.[5] Indeed, this author himself has been guilty of such lazy stereotyping, once cruelly describing the series in *DreamWatch* magazine as '*Buffy*-lite for those who can't afford a real imagination.' This isn't the first time that I've dismissed a series at first glance only to return later as a fan. It *is*, however, the most spectacular misreading of a show's strengths that I've ever made. What can I say? We *all* make mistakes.

The series that *Charmed* most closely resembles, for obvious reasons, is the WB's former jewel in the crown, *Buffy the Vampire Slayer*.[6] Whilst *Charmed* lacks the deadly quick-fire humour of Buffy and her Scooby Gang friends, it *does* possess its own, quietly confident and acid-tongued wit.[7] It's true that *Charmed*'s ambitious attempts to straddle two vastly different genres have led to some gross miscalculations of taste. At its worst, *Charmed is* undeniably cosy and undemanding. However, *Charmed*'s coy

---

[3] Basically, the *Charmed*-universe's version of an *It's a Wonderful Life*-style guardian angel.

[4] This trend has continued with more recent WB shows like *Angel*, *Roswell*, *Popular*, *The Gilmore Girls* and *Smallville*. The WB remains, to this day, the first stop for every US advertiser looking to sell clothes, cosmetics, CDs and cell-phones on television. Put it another way, there are plenty of adverts for the Gap and Maybelline broadcast during *Charmed*'s timeslot, but very few for life assurance.

[5] *SFX* magazine has described *Charmed* as: 'TV's answer to easy listening. You'd be hard pressed to find anyone who'd call themselves a committed fan, but you'd be even harder pressed to find someone who loathes it.' Ignoring the statement's grammatical error, it's also inaccurate. *Charmed has* a very devoted online fandom, and a pretty lively and vocal one at that.

[6] A stablemate for three years, *Buffy* left the WB amid much acrimony in 2001 and was subsequently broadcast on the rival UPN. See 'Bite Me'.

[7] It's also worth pointing out, of course, that *Charmed* always got higher ratings than *Buffy* – on average a million more viewers per episode. Not that this is, necessarily, an indication of superior quality. In 1965, Herman's Hermits sold more records, worldwide, than the Beatles and the Rolling Stones put together. Which only proves one thing – you can fool all of the people some of time …

INTRODUCTION

aloofness and its frequent nods toward dysfunctional family values and relationships in crisis can be its salvation in the often sterile, antiseptic world of TV drama. Sometimes the series' pat characterisations and *deus ex machina* plots involving angels and demons render it gauche beside, for example, *Stargate SG-1*'s groundbreaking and urbane recontextualisation of classic myths, and positively anaemic compared to the sophisticated /metaphors of *Buffy*. Nevertheless, there is *much* to admire here. Hence, this book.[8]

A bit of information specifically for those readers who didn't realise that Pagan Man wasn't *just* a nasty 1970s aftershave: recognised by both the Home Office and the Church of England as a bona-fide religion, Paganism involves a wide body of beliefs, including Wicca, Druidry and Shamanism, most of which have their roots in the world's pre-Christian nature religions. The Pagan Federation was set up in 1971 to help counter Sunday-supplement-type misconceptions about Satanism: naked-romps on the heath and so on. It is estimated that, today, there are over 60,000 practicing Pagans in the UK alone. Federation spokesperson Andy Norfolk noted, in *Alternative Metro*, that series like *Buffy the Vampire Slayer* and *Charmed* had greatly helped to increase the profile of Paganism in recent years: 'Stories about young women who use magic to battle bad guys could be seen as positive role models.' However, there is a downside to all this feminist empowerment and getting-in-touch-with-your-inner-broomstick. The *Buffy* character Willow neatly sums up the current, rather trendy, nature of much of the interest in new-age religions and of a generation of *'Wanna-Blessed-Be*s', noting: 'Nowadays, every girl with a henna tattoo and a spice rack thinks she's a sister to the Dark Ones.' *Charmed*, to its credit, has also acknowledged this embarrassing dichotomy. (Frivolous characters seen in 'The Fourth Sister' and 'Ms Hellfire' are good examples.)

HEADINGS

Dreaming (As Blondie Once Said) is Free: Dream sequences and hallucinations, described in full, surroundsound detail.

It's Witchcraft: Observations on *Charmed*'s use of magick and lore.

---

[8] The author feels duty-bound at this juncture to point out what should be patently obvious from reading his books – he's a fan of both *Charmed* and *Buffy the Vampire Slayer*. A deep admiration for one of the two series is not, despite what you may have heard to the contrary, mutually incompatible with a similar feeling toward the other.

INTRODUCTION

The Conspiracy Starts at the Witching Hour: Ever since *The X-Files*, it's virtually impossible to find a telefantasy show that *doesn't* feature some form of shadowy, secrecy-based shenanigans going on somewhere in the background. *Charmed* is no different.

Work is a Four-Letter Word: This category lists the various, mostly disastrous, vocational activities of the Halliwells.

References: Notes allusions to literary sources, references to pop-culture, 'Generation X' moments and general homages to all things esoteric.

'You May Remember Me ...' and **Behind the Camera:** These detail the past and future CVs of the cast and crew and will, hopefully, be useful in solving many of those 'Where have I seen his/her face before?' questions.

Cigarettes and Alcohol: Naughtiness of the nicotine and lager variety.

Logic, Let Me Introduce You to This Window: A section that, *gleefully*, details all the apparent mistakes, the continuity errors, the geographical absurdities, and the bits of the plot that simply make no sense.

Quote/Unquote: Samples of the dialogue that it's worth rewinding the video or DVD for.

Other categories will appear from time to time. Most should be fairly self-explanatory, **Continuity** for instance.
    Each episode concludes with a brief review and copious notes on other assorted trivia, which are really useful for boring your friends rigid with at parties and conventions. Mine have all suffered for my art already. Now it's your turn.

Keith Topping
Escaping By Canoe
Merrie Albion
March 2005

SISTERS OF THE 'CRAFT

During the mid-to-late 1990s there was a creative explosion within the many-roomed mansion of US telefantasy. The enormous mainstream crossover success of two shows – Star Trek: The Next Generation and The X-Files – had, it appeared, finally demonstrated to the jaded and cynical collective middle-management of television executives that intelligent, well-written and occasionally wryly self-deprecating TV shows that dealt with subject matter like science fiction and the paranormal could produce the ratings; that they could get not only a dedicated *cult* audience (for which read 'two or three highly vocal young men with anoraks and their equally vocal dog') but many 'normal' viewers as well. Inevitably, this juxtaposition produced two distinct types of shows over the subsequent decade as several different US TV networks tried to access the genre – with, admittedly, varying results.

On the one hand there were a bunch of rather fine quasi-futuristic SF series that looked and sounded a lot like the classier end of the *Trek* franchise – and particularly its most underrated offspring, *Deep Space Nine*. *Babylon 5*, *Andromeda*, *Farscape* and *Stargate SG-1*, for instance. On the other hand, there was a trend toward pre-millennial, politically-tinged paranoid angst, which recalled the best of 1950s Cold War SF, in the style of the more po-faced *The X-Files* stories and best exemplified by Chris Carter's follow-up series, *Millennium*. See *First Wave*, *Dark Skies* and *Brimstone* for further examples.

At the same time, another media-generated movement, the faintly ridiculous generic concept of 'girl power', was being rather cynically used as a specific marketing tool in and of itself. Riding on the back of the enormous success of a variety of – vastly different – female pop acts (Madonna, the Spice Girls, Natalie Imbruglia, Courtney Love's Hole, Dido), marketers began to see the potential for television shows that, rather than simply featuring strong female characters, also emphasised such women's empowerment in an ostensibly male world.

Thus, *Xena: Warrior Princess* and *Buffy the Vampire Slayer*, which began in 1995 and 1997 respectively, featured emotionally and physically strong, intelligent and capable young women in positions of great power (and, in the case of Gabrielle and Willow, with a dose of great wisdom too). This, of course, had previously been the sole province of the dominant males in drama generally and telefantasy in particular. That both these shows also, clearly, had more in common with *The Simpson*, *Friends* and *Ally McBeal* than with either *The X-Files* or *Star Trek: The Next Generation* was an additional selling point to the masses.[9]

It's very probable that without the success of *Xena* and, particularly, *Buffy* - at least in artistic and critical terms - *Charmed* would never have happened. 'I had come in to pitch on an entirely different project,' the series creator Constance Burge told *TV Zone* in 2000. 'At the time, *Buffy* [was] a huge success and the WB was looking for a companion piece. They thought the area of witches might be interesting to explore. Burge admits that she knew almost nothing about the subject of witchcraft prior to being commissioned to create *Charmed*[10] but, coming from a family that included two older sisters, the issues that surround living with siblings was a dramatic field that needed little research for her.[11] Burge, who had previously created the short-lived soap *Savannah* (1996) for the WB, initially conceived a story about three sisters who were the latest in a long-line of Wiccan women living in Boston. This was soon changed to San Francisco, which was felt to be more location friendly.[12]

'Ever since we realised that we have all these teenage girls as fans, we've tried to somehow put a moral message in, a family message or a value message in with, you know, our witchcraft,' Holly Marie Combs suggests.

Of course, with any show featuring three beautiful female leads - and especially considering his involvement in the production - a comparison with one of Aaron Spelling's previous TV triumphs is,

---

[9] 'We're in a time [of] girl power,' Alyssa Milano noted in an interview in 2001. '*Charmed* is [about] three very strong women fighting evil and trying to save people.'

[10] 'I had only preconceived emotions about what a witch was and, frankly, [those included] the pointed hat and the wart on the nose, so I bought an inordinate amount of books on the history of witchcraft,' Burge stated in the 2001 *Women of Charmed* documentary.

[11] 'My older sister, Laura is very strong and so I attributed the characteristics [she] has to Prue' noted Burge. 'The middle sibling typically tends to deal with life with a lot of humour. That really applied to my sister, Edie, and so I could see the character of Piper. Phoebe was, honestly, the easiest. It just grew from within.'

[12] Almost all of *Charmed* is actually filmed in Los Angeles, with just some occasional - admittedly very beautiful - stock footage of various San Francisco landmarks helping to create the illusion.

inevitably, never too far away. 'We have three attractive women doing good things every week,' Constance Burge once noted. 'I've been told that this feels like *Charlie's Angels* with broomsticks!'

In spite (or, perhaps, *because*) of this, *Charmed* was quickly picked up and, after just two episode had been produced (and before the first had even been broadcast), the WB network were confident enough in Spelling's proven record of success and Burge's intriguing format, to commission an entire season of 22 episodes.

WHICH WITCH IS WHICH?

Shannen Doherty: One of TV's most famous faces for the past decade, Shannen Maria Doherty was born in April 1971, in Memphis. Her parents moved to Los Angeles when she was seven.[13] She made her acting debut aged 11, when she was talent-spotted by Michael Landon and cast as Jenny Wilder in *Little House on the Prairie: A New Beginning* (1982-83), a role she subsequently reprised in several sequels. After appearing in her first movie, *Night Shift* (1982), Doherty featured in the 1986 cult black-comedy *Heathers*, opposite Christian Slater and Winona Ryder. She also appeared in *Girls Just Want to Have Fun* (1985) and, later, *Mallrats* (1995), played the title role in *A Burning Passion: The Margaret Mitchell Story* (1994), worked on mini-series like *Gone in the Night* (1996) and *Robert Kennedy and His Times* (1985) and the TV movies *Sleeping With the Devil* (1997), *The Ticket* (1997) and *Friends 'Til the End* (1997).

On television, Doherty made a guest appearance on *Parker Lewis Can't Lose* (1992), starred as Kris Witherspoon in *Our House* (1986-88) and, most famously, played the notorious teenage bad-girl Brenda Walsh in the popular *Beverly Hills, 90210* from 1990 to 1994. She then left the show acrimoniously. 'It wasn't like I walked out one day and said, "I quit,"' she told *Cleo* magazine in 2000. 'It was a long process. I think it was because the notoriety was too much. People hated the character and I couldn't take the abuse [that] came with that. I got sick of people assuming that I was as naughty as Brenda.' According to official sources, including Executive Producer Aaron Spelling, Doherty's leaving had more to do with behind the scenes problems. Doherty reportedly infuriated director William Friedkin when she failed to turn up for the first day of shooting on her post-*90210* movie, *Jailbreakers* (1994). As it turned out, she had just returned from Italy and was said to be jet-lagged. She also posed nude for *Playboy* in December 1993 and March 1994. On a personal level, Doherty has been

---

[13] Doherty's father, Tom, was a banker, whilst her mother, Rosa, owned a beauty parlour.

involved in a series of tempestuous relationships and public bust-ups with numerous boyfriends. Following the break-up of her engagement to Dean Factor in 1991, she was reportedly issued with a restraining order. Her next fiancé was Judd Nelson, whom she met on the set of *Blindfold: Acts of Obsession* (1994). She married Ashley Hamilton, the son of actor George Hamilton, just two weeks after meeting him in September 1993. The marriage lasted 18 months, with Doherty subsequently quoted as saying that she would gladly throw her former husband off a plane. Shortly after the divorce, she was back in the headlines with rumours of extensive cosmetic surgery.

Shannen has, subsequently, been romantically linked with Dean Cain, Jason Priestly and Counting Crows frontman Adam Duritz, and was briefly engaged to director Rob Weiss. She married her second husband, Rik Salomon, in February 2002, but the marriage was annulled a year later. In 1997, Doherty was reportedly ordered to attend a course of anger-management counselling by the Beverly Hills Municipal Court after a widely-publicised altercation with 22-year-old Corey Hanker. In June 2001, she was reportedly sentenced to three years probation and 20 days' work-release duty and fined $1500 for a drunk driving offence. Allegedly, Doherty was released from her *Charmed* contract because of persistent arguments between herself and co-star Alyssa Milano.[14] Since leaving *Charmed*, she has become the presenter of the quasi-reality show *Scare Tactics* (2003-4).

Holly Marie Combs: Combs was born in December 1973 in San Diego. Her mother, Lauralei, was just 14 when she became pregnant. Although Combs's parents did subsequently marry, they separated two years later. Mother and daughter subsequently moved to New York when Combs was eight, and she was enrolled in stage school soon afterwards. Her first TV appearances came when she was 10 in various commercials, while her mother followed her own ambitions to become an actress. Combs's movie debut was as an extra on *Walls of Glass* (1985), a film in which her mother also appeared. At the age of 13, she landed the role of Debs Boon in *Sweet Heart's Dance* (1988) and, a year later, she appeared in *Born on the Fourth of July* (1989). Other credits include a cameo in *Ocean's Eleven* (2001). She also appeared in *New York Stories* (1989), *Swearing Allegiance* (1987), *Dr Giggles* (1992) and as Natasha Nutley in *See Jane Date* (2003). Another role came in heavy-metal band Slaughter's video 'Real Love' (1992).

Combs's big break came with the role of Kimberly Brock in *Picket*

---

[14] These days, Doherty appears to bitterly regret her involvement with *Charmed*, unflatteringly describing the series in one post-departure interview as 'a show for 12-year-olds.'

WHICH WITCH IS WHICH?

Fences (1992-96) when she was 18. Her performance earned her a *Young Artist Award* for 'Best Young Actress in a Television Series'. She began a relationship with actor Bryan Smith in 1993, the couple eloping amid much publicity to get married in Las Vegas. They divorced in 1997. A year later, she became engaged to Storm Lydon, a Venice schoolteacher whom she met in Mexico, but she subsequently called-off the engagement and began a relationship with David Donoho, a technician whom she met on the set of *Charmed* and with whom she had a son, Finlay, in 2003. Combs, along with fellow actresses Tangi Miller and Alyson Hannigan, is a spokesperson for various breast cancer charities, and she has appeared in *Vogue*, *Glamour*, *Self* and *Mademoiselle* to raise awareness about the disease. She is also on the board of Thursday's Child, a charity working with teenage runaways. Her hobbies include gardening and horse riding. She was a bridesmaid at the wedding of Alyssa Milano in 1999.

Alyssa Milano: Milano was born in December 1972 in Brooklyn. Her acting career started when her parents took her to see a stage production of *Annie* when she was seven. She precociously told them, 'I could do that,' and, a year later, she landed the part of July in a touring version of the same play. Having moved to Los Angeles to further her career, she attended the Buckley School in Sherman Oaks. Her screen debut came in 1983 when she appeared in *Old Enough*. Soon afterwards, she was cast as Samantha, Tony Danza's daughter, in the popular sitcom *Who's the Boss?* (1984-92). Enjoying much small-screen success, Milano ventured back into movies, playing Arnold Schwarzenegger's daughter in *Commando* (1985), and appearing in *Crash Course* (1988) and *Dance til Dawn* (1988). A picture of her was allegedly used to create Ariel, the title character in the Disney cartoon *The Little Mermaid* (1992). After eight years on *Who's the Boss?*, she reinvented herself, shedding her child-star image, making the transition to adult films like *Embrace of the Vampire* (1994) and brilliantly portraying teenage murderess Amy Fisher in *Casualties of Love: The Long Island Lolita Story* (1993). Her other credits include *The Surrogate* (1995), *Candles in the Dark* (1993), *Where the Day Takes You* (1992) and *Glory Daze* (1996). Milano's role in the soft-core movie *Poison Ivy 2* (1996) caused much subsequent controversy, and her mother, Lin, has since waged war on numerous websites that have reproduced pictures of Milano in various states of undress. This included successfully suing a webmaster in Minnesota for $230,000. Milano herself is quoted as saying that she doesn't regret any of her nude work, although her TV dad, Tony Danza, wasn't impressed when she posed naked in *Bikini* magazine whilst still playing a 15 year old in *Who's the Boss?*. 'I worried about her,' noted Danza, 'but it wasn't my place to say anything.'

In 1996, Milano starred alongside Reese Witherspoon and Mark

WHICH WITCH IS WHICH?

Wahlberg in *Fear*. Soon afterwards, she returned to television in Aaron Spelling's *Melrose Place* (1997-8), as Jennifer Mancini. After keeping a low-profile love-life for several years, she complained publicly about the lack of men in her life. She eventually met Cinjun Tate, singer with the band Remy Zero, and the couple were married on New Year's Day 1999. Milano filed for divorce 11 months later, citing irreconcilable differences. The marriage, however, lasted long enough for paparazzi to snap the honeymooning couple naked on the isle of St Barts, applying sun-cream on each other's naughty bits. Her brief engagement to *Double Dragon* co-star Scott Wolf also ended in tears. Other boyfriends have included her *Charmed* co-star Brian Krause and N'Sync's Justin Timberlake.[15] Another important string to Milano's bow was her singing career. She recorded five albums in Japan during the early '90s, all of them – *Alyssa*, *Look In My Heart*, *Best in the World*, *Locked in a Dream* and *Do You See Me?* – going platinum. She once performed live at a Japanese festival in front of 40,000 people. She also appeared in Blink 182's video 'Josie' as a cheerleader in 1998. Her distinguishing features include several tattoos, a few of which can be seen in *Charmed*: the Hindu symbol *Om* on her wrist, a fairy kneeling in grass on her hip, rosary beads on her back, an angel on her left ankle and a garland of flowers around her right ankle. She also, reportedly, has a sacred-heart tattooed on her bottom.[16] She caused something of a stir with her commercials for Candies perfume in 2000. These, tagged *Anywhere You Dare*, featured a lingerie-clad Milano and a man perfuming her cleavage. The ads were turned down by youth-orientated magazines *Seventeen* and *Teen People* on taste grounds.

Rose McGowan: 'You have to work to carve out your own little corner, and I'm certainly smacking my head against the wall trying to make a dent,' Rose McGowan once told an interviewer. 'I just hope I don't get brain-damaged before I get there.' McGowan had something of an unconventional upbringing. The eldest daughter of six children, she was born in September 1973 in Florence.[17] Her mother was French and she spent much of her childhood travelling throughout Europe and living in communes as part of the Children of God cult. When she was nine, the family moved to the US, and McGowan attended school in Seattle before running away to Los Angeles when she was 16.

After working in various menial jobs and occasionally sleeping rough, she was spotted by a casting agent and won the role of Amy Blue in

---

[15] 'Every time I decide I want a child I get another pet,' Milano once noted. 'I have three dogs, 13 birds and three horses. What does that tell you?'
[16] That one, somewhat inevitably, *hasn't* featured in *Charmed*.
[17] Some sources give McGowan's birthday as 13 December 1974.

WHICH WITCH IS WHICH?

The Doom Generation (1995), where her performance earned several Best Newcomer nominations. In 1996, she appeared in *Scream* as Tatum. She also co-starred with Ben Affleck in *Phantoms* (1998), played Courtney in *Jawbreaker* (1999) and was in *Monkeybone* (2001), *Vacuums* (2002), *Ready to Rumble* (2000), *Devil in the Flesh* (1998), *Seed* (1997) and *Bio-Dome* (1996). On television, she guest-starred in 2001 on *What About Joan?*[18] McGowan has dated both Ryan Phillippe and Matthew Lillard, and was engaged for three years to notorious shock-rocker Marilyn Manson (Brian Warner). After the couple split in 2001, she told Howard Stern that their relationship fractured because she had become tired of Manson's 'rock n roll lifestyle.'[19] During early, McGowan Rose was dating Ahmet Zinczenko, the editor of *Men's Health Magazine*. In 1998, she wore a dress to the MTV awards ceremony that was so revealing that she could be photographed only from one side. She also auditioned for the role of Lisa in *Girl, Interrupted*. 'I think if I had lived back in Salem, I would have been burned at the stake,' she notes.

---

[18] McGowan also spent 1998 as fashion house Bebe's spokesmodel.
[19] When pressed further by Stern on the subject, McGowan admitted that drugs use was a major part of their lives and that this had been a factor in her decision to end the relationship.

THREE, THAT'S THE MAGIC NUMBER

Dorian Gregory: Gregory was born in January 1971, in Washington DC, and raised in Cleveland. When he was aged nine, his family moved to Los Angeles. He began his acting career with roles in shows including *Baywatch* (1991), *Pacific Blue* (1997), *3rd Rock From the Sun* (1999) and *Moesha* (1998). His CV also includes appearances in *Stop! Or My Mom Will Shoot* (1992), *The Barefoot Executive* (1995), *Baywatch Nights* (1996-7) (as Diamont Teague) and a period as co-host of *The Other Half* (2002-3). An active humanitarian, Gregory is involved in the Jeopardy programme, sponsored by the Los Angeles Police Department for youth at risk, and serves as the national spokesperson for the American Diabetes Association. He can be seen in the kick-boxing video *Kick Butt II* (1999).

TW King: Born in October 1965, in Hollywood, Ted King was raised in Bethesda, Maryland. He attended the Tisch School of the Arts in New York where he studied film direction. King then co-founded the New York Portal Theatre Company and has been a strong presence in the New York theatre scene for several years. He also worked as a film and video editor before landing his first lead acting role, as Danny Roberts in the TV series *Loving* (1995) and, subsequently, its spin-off, *The City* (1995). Thereafter, he appeared as Jack Logan in *Timecop* (1997) and had guest roles in *Frasier* (2002), *Law & Order: Special Victims Unit* (2001), *Sex and the City* (2001) and *JAG* (2000). His movies include *The X-Files* (1998), *Impostor* (2002) and *Hoodlum & Son* (2003). He is currently playing Luis Ramon Alcazar in *General Hospital* (2002-).

Brian Krause: Born in February 1969 in El Toro, California, Krause was a football star at Orange Coast College in 1987, where he initially considered a career in sports medicine. That's *real* football, or *soccer* for our American readers. Krause had already made his TV debut, appearing in *Highway to Heaven* (1989) as a child actor and, at the age of 16, he enrolled in his first professional acting class. He played Mike in *Earth Angel* (1991), Richard in *Return to the Blue Lagoon* (1991), Tim in *December* (1991), Charles Brady in *Sleepwalkers* (1992), Matthew Cory in the soap *Another World* (1997-8) and Lynn in the *Bandit* series of TV movies (1994). His CV also includes *The Liars' Club* (1993), *An American Summer* (1991), *Naked Souls* (1995), *Breaking Free* (1995), *Mind Games* (1996), *Get a Job* (1998), *Trash* (1999), *Dreamers* (1999) and *Return to Cabin by the Lake* (2001). He also appeared in *Walker, Texas Ranger* (1995). Krause and his wife, Beth, divorced in 2000. The couple have a daughter. During 2001, Krause was rumoured to be dating his *Charmed* co-star Alyssa Milano.

Greg Vaughan: Vaughan was born in June 1973 and raised in Dallas. Shortly after graduating from high school, he travelled to Italy, where he modelled for legendary designer Giorgio Armani. Work for other design houses Gianni Versace, Tommy Hilfiger, Banana Republic and Ralph Lauren followed. After several years in modelling, Vaughan's interests turned to acting, initially with roles in the Aaron Spelling-produced soaps *Malibu Shores* (1996) (as Josh Walker) and *Beverly Hills 90210* (1996-7) (as Cliff Yeager). He also made guest appearances in *Baywatch* (1996), *Buffy the Vampire Slayer* (1997), *Will & Grace* (2002) and *Sabrina, the Teenage Witch* (2002). Vaughan's movies include *Poison Ivy: The New Seduction* (1997), *No Small Ways* (1997) and *Children of the Corn V: Fields of Terror* (1998). He starred as Diego Guittierez in *The Young and the Restless* (2002-3). When he's not working, Vaughan enjoys golf, basketball, windsurfing and hiking. He's also a fine singer and guitarist.

Julian McMahon: The son of former Australian Prime Minister the late Sir William McMahon, Julian studied law at the University of Sydney. However, he left after his first year and began a career in modelling, working primarily in commercials. In 1987 alone, he travelled to Los Angeles, New York, Milan, London, Rome and Paris. His appearance in a TV commercial promoting jeans in Australia led to him being cast in *The Power, The Passion* (1989) as Kane Edmonds. After this, he achieved international recognition as Ben Lucini in *Home and Away* (1989-91). It was whilst working on the popular teenage soap that he met his future first wife, actress and singer Dannii Minogue.[20] The couple married in 1994, but divorced just over a year later.

McMahon has been quoted in an Australian magazine as saying that, to him, acting was just another way to bring in money. He subsequently spent a year performing on stage, appearing in *Love Letters*

---

[20] Yes, that *does* mean he was Kylie's brother-in-law.

in Sydney and Melbourne. After a lead role in the feature film *Wet and Wild Summer!* (1992), he relocated to Los Angeles. In 1992, he was cast as Ian Rain on NBC's daytime drama *Another World* (1992-4). He also appeared in the films *Magenta* (1996) and *Chasing Sleep* (2000) and played John Grant in the TV series *Profiler* (1996-2000). Following his departure from *Charmed*, he starred as the amoral plastic surgeon Christian Troy in *Nip/Tuck* (2003) and as Dr Doom in *The Fantastic Four* (2005). He was also, reportedly, under consideration for the role on James Bond in 2004. In his spare time, McMahon enjoys surfing, biking and cooking, and is an avid collector of rare books. His second marriage, to Brooke Burns, ended in 2001. The couple have a daughter called Madison.

Drew Fuller: Born in Los Angeles in May 1980, Fuller was discovered by an agent when he was 12 years old after a family friend put him on the cover of UCLA magazine. Fuller began modelling at the age of 16 and quickly became a top male model for Tommy Hilfiger, Prada and Club Med, amongst others. He subsequently made the transition to TV commercials for companies like Subway and Toyota and – famously – Pepsi acting opposite Britney Spears. He also appeared in Jennifer Love Hewitt's video for the song 'Barenaked'. He made his acting debut in the movie *Voodoo Academy* (2000) and played Rod Farrell in *Vampire Clan* (2002). His other movies include *One* (2001), *Angels Don't Sleep Here* (2001) and *Close Call* (2004) and, and he has had roles in the TV series' *Home of the Brave* (2002) and *Black Sash* (2003).

In his spare time, Fuller enjoys playing basketball, surfing, rock climbing, snowboarding and tennis as well as watching movies and hanging out with friends. At the time of writing, he is dating his *Black Sash* co-star Sarah Carter.

THE POWER BEHIND THE POWER OF THREE

Aaron Spelling: One of the most famous names in television history, Aaron Spelling was born in April 1923 and graduated from the Southern Methodist University, Dallas, with a Bachelor of Arts Degree. Spelling started his media career as a writer, selling his first TV script to *Jane Wyman Theater* in 1951. He subsequently wrote for *Playhouse 90*, *Johnny Ringo* and *The Dick Powell Show*. He was also an occasional actor in the 1950s, appearing in *Dragnet* (1953-4), *I Love Lucy* (1955) and *Alfred Hitchcock Presents* (1955) and in the films *Mad at the World* (1955), *Target Zero* (1955), *Black Widow* (1954), *Alaska Seas* (1954) and *Vicki* (1953). Towards the end of the decade, Spelling became a producer, initially for Four Star Productions. He subsequently went in partnership with Danny Thomas for several years before forming his own company, Aaron Spelling Productions, in 1972. Amongst the dozens of classic TV series that he has produced are: *Burke's Law*, *Honey West*, *Daniel Boone*, *The Mod Squad*, *Chopper One*, *S.W.A.T*, *Starsky and Hutch*, *Charlie's Angel*, *The Love Boat*, *Fantasy Island*, *Hart to Hart*, *Dynasty*, *T.J. Hooker*, *Beverly Hills 90210*, *Melrose Place*, *Malibu Shores* and *7th Heaven*. Spelling also produced almost 100 TV movies, including *Carter's Army*, *But I Don't Want to Get Married!*, *Wild Women*, *Crowhaven Farm*, *A Taste of Evil*, *The Daughters of Joshua Cabe*, *Rolling Man*, *Satan's School for Girls*, *The Girl Who Came Gift-Wrapped*, *California Split*, *The San Pedro Bums*, *Cruise Into Terror* and *Velvet*.

He is the father of actors Tori and Randy Spelling, and his six-acre mansion 'The Manor', at 594 Mapleton Drive in Bel-Air, has 123 rooms, a bowling alley, swimming pool, gymnasium, tennis court and screening room.[21]

---

[21] Allegedly the largest family home in California, the property was bought by Spelling in 1983, having previously belonged to Bing Crosby.

A BOOK OF SHADOWS

The Untransmitted Pilot

Writer: Constance M Burge
Director: Bruce Seth Green

Cast: Shannen Doherty (Prue Halliwell), Holly Marie Combs (Piper Halliwell), Dorian Gregory (Darryl Morris), Lori Rom (Phoebe Halliwell), Chris Boyd (Andy Trudeau), Eric Scott Woods (Jeremy Burns), Matthew Ashford (Roger), Lonnie Partridge (Woman)

Following the recent death of her beloved grandmother, Phoebe Halliwell returns from New York to San Francisco and to the family home in which she grew up with her two older sisters, Prudence and Piper. During their first night together at the Manor, Phoebe finds a mysterious book of witchcraft in the attic and recites an incantation from it. This leaves the three sisters with the awesome powers that they were always destined to have, but also makes them a target for a supernatural serial-killer.

'You May Remember Me ...': Lori Rom played Laura in *Party of Five*. Chris Boyd appeared in *Shrieker*.

Behind the Camera: Charmed's creator, Constance M Burge, also worked on *Boston Public*, *Ally McBeal* and *Savannah*. Producer Brad Kern's other TV credits include *Nash Bridges*, *The Adventures of Brisco County Jr.*, *Carly's Web* and *Remington Steele*. E Duke Vincent was executive producer on *All Souls*, *Satan's School for Girls*, *Rescue 77*, *Sunset Beach*, *7th Heaven*, *Models Inc.*, *Melrose Place*, *Beverly Hills 90210*, *Hollywood Wives*, *Hotel*, *Dynasty* and *Gomer Pyl, U.S.M.C*. Bruce Seth Green's CV includes *Knight Rider*, *Airwolf*, *MacGyver*, *She-Wolf of London*, *V*, *Buffy the Vampire Slayer*, *SeaQuest DSV*, *Xena: Warrior Princess*, *Hercules: The Legendary Journeys*, *American Gothic* and *Jack & Jill*.

Notes: 'I shield you in my Wiccan way, here in my circle round, asking you to protect this space.' The unaired pilot was shot in March 1998 and was presented to the Television Critics Association in Los Angeles during the summer. Following the sale of *Charmed* to the WB network, portions of the episode were hastily refilmed in August 1998 to transform it into the first transmitted episode, 'Something Wicca This Ways Comes'. The pilot has the same basic script as the transmitted episode, and includes large chunks of what, subsequently, became that episode. However, those scenes featuring the characters Phoebe and Andy Trudeau were entirely refilmed, the roles having been recast. Contemporary publicity stated that Lori Rom, the original Phoebe, left the production due to 'personal reasons.' Additional sequences dropped for the refilmed episode include a telephone conversation between Jeremy and Piper from outside Serena Fredrick's apartment in North Beach and a much lengthier introductory scene for Andy.

CHARMED SEASON 1 (1998-99)

Co-ordinating Producers: Robert Del Valle (1), Betty Reardon (7-22)
Consulting Producers: Jonathan Levin (9-22), Tony Blake (11-22), Paul Jackson (11-22)
Producers: Les Sheldon (1), Sheryl J Anderson (2-22), Jon Paré (18-22)
Supervising Producer: Les Sheldon (2-22)
Executive Producers: Brad Kern, Constance M Burge, Aaron Spelling, E Duke Vincent
Associate Producer: Peter Chomsky

Regular Cast:
Shannen Doherty (Prue Halliwell)
Holly Marie Combs (Piper Halliwell)
Alyssa Milano (Phoebe Halliwell)
T W King (Andy Trudeau 1-16, 18-22)
Dorian Gregory (Darryl Morris, 1-2, 5-6, 9-10, 13-15, 18-22)
Brian Krause (Leo Wyatt, 3, 7-10, 14, 21)

1: SOMETHING WICCA THIS WAY COMES

7 October 1998 [22]

Writer: Constance M. Burge
Director: John T Kretchmer

Cast: Eric Scott Woods (Jeremy Burns), Matthew Ashford (Roger), Chris Flanders (Chef Moore), Francesca Cappucci (News Reporter), Charmaine Cruz (Admitting Nurse), Hugh Holub (Pharmacist), Lonnie Partridge (Woman)

> Phoebe Halliwell returns to San Francisco to live with her older sisters, Prue and Piper, in their late grandmother's home. In the attic, Phoebe finds an ancient volume of witchcraft, *The Book of Shadows*. She recites from it, an incantation that leaves the sisters with paranormal powers. As they come to terms with the advantages and disadvantages of their new-found abilities, the girls also learn that a warlock has been killing local witches. And, he seems to have targeted the Halliwells as his next victims.

It's Witchcraft: The inscription on the family's Ouija board says *To my three beautiful girls. May this give you the light to find the shadows. The power of three will set you free. Love Mom.* Phoebe reads the following from *The Book of Shadows*: 'Hear now the words of the witches, the secrets we hid in the night, the oldest of gods are invoked here, the great work of magic is sought. In the night and in this hour, I call upon the ancient power, bring your powers to we sisters three, we want the power, give us the power.'

The book suggests that there are three essentials of magic: timing, feeling and the phases of the moon.

---

[22] *Charmed* is made by Spelling Television Inc., a Paramount/Viacom Company. The series is broadcast in the US on the WB network and all transmission dates refer to these initial broadcasts. Thereafter, repeats are shown on TNT, which also syndicates old episodes. Overseas, *Charmed* is broadcast by Living TV and Channel 5 in the UK, Channel 10 in Australia, TV3 and Sky 1 in New Zealand, CTV and Showcase Diva in Canada, M6 in France, TV3 in Norway and Denmark, Net5 in the Netherlands, Canal Sony in Latin America, Tele5 in Spain, ZTV in Sweden, TV3 in Ireland, Pink TV in Serbia-Montenegro, BS2 in Japan and in many other countries.

SEASON 1: SOMETHING WICCA THIS WAY COMES

Work is a Four-Letter Word: Prue is employed at the Museum of Natural History as a fund-raising co-ordinator although she, satisfyingly, resigns in this episode. Piper is a chef in a restaurant.

It's a Designer Label!: The undoubted highlight is Phoebe's extremely tight shorts in the final scene. They're certainly more impressive than the pair of check trousers she wears earlier. Phoebe describes Prue's ex-boyfriend, Roger, as an 'Armani-wearing, Chardonnay-slugging, trust-funder.'

References: The title alludes to Ray Bradbury's classic carnival horror *Something Wicked This Way Comes* (filmed by Disney in 1983). The source for *that* is a quotation by one of the three witches in Shakespeare's *The Tragedy of Macbeth* (Act IV, Scene I: 'By the pricking of my thumbs/Something wicked this way comes'). The headline on the copy of the *San Francisco Gazette* that Prue holds is POLICE DOUBT FIRE WAS ACCIDENTAL. This was a prop from the movie *Mrs. Doubtfire*, which also took place in San Francisco. Robin Williams's character used the second and third words of the headline to create his transvestite pseudonym. Jeremy is said to work for the *San Francisco Chronicle*. Also, allusions to: 'Do what thou whilst,' the avocation associated with English writer and magus Aleister Crowley (1875-1947); the character Chicken Little who – according to the folk-tale – believed that the sky was falling; Dutch artist Hieronymous Bosch (c.1460-1516); *The Exorcist*; *Lethal Weapon*; *Bewitched*; and teenage detective Nancy Drew; and a visual reference to *Raiders of the Lost Ark*. The Yung Lee market in Chinatown is mentioned.

'You May Remember Me ...': Eric Scott Woods appeared in *Quantum Leap*, *Ally McBeal* and *Another World*. Matthew Ashford played Jack Devereaux in *Days of Our Lives*. Francesca Cappuncci's movies include *Beverly Hills Ninja*. Chris Flanders was in *Reasonable Doubt* and *Grounded For Life*. Hugh B Holub appeared in *Desire*. Charmaine Cruz was the writer/director of the movie *Pissed*.

Behind the Camera: John Kretchmer started his career as a set dresser on *Manhunter*. He was an assistant director on the first two *Naked Gun* movies and *Jurassic Park*. His CV also includes directing episodes of *One Tree Hill*, *The Lone Gunmen*, *Dark Angel*, *Buffy the Vampire Slayer*, *Early Edition*, *Xena: Warrior Princess* and *Star Trek: Deep Space Nine*.

Logic, Let Me Introduce You to This Window: An exterior establishing shot of the Halliwell house shows Piper going in through the door with a black umbrella with a white stripe around the edge. The interior shot shows her hanging up a different umbrella with a floral print. The tree in front of the Halliwell house has leaves in some shots but is bare in others. Obviously, some footage was used from the original pilot, which had been filmed during spring. All scenes featuring Alyssa Milano and Ted King, however, were reshot later in the year. Phoebe's hair is very different in her first scene from the rest of the episode. Piper surely shouldn't be wearing nail polish during her cooking interview. Does Piper use her power for 'personal gain' when she freezes Moore before he tastes her incomplete meal? Whilst not understanding why Moore is frozen, Piper gratefully adds a splash of port before he unfreezes and, *technically*, she *does* gain from this, by getting the job.

It's established elsewhere in the series that all demons and warlocks can magically transport themselves from place to place (either by what becomes known as 'shimmering' or by 'blinking'). Jeremy, therefore, looks about as dangerous as a chicken vol-au-vent when *running* from the warehouse to the Manor. By the time he arrives at his destination, he's extremely out of breath. Jeremy throws two fireballs when he breaks into the attic, but only one lands and surrounds the girls with fire. What happened to the other one? Prue talks to Andy at the end of the episode and picks up the newspaper. In some shots, Prue holds the paper with the headline visible towards the camera. In others, it's turned the other way around. When we first meet Piper, she wears her watch on her right wrist. Later, whilst preparing the meal at the restaurant, it's on her left wrist.

In the stock-footage exterior of the Manor used in this and most subsequent episodes, it doesn't appear that the house has room for an attic.

Continuity: Before the recent death of their grandmother, Prue and Piper shared an apartment, whilst their younger sister Phoebe – with whom Prue has an awkward relationship – lived in New York (see 'PreWitched'). Their mother died when they were young, their father having already left prior to this, and they were raised by their grandmother. It sounds as though the Halliwells are something of a dysfunctional family all round as, in addition to an invisible father, they, according to Piper, have an alcoholic cousin and a manic aunt. They also, as Phoebe discovers, have an ancestor called Melinda Warren (see 'The Witch is Back'), a witch who was burned at the stake. Prue, at some stage in her past, dated Andy Trudeau, a third generation police officer (see 'I've Got You Under My Skin'). She subsequently had a lengthy relationship with her (disgracefully manipulative) colleague Roger, including a period when they were actually engaged. Part of the reason for her fractious relationship with Phoebe appears to have been various lies that Roger told Prue about Phoebe. Piper met her boyfriend, Jeremy, six months earlier at the hospital on the day that their grandmother was first admitted. Phoebe's bedroom

SEASON 1: SOMETHING WICCA THIS WAY COMES

was always considered the coldest room in the house. Andy's partner, Darryl Morris, doesn't believe in either UFOs or the occult.

A Sinister Animal: Having seen its previous mistress horribly murdered, Kit the cat subsequently foists itself upon the unsuspecting Halliwell sisters (however, see 'PreWitched' and 'Cat House').

Quote/Unquote: Phoebe, using the Ouija Board: 'I forgot your question.' Piper: 'I asked if Prue would have sex other than [with] herself this year.' Phoebe: 'That's disgusting. *Please* say "yes".'

Prue: 'We're perfectly safe here.' Piper: 'In horror movies, the person who says that is *always* the next to die.'

Prue, concerning Roger: 'How did you know about him?' Andy: 'I know people.' Prue: 'You checked up on me?' Andy: '... What can I say? I'm a detective.'

Notes: 'The Power of Three will set us free.' A rather smart beginning, which nicely illustrated the main asset that the show had going for it – namely, the terrific interplay between the three sisters. If you can tear your attention away from their bosoms for a few moments – and, let's face it, at times that's *difficult* if you're either male or of the Sapphic persuasion – then there's much fun to be had in their pithy dialogue and cunningly constructed characterisation. Which is a good job because, frankly, most of the other characters are little more than ciphers (especially that awfully stereotypical French chef and Prue's smarmy-but-dim ex-fiancé) and the plot is very thin and one-dimensional.

Nevertheless, when *Charmed* works, it usually works well, and this is an example of it working effortlessly. Best bits: the changing photograph; the scene in the chemist's between Phoebe and Prue; the girls first entering the attic. And that wonderful closing shot of Prue shutting the front door of the Manor with a wave of her finger that would subsequently be used as the final image of the series' much-admired title-sequence for its first three seasons. The addition of much well-shot San Francisco location footage (particularly the night views) is a real bonus. There are, genuinely, few more beautiful cities in the world.

With the popular teen-drama *Dawson's Creek* airing immediately prior to this episode, *Charmed*'s debut gained 7.7 million viewers. This was, and remained for a long time afterwards, the highest rating figures for any show in the history of the WB.[23]

Soundtrack: *Charmed*'s title theme is a cover version of the Steven

---

[23] It was eventually beaten by the debut episode of *Smallville* in 2001.

Morrisey and Johnny Marr epic torch-song 'How Soon Is Now?'[24] performed by the band Love Spit Love.[25] This recording had previously featured on the soundtrack of *The Craft* (1996), a movie that also concerned teenage witches, albeit rather more naughty ones than the Halliwell sisters.

Did You Know?: The house used for exterior shots of the Manor is located at 1329 Carroll Avenue in Angelino Heights, part of Echo Park in Los Angeles.[26] The major cross streets, if you're planning to seek it out next time you're in the area, are Douglas Street and West Sunset Boulevard[27] at one end, and Edgeware Road and Temple Street at the other.

---

[24] Originally recorded by Morrisey's and Marr's band, The Smiths, 'How Soon is Now?' was a minor British hit in the spring of 1985. It is now regarded as one of the most influential records of all time. Smiths biographer Simon Goddard noted the *Charmed* connection to 'How Soon is Now?' in his book *Songs That Saved Your Life*, describing the show as a 'cult US lipstick 'n' witchcraft series.'

[25] Love Spit Love included former Psychedelic Furs lead singer Richard Butler.

[26] Echo Park is a 26-acre area in Westlake that will be familiar to moviegoers as a location from Roman Polanski's *Chinatown*. It has also featured, more recently, in both 24 and *Angel*. The area takes its name from a tranquil collection of lotuses and palm trees set around the idyllic eponymous lake itself.

[27] Possibly the most famous street in the world, Sunset Boulevard runs through Hollywood into West Hollywood, where it becomes the even more legendary Sunset Strip, a two mile conglomeration of chic restaurants, expensive hotels and 'you can't come in here dressed like that'-type nightclubs. This is home to the Comedy Store, the Whisky-a-Go-Go, the Roxy and the Viper Room. And, most notoriously, the Sunset Hyatt Hotel, the staging area for the wild and lurid antics of several generations of rock stars from Led Zeppelin, the Rolling Stones, the Who and Hawkwind onwards. A flavour of the Hyatt's colourful past can be glimpsed in Cameron Crowe's seminal *Almost Famous* (2000).

2: I'VE GOT YOU UNDER MY SKIN

14 October 1998

Writer: Brad Kern
Director: John T Kretchmer

Cast: Barbara Pilavin (Older Brittany Reynolds), Cynthia King (Brittany Reynolds), Michael Philip (Stefan/Javna), Neil Roberts (Rex Buckland), Leigh Allyn-Baker (Hannah Webster), Marc Shelton (Father Williams), Bailey Luetgert (Alec), Julie Araskog (Darlene), Todd Feder (Clerk), Tamara Lee Krinsky (Tia), Ralph Manza (Elderly Man), Ben Caswell (Max Jones), Lou Glenn (Carpenter)

> Andy and Darryl investigate the abduction of several young women, including the girls' friend Brittany. Phoebe catches the eye of a photographer whose interest in her extends beyond taking her picture. Meanwhile, Piper faces a personal crisis when she fears that her powers may have come from the Dark Side.

The Conspiracy Starts at the Witching Hour: Stefan is a renowned photographer who is in town to do a Porsche shoot. He invites Phoebe along to his studio – 78 Waterfront Boulevard – to pose for him. In reality, Stefan is Javna, a demon who, one week each year, steals the life-force from the young to sustain his own eternal youth. Prue asks if there is some kind of incantation to reverse these effects and Piper confirms there is, the Hand of Fatima. The prophet Mohammed banished Javna centuries ago using this.

A Little Learning is a Dangerous Thing: Phoebe has a premonition that the $10 million state lottery will be won by the following numbers – 4, 16, 19, 30, 32 and 40. She advises an old couple who are about to lose their house accordingly. She also buys a ticket for herself but, since that's a clear example of using the powers for self-gain, her ticket changes after the winning numbers have been called.

It's Witchcraft: Having watched a disturbingly inaccurate television documentary about the Salem Witch Trials[28] (see **Logic, Let Me Introduce You To This Window**) Piper frets about whether her powers are the work of evil or not. She finally walks into a church and is patently relieved when no divine retribution visits itself upon her.

The full text of the spell that the girls use to destroy Javna is: 'Evil eyes look unto thee, may they soon extinguished be, bend they will to the power of three, eye of Earth, evil and accursed.'

Work is a Four-Letter Word: Prue has an interview at Buckland's Auction House with the dishy (if wet-as-a-kipper-in-the-face) Rex Buckland, who has recently taken over the business from his father. Despite a less-than-successful first impression and the attempted intervention of Horrible Hannah Webster (one of the firm's Assistant Specialists), Prue gets the job.

Phoebe has always dreamed of being a model. Subsequent to this episode, she having learned her lesson, her dreams change somewhat.

It's a Designer Label!: Check out Phoebe's figure-hugging dress in the opening scene.

---

[28] One of the most infamous outbreaks of witch-hunting, this took place in colonial Massachusetts in 1692. It led to the execution of 20 suspected witches – men *and* women – all seemingly falsely accused. The saga began in January when 9-year-old Elizabeth Parris and 11-year-old Abigail Williams exhibited strange behaviour, such as blasphemous screaming and convulsive seizures. Soon, the phenomena spread to other young girls, including Sarah Churchill. Unable to determine a cause, physicians concluded the girls were bewitched. Pressured to identify the source of their affliction, the girls named Tituba, an Indian slave, who confessed to consorting with Satan and testified that there was a conspiracy at work in Salem. Over the following weeks, other townspeople stated that they, too, had been witness to devilish activities. Amongst those denounced were several women whose economic circumstances were disturbing to the accepted social order. Some of the accused had previous records of criminal activity, but many others were faithful churchgoers of high standing within the community. The subsequent trials took place within the context of a schism between the church and a controversial local minister, Reverend Samuel Parris, Elizabeth's father. Personal differences were exacerbated in a small, isolated community in which religious beliefs were deeply held. A court was convened in May by Governor Phips. The trials quickly succumbed to outbreaks of mass hysteria, during which even the Governor's wife was implicated. By October, however, community leaders were casting doubts upon the evidence, the courts were dissolved and those imprisoned were pardoned. Eventually indemnities were paid to the families of those executed, although of the presiding judges only one, Samuel Sewall, ever publicly admitted error. For a disturbing fictionalisation of the Salem tragedy, see Arthur Miller's 1953 play *The Crucible*.

SEASON 1: I'VE GOT YOU UNDER MY SKIN

References: The title is a Cole Porter song, most famously recorded by Frank Sinatra in 1954. Andy's favourite movie when growing up was Sam Raimi's *Evil Dead II* (and not *Ghostbusters* as Darryl suggests). Also, *Romeo and Juliet*; fashion designer Georgio Armani; TV chat show hostess Rosie O'Donnell; and a quotation from Exodus 22:18 ('Thou shalt not suffer a witch to live'). Prue claims that her area of expertise ranges from the Ming Dynasty to a Mark McGuire rookie baseball card. Buckland shows Prue *The Madonna of the Meadow* by Giovanni Bellini (c. 1430-1516) which, she notes, would be worth around $4 million if it wasn't a copy. She also, correctly, identifies a sculpture by Louis Jacques Mandé Daguerre (1789-1851). Among popular San Francisco landmarks seen in stock footage in this, and many future, episodes are the Golden Gate Bridge, Fisherman's Wharf, the TransAmerica Pyramid and the city's famous Powell-Hyde cable cars.

'You May Remember Me ...': Barbara Pilavin's movies include *Sweet Jane*, *Vice Squad* and *Red Shoe Diaries*. Cynthia King appeared in *Shrink Rap*. Bailey Chase played Graham in *Buffy the Vampire Slayer* and was in *Sweet Valley High*. Leigh Allyn Baker's CV includes *Will & Grace* and *Very Mean Men*. Julie Araskog has appeared in *Freeway*, *Nixon*, *Se7en* and *Angel*. Ben Caswell was in *JAG*. Todd Feder's movies include *The Lost Boys*. Marc Shelton was in *Agent Cody Banks*. Neil Roberts appeared in *Family Affairs*. Michael Philip was a regular in the soap *The Guiding Light*. Ralph Manza's extensive CV includes *Get Shorty*, *The Cat from Outer Space*, *The High Chapperal*, *Soap*, *Get Smart* and *Chico and the Man*. Tamara Lee Krinsky appeared in *Star Trek: First Contact*.

Cigarettes and Alcohol: Alec buys Phoebe a Martini in the (oddly named) [quake] restaurant.

Sex and Drugs and Rock n Roll: Immediately after the previous episode, Prue slept with Andy. She spends this episode suffering from obvious post-coital guilt. Piper *never* has sex on a first date. Phoebe, though, has. And not infrequently, either.

Logic, Let Me Introduce You To This Window: Because this episode was made some time after 'Something Wicca This Way Comes', there are inevitable visual continuity errors. For example, the restaurant in which Piper works bears no resemblance to the one seen during the pilot. In the previous episode it had a different name: *L'Opera Ristorante* as opposed to [quake]. At the restaurant, when Phoebe is talking to Alec, in some shots Phoebe's face is resting on her hand, whilst in others, it isn't. Rex Buckland, seemingly owns the entire 12-storey building that we see Prue go into, judging from the large sign at the door – which seems somewhat ostentatious for an auction house. In the restaurant, Stefan looks at his left hand as it begins to age. However, when he grabs Phoebe in the car after she has her premonition, the same hand is normal-looking again.

Piper watches a documentary about Salem that claims Mary Easty was struck by a bolt of lightning when she tried to enter a church to protest her innocence and was subsequently burned at the stake. That's *all* complete nonsense. None of those executed at Salem was burned. In reality, 19 were hanged and one, Giles Corey, was crushed to death by having a large stone placed on him. Mary Towne Easty *was* one of three sisters in Salem who found themselves accused. Mary was tried, declared innocent, and freed. However because of a public outcry against her release from prison, she was re-arrested and, subsequently, hanged.[29]

Continuity: Since the last episode, Chef Moore (he of the phoney accent) has quit at the restaurant, [quake] (established 1987), to open his own place, leaving a reluctant Piper in charge. Prue and Andy went to high school together and it was then that they were an item. Prue hasn't seen Andy for seven years. The loathsome Roger gave Prue exactly the sort of dreadful reference that she predicted he would in the previous episode. Piper's power of freezing time doesn't work on her sisters. Piper is envious of Phoebe's lack of fear. Phoebe notes that this does have certain disadvantages, however, as it often gets her into trouble.

Motors: Piper drives a black Cherokee Jeep (3B583Y8). Prue's car is a rather nice black Sebring (2WAQ233).

Quote/Unquote: Prue, to Andy: 'Do you want me to toss you a life preserver now, or just let you sink on your own?'
Piper: 'Andy called … Bad date?' Prue: 'Not at all. You know, dinner, movies, sex.' Piper: 'On your *first date*? You *sleaze*.'
Piper: 'Prue slept with Andy.' Prue: 'Thanks a lot, *mouth*.' Phoebe: 'You were gonna tell her but not me? *Family meeting*.'
Piper: 'Don't put me in the middle.' Prue: 'You were *born* in the middle.'

---

[29] Mary's sisters were Rebecca Nurse and Sarah Cloyce. All were, apparently, intelligent, well-educated and devoutly religious women. They could easily have saved themselves by confessing to the charges but they chose, instead, to protest their innocence. Rebecca, one of the first to be accused, was hanged in July 1692. Sarah was cleared by the court the following year, but she was damaged by her ordeal and died soon afterwards. Descendants of all three women still live in Massachusetts today.

SEASON 1: I'VE GOT YOU UNDER MY SKIN

Notes: 'Yeah, I'm charmed all right.' Essentially, a second pilot episode, with a few subtle characterisation tweaks (Prue is far less of the mother-figure than she was in 'Something Wicca This Way Comes' and much more the kind of girl who hops into bed with the first badge who comes along). The plot is *really* uninvolving, with exposition overloads and dramatic clichés that are painfully obvious in places. (The prominence given to Brittany's tattoo in the opening scene tells the viewer exactly how the *denouement* is going to be reached 40 minutes later.) Yet, despite some inept flourishes, it's hard not to love any episode that features Phoebe getting herself tied up in such a fetishistically *The Avengers*-like fashion. Best bits: Piper's panic attack after she freezes everyone in the kitchen; and her joy at *not* being struck by lightning when she enters the church.

Soundtrack: Natalie Imbruglia's 'Torn' features prominently. Also, Smash Mouth's 'Walkin' On The Sun' and Phil Collins's 'Another Day In Paradise'.

Did You Know?: *The Book of Shadows* prop weighs nine pounds, six ounces and is easily the most valuable item on set, having cost approximately $20,000 to make.

3: THANK YOU FOR NOT MORPHING

21 October 1998

Writer: Chris Levinson, Zach Estrin
Director: Ellen Pressman

Cast: Tony Denison (Victor Halliwell), Markus Flanagan (Marshall), Eric Matheny (Fritz), Mariah O'Brien (Cyndra), James Dineen (Mailman)

> The sisters' father, Victor, drops in for a surprise visit after something like a 20 year absence. When the Manor is broken into – with *The Book of Shadows* the apparent target for the intruder – Prue believes that her father is obviously responsible. But it turns out that the Halliwells' new neighbours are demons who are desperate to gain the power of the book.

The Conspiracy Starts at the Witching Hour: Marshall, Fritz and Cyndra are a trio of shapeshifters. If Phoebe's comments are accurate then, in addition to wanting *The Book of Shadows*, one of them may also have stolen Phoebe's Pat Boone Christmas CD.

It's a Designer Label!: You just gotta love the girls' party clothes – particularly Prue's insanely tight black miniskirt. It must cut off the blood-flow to the poor girl's brain, that.

References: Allusions to Shakespeare's *Julius Caesar*; the basketball teams the San Francisco Warriors and the Los Angeles Lakers; the advertising slogan of *Yellow Pages* ('Let your fingers do the walking'); the character Tabitha from *Bewitched*; and the *Star Trek* episode 'The Enemy Within' ('Kill us both'). The fake Piper reads a copy of *Living Times* magazine. There's a visual reference to the schlock horror classic *Zoltan, Hound of Dracula*.

'You May Remember Me ...': Tony Denison appeared in *Road Kill, A Brilliant Disguise, Wiseguy* and *The Lone Gunmen*. Markus Flanagan's CV includes *Holiday in the Sun, Biloxi Blues, Apollo 11* and *Melrose Place*. James Dineen was in *ER*. Marian O'Brien's movies include *Ordinary Madness* and *Being John Malkovich*. Peter Blackwell was in *Passions*. Eric Matheny has appeared in *CSI*, *Buffy the Vampire Slayer* and *Early Edition*.

Behind the Camera: The writing team of Chris Levinson (the daughter of legendary TV writer Richard Levinson, co-creator of *Columbo* amongst many other achievements) and Zach Estrin subsequently worked on *Miracles* and *Tru Calling*.

Logic, Let Me Introduce You To This Window: At the beginning of the episode, Prue comes home to find a dog in the Manor, which is subsequently revealed to be a shapeshifter. The dog is also shown lurking outside the house before the girls leave but, when they get to the party opposite, all three of the shapeshifters are there. So, who was the dog? In this episode, the sisters' father is credited, on-screen, as 'Victor Halliwell'. However, subsequently in 'That 70s Episode' it's established that Halliwell is Patty's maiden name and, thereafter, Victor is renamed. Victor mentions at dinner that he last saw Piper and Phoebe when they were four and one respectively. Yet in flashback scenes in 'That 70s Episode', Piper appears to be about three, Phoebe hasn't even been born yet and Victor has already left. To further complicate matters, it would have been impossible for Victor to have abandoned the family before Phoebe was born because at the end of this episode he gives Prue a videotape of the whole family at Christmas. In this, Phoebe looks to be about two years old. In 'Something Wicca This Way Comes,' Phoebe knew enough about her father to tell Prue that he was living in New York, and the strong implication is that she moved there either to be with him or, at least, to see him. This episode suggests quite the opposite.

When Piper freezes time in the restaurant, the flame on the dessert starts moving again when Piper grabs it a split second before she unfreezes everything. The shapeshifter unlocks the front door by changing his finger into a key. He then goes to the attic door and, finding it locked, gets frustrated and bangs down the door. Why doesn't he do the finger-into-key trick again? When Prue finds 'Andy' in her house, someone is sitting in the kitchen in the background, probably a member of the production team. Phoebe has a newspaper in her hand when she is talking to her father outside the Manor. When she runs inside having realised that Marshall, and not her father, is the one after *The Book of Shadows*, the paper has disappeared. Could Victor's sideburns in the '70s video *be* any more fake?

Continuity: As a child, Prue played the piano. She also once broke her arm. Phoebe could swim before she could walk. She says that she is 'barely legal' which, thankfully, seems to refer to her status with regard to alcohol rather than sex. Thus, she's 21. Piper is three years older than Phoebe (something subsequently contradicted). Grams always told Prue, Piper and Phoebe that their father was a threat to them. *The Book of Shadows* can, it seems, protect itself from theft. It also has the uncanny knack of finding the very spell that the girls need at any given moment, which, they subsequently discover, is often down to their grandmother's otherworldly intervention.

Quote/Unquote: Prue: 'We could rely on our vicious guard-cat to protect us. Or we could remember to lock the doors.'

Victor: 'I can see we have some issues to work through.' Prue: 'We've got the whole subscription.'

Phoebe: 'One day I'm a member of the Y-Generation with average hair and a thing for caffeinated beverages. The next, I'm a witch.'

Piper: 'First we didn't *have* a dad, and now we have *two*?'

Note: 'There's a good chance dad doesn't even know we're charmed.' This is not a patch on the previous episodes. Any suspense and intrigue that the story could have potentially generated is destroyed when, having raised the possibility that Victor may be working with the shapeshifters, the next scene reveals that, actually, he isn't. Ugly special effects, and very poor performances from some of the guest cast, don't help either.

Did You Know?: This episode sees the first appearance of future regular Brian Krause, who had originally auditioned unsuccessfully for the role of Andy.

Soundtrack: Remy Zero's 'Prophecy'.

4: DEAD MAN DATING

28 October 1998

Writer: Javier Grillo-Marxuach
Director: Richard Compton

Cast: Todd Newton (Yama), John Cho (Mark Chao), Patricia Harty (Mrs Correy), Elizabeth Sung (Mrs Chao), William Francis McGuire (Nick Correy), Joe Hoe (Tony Wong), Sherrie Rose (Susan Trudeau), Randelle Grenachia (Frankie)

> When Mark, a young man unjustly murdered, returns from the grave as a ghost, he seeks Piper's help to get his body buried before his soul is claimed by a Chinese demon and he is cast into Hell. With Prue's birthday coming up, Phoebe takes a job to earn money to buy her a gift, and becomes involved in a quest to save an ungrateful man's life.

Work is a Four-Letter Word: Phoebe gets herself a job as a lobby psychic at the Hotel Neptune.

A Little Learning is a Dangerous Thing: Picking up the wallet of a man drinking at the bar, Phoebe has a vision of him dying when hit by a car. She finally tracks down the man, Nick Correy, but is unable to convince him that she is anything other than a lunatic. Nevertheless, she manages to save his life. And she charges him 20 dollars for the privilege.

References: The title alludes to Tim Robbins's powerful 1995 exposé of death row, *Dead Man Walking*. Mark thinks his mother is like actress Shirley MacLaine. There is a possible oblique allusion to the *Buffy the Vampire Slayer* episode 'Becoming' ('Close your eyes'). A copy of the *San Francisco Herald* features the headline TONY WONG FOUND DEAD. Piper reads a beautiful passage from Albert Camus's THE PLAGUE ('A loveless world is a dead world. And always there comes an hour where one is weary of prisons and all one craves for is a warm face. The warmth and wonder of a loving heart.') The costume Phoebe wears at her job was obviously inspired by that of the title character in *I Dream of Jeannie*.

'You May Remember Me ...': Todd Newton is the host of *Hollywood Showdown*. Joe Hoe appeared in *Green Dragon*. William McGuire was in *Tru*

SEASON 1: DEAD MAN DATING

Confessions. John Cho is the lead singer with LA band Left of Zed. He played John in the *American Pie* trilogy. Elizabeth Sung was in *Lethal Weapon 4* and *Restless* and directed the film *Requiem*. Sherrie Rose's CV includes *The Girl's Life, Guns and Lipstick* and *After School*. Patricia Harty was the eponymous star of *Blondie* and appeared in *The Virginian, The Odd Couple* and *Route 66*.

Behind the Camera: Javier Grillo-Marxuach's CV also includes scripts for *Lost, Boomtown, Dark Skies, Law & Order: Special Victims Unit* and the movie *Cops On the Edge: Episode 89* (which he also directed). Richard Compton was originally an actor who appeared in *Star Trek*. As a director he worked on *LA Law, The X-Files, Babylon 5* and *The Sentinel*.

Logic, Let Me Introduce You To This Window: Despite Prue's assertion that Tony Wong killed Mark because they look like each other, they *really* don't. The differences are not only facial – burning Mark's body takes care of that – but Mark is *much* taller than Wong. Mark is non-corporeal and can move through objects. Yet he needs Piper to open the car door so he can get in. Indeed, *Charmed*'s presentation of ghosts is somewhat inconsistent. In addition to Mark, we see numerous subsequent examples – Jackson ('The Power of Two') and Charlene ('Ex Libris') for instance, not to mention Grams and Patty. Sometimes they can touch objects, sometimes they can't. Doesn't anyone at Mark's funeral notice Prue, Piper and Phoebe talking to thin air? Phoebe and Prue are in Prue's bedroom watching television. In the next scene, Piper and Mark arrive at the Manor, and then Piper is kidnapped. Phoebe and Prue rush downstairs, and they're wearing clothes completely different from those seen in the previous scene. There is no channel ID on the TV news as there are on all US networks.

Continuity: Prue likes honest men, but hates surprises. Piper – despite her professional chef credentials – has never made Peking duck. She says that her grandmother taught her to cook. She has also never seen someone killed before Andy shoots Tony Wong. At least, not anyone *human*. Andy has an ex-wife called Susan with whom he still gets on quite well.

Motors: A pink Cadillac (2QR1445) makes a significant contribution to the episode.

Quote/Unquote: Andy: 'I was nowhere near the neighbourhood. Thought I'd stop by.'
    Piper: 'At least tell me you've managed to get Prue something other than your traditional birthday gift ... A card, three days late.'
    Phoebe: 'We're the Charmed Ones, Prue, not the Doomed Ones. We

have lives just like everyone else.'

Notes: 'Birthdays are important. I know, I walked out of my last one and it never occurred to me that I wouldn't get another.' Something of a shameless tear-jerker that, quite remarkably, transcends its manipulative origins to become a beautiful, redemptive essay on hope. 'Dead Man Dating' could have been *horrible*, mawkish and trite, but the emotion that Holly Marie Combs and John Cho give to their scenes raises it far above expectations. Not only that, but the Phoebe subplot is rather good, too – a nice mixture of silly humour and profundity. All in all, an early sign of *Charmed*'s potential. Best bits: The wonderfully played Piper/Mark relationship. Piper freezing Wong's bullet in mid-air.

Soundtrack: Includes 'Secret Smile' by Semisonic, Paula Cole's 'Hush Hush Hush' and Beth Nielsen Chapman's 'Sand And Water'.

Did You Know?: The telephone number that Piper finds circled in the newspaper is 415-555-0163. If you've ever wondered why 555 is used so often as a telephone prefix in US TV shows, the answer is that when exchange names were part of phone numbers, digits also corresponded to letters, the first three signifying the exchange that the caller was dialling. 5 was J K and L and there aren't many American place-names that use only a combination of those letters. Due to the low number of 555 codes, Hollywood was encouraged to quote them in their productions to prevent real telephone subscribers being harassed by people trying out numbers they'd heard in the movies. Now the 555 code *is* used by various Internet service providers, and 555-0100 to 555-0199 are specifically set aside by Bellcore for the entertainment industry.

5: DREAM SORCERER

4 November 1998

Writer: Constance M Burge
Director: Nick Marck

Cast: Matt Schulze (Whitaker Berman/Dream Sorcerer), Neil Roberts (Rex Buckland), J Robin Miller (Skye Russell), Alex Mendoza (Jack Manford), Tim Herzog (Hans), James Howell (Technician #1), James O'Shea (Goatee Guy), Marie O'Donnell (Dr Black), Todd Howk (ER Nurse), Trish Suhr (Paramedic #1), Doug Spearman (Nurse),Bo Clancy (Businessman), Rainoldo Gooding (Guy #1)

> Prue finds her sleep disturbed by strange visions in which she's taunted by a man. Capable of subconscious stalking, the Dream Sorcerer has already four killed women while they sleep. Elsewhere, Phoebe and Piper cast a spell to attract men. Unfortunately, it has side effects, and they must deal with a plethora of amorous admirers.

Dreaming (As Blondie Once Said) is Free: The episode includes a series of sinister and erotic dreams – in the best, Prue falls asleep in the bath and finds herself at the mercy of the Dream Sorcerer, who tries to drown her.

A Little Learning is a Dangerous Thing: Piper know that while this may not sound very PC, she wants romance in a relationship. Long, slow kisses, late-night talks, candlelight. She loves love and wants a man who is single, smart and employed (and, possibly, well-endowed). A man who loves sleeping in on Sunday, sunset bike rides and cuddling by a roaring fire. Phoebe, by contrast, is seeking the sexy, silent type who will take her driving through town on the back of a Harley at 3:00 am. A man who appreciates scented candles, body oils and Italian sheets. He must also be about hunger, lust and danger, recycle frequently (and *definitely* be well-endowed).

It's Witchcraft: Phoebe notes that the girls are lucky. If they were men looking for women, the spell would require them to put a piece of honey cake in a sweaty armpit for day. As it is, she and Piper must still intone a very silly spell. ('I conjure thee, I conjure thee/I am the queen, you're the bee/As I desire, so shall it be.')

SEASON 1: DREAM SORCERER

The Conspiracy Starts at the Witching Hour: Whitaker Berman runs a privately-funded research facility studying the possibilities of so-called 'dream-leaping', the ability to project oneself into someone else's dreams. Andy and Darryl speculate that Berman has found a way to do exactly this into the dreams of women who reject him. The first victim was Julie Derrickson, Berman's girlfriend. She broke up with him whilst they were driving. This caused an accident that left Berman paralysed. The day after Berman went back to work at the lab, Julie died in suspicious circumstances. Three further victims have died in the six months since, including Skye, a waitress at [quake]. All were, apparently, crushed to death as though they had fallen from a tall building, despite being found in their own beds.

It's a Designer Label: Phoebe's fluffy pink jumper.

References: *A Nightmare on Elm Street*. There's an oblique reference to The Doors' 'Celebration of the Lizard' ('I can do *anything*'). Also allusions to: *The Burns and Allen Show*; *The Godfather* (Prue stabbing the Dream Sorcerer in the hand); Oliver Cromwell (1599-1658); Dutch painter Rembrandt Harmensz van Rijn (1606-69); and novelist Ernest Hemingway (1899-1961).

'You May Remember Me ...': Matt Schulze played Crease in *Blade*. J Robin Miller was in *S Club 7 in Hollywood*. Alex Mendoza's CV includes *Crusade* and *Xena: Warrior Princess*. Tim Herzog appeared in *The Animals*. Bo Clancy was in *Roswell*. Doug Spearman appeared in *Star Trek: Voyager*. Marie O'Donnell was in *7th Heaven*. James O'Shea played Mac in *Slash* and Racer in *The Forsaken*. James Howell's CV includes *Flipping* and *The X-Files*. Rainoldo Gooding was in *To Protect and Serve*. Trish Suhr appeared in *Spiral*.

Behind the Camera: Nick Marck began as an assistant director on *10*, *Battlestar Galactica*, *The Postman Always Rings Twice* and *Rehearsal for Murder* before becoming a director on *The Wonder Years*, *The X-Files*, *Dawson's Creek* and *Malcolm in the Middle*.

Sex and Drugs and Rock n Roll: Phoebe and Hans, her new spell-induced boyfriend, have safe sex. *Lots* of it, apparently.

Logic, Let Me Introduce You to This Window: If the Dream Sorcerer knew what Prue was thinking whilst she was dreaming, shouldn't he also have realised that she's a witch? Phoebe goes to [quake] to see if the spell worked. Why isn't Piper already there?

SEASON 1: DREAM SORCERER

Cruelty To Animals: The Halliwells' cat (see 'Something Wicca This Way Comes') is in the same room as Phoebe and Piper when they cast the love-spell and has its life made miserable by 'horny' tom-cats.

Continuity: Prue is 27 (and, thus, three years older than Piper and six years older than Phoebe). Her favourite meal is cheeseburger and fries (with *her* figure, surely not ...?) Piper suggests that when she gets stressed, she get hives in strange places. Which is nothing compared to what happens when she panics.

Quote/Unquote: Dream Sorcerer: 'It's your dream. But it's *my* fantasy.'
    Phoebe: 'How is asking for what you want being desperate? I say it's empowering.'
    Piper: 'Love is a magic between two people that cannot be explained [or] conjured.'

Notes: 'You're in my world now.' Taking the popular maxim 'Be careful what you wish for, it might just come true' to a logical extreme, 'Dream Sorcerer' is very much a game of two halves. The 'Prue's nightmare' plot is rather good, with red-filtered dreamy eroticism and, despite some scenery chewing by Matt Schulze, a hint of genuine menace. Unfortunately, the 'Phoebe and Piper try a love-spell' conceit is hackneyed and obvious. There's also a completely undramatic *deus ex machina* conclusion that undercuts the carefully built tension of what's gone before. Despite this, and some *Nightmare on Elm Street* riffs that betray a lack of imagination, the episode at least has good direction and Shannen Doherty acting her little cotton socks off to its credit.

Soundtrack: The song heard during the dream sequence is 'A Stroke of Luck' by Garbage.

Did You Know?: Alyssa Milano liked the drawings made for *The Book of Shadows* so much that she had the artist who designed them paint murals on the walls of her spacious Malibu home.

6: THE WEDDING FROM HELL

11 November 1998

Writer: Greg Elliot, Michael Perricone
Director: Richard Ginty

Cast: Sara Rose Peterson (Jade D'Mon/Hecate), Barbara Stock (Grace Spencer), Deeny Consiglio (Kirsten), Neil Roberts (Rex Buckland), Christie Lynn Smith (Allison Michaels), Leigh Allyn-Baker (Hannah Webster), Todd Cattell (Elliott Spencer), Jeffrey Hutchinson (Father Trask), Roy Abramsohn (Doctor), Jennifer Badger (Bridesmaid #1), Eileen Weisinger (Bridesmaid #2), Bill Ferrell (Security Guard #1), Thomas Crawford (Security Guard #2), James Geralden (Justice Of The Peace), David Moreland (Charles), Phoenix Nugent (Seamstress), Leon Franco (Male Stripper)

> Grace Spencer made a promise to marry her son, Greg, to Hecate, Queen of the Underworld, many years ago in return for power and wealth. Now, on the eve of Greg's wedding to his beloved fiancée, Allison, Hecate is back to claim her husband. Piper, catering at the wedding with help from Phoebe, inevitably becomes involved. A priest attempts to vanquish the demon. When he falls to his death, Andy takes his sacrificial knife to Prue to establish its historical purpose. Meanwhile, Phoebe has a premonition that Piper is pregnant with a demon child.

It's Witchcraft: The knife is, Prue suggests, a 14th Century Italian jewelled *poignard* with the inscription *NEC PRIUS ABSISTIT QUOAD PROTERO PRODIGIUM* on the blade. Translated from Latin, this reads, 'I shall not rest until the demon is vanquished.'

The Conspiracy Starts at the Witching Hour: Hecate comes to Earth each 200 years to wed an innocent. Once the marriage is consummated, Hecate will be impregnated.

Rex Buckland and Pouty Hannah (see 'I've Got You Under My Skin') deliver a rare fertility statue to Hecate as a wedding gift. Both seem to have some dark and nefarious secret to hide from Prue. They cannot risk going to the wedding, for a variety of reasons, but Rex offers to take Heather to a football game instead, so she can enjoy watching players getting injured.

SEASON 1: THE WEDDING FROM HELL

Work is a Four-Letter Word: Phoebe is hired to help Piper with the wedding catering at $10 per hour.

It's a Designer Label!: Piper's and Phoebe's somewhat less-than-practical low-cut waitress outfits. Phoebe recognises that Jade's wedding dress is a Shiro.

References: Conceptually influenced by the 'devil-child' school of schlock horror (*I Don't Want to Be Born*, *The Omen*, *Rosemary's Baby*). Greg reads a copy of *Honeymoon* magazine. There are oblique allusions to *Touched By An Angel* and *Honey, I Shrunk the Kids*. One of the presents that her carnivorous bridesmaids give Hecate is a copy of *Faust* by Johann Wolfgang von Goethe (1749-1832). Stock footage features San Francisco landmarks Pier 39 and the Coit Tower.

'You May Remember Me ...': Sara Rose Peterson appeared in *Friends*. Barbara Stock played Nicole Devlin in *Port Charles* and was in *Dallas* and *MacGyver*. Deeny Consiglio appeared in *Grand Avenue*. Christie Lynn Smith's CV includes *CSI* and *Malcolm in the Middle*. Todd Cattell appeared in *Special Unit 2*. Jeffrey Hutchinson's movies include *Lingerie Kickboxer*. Roy Abramsohn was in *Picket Fences*. Jennifer Badger was Charisma Carpenter's stunt-double on *Buffy the Vampire Slayer* and *Angel* and also appeared in *Summer of Sam*. David Moreland was in *Legally Blonde* and *Becker*. Thomas Crawford's CV includes *Catch Me if You Can*, *Apollo 13*, *The Net* and *The West Wing*. Bill Ferrell was in *Blue Streak*. James Geralden appeared in *The X-Files*. Eileen Weisinger is a stuntperson who had worked on *Not Another Teen Movie*, *Charlie's Angels* and *The Faculty*.

Behind the Camera: Michael Perricone was an assistant engineer on *The Muppet Movie*.

Logic, Let Me Introduce You To This Window: 'The Wedding From Hell' was actually the second episode into production, but was subsequently broadcast sixth. This accounts for several pieces of discontinuity. For example, Piper has to substitute for Chef Moore, who was said to have left [quake] in 'I've Got You Under My Skin'. Also, Piper takes a pregnancy test after her fling with Jeremy that, according to various on-screen references, ended with his death between six and eight weeks earlier. Jade's assistant manages to haul Allison out of the mansion and be upstairs attacking Father Trask more or less simultaneously. When the demon-bridesmaids push the Halliwells into the bedroom, Prue drops her purse. In the next shot, she still has it in her hand. Subsequently, Elliott picks up the dagger lying next to the purse on the floor. Yet, Prue had the dagger when it was last seen, and she entered the bedroom from a different direction. When Jade summons storm clouds to block the sun, the lighting on the outdoor set of the wedding never changes.

Continuity: Phoebe has previously attended college and is thinking about going back. Prue has a Toshiba laptop in her office at Buckland's. Andy can read lips.

Quote/Unquote: Prue, banging on the bathroom door: 'You're positive?' Piper, looking at her pregnancy test: 'I hope not.'
    Andy: 'Sorry the dead man on your driveway is such an inconvenience.' Darryl: 'Welcome to the lifestyles of the rich and shameless.'
    Piper: 'You'll never greet your husband with "Hon, I think I froze the kids again."' Prue: 'No, I just accidentally moved them to another zip code.' Phoebe: 'But I'll see them, find them and bring them home safely.'

Notes: 'There are many things about our family that you will never understand.' It's not hard to see why this episode was held back in the transmission order. Because it's absolute rubbish, basically. It's quite *appallingly* over-acted by the guest cast, features crass dialogue and a pair of tissue-paper-thin lovers, has a plot that runs, almost entirely, on co-incidences, and a hugely contrived ending. Easily the worst episode of *Charmed* thus far.

Did You Know?: The names of the lovers in this episode – Allison Michaels and Elliott Spencer – derive from the names of the two scriptwriters.

Soundtrack: 'Evidence' by Tara MacLean, 'Your Woman' by White Town, and the Goo Goo Dolls' 'Slide'.

7: THE FOURTH SISTER

18 November 1998

Writer: Edithe Swensen
Director: Gilbert Adler

Cast: Danielle Harris (Aviva), Rebekah Carlton (Kali), Rebecca Balding (Aunt Jackie), Michael LeBlanc (Video Clerk)

> Prue tries, repeatedly, to spend time with Andy, while Phoebe and Piper battle for the attention of Leo. A troubled teenager, Aviva, befriends Phoebe after finding the sisters' missing cat. But Aviva is being manipulated by Kali, a sorceress who appears through a mirror. Her mission is to gain the Halliwell sisters' trust and steal their powers.

It's Witchcraft: Kali is, according to *The Book of Shadows*, a sorceress cursed into her own dimension. She has the power to possess innocents and use them as pawns to steal another witch's power. To vanquish Kali, her reflection must be shattered.

A Little Learning is a Dangerous Thing: Aviva sneaks out of school to meet Phoebe. She guesses (correctly) that Phoebe used to do similar things when she was Aviva's age.

The Conspiracy Starts at the Witching Hour: Andy finally grows tired of Prue not trusting him enough to tell him the reason why she is constantly calling off dates at the last moment.

It's a Designer Label!: Prue's leather skirt and Phoebe's incredibly tight, sky blue T-shirt take the immediate attention. Several minus points, however, for Aviva's general Goth-chick look.

References: The title may be drawn from Paul Verhoeven's 1983 art-house black-comedy *The Fourth Man*. Kali is named after the Hindi mother-Goddess.[30] Andy and Prue, hiring a video, can't decide between *Lethal*

---

[30] The consort of Shiva, Kali is frequently depicted as a laughing, naked hag with blood-stained teeth. Kali's worshipers purportedly appeased her with human sacrifices (see the shenanigans of *Help!* for a comic western take on this). As Bhavani, she was invoked by the secret brotherhood of 18th Century assassins and scoundrels called Thugs. Calcutta gets its name from Kalighata, a temple dedicated to Kali.

SEASON 1: THE FOURTH SISTER

Weapon III (not very romantic) and Billy Wilder's *Double Indemnity* ('In black and white!'). In the end, the store clerk chooses *Body Heat* for them. Also, *The Simpsons* ('Your point being ...?') and *Sibling Rivalry*. Leo tells Piper that in Mayan culture, the cook was second in hierarchy only to the medicine man. Aviva has posters with the slogans 'Creepy Crawlings' and 'Live Monsters' on her bedroom wall. There's stock footage of Bay General Hospital.

'You May Remember Me ...': Danielle Harris played Suzi in *Poor White Trash* and also appeared in *City Slickers*, *The West Wing* and *Roseanne*. Rebekah Carlton was Tracy in *Baywatch*. Rebecca Balding's CV includes *Silent Scream*, *Lou Grant* and *Starsky and Hutch*.

Behind the Camera: Edithe Swensen also worked on *Odyssey 5*, *Witchblade*, *Xena: Warrior Princess* and *Star Trek: The Next Generation*.

The Drugs Don't Work: Aviva's mother is currently in rehab.

Sex and Drugs and Rock n Roll: Piper and Phoebe spend a few blissful seconds staring, lovingly, at Leo's bottom.

Logic, Let Me Introduce You To This Window: If Aviva had evilly-induced powers, wouldn't she have been frozen when Piper froze the room? Aviva's black lipstick occasionally disappears and reappears between shots. If Kit always hisses at anyone evil, why doesn't it react when Aviva picks it up and Kali is watching from the mirror? People with concussion, like Aviva's aunt, usually experience considerable disorientation if they attempt to sit upright. When Kali appears in Phoebe's mirror while Phoebe is sleeping, in one shot the bed is empty. Aviva leaves her sweater in the sun room but later we see it lying in the kitchen. Do Leo's handyman duties really include both putting up and taking down 'Missing Cat' flyers? Phoebe's hair length changes between scenes. Piper accuses Phoebe of kissing her boyfriend, Billy Wilson 'at Homecoming'. Given that Piper is two or three years older than Phoebe, and that Phoebe mentions she was in 8th Grade when this happened, she'd have been 13 at the time. What was a 13 year old doing at a Homecoming Prom?

Cruelty To Animals: Kit has disappeared. In actual fact, Aviva stole the cat so that she could use the pretext of returning it to become friendly with the sisters.

Continuity: The Halliwells' address is 7571 Prescott Street (however, see 'Is There a Woogy in the House?'). Their telephone number is 555-0198.

SEASON 1: THE FOURTH SISTER

Both Prue and Piper consider Phoebe a 'boyfriend thief.' The former, regarding Roger (see 'Something Wicca This Way Comes'), the latter over Billy Wilson. Prue, apparently, sleeps with the light on.

Quote/Unquote: Leo: 'Does Phoebe work here, too?' Piper: 'Phoebe? Work? No, no, no. She's probably at her Gay and Lesbian support group.'

Piper: 'You were all over him with your breasts all … whatever.' Phoebe: 'I didn't even have breasts back then.' Piper: 'Phoebe, you've *always* had breasts.'

Leo: 'Are you and Aviva …? Piper said …' Phoebe: 'You should probably take it with a grain of salt, because sometimes her medication makes her say the strangest things. But don't worry, her shrinks are on it.'

Notes: 'She's a strange kid. Into all sorts of weird stuff … No wonder she doesn't have any friends.' This episode features a thoroughly rotten attempt at Generation X – Aviva's entire 'I'm a moody outsider' thing grows old *very* quickly. Edithe Swensen appears to have picked up all her ideas on how '90s teenagers behave – as sulky brats who, in reality, just wanna be loved – exclusively from a bunch of Nirvana CDs. Nevertheless, 'The Fourth Sister' actually isn't bad dramatically, and the deeper characterisation of the sisters is quietly impressive. It could've done with a bit more reality in its presentation of adolescence, however.

Soundtrack: 'Wheel' by UMA and 'Lady in the Lake' by Elysian Fields.

8: THE TRUTH IS OUT THERE ... AND IT HURTS

25 November 1998

Writer: Zack Estrin, Chris Levinson
Director: James A Contner

Cast: Brad Greenquist (Warlock), Michelle Brookhurst (Tanya Parker), Leigh Allyn-Baker (Hannah Webster), Neil Roberts (Rex Buckland), Jason Stuart (Martin), Richard Gilbert-Hill (Dr Oliver Mitchell), Craig Thomas (Alex Pearson)

> Acting on a premonition of Phoebe's, the sisters race to stop the murder of a pregnant woman. Meanwhile, Prue discovers a temporary truth spell and uses it to observe Andy's reaction to her being a witch. Unfortunately, it doesn't affect just her and Andy, but also her sisters. And everyone with whom they come into contact.

Dreaming (As Blondie Once Said) is Free: Phoebe has a vision of the murder of Tanya, the sandwich girl who works at Buckland's.

The Conspiracy Starts at the Witching Hour: The sinister killer with the third eye in the middle of his forehead is, in reality, a warlock from the future who had come back in time to destroy all those who will, at some stage, contribute toward creating a vaccine deadly to those like him.

The man found murdered in the movie theatre parking lot was Dr Oliver Mitchell, whose work, specifically on cell degeneration, is considered ahead of its time. At some stage in the future, Mitchell will have an article on the mutant retina gene published (seemingly posthumously). The second victim was an Oakland lab technician, Alex Pearson. Tanya Parker's unborn child will use the pioneering work of Mitchell and Pearson to create the vaccine.

It's Witchcraft: The truth spell begins: 'For those who want the truth revealed, open hearts and secrets unsealed ...'

A Little Learning is a Dangerous Thing: Hannah Webster suggests that it's her mission in life to destroy Prue. Rex Buckland hustles her out of the room before she can add that she is talking literally, not metaphorically.

SEASON 1: THE TRUTH IS OUT THERE ... AND IT HURTS

The implication that's been brewing since 'I've Got You Under My Skin' that either Hannah, or Rex, or both are demons is partially confirmed when Hannah lights Rex's cigar with her breath.

References: The title refers to a phrase made famous by *The X-Files*. Phoebe has a Magic 8-ball toy. Someone from the future travelling back in time to kill a woman who will give birth to an, as yet unborn, child is an age-old SF standard central to, for example, *The Outer Limits* episodes 'Soldier' and 'Demon with a Glass Hand', not to mention *The Terminator*.

'You May Remember Me ...': Brad Greenquist appeared in *Crime And Punishment in Suburbia*, *Gang Related* and *Stargate SG-1*. Michelle Brookhurst played Molly in *Can't Hardly Wait* and Cindy in *Foxfire*. Craig Thomas was in *Babylon 5* and *NYPD Blue*. Jason Stuart's CV includes *Bad Boy* and *Murder One*. Richard Gilbert-Hill appeared in *The Bonfire of the Vanities* and *Star Trek: The Next Generation*. He also wrote episodes of *Highlander*.

Behind the Camera: Jim Contner's CV includes *Midnight Caller*, *21 Jump Street*, *Wiseguy*, *The Equalizer*, *Miami Vice*, *The Flash*, *SeaQuest DSV*, *Roswell*, *Dark Skies*, *American Gothic*, *The X-Files*, *Smallville*, *Enterprise*, *Firefly*, *The Dead Zone*, *Buffy the Vampire Slayer* and *Angel*. He was a cinematographer on movies like *Heat*, *Monkey Shines*, *Jaws 3-D*, *The Wiz*, *Superman* and *Times Square*. It's his camerawork on the concert footage in *Rock Show: Wings Over the World* (1976).

Cigarettes and Alcohol: Rex smokes cigars.

Logic, Let Me Introduce You To This Window: When Andy asks Prue if her children will inherit her powers, she replies, 'If they're girls ...' Of course, as we subsequently discover, Piper's *sons* also inherit their mother's and father's abilities. Andy claims that the victims of the time-travelling killer had all the colour drained from their eyes. The first victim, Mitchell, *is* left in such a condition, but the subsequent victim's eyes remain normal. How does Piper know where to find Prue and the time-travelling killer in the storage basement at Buckland's?

Continuity: The movie that Prue, Piper and Phoebe are waiting in line to see at the beginning of the episode is called *Love's Deadly Desire*. Prue secretly admires Phoebe's confidence and fearlessness. However, her younger sister's utter lack of responsibility frustrates Prue no end. Her favourite type of sandwich is turkey with no mayonnaise. Andy notes that Prue has a fondness for twizzers (a slang expression for Twizzlers – a

SEASON 1: THE TRUTH IS OUT THERE ... AND IT HURTS

candy bar made by Hershey) and that she cannot stand people who talk at previews. He also comments on how she likes to argue to win and that she picks her cuticles when she is nervous. Phoebe claims that Internet chat rooms saved her life. Piper's boss at [quake] is the camp and manipulative Martin.

Quote/Unquote: Phoebe to Piper after the truth spell begins working: 'We both know I only like Leo because you do.'
Phoebe: 'What do you think of your boss?' Piper: 'He's a self-centred jerk who must have a *very small penis.*'

Notes: 'The biggest pooper at the Wicca party has finally used her power for personal gain. About time.' A fast-paced episode that neatly balances a serious subplot with another, much funnier, one. The consequences of Prue's use of a truth spell on all concerned are often hilarious and, occasionally, very insightful. The killer-from-the-future story is less involving, although for the most part it's well-realised apart from a somewhat rushed ending (something of a recurring problem on *Charmed* during this period). Best bit: Piper's and Leo's first kiss.

Soundtrack: Merril Bainbridge's 'Love and Terror', and 'One More Murder' by Better Than Ezra.

9: THE WITCH IS BACK

16 December 1998

Writer: Sheryl J Anderson
Director: Richard Denault

Cast: Billy Wirth (Matthew Tate), Tyler Layton (Melinda Warren), Neil Roberts (Rex Buckland), Leigh Allyn-Baker (Hannah Webster), Michael Mitz (Cafe Patron), Terry Bozeman (Arnold Halliwell), Catherine Kwong (Waitress), Jodi Fung (TV Reporter)

> In the 17th Century, the Halliwells' ancestor Melinda Warren cursed a warlock to spend eternity trapped in an amulet after stealing her powers and betraying her love. Three hundred years later, Prue accidentally frees the warlock. The sisters summon Melinda from the past to re-imprison her nemesis, Matthew Tate. Meanwhile, Andy becomes frustrated by Prue's continued involvement with bizarre police investigations.

It's Witchcraft: The spell that Melinda uses to trap Matthew in the amulet begins, 'Outside of time, outside of gain, know only sorrow, know only pain.'
To bring Melinda to the 20th Century, *The Book of Shadows* has a spell of blood-calling-blood. It shouldn't hurt too much, says Phoebe hopefully.

A Little Learning is a Dangerous Thing: Arnold Halliwell (no relation) of Halliwell, Rossen & Haas Attorneys, and the unfortunate owner of Halliwell's Hardware & Appliance (also no relation), are killed by Matthew for the simple bad luck that they share a surname with Prue, Piper and Phoebe.

The Conspiracy Starts at the Witching Hour: Rex implies that he and Hannah work for some greater power in attempting to destroy the Charmed Ones. He comments about Hannah having (seemingly invisible) horns and notes that he hasn't mastered teleportation himself. Hannah can also read minds.

Work is a Four-Letter Word: Prue's office is on the twelfth floor of the Buckland's building.

References: The title alludes to Elton John's song 'The Bitch is Back'. Leo and Melinda quote from Shakespeare's *As You Like It* ('I earn that I eat, get that I wear, own no man's hate, envy no man's happiness.') Also, Robin Hood; and

SEASON 1: THE WITCH IS BACK

the Beatles' 'Tell Me What You See'.

'You May Remember Me ...': Michael Mitz's CV includes *Frasier* and *thirtysomething*. Terry Bozeman appeared in *CSI*, *24* and *Matlock*. Catherine Kwong played Lauren Chin in *The West Wing*. Tyler Layton was Detective Holly Rawlins in *Silk Stalkings* and also appeared in *Dark Skies*. Billy Wirth was in *Venus Rising* and *Sex and the City*.

Behind the Camera: Sheryl J Anderson's CV also includes scripts for the early '90s high school comedy classic *Parker Lewis Can't Lose*.

Sex and Drugs and Rock n Roll: Piper tells Phoebe that she has never asked a man out on a date before, although she overcomes that flaw in her character by asking Leo.

Logic, Let Me Introduce You To This Window: The shot of the lawyer's office is the same piece of stock footage used for Skye's apartment in 'Dream Sorcerer'. Again, no witches were burned in Salem, they were mostly hanged (see 'I've Got You Under My Skin'). Neither Melinda nor Matthew talks particularly like a 17th Century New Englander. Melinda claims that if she had used her powers to escape from Salem, it would have endangered her daughter, Prudence. Why, in that case, didn't she simply escape *with* Prudence? Melinda says that Matthew probably stole his transportation powers from another witch. We later discover that blinking is actually a warlock trait and that witches don't have it. When Prue lets Matthew out of the amulet in her office, her hand keeps moving from being by her side to her stomach between shots.

Phoebe notes that when they bring Melinda forward in time, she has all the various abilities that Prue, Piper and Phoebe possess. So, when Matthew comes to the Manor, why doesn't she used them on him? When Matthew breaks the window in Prue's office, the glass falls toward the street below. However, when the camera shows a top view of the sidewalk, it's devoid of glass. The potion for the vanquish spell is the same one that Melinda used 300 years previously. It requires a feather from an endangered spotted owl. There weren't any such owls, endangered or otherwise, on the US East Coast during the 1690s.

Continuity: When Phoebe discovers she can also see the past, Prue notes that the sisters' powers are growing. Phoebe then says that she wants to learn to fly – something she will ultimately do in season three. When the sisters are chanting to bring forth Melinda, Phoebe and Prue say six 'greats' before grandmother and Piper adds a seventh. Melinda says that *The Book of Shadows* has grown considerably since her day – each new generation adds its own spells to it. None of the sisters realised that she could do that, but Melinda tells them that as their powers grow, the book will grow with them. Piper notes that Grams must have added a spell to increase patience. Phoebe believes Grams probably used it a lot on the girls, though Prue and Piper argue that *they* weren't troublemakers. Phoebe says that, on the contrary, she was a free spirit (see 'PreWitched'). Melinda adds this is a Warren family trait. So are short tempers, great cheekbones and strong wills. One summer, when the girls were children, they were on holiday at a lake and made a blood oath to be friends forever (possibly this was Camp Skylark – see 'P^3 H^{2}O' – although if it was then it must mean they went back there after their mother died, which seems a very strange place for a family holiday). Piper's finger became infected and she couldn't go in the water for three weeks. Melinda uses Phoebe's power to see into the future and predicts many more generations of daughters after Prue, Piper and Phoebe.

Quote/Unquote: Phoebe: 'Am I the only one in this family who has inherited the "take the chance" gene?' Piper: 'Probably. Because, if I remember my biology correctly, it was connected to the "can't mind my own business" gene.'

Melinda: 'Which sheep has wool so soft?' Phoebe: 'A synthetic one.'

Melinda: 'How do you keep your legs warm?' Prue: 'We drink coffee.'

Notes: 'Great, so now I'm being hunted by a warlock *and* the San Francisco PD.' This one probably looked good on paper and, indeed, what emerges *is* a very entertaining romp – but mostly for all the wrong reasons. There's a nice performance by Tyler Layton and a completely over-the-top one from Billy Wirth and, together with some pithy dialogue, the whole thing rattles along at a fair old pace. It's only when you stop to think about some of the plot elements that it all threatens to fall to pieces in your hands like so much wet cardboard. Once again, a fundamentally good episode is let down by a weak and inelegant *denouement*. Best bits: Hannah, her sexuality barely repressed, trying to remain calm as Matthew dresses, and attempting to explain narrow and cerebral 20th Century values like political correctness and sexual harassment to him.

Soundtrack: Holly McNarland's version of 'In The Air Tonight', and 'Around Here' by Counting Crows.

Did You Know?: *Charmed*'s popularity inspired the company SOTA Toys to create 6.5 inch action figures of the characters Piper, Phoebe and, subsequently, Paige and Belthazor. These come with interlocking attic walls and a miniature *Book of Shadows*. Originally a Prue figure was envisioned, but Shannen Doherty declined to allow her likeness to be used.

10: WICCA ENVY

13 January 1999

Writers: Brad Kern, Sheryl J Anderson
Story: Brad Kern
Director: Mel Damski

Cast: Neil Roberts (Rex Buckland), Leigh Allyn-Baker (Hannah Webster), Al Rodrigo (Jaime), Tim Stark (Super)

> Prue is framed by Rex and accused of stealing from the auction house and murdering to cover up her theft. Piper and Phoebe conclude that Rex is a warlock and break Prue out of jail to help defeat him. Their plans are, apparently, ruined as Rex photographs their crime and blackmails them into giving up their powers in exchange for Prue's freedom.

It's Witchcraft: The full extent of Rex's and Hannah's powers is revealed. Both appear to be warlocks, although they could well be demons – Rex says that he misses Hell terribly. And, indeed, after Hannah kills him in her panther form, she is engulfed in flames and appears to have been taken back there for punishment. Good. Hope it hurts.

Rex has the power of astral projection, can create illusions and possesses a form of auto-suggestion to implant ideas subconsciously in people's minds. He uses this for a variety of nefarious activities, not least of which is getting Hannah to take off all her clothes in his office.

The Conspiracy Starts at the Witching Hour: We see for the first time that Leo has some form of magical power (shortly after Phoebe has speculated, less than seriously, that he might be a warlock). As he leaves the Manor, after he has (anonymously) restored the sisters' powers, he dissolves into a cascade of blue-white light. It's a while before we discover the full meaning of this, however.

Work is a Four-Letter Word: Rex says that he has set up an interview for Phoebe with the fashion department of *Zeitgeist* magazine.

It's a Designer Label!: Phoebe wants to buy an exclusive Betsy Johnson dress, despite Prue's protests about the cost. There's a lengthy – and rather effective – montage sequence during which Prue tries on most of the

SEASON 1: WICCA ENVY

contents of her wardrobe.

References: The title alludes to the sexual/psychoanalytical concept of penis envy, first postulated by Sigmund Freud (1856-1939). The episode's *MacGuffin* is a tiara said to have belonged to the Romanovs – the Russian royal family. Rex claims to be friends with British rock group The Verve. Phoebe is a big fan, considering their single 'Bittersweet Symphony' to be 'the best song ever.' Also, an allusion to *Single White Female*.

'You May Remember Me ...': Al Rodrigo appeared in *Under Suspicion* and *Star Trek: Deep Space Nine*.

Behind the Camera: Mel Damski also worked on *1-800-Missing*, *Without a Trace*, *Everwood*, *Boston Public*, *Jack & Jill*, *Ally McBeal*, *The Practice*, *American Gothic*, *Nowhere Man*, *Picket Fences*, *Lou Grant*, *The Bionic Woman*, *Barnaby Jones* and *M*A*S*H*. His CV also includes the movies *The Girl Who Came Between Them*, *Badge of the Assassin*, *Yellowbeard* and *For Ladies Only* and second unit status on *Cover Girl Models* and *Summer School Teachers*.

Cigarettes and Alcohol: Rex offers Phoebe a glass of champagne at his spectacular – if fake – apartment. She asks what the catch is and Rex says, jokingly it appears, that she has to sleep with him. He then offers her some sushi, imported fresh from Kyoto.

Sex and Drugs and Rock n Roll: The opening sequence features in a semi-clothed Piper and Leo in, very obvious, giggly pre-coital excitement. Subsequently, after a night of apparent passion, a glowing Piper rushes her sisters out to work noting that she hasn't had sex for a while.

Logic, Let Me Introduce You To This Window: Shouldn't a female officer automatically accompany Andy and Darryl when they come to search Prue's bedroom? When Piper and Phoebe break Prue out of prison, Piper stands outside and freezes the guards inside the building. This should be impossible. In several episodes – 'I've Got You Under My Skin' and 'The Wendigo' are two obvious examples – Piper demonstrates that she can freeze only things that are in the same room as she is. When the sisters look in *The Book of Shadows*, Phoebe asks if the relinquishing spell is reversible, and Piper replies 'It doesn't say.' Yet the book quite clearly states, 'This spell is to be used in dire emergency; not lightly, only by choice. *This spell is irreversible.*' When the girls get their powers back and return home, Prue rips the relinquishing spell out of the book and sets fire to it. This presumably means that she has also destroyed the spell written on the other side of the page?

SEASON 1: WICCA ENVY

During the scene where Piper is running with Leo, her blouse goes from open to buttoned and then back again. Why is the door to the prisoner lockup area unlocked, and why are men and women kept in the same cells? After freezing the guards, Piper grabs a keyring full of keys and immediately starts unlocking doors. How did she know which key to use? If Phoebe stayed outside the prison to keep watch while Piper freed Prue, then why doesn't she spot Rex standing next to his car? After Rex takes the photograph, couldn't Piper have simply frozen him and pinched his camera? According to the police computer file that Andy accesses, the real Rex Buckland's birthdate is given as 12 July 1974 which would make him approximately 24. However, the photograph shown is of a much older man.

Continuity: The Halliwell sisters' powers are manifested as shiny blue-glowy things, seemingly. The real Hannah Webster was born on 27 November 1976. Both she and the real Rex Buckland were found dead on 20 August 1998 (in other words, a few weeks before the events of 'Something Wicca This Way Comes').

Quote/Unquote: Piper: 'What the hell was that?' Phoebe: 'I think you've just answered your own question.'
Phoebe: 'If you ran an employment agency wouldn't you want me?' Prue: 'Maybe. But I would definitely want my suit back.' Phoebe: 'This is part of your old wardrobe. I'm just recycling.' Prue: 'Well, the environment thanks you …' Phoebe: 'But take it off? I know.'
Phoebe: 'Prue was right, which means I'm dating a warlock.' Piper: 'Been there, done that.'
Prue, on being broken out of jail: 'This isn't right.' Piper: 'Neither is the gas chamber.'

Notes: 'Somebody is obviously trying to set me up, and they're using magic to do it.' Basically, this episode sees the end of *Charmed*'s opening gambit, with the vanquishing of Rex and Hannah, the recurring villains of the early episodes. It's a pretty good effort, too, with lots of amusing lines and, in the subplot concerning Leo, the *next* major revolution in *Charmed*'s development. Yet again, the end is somewhat rushed, but otherwise 'Wicca Envy' is a good example of the series' many positive aspects. Best bits: Prue's barely-concealed jealousy when Rex comes on to Phoebe. Hannah turning into a black panther.

Soundtrack: 'She's So High' by Tal Bachman.

11: FEATS OF CLAY

20 January 1999

Writers: Michael Perricone, Greg Elliot, Chris Levinson, Zack Estrin
Story: Javier Grillo-Marxuach
Director: Kevin Inch

Cast: Victor Browne (Clay), Stacy Haiduk (Guardian of the Urn), Eddie Bowz (Palmer Kellogg), Allen Cutler (Doug), Niklaus Lange (Wesley), Carolyne Lowery (Sheila), Ming Lo (Police Officer), Cristine Rose (Claire Pryce), Allan Hunt (Auctioneer), Sean Moran (Custom Officer)

> Phoebe's caddish ex-boyfriend, Clay, comes to town looking for a reconciliation. But his attentions have always come with strings attached. In this particular case, a stolen Egyptian urn that carries a mortal curse. Prue's protective instinct is to help her sister, but she must deal with problems of her own – trying to save Buckland's auction house from bankruptcy. Meanwhile, Piper uses her powers in a misguided attempt at matchmaking.

A Little Learning is a Dangerous Thing: Sour-faced Claire Pryce has taken over the almost-bankrupt Buckland's in the aftermath of Rex's disappearance. She has Prue arrange an auction at very short notice. Luckily, it makes enough money to keep the company afloat. For this week, at least.

The Conspiracy Starts at the Witching Hour: Prue notes that there is a curse attached to the urn. Anyone who steals it ends up dead – a victim of the guardian who protects it, who feeds off the would-be thief's greed.

Work is a Four-Letter Word: When she lived in New York, Phoebe had a number of jobs to pay for her party-girl lifestyle – these included working at the Rainbow Rooms and the Chelsea Pier.

References: The episode begins with some stock footage of Cairo and the Sphinx. The central theme of the curse of the dead, and much of the imagery, comes from a variety of Egyptian myths and horror texts (the *Mummy* films, *Stargate SG-1*, the *Blue Beetle* comic etc.). Allusions to Tony Bennett's 'I Left My Heart in San Francisco'; the Cowardly Lion from *The Wizard of Oz*; Tom Cruise and his performance in the movie *Cocktail*; and

SEASON 1: FEATS OF CLAY

novelist F Scott Fitzgerald (1896-1940).

'You May Remember Me ...': Victor Browne appeared in *Rescue 77*. Stacy Haiduk's CV includes *Brimstone*, *SeaQuest DSV* and *Due South*. Eddie Bowz was in *The Fear*. Allen Cutler appeared in *The Sculptress*. Niklaus Lange was in *Legally Blonde* and *Dawson's Creek*. Carolyne Lowery's movies include *Vicious Circle* and *Octopus*. Ming Lo appeared in *Boomtown*, *Alias* and *Doctor Doolittle*. Cristine Rose played Jackie Kennedy in *The Trial of Lee Harvey Oswald* and appeared in *What Women Want* and the *Ferris Bueller* TV series. Allan Hunt's CV includes *The Munsters*, *Ironside* and *Centennial*. Sean Moran appeared in *Drive*, *Grease*, *The West Wing* and *Sliders*.

Behind the Camera: Kevin Inch also worked on *Monk*, *Strange Frequency*, *Queer as Folk*, *7th Heaven*, *Party of Five*, *Baywatch*, *Remington Steele* and *MacGyver*. Greg Elliot's CV includes *Star Trek: Voyager*.

Sex and Drugs and Rock n Roll: When Clay first turns up and Phoebe kisses him, she has a vision of herself in bed with him. Prue asks if Piper heard Phoebe and Clay going at it the previous night. There was music and there was wine, she continues. Piper asks how she's so sure about the wine and Prue confesses that, actually, she peeked.

Logic, Let Me Introduce You To This Window: Doesn't *anyone* notice a bejewelled ancient Egyptian wandering around San Francisco? And one with a decidedly American accent, at that.

Continuity: When Phoebe first moved to New York, she was angry and scared. Then, she met Clay, a musician, and he was really good to her at a time in her life when no-one else was. However, he kept living beyond his means and never thought of the future. Eventually he got involved with some bad people and Phoebe left him. Piper believes that Prue is a bit judgmental. She also believes in giving people second chances. Phoebe thinks that she is a sucker for punishment, but Piper argues that, actually, Phoebe tries to see the good in people and that's never wrong. Besides, the wrong guys are usually the most interesting. Prue implies that Phoebe is a terrible cook.

Quote/Unquote: Doug, to Phoebe: 'I don't believe I've had the pleasure.' Piper: 'I don't think you will. Get back to work, she's off limits.'

Phoebe: 'Do we expect to be sixty years old and still be sharing clothes and a cat.' Piper: 'Now that you put it *that* way, no! I don't want to live with you anymore.'

Prue: 'Seasons change, people don't.' And: 'Maybe there are some things that we're not supposed to save.'

Notes: 'The urn. It's cursed.' A horrible, banal episode – sloppy in terms of plot-holes big enough to push a pyramid through, with shallow characterisation and a perfectly dreadful attempt at a moral ending. When series like *Angel*, for example, do the 'road to redemption is a rocky path' storyline, they usually do so with some wit, imagination and integrity. *Charmed* has many things going for it, but a sense of *realpolitik* just isn't one of them. Virtually every time that the production tries to present serious issue-based episodes – like this – it ends up looking silly, inconsequential and hopelessly naïve. If 'Feat of Clay' has one, overriding, message for *Charmed*'s creators it's to stick to what you're good at.

Soundtrack: 'Inside Out' by Eve 6, Sarah McLachlan's 'Good Enough', and 'Hey Pachuco!' by Royal Crown Revue.

12: THE WENDIGO

03 February 1999

Writer: Edithe Swensen
Director: James L Conway

Cast: Christina Milian (Teri Lane), Jocelyn Seagrave (Ashley Fallon), Billy Jayne (Billy Waters), J Karen Thomas (Harriett Lane), Charles Chun (Lawrence Beck), Cristine Rose (Claire Pryce), Richard S Wolf (Auctioneer), William Dixon (ER Doctor)

> Piper is attacked by 'a cross between a werewolf and Charles Manson.' Andy goes on a stakeout with an FBI agent who is hunting the creature. Prue hires Phoebe to work at the auction house, but Phoebe's vision of a terrible car crash immediately sends her on a mission to find a long-lost child.

Dreaming (As Blondie Once Said) is Free: After she is attacked by the creature, Piper has a horrific dream about turning into it and attacking Andy.

It's Witchcraft: Piper tells Billy that the creature is called a Wendigo. According to *The Book of Shadows*, it looks like a normal person during the day but transforms at night and survives by eating human hearts during the three phases of the moon. The first Wendigo was a mortal who was betrayed by its lover. When it took revenge by ripping out the lover's heart, its own heart turned to ice and it became a monster. In reality, the Wendigo is FBI Special Agent Fallon. Prue discovers that killing the Wendigo by melting its ice heart will cure Piper (and, indeed, Andy).

A Little Learning is a Dangerous Thing: Phoebe used to date a mechanic and therefore knows how to jack up a car.

The Conspiracy Starts at the Witching Hour: There have been a series of killings in Chicago – including that of Billy Waters' fiancée, Laura – and in New Orleans, and at least one previous death in San Francisco.

Work is a Four-Letter Word: Phoebe tells Prue that she is good on the telephone and better with people and, thus, manages to get herself hired as Prue's new assistant at Buckland's. And, she's actually rather good at the

SEASON 1: THE WENDIGO

job but, ultimately, quits because the risk of her having another vision when touching items in the auction house is too great.

References: Influenced – hugely – by just about every werewolf film ever made (see also 'Once Upon a Blue Moon'). The episode is, also, very *The X-Files*-like.

'You May Remember Me ...': Christina Milian's CV includes *American Pie* and *Get Real*. She wrote Jennifer Lopez's 'Play', featured on Ja Rule's 'Between Me And You' and has enjoyed chart success herself with singles including 'AM to PM'. Jocelyn Seagrave played Rita Winsler in *Savannah*. Billy Jayne was a cult figure as Mikey Randall in *Parker Lewis Can't Lose*. J Karen Thomas appeared in *Go* and *Sunset Beach*. Charles Chun was in *Dumb and Dumber* and *Star Trek: Deep Space Nine*.

Behind the Camera: James L Conway also worked on *Enterprise*, *Kindred: The Embraced*, *Legend*, *Star Trek: Deep Space Nine*, *The Life and Times of Grizzly Adams* and the movies *Hangar 18*, *The Lincoln Conspiracy* and *In Search of Noah's Ark*.

Sex and Drugs and Rock n Roll: Fallon tells Andy that she was once engaged. After a tortuous break-up, she did what she needed to make herself strong, so that no-one could ever hurt her like that again. All she is interested in now, she notes, is sex. Andy idly wonders where she was when he was in college.

When looking for something with which to restrain Piper, Phoebe produces a pair of handcuffs (see 'When Bad Warlocks Turn Good'). Prue asks where Phoebe got those, then, presumably before getting a 10-minute lesson on the BDSM community, she shuts up.

Logic, Let Me Introduce You To This Window: Piper says that it may be hard to find a match for her blood-type. However, AB- patients can receive O-, A- or B- transfusions quite safely. Moreover, shouldn't Prue and Piper have the same blood type as their sister? Isn't that telephone box in a rather convenient place when Piper is attacked? When Agent Fallon arrives at the hospital, Andy introduces her to the Halliwell sisters, but he points to the wrong ones as he says their names. When Piper changes into a Wendigo, we see her clothes ripping. Yet once the camera pans around, there are no clothes lying on the floor. Similarly, when Fallon changes, her ripped jacket and skirt can be seen, but seemingly she was wearing no underwear. When the Wendigo is about to slash Andy, we see it rip his shirt open. A subsequent shot shows an unconscious Andy with his shirt still undamaged. Doesn't Andy find it strange that Agent Fallon missed such an obvious clue as all of the murder victims having the same blood type? Or, shouldn't he at least make some sarcastic comment like, 'Agent Scully wouldn't have missed that.' Phoebe suggests that her résumé is only three sentences long. We know from previous episodes that she's had plenty of previous jobs. She might not have kept most of them very long, but still ...

Continuity: Phoebe's first boyfriend was called Jimmy and drove a 1965 Lincoln. When she touches the bracelet in Buckland's, Phoebe has a flashback to a similar car running over a cliff. Investigating, she discovers that the car owner was one Franklin Bates, a private investigator in San Jose, who died in an accident on the Pacific Coast Highway near Carmel in February 1989. The bracelet belongs to a five year old girl, Teri Lane, who was kidnapped by her father. This was the case Bates was working on when he died. Subsequently, Phoebe finds Teri, living in Oakland, and is able to reunite her with her mother. Like Piper, Andy has an AB- blood-type.

Quote/Unquote: Prue: 'Can you start tomorrow?' Phoebe: 'Yes. Can you give me a ride?'
 Piper: 'I have the power to freeze. I'll be fine – it's better than mace.'
 Health Inspector: 'Excuse me, what are you doing with that meat?' Piper: 'Dying.'

Notes: 'You're the only one to survive the attacks. Hope you didn't get infected by it.' A beautifully-directed and nicely-assembled shocker with some really scary moments. The minor, and somewhat heavy-handed, subplot about Phoebe and Prue finding the kidnapped little girl takes some attention away from the episode's real strength – Piper becoming a werewolf. But overall this is one of *Charmed*'s first real moments of greatness, featuring a superbly schizophrenic performance by Holly Marie Combs.

Soundtrack: Jewel's 'Down So Long'.

13: FROM FEAR TO ETERNITY

10 February 1999

Writers: Tony Blake, Paul Jackson
Director: Les Sheldon

Cast: Billy Drago (Barbas), Kimberley Kates (Tanjella), Steve Wilder (Lucas Devane), Allen Cutler (Doug), Jodie Hanson (Zoe), Linda Kim (Monique), Dailyn Matthews (Susan Warner), Evan O'Meara (Richard Warner).

> Every 1,300 years on Friday the 13th, Barbas the Demon of Fear scares 13 witches to death by feeding on their hidden terrors. And it seems that the day has rolled around again. Meanwhile, Phoebe has misgivings about her duties at a new job; Piper's superstition about relationships starting on Friday the 13th has her frustrated; and Prue can't seem to tell anyone that she loves them.

Dreaming (As Blondie Once Said) is Free: Prue had a dream about her mother, in which she was around four or five years old. Phoebe wishes she had dreams like that. Piper notes that their mother would have to knock before she came into Phoebe's dreams.

It's Witchcraft: There's a strong implication that the ghost of the girl's mother came to the attic and made an entry into *The Book of Shadows* to help Prue defeat the Barbas – see 'That 70s Episode.'

It's Big and It's Hairy and I Be Afeared of It: Piper is afraid of flying. Phoebe's big terror is said to be getting trapped in an elevator, although Barbas knows that, secretly, she is more afraid of losing a sister. Prue is afraid of water – a psychological consequence of her mother having drowned.

The Conspiracy Starts at the Witching Hour: Barbas feeds on the fears of young witches for his survival, by turning a witch's greatest fear against her. Because of this, the witch's powers are temporarily paralysed until she can release her fear. To do this, she must 'trust in the greatest of all powers,' which, Prue discovers, is love.

Work is a Four-Letter Word: Phoebe starts a new job as a secretary at SWA Properties. However, one of her responsibilities to is cover for her new boss, Susan, who is having an affair. Phoebe finds that she is unable to do so when she meets Susan's husband, Richard.

It's a Designer Label: Piper says that she hasn't worn white cotton underwear since high school.

References: The title alludes to Fred Zimmerman's 1953 Pearl Harbor epic *From Here To Eternity*. A clock striking thirteen is an element used in both *1984* and *Tom's Midnight Garden*.

'You May Remember Me ...': Billy Drago played Frank Nitti in *The Untouchables* and appeared in *Welcome to America*, *Never Say Die* and *Moonlighting*. Kimberley Kates was one of the medieval princess babes in *Bill & Ted's Excellent Adventure*. Her CV also includes *Highway* and *The Pornographer*. Steve Wilder was Alex Bastian in *Melrose Place*. Jodie Hanson played Marianne Dwyer in *Brookside* and also featured in *The West Wing*. Linda Kim's movies include *Austin Powers in Goldmember* and *Dude, Where's My Car?*. Dailyn Matthews was in *Weapons of Mass Destruction*. Evan O'Meara's CV includes *When Billie Beat Bobby* and *Jacob's Ladder*.

Sex and Drugs and Rock n Roll: Piper, despite reservations, goes on a date with one of the Bay Area's most eligible bachelors, Lucas Devane. She blows any chance of a lasting relationship with him, however, as his last girlfriend was also heavily influenced by superstition.

Logic, Let Me Introduce You To This Window: Are occult shops routinely open until 1 am? Prue gets pushed into a pool, yet when she arrives home, her hair is not only dry but also perfectly styled, and her clothes don't seem even a little bit damp. When Andy bursts in on Prue in the shower there is no white in her hair, but when Phoebe comes home the streak has suddenly materialised. During the following scene, it changes position in Prue's hair at least twice and then vanishes. Why does Phoebe write both her name and Prue's on the store list when they both live at the same house? Why does the store manager put Phoebe's good luck charm in a really large carrier bag? When Prue is in the swimming pool, her bra strap is clearly white. When she gets out of the pool, it has changed to a black one. When Phoebe is debating with herself whether to lie to her new boss's husband, there is no water in the water bottle on her desk. In the next shot, she knocks over the bottle, which is now full of water.

Continuity: Piper is the most superstitious of the Halliwell sisters by some distance. She met Jeremy (see 'Something Wicca This Way Comes') on Friday 13th (presumably the previous year). Prue notes that her mother wore a fragrance like Sandalwood. Phoebe says that she was too young to remember such details. Prue's fear of water explains why she never took swimming lessons with her sisters. They always knew the real reason but never said anything to spare her feelings. By the same token, the reason why Prue never tells anyone that she loves them is that those were her final words to her mother before she drowned. There is due to be a Wicca gathering at 5871 Stanton Avenue (Apartment 1951). The address at which Barbas attempts to kill two witches with one stone is 1312 Napper Avenue.

Quote/Unquote: Prue: 'If he can kill 13 unmarried witches by midnight, he'll be free from the underworld to wreak his terror every single day.' Piper: 'Like being single doesn't have enough problems.'

Notes: 'If I didn't know any better, I'd say [she was] literally scared to death.' 'From Fear to Eternity' starts like a locomotive, with an exciting and genuinely scary plot about hidden fears and a neat allegory concerning how superstitions often cause more problems than the peace of mind they offer. It briefly threatens to become a train-wreck via the complete *deus ex machina* conceit of the girls' mother appearing to Prue as she's about to drown. Nevertheless, although it's a bit simplistic, this is again fundamentally a tale well told, introducing a genuinely powerful returning nemesis for the sisters.

Soundtrack: Brooke Ramel's 'The Answer', 'Enchanted' by Chasing Furies and Khaleel's 'No Mercy'.

14: SECRETS & GUYS

17 February 1999

Writers: Constance M Burge, Sheryl J Anderson
Story: Brad Kern, Constance M Burge
Director: James A Contner

Cast: Richard Cody (Danny), Robert Gossett (Mr. Franklin), Brad Tatum (Mickey Jackson), David Netter (Max Franklin), Will Stewart (Harry), Michael Brunin (Security Guard)

> When Max Franklin, a young witch, is kidnapped by thieves who want to use his power to stage a robbery, he contacts Prue through the spirit-board for help. Phoebe learns that Leo is a Whitelighter, a guardian angel for witches, and has returned to make sure that Max's call for help reached the Charmed Ones.

It's Witchcraft: Leo's Whitelighter powers include levitation, heat-touch and healing hands. He notes that Whitelighters answer to a group known as the Founders (subsequently known as the Elders).

Max's power is psychokinesis, which he seemingly inherited from his dead mother.

A Little Learning is a Dangerous Thing: Leo implies that angels exist – establishing the fundamentally Judaeo-Christian nature of the *Charmed* universe (see also 'When Bad Warlocks Turn Good'). Despite all that awkward stuff in Exodus about not suffering a witch to live.

Work is a Four-Letter Word: Prue suggests that, with Phoebe's imagination, she should write children's books. Piper's job title at [quake] is manager, but she seemingly cannot sack the full-of-himself new chef, Harry.

References: The title alludes to Mike Leigh's Oscar-winning 1996 film *Secrets & Lies*. Phoebe bemoans the misfortunes of the San Francisco '49ers. The spring-cleaning sequence appears inspired by the *Sorcerer's Apprentice* segment of *Fantasia*. Further examples of stock footage of San Francisco landmarks occur – including a stunning aerial shot of the Coit Tower and its surrounding area. Also seen, Alcatraz Island and Russian Hill. Max has an Etch-a-Sketch in the opening scene; Piper also has one

SEASON 1: SECRETS & GUYS

'You May Remember Me ...': Richard Cody was in *Ivory Tower*. Robert Gossett appeared in *Dark Angel*, *Phoenix* and *Pacific Palisades*. Brad Tatum's movies include *The Burning Zone* and *The Stöned Age*. David Netter played Nigel Hamilton in *7th Heaven*. Will Stewart was in *Playing God*.

Behind the Camera: Shannen Doherty's stunt double, Julie Adair, also worked on *Malcolm in the Middle*, *The Patriot*, *Raven*, *Bad Girls*, *Rescue 911* and *The Red Shoe Diaries*.

Sex and Drugs and Rock n Roll: Leo intends to tell Piper the truth – that, as much as he loves her, he must leave and doesn't know how long his work will keep him away. Phoebe notes that such a line sounds like Leo would like to stay and have sex with Piper, but he has a wife and kids in another part of the country.

Logic, Let Me Introduce You To This Window: Leo says that he needs to keep the fact that he's a Whitelighter a secret. In future episodes, all sorts of people discover his true nature – Dan, Victor and Cole, for example. Using Prue's powers to do the spring cleaning – isn't *that* personal gain?

Continuity: Phoebe advises Leo on the best way for him to break up with Piper, as Whitelighters and witches are not allow to fall in love. She seems to be something of an expert on dumping and being dumped. Phoebe wrote diaries as a teenager. These were, she notes, the place where she kept her secrets. Her sisters are amused by the idea that Phoebe could *ever* keep secrets. When Phoebe tells her sisters about Leo's true nature, neither seem to believe her.

Quote/Unquote: Harry: 'You must be Pippy.' Piper: 'Piper.' Harry: 'Your voice doesn't do you justice. You're actually attractive.'
Leo: 'Think of us as guardian angels for good witches ... ' Phoebe: 'You *are* handy.'
Piper: 'Let's face it, you're geographically undesirable. I mean, you said you live really far away, right?' Leo: 'Pretty far.'

Notes: 'One day, I'm going to figure out your secret, Prue. Count on it.' An interesting mixture of heist movie and doomed love story, 'Secrets & Guys' contrasts the life of a lonely little boy with powers neither he nor his grief-stricken father understand and the experiences of Prue and Piper discovering important things about themselves. Some crap-awful dialogue aside (particularly for the pretty-boy robbers), it's a rather effective episode with some nice depth in Prue's relationship with Max.

Soundtrack: Fuel's 'Shimmer', Liz Phair's 'Baby Got Going', 'Know You Better' by Reality Check, DC Talk's 'Day By Day', and 'Anything' by PFR.

15: IS THERE A WOOGY IN THE HOUSE?

24 February 1999

Writers: Zack Estrin, Chris Levinson
Director: John T Kretchmer

Cast: Jennifer Rhodes (Penny Halliwell), Michael Mantell (Gasman), Richard McGonagle (The Woogyman), Shawn Christian (Josh), Nancy Moonves (Professor Whittlesey), Cristine Rose (Claire Pryce), Tait Ruppert (Joe)

> Phoebe's childhood fear of the Woogyman greatly amuses Prue and Piper. But, when an earthquake releases a shadow demon, Phoebe, under its control, tries to kill her sisters. As if that doesn't make them stressed enough, they have a very important dinner party.

It's Witchcraft: Some considerable time ago (see **Continuity**), Grams Halliwell battled a demon that emerged from the Manor's basement. Phoebe caught sight of this battle and was so traumatised by the experience that Grams had to convince her it had been a dream. Wrapping up the story in fairy-tale language, however, she left Phoebe, Piper and Prue clues as to what to do should the Woogyman ever return. ('I am light. I am one too strong to fight. Return to dark where shadows dwell. You cannot have *this* Halliwell.')

The Conspiracy Starts at the Witching Hour: Professor Whittlesey notes that the original house that stood on the spot of the Manor was a masterpiece, but had to be rebuilt after the 1906 San Francisco earthquake. Shortly afterwards, the Halliwells' great-grandparents moved in (i.e. Grams' parents). Whittlesey says that metaphysicists believe the land to be a spiritual nexus (see 'The Importance of Being Phoebe'). It is believed that when a geographical point is an equal distance from the five spiritual elements, it's a place of great power. Prue and Piper subsequently discover that the house is not just a spiritual nexus, but a Wiccan one as well. Which means that it is, and always has been, a battle ground for good and evil.

It's a Designer Label!: Evil-Phoebe's evil red dress.

SEASON 1: IS THERE A WOOGY IN THE HOUSE?

References: Another episode that depends for much of its concept and almost all of its visuals on a horror movie sub-genre (in this case the haunted/evil house). And *Ghostbusters*. Piper alludes to the jewellery chain Tiffany's. The San Francisco landmarks Mountain Lake Park and Twin Peaks are mentioned. Two others (Kenwood Park and Potrero Hot Springs) are fictitious. There's an oblique reference to a Biblical verse, Matthew 7.

'You May Remember Me ...': Jennifer Rhodes's extensive CV includes *Heathers*, *Popular*, *3rd Rock from the Sun*, *LA Law* and *The Rockford Files*. Michael Mantell's movies include *The Velocity of Gary*, *Quiz Show*, *Passion Fish*, *A Mighty Wind* and *The Brother from Another Planet*. He's also appeared in *Angel*, *Gilmore Girls*, *The X-Files* and as Howard Sewell in *Space: Above and Beyond*. Richard McGonagle was in *Mighty Joe Young* and *The American President*. Nancy Moonves played Nicki Long in *Beverly Hills 90210*. Shawn Christian appeared in *as The World Turns* and *Birds of Prey*. Tait Ruppert appeared in *Swordfish* and *The General's Daughter*.

Behind the Camera: Alyssa Milano's stunt double, Laura Lee Connery, also worked on *Dead Like Me*, *The X-Files*, *Buffy the Vampire Slayer*, *Molly*, *Hollow Man*, *CSI*, *Mulholland Dr*, *Wolf Lake* and *Catwoman*.

Cigarettes and Alcohol: Piper has a lengthy argument with Josh over which of them has the greater need for a '93 bottle of Callara Jensen.

Logic, Let Me Introduce You To This Window: Twin Peaks isn't the highest point in San Francisco, Mount Davidson is. When Phoebe clouts the gasman over the head with a baseball bat, there's a remarkable lack of blood or any sign of blunt-force trauma. In 'The Fourth Sister', the Halliwell's address was 7571 Prescott Street. Here, Phoebe says it's 1329 Prescott Street. Unusually, Kit wasn't wearing a collar when it ran out of the house. The gasman never told Piper that Phoebe was in the basement. Water, wood, fire, earth and metal are the five Chinese elements and not the Wiccan ones. Why does Prue draw a pentagram? There are, after all, many different ways of connecting five dots on a map. Prue and Piper spend the night outside. The previous evening Prue was wearing a black choker around her neck. In the morning this has changed to a silver necklace, until Piper attempts to throw a brick through the window. In the next shot, Prue has the distinctive choker on again. When Piper puts her jacket on in the morning, a rear shot shows the collar turned up but, from the front, it's down.

Continuity: Phoebe uses the fake name Chander Lear to order some free

SEASON 1: IS THERE A WOOGY IN THE HOUSE?

CDs. She had buck teeth when she was five (and was, thus, unable to pronounce the word 'bogeyman' correctly). As a consequence of her experience seeing Grams battling with the shadow demon, Phoebe hasn't been in the basement since. (Prue says this is a period of 18 years – given that Phoebe was five at the time, it's probably closer to 16.) Phoebe was the only sister who was actually born in the Manor. The earthquake that has just hit San Francisco had a magnitude of 4.5 on the Richter scale.

Cruelty to Animals: Kit runs out of the house after Phoebe is possessed.

Quote/Unquote: Phoebe: 'They give me the jeebies.' Prue: 'Would that be the Phoebe-jeebies?'

Piper: 'You're the only Halliwell that actually likes earthquakes.' Prue: 'I don't *like* them. But I don't go running through the house, naked, screaming "Run for your life."' Phoebe: 'That is *such* an exaggeration. I was wearing slippers.'

Phoebe: 'Prue's just pissy because this time she didn't get to play Wonder Woman.'

Darryl: 'Why do I feel like we live here?'

Phoebe, to Prue: 'Any fantasies about how you wanna die?'

Notes: 'I'm a good person. What did I do to deserve this?' Very silly ... and also very funny. 'Is There a Woogy in the House?' is, rightly, a popular episode with fans. It's played gloriously over-the-top – with Alyssa Milano's Evil-Phoebe acting like a character straight out of *Dynasty* – and with its sitcom conceit of the boss bringing an important client to dinner, it's just impossible not to admire this episode. Arguably, the series would do more subtle versions of basically the same plot again in future years. But none of them was ever this much fun! Best bits: Prue being thrown backwards in a flash of lightning as she tries to enter the house. The Manor destructively reacting to Phoebe's possession.

Soundtrack: Owsley's 'Zavelow House'.

16: WHICH PRUE IS IT, ANYWAY?

03 March 1999

Writer: Javier Grillo-Marxuach **Director:** John Behring

Cast: Alex McArthur (Gabriel), Shannon Sturges (Helena Statler), Cristine Rose (Claire Pryce), Mongo Brownlee (Luther Stubbs), Susan Chuang (Monique), Bernie Kopell (Coroner)

>Gabriel, an outcast Lord of War, intends to kill Prue to regain his position taken from him by one of her ancestors. To increase her power, and vanquish Gabriel, Prue takes Phoebe's advice and recites a spell to multiply her power. Unfortunately, it creates two duplicate Prues.

It's Witchcraft: Phoebe finds an incantation in *The Book of Shadows* that can be used to multiply Prue's strength. 'Take my powers blessed be. Multiply their strength by three.'

Prue, unlike many witches, channels her power through her eyes rather than her hands.

The Conspiracy Starts at the Witching Hour: The crystal sword that Phoebe saw in her vision killing Prue is the symbol of The Lords of War, a clan of supernatural warriors who have existed since the dawn of time. They have been responsible for most of the major wars in history. Once they achieve their purposes, they are reincarnated in another part of the world and start all over again. Although human, as long as they retain their sword they are immune to the weapons of man. They do, however, have a code of honour, and when one of the Lords is disgraced, as Gabriel was, he has to steal his abilities back. One of these is 'the magic of a first born witch.'

A Little Learning is a Dangerous Thing: Gabriel steals the killer instinct from a boxer who once caused the death of an opponent in the ring.

Work is a Four-Letter Word: Visiting Helena, Gabriel's sister, Prue correctly identifies a Roman vessel. The handles represent Venus and the relief details scenes of Roman life. It probably dates from 210 BC.

It's a Designer Label!: Phoebe's red trousers.

SEASON 1: WHICH PRUE IS IT ANYWAY?

References: The title is a probable allusion to the improvisation/comedy show *Whose Line Is It, Anyway?* Also, abstract-impressionist artist Jasper Johns; the Spanish Inquisition; Christie's auction house; *The Parent Trap*; *Reversal of Fortune*; GI Joe dolls; Thor's Hammer from Norse mythology; Ripley's *Believe It Or Not!*; and Bruce Springsteen's 'Blinded By the Light' (a cover version of which by Manfred Mann's Earth Band was a transatlantic hit in 1976). Prue reads a copy of *Living Times* magazine. Andy has tickets for the Bay Area Music Awards. The body of the Prue-clone was found in the Presidio: the national park next to the Golden Gate Bridge.

'You May Remember Me ...': Shannon Sturges played Molly Brinker in *Days of Our Lives* and appeared in *Herman's Head*. Mongo Brownlee's CV includes *Bulworth*, *Con Air* and *The West Wing*. Susan Chuang played Susan in *Dharma & Greg* and featured in *Buffy the Vampire Slayer* and *CSI*. Alex McArthur appeared in Madonna's video for 'Papa Don't Preach', and also in *Route 666* and *Conspiracy Theory*. Bernie Kopell was in *Missing Pieces*, *Get Smart*, *The Love Boat*, *Scrubs* and *Bewitched*.

Behind the Camera: John Behring's CV also includes *One Tree Hill*, *Resurrection Blvd*, *Roswell*, *Dawson's Creek*, *The Lazarus Man* and *The Cape*.

Sex and Drugs and Rock n Roll: Phoebe is said to have at least eight 'bouncer friends.'

Logic, Let Me Introduce You To This Window: When Prue leaves Piper and Phoebe to go to the attic, Piper's hair is down. However, when Piper and Phoebe run upstairs a moment later, it's in a ponytail. When Gabriel kills the Prue-clone, the sword is aimed toward her knees. Yet she is stabbed in the stomach. The pathologist says that he cross-referenced the fingerprints from the Prue-clone with prints for Prudence Halliwell that 'came from her birth certificate from the archives.' Since when do birth certificates include fingerprints? The case officers said that Andy might be able to ID the Prue-clone's body. This suggests they knew of Andy's and Prue's prior relationship. Yet seemingly no-one has had the decency to *tell* Andy that he's going to the morgue to identify the body of his former girlfriend. Piper initially touches Prue's head with the boxing glove with her left hand. In the next shot, she's using her right hand.

Continuity: Sick of being the only sister with a non-combative power, Phoebe has been taking self-defence classes. Prue says that she doesn't scare easily. Andy has a large file on Prue, which contains a newspaper article on witchcraft. One of the Halliwells' ancestors, Brianna (their great-

SEASON 1: WHICH PRUE IS IT ANYWAY?

great-great aunt), had powers similar to Prue's. She disgraced Gabriel during the Crimean War and used her powers to take away his sword.

Quote/Unquote: Prue: 'So, some guy couldn't keep it in his sheath and now I'm marked for death.' Piper: 'Well, some men are very sensitive about their weapons.'

Piper: 'This is like *The Parent Trap* with a B-cup.' Phoebe: 'I think I might've found a way to take some of the Disney out of our life.'

Prue: 'Phoebe, I'll have to call you back. I have to go yell at myself.'

Prue: 'One day you might actually hear what you sound like when you say stuff like that.' Phoebe: 'And I will find myself sassy and delightful.'

Notes: 'I'm not talking to that *clone*.' Somewhat farcical but – again – rather fun, 'Which Prue Is It, Anyway?' takes an age-old dramatic idea and plays lots of cute, intertextual games with it. Parts of the plot are, frankly, ludicrous, but it doesn't really matter as the humour is terrific. Good special effects, too. Best bit: The various Prues and their interaction.

Soundtrack: Massive Attack's classic 'Teardrop'.

17: THAT 70S EPISODE

07 April 1999

Writer: Sheryl J Anderson
Director: Richard Denault

Cast: Jennifer Rhodes (Penny Halliwell), Finola Hughes (Patty Halliwell), Andrew Jackson (Nicholas), Jake Sakson (Little Andy), Megan Corletto (Little Piper), Emmalee Thompson (Little Prue), Sally Ann Brooks (Officer at Jail), Rey Silva (Officer at Park)

> A powerful warlock claims that he made a pact with the Halliwells' mother in which he spared her life in exchange for the girls' powers. Fleeing from him, the three sisters go back in time to the 1970s when their mother was still alive and try to prevent the pact from happening.

Dreaming (As Blondie Once Said) is Free: The as-yet-unborn Phoebe, in utero, gives her mother a vision of the attempted kidnap of her sisters by three female warlocks. Which turns out to be the three sisters' own future selves.

It's Witchcraft: Phoebe finds an unbinding spell in *The Book of Shadows* – 'The bond which was not to be done, Give us the power to see it undone, And turn back time to whence it was begun.' This succeeds in sending Prue, Piper and Phoebe back to 1975. The spell to return them to the present begins, 'A time for everything, and to everything its place. Return what has been moved, through time and space.'

Grams also concocted the 'Nicholas Must Die' spell, which she wrote into *The Book of Shadows* and which the sisters use to vanquish him. ('Cleanse this evil from our midst, scatter its cells throughout time, let this Nick no more exist'.)

A Little Learning is a Dangerous Thing: The girls all had their powers at a young age but, after these events, Grams suspended them to prevent Nicholas from attempting to kill the girls. This suspension was only lifted when Grams herself died.

The Conspiracy Starts at the Witching Hour: After Piper has left the young Andy (whom Phoebe considers to be really cute) in a frozen state,

SEASON 1: THAT 70S EPISODE

Prue suggests that maybe this childhood trauma explains why Andy will be so suspicious of the sisters twenty odd years hence.

Work is a Four-Letter Word: After Victor left, Patty worked as a waitress at a diner called Buddies.

References: The title alludes to the NBC comedy series *That 70s Show*. Along with much stock footage of the 1970s (discos, roller-skating, etc), and a magnificent lava-lamp that decorates the Manor, there are numerous allusions to of-the-era items like 8-Track cassettes (one of the two Prue picks up is seemingly a compilation of love songs entitled *Some Enchanted Evening* – see also 'Witchstock'). Also, Mr Spock from *Star Trek*; *The Stepford Wives*; Charles Dickens' *A Christmas Carol*; cookery icon Betty Crocker, star of the long-running radio show *The Betty Crocker School of the Air*; and IBM. One of the spells includes an allusion to the Biblical verse Ecclesiastes 3.

Finola Hughes: Born in London, as a child Finola studied ballet and made her first appearance at the Royal Opera House at the age of 11. In 1980, she played Victoria in the original West End production of *Cats*. Sylvester Stallone received a tape of Finola's work and cast her in *Staying Alive*, opposite John Travolta. Finola later returned to London, where she starred in *The Hot Shoe Show*. Her other TV credits include *The Master of Ballantrae*, *The Prime of Miss Jean Brodie* and *Grace Kennedy*. She also appeared in the movies *The Apple* and *The Bride in Black*. Finola is married to photographer Russell Young and they have a son, Dylan.

'You May Remember Me ...': Andrew Jackson played Buddy in *Taken* and appeared in *Millennium Man* and *Andromeda*. He is the opening credits narrator on *Earth: Final Conflict*. Jake Sakson was in *Chicago Hope*. Sally Ann Brooks was a voice artist on *Josie & The Pussycats*. Megan Corletto appeared in *The X-Files*. Emmalee Thompson's movies include *Halloween H20*. Rey Silva was in *Sexual Roulette*.

Behind the Camera: Holly Marie Combs' stunt double, Nancy Thurston, also worked on *Artificial Intelligence: AI*, *Charlie's Angels*, *Freeway*, *The X-Files* and *Titanic*.

The Drugs Don't Work: When Piper says that she's getting a migraine, Phoebe notes that it might be an idea not to as, they are stuck in the past before the painkiller Advil has been invented.

Cigarettes and Alcohol: Patty smoked – at least, before Phoebe was born.

SEASON 1: THAT 70S EPISODE

Logic, Let Me Introduce You To This Window: Piper tells her sisters that she found a payphone and that their mom is at work until five and Nicholas is on duty till six. One can, perhaps, accept that someone at the diner may have given out such information, if someone rang and asked 'What time does Patty's shift end?' (even given that the woman in question had recently been through a messy separation from her husband). However, what kind of police station casually gives out details when someone asks about one of their officers' shift patterns? (And, an officer whom the caller doesn't know the surname of, at that.) When Nicholas tells Piper that he knows she froze time, the clock behind the girls reads 12:25, even though it is supposed to be noon. The note that Phoebe writes to her mother says: 'Be careful on February 28, 1978, or a Warlock will drown you.' However, 'P^3 H^2O' establishes that Patty was murdered at a summer camp by the Water Demon.

There are numerous timing and continuity problems. Piper is said to have graduated from high school in 1992 (see 'Déjà Vu All Over Again', 'Pardon My Past'), which would mean that she was born in either 1973 or 1974. The latter date would – just – fit in with her being 24 in 'Thank You For Not Morphing'. But in this episode, which takes place on 24 March 1975, Piper appears to be about four years old. By the same token, Phoebe sees a photograph of herself with her mother when she was about two years old and notes that a year later, her mother died. This (along with Patty being pregnant with Phoebe in March 1975) means that Phoebe was born in late 1975. In 'Thank You For Not Morphing', which takes place in early 1999, she was said to be 21 years old. A movie marquee is seen with *Jaws* on it, but that movie wasn't released until July 1975. Conversely, the final episode of *The Mod Squad* was broadcast on 23 August 1973. Victor had already left Patty before Phoebe was born (flatly contradicting 'Thank You For Not Morphing').

Continuity: Andy seemingly has known Prue since they were both very young – and, presumably, lived close to the Halliwells. Phoebe says that she used to listen when Prue sneaked Andy up to her room when they were in high school. Phoebe was named after Patty's favourite aunt (presumably, Grams' sister?). Grams was born in a hotel room in Boston. There's a reference to Melinda (see 'The Witch is Back'). Phoebe can pick locks. She has seemingly inherited her occasional clumsiness from her mother. The secret ingredients in Grams' blueberry cobbler were, according to Piper, honey and a splash of rum. Piper confesses to her grandmother that she never learned to like lima beans.

Quote/Unquote: Prue: 'If we stayed in our own time, Nick would have killed us. We barely got away as it was ... is ... will be ... You know I've never been good at tenses!'

Grams: 'If husbands were supposed to stay married, God would have made them live longer.' And: 'Destiny always gets its own way.'

Grams: 'I can't stop you. But I also can't promise I won't teach the girls a new spell.' Patty: 'Can't you bake cookies with them like all the other grandmothers?'

Prue: 'What are we gonna do when we see a bad guy?' Little Prue: 'She's going to cry.' Little Piper: 'Am not. I'm gonna freeze him.' Little Prue: 'And *I'm* gonna move him.'

Notes: 'I want your power, Patty.' The episode that, almost single-handedly, marked out *Charmed* for greatness. It's a bit mawkish and calculating in places, but the cunning mixture of time paradoxes, nostalgia and future-imperfect metaphors give the audience a double-whammy of emotions to play with. It was noticeable that in this period of pre-millennium angst a lot of series were doing this kind of reference-dripping blast-from-the-past idea (*Stargate SG-1* and *The X-Files*, for example, both did episodes at almost exactly the same time with similar conceits). Crucially, where 'That 70s Episode' scores more tellingly than some other examples is the way in which it uses personal core values like loss and need in such a context. Great performances and a super script combine to produce something greater than the sum of its parts. *Charmed*'s first 24-carat classic.

Soundtrack: Some classics in this one: Gloria Gaynor's 'Never Can Say Goodbye', Cher's 'Gypsies, Tramps & Thieves', 'Heat Wave' by Linda Ronstadt and 'S.O.S' by ABBA.

18: WHEN BAD WARLOCKS TURN GOOD

28 April 1999

Writer: Edithe Swensen
Director: Kevin Inch

Cast: Michael Weatherly (Brendan), Shawn Christian (Josh), Nick Kokotakis (Greg), David Kriegel (Paul), Frank Birney (Father Austin), Andrea E Taylor (Girl Victim), Stacie Chan (Little Girl), Dathan Hooper (Officer), Ann Vareze (Nun)

> Brendan Rowe wishes to become a priest to avoid fulfilling his destiny as a warlock, completing an evil triad with his half-brothers Greg and Paul. Prue tries to help Brendan resist his dark side. Meanwhile, Phoebe tries to get Piper to date the dishy Josh.

It's Witchcraft: It's stated that once Brendan is ordained, he can never become a warlock.

The Conspiracy Starts at the Witching Hour: Brendan's brothers want to accept his heritage and fulfil the prophecy of the rogue coven. This states that three brothers, descended from an ancient warlock line, are destined to become the most powerful force of evil the world has ever known. Ever since the 10th Century, each generation of the coven has grown stronger. Brendan, with his human mother's blood nullifying some of his more desperate urges, went into hiding from his brothers some years earlier and has dedicated his life to God, hoping to make some amends for all that his family has done.

It's a Designer Label!: Prue's hip-hugging red leather trousers.

References: The title alludes to a Fox video clip-show, *When Good Pets Go Bad*. Also, Nina Simone's 'I Put a Spell on You' and the Biblical verse Matthew 6.

'You May Remember Me ...': David Kriegel appeared in *Sticks*, *Speed* and *Quantum Leap*. Michael Weatherly was Logan Cale in *Dark Angel*. Nick Kokotakis's movies include *The Nutty Professor*. Frank Birney appeared in

SEASON 1: WHEN BAD WARLOCKS TURN GOOD

Jane Austen's Mafia!, *Dave* and *Mr Mom*. Andrea Taylor was in *What Women Want* and *Pleasantville*. Stacie Chan was the voice of Jade on *Jackie Chan Adventures*. Dathan Hooper appeared in *Eclipse*. Ann Vareze was in *Armageddon*.

Behind the Camera: Leadperson on the *Charmed* production crew for the first two seasons, Rocky Slaymaker's CV also includes *Dante's Peak*, *Turbulence*, the *Buffy the Vampire Slayer* movie and acting roles in *Tour of Duty*.

Sex and Drugs and Rock n Roll: Piper notes that, at least after seeing Andy, Prue is not handcuffed, which she adds is a good thing. Phoebe replies that this rather depends on who is cuffing whom and why (see 'The Wendigo').

Logic, Let Me Introduce You To This Window: The intended sacrifice victim tells the police that she felt the knife on her skin when it never actually touched her. Phoebe emerges from [quake] completely dry, even though she was soaked inside whilst looking for the water valve.

Continuity: Prue lets Brendan stay in her room and says that she will sleep with Piper (because Phoebe kicks in bed). When discussing Brendan's internal struggle, Prue mentions Piper becoming a Wendigo and Phoebe being possessed by the Woogyman. Andy is Catholic. Josh (see 'Is There a Woogy in the House?') takes Piper rock climbing whilst Phoebe, incompetently, looks after [quake].

Cruelty to Animals: Brendan is the kind of guy who wouldn't hurt a spider. Until his baser instincts kick in, at which point viciously crushing one is his idea of fun.

Quote/Unquote: Phoebe: 'Out of curiosity, if you were the shut-off valve, where would you be?'
   Phoebe: 'God's got all the studs.'

Notes: 'You're praying to the wrong deity.' After such a good run of half-a-dozen episodes, what a right *load* this waste of time and talent is. Visually, the episode is often stunning – particularly the scene of Brendan and Prue riding horses. The idea of an evil (male) equivalent of the Charmed Ones is quite clever, but the three actors involved have the collective charisma of an ashtray. Complete with one of the most disgracefully bland endings of any *Charmed* episode, this is a real disappointment of half-baked ideas and crass execution. Dreadful.

Soundtrack: 'A Charming Spell' by Splashdown.

19: BLIND SIDED

05 May 1999

Writers: Tony Blake, Paul Jackson
Director: Craig Zisk

Cast: Matt George (Grimlock #1), Shawn Christian (Josh), Scott Terra (David), Scott Plank (Eric Lohman), Raphael Sbarge (Brent Miller), Maureen Muldoon (Dee), Michael O'Connor (Jerry Cartwright), Dennis Keiffer (Grimlock #2), Lucy Rodriguez (Housekeeper)

> When a young boy is kidnapped at his birthday party, Prue's powers are observed by an unscrupulous journalist who threatens to expose her secret. Phoebe and Piper learn that Grimlocks kidnap children every 20 years to steal their eyesight, and Phoebe seeks out one of their former victims.

A Little Learning is a Dangerous Thing: Piper spends an hour searching *The Book of Shadows* for any reference to demons with whirling eyes. She doesn't find any, but does come across demons with no eyes, four eyes and eyes that grow legs.

The Conspiracy Starts at the Witching Hour: Grimlocks are underground demons who roam from city to city killing powerful forces of good by seeing the unique auras that surround them. They are able to do so by stealing the sight from innocent children. The stolen eyesight will last for 24 hours, but only if the children remain alive.

It's Witchcraft: The only way to kill a Grimlock is to blind it with a potion made from Chisandra root.

References: The loathsome Eric Lohman works for the *Bay Weekly*, which he describes as 'the alternative press.' He mentions the magicians David Copperfield and Lance Burton. The murder of Jerry Cartwright takes place outside a charity concert given by the San Francisco Philharmonic Orchestra. Also, *E.T. The Extra-Terrestrial*; and *Julius Caesar*.

'You May Remember Me ...': Matt George played Charlie Flanagan in *Wind on Water*. Scott Terra's CV includes *Daredevil* and *Firefly*. Scott Plank was in *The Division*, *Co-ed Call Girls* and *Baywatch*. Raphael Sbarge was Jake

SEASON 1: BLIND SIDED

Straka in *The Guardian* and appeared in *Independence Day* and *Star Trek: Voyager*. Maureen Muldoon was in *Venus Envy* and *CSI*. Michael O'Connor appeared in *Dance of the Pendulum*. Dennis Keiffer is a stuntman who had worked on *X-Men*, *Minority Report* and *Alias*. Lucy Rodriguez played Nurse Bjerke in *ER*.

Behind the Camera: Craig Zisk also worked on *Wonderfalls*, *Las Vegas*, *Nip/Tuck*, *My Guide to Becoming a Rock Star*, *The Tick*, *Smallville*, *Scrubs*, *Alias*, *Grounded for Life*, *Shasta McNasty*, *Popular*, *Felicity*, *Just Shoot Me!*, *The Larry Sanders Show* and *NYPD Blue*. He was editorial co-ordinator on the movie *Less Than Zero*.

Sex and Drugs and Rock n Roll: Josh and Piper have now had three dates all without any sex taking place. Josh has been offered a job in Beverly Hills that he considers a good opportunity, but he's not prepared to take it so long as he believes that he and Piper have a future together. When Piper was injured in the storm-drain, she was constantly thinking of Leo. She therefore decides to call Josh and tell him to take the job.

Logic, Let Me Introduce You To This Window: Lohman's digital camcorder is clearly turned off when he's supposed to be recording Prue and Piper using their powers. When Prue is making the potion, she begins to pour it into a jar when the telephone rings. Returning, she picks up two full, capped jars.

Continuity: Andy finds out about the powers of Prue and her sisters when Prue saves him from the Grimlocks. Prue now apparently channels her power through her hands (see 'Which Prue Is It, Anyway?'). Brent Miller, one of the Grimlocks' victims from 20 years earlier, survived his ordeal, albeit with the loss of his sight. He subsequently designed software for the visually impaired and apparently made a lot of money doing so. After the Grimlocks are destroyed, he regains his sight.

Cruelty to Animals: Andy's 'official' explanation for the events was that there was no kidnapping, the two boys merely followed a kitten into the storm-drain and then got lost.

Quote/Unquote: Lohman: 'Prue, be smart. I'm gonna break this story one way or another. I can either make you sound like Wonder Woman or the devil incarnate.'

Phoebe's description of the Grimlocks: 'They're, like, hitmen for the Dark Side.'

Prue, mixing the potion: 'I feel like I should be cackling.' And when using it, successfully, against the Grimlocks: 'Just what we need, more toxic waste in our sewers.'

Notes: 'A demon who steals kids. Does it get any worse?' Well, this is a real surprise. The revelation of the sisters' powers to an outsider had the potential to be a blind alley that is given far more emphasis than necessary. Instead, *that* (and, indeed, Andy finding out the same information) is the throw-away element in a rather cruel but effective plot about child kidnapping. Again, some parts are more effective than others, but the sum is an episode that shifts the series, subtly, in a new direction. Best bits: Piper stopping the truck from crashing into the runaway pram. The sweet and effective Phoebe/Brent scenes. Some of the series' best special effects so far.

Soundtrack: 'Hermes Bird' by series favourites Remy Zero.

20: THE POWER OF TWO

12 May 1999

Writer: Brad Kern
Director: Elodie Keene

Cast: Jeff Kober (Jackson Ward), Brenda Bakke (Soul Collector), Sean Hennigan (Alcatraz Guide), Carlos Gomez (Inspector Rodriguez), Cristine Rose (Claire Pryce), Susan Chuang (Monique), Don Brunner (Inspector Anderson), Lesley Wood (Iris Beiderman), Jack Donner (Judge Renault), Michele Harrell (Inspector Blakely), Gregg Monk (Officer), Jim Hanna (CSI Detective), Victoria Fang (Marianne), Yuji Hasegawa (Mr Yakihama)

> At Alcatraz, Phoebe sees a murderer's ghost use a dead guard's body to escape. Once free, the ghost seeks blood vengeance on those who played a part in his conviction. With Piper out of town, Prue and Phoebe discover that the only way to destroy the ghost is for one of them to die and recite a spell whilst on the astral plane.

Dreaming (As Blondie Once Said) is Free: Phoebe has been practicing calling premonitions using meditation techniques and, in the opening scene, she sees a future event by touching Piper's plane ticket. Unfortunately, it shows Piper missing her forthcoming flight. Prue notes that they have stopped Phoebe's premonitions from coming true before and, hopefully, can do so again (which they do).

Phoebe later notes that in one of her visions, she experienced the victim's fear and pain as well as observing it, and that her powers seem to be growing as she was assured they would.

It's Witchcraft: Serial-killer Jackson Ward, executed in 1963 for his crimes, has been trapped between life and death in a state of ghostly limbo ever since. With help from the mysterious Soul Collector, he escapes from his netherworld existence.

According to *The Book of Shadows*, to lure an evil spirit, a witch must mix mercury and acid with the blood of one of the spirit's victims and pour it over the spirit's grave. Phoebe comments that this is disgusting.

Killing a malevolent spirit can be done only from the astral plane. To get there, Prue concocts a 'killer cocktail', which includes oleander, St Jensen weed and bloodwurt. This stops her heart when she drinks it, allowing her to enter Ward's realm and cast the spell, which begins 'Ashes to ashes, spirit to spirit,

SEASON 1: THE POWER OF TWO

take his soul, banish this evil.' This successfully vanquishes Ward.

A Little Learning is a Dangerous Thing: Phoebe's extensive Internet research leads her to discover that some evil spirits need a dead body to transport them across water.

The Conspiracy Starts at the Witching Hour: Internal Affairs – in the shape of Anderson and Rodriguez – are conducting an investigation into the unsolved cases that Andy has been involved with recently. Having grilled Darryl for information, they interview Andy himself. Among the cases referenced are a series of women murdered with an occult knife ('Something Wicca This Way Comes'), victims with curious holes burned into their foreheads ('Secrets & Guys'), victims found in a locked room with every bone broken ('The Dream Sorcerer') and victims, literally, scared to death ('From Fear to Eternity').

Work is a Four-Letter Word: Piper spends most of the episode at a business convention in Honolulu. Prue says that *her* job is hanging by a thread due to the extensive demon-hunting time-off she's taken lately – which she has excused as being necessitated by family emergencies. Subsequently, sour-faced bully-woman Claire does, indeed, fire her. Andy promptly gets Prue her job back, with a highly dubious cock-and-bull story about Prue helping a police sting operation involving an Asian gang smuggling exotic jewellery and antiques.

Phoebe complains that Prue and Piper automatically assume she will take care of the house because she doesn't have a *real job*. She asks when was the last time either of her sisters went grocery shopping, vacuumed the house or waited in for the cable guy. She notes that if she were being paid by the hour for such tasks, she'd be a millionaire.

It's a Designer Label!: Spectacular highlights include Prue's incredibly short miniskirt and a pair of light brown jeans. Also, Phoebe's peach sweater.

References: There are several visual and dialogue allusions to *Ghost*. Also, *Charmed*'s first direct reference to *Buffy the Vampire Slayer*; Dr Jack Kevorkian, the advocate of doctor-assisted suicide; the 'Get Out of Jail Free' card in *Monopoly*; *The Little Shoppe of Horrors*; and *The Jazz Singer* via Bachman Turner Overdrive ('You ain't seen nothing yet'). The episode's stock footage includes an aerial shot of Alcatraz Island.

'You May Remember Me ...': Sean Hennigan appeared in *Space Marines* and *Walker, Texas Ranger*. Jeff Kober played Bear in *The X-Files*, Dodger in *China Beach*, Booga in *Tank Girl* and both Zackary Kralik and Rack in *Buffy the Vampire Slayer*. He also appeared in *Enough*, *Coyote Moon*, *The Shield* and

SEASON 1: THE POWER OF TWO

Enterprise. UK readers may recognise him as 'Ray, the voice of Reef Radio' in a series of Bacardi adverts. Brenda Bakke was Joyce in *Groom Lake* and appeared in *LA Confidential*. Carlos Gomez's movies include *That Summer in LA*. Don Brunner was in *CSI: Miami*. Lesley Wood appeared in *Nurse Betty, Falcon Crest, Dallas* and *Bonanza*. Jack Donner's lengthy CV includes appearances in *Stigmata, Soulkeepers, Mission: Impossible, The Monkees* and *Star Trek*. Michele Harrell was in *Married ... with Children*. Gregg Monk was a producer of *Rice Girl*. Jim Hanna appeared in *Alias*. Victoria Fang played Gwen in *Once and Again*. Yuji Hasegawa appeared in *Net Games*.

Behind the Camera: Brian Krause's stunt double, Zach Hudson, also worked on *American Wedding, Grosse Pointe, Angel* and *Buffy the Vampire Slayer* (doubling for James Marsters on the latter series).

Cigarettes and Alcohol: Piper appears to be enjoying an exotic cocktail when she phones her sisters from Hawaii.

Logic, Let Me Introduce You To This Window: No prisoners were *ever* executed at Alcatraz. When Jackson grabs the candlestick the candle can be seen on the table. When he subsequently attacks Andy, it's vanished. Prue drinks the full glass of the death potion. A later shot of the glass reveals some of the red liquid still in it.

Continuity: This episode confirms the Halliwells' address as 1329 Prescott Street (see 'Is There A Woogy In The House?'). Prue confesses to Andy that she used a truth spell on him the previous year and, because of his reaction to her powers then, their relationship floundered (see 'The Truth Is Out There ... And Hurts'). Andy gives Prue the file he compiled on her (see 'Which Prue Is It, Anyway?') and suggests she burn it. Which she does. Prue asks Phoebe to buy her some tampons at the market. Ward's intended victims include the judge at his trial, the foreperson of the jury and the son of the District Attorney who prosecuted him.

Quote/Unquote: Phoebe: 'If we've learned anything by now, it's that there aren't any coincidences.'
Prue: 'I hate cemeteries at night.' Phoebe: 'I hate cemetery's at day. What was that?' Prue: 'Probably a zombie or vampire.' Phoebe: 'Great, where's Buffy when you need her?'
Phoebe: 'Is the ghost toast?'

Notes: 'It looks like your soul is safe. For now.' An interesting mix of ghost story and revenge tragedy, with some nice conspiracy drama thrown in, 'The Power of Two' manages to tell its story in an impressively minimalist way.

SEASON 1: THE POWER OF TWO

Helped by some terrific actors – Jeff Kober's always a great villain – it chugs along only occasionally threatening to become derailed by spurious plot-points or the odd bit of overt exposition. Retrospectively, it's yet another first season episode that deserves repeated viewing to allow the audience to catch the more subtle elements.

Soundtrack: Beth Orton's 'Stolen Car'.

21: LOVE HURTS

19 May 1999

Writers: Chris Levinson, Zack Estrin, Javier Grillo-Marxuach
Director: James Whitmore

Cast: Michael Trucco (Alec), Carlos Gomez (Inspector Rodriguez), Lisa Robin Kelly (Daisy), Don Brunner (Inspector Anderson), Tom Yi (Motel Manager)

> The sisters' vacation is cancelled at short notice when a dying Leo crashes back into their lives, the victim of a Darklighter's poison arrow. Leo says that the sisters must protect a girl, Daisy, who has become a fatal obsession for the Darklighter, Alec. To save Leo, Piper casts a spell that switches her powers with his. Unfortunately, the spell causes Prue and Phoebe to swap powers too.

It's Witchcraft: Whitelighters cannot use their healing powers on themselves. Their nemeses are called Darklighters who seduce innocent women to achieve their goal of creating evil through reproduction. Alec broke Darklighter rules by falling in love with one of his victims, Daisy, who is herself destined to become a Whitelighter.

The power-switching spell begins, 'What's mine is yours, what's yours is mine, let our powers cross the line. I offer up this gift to share, switch our powers through the air.'

A Little Learning is a Dangerous Thing: Love is said to be the trigger for Leo's various powers, just as hate is at the root of Alec's powers (and presumably this is true of all White and Darklighters). After they have switched powers, Prue asks if Phoebe too experiences ringing in her ears when she has a vision. Phoebe confirms that she does.

The Conspiracy Starts at the Witching Hour: To protect Prue, Andy surrenders his badge and weapon to the Internal Affairs officers, which means that he is automatically suspended. At the end of the episode, it is revealed that Inspector Rodriguez is a demon.

It's a Designer Label!: Best thing on view, Prue's green dress.

References: Allusions to *It's a Wonderful Life*; Kevin Costner; *How Stella Got*

SEASON 1: LOVE HURTS

Her Groove Back; *Freaky Friday*; Billy Bragg's 'Greetings to the New Brunette'; the *Yellow Pages*; and the Biblical verse *Revelations* 13:18. The opening scene was filmed at Freddy's Mini-Market on Belmont Street in Castro. There's a reference to Heroes Grove in Golden Gate Park.

'You May Remember Me ...': Michael Trucco played Tucker in *Pensacola: Wings of Gold* and also appeared in *Sabrina, the Teenage Witch*. Lisa Robin Kelly's CV includes *Jawbreaker, Payback, The '70s Show*.

Behind the Camera: James Whitmore's credits include *Melrose Place, Quantum Leap, The X-Files, Nowhere Man* and *The Pretender*. He was also an actor playing Bernie Terwilliger in *Hunter*.

Cigarettes and Alcohol: Despite having to postpone their 48 hours in Cabo, Prue and Phoebe still end the episode drinking something pineapple-y with little umbrellas in it.

Sex and Drugs and Rock n Roll: Prue remembers an occasion in high school when Phoebe was caught making out with someone under the bleachers. Her nickname, thereafter, was 'Freebie'. Phoebe says that was just a rumour.

Logic, Let Me Introduce You To This Window: Why is there a California poster on the wall of a San Francisco bus station? Leo tells the sisters that they mustn't touch the arrow because it's poisoned. However, it's already been stated that the poison is lethal only to Whitelighters. Given that Leo was dead for some considerable time before Piper discovered how to use his healing powers, how is she able to bring him back? It is subsequently established that Leo cannot heal the dead (see, for example, 'Be Careful What You Witch For', 'Coyote Piper').

Continuity: Prue mentions that Piper's recent romantic attachments have included a warlock ('Something Wicca This Way Comes'), a ghost ('Dead Man Dating'), a geographically undesirable handyman ('Secrets & Guys') and a very dorky grad student. Prue once borrowed Grams' car and dented the fender. Phoebe got blamed for this and was grounded. Prue has a colleague in accounting who owns a condo in Cabo.

Leo was born a human in San Francisco. He left medical school and enlisted as a medic during World War II because he wanted to save people rather than shoot them. He was killed whilst treating an injured man (see 'Ex Libris', 'Saving Private Leo') and was offered immortality as a Whitelighter. He has never doubted for a second that he made the right choice until he met Piper. He notes that he could have a mortal life again.

However, this would mean that he couldn't help other witches or future Whitelighters again. The Halliwells' have a very well-stocked bathroom medicine cabinet, the contents of which includes a box of Tampax (seemingly, Phoebe finally went down the market – see 'The Power of Two').

Quote/Unquote: Leo: 'If you know I cloaked her, then you also know you won't find her for as long as I live.' Alec: 'I have a solution for that.'
Phoebe, on Whitelighters: 'You know how Peter Pan has Tinkerbell? They're sort of like that. Minus the tutu and the wings.'
Leo: 'How's Piper?' Phoebe: 'She's dealing. I mean, it's not everyday that you find out that the guy you're seeing isn't human. Although, in Piper's case ...'

Notes: 'I'm gonna die and there's nothing you can do about it.' An important episode, as much for its confirmation of the Leo/Piper relationship as for the wealth of new lore that the script provides. The strength of 'Love Hurts' lies in its clever deconstruction of some traditional genre clichés. It's also terrifically well-acted and, despite a couple of cul-de-sacs along the way, the plot resolves itself in a satisfyingly complete way.

Soundtrack: 'Human' by The Pretenders and 'Human (On The Inside)' by Nine Inch Nails.

22: DÉJÀ VU ALL OVER AGAIN

26 May 1999

Writers: Brad Kern, Constance M Burge
Director: Les Sheldon

Cast: David Carradine (Tempus), Carlos Gomez (Inspector Rodriguez), Wendy Benson (Joanne Hertz),
Nancy O'Dell (Weatherperson)

> The warlock impersonating Rodriguez plans to kill the Charmed Ones. Tempus, a time-manipulating demon, guarantees that Rodriguez will be given every opportunity to succeed. Stuck in a time-loop, repeating the same day over and over with minor variations, Phoebe begins to experience a strange sense of *déjà vu*.

Dreaming (As Blondie Once Said) is Free: Phoebe has a vivid premonition of Andy's death. Again, and again, and again.

It's Witchcraft: *The Book of Shadows* contains a spell to accelerate time, which the sisters eventually use to end Wednesday, even though it means that Andy must stay dead. The spell begins: 'Winds of time gather round, give me wings to speed my way.'

The Conspiracy Starts at the Witching Hour: Tempus is described as 'The Devil's Sorcerer'. To vanquish him, *The Book of Shadows* requires that he be taken out of the time he's in. There is a vague suggestion that Tempus is sent to help Rodriguez by a higher demon power.

Work is a Four-Letter Word: At the end of the episode, Piper is planning to give up her job at [quake] and fulfil her dream of owning a restaurant (however, see 'Witch Trial').

It's a Designer Label!: The award for this season's Fashion Victim of the Year goes to Tempus's Duran Duran-look.

References: There are allusions to *The Wizard of Oz*; *Batman*; The Food Channel; and Celine Dion. Most of the great US telefantasy shows of the last decade have done *Groundhog Day*-style plots including *Star Trek: The Next Generation* ('Cause and Effect'), *The X-Files* ('Monday'), *Stargate SG-1* ('Window of Opportunity') and *Buffy the Vampire Slayer* ('Life Serial'). The Andy-and-Prue-in-a-white-void scene is a conceptual and visual steal from the Michael Powell and Emeric Pressburger 1946 masterpiece *A Matter of Life and Death*.

The Legend That Is ...: David Carradine made his movie debut in 1964 in *Taggart* and appeared in the TV adaptation of *Shane*. His roles in Martin Scorsese's *Boxcar Bertha* (1972, co-starring Carradine's then-wife Barbara Hershey) and *Death Race 2000* brought him cult status. A student of martial arts, Carradine was perfectly cast as the existential drifter Kwai Chang Caine in *Kung Fu*, whilst his background in the LA counterculture scene was key to his performance as Woody Guthrie in *Bound for Glory*. His other movies include *Mean Streets, Cannonball, The Long Riders, Hammer House of Mystery and Suspense: A Distant Scream, I Saw What You Did, Bird on a Wire, Field of Fir* and *Roadside Prophets*. He also directed the movies *You and Me, Mata Hari* and *Americana* and played the title role in Tarantino's *Kill Bill*.

'You May Remember Me ...': Nancy O'Dell appeared in *Scream 3*. Wendy Benson's CV includes *Bobby's Whore, Bull* and *The X-Files*.

Behind the Camera: Stunt co-ordinator Noon Orsatti's CV also includes *Not Another Teen Movie, The Limey, Pleasantville* and *Alien: Resurrection*.

Classic *Double Entendre*: Rodriguez, to Andy: 'Prue Halliwell is a witch. You're gonna arrange a meeting with her tonight, you understand? Or else I'm gonna bust your ass and expose hers.' More of a *single entendre* when you think about it.

Logic, Let Me Introduce You To This Window: How do the sisters explain Andy's death in their living room? (A sort-of answer is given by Darryl in 'Witch Trial' but it's not very satisfying.) The paperboy delivers only to the Halliwells in their entire street. When Piper and Phoebe are in the kitchen talking, Phoebe's hair is in a bun. As they emerge to see Prue, her hair is down. During the same sequence, Piper is wearing a cross. Subsequently, she's wears a butterfly necklace. There is no station ID on the TV weather report. There are more dating problems. Given that Piper was in the same class as Joanne, who is 26, she must be roughly the same age. She should, however, be 25 at most.

Continuity: Sometime between the final scene of the last episode and the beginning of this one, Rodriguez killed his partner, Anderson, and laid the blame on Andy. The headline in the *San Francisco Ledger* report that Prue and Phoebe read is SAN FRANCISCO INSPECTOR SUSPECTED IN I.A. MURDER. (Other headers briefly glimpsed include LOCAL RESIDENT

SEASON 1: DÉJÀ VU ALL OVER AGAIN

DAVE MAGNO FOUND DEAD, and NEW FACTORY BOOSTS STATE ECONOMY.) Joanne Hertz was in the same graduating class as Piper in 1992 at Baker High School. Joanne subsequently went to New York, married into money, and is now a TV producer.

Cruelty to Animals: Kit knocks over a pepper pot and ends up sneezing. Again, and again, and again.

Quote/Unquote: Piper: 'What am I supposed to say? I'm a cash-strapped, single restaurant-manager who still lives in the same house I grew up in with my sisters.' Phoebe: 'And the cat. Don't forget the cat!'
    Phoebe: 'Prue, I am *not* nuts. Okay, maybe a little bit, but that's irrelevant here.'
    Tempus: 'Hurts to die, doesn't it?'
    Rodriguez: 'I know my partner was killed by a supernatural being. I think Prue Halliwell could help me find out who did it.' Andy: 'Really? I'll get the commissioner to signal Batman.'
    Piper, to Joanne: 'Just because I may not have realised my dreams yet, like you think you have, it doesn't mean I won't ... And I'm damn sure I'll be doing it with my own nose, not one some discount doctor gave me.'

Notes: 'Let's just get this day over with.' A visually stimulating intellectual parallelogram to *Groundhog Day*, 'Déjà Vu All Over Again' is a critical summation of all the best elements of *Charmed*'s first year. Like most of the previous episodes, bits of it are great, some stuff is less impressive but, overall, it works really well. It has a confident swagger, some humane conceits and a bit of required compassion at, crucially, a level just below the manipulative. Behind the scenes circumstances, it is alleged, dictated the departure of Ted King, but Andy's death is stunningly handled and played. One of the highlights of the episode is watching a genuine legend like David Carradine hamming it up for all he's worth. Even here, you sense that he was having a great time doing so. Best bits: Phoebe and Piper's 'death scenes'; Rodriguez's pyrotechnic demise; Tempus reversing time with San Francisco at night as his backdrop. The season ends in the same way as the first episode, with Prue using her power to gently close the Manor's door behind her. Magical.

Soundtrack: The episode begins to the wail of the Cranberries' indescribably annoying 'Animal Instinct'. Thereafter, it gets better: Citizen King's 'Better Days'; 'Calling All Angels' by Jane Siberry; and Beth Hart's gorgeous 'Delicious Surprise'.

Did You Know?: No *official* explanation was ever given for TW King's departure from *Charmed* after this episode.

CHARMED SEASON 2
(1999-2000)

Coordinating Producers: Jonathan Levin, Betty Reardon
Producers: Sheryl J Anderson, Jon Paré
Co-Executive Producer: David Simkins
Co-Producers: Javier Grillo-Marxuach, Vivian Mayhew (23-35), Valerie Mayhew (23-35),
Chris Levinson (36-44), Zack Estrin (36-44)
Executive Producers: Brad Kern, Constance M Burge, Aaron Spelling, E Duke Vincent
Associate Producer: Peter Chomsky

Regular Cast:
Shannen Doherty (Prue Halliwell)
Holly Marie Combs (Piper Halliwell)
Alyssa Milano (Phoebe Halliwell)
Greg Vaughan (Dan Gordon, 23, 25-36, 38-41, 44)
Dorian Gregory (Darryl Morris, 23, 27, 31, 33, 35-38, 40-44)
Brian Krause (Leo Wyatt, 24, 26, 28, 30, 34-38, 40-44)

23: WITCH TRIAL

30 September 1999

Writer: Brad Kern
Director: Craig Zisk

Cast: Jennifer Rhodes (Penny Halliwell), Sibila Vargas (Sierra Stone), Greg Cromer (Rob), Karis Paige Bryant (Jenny Gordon), Janet Wood (Mrs Milton), Rich Cramer (Nicholas),[31] Jesse D Goins (Doctor), Walter Phelan (Abraxas), Matt Entriken (Assistant), Mark Nearing (Paramedic), Eric Scott Woods (Jeremy),[32] Amanda Wyss (Stevie)[33]

> On the first anniversary of the Halliwell sisters becoming witches, the demon Abraxas steals *The Book of Shadows* into another dimension and begins to reverse all the spells they've cast. This causes several vanquished demons to return. Meanwhile, Prue's guilt over Andy's death leaves her reluctant to save their powers.

It's Witchcraft: At the end of the episode, it's revealed it is Grams' spirit that has been turning the pages of *The Book of Shadows* to reveal spells over the past year. Abraxas is a demon from the astral plane who destroys witches by demonising their powers.

The Rite of Passage spell from *The Book of Shadows* states: 'Fight it with The Power of One, or else a more powerful evil that awaits will destroy you.' The sisters vanquish Abraxas with a spell that begins: 'The oldest of Gods are invoked here, the great work of magic is sought. In this night, and in this hour we call upon the ancient power.'

A Little Learning is a Dangerous Thing: The Halliwells' new neighbours are Dan Gordon and his teenage niece, Jenny, whose parents are currently in Saudi Arabia (where her father works for the State Department).

The Conspiracy Starts at the Witching Hour: Three of the Charmed Ones' former enemies return: Jeremy ('Something Wicca This Way Comes'), Nicholas ('That 70s Episode') and the Woogyman ('Is There A

---

[31] Note that Nicholas is played by a different actor from 'That 70s Episode'.
[32] Uncredited.
[33] Uncredited.

SEASON 2: WITCH TRIAL

Woogy In The House?').

Work is a Four-Letter Word: Piper has now decided that she wants to open a night-club rather than a restaurant and has selected one, The Industrial Zone, the last two owners of which went bankrupt. After Piper fails to secure a loan from Rob, largely because of Jeremy's attack, Prue and Phoebe acquire the $60,000 needed from Home Equity Loan by taking out a second mortgage on the Manor. Thus, technically, the club will be jointly owned by all three sisters.

It's a Designer Label!: Two outstanding dresses – Phoebe's light blue one and Prue's long black number.

References: Phoebe acquires several books including *Wiccan*, *Wicca Garden*, Montague Summers' *Encyclopaedia of Witchcraft and Demonology* (see 'Ex Libris') and *Goddess Spirituality Rites*. Also, allusions to *Fawlty Towers* and *Bill & Ted's Excellent Adventure*. Phoebe quotes the popular aphorisms 'Forewarned is forearmed' and 'When in Rome do as the Romans do.'

'You May Remember Me ...': Rich Cramer appeared in *Terminal Error*, *Spy Hard* and *The West Wing*. Karis Paige Bryant's CV includes *While Justice Sleeps*. Janet Wood played Sweet Lil'l Alice in *Up!* and appeared in *The Centrefold Girls*. Greg Cromer was in *Mother Ghost*. Jesse D Goins appeared in *Soldier*, *Patriot Games* and *24*. Walter Phelan's movies include *from Dusk Till Dawn*. Matt Entriken was in *Starship Troopers*. Mark Nearing appeared in *Terrorgram*. Amanda Wyss played Randi MacFarland in *Highlander* and was in *To Die For* and *Buck Rogers in the 25th Century*.

Cigarettes and Alcohol: The Halliwells are out of wine ... Until the obliging Dan calls round with a bottle.

Sex and Drugs and Rock n Roll: Finding Piper kissing her 'banker friend', Rob, Phoebe considers that her sister is single, responsible *and*, 'way overdue in the sex department.' Piper says she would never sleep with a guy simply to get something. There's yet another excessively long discussion about tampons (see 'The Power of Two').

When Phoebe and Piper attend a meeting of fellow witches and believers in a – presumably well-hidden – wooded area, inevitably, it ends with them taking their clothes off. And, hey, why not?

Logic, Let Me Introduce You To This Window: Phoebe describes Jenny

SEASON 2: WITCH TRIAL

as 'a great kid.' Surely that should be 'whiny, self-involved, obnoxious brat' or something similar? In 'That 70s Episode,' a pouch full of various ingredients was needed to vanquish Nicholas along with a spell. In this episode, Prue vanquishes him using *just* the spell.

Continuity: Given that the anniversary of the sisters becoming the Charmed Ones falls on the autumnal equinox, that would place the events of 'Something Wicca This Way Comes' on 21 September 1998. Prue says that they have been demon-free for a month, and it is later stated that Prue hasn't faced a demon since Andy died. Thus, 'Déjà Vu All Over Again' appears to have taken place in mid-August 1999. Piper hasn't heard from Leo in 'weeks' (see 'Love Hurts'). Darryl hasn't been assigned a new partner to replace Andy yet. It's SWA Properties (see 'From Fear to Eternity') that's selling the nightclub Piper wants to buy.

Motors: New season, new car – Piper has a replacement Jeep, a dark green model (2CON654), although viewers don't really get a decent look at it until 'P^3 H^{2}0'.

Quote/Unquote: Piper, as Phoebe lusts after Dan: 'Demons now, drooling later.'
Rob, asking why Piper would want to risk the financial burden of the club: 'You could lose your shirt.' Piper: 'Wouldn't be the first time today.'

Notes: 'Without *The Book of Shadows*, we're not the Charmed Ones anymore.' A new season and, with it, a new set of challenges to be faced. One of which may well have been finding out whose bright idea it was to introduce the character Jenny – a gross miscalculation, which fortunately the production team recognised after four episodes. That apart, 'Witch Trial' is a pretty decent start to the series' second year, with a plot that looks to the past and, having re-established who the sisters are and how they came to be, pointing a way to the future. Mostly good stuff, actually, although not without some flaws.
Switched to Thursday nights for this season, *Charmed*'s new lead-in show was the high school drama series, *Popular*.

Did You Know?: The symbol on the cover of *The Book of Shadows* is referred to in this episode as a triquetra – which, Prue suggests, represents the Power of Three working together as one. In fact, in runic lore, the triquetra is a feminine symbol of protection from evil, formed by three yonic vesicas. These represent the triple Goddess and, if used, the circle represents eternity. The same symbol appears on the cover of Led Zeppelin's fourth LP (you know, the one with 'Stairway to Heaven' on it), released in 1971. Each symbol was supposed to represent one member of the band, and the triquetra was chosen by bassist John Paul Jones from a book of runes. In contemporary publicity, the symbol was said to represent confidence and competence.

Soundtrack: 'Ladyfingers' by Luscious Jackson.

24: MORALITY BITES

07 October 1999

Writers: Chris Levinson, Zack Estrin
Director: John Behring

Cast: Pat Skipper (Nathaniel Pratt), Clara Thomas (Melinda), Lisa Connaughton (Anne), Jennifer Hale (Carpool Neighbor), Sibila Vargas (Sierra Stone), Dan Horton (Cal Greene), Michael Brownlee (Sports Reporter), Richard Saxton (TV Anchor From 2009), Claudia Gold (Screaming Woman), Darron Johnson (Hallway Guard), Tina Thomas (Assistant #1), Taili Song (Assistant #2)

> When Phoebe has a vision of her future self being burned to death, the sisters must travel forward a decade to learn what happened. There, they discover that Phoebe has used her powers to kill someone. A local DA has initiated a witch trial as a platform for political office. As Prue and Piper try to save Phoebe, they both are surprised – and somewhat disappointed – to learn how their own lives will turn out.

Dreaming (As Blondie Once Said) is Free: Phoebe has a premonition of her own death, burned at the stake on 26 February 2009.

Future-Imperfect: Six months prior to the future events (so, approximately August 2008), Phoebe used her magic powers to kill baseball player Cal Greene. Greene was, himself, a murderer – he killed a friend of Phoebe's, but got off on a technicality. Phoebe was outraged and crossed the line from protecting the innocent to punishing the guilty. She was caught, and her magic exposed by ambitious District Attorney Nathaniel Pratt.

It's Witchcraft: The Move Ahead In Time Spell begins: 'Hear these words, hear the rhyme. We send to you this burning sign. Then our future selves will find. In another place and time.' Among the other spells used are one to create a door. The spell to return the sisters to the present should be in *The Book of Shadows* between one concerning a demon with a tusk and another designed to discourage a lover.

At the conclusion, Leo appears to suggest that it was the Whitelighter Elders who sent Prue, Piper and Phoebe back to the present, having satisfied themselves that the sisters had learned their lesson not to use magic for revenge.

The Conspiracy Starts at the Witching Hour: It was seemingly the random – if amusing – revenge that Piper and Prue played on Nathaniel Pratt after he allowed his dog to defecate on the Halliwells' front path that set Pratt on a road that would, a decade later, end in Phoebe's horrific death.

Work is a Four-Letter Word: In 2009, Prue runs Buckland's – which now has offices in Tokyo, London and Paris.

It's a Designer Label!: There's nowhere else to start (or, indeed, finish) but future-Prue's leather miniskirt.

References: The title alludes to Ben Stiller's cult 1994 examination of Generation X, *Reality Bites*. The episode, conceptually, bears strong resemblance to *Quantum Leap* (and specifically that series' episode 'Last Dance Before the Execution'). The – terrific – passage-of-time special effects seem to have been inspired by scenes in the 1960 film adaptation of HG Wells's *The Time Machine*. When Phoebe is channel surfing she briefly passes *Justice Today*. In 2009, the scheduled programme that the live execution of Phoebe Halliwell is due to replace is MTV's *Real World 18: On the Moon*. There's an allusion to the philosophy of Marcus Cicero (106-43BC), whilst Pratt paraphrases *Apocalypse Now* ('I love the smell of burnt witch in the morning').

'You May Remember Me ...': Pat Skipper's movies include *Seabiscuit* and *Erin Brokovitch*. Clara Thomas was in *What Dreams May Come*. Lisa Connaughton appeared in *Skeleton Woman*. Jennifer Hale is a voice artist who had worked on *Justice League*. Sibila Vargas is best known as the host of *Hollywood Insider*. Dan Horton appeared in *The West Wing*. Michael Brownlee was in *Bruce Almighty*. Richard Saxton's CV includes *Wag the Dog*, *Girls in Prison* and *Ellen*. Claudia Gold was in *Hang Time*. Darron Johnson appeared in *God's Army*. Tina Thomas's movies include *Fever*. Taili Song was in *Very Mean Man*.

Logic, Let Me Introduce You To This Window: If the sisters are sent back in time to a moment just before they first encountered Nathanial Pratt, then why does the news story about Cal Greene appear *before* they encounter him in the revised timeline? Previously, it was only *after* magicking dog-shit onto Pratt's shoe that Phoebe went channel surfing and saw the story that triggered her premonition in the first place. When future-Prue looks through *The Book of Shadows* and notices all the personal gain spells, she passes the return spell that had supposedly disappeared. If future-Prue owns Bucklands, why does she still have the same office? Piper currently cannot freeze anything outside the room that she's in – however, if the window is open, she can freeze someone outside as well. When Piper and Prue are looking through *The Book of Shadows*, on the page next to the binding spell is another spell. When Prue subsequently rips out the binding spell page, the page opposite is blank. All the cars seen in the 2009 sequences seen to be of a 1999 vintage. Quick, somebody inform the witch-hunters that a furry animal is attacking Shannen Doherty's head ... Oh, hang on, it's a wig.

Continuity: When discussing going forward in time with her sisters, Phoebe reminds Prue and Piper that they almost died travelling to the past (see 'That 70s Episode'). In the future, at the age of 38, Prue will become a wealthy woman so buried in her work that she has no social life. She has – really scary – blonde hair and her powers are considerably enhanced. Piper, again with much greater powers than currently, married Leo but is now about to get a divorce. They were happy for a while and tried to make the marriage work whilst both retained their powers, but eventually a schism occurred (seemingly due to Phoebe's predicament). The couple have a daughter, Melinda, who also has powers (as the daughter of a witch and a Whitelighter, you'd expect nothing less) but has been told by her mother never to use them. Phoebe is able to levitate herself (a power that she *will* eventually attain in 'The Honeymoon's Over'). However this future will now never happen: Prue died in 2001 (see 'All Hell Breaks Lose'), Phoebe will die at an old age from a warlock attack (see 'The Three Faces of Phoebe') and Piper's first child is not a girl, but a boy (see 'The Day The Magic Died'). This is the first episode in which Whitelighters' powers of teleportation are referred to as 'orbing'.

Quote/Unquote: Piper: 'What a difference a decade makes.'

Prue: 'Do you know if my husband called by any chance?' Anne: 'Husband? Good one! Like *you* have the time.'

Phoebe, to Pratt: 'At least I'm paying for my crime. There'll come a day where you have to pay for yours.'

Notes: 'I saw my future. I was being executed.' A beautiful meditation on fate, causality, crimes of passion, the thirst for vengeance and, magnificently, redemption. 'Morality Bites' is an outstanding example of *Charmed*'s occasionally-displayed ability to create big dramatic ideas from a minimalist setting. A piece of *bijoux* death-row theatre that could have drowned in a *faux-naïf* avalanche of cheap slogans in lesser hands. Instead, thanks to some great performances, suspension of disbelief is not a problem here. It's fair to say that, often, *Charmed* can be dismissed as mildly entertaining fluff – this episode proves that, when they put their mind to it, the production team can fashion something much deeper and more impressive than the norm.

Soundtrack: Stroke 9's 'Tail of Sun'.

25: THE PAINTED WORLD

21 October 1999
Writer: Constance M Burge
Director: Kevin Inch

Cast: Karis Paige Bryant (Jenny), Paul Kersey (Malcolm), Holly Fields (Jane Franklin), Damian Perkins (Joe), Cindy Lu (Receptionist), Anthony Deane (Applicant #1), Rebecca Jackson (Applicant #2), Tate Taylor (Applicant #3), Ryan Notch (Seth), J R Richards (Himself)

> Appraising a painting, Prue discovers a man trapped inside it. Believing him to be an innocent, Prue attempts to free him but, instead, becomes trapped within the painting herself. Meanwhile, Phoebe casts a spell to increase her intelligence.

It's Witchcraft: In the 1920s, a witch named Nell tricked a warlock, Malcolm, into a painting using a hidden spell that only his X-ray-vision could see (*Absolvo amitto amplus brevis semper mea*). The Latin chant *Verva omnes liberant* ('Free us all') will release anyone trapped inside the painting, but only if *they* say it.

Phoebe's 'smart spell' begins: 'Spirits, send the words from all across the land. Allow me to absorb them through the touch of either hand.'

A Little Learning is a Dangerous Thing: Prue can read Latin. Phoebe can't. Usually. Piper has a four-year degree, which has, it seems, inspired Phoebe to think about either taking night classes or, perhaps, returning to college. After making herself incredibly smart for 24 hours with an embiggened-brain-spell, Phoebe tells Piper, who's worrying that Prue didn't come home the previous night, that 63% of all adults believed to be missing show up within a day. If Piper factors in Prue's good health, a life expectancy of 78.5 years and her defensive powers of telekinesis, the odds are less than 4% that anything nasty has happened to Prue. Later, Phoebe watches a TV quiz show and knows that: the science primarily concerned with blood and blood-forming organs is haematology; Oona Chaplin, the wife of Charlie Chaplin (1889-1977), was the daughter of American playwright Eugene O'Neill (1888-1953); and the country that now occupies the Peninsula once known as Asia Minor is Turkey.

The Conspiracy Starts at the Witching Hour: There is said to be a history of insanity linked to ownership of the painting. In reality, however, the painting is owned by Jane, Malcolm's warlock lover, who has been trying to release Malcolm for the last 70 years.

Work is a Four-Letter Word: Phoebe takes an aptitude test for a job with an interactive network company called Web San Francisco, having faxed them her résumé.

It's a Designer Label!: Highlights include Prue's mega-revealing black dress and Phoebe's tight white top (the yellow hard-hat she also wears, actually, makes it *more* sexy). However, Piper's frumpy shoes really don't go with her green miniskirt.

References: Allusions to *Good Will Hunting*; *Rain Man*; Tolstoy's *War and Peace*; the universities of Havard and Stanford; Oasis's 'Live Forever'; physicist Albert Einstein (1879-1955), one of the great revisers of mankind's understanding of the universe; and pianist Wladziu Liberace (1919-87). A copy of the book *The Complete Astrologer* is seen in the Manor.

'You May Remember Me ...': Paul Kersey was in *Forbidden Island*. Holly Fields appeared in *Hip Edgy Sexy Cool* and *Runaway Daughters*. Damian Perkins was in *CSI: Miami*. Cindy Lu's movies include *Rush Hour 2*. Anthony Deane appeared in *Becoming Marty*. Rebecca Jackson was in *Batty*. Tate Taylor's CV includes *Planet of the Apes* and *Chicken Party*, which he also wrote and directed. Ryan Notch was in *Sex and the City*. J R Richards played Derek in *Almost Anything*.

Cigarettes and Alcohol: Piper met Prue's personable colleague Joe Lyons at a wine auction.

Sex and Drugs and Rock n Roll: Dan asks Piper for a favour. Jenny needs help with a paper for Biology relating to the human reproductive system. This is a subject, he notes, that is awkward for him to talk to his niece about. Piper agrees to help as she has plenty of experience of talking about sex. Jenny subsequently tells Phoebe that she was too embarrassed to tell Dan that she already knows all about the subject.

Logic, Let Me Introduce You To This Window: Phoebe speed-reads *Webster's Dictionary* by opening the book approximately a quarter of the way through (somewhere towards 'D', probably). She therefore shouldn't be able to recite the definition for 'abaca' (a strong fibre obtained from a banana leaf). When Phoebe is writing the spell in her room, as Piper enters and Phoebe quickly hides the spell, the piece of paper on which she's writing is in the middle pages. When Piper leaves and Phoebe takes out

SEASON 2: THE PAINTED WORLD

the book, the paper is just inside the cover.

Continuity: Prue notes that obsession runs in the Halliwell family. Piper's new (and, as yet, unopened) club is called P³ (see 'The Devil's Music').

Motors: Phoebe has recently backed Prue's car into a pole. This will cost $1,200 to repair.

Cruelty to Animals: To send her sisters the release spell, Phoebe pushes Kit into the painting with the three-word spell attached to the cat's collar.

Quote/Unquote: Phoebe: 'Smart people don't do stupid things. Only stupid people do.'
Piper: 'What's up?' Phoebe: 'The Dow Jones, housing prices and space shuttle Discovery.'
Piper on Phoebe's new abilities: 'She's a walking brain trust. Einstein with cleavage.'

Notes: 'I just want you to sell that painting as soon as you can.' An amusing pastiche of haunted house movies. The idea of trapping first Prue and then Piper in a gothic castle within a painting is a clever dramatic device that pays off with some witty interplay between them (particularly when they're being attacks by elemental forces). However, 'The Painted World' is very much Phoebe's episode – with an intelligent use of intelligence itself amid Alyssa's usual wise-cracking delivery. Best bit: Phoebe's biologically accurate, if somewhat adult, drawing to help Jenny with her homework.

Soundtrack: 'Needs' by Collective Soul.

Did You Know?: We all know what happens when you put Tara Reid and Shannen Doherty in a room together. According to the *New York Metro*'s 'Intelligencier' section, their South Beach spies reported that on 21 February 2004, Reid and Doherty were sitting at adjacent tables at the opening of a new club, Mansion. 'They were squabbling,' said a source. 'Tara tried to get Nicole Richie's bodyguard to throw Shannen out.' Doherty was apparently unfazed. 'She said, "She needs to go to rehab".'

26: THE DEVIL'S MUSIC

14 October 1999

Writer: David Simkins
Director: Richard Compton

Cast: Karis Paige Bryant (Jenny), David Haydn-Jones (Chris Barker), Larry Holden (Jeff Carlton), Alexandra Picatto (Tina Hitchens), Chris Nelson (Masselin), Ralph Garman (DJ), Robert Madrid (Roadie #1), Smalls (Bouncer), Dishwalla (Themselves)

> Leo lures the manager of rock band Dishwalla to P^3, aware that the man has made a pact with a demon that grants him fame and fortune in exchange for innocent souls. However, Darryl becomes involved when he investigates the disappearance of young women from many of Dishwalla's concerts.

It's Witchcraft: The demon, Masselin, made a bargain with Jeff Carlton. The latter will become rich and powerful by attracting successful bands to his management company, whilst the demon is provided with a steady stream of rock chicks to devour. Trapped within the demon, his unfortunate victims are still alive, their souls tortured for pleasure. A strong antacid, supplied by the Halliwells, vanquishes the demon and frees his victims.

Leo has the power to erase memories (or, as he puts it, to make pain go away).

A Little Learning is a Dangerous Thing: Loathsome and slimy Chris Barker appears at first to be an investment banker with a simple crush on Prue. (He'd like to take her to dinner ... in Paris.) When Prue plays hard to get, his true motives become clear. He's after a controlling interest in P^3 and, to this end, is prepared to loan Prue money. Once the Dishwalla booking is confirmed, and his loan is no longer required, Barker approaches the Halliwells' bank, offering a hostile takeover of the debt that Prue and Phoebe secured in 'Witch Trial'. Fortunately his encounter with the Power of Three and the sisters' vanquishing of Masselin prove that Barker doesn't have the stomach for gruesome stage theatrics, and he withdraws his offer.

The Conspiracy Starts at the Witching Hour: Among various theories that

SEASON 2: THE DEVIL'S MUSIC

Darryl has formulated concerning the sisters is the idea that they work for the CIA.

It's a Designer Label!: Impressive item: Piper's lovely purple dress. Less impressive: Prue's sparkly trousers and Jenny's rather disturbing minxy jailbait look. That's a nice silver nothing that Phoebe is almost wearing in the club.

References: Band posters seen both in P³ and Butterfly's Cocoon include ones of the B-52s, REM, Depeche Mode, Green Day, New Order, Iron Hand, Sulphur and the Cruel Shoes. There are allusions to *Jaws* ('We need a bigger balloon'); MTV; *The Sound of Music*; and *Elvis: That's The Way It Is*. The offices of San Francisco radio station KJCH-FM are seen.

'You May Remember Me ...': David Haydn-Jones was in *Double Take*. Larry Holden appeared in *Ted*, *Memento* and *CSI*. Alexandra Picatto's CV includes *Teen Angel*, *Malcolm in the Middle* and *Get Real*. Ralph Garman was in *NYPD Blue*. Robert Madrid appeared in *Coyote* and *Angel*.

Behind the Camera: David Simkins also worked on *FreakyLinks*, *Dark Angel*, *Roswell*, *Lois & Clark: The New Adventures of Superman*, *The Adventures of Brisco County Jr.*, *Beyond Our Control* and, for a very brief period, *Angel*.

Sex and Drugs and Rock n Roll: Carlton tells a bouncer that Phoebe has something illegal in her purse. He asks if Darryl has any idea how many girls show up to an average rock show. They all look the same – short skirts and tight tops. Like sexy little peas in a pod.
 Carlton notes that Dishwalla: '... want to reacquaint themselves with the personal side of performing. They want to connect again.' Pretentious, or what?

Logic, Let Me Introduce You To This Window: When Carlton takes Jenny backstage to meet the band, Dishwalla are still onstage. Doesn't she want to stay and see the rest of the gig before meeting them? Shouldn't the sisters be a shade more worried about what Barker thinks when he ends his night covered in demon crud? If, after Leo's intervention, none of Messalin's victims has any memories, then isn't prosecuting Carlton as a kidnapper going to somewhat difficult? It's very obvious that the Butterfly Cocoon dressing room in which the first victim is killed and the room in P³ are, in fact, the same set slightly (but only *very* slightly) redressed.

Continuity: Leo confirms that he looks after other witches beside the sisters. He is a big baseball fan and knows that Dan Gordon used to play second base for the Seattle Mariners before he injured his knee.

Cruelty to Animals: Piper notes that the sisters have difficulty giving their cat a vitamin pill.

Quote/Unquote: Phoebe: 'This place couldn't be more dead if I was embalmed.'
Jenny: 'Do you think it'll be possible for me to meet the band? I'd do almost anything.' Carlton: 'Be careful what you wish for, sweetheart.'
Piper, to Carlton: 'Listen up, skidmark. Tell us how to save Jenny and get Elvis out of the building, or spending an eternity in Hell is gonna be the least of your worries.'

Notes: 'All this freeing and destroying, is this in-between sets or during the encore?' A well-fashioned exposé of dodgy music business shenanigans (with an amusing supernatural twist) that works for the most part but is almost fatally ruined by the inclusion of Jenny. The dramatic potential for a story that, basically, involves a 13 year old girl gatecrashing a nightclub and ending up as (metaphorical) rape fodder is serious and needed a far stronger platform than this to work with anything like the necessary impact required. It also needed a far better performance than the one that Karis Paige Bryant was able to supply. That apart, there's some fun to be had (particularly in the Prue subplot).

Soundtrack: 'Fortified Grapes' by Gordon and four songs by guest band Dishwalla – 'Counting Blue Cars', 'Find Your Way Back Home', 'Stay Awake' and 'Until I Wake Up'. This was the first of what was to become a recurring motif over the next couple of seasons – having a musical guest in many episodes.

27: SHE'S A MAN, BABY, A MAN!

04 November 1999

Writer: Javier Grillo-Marxuach
Director: Martha Mitchell

Cast: Lex Medlin (Alan Stanton), Michael McLafferty (Stein), Heidi Mark (Darla), Nick Stabile (Owen Grant), Georgia Emelin (Jan), Jamison Yang (Coroner), Dean Kelly (Gorgeous Man), The Cranberries (Themselves)

> As San Francisco stews in its own heatwave, Phoebe experiences several vivid dreams of seducing men before murdering them. The sisters discover that Phoebe is psychically linked to a female demon known as the Succubus. To lure the demon, Prue casts a spell, which turns her into a man.

Dreaming (As Blondie Once Said) is Free: Phoebe tells Piper that she's in a highly excited state. She has been having sexually explicit dreams. This takes place in a swanky penthouse love den, with candles, satin sheets, the full sensual experience. But every night it's with a different man, each of whom tells Phoebe that she is irresistible. Then, they have wild and abandoned sex, after which, Phoebe kills the man. Piper suggests that there is nothing wrong with Phoebe – the dream is just a metaphor for extreme sexual frustration.

It's Witchcraft: When a witch renounces all human emotions and makes a pact with darkness to protect herself from heartbreak, she becomes a Succubus, a sexual predator. The Succubus seeks out powerful men who become helpless against her magic. She then feeds on the victim's testosterone with her razor-sharp tongue. (Suggests a whole new meaning to 'giving tongue,' doesn't it?) The spell to reveal the Succubus that turns Prue into a man begins: 'By the forces of heaven and hell, draw to us this woman fell, rend from her foul desire, that she may perish as a moth of fire.'

A Little Learning is a Dangerous Thing: Phoebe suggests that what really makes a man is the clothes he wears, the car he drives and the money he earns.

The Conspiracy Starts at the Witching Hour: All the murder victims were

SEASON 2: SHE'S A MAN, BABY, A MAN!

members of the Fine Romance Dating Agency.

It's a Designer Label!: It's difficult to look beyond Phoebe's shorts. But, perseverance will be rewarded, with Piper's bosom-busting red dress.

References: Allusions to notorious erotic drama *The Red Shoe Diaries*; *Playboy* creator Hugh Hefner; *Cosmopolitan*; actor Tom Hanks (*Forrest Gump*, *Apollo 13*, *Saving Private Ryan*); the San Francisco 49ers; Cheap Trick's 'I Want You To Want Me'; and camp fitness expert Richard Simmons.

'You May Remember Me ...': Lex Medlin appeared in *Film Club*. Michael McLafferty's movies include *Jawbreaker* and *Poison Ivy: The New Seduction*. Heidi Mark's CV includes *Rock Star* and *Married ... With Children*. Nick Stabile played Jamie Roth in *Popular*. Georgia Emelin appeared in *Space Cowboys*, *Daddy* and *Frasier*. Jamison Young's movies include *Godzilla*.

Sex and Drugs and Rock n Roll: Phoebe's libido is said to be connected to the Succubus. It's not like she hasn't dreamed about sex before, she confesses.

Gosh, but Heidi Mark is a well-built young woman.

Logic, Let Me Introduce You To This Window: Manny's manly man-boobs are a bit bigger than one might expect in a svelte little chap such as he.

Weird, But True: When Shannen Doherty is playing Manny she looks *uncannily* like Sean Penn.

Continuity: Phoebe refers to the time that Piper became a werewolf (see 'The Wendigo'). Prue's latest romantic interest is a colleague, Alan, with whom she had a cosy dinner but who seems a bit stand-offish despite her putting out the signals. It turns out he *is* interested, but was unsure of how Prue would react to a more forward approach. Meanwhile, Piper is busy making a play for hunky neighbour Dan, and Phoebe is getting on *really* well with Dr Owen Grant, whom she met whilst staking out the dating agency.

Quote/Unquote: Prue, as a man: 'I'm wearing clothes from the ex-boyfriend's pile. I have hair in strange places. I have a penis. This is *not* funny.'

Jan: 'Can I just say that you are *really* in touch with your feminine side.'
Prue: 'You have *no* idea.'

SEASON 2: SHE'S A MAN, BABY, A MAN!

Phoebe: 'Did Manny just check out that girl's butt?' Piper: 'Oh God, this is starting to get weird.' Phoebe: '*Starting*? Where've ya been?'

Notes: 'I tell you that, maybe, I'm some kind of man-killing demon, and you want me to go to the bachelor central?' On one level, a simple – but very effective – episode about gender politics. This is nicely articulated in the lovely scene in which Alan and 'Manny' discuss the fact that this is a really confusing time to be a man. However, 'She's a Man, Baby, a Man!' is actually a much deeper, cleverer and more acute investigation of desire-versus-need and, one of *Buffy the Vampire Slayer*'s favourite allegories, 'When we stop talking, we start to communicate.' An episode of *Charmed* is such an unexpected place to find a slice of theoretical McLuhanism[34] that it actually takes a while for the viewer to get to grips with the deep issues that it's addressing. There are numerous clever moments (and brave ones, too, in an episode in which penis envy and impotence metaphors happy co-exist). Best bit: The sisters happily dancing with their respective blokes at the end (if you ignore the dreadful soundtrack).

Soundtrack: Filter's 'Take A Picture', an interesting cover of New Order's 'Blue Monday' by Orgy and those earache-inducing Cranberries again (see 'Déjà Vu All Over Again') performing 'Promises' and 'Just My Imagination', the latter featuring some of the worst miming ever seen on television.

---

[34] McLuhanism: The philosophy contained in the writings of Canadian media guru Marshall McLuhan (1911-80), author of *The Medium is the Message*, which states that the *way* people communicate with each other is actually far more important than *what* they communicate.

28: THAT OLD BLACK MAGIC

11 November 1999

Writers: Vivian Mayhew, Valerie Mayhew
Director: James L Conway

Cast: Karis Paige Bryant (Jenny), Lochlyn Munro (Jack Sheridan), Brigid Brannagh (Tuatha), Jay Michael Ferguson (Kyle Gwideon), John Johnston (Joshua), Pamela Koch (Betty), Teddy Lane Jr. (Director), Maulik Pancholy (Treasure Hunter #1), Jeremy Rowley (Treasure Hunter #2), Liz Boughn (Heather), Matthew Senko (Michael)

> Tuatha, entombed for 200 years, is set free. The sisters learn that only the Chosen One – a teenage boy named Kyle – has the ability to destroy Tuatha, by using the evil witch's magic wand against her. Prue deals with an Internet auction site trying to purchase the wand, whilst Piper must decide between continuing to see Leo or starting a new relationship with Dan.

It's Witchcraft: Tuatha has her own – evil – version of *The Book of Shadows*. This includes a spell designed to 'Disempower a Witch', which involves a red ribbon tied around a fresh human heart. *The Book of Shadows* contains a variant on the same spell. A once-good witch turned evil, Tuatha started using her craft against innocents. Fortunately she was tricked by a previous Chosen One and entombed approximately two centuries earlier. Her powers include a bag of magic dust that she can use to disappear and to shrink others (the latter really impresses Phoebe).

A Little Learning is a Dangerous Thing: Phoebe finds a scrying spell in *The Book of Shadows*. Witches use this technique to find something lost. The process requires a map, a piece of string and a crystal and would, over the following years, become one of *Charmed*'s most regularly used plot-devices when they needed to – quickly – move the story along.[35]

Work is a Four-Letter Word: The KMAB Channel 10 show *What's It Worth?* (a variant on *The Antiques Roadshow*, seemingly) is broadcast, live, from

---

[35] In a wider mystical context, scrying means to divine – especially by means of crystal-gazing, or by candlelight on water. This was the process that Michel Nostradamus (1503-66) used to envision his famed prophecies.

SEASON 2: THAT OLD BLACK MAGIC

Buckland's. Prue's $5,000 valuation of the wand (the pewter and ebony is said to be distinctly 18th Century European) is challenged by the witty, but full-of-himself, Jack Sheridan, who notes that an item is only ever worth as much as someone is willing to pay for it. Jack runs his own Internet auction company. He's a big fan of Prue, noting that if the other specialists at Buckland's have her expertise and talent, he may reconsider a standing job offer that he has from the firm.

It's a Designer Label!: Top marks for Phoebe's pretty, Japanese-style top.

References: The title is that of a song written by Harold Arlen and Johnny Mercer for the 1942 movie *Star Spangled Rhythm*, which subsequently was a hit for the Glenn Miller Orchestra and Frank Sinatra. Allusions: *The Blair Witch Project*; *Indiana Jones and the Last Crusade*; *Star Wars* (Obi Wan); *The Wizard of Oz*; the Lovin' Spoonful's 'Do You Believe in Magic?'; and the comic character Jungle Jim.

'You May Remember Me ...': Lochlyn Munro appeared in *A Guy Thing*, *Scary Movie* and *Dead Man on Campus*. Brigid Brannagh played Wesley's girlfriend, Virginia, on *Angel* and was in *Hyperion Bay*, *Enterprise*, *The West Wing*, *CSI* and *Early Edition*. Jay Michael Ferguson's CV includes *Reality School*, *The Girl's Room* and *Possums*. John Johnston was in *Johnny Bagpipes*. Pamela Kosh played Miss Simpson on *Saved By The Bell*. Teddy Lane's movies include *Red Letters* and *The Apocalypse*. Jeremy Rowley was in *Coyote Ugly*. Maulik Pancholy appeared in *Felicity*.

Behind the Camera: Vivian and Valerie Mayhew also wrote for *The X-Files*.

Cigarettes and Alcohol: Prue has a drink with Jack at P^3.

Logic, Let Me Introduce You To This Window: Exactly how 'lost' are 'the lost caves of Muir Park' if a standard city map contains their location for all to see? Jenny sees Kyle walking down the street when she and Dan are coming home in the car. However, the vehicle is moving away from their house rather than towards it. When Prue, Piper, and Phoebe return from their encounter with Tuatha, Leo notices that Piper is bleeding on the right of her forehead. When Piper walks into the kitchen, the wound has moved.

Continuity: Prue wears Cartier perfume. Kyle is the seventh son of a seventh son (and his brothers include Shaun, Ian and Dylan). Leo notes that the Whitelighters have been watching him since he was a young boy. Piper tells Dan that her relationship with Leo is over.

SEASON 2: THAT OLD BLACK MAGIC

Cruelty to Animals: When Tuatha was entombed, her evil pet snake was entombed with her. Subsequently, when it menaces the sisters at the Manor, Prue spears it with a poker, at which point it duplicates itself. Eventually, Kyle destroys both snakes with the wand.

Quote/Unquote: Phoebe: 'Tuatha? Who *wouldn't* go bad with a name like that?'

Betty: 'My God, who are you?' Tuatha: 'The last being you will ever see.'

Dan, to Leo: 'Don't you have some other house to repair?'

Phoebe: 'I did find one spell, but it requires a human heart, and unfortunately we're still using ours.' Piper: 'Take mine. All it does is get me in trouble.'

Notes: 'This is wrong. He should be battling acne at his age, not evil witches.' Another example of the 'Be careful what you wish for ...' school of dramatic licence. This one's pretty good, actually. Particularly effective is Brigid Brannagh's so-over-the-top-she's-down-the-other-side performance. The episode's flaws are mostly aesthetic, though the pointless subplot involving Jenny could've been jettisoned without losing anything significant. This was, in fact, Karis Paige Bryant's last appearance – the production team having seemingly realised that a significant mistake had been made. Something of a fish-supper special, stripped of the last few episodes' more conceptually deep jiggery-pokery, but with plenty to keep the casual viewer entertained.

Soundtrack: Paula Cole's 'Free', and 'Show Me' by Bree Sharp.

29: THEY'RE EVERYWHERE

18 November 1999

Writer: Sheryl J Anderson
Director: Mel Damski

Cast: Lochlyn Munro (Jack Sheridan), Jim Antonio (Collector #2), Misha Collins (Eric Bragg),
Dean Morris (Ben Bragg), Eddy Sadd (Collector #1), Marcelo Tubert (Museum Tour Guide)

> Phoebe has a vision of a young man, Eric, being pursued by two warlocks. The sisters learn that these warlocks are trying to acquire the location of the Akashic Records, which are believed to contain a complete written account of history – including the future. Meanwhile, Piper and Prue believe the new men in their lives may *both* be warlocks and cast a spell to discover their secrets.

It's Witchcraft: There are said to be 19 warlock-specific death spells in *The Book of Shadows*. The 'Hear Secret Thoughts' spell begins: 'As flame lights shadow, as truth ends fear, open locked thoughts to my mind's willing ear, may the smoke from this candle into everywhere creep, bring innermost voices to my mind in speech.'

A Little Learning is a Dangerous Thing: The Akashic Records are, according to legend, buried in the Iraqi desert. A fabled book, penned by ancient mystics, it's a written account of all significant events throughout time. A sandstone tablet found on the Ivory Coast the previous year is believed to be a map to locate the burial place of the artefact. The engravings are in an indecipherable language.

The Conspiracy Starts at the Witching Hour: The Collectors are a warlock breed that drain the knowledge from people's brains.

Work is a Four-Letter Word: Phoebe has begun working as a medical volunteer at the Bayridge Convalescent Hospital. Jack Sheridan's company handled a collection for Verswang Publications, a German conglomerate.

It's a Designer Label!: Piper's 'tennis' negligee. Contrast this with Jeff's vile shirt and shorts combination.

SEASON 2: THEY'RE EVERYWHERE

References: There are allusions to *The Godfather* (a sick father in an empty hospital); Herod the Great (74-4 BC); Adolf Hitler (1889-1945); and *Indiana Jones and the Last Crusade*.

'You May Remember Me ...': Dean Morris was in *Leap of Faith*. Jim Antonio appeared in *Outbreak*, *Edge of Destruction*, *Little House on the Prairie* and *Mannix*. Misha Collins played Tony in *Girl, Interrupted* and Alexis Drazen in *24*. Edouard Sadd was Mono Shabong in *Action*. Marcelo Tubert played Bob Porter in *The Young and the Restless*.

Behind the Camera: Costume Designer Eilish Zebrasky previously worked on *Hart to Hart*, *Charlie's Angels* and *Murder, She Wrote*.

Sex and Drugs and Rock n Roll: Dan has a friend who is getting married in Tahowan, and he invites Piper to attend this with him. In the same hotel and the same bed type-of-thing?, wonders Prue. Piper notes that this is yet to be decided.

Logic, Let Me Introduce You to This Window: Prue worries that Jack is a warlock because she believes that he can blink. In 'The Witch is Back', Melinda stated that Matthew copied his ability to blink from a witch so, at least at this stage of the series' development, blinking is not necessarily a sign of being a warlock. When the sisters are in the park and the warlock appears behind Prue, Piper freezes him after he puts his finger up to Prue's head. Prue then steps directly to the side. The warlock's hand should have prevented her from doing so. When Prue hangs up on Jack, he gets a dial-tone on his cellphone. Phoebe tells Piper and Prue that a way to find out if someone is a warlock is just to prick them, because warlocks don't bleed. Jeremy certainly did (see 'Something Wicca This Way Comes'). After Eric shoots the Collectors, Phoebe hustles him out of the room. Note that the gun is no longer in his hand. San Francisco must have the least secure museum in the world, judging by the ease with which Eric breaks into a display case, destroys a priceless exhibit and then escapes with Phoebe.

Continuity: Prue mentions the occasion on which the sisters helped a troubled priest with warlock brothers ('When Bad Warlocks Turn Good'). She kept the sacrificial dagger used in that episode in case of emergencies. Prue accuses Piper of being a warlock magnet. Piper wonders if she is ever going to live her relationship with Jeremy down, and reminds Prue that she had 'that Rex and Hannah thing at work.' Jack has an identical twin brother, Jeff, who owns a chain of mortuaries. Phoebe loses three weeks' memories at the end of the episode. (The last thing she remembers is a party at Halloween.)

SEASON 2: THEY'RE EVERYWHERE

Cruelty to Animals: Prue almost vanquishes a poor defenceless peacock. A hornet's nest above the Manor's door seems to be what scares Kit on two occasions. Alternatively, maybe the cat just *doesn't like* Dan. It is, after all, a very perceptive cat.

Quote/Unquote: Prue, finding Phoebe sitting astride Eric: 'Entertaining guests, I see.'

Piper, on Dan: 'He's not a warlock. No cats have hissed at him, he hasn't blinked, he hasn't tried to kill me or my sisters and steal our powers. Which, as you know, is a key indicator.'

Prue, on Jack and his twin brother: 'Okay you unfreeze them. If that prick doesn't bleed, then that one's dead too.'

Phoebe: 'I'm no angel. I could probably introduce you to one, though.'

Prue: 'They really shouldn't have given us the finger.'

Notes: 'To know the future brings, obviously, ultimate power.' A disappointingly incomplete episode that flirts with having really important things to say – particularly in some of the *Electra complex* issues articulated. Throughout the episode, Eric's close relationship with his father is used as a pointed contrast to the sisters' unresolved issues with their own. (Piper and Prue both, to a greater or lesser degree, seem to miss their father; Phoebe suggests that she is not interested in Victor.) Unfortunately, these potentially fascinating avenues aren't really matched elsewhere, and the episode meanders about spending far too much time on less worthy subject matter. Best bits: An annoyed Phoebe slapping Prue's bottom as she passes. Phoebe's discombobulated thoughts as heard by her sisters.

Soundtrack: Sugar Ray's 'Falls Apart' and 'Early Morning'.

30: P³ H²O

09 December 1999

Writers: Chris Levinson, Zack Estrin
Director: John Behring

Cast: Finola Hughes (Patty Halliwell), Lochlyn Munro (Jack Sheridan), Scott Jaeck (Sam Wilder), Pat Crowley (Mrs Johnson), Lucky Luciano (Kid #1), Ferrell Barron (Medic), Emmalee Thompson (Young Prue Halliwell)

> Whilst visiting the summer camp where her mother died, Prue witnesses a man drowning, he having been dragged beneath the surface of the lake by something lurking beneath. She then encounters an old man telling her to leave. The sisters learn that the man, Sam, was their mother's Whitelighter, who has been living near the lake for the past 20 years trying to prevent history from repeating itself. Meanwhile, Piper discovers love letters written by her mother to Sam and is forced to re-evaluate her relationships with Leo and Dan.

Work is a Four-Letter Word: Jack Sheridan has joined Buckland's. Prue misses her 12 o'clock lunch appointment with Mr Fujimoto. Jack steps in, successfully negotiates a deal (the fact that he speaks fluent Japanese helps) and then makes sure that Prue is credited with the sale. His reward is dinner.

It's a Designer Label!: Phoebe's pyjamas are that special kind of adorable that poets traditionally write their more flowery stuff about.

References: Much visual imagery taken, without apology, from *Jaws*. Phoebe impersonates Elmer Fudd. Also, the children's game Red Rover; and Ray Charles's 'I Can't Stop Loving You'.

'You May Remember Me ...': Scott Jaeck played Commander Dooley in *JAG* and Dr Flint in *ER*. Pat Crowley was Emily Fallmont in *Dynasty* and appeared in *Hawaii 5-0*, *Happy Days* and *Alias Smith and Jones*. Lucky Luciano's movies include *Courage Under Fire*.

Sex and Drugs and Rock n Roll: Could the embarrassingly twee initial scenes between Piper and Dan *be* any more annoying?

SEASON 2: P³ H²O

Logic, Let Me Introduce You To This Window: In 'That 70s Episode', the note that Phoebe attempted to leave for Patty told her to stay away from water during February. However, here it's revealed that Patty was killed at a summer camp. Camp Skylark has been closed since the summer that Patty died (1978). What source of income, therefore, has Mrs Johnson, the camp's owner, had for the last 21 years? And, did she really leave the 'Welcome Campers' sign up for all that time? When Prue and Phoebe leave their car, the camera crew can be clearly seen reflected on the car door. Leo's healing powers work only when they are 'meant to', something never previously mentioned, never alluded to again, but a nice little cop-out to explain a few potential loopholes from now on. You've got to wonder, too, why the Whitelighters would want Piper not to be healed of poison ivy – hitherto undisclosed sadism, perhaps? Why would Patty *write* to Sam when she could simply have called for him? More to the point, *where* did she send these letters to? Do Whitelighters have homes? Prue touches Sam mere seconds after he's been shocked by a massive voltage – he should still be 'live' and very dangerous. In 'They're Everywhere', Phoebe said that the last thing she remembered was a Halloween Party three weeks earlier. This episode appears to take place in mid-summer.

Continuity: The sisters meet Sam Wilder, their mother's Whitelighter, and learn that Patty had a relationship with him (see 'Charmed Again'). Sam was a teacher in New York in the 1870s before becoming a Whitelighter. After Patty's death, he had his wings clipped and returned to life as a human. He has spent the 21 years since tormented over the death of his lover. Prue once got poison ivy at Camp Skylark – something Piper repeats in this episode.

Quote/Unquote: Phoebe, seeing children playing near the water: 'Pre-pubescent demon food!'

Prue: 'If you're gonna defeat your demons, Sam, then you have to help us defeat the one out there.'

Notes: 'Can't let it happen again.' Mostly terrific, 'P³ H²0' is one of the most dense and obstinate of *Charmed* episodes – lots of little things in it aren't very good (most of which surround Piper's and Dan's growing relationship). Yet it's impossible not to be affected by the dramatic opening and closing acts – particularly the stunningly directed pre-title sequence, with its weird camera angles and monochrome flashbacks to Patty Halliwell's death. The episode's middle section is somewhat sluggish (and, worse, melodramatic) but the ending more than makes up for these flaws.

Soundtrack: Melissa Etheridge's 'Angels Will Fall' and Sarah McLachlan's 'I Love You'.

31: MS HELLFIRE

13 January 2000

Teleplay: Constance M Burge, Sheryl J Anderson
Story: Constance M Burge
Director: Craig Zisk

Cast: Billy Drago (Barbas), Lochlyn Munro (Jack Sheridan), Antonio Sabato Jr (Bane Jessup), Courtney Gains (DJ), Hynden Walch (Marcy Steadwell), Carlo Castronovo (Wills), Tom Simmons (Coroner), Wendi Bromley (Ms Hellfire)

> After Prue kills a hit-woman who attacks the sisters, the Halliwells learn that they were just one of the targets the assassin was hired to murder. Enlisting the help of Darryl to cover up the woman's death, Prue tries to discover who hired the assassin, Ms Hellfire, by assuming her identity.

It's Witchcraft: The hyperactive Wicca practitioner Marcy Steadwell runs the *New Age Books* store. She warns Piper and Phoebe that they shouldn't keep wolfsbane and holy thistle on the same shelf – their harmonics are in complete opposition.

A Little Learning is a Dangerous Thing: Piper convinces Dan that they were victim of a drive-by shooting.

Work is a Four-Letter Word: Prue's busy work day is scheduled to include a meeting with the Curzon Foundation at noon, a 1 o'clock lunch regarding the Lowe estate, a slide presentation, a 4:30 meeting with the new printers, then a walk to the Royal Hotel for her 5:30 with Mrs Swansen. This will leave her just enough time to make a kick-boxing/Tae Kwan Doe class that she takes with Phoebe. All this goes out the window when the office of Mr Caldwell, Buckland's new Vice President, rings, ordering her to attend an emergency staff meeting at 9:30 – be there, or be fired. Prue arrives late and sneaks into the meeting, at which she is paired up with Jack and given the task of raising $100,000 of auction material by the following night.

It's a Designer Label!: This features the most leather seen in a single TV episode since the heyday of *The Avengers*. Watch Prue's delight when being

SEASON 2: MS HELLFIRE

let loose in Ms Hellfire's wardrobe.

References: Among the gifts lavished on Ms Hellfire by Bane were paintings by David Hockney (1937-) and Salvador Dali (1904-89), which she intends to use to help keep her job at Buckland's. The whole set-up is very reminiscent of *La Femme Nikita*. Also, Lou Reed's 'Walk on the Wild Side'; *Pulp Fiction*; *Shane*; and the advertising slogan of Avon Cosmetics ('Avon calling').

'You May Remember Me ...': Courtney Gains played Malachai in *Children of the Corn* and appeared in *Sweet Home Alabama* and *Memphis Belle*. Hynden Walch's movies include *Jerry Maguire* and *Groundhog Day*. Carlo Castronovo was in *Grownups*. Tom Simmons appeared in *The Truman Show* and *The Adventures of Brisco County Jnr*. Antonio Sabato's CV includes *Longshot*, *Goosed* and *Earth 2*.

Behind the Camera: Wendi Bromley, one of *Charmed*'s stunt-drivers, also worked on *Gone in Sixty Seconds*.

Cigarettes and Alcohol: Piper shares a glass of champagne with Bane, much to Jack's surprise.

Sex and Drugs and Rock n Roll: Prue mentions that Piper has fallen 'in lust' with Dan.

Logic, Let Me Introduce You To This Window: 'From Fear to Eternity' appeared to establish that Barbas kills by fear of what is actually happening. In this episode most of the fear is, clearly, illusionary. (The doctor wasn't autopsied, he merely believed he was.) Would a professional assassin *really* carry a purse containing her personal details? To avoid investigation, Darryl helps the sisters place Ms Hellfire's body in the store, which is then blown up. Any forensic examination of the body would discover injuries inconsistent with the apparent cause of death. Admittedly *CSI* hadn't yet started, but didn't the writers ever watch *Quincy*? Phoebe claims to have taught Prue how to French kiss. Given that Phoebe is five years younger than Prue, this suggests either a precocious teenage promiscuity hitherto unsuspected in Phoebe or that Prue had a *very* sheltered upbringing.

Continuity: Darryl discovers the sisters' secret. Prue prefers orchids to roses. Prue gave Piper chicken pox when they were children. Prue also broke her ankle when she was seven. Piper and Prue went to see Duran Duran together and Prue stretched Piper's leg warmers. Which were then passed on to Phoebe. Ms Hellfire's list of the sisters' powers reads: 'Prue – Telekinesis, Piper – Power to freeze, Phoebe – Negligible.'

Prue has conquered her fear of water (see 'From Fear To Eternity'). However, she now shares Phoebe's phobia of someone hurting her sisters. Once again Barbas appears on Friday 13th, having made a deal that gave him a 24 hour window to break free from Hell. But he can do so only by killing 13 witches. It is mentioned that Jenny went to live with her parents, so her sudden departure is explained. Prue gains a new power – astral projection. The names of the assassinated witches on Ms Hellfire's list include: J Cocheren, S Petty, I Chee, R Chillet, B Reardon and B Napoli. Hellfire lives at 2498 Brook Street, Apartment 25.

Motors: Ms Hellfire drove a Porsche.

Quote/Unquote: Prue: 'Who else would want to kill us?' Phoebe: 'You were a little sharp to the mailman yesterday. We all know how testy they can be.'

Marcy, singing: 'Save your sisters, Moon, with your protective beans.' Piper: 'Oh, please stop.'

Phoebe: 'We need you to babysit.' Darryl: 'Is this one breathing?'

Notes: 'One develops a sixth sense about such things when you've been in purgatory for as long as I have.' What starts off as a straightforward tale of undercover investigations and assumed identities rapidly spins off into half-a-dozen separate plot strands, each with its own positives and negatives. 'Ms Hellfire' includes some of *Charmed*'s most memorable moments – the brilliant pre-title sequence and the incredible slow-motion shot of Prue entering the Reptile Room, leather coat billowing behind her.

Soundtrack: 'Earth to Andy' by Chronicle Kings and Moby's 'Find My Baby'.

Did You Know?: Originally the role of Bane Jessup was scheduled to be played by Richard Grieco. However, Shannen Doherty reportedly strongly objected to the casting – for unknown reasons – and was supported by both Alyssa Milano and Holly Marie Combs.

32: HEARTBREAK CITY

20 January 2000

Writer: David Simkins
Director: Michael Zinberg

Cast: Lochlyn Munro (Jack Sheridan), Clayton Rohner (Drazi), Michael Reilly Burke (Cupid),
Tiffany Salerno (Cindy), Brody Hutzler (Max), Jonathan Aubé (Kevin)

Drazi, a demon of hate, steals a ring from Cupid in order to destroy him by undoing his recent love matches. Cupid seeks out the Charmed Ones to help banish Drazi, but Prue's and Piper's relationships both fall victim to Drazi's magic. Meanwhile Phoebe learns from Cupid why she is so unlucky in love.

It's Witchcraft: Cupid has Phoebe prepare 'a travel potion with an aphrodisiac.' This contains lavender, oysters, rosemary, chocolate and basic caris compound. The key ingredient, however, is desire.

A Little Learning is a Dangerous Thing: Drazi once fell in love with a mortal woman. Cupid redirected the woman's love towards another mortal – she's married and happy now. But Drazi blames Cupid for denying him love. Phoebe is surprised that demons *can* love. Cupid notes that they usually love frightening stuff like evil and fear. But sometimes they love the very things they hate. He also says that if a demon can open his heart, there's hope for Phoebe.

The Conspiracy Starts at the Witching Hour: Cupid is one of many agents of love who work in secret all over the world making connections. (He is mortal and has been in his current position for two years.) Piper asks if he connected her and Leo. Cupid says, no, that was the work of the two of them alone. The Cupids are forbidden to make such connections, for obvious reasons. Their power is in their ring.

References: The reference to the 'Y2K' computer scare and how it all turned out to be a bunch of hype suggests that this was the first episode to be completed in the days immediately after 1 January 2000. Piper, Dan, Jack, Prue and Phoebe attend a Warner's cinema to watch the 1970 weepy *Love Story*. At the end of the episode they, together with Phoebe's friend

Kevin, go to the same venue to watch Robert Aldrich's classic 1967 war movie *The Dirty Dozen*. Posters for the B-52s and Soul Coughing can be seen in the P³ ladies' loo. Dan has several tasteful art prints on his bedroom wall, including vintage posters for Cinzano, Bughatti and Air France. Also allusions to Charles Bronson; *Deathwish*; *The Terminator*; *Judge Dredd*; Sam Cooke's 'Twisting the Night Away'; Shakespeare's *Twelfth Night* ('If the food of love is Cheetos and soda, then play on'); Alfred Lord Tennyson's *In Memoriam* ('It's better to have loved and lost than never to have loved at all'); Soft Cell's 'Where The Heart Is'; Rodgers and Hammerstein's 'Hello, Young Lovers' (from *The King And I*); and the 1980s TV dating show *The Love Connection*

'You May Remember Me ...': Clayton Rohner played Chandler Smythe in *G vs E*. He also appeared in *Jack and Jill* and *Murder One*. Michael Reilly Burke's CV includes *Providence*, *Mars Attacks!* and *Star Trek: The Next Generation*. Tiffany Salerno was in *Forrest Gump*. Brody Hutzler played Landok in *Angel* and appeared in *Legally Blond*. Jonathan Aubé was in *Ocean Park*.

Behind the Camera: Michael Zinberg's CV includes *Lost*, *Navy NCIS*, *Everybody Loves Raymond*, *Midnight Caller* and *Quantum Leap*.

Cigarettes and Alcohol: Jack, Dan, Piper and Prue all seem to be drinking the popular (and rather tasty) Mexican beer Corona at P³.

Logic, Let Me Introduce You To This Window: This cinema seems to specialise in oldies – don't they have any *new* films to show? Why is Shannen Doherty dressed as Hiawatha in the opening scene? Alyssa Milano's hairstyle changes, radically, between scenes that take place on the same day. There is no number plate on the car that hits Max. P³ seems to have the most luxurious washrooms of any night-club in the world (complete with posters on the wall – including the same B-52s one previously seen in the dressing room in 'The Devil's Music').

Continuity: When the sisters ask Cupid to back up his claims concerning his identity, he knows that Piper's current *beau* is Dan, Prue's is Jack and that Phoebe once went out with a guy called Clay (see 'Feats of Clay'). He then gives Prue his sincerest condolences in relation to Andy (see 'Déjà Vu All Over Again') and mentions previous boyfriends Eric in London and Alec in college. Jeremy the Warlock (see 'Something Wicca This Way Comes') was, he suggests, nothing to do with him. But Piper's other boyfriends – Joe in college, Barry in high school and Tim in eighth grade – were. Phoebe's boyfriends have apparently included Ken, Kyle, Steve,

Mike, Ken again, Brian, Joel, Martin, Peter, Paul and Tony. Phoebe says that she didn't love all those guys. Cupid notes that *they* all wanted to love her but she is closed hearted, and that's what sent them away. This is Prue's second date with Jack (and she doesn't sleep with people on second dates). Prue says that she doesn't love him but, Cupid notes, she does like him a lot (she finds him amusing) and she's open to their relationship progressing further.

Quote/Unquote: Prue: 'Where's Piper?' Phoebe: 'She's still at Dan's. If only I'd bagged Mr Creepy, we could have scored a Halliwell hat-trick last night.'

Prue: 'Everybody has secrets, including Jack and Dan.' Piper: 'Unless they're transvestite-Nazi-war-criminals with great face-lifts, I think we've got them beat.'

Cupid: 'Don't confuse the message with the messenger, Phoebe. It's what you've always done. Messengers make mistakes, they get lost, they run away, they even die. But the message – open your heart – comes from life itself. Hear it.'

Phoebe, to Cindy: 'Fear and love cannot live in the same house.'

Notes: 'Thanks to you, I know what it feels like to have your heart ripped out.' A quiet, and rather sweet, meditation on all aspect of love. As with a fair few other *Charmed* episodes, some of the material on display could, in lesser hands, have been wretched. But, thanks to completely sincere performances (in this case, one of Alyssa Milano's finest 42 minutes, together with a charismatic partnership with Michael Reilly Burke), it often seems to work. There are some fine effects, too (notably the apparent vanquishing of Drazi).

Soundtrack: 'I Wanna Be Moved' by Ginny Owens and 'Ga Ga' by Melanie C.

Did You Know?: This episode features the on-screen caption 'Dedicated, with love, to Doug Wood, a special member of our crew.'

33: RECKLESS ABANDON

27 January 2000

Writer: Javier Grillo-Marxuach
Director: Craig Zisk

Cast: Lochlyn Munro (Jack Sheridan), Hilary Danner (Alexandra van Lewen), Stephanie Beacham (Martha van Lewen), J Kenneth Campbell (Elias Lundy), Rick Coy (Gilbert), Rolando Merlina (Hernandez), Albert Stroth (Uniform Cop)

> Phoebe brings home an abandoned baby after she has a vision of a ghost that was trying to kill it. As the sisters attempt to find the baby's parents, they discover that, even with witchcraft, it's not easy to care for a child. They soon learn that a vengeful spirit is killing all the male members of a rich family after its own murder at the hands of the woman it once loved.

It's Witchcraft: At the end of the lengthy spell (apparently written by Patty) in *The Book of Shadows* is a note that states 'Sometimes a baby just *has* to cry.'

The Conspiracy Starts at the Witching Hour: The van Lewens' chauffeur, Elias Lundy, disappeared suddenly some years ago. He had become obsessed with Martha van Lewen. After apparently attacking Martha, he was shot in the back. (Martha subsequently confirms that she, and not her husband, was responsible.) Lundy was buried on the grounds, where his vengeful spirit remains, tied to the house and with fearsome psychic powers. A week afterwards, Martha's husband was mysteriously killed. In the following years, every male member of the van Lewen household has also died. Gilbert says that Lundy strikes at moments of greatest joy.

Work is a Four-Letter Word: Mr Caldwell (see 'Ms Hellfire') is sending the two Buckland's employees with the best presentation to New York for a conference, all expenses paid. Due to Prue's never-ending run of 'family crises', Jack takes over the presentation on her behalf and is successful. However, despite having argued for Prue to be allowed to accompany him to New York, in the end neither goes, and they have to make do with a night at P³ instead.

Phoebe tries to persuade Darryl to get her a job with SFPD as a psychic.

SEASON 2: RECKLESS ABANDON

It's a Designer Label!: What on earth is Phoebe's nothing-goes-with-anything pink, purple, light blue and white top all about?

References: There are allusions to *Rugrats*; *Mr Mom*; *Casper the Friendly Ghost*; *Three Men and a Baby*; *Cosmopolitan* magazine; and paediatrician Dr Benjamin Spock. The episode's *denouement* appears to be inspired by the final sequence of *Hands of the Ripper*.

'You May Remember Me ...': Hilary Danner appeared in *Homicide: Life on the Streets*. Stephanie Beacham played Dr Westphalen in *SeaQuest DSV*, Mrs Peacock in *Cluedo*, Jessica Van Helsing in *Dracula AD 1972*, Rose Millar in *Tenko*, Phyl Oswyn in *Bad Girls* and Sable Colby in *Dynasty* and *The Colbys*. She also appeared in *Saving Grace*, *The Wolves of Willoughby Chase*, ~ ~ ~ *And Now The Screaming Starts!*, *UFO*, *Callan*, *Schizo*, *The Confessional*, *The Aries Computer*, *The Rag Trade* and *Star Trek: The Next Generation*. J Kenneth Campbell was in *Collateral Damage*, *Bulworth*, *Angel* and *The Abyss*. Rick Coy appeared in *Cheers* and *Murphy Brown*. Rolando Molina's CV includes *Kingpin*, *Gun* and *ER*.

Sex and Drugs and Rock n Roll: When Prue tells Piper that she and Jack may be going to New York, Piper asks if Prue intends to sleep with Jack. Prue replies that it's merely a business trip.

Logic, Let Me Introduce You To This Window: When Piper and Prue change the baby's nappy, a clearly visible plastic hand gives away the fact that the baby is a doll. 'Dead Man Dating' established that when people die, their spirit does not pass over until they have been properly buried. However, in this episode this no longer applies. Prue exhibits a great deal more control over her powers than previously (or, indeed, subsequently).

Continuity: Prue says she hates guys who are afraid to commit, though it's probable she's merely teasing Piper. It's established that Darryl is a father. In relation to babies, Piper notes that she 'isn't good with these things', though she does refer to the future events seen in 'Morality Bites' and her impending motherhood. Phoebe, it appears, is a natural at the maternal stuff ... for a while, at least. She says that she can't wait to have a baby of her own. Piper knits, something Prue was unaware of. The sisters have a friend called Lisa Kreager, who has just had a baby.

Quote/Unquote: Prue: 'We have a baby?' Piper: 'Phoebe picked it up at the police station.' Prue: 'I thought you were going to ask about a job, not a kid.'

Piper, impressed by Dan's ease with the baby: 'You're like MacGyver with oestrogen.'

Prue: 'I thought that babies slept a lot.' Phoebe: 'Obviously one of those lies they'll tell you so you want to get pregnant.'

Notes: 'Every time I get close to the little guy, he either opens his mouth or his bowels. Call me kooky but that feels like rejection.' Insubstantial and lightweight, 'Reckless Abandon' is fatally compromised by some scenery chewing performances from members of the guest cast. (Stephanie Beacham seems to be under the impression that she's wandered back onto the set of *Dynasty*.) It's not a bad episode, *per se*, but it's powder-puff in relation to some of the more dense and interesting episodes that surround it. Best bit: Prue's and Piper's ineptitude at changing Matthew's nappy.

Soundtrack: 'Human Touch' by Pocket Size and 'I Love You' by Martina McBride.

Did You Know?: The extremely good ratings for this episode – *Charmed*'s second best ever after its debut – are somewhat deceptive. Instead of regular programmes airing on NBC, CBS, ABC and FOX, those networks aired President Clinton's final State of the Union address during this hour.

34: AWAKENED

3 February 2000

Writers: Vivian Mayhew, Valerie Mayhew
Director: Anson Williams

Cast: Lochlyn Munro (Jack Sheridan), Matthew Glave (Dr Curtis Williamson), Andrew Ducote (Nathan), Daniel Reichert (Dr Seigler), Monica Allison (Nurse), Faith Slie (Second Nurse), Chuti Tiu (Asian-American Nurse), Louisa Abernathy (Angie), Lisa Ann Grant (Female Reporter #2), Jennifer Massey (Female Reporter #1)

> Piper contracts a life-threatening tropical virus from some illegally-imported fruit. To save her life, Prue and Phoebe cast an awakening spell. However, since the spell was used for personal gain, the sisters can no longer sleep, and Piper's sickness spreads into an epidemic.

It's Witchcraft: The Awakening spell begins: 'Troubled blood with sleeps unease, remove the cause of this disease.' The reversal for this is: 'What was awakened from its sleep, was once again slumbered deep.'

A Little Learning is a Dangerous Thing: Piper has contracted arroyo fever, a blood disease rarely seen in the United States. This is transmitted through the bite of a sandfly. It attacks the immune system. Piper believes that she may have mono or Epstein-Barr.[36]

Work Is A Four Letter Word: Prue quits her job at Buckland's in this episode over ethical issues. Meanwhile, Phoebe enrols in college. She has signed up for two general courses and seven electives.

It's a Designer Label!: Check out Phoebe's pink fluffy shawl and tea-cosy hat. Much easier on the eye is her electric blue miniskirt. Prue's leather trousers, black roll-neck sweater and oddly-styled fur coat are also eclipsed by her backless silver top.

---

[36] Infectious mononucleosis ('mono' or 'the kissing disease') is a common illness caused by the Epstein-Barr virus (EBV). Mono is most often diagnosed in adolescents and young adults.

SEASON 2: AWAKENED

References: Prue gives Jack a precise little essay on the French Impressionist Claude Monet (1840-1926) and the first *Exposition de Versaille* (1874). There are several visual references to *The West Wing* (notably the shot in the hospital in which the camera circles around the Halliwells as they discuss the reversal spell). Also, allusions to the *San Francisco Weekly*; Bugs Bunny's catchphrase 'What's up, Doc?'; the Beatles' 'Let it Be'; and Ricky Valance's 'Tell Laura I Love Her'.

'You May Remember Me ...': Matthew Glave's CV includes *Rock Star*, *The Wedding Singer*, *The Lyons Den* and *Millennium*. Andrew Ducote was in *The Secret Life of Girls*. Daniel Reichert's movies include *Batman Forever*. Monica Allison appeared in *Virtuosity* and *Seinfeld*. Faith Slie was in *Alien Avengers* and *Start Trek: Deep Space Nine*. Chuti Tiu appeared in 24 and *The West Wing*. Louisa Abernathy was in *Another Day in LA* and *Roseanne*. Lisa Ann Grant's movies include *Deep Impact*. Jennifer Massey was in *Orphelia Learns to Swim* and *The Practice*.

Behind the Camera: The nephew of Dr Henry Heimlich, Anson Williams is best known for his performance as the nice-but-dim Potsie in *Happy Days*. He later became a director working on *Sabrina, the Teenage Witch*, *Clueless*, *The Cape*, *Xena: Warrior Princess*, *Star Trek: Voyager*, *Diagnosis Murder*, *Melrose Place* and *L.A. Law*.

Sex and Drugs and Rock n Roll: Jack asks if Monet was a 'randy little painter'. He's probably thinking about Eugène Henri Gauguin (1848-1903), who was. Allegedly. 'Is everything with you sexual?' asks Prue.

Logic, Let Me Introduce You To This Window: How did the Halliwells arrange to have such stylish and figure-hugging hospital gowns? Does San Francsico Mercy really use designer pink sheets? Shouldn't the nurse be more concerned when she feels a sharp prick in her leg whilst standing next to a biohazard bag? Kiwano fruit is grown in New Zealand and parts of Africa but not in South America. It's also quite a bitter fruit and, therefore, doesn't really go with a Mai-Tai. Note that the reversal spell switches tense half-way through.

Continuity: Piper hates hospitals. Leo has his Whitelighter wings clipped for saving Piper's life, although he says this is not a permanent situation.

Quote/Unquote: Jack: 'The world is made up of "almost perfect". It's nothing but near misses and necessary compromises ... I'm just asking you not to look so close. Nothing bears up under that kind of scrutiny.' Prue: 'Are you talking about the Monet?' Jack: 'Yeah, that too.'

Piper: 'What's the matter, doctor? You don't believe in miracles?' Dr Williamson: 'Not the kind that don't leave traces.'

Notes: 'Either Piper pulls out of the coma on her own or, I'm afraid, your sister's not going to survive.' The first half of 'Awakened' is a rather obvious medical drama story with little to recommend it. Then, suddenly, straight out of left-field, it becomes in the final 20 minutes, a pointed and admirable essay on ethics, consequences and sacrifice. How did *that* happen? Anson Williams' direction is superb, with a truly thrilling tracking shot of dawn over San Francisco and a classic presentation of Piper's out-of-body experience – beautifully lit and filmed. Best bits: Prue dee-jaying and Phoebe dancing. Prue's heart-to-heart with Jack, ostensibly about the Monet painting but actually about their relationship.

Soundtrack: Citizen King's 'Under the Influence', 'Lust' by Tori Amos, 'The Chemical Between Us' by Bush and Everything But the Girl's 'Five Fathoms'.

35: ANIMAL PRAGMATISM

10 February 2000

Writers: Chris Levinson, Zack Estrin
Director: Don Kurt

Cast: Janice Robinson (Herself), Katie Johnston (Brooke), Kelly McNair (Andrea), Rafer Weigel (Ethan), Steve Monroe (The Pig), Tim Griffin (The Rabbit), Christopher Wiehl (Snake), Lela Lee (Tessa), Richard Wharton (Professor), Benton Jennings (Concerned Citizen), Amber Skalski (Girl)

> A trio of college girls, desperate for love on Valentine's Day, transform three animals into the men of their dreams, with some indirect help from Phoebe. The former animals, however, soon decide that they wish to remain human, and seek Phoebe to prevent them from returning to their true form. Piper's relationship with Dan is strained when she gives Leo a Valentine's card.

Dreaming (As Blondie Once Said) is Free: The episode ends with a fabulous sequence in which Piper and Leo embrace ... which, inevitably, turns out to be fantasy of one or both.

It's Witchcraft: Brooke, Andrea and Tessa purchase a book of love spells from the campus bookstore. Phoebe reads one and notes that you would never say the spell in that particular order. First you note what's lacking and then ask for what's needed. She suggests they try: 'From strike of 12, count 24, that's how long the spell is for. If to abate my lonely heart, enchant these gifts I thee impart.' She hurriedly adds that she's doing a paper on the growing popularity of witchcraft.

A Little Learning is a Dangerous Thing: Phoebe tries a spell to return the three animals to their true nature with: 'Something wicked in our midst, in human form these spirits dwell.' This promptly turns everyone in P^3 into an animal. She is eventually able to reverse the spell.

Work Is A Four Letter Word: Prue discovers that unemployment can be a bit boring.

References: Allusions to *Superman*; *All of Me*; James Brown's 'Papa's Got a Brand New Bag'; *A Matter of Life and Death*; Woody Allen's *Love and Death*;

SEASON 2: ANIMAL PRAGMATISM

Hallmark Cards; Thumper the rabbit in *Bambi*; US home and garden guru Martha Stewart; and the popular aphorism 'Rome wasn't built in a day.'

'You May Remember Me …': Katie Johnston's CV includes *Once and Again* and *Star Trek VI: The Undiscovered Country*. Kelly McNair appeared in *Come On, Get Happy: The Partridge Family Story*. Tim Griffin was in *Lover Girl*. Benton Jennings appeared in *Shoo Fly* and *Highway to Hell*. Steve Monroe's movies include *8 Mile*, *Miss Congeniality* and *Can't Hardly Wait*. Lela Lee was in *Rave* and *Scrubs*. Rafer Weigel appeared in *Free Enterprise*. Richard Wharton's CV includes *The Borrower*, *Running Scared* and *Buffy the Vampire Slayer*. Christopher Wiehl played Hank Peddigrew in *CSI* and appeared in *Hollywood Homicide* and *Space: Above and Beyond*.

Cigarettes and Alcohol: Dan gets a bottle of *Piper-Heidsiect* champagne for his proposed Valentine dinner with Piper.

Sex and Drugs and Rock n Roll: The episode begins with a pointed essay on the mating habits of lions. Those observed in the Ingorogoro crater of Tanzania mated, on average, once an hour for a week. Before Phoebe's professor loses half the room to that thought alone, he tells his class that the purpose of all animals is the proliferation of the species. However, it usually isn't simply a case of 'Your nest or mine?'. It starts with a series of mating rituals. First, the animal must get the attention of the object it desires. Next, there must be a sign that the interest is mutual. Whilst all this is going on, Phoebe is sharing mutual admiring looks with Ethan.

Logic, Let Me Introduce You To This Window: A vicious, bloodthirsty killer Rabbit? Had someone been watching *Monty Python's Holy Grail* recently? When the Snake advances on Brooke and Andrea at the Manor, the door behind him is open. Next shot, it's closed. It's lucky that the Rabbit and the Pig appear to have elasticated collars so that, when they become human, they don't choke to death. The Snake attacks using both poison and constriction. Real snakes kill their prey using one or the other but never both. Why did Phoebe's spell at P^3 affect the clientele *and* their clothing? The Snake's contact lenses appear misaligned in at least two shots.

Continuity: Phoebe is a vegetarian and claims that she doesn't handle pressure well. When Phoebe notes that true love needs a backseat, Prue alleges that Phoebe was conceived in one. (One has to wonder how Prue would know this.) Piper's Valentine gift to Dan is a copy of *Above San Francisco* by Robert Cameron and Arthur Hoppe. Since returning to mortality, Leo is working at (and, indeed, sleeping in) P^3.

SEASON 2: ANIMAL PRAGMATISM

Cruelty to Animals: When the Pig sees a guy frying hot dogs on campus he is outraged, grabbing a handful of his 'brothers' and telling them to flee.

Quote/Unquote: Piper: 'You can't finish doing nothing.' Prue: 'So then how do you know when you're done?'

Piper: 'Why don't they make a card that says, "You used to be my Whitelighter and now your wings are clipped and you're sleeping in my club."' Phoebe: 'Or, how about "You snooze, you lose, and now I'm getting naked with the neighbour."'

Piper: 'Why do we seem to have a habit of gathering our men at the scene of the supernatural smack down?' Phoebe: 'It's part of our charm.'

Piper: 'Prue, the place is full of snakes. How am I suppose to pick out the right one?'

Notes: 'We've been given a gift. It's time to take it out for a test drive.' A crude, and somewhat nasty metaphor for male sexual aggression, 'Animal Pragmatism' is similar to the average Marti Noxon-penned *Buffy* episode in which sexuality and rad-fem agenda squat awkwardly together in the dark whilst dreaming up various forms of punishment for mankind. This author, genuinely, doesn't want this to sound like a betrayal of the Sisterhood, but there are, he would like to assure his readers, men out there who *aren't* raging bags of suppressed misogyny. One or two, anyway. One major plus point is the sequence in which Phoebe's spell in P³ goes horribly wrong, which helps to restore the balance. But it's still a pretty awful episode.

Soundtrack: Three songs by guest artiste Janice Robinson – 'Nothing I Would Change', 'Finally Taking Over You' and 'The Search For Love'. Plus 'I Promise You' by Judith Owen used for the Piper/Leo fantasy sequence. Alyssa Milano sings a brief snatch of 'Old MacDonald Had a Farm'.

36: PARDON MY PAST

17 February 2000

Writer: Michael Gleason
Director: Jon Paré

Cast: Tyler Christopher (Anton), Jeanette Miller (Adult Christina Larson), Daveigh Chase (Young Christina), Susan Savage (Classy Woman), Lauri Hendler (Socialite), Greg Kovan (Bouncer)[37]

> Phoebe experiences visions relating to a past life in which she and her sisters were cousins in the 1920s. However, in this past, Phoebe was an evil witch.

It's Witchcraft: The Entering a Past Life spell begins: 'Remove the chains of time and space and make my spirit soar. Let these mortal arms embrace the life that haunts before.' The spell that past-Prue and past-Piper use to curse their cousin beings: 'Evil witch in my sight, vanquish thyself, vanquish thy might, in this and every future life.'

A Little Learning is a Dangerous Thing: A witch who uses his or powers for evil will have weaker powers in the next life.

The Conspiracy Starts at the Witching Hour: Dan had his brother-in-law – who works for the State Department – check out Leo's army records. However, the only Leo Wyatt that can be found died almost 60 years earlier in World War II.

It's a Designer Label!: Prue's brown party dress and Phoebe's Japanese-style night-shirt.

References: Conceptual elements of the 'past lives' plot are similar to *The X-Files* episode 'The Field Where I Died' (groups of souls travelling in the same circle of family, friends and enemies throughout their various lives). Some of the visuals also appear influenced by *The Entity*. The sepia-tinged flashback scenes of the 1920s could have come straight from Sergio Leone's *Once Upon a Time in America*. Also, allusions to Shirley MacLaine (see 'Dead Man Dating'); 1940s baseball legend Joe Dimaggio; *Sleeping Beauty*; and The Beatles' 'Here,

---

[37] Uncredited.

There and Everywhere'.

'You May Remember Me ...': Tyler Christopher played Nikolas Cassadine in *General Hospital*. Jeanette Miller's movies include *Stuck* and *Austin Powers: The Spy Who Shagged Me*. Daveigh Chase appeared in *Beethoven's 5th* and *The Ring*. Susan Savage was in *Cadillac* and *Baywatch*. Lauri Hendler appeared in *The Big Hex of Little Lulu* and *Eerie, Indiana*. Greg Kovan was a production assistant on *Die Hard 2*.

Behind the Camera: Michael Gleason was the creator of *Remington Steele*. Jon Paré also worked on *The Love Boat: The Next Wave* and *Beverly Hills 90210*. He was an assistant director on *Masters of the Universe II: The Cyborg*.

Sex and Drugs and Rock n Roll: Phoebe is studying phobias for her midterm psychology exam. In relation to this, she mentions that she had no idea there were so many and gives several examples, one of which is 'phallusphobia' (a fear of penises). This isn't something that past-Phoebe worried too much about, if her and Anton's kissing-with-tongues is anything to go by.

Logic, Let Me Introduce You To This Window: Despite the broadly Judaeo-Christian nature of the *Charmed* universe's take on heaven, hell and the afterlife, this episode appears to suggest that the Buddhist concept of reincarnation is also a key aspect. ('That's how our souls evolve, we grow as individuals from one lifetime to the next' notes Leo.) When looking at the family tree, Phoebe realises that she will die by midnight on 17 February 2000 if she doesn't stop the curse, mentioning that she was the same age as Phoebe Russell when *she* died. According to the tree, Phoebe Russell was born on 2 July 1895 and died on 17 February 1924. However, Phoebe was born on 2 November 1975, making her 24, whereas Phoebe Russell died aged 28.

When Anton puts the necklace on Phoebe's neck in Christina's hospital room, he doesn't lift her hair to secure it around the back. The family tree says that Grams (Penelope Johnson) was born on 23 June 1937 and that her daughter, Patricia Halliwell, was born on 5 May 1950. That would have made Grams 12 when Patty was conceived. It also erroneously states that Grams died in 1963. In 'That 70s Episode', Patty mentioned that her favourite aunt was called Phoebe. Presumably this was a reference to Phoebe Russell – who died in 1924, 36 years before Patty was born. Prue Bowen, by contrast, died in 1977, seven years *after* Prue was born. Further to the confusion surrounding Victor's surname (see 'Thank You For Not Morphing'), here – and in 'Baby's First Demon' – it's given as Jones. Leo says the cousins in the past look like Prue and Piper to Phoebe because she recognises their souls. So, why does Anton look like Leo? When Phoebe comes down the stairs, her nightshirt is buttoned. When she gets to the bottom, it's unbuttoned. Note that when

SEASON 2: PARDON MY PAST

Gordon Johnson plays the piano and Phoebe enters the room, he seems to stop playing whilst looking at her. On the soundtrack, however, the piano can still be heard. Keep an eye open, also, for past-Prue's and past-Phoebe's decidedly un-1920s underwear, glimpsed briefly during the fight sequence. And then there's the dreadful ginger flapper-wig that Shannen Doherty wears ...

Continuity: In a past life, Piper was Piper Baxter-Johnson (i.e. her own great-grandmother). Born in September 1897, she died in December 1970. In the 1920s, she ran a speakeasy in the Manor and had more or less the same powers as her present-day counterpart. Prue was Prudence Bowen (born June 1895, died May 1977), Piper's cousin, a celebrated photographer with the power to exhale freezing winds. Phoebe was Phoebe Russell (born 2 July 1895, died 17 February 1924), another cousin, with the power to throw fire. Dan was Gordon Johnson (born September 1895, died August 1965), Piper's husband (and, therefore, the sisters' great-grandfather). Leo was Piper's former lover, though his name is not revealed. Grams' first husband (the sisters' grandfather) was called Jack Halliwell (born 1930, died 1963 – however, see 'Witchstock'). Piper's date of birth is given as 7 March 1973.

Phoebe says that she has not needed her big sister to walk her to class since she was in the 1st Grade. At the party, Leo and Dan seem to be getting along reasonably well – due, it would seem, to their shared love of baseball (see 'The Devil's Music'). When someone becomes a Whitelighter, the Elders let him see all his past lives for perspective. Thus Leo knew that he and past-Piper had a relationship before he even met Piper herself. Seemingly there is no support group for fallen Whitelighters.

Quote/Unquote: Phoebe: 'Dying is one experience I don't plan on reliving.'

Phoebe: 'Can we get back to my problem since, at best, I only have till midnight to live?'

Notes: 'Bright side, at least I won't have to worry about ending up in a place like this in my golden years.' One of the cleverest and most unusual of *Charmed* episodes – a structurally fascinating, multi-layered plot, complete with some linguistic brilliance and the series' usual intertextual games. Particularly impressive are the flashback sequences to some visually-stimulating past-lives. Not, perhaps, the most logical of episodes, but impressive nonetheless.

Brian Krause joins the regular cast on the opening credits from this episode.

Soundtrack: Owsley's 'The Homecoming Song', and 'Can't Stand It' by Wilco. The episode's key song, performed by several different characters, is Clifford Gray's and Nat Ayer's 1916 standard 'If You Were The Only Girl in the World.'

37: GIVE ME A SIGN

24 February 2000

Writer: Sheryl J Anderson
Director: James A Contner

Cast: Keith Brunsmann (Litvack's Assistant), Steve Railsback (Litvack), Antonio Sabato Jr (Bane Jessup), Geoff Mead (Guard #1), Janis Chow (Newscaster), Gwen McGee (TV Anchor), Sean Christopher Davis (Delivery Guy), Anthony Holiday (Other Guard), Sal Rendino (Guard #2)

> A demon, Litvack, orders his henchmen to kill Bane Jessup, whom Prue helped to put in prison. Bane escapes from jail and kidnaps Prue, hoping that her powers will protect him. Meanwhile, seeing Piper's anguish in choosing between Leo and Dan, Phoebe works a little magic to help her sister find her true love.

It's Witchcraft: The spell that Phoebe casts which, she hopes, will give Piper a sign as to whether she should chose Leo or Dan, begins: 'I beseech all powers above, send a sign to free my sister's heart, one that will lead her to her love.'

The Conspiracy Starts at the Witching Hour: Leo notes that there is a hierarchy of demons. They try to work their way up various levels by destroying good, promoting evil. (Litvack, for instance, is described as a 'level two demon'.) Litvack also refers – for the first time in the series – to an entity who will eventually be revealed as the *Charmed* universe's ultimate Big Bad, the Source. Litvack says that the Source likes to be fed witches.

Litvack himself lives in a mausoleum for one William Bowen (1889-1979). Entry to this is gained by turning the three nine figures upside down to create 666.

Work Is A Four Letter Word: Since leaving her job at Buckland's, Prue has decided to attempt a career as a freelance photojournalist. Although she was, perhaps, inspired in this by what she saw in her past life (see 'Pardon My Past'), Piper notes that Prue was dreaming of winning a Pulitzer Prize for her photography whilst in college and she took her first job, at the museum (see 'Something Wicca This Way Comes'), only to help out with her sisters' education.

SEASON 2: GIVE ME A SIGN

It's a Designer Label!: Piper's Nike jogging shirt is *very* tight-fitting. There's also Phoebe's red dress, which is worth a second glance.

References: There are allusions to Chicago Cubs baseball star Sammy Sosa; The Blue Aeroplanes' 'Jacket Hands' ('Pick a card, any card'); Cindi Lauper's 'True Colours'; and *Scooby Doo Where Are You?*

'You May Remember Me ...': Keith Brunsmann played Mr Smith in *Lois & Clark*. Steve Railsback made something of a career portraying serial killers; he was Ed Gein in *In the Light of the Moon*, Charles Manson in *Helter Skelter* and Duane Berry in *The X-Files*. He also appeared in *Calendar Girl* and *Blue Monkey*. Geoff Mead was in *Buffy the Vampire Slayer*. Janis Chow appeared in *Party of Five*. Gwen McGee's movies include *Malevolent*, *Mercury Rising* and *Do The Right Thing*. Sean Davis was in *CSI*. Anthony Holiday appeared in *Star Trek: Voyager*. Sal Rendino played John Wade Bobbit in Weird Al's eponymous video.

The Drugs Don't Work: Bane uses chloroform to kidnap Prue.

Sex and Drugs and Rock n Roll: Prue and Bane sleep together, much to the shock of Piper and Phoebe, who point out the location of Prue's discarded panties, to their sister's obvious embarrassment.

Logic, Let Me Introduce You To This Window: After Bane takes the blindfold from Prue, her hair is all over the place. In the next scene, despite her hands being tied, she now has a nicely-groomed look. When Prue, Piper and Phoebe enter the cemetary room, they walk directly behind Bane to get behind a wall. Litvack, who is looking directly at Bane, should have seen them the instant they crossed his line of vision. Given how easily Prue magicked the ropes from Rodriguez in 'Déjà Vu All Over Again', why doesn't she free herself when she pushes Bane into the wall? When Piper and Phoebe discover Prue's location, Phoebe looks at a map and Piper says: 'You drive, I'll navigate.' Phoebe folds up the map and puts it in her pocket. They then leave as the camera goes into a close-up of the map that Phoebe took which is now lying on the table.

Continuity: Dan and Piper recently visited Leonardo's Boutique in Bodega Bay, north of San Francisco. Piper ordered some earrings from the store.

Quote/Unquote: Piper, to Phoebe: 'You're overreacting. That's *my* department.' And: 'Don't act blonde!'
Prue: 'What are you guys doing here?' Phoebe: 'We're rescuing you ... from the tall, dark, and naked man.'

SEASON 2: GIVE ME A SIGN

Prue, on Litvack: 'He lives in a cemetery? How clichéd.'

Notes: 'To find a mortal? All you need to do is follow his dreams. That's where they always escape to.' An ambitious story about both the positive and the negative aspects of a person's dreams. The main drawbacks are some rather inept performances from members of the supporting cast. Steve Railsback – a *great* actor – seems to have taken David Carradine's appearance in 'Déjà Vu All Over Again' as his inspiration and, on this occasion, the snarling, eye-rolling, over-the-top baddy act doesn't come even close to working. Nevertheless, there is much to admire in an episode that, apart from a somewhat shallow last few minutes, rattles along at an impressive pace.

Soundtrack: Marie Wilson's 'Making It Up As I Go Along', and 'Just A Little Hole' by Beth Hart.

38: MURPHY'S LUCK

30 March 2000

Writer: David Simkins
Director: John Behring

Cast: Arnold Vosloo (Darklighter), Amy Adams (Maggie Murphy), Kent Faulcon (Gil Corso)

Prue's first photojournalism assignment is to photograph Maggie Murphy, the unluckiest woman in San Francisco. Prue saves Maggie from attempted suicide and casts a spell to remove her bad luck. However, Maggie's misfortune was actually caused by a Darklighter. And he now wants to eliminate Prue to remove the spell. Leo discovers Piper's true feelings, but isn't pleased when she wants to tell Dan in person that she is breaking up with him.

It's Witchcraft: *The Book of Shadows* notes: 'Spirit Killer Classification: Darklighter: Method: Forces good souls into suicide through telepathic suggestion. Very Dangerous.' (This is an allusion to *Raiders of the Lost Ark*.) When Piper is searching through the book, she comes across the Multiplicity Spell (see 'Which Prue is It, Anyway?). After Prue tries her first solo spell, Phoebe notes that it took her a few tries before she got the hang of it.

The Conspiracy Starts at the Witching Hour: Until three months earlier, Maggie Murphy was regarded as something of a saint – she helped the homeless and did much selfless charity work. Then, almost overnight, everything started going bad for her. It was at this point that she crossed paths, unknowingly, with a Darklighter. There is, Leo notes, a certain type of Darklighter that drives future Whitelighters to commit suicide and lose their souls forever. The Darklighter curses his unfortunate victim with self-doubt and bad luck – the kind that hurts other people.

Work Is A Four Letter Word: Prue has been hired by *415* magazine.

It's a Designer Label!: Highlights include Prue's red leather trousers and Phoebe's 'Ming's Tattoo' T-shirt.

References: Aspects of the plot, and a healthy proportion of the visuals, appear influenced by Hitchcock's *Vertigo* (1958). Also, a reference to actress Della Reese and her performance in the series *Touched By An Angel*; and an oblique allusion to *It's a Wonderful Life*.

'You May Remember Me ...': Arnold Vosloo played Imhotep in *The Mummy* and also appeared in *Strange World* and *Steel Dawn*. Amy Adams was Alex in *Pumpkin*. Her other movies include *Drop Dead Gorgeous* and *Psycho Beach Party*. Kent Faulcon appeared in *Solaris* and *American Beauty*. The band Four Star Mary (best known for their regular work on *Buffy the Vampire Slayer*) appear, uncredited, in the opening sequence.

Logic, Let Me Introduce You To This Window: When Prue goes missing, Leo suggest her sisters find her by scrying (see 'That Old Black Magic'). This is rejected because, Phoebe notes, they don't have time. However, they seemingly *do* have time to leave the house, go to the nursing home and find Maggie. When Prue burns the photograph, she places it into the fire with the image facing down. After a change of camera angle, the photo is facing upwards. Why would Prue be taking Maggie's photo with such a lot of movement in the background? At P^3, when Prue and Phoebe are about to leave, Prue backs into a tray of glasses and Piper freezes the room. But Leo doesn't freeze.

Continuity: When Prue was 20 (approximately nine years earlier) she was driving her sisters and accidentally ran a red light, crashing into another car. Phoebe was hurt and spent a week in hospital. Prue had a severe depression afterwards and has never fully forgiven herself. Piper notes that when the girls were younger, Grams was extremely over-protective, especially towards her eldest granddaughter – for instance she would not let Prue go away to school. (Prue had wanted to go to a college in the East to become a photojournalist – see 'Give Me a Sign'.) Leo becomes a Whitelighter again to save Prue's life. Dan is currently in New York – Piper still hasn't told him that she has decided to end their relationship in favour of Leo (see 'Give Me a Sign').

Quote/Unquote: Corso, on Maggie: 'She's gonna be featured in our St Paddy's day issue, something about being the unluckiest woman in San Francisco. And she's Irish. Down the hall where they do the writing, they call that irony.'
Phoebe: 'Stop trying to predict the future, that's my job.'

Notes: 'Maybe you should just stay away from me. People get hurt.' A deeply and painfully awful episode with a banal central idea and not even the saving grace of a clever twist in the plot or the odd good line of dialogue. 'Murphy's Luck' is something of a paradox in relation to the surrounding episodes – all of which at least tried to be inventive and occasionally surprising. This, sadly, is *Charmed* on autopilot. More worrying, several of the performances seem equally phoned-in.

Soundtrack: Bif Naked's epic 'Lucky', and 'Higher' by Tara MacLean.

39: HOW TO MAKE A QUILT OUT OF AMERICANS

6 April 2000

Teleplay: Javier Grillo-Marxuach and Robert Masello
Story: Javier Grillo-Marxuach
Director: Kevin Inch

Cast: Cameron Bancroft (Cryto), Anne Haney (Gail Altman), Pamela Gordon (Amanda), Lucy Lee Flippin (Helen), Julia Lee (Young Gale), John Gowans (Mr York), Bill Wiley (Caddie Guy #1), Charles C Stevenson Jr (Caddie Guy #2)

> The sisters' aunt asks for help when a number of corpses turn up in her town. But Aunt Gail is actually intent on stealing the powers of the Charmed Ones in order to regain her youth from the demon Cryto. When the sisters discover that their powers have been taken, Piper sees this as a way to regain a normal life without witchcraft.

It's Witchcraft: The page that Gail rips from *The Book of Shadows* contains two spells – the first detailing how to separate a witch from her powers, the second how to restore them. Both are variants on the same chant, which begins: 'Powers of the witches rise, course unseen across the skies. Come to us who call you near, come to us and settle here.' To destroy Cryto, Phoebe chants: 'What witches done and then undone, return this spirit back within, and separate him from his skin.'

The Conspiracy Starts at the Witching Hour: In the 16th Century, Cryto the Demon of Vanity travelled from dukedom to dukedom in Europe, bestowing youth and beauty in exchange for people's souls. Cryto's activities were discovered and he was skinned alive by a group of witches who believed this would keep his spirit from being resurrected.

A Little Learning is a Dangerous Thing: Cryto notes that it takes three witches to summon him and three to banish him. Having killed Gail and her friends, he assumes – incorrectly – that he's invulnerable to the Charmed Ones. He isn't, as he painfully discovers.

It's a Designer Label!: An entire scene is taken up in a discussion about the demon blood stains that have wrecked Piper's tan boots. A replacement pair are bought for her by her sisters at the end of the episode.

References: The title (and aspects of the plot) allude to Jocelyn Moorhouse's movie *How To Make An American Quilt*. Phoebe has trouble deciphering an AAA California State map. There is a possible allusion to *Father Ted*. Also, The Faces' 'Gasoline Alley'.

'You May Remember Me ...': Cameron Bancroft was in *She's No Angel* and *The Cape*. Anne Haney appeared in *Liar Liar*, *Mrs Doubtfire*, *The Bad Seed* and *LA Law*. Pamela Gordon's CV includes *Another Day in Paradise*, *Weird Science* and *The Wonder Years*. Lucy Lee Flippin was in *Soccer Dog: The Movie*, *My Mom's a Werewolf* and *Annie Hall*. Julia Lee played Anne Steele in *Buffy the Vampire Slayer* and *Angel*. John Gowans was Mr Levin in *Crossing Jordan*. Bill Wiley appeared in *That Thing You Do!*, *Taxi* and *Knight Rider*. Charles Stevenson was in *Ghost World*, *Ed Wood* and *Spin City*.

Classic *Double Entendre*: Watch closely the scene in which Cryto and Gail are in the garage shop. Behind Cryto on the wall are several post-it notes, one of which says 'Lost Dog – Willy'. One hardly dares to ask ...

Logic, Let Me Introduce You To This Window: Is Gail the sisters' actual aunt or not? The script is never entirely clear on this point. Her surname notwithstanding, the fact that she and Grams first met when they were both at college suggests that Gail and Penny were friends rather than relatives. However, Gail's observation to Amanda that the girls are 'family' muddies the water somewhat. The potion ingredients to strip a witch of her powers includes gypsy blood. Unless something remarkable happened off-screen (twice) then it seems this ingredient was never obtained. In 'That Old Black Magic', the same spell was said to require a fresh human heart. When the girls arrive at Gail's house and are drinking lemon tea, Amanda pours them a refill. However, the level of tea in Piper's cup stays more-or-less the same. Subsequently, when the sisters are about to leave, Piper's cup is suddenly almost full. The potion contains hemlock root, a poison that is deadly in even tiny amounts. Gail and her friends had to wait some time for the potion to work on Pheobe, Piper and Prue, but it works instintly on Cryto. It seems that SWA Properties (see 'From Fear to Eternity', 'Witch Trial') also have an office in Santa Costa – one with the same phone number as the San Francisco branch.

Continuity: Piper breaks up with Dan in this episode. Piper tells Prue that she knows she's been something of a drag lately, however she's confused and frustrated. Nothing has changed since she and Leo met except that

SEASON 2: HOW TO MAKE A QUILT OUT OF AMERICANS

Piper is two years older. Sometimes, she continues, she worries that they will all end up like Aunt Gail.

Grams was a member of a coven whose activities were hidden using the front of a bridge club. There is a further reference to the fact that Grams had several husbands. Phoebe needs spectacles for reading.

Cruelty to Animals: It's Piper's inability to freeze a rat that first alerts the sisters to their sudden lack of powers.

Quote/Unquote: Prue, on Gail: 'She was like a second Grams to us.' Phoebe: 'Yeah, only a nice one. One that never said no.'

Prue: 'There's nothing wrong with wearing glasses. I wear them.' Phoebe: 'But you're *older*.'

Piper: 'Aunt Gail was Grams' best friend. She used to bake us cookies.' Phoebe: 'And now she's spiking our tea.'

Notes: 'Sometimes, being a witch sucks.' Good God, what have we here? A morally ambiguous *Charmed* episode? Well, *that's* a first. Taking some inspiration from *Cocoon*, the episode plays around the periphery of interesting subject matter (growing old is horrible and unfair, and the young don't exactly help). Sadly, it's too shallow an exercise to overcome some obvious limitations. Nice performances though, especially from Anne Haney and Julia Lee. It's just a shame that the villain is so utterly one-dimensional. The subplot about Piper's unhappiness at the prospect of remaining a witch, and the problems that this presents in having a 'normal' life, would be attempted again – and more successfully – in many subsequent episodes.

Soundtrack: Catatonia's 'Bulimic Beats' and the Eurythmics' '17 Again'.

40: CHICK FLICK

20 April 2000

Writer: Chris Levinson, Zack Estrin
Director: Michael Schultz

Cast: Chris Payne Gilbert (Billy), Robin Atkin Downes (Demon of Illusion), Mark Lindsay Chapman (Finley Beck), Kent Faulcon (Gil Corso), Olivia Summers (Bloody Mary), Alec Ledd (Film Geek), Leslie Lauten (Sally Mae), Michael Rivkin (Cell Phone Guy), Dale Fabrigar (Irritated Guy), August Amarino (Projectionist), J P Romano (The Slasher)

> Phoebe's infatuation with a fictitious character in a horror movie leads the sisters to encounter the Demon of Illusion. When Phoebe attempts to banish him, the demon discovers that he can move fictional celluloid characters into the real world. The sisters soon find themselves facing real-life horrors, an axe murderer and knife wielding maniac, upon whom their powers have no effect. Meanwhile, Prue finds that a chance to work with her photographer hero isn't what she thought it would be.

It's Witchcraft: The spell Phoebe uses to vanquish the demon at the movie theatre begins: 'Evil that has travelled near, I call on you to disappear. Elementals hear my call, remove this creature from these walls.' She admits that this is actually something she cobbled together from two previously-successful spells.

The Conspiracy Starts at the Witching Hour: Leo notes that the Demon of Illusion uses magic to create violence in society – by entering movies and affecting the audiences' reactions to the stimulus they receive.

Work Is A Four Letter Word: Prue is given the opportunity to work with her hero, a gifted photojournalist Finlay Beck. Inevitably, he turns out to be nothing like she expects – instead of a warm and humane person, she meets a cynical and aggressively egotistical man.

It's a Designer Label!: Outstanding highlights include Piper's date dress, Phoebe's Miami High Mermaids T-shirt and Prue's extraordinary red vest-type top. By contrast, Prue's shocking stretchpants appear to have escaped from the 1970s, the era that taste forgot.

SEASON 2: CHICK FLICK

References: An episode full of neat subversions of horror movie clichés, 'Chick Flick' includes direct allusions to *The Shining* and *Psycho*, together with more oblique paraphrasing of *I Married a Teenage Werewolf*, *The Howling* and Michael Jackson's *Thriller* video. Also, *A Matter of Life and Death* ('Add a little Technicolor to him'); and the US folk-tale axeman Paul Bunyan.

'You May Remember Me ...': Chris Payne Gilbert's movies include *Story of a Bad Boy*. Leslie Lauten was in *The Woman Chaser*. Alec Ledd appeared in *Can't Hardly Wait*. Robin Atkin Downes played Byron in *Babylon 5*. Mark Lindsay Chapman was in *Titanic*, *American Gothic* and *Dallas*. Olivia Summers appeared in *The Deep End of the Ocean*. Michael Rivkin's CV includes *Cradle Will Rock*. August Amarino was in *I'm Losing You*. J P Romano is a stuntman who has worked on *Pirates of the Caribbean*, *24* and *CSI*.

Cigarettes and Alcohol: Piper's first date with Leo is interrupted by the couple's embarrassment at finding Dan, on a date of his own, sitting at the next table. Piper freezes the restaurant and she and Leo share a glass of white wine before he is called by the Whitelighters on an emergency.

Sex and Drugs and Rock n Roll: Phoebe's latest lunch date with a college boy doesn't go very well. She describes him as 'totally Melatonin-boy', referring to a popular US over-the-counter sleeping pill.

Logic, Let Me Introduce You To This Window: The episode features the worst-staged movie theatre riot in the history of this small-but-interesting sub-genre. Amelia, Dan's date, drinks water. This magically changes to coke in a subsequent scene. Would any chef really ask for salt before she had even tasted the food? Prue tells the Demon of Illusion that if you leave a subject under the light too long it burns, information she received from Finley Beck. Piper subsequently notes that at least Prue got *something* useful out of Beck. When, exactly, did Prue *tell* Piper what Beck said? Did Phoebe get Billy coloured contact lenses and dye his tongue pink?

Continuity: The classic black and white horror movie from which Billy emerges, *Kill It Before It Dies*, is a particular favourite of Phoebe's. (She's subsequently seen watching it again during 'Sense and Sense Ability' and it's also briefly glimpsed in 'Bride And Gloom'.) Phoebe first saw the film when she was 12. On this occasion, she sees it at a revival theatre on Larkin. (At the end of the episode, Prue buys Phoebe a video copy – although you've got to wonder, if Phoebe's *such* a fan, why she hasn't got one of those already?) Phoebe seems to be a big fan of horror movies generally – 'We *so* have to monitor your viewing habits,' notes an exasperated Prue. For example, Phoebe saw *Axe Husband*, the movie from which the Slasher emerges, just the previous week, and knows that his death in the movie is caused by electrocution. She also remembers that the eponymous Bloody Mary was pushed out of a window to her death.

In 'Morality Bites', when future-Prue and future-Piper read *The Book of Shadows*, they flipped past a page concerning the Bunyip, a demon to which Phoebe refers to this episode.

Quote/Unquote: Phoebe, on the demon: 'How am I supposed to know what his deal is? He likes moonlit walks, thinks holding hands is underrated and enjoys, in his spare time, killing witches.'

Phoebe: 'When we last saw the demon, we vanquished him at 9:06.' Prue: 'And now he's in Act Three.'

Demon of Illusion, to the Slasher: 'I can get you out of here. Take you to a place where the movie never ends.' And, to the movie audience: 'Ladies and gentlemen, let's make your PG lives rated R.'

Billy: 'This is around the second act, right? When everything's about to be explained. Where's the music we're supposed to talk over, to build suspense and hide the exposition? Don't you just hate exposition?'

Piper: 'I'm a romantic comedy girl. Why go to horror movies when they come to *us*?'

Notes: 'This is the world of illusion and you girls are reality.' A beautifully constructed pastiche of the horror genre that is, at the same time, a celebration of it. Postmodernism of this kind can seem dreadfully arch if it's not done well, but 'Chick Flick' takes all the best bits of 50 years of dark fantasy and reassembles them as a witty and, importantly, *informed* comment on the genre. Full of clever, self-aware dialogue – 'Check me out, I'm retro,' notes Phoebe as she enters the movie and becomes monochrome – 'Chick Flick' also contains some complex ideas. Phoebe becoming infatuated with a fictional character is an ingenious comment on the various 'Mary Sue' strands of popular fan-fiction, where fans write themselves into the stories. The episode includes much discussion about free will and allegories towards reality-versus-illusion as a preferred state. Never has *Charmed* so resembled the Joss Whedon school of horror deconstruction-via-celebration as here.

Soundtrack: Nina Gordon's 'Bad Way'.

41: EX LIBRIS

27 April 2000

Teleplay: Brad Kern
Story: Peter Chomsky
Director: Joel J Feigenbaum

Cast: Cleavant Derricks (Cleavant Wilson), Peg Stewart (Lillian), Rebecca Cross (Charlene Hughes), Molly Chance (Young Lillian), Scott Lincoln (Libris)[38], Jeremy Roberts (Gibbs)[39], The Goo Goo Dolls (Themselves)

> When one of Phoebe's classmates, Charlene, is murdered, she has a hard time accepting her new status as a ghost. Whilst Phoebe tries to obtain justice for Charlene's untimely death, Prue helps a father incriminate his daughter's killer. Meanwhile, a green-eyed Dan tells Piper that Leo was once married.

It's Witchcraft: When Prue proposes using the truth spell (see 'The Truth is Out There ... And It Hurts') on Gibbs to make him confess to Tyra's murder, Phoebe reminds her sister that the Charmed Ones can't use their power to punish the guilty, only to protect the innocent (see 'Mortality Bites'). The spell to vanquish Libris begins: 'Demon hide your evil face, Libris die and leave no trace.'

A Little Learning is a Dangerous Thing: Phoebe tells Charlene that neophyte ghosts cannot channel their anger into moving material objects.

The Conspiracy Starts at the Witching Hour: Leo notes that evil doesn't want anyone to know about its existence and has a system for covering its tracks. Amongst other things, that's the reason why demons disappear when they are vanquished. There are, Prue subsequently discovers, a group of Libris demons. Wherever a human has the potential to discover unequivocal proof of the existence of demons, the Libris kill the unfortunate victim – usually by decapitation.

Work Is A Four Letter Word: Prue's latest assignment for *415* is called 'Faces in the City'. It's whilst photographing street scenes in Haight-

---

[38] Uncredited.
[39] Uncredited.

Ashbury that she encounters grief-stricken Cleavant Wilson, whose daughter, Tyra, was murdered on 18 October 1999 at the corner of Post and Mason. The police are certain she was killed by a pawn shop owner, Gibbs, but have no evidence on which to charge him.

It's a Designer Label!: Best items on display, Prue's shorts and Phoebe's figure-hugging dress in the final scene.

References: An allusion to Electronic's 'Get the Message'. The two books Charlene has at the library are *The Encyclopaedia of Witchcraft and Demonology* by Montague Summers (see 'Witch Trial') and *The Complete Book of Devils and Demons* by Leonard R N Ashley.

'You May Remember Me ...': Cleavant Derricks appeared in *Sliders*, *Moonlighting* and *Fort Apache The Bronx*. Peg Stewart's CV includes *Buffy the Vampire Slayer*, *The A-Team*, *The Rockford Files* and *CHiPs*. Rebecca Cross was in *I Love Trouble*. Scott Lincoln appeared in *Tom Cats* and *How High*. Jeremy Roberts's movies include *The Mexican*, *Sister Act* and *Phoenix*.

Behind the Camera: Joel J Feigenbaum previously worked on *Hotel*, *Dallas* and *7th Heaven*. Peter Chomsky's CV includes *Pacific Palisades*.

Sex and Drugs and Rock n Roll: When leaving Piper and Leo alone, Prue whispers some useful advice to her sister: 'No sex without safe sex!' The next morning, when she catches a glimpse of Leo naked in the shower, Prue's only comment is an appreciative 'Nice orbs!'

Logic, Let Me Introduce You To This Window: Are Phoebe's books library books? If so, is she really supposed to be highlighting sections of them? The ghost, Charlene, is non-corporeal and passes through a library cart. Later, however, she can pick up objects – including some quite heavy ones – with no apparent difficulty. She might be a 'quick study' as Phoebe notes, but *that* quick? The Libris's sickle appears and disappears in his hand with alarming regularity during the scene when he's trying to kill Phoebe. How many different pairs of spectacles does Phoebe have? When Leo and Piper wake her up in the kitchen, she's wearing the square-framed pair seen in 'Chick Flick'. When she's in the library with Charlene, she's wearing the round wire-rim glasses from 'How To Make A Quilt Out Of Americans.'

Continuity: Phoebe and Charlene were in the same Metaphysics 301 class, in which Charlene's father was the lecturer. (They also car-pooled together on occasion.) Charlene appeared to have an awkward relationship with her father and was driven to get her thesis – concerning the existence of demons – published so that Mr Hughes would take her seriously. She's actually quite surprised to find that her death upset him greatly. At the end of the episode, we discover that Phoebe has aced her final exams. Piper has bought a birthday card for Victor. Both Phoebe and Prue refuse to sign it (although Phoebe does, subsequently, relent).

In the 1940s, Leo was married to a woman named Lilian, whom Piper meets. After Leo's death trying to help a wounded man (for which he was rewarded with a posthumous Purple Heart – see 'Love Hurts', 'Saving Private Leo'), he visited Lilian in a dream bathed in the most brilliant white light and told her not to worry about him, that he was in a good place. He also told Lilian to move on, and that there was another love out there for her to find. Which she subsequently did, marrying a doctor and having two children and several grandchildren.

Quote/Unquote: Phoebe: 'Contrary to popular belief, not every crime in this city is demonically-related. Or Halliwell-related for that matter.'

Phoebe: 'Charlene's spirit can't move on unless I get justice for her murder.' Prue: 'By getting murdered yourself?' Phoebe: 'Well, hopefully not. On the bright side, I won't have to suffer through flunking out of college. So how was your day?'

Prue, on Charlene's murder: 'He must've grabbed her in the aisle and taken her somewhere else to, you know [mimes decapitation] … Sorry.' Charlene: 'That's okay. I'm over the shock.'

Notes: 'I hate to top that, but I am dealing with a ghost who doesn't know she's a ghost.' Something of a dry remake of 'Dead Man Dating', which has some nice characterisation (particularly Prue's determination to help someone who very definitely *doesn't* remind her of her own father) but never really hits the emotional level required. Piper's tracking down of Leo's – now aged – ex-wife is case in point. It's a beautifully played scene but, somehow, hollow. Best bit: Dan's and Leo's bar-room brawl. Which says a lot, frankly.

Soundtrack: Faith Hill's 'That's How Love Moves', and 'January Friend' By the Goo Goo Dolls. The latter also perform 'Broadway' at P^3.

42: ASTRAL MONKEY

4 May 2000

Teleplay: Constance M Burge, David Simkins
Story: Constance M Burge
Director: Craig Zisk

Cast: Jim Davidson (Evan Stone), Matthew Glave (Dr Curtis Williamson), Milt Tarver (Dr Jeffries), Susan Martino (Lucy), Jack Maxwell (Barry), Dierdre Holder (Nurse #1), Gary Douglas Kohn (Benny Ritter), Karen James (Sally 'Bones' Dopler), Lina Patel (Doctor #1)

>Piper's former doctor, Curtis Williamson, has been experimenting with the blood of the Charmed Ones on chimpanzees. When he is, himself, injected with some of the sisters' blood, he discovers that he now has the magical powers of Prue, Piper and Phoebe. However, because the doctor is mortal, the powers slowly drive him insane – causing him to remove the vital organs of a number of criminals to save needy patients. Meanwhile, Prue finds herself mobbed by the tabloid press when she's linked romantically to a well-known actor.

A Little Learning is a Dangerous Thing: Evan Stone is a publicity-hungry actor who starred in a movie called *Red Death* that Phoebe has seen five times. He takes a real shine to (a somewhat uninterested) Prue when she is hired to take some photos of him.

References: Allusions to *The Karate Kid* ('The whole wax-on, wax-off approach'); *Jeopardy* and it's host Alex Trebek; and *Notting Hill*. The TV show that exposes Prue's supposed relationship with Evan Stone is called *Showbiz Tonight*.

'You May Remember Me ...': Jim Davidson appeared in *Crocodile Dundee in Los Angeles*. Milt Tarver's movies include *Fear and Loathing in Las Vegas* and *Total Recall*. Susan Martino was in *The Shield* and *Angel*. Jack Maxwell's CV includes *The Pharaoh Project*. Dierdre Holder appeared in *The Guardian*. Gary Kohn was in *Almost Famous* and *Girl X*. Karen James played Dotty in *Reform School Girls*. Lina Patel appeared in *Saving Jessica Lynch* and *Alias*.

SEASON 2: ASTRAL MONKEY

The Drugs Don't Work: Williamson obtains a new kidney for his ailing sister by removing one from a rather scummy drug dealer named Barry Ritter.

Sex and Drugs and Rock n Roll: Leo has been having breakfast at the Manor a great deal recently. To such an extent that both Phoebe and Prue suggest to Piper that perhaps some ground rules should be drawn up. Phoebe is particularly keen on 'No orbing in unannounced' after Leo arrives in Piper's bedroom, mistakes Phoebe for Piper and ask if she's ever 'done it on a cloud' before. Phoebe asks if a feather bed counts.

Logic, Let Me Introduce You To This Window: If Williamson was attempting to find some unique property in the Halliwells' blood, mixing the three samples together and injecting it into a chimp doesn't seem a particularly scientific way of achieving much. That is always assuming that all three sisters share the same blood type (see 'The Wendigo'), as mixing different blood types would merely coagulate the specimen. The sticking plaster on Williamson's neck switches from the left side to the right for one shot. A chimpanzee is an ape, not a monkey. Leo says that once the sisters' cast the awakening spell, their powers could be passed on through their blood. But, in 'Awakened', once they reversed that spell, this should have nullified any side effects. It took the Charmed Ones some time to learn how to use their powers properly (see 'Something Wicca This Way Comes' and subsequent episodes). How, therefore, do Williamson and, indeed, *some chimpanzees*, master them in a few days? Jack Maxwell's character is credited as Barry, but Williamson refers to him as Larry. If the sisters' blood is so detrimental to Williamson's sanity then shouldn't it also be to the chimpanzees'? Dr Jeffries clearly moves when he's supposed to be frozen.

Continuity: Prue says she knows Aikido. (Wasn't Phoebe the martial arts expert in the family?) This episode takes place shortly after 1 May 2000 (the date of Williamson's letter to Piper), and approximately 90 days after the events of 'Awakened'. The address of San Francisco Memorial Hospital is 25173 Chambers Drive. Curtis Williamson works in Lab B-111. The list of recently released criminals that Williamson obtains contains the names Benny Ritter, Trey Sullivan, Frank McNamara, Arlen Jackson and Sally Dobler.

Motors: A first decent look at Prue's new black BMW (3EXQ 691).

Cruelty to Animals: Chimps in cages. Enough said. Having staged a daring hospital-break with her sisters, Phoebe intends to give the animals to a wildlife reserve.

Quote/Unquote: Phoebe, to Leo: 'He's like the big brother I never wanted. I mean, had.'
Prue: 'Mr Corso, you know that I'm not Evan Stone's girlfriend. Are you laughing at me?'
Leo: 'You okay?' Piper: 'Well, considering our powers have combined to drive a man crazy and put who knows how many other people in danger, I'm terrific.'

Notes: 'Prue, honey, I don't think monkeys can astral project.' Another *Charmed* first – a realisation that the sisters can't always do the right thing (or, that they *can*, but that the right thing isn't always the *easy* thing). Piper's heartbreak that she was unable to save an essentially decent man destroyed by his obsessive need to help others is wonderfully played – this is Holly Marie Combs' best episode thus far by a considerable distance. The lighter subplots (the chimpanzees, chiefly) are more hit-and-miss, although the Halliwells trying to sneak the chimps out of the hospital, freezing people as they go, is one of the best comedy moments *Charmed* ever attempted.

Soundtrack: Grunge overload! Smash Mouth's 'When The Morning Comes', and 'Let the Cables Fall' by Bush.

43: APOCALYPSE, NOT

11 May 2000

Teleplay: Sheryl J Anderson
Story: Sanford Golden
Director: Michael Zinberg

Cast: Brian Thompson (War), Geoffrey Blake (Strife), Jeff Ricketts (Famine), Patrick Kilpatrick (Death), Kevin Ramsey (Bartender), Kenneth Cortland (Assistant), Gannon Brown (Worker #1), Peter Asle Holden (Worker #2)

> A sudden outbreak of street violence in San Francisco – mirroring other events around the world – may have a supernatural root. The sisters cast a spell to vanquish the suspected cause of this but, unbeknown to them, they are actually facing the Four Horsemen of the Apocalypse. The Charmed Ones' magic causes Prue and one of the Horsemen, War, to be banished to another plane of existence. Phoebe and Piper learn that the only way to save Prue is to work with the evil trio. But that might mean rescuing their sister just in time for the end to the world.

It's Witchcraft: The Demon of Anarchy can be vanquished with a basic iambic pentameter chant.[40] (The spell that the sisters cast is: 'Sower of discord, your works now must cease. I vanquish thee now, with these words of peace.') The Demon of Cruelty is a woman who is said to harden the heart and corrode the soul.

A Little Shopping is a Dangerous Thing: The episode begins with the Halliwells having spent an enjoyable day together attending their yoga class, getting pedicures, shopping for shoes and then doing lunch.

The Conspiracy Starts at the Witching Hour: The Source is mentioned again (see 'Give Me a Sign'). Leo notes that the Horsemen wear the mark of the Anointed Ones – the Omega tattoo. Only the Source can destroy the Horsemen. Each time the world has been on the brink of Armageddon – Hitler or the 1962 Cuban missile crisis, for instance – a team of Horsemen has been vanquished by the Source for their failures and replaced. The current Horsemen are said to be closer to succeeding that any previous collective.

---

[40] Iambic pentameter: a verse line consisting of five metrical iambic feet – including two dactyls and one stressed syllable.

Subsequently, Leo tells the sisters that it was Piper's and Phoebe's act of selflessness that stopped the Source's plans. It was acknowledged to be a sign that there was still too much good in the world to make the apocalypse successful. Piper asks if this means that evil is going to give up. Leo doubts it – indeed, it will probably try harder from now on.

Work Is A Four Letter Word: The Death Horseman is responsible for outbreaks of cholera in Central Asia and smallpox in Venezuela.

References: The title alludes to Francis Ford Coppola's epic 1979 Vietnam odyssey, *Apocalypse Now*, starring Martin Sheen and Marlon Brando. Phoebe possibly makes an oblique reference to *Doctor Who* ('reverse polarity'). The – seemingly fictitious – book *Ask Me a Tough One* also features heavily.

'You May Remember Me …': Brian Thompson will be familiar to most readers as the sinister Alien Bounty Hunter in *The X-Files*. He's also appeared in *Buffy the Vampire Slayer* and *Star Trek: Generations*. Geoffrey Blake's movies include *Life Without Dick*, *Apollo 13* and *Young Guns*. Jeff Ricketts played Malcolm in *Chance* and was also in *Firefly*, *Angel* and *Enterprise*. Patrick Kilpatrick's CV includes *Minority Report* and *The X-Files*. Kevin Ramsey appeared in *24*. Kenneth Cortland was in *The Boy Next Door*. Gannon Brown appeared in *Sister Sister*. Peter Asle Holder was in *The Victim* and *The Wonder Years*.

Behind the Camera: Sanford Golden also wrote for *Mr & Mrs Smith*.

Logic, Let Me Introduce You To This Window: When Phoebe and Piper place several objects on the table, the pyramid and candle change places between shots. Twice. Leo explains why nothing supernaturally horrid happened on New Year's Eve 1999; because the monks who converted the Julian calendar to the Gregorian calendar made some errors.[41] Actually, it was largely the Venerable Bede's fault.[42] Christ's birth, most historians now believe, took place in or prior to 4 BC (the year in which Herod the Great died).[43] Therefore, the actual second millennium of this event would have been circa 1996 not in May 2000. The Four Horsemen of the Apocalypse wear

---

[41] The Gregorian Calendar was adopted in 1582 and represented a change of 10 days from the Julian Calendar, which had remained unchanged since its adoption by Julius Caesar in 46 BC.
[42] Bede, an English cleric, made a calculation of the birth of Christ occurring in the year 1 *Anno Domini* in his *Ecclesiastical History of the English People*, which he completed in 731.
[43] Matthew's gospel reports that Herod was still alive when Christ was born.

colour-coded ties, and at least one of them, Strife, can't outrun a girl. Which probably explains why the world hasn't ended yet.

Continuity: Piper is surprised when Leo rings the bell instead of merely orbing into the Manor. Leo notes that he is trying to respect everyone's space (see 'Astral Monkey'). Phoebe suggests there are 11 planes of existence.

Quote/Unquote: Phoebe: 'Random social violence is encouraged by a general decline in ethical thinking, according to my sociology professor. He said that we don't think about the big questions enough.' Prue: 'The big question is, how did you stay awake through his class?'
Leo: 'This is why evil loves free will so much. Because humans use it to follow their heart.'
Assistant: 'You should know we're losing momentum across the board, especially in war. Peace has broken out in several areas this afternoon.'
Phoebe: 'Are you telling me evil called good and good answered?' Leo: 'These suits that you're dealing with have the highest possible connections. Their bosses talk to my bosses.'

Notes: 'I think we just vanquished our sister.' You've just got to love the idea of the Four Horsemen of the Apocalypse running the countdown to Armageddon from a multi-national company headquarters with a team of minions watching events around the world on TV. It's *so* 21st Century. 'Apocalypse, Not' is a terrific example of ambition outstripping ability but coming out punching. Making the Horsemen themselves a kind-of dark version of the sisters, full of bickering sibling rivalries, was a really clever move. The stock footage of world chaos also works nicely. Ultimately, it's really only the small-scale nature of the girls' victory that disappoints – although one suspects this may have been the whole point of the episode; that in the face of overwhelmingly enormous events, it's the little victories that actually matter most.

Soundtrack: Paula Cole's 'Amen' and 'Be Somebody' (performed in P^3), and 'Compression' by Everything But the Girl.

44: BE CAREFUL WHAT YOU WITCH FOR

18 May 2000

Teleplay: Brad Kern, Zack Estrin, Chris Levinson
Story: Brad Kern
Director: Shannen Doherty

Cast: French Stewart (Genie), J G Hertzler (Council Member), Jeff Corey (Council Member), Zitto Kazann (Council Member), Marcus Graham (Dragon Warlock), Joshua Hutchinson (Dick)

> The Council, a cabal of five senior figures in the demon hierarchy, send a mischievous Genie to grant the Charmed Ones their desires. The sisters are cautious but – accidentally – make wishes that, respectively, turn Prue into a teenager, allow Phoebe to fly and cause Dan to rapidly age. As the girls try to undo the harm that they have caused, their weakened state makes them easy targets for the Dragon Warlock.

It's Witchcraft: This episode sees the first use of 'The Power of Three' chant (see 'Something Wicca This Way Comes') since 'Witch Trial'.

The Conspiracy Starts at the Witching Hour: The Dragon Warlock is descended from a long line of ancestors with similar abilities. His father left him with a passionate hatred of witches. *The Book of Shadows* confirms that the Dragon Warlock is a feared witch-killer. In addition to having the power of flight, he can breathe fire and has supernatural strength.
   The Genie tells the sisters about the Council, describing them as 'very high up on the evil food chain.' It is, he believes, only a matter of time before they send someone looking for the Charmed Ones. Prue notes this means they're clearly doing something right if they got the evil underworld's attention. Phoebe is pleased to discover that there is some method to their Wiccan madness, a greater purpose. 'Be careful what you wish for,' adds Leo, wisely.

It's a Designer Label!: Teenage-Prue's silver miniskirt.

References: The episode contains dialogue allusions to 'Puff the Magic Dragon' and the *Monty Python's Flying Circus* Spanish Inquisition sketch. A briefly glimpsed headline in the *San Francisco Chronicle* is WORLD MARKET

SEASON 2: BE CAREFUL WHAT YOU WITCH FOR

TURMOIL.

'You May Remember Me ...': French Stewart is perhaps best known as Harry Solomon in *3rd Rock from the Sun* and as Major Ferretti in *Stargate*. J G Hertzler was Martok in *Star Trek: Deep Space Nine*. Jeff Corey's impressive CV includes *Bird on a Wire*, *Santa Barbara*, *Butch Cassidy and the Sundance Kid*, *Seconds*, *In Cold Blood* and *The Outer Limits*. Zitto Kazann appeared in *Thirteen Days*, *Red Dawn*, *Starsky and Hutch* and *Buffy the Vampire Slayer*. Josh Hutchinson was in *Roswell*. Marcus Graham's movies include *Mulholland Drive*.

Sex and Drugs and Rock n Roll: Piper wonders what she will tell Dan, considering that he has provided her with proof that Leo was killed in 1942. 'How about "Hey Dan, I'm a necrophiliac",' suggests Phoebe, less than helpfully. Phoebe is given a terrific foot-massage by the Genie, who says he learned it from a Sultan.

Classic *Double Entendre*: Prue has a lunch date (her third) with a dull guy named Dick. Two subsequent scenes are full of over-the-top *Carry On*-style innuendo (e.g. Prue: 'I gotta figure out a way to put some more balance in my life.' Piper: 'Yeah, but you don't need Dick.')

Logic, Let Me Introduce You To This Window: How did Piper know that Prue had made her wish at the restaurant and that she and Leo could subsequently find the Genie there? Teenage-Prue certainly didn't tell her. Furthermore, how did Piper and Prue know what their own wishes were? They clearly weren't conscious of the fact that they were making a wish when doing so. When Prue was stabbed by the demon in the park, Piper and Phoebe dragged her back home and *then* called for Leo to heal her. Why didn't they call for him in the park? How long did it take Piper and Phoebe to get to the park to rescue Prue? When Prue called the Manor for help, it was dark, yet when Piper and Phoebe arrive, it's broad daylight. A line of dialogue seems to have been inserted in post-production – Phoebe noting that 'It'll be dawn soon' – to cover this error. But that clearly isn't an immediate post-dawn sky; it looks more like mid-afternoon. Why didn't Leo heal Phoebe's foot? She injured it whilst fighting a demon, which appears to satisfy established Whitelighter criteria.

If Piper wished for Dan to forget everything that had happened to him over the past couple of days, wouldn't he also have forgotten about the job offer in Portland? When the Dragon Warlock's fire unfreezes and it hits the picture, a subsequent shot shows the picture undamaged. Later, it's badly burned. The Genie tells the Halliwells that he's been stuck in a bottle for 200 years. However, within moments, he's making references to telephone calls and CDs. Surely *that* alone should tip Prue, Piper and Phoebe off as to his duplicity? Phoebe asks, in relation to teenage-Prue, whether cellphones were even invented 10 years

SEASON 2: BE CAREFUL WHAT YOU WITCH FOR

earlier. They were – mobile-phones have existed since the early 1980s. However, 10 years earlier Prue wasn't 17, she was 20. SWA Properties (see 'From Fear to Eternity', 'Witch Trial', 'How To Make a Quilt Out of Americans') appears to be the only real estate company in California – they're handling the sale of Dan's house.

Continuity: Piper asks Leo about his life when he orbs away. Does he have a house? Friends? A CD player? Leo changes the subject but, at the end of the episode, when he's called by the Whitelighters, Piper goes with him, leaving her sisters to speculate on when, indeed *if*, she'll be back (see 'The Honeymoon's Over'). A brace-wearing 17 year old Prue was, according to Phoebe, 'a nightmare'. Piper adds that she was lucky to make 18. It was Prue's rebellious stage – she thought everything bad was good, especially the guy she thought she was in love with. Victor used to take the girls fishing in Golden Gate Park.

The Dragon Warlock notes that genies are notorious for being interested only in themselves. Leo subsequently confirms that genies are tricksters by nature. They can and will do anything to be free. They're not evil *per se*, and can't actually harm someone unless they wish for something dangerous – but genie-wishes always come with an unseen consequence, as all three sisters discover. Fortunately, this Genie has one of those sudden changes of character motivation that happen only in television shows, helps the girls to defeat the Dragon Warlock and is rewarded with his freedom.

Quote/Unquote: Phoebe: 'Check my to do list. It says bank, dry cleaners, pedicure. Nowhere on the list does it say kick-box a beast. Just walking along, minding my own business and "wham!" it was like a random attack, a demonic drive-by.'

Genie: 'The only way to get rid of me is to make three wishes. Come on, large or small, I do all kinds. Only no "world peace", I can't do *that*.'

Genie: 'They'll kill me.' Piper: 'They're gonna have to wait in line.' And, Genie: 'You're probably a bit upset?' Piper: 'I've moved *past* upset and straight to *pissed off*.'

Phoebe, on her new power: 'Flying's awesome! It's the landing part that's a bitch.'

Darryl, concerning an incident report he's recently received: 'She swore she saw a brown haired, young woman fly over the house earlier. Without a plane.'

Notes: 'I will not rest until I put all witches to rest.' This episode, which marked Shannen Doherty's directorial debut, works mostly because French Stewart's lithe clowning antics suit the ridiculousness of the plot. Thus, we have a *Charmed* episode in the tradition of 'The Theatre of the Absurd', with one ludicrous plot device after another heaped on top of each other to, frankly, brilliant effect. You can imagine the discussions in the writers' room: 'Let's have Phoebe fly for an

SEASON 2: BE CAREFUL WHAT YOU WITCH FOR

episode ...' etc. But there's some depth, too; this is a very literal 'Be careful what you wish for' conceit with some surprisingly perceptive things to say about free will. Once again, the season ends with Prue closing the door of the Manor (see 'Something Wicca This Way Comes', 'Déjà Vu All Over Again'), a suitably respectful note on which to end 22 weeks of *fine* television.

Soundtrack: Filter's 'I'm Not The Only One', Beth Hart's 'Delicious Surprise', and 'Met With You' by Modern English.

CHARMED SEASON 3
(2000-2001)

Executive Consultants: Chris Levinson (45-49), Zack Estrin (45-49)
Supervising Producers: Sheryl J Anderson (45-58), Peter Hume (48-58)
Consulting Producers: James L Conway, Jonathan Levin
Coordinating Producer: Betty Reardon
Co-Executive Producers: William Schmidt (45-58), Nell Scovell (59-66), Sheryl J Anderson (59-66)
Producer: Jon Paré
Executive Producers: Brad Kern, Aaron Spelling, E Duke Vincent
Creative Consultant: Constance M Burge (45-47)
Executive Consultants: Constance M Burge (48-66), Peter Hume (59-66)
Associate Producer: Peter Chomsky

Regular Cast:
Shannen Doherty (Prue Halliwell)
Holly Marie Combs (Piper Halliwell)
Alyssa Milano (Phoebe Halliwell)
Dorian Gregory (Darryl Morris, 45, 48-49, 56, 59, 62, 66)
Brian Krause (Leo Wyatt)
Julian McMahon (Cole Turner, 45-52, 57-60, 63-66)

45: THE HONEYMOON'S OVER

05 October 2000

Writer: Brad Kern
Director: James L Conway

Cast: Harry Danner (Judge William Harrison), Fleming Brooks (Emilio Smith), A T Montgomery (Paramedic), Stoney Jackson (Alan Sloan), Bakenaked Ladies (Themselves).

> Whilst Piper is on another plane with Leo, Prue and Phoebe face a series of demons known as Guardians, who protect mortal murderers in exchange for the souls of innocents. After saving Darryl, Prue and Phoebe must testify in court, where they stumble upon an evil conspiracy. Phoebe, meanwhile, falls head over heels for a handsome Assistant District Attorney, Cole Turner. Piper returns and reveals that the Elders have delivered an ultimatum.

A Little Learning is a Dangerous Thing: Prue believes – erroneously – that Guardians can be killed with a stake, like vampires (the first *Charmed* reference to the latter since 'The Power of Two').

The Conspiracy Starts at the Witching Hour: A spate of recent attacks on Phoebe and Prue are said to be have been the work on an Evil Triad (see 'Magic Hour'). No further information is given as to what sort of attacks these were (and indeed, at one point, Phoebe contradicts Prue's earlier statement, saying that they're lucky they *haven't* been attacked). Presumably, any attacks that did take place weren't *that* serious as, even without the Power of Three, Prue and Phoebe are still alive. Meanwhile, Darryl has been tracking a murder suspect who, he believes, is in league with a demon. This turns out to be Emilio Smith. Subsequently, Leo speculates that the sisters may have stumbled across an evil conspiracy in the court – where an upper level demon assigns Guardians to the criminals who are set free.

Piper notes that the longer she is back from wherever it was that she and Leo went, the fuzzier the details of her time there seems to get. She believes that the Elders do this on purpose, as they are very big on mystery. All she remembers are feelings – mostly good ones. But then it all went to crap when the Elders said that Leo and Piper had to stop seeing each other. If they failed to do so, Leo would be reassigned and the

SEASON 3: THE HONEYMOON'S OVER

Charmed Ones would never see him again. Piper believes that she is being punished for the relationship between her mother and her Whitelighter (see 'P^3 H^{2}0').

Work Is A Four Letter Word: Prue has a home fax machine – ostensibly for work-related stuff but, in this episode, used by Darryl to send over a crime scene photograph.

It's a Designer Label!: The production's pair of leather trousers are worn this week both by Darryl (see **Logic, Let Me Introduce You To This Window**) and, slightly more effectively, by Prue. The more discerning viewer is, instead, pointed in the direction of Prue's very tight white sweater and Phoebe's even tighter star T-shirt.

References: Allusions to *Night Court*; Barry Manilow; *Free Willy*; *Cinderella*; and the Salem witch trials (see 'I've Got You Under My Skin', 'The Witch is Back', 'All Halliwell's Eve'). There's a possible visual reference to *Highlander*. A couple of California state flags are visible in the court house. 'We are not alone' was the poster tagline for *Close Encounters of the Third Kind* and was also, frequently, used in dialogue in *The X-Files*. In P^3, posters for Muzzle, the Goo Goo Dolls and the Pretenders, amongst others, can be seen.

'You May Remember Me ...': A T Montgomery is now best known as Travis Mayweather on *Enterprise*. He also appeared in *Popular*. Harry Danner's movies include *The Wedding Planner*. Stoney Jackson was in *Carnival of Wolves*, *The Fan* and *M*A*S*H*.

Behind the Camera: Stuntman Roger Stoneburner also worked on *The X-Files*, *Angel* and *Nash Bridges*.

Cigarettes and Alcohol: Piper is seen mixing a lethal-looking cocktail for someone (possibly herself) in P^3 towards the end of the episode.

Logic, Let Me Introduce You To This Window: When Phoebe kicks Cole, he catches her leg at his chest's height. However, in the next shot, he's holding her foot much lower down. When the sisters and Leo enter the courtroom, a prison guard is standing directly behind them. In the next shot, he's gone. When Piper orbs in with Leo, she's wearing different hair-clips to those she wore when she left in 'Be Careful What You Witch For'. When Phoebe says, 'What if she doesn't come back?', a member of the production crew can be seen moving in the background. Cole's destructive power would eventually be shown as a blue electric-like light stream, but

SEASON 3: THE HONEYMOON'S OVER

in this episode he simply lifts up his hand and the judge bursts into flames. When the sisters are in the court room, Piper freezes Cole immediately, but it takes a further few seconds to freeze Darryl and Leo. Of course, Cole only *pretends* to be frozen. When Phoebe tries to call and warn Cole not to leave the police station, Pure tells her that it will take them at least 10-15 minutes to get there. But when Cole is attacked by Emilio, almost immediately afterwards, the sisters arrive within seconds. Darryl trying to look inconspicuous in his leather trousers at the Pier Street rave must be one of the most incompetent bits of undercover work in the history of policing. Some of the dancing in P^3, when Barenaked Ladies are doing their stuff, is hilarious – looks like a bunch of people trying to crush cockroaches.

Continuity: This episode begins in early October, approximately one month after the events of 'Be Careful What You Witch For,' although, as far as Piper's concerned, merely a day has passed. (She notes that time must run differently on other planes.) Phoebe now has prominent blonde highlights in her hair and, though asked for an explanation on several occasions, waffles around the subject. In Piper's absence, and since school is about to restart, Phoebe has been taking care of P^3 whilst Prue looks after the house. Phoebe gains a new power, levitation. Piper appears to gain the ability to selectively freeze people based on their morality. Piper (eventually) accepts Leo's proposal of marriage.

Motors: New season, new car. Prue drives a BMW SUV.

Quote/Unquote: Leo: 'I thought this whole thing through.' Piper: 'Is that why you asked me to marry you in *a toilet*?'
Darryl, on Emilio: 'He's not talking.' Cole: 'It seems to be an epidemic.'
Prue: 'Can't you just freeze them?' Piper: 'No. Once they're immune to it, they stay that way. That's why it's called *immunity*.'

Notes: 'You have no idea who you're dealing with.' Ah, major change of emphasis here – the introduction of Julian McMahon is the point at which *Charmed* went from being a pretty reasonable show with the occasional ability to surprise to a frequently excellent show with the occasional ability to *astonish*. It's a credit to this fine actor that he underplays his introduction to such an extent. The episode itself isn't the greatest ever made; it goes somewhat flat after an exciting opening. But in terms of neat characterisation and great one-liners, it's a sign of the way in which the show would develop over the coming year. Best bits: The lengthy pre-title sequence. Piper catching an embarrassed Leo practising his proposal to her in the bathroom. Phoebe's little squeak when Piper tells her sisters that Leo has asked her to marry him.

Soundtrack: The pre-title sequence piano theme is remarkably similar to the opening notes of Roy Budd's legendary score for the movie *Get Carter*. Bakenaked Ladies perform 'Pinch Me' at P^3.

Did You Know?: The impressive ratings for this episode – approximately 7.2 million viewers – are somewhat deceptive, for two reasons. First, the episode followed the premiere of *The Gilmore Girls*, the WB's replacement for *Popular*. Secondly, other networks broadcast the Vice Presidential debates and major league baseball instead of normal programming.

46: MAGIC HOUR

12 October 2000

Writers: Chris Levinson, Zack Estrin
Director: John Behring

Cast: Elisabeth Harnois (Brooke), Michael Dietz (Christopher), Erik Passoja (The Boss), Jennifer Rhodes (Penny Halliwell), Amir Aboulela (Evil Triad Member #1), Rick Overton (Evil Triad Member #2), Shaun Taub (Evil Triad Member #3), Madoka Raine (Bookseller), Billy Ray Gallion (Assistant #1), Keith Allan (Assistant #2)

> Piper learns that she and Leo have just 24 hours to marry in secret before his superiors discover their plan. The sisters find a ritual to perform the ceremony, but Phoebe believes that using it may have further consequences. As the Halliwells seek an answer to Piper's dilemma, they encounter a couple, Christopher and Brooke, who are the victims of a jealous warlock. Christopher is cursed to be an owl during the day and Brooke to be an wolf during the night.

It's Witchcraft: 'Handfasting' is the eternal joining of two people in love. It is a sacred ceremony of commitment presided over by a High Priestess and is best performed at a time of sunrise or sunset when both the sun and moon are present in the sky.

The Conspiracy Starts at the Witching Hour: Piper suggests that if the Elders find out about her and Leo's plan, they can break the pair into a thousand little pieces. She notes that the exact phrase used was 'unspeakable wrath.'
  Cole is a demon and seems to have been sent to find a way of destroying the Charmed Ones.

It's a Designer Label!: Definite highlight, Phoebe's red leather jacket.

References: Amongst the magazines an annoyed Piper sees in the opening scene are *Tomorrow's Bride*, *Bridal Guide* and *Modern Bride*. The two books that Piper buys are *How To Keep Your Marriage Hush-Hush* by Linda Ferrington and *The Secret of Eloping* by Stanley Kaufman. Also, allusions to Spike Lee's *Do The Right Thing*; and Attica state prison.

SEASON 3: MAGIC HOUR

'You May Remember Me …': Amir Aboulela appeared in *Gods and Monsters*. Elisabeth Harnois played Sarah Livingstone in *All My Children*. Michael Dietz was Mark Maclane in *The Bold and the Beautiful*. Erik Passoja played Charles Manson in *The Beach Boys: An American Family*. Shaun Taub's movies include *Stigmata* and *Hot Shots! Part Deux*. Rick Overton appeared in *Eight Legged Freaks*, *My Giant* and *Groundhog Day*. Madoka Raine was in *Whitewood Crossing*. Billy Ray Gallion appeared in *Some Body*. Keith Allan's CV includes *CSI* and *Will & Grace*.

Behind the Camera: Julian McMahon's stunt double, Allen Robinson, also worked on *The Ladykillers*, *Analyze That*, *Bedazzled* and *Scream*.

Sex and Drugs and Rock n Roll: Grams suggests that although the Charmed Ones are destined for greatness, that fact doesn't keep a girl warm on a cold winter's night.

Logic, Let Me Introduce You To This Window: At the beginning of the episode, Piper closes the door of her car, but when the car with a new-married couple drives by, she is in the process of closing it again. For someone who 'rarely misses' with the crossbow, this must have been a bad day for the first assistant … After Cole's shadow departs to give his report to the Triad, a shadow can still be clearly seen on Cole's shoulder. One shot shows a full moon. The next day there is a total eclipse of the sun, which requires a new moon. Prue says that she was three and Piper was one when Phoebe was born, contradicting information given in both 'That 70s Episode' and 'Pardon My Past'. Phoebe introduces Leo to Cole, they shake hands and Leo says, 'It's nice to meet you.' But they met in the previous episode in the court room. When owl-Christopher changes back into his human form, he has a chest bandage covering the wound he suffered when he was an owl. Total eclipses usually last about five minutes or so, and even partial eclipses are normally over within an hour – this one lasts long enough for the girls to get to the Boss's office, have a two minute conflab about their priorities, vanquish the Boss, unite Christopher and Brooke, get back home, change, contact Grams, find Leo a tux(!) and start the wedding ceremony. Also, if the eclipse turned Christopher back from an owl into a man, then shouldn't it have simultaneously changed Brooke into a wolf?

Continuity: It has been previously established that Grams was married more than once – this episode confirms that she actually had four husbands.

Cruelty To Animals: The episode begins with Kit menacing an owl on the

Halliwells' doorstep. That's hard to top, really, but the Boss's instruction to his crossbow-wielding minion to kill every owl he sees, then said minion's return to the office with something very bloody-looking and owl-sized in a sack, and then the really manipulative scenes of Brooke cradling the injured owl-Christopher, manage it – especially as Leo can't heal animals. A solemn note on the end credits informs viewers that no animals were injured during the filming of this episode. Presumably, none of the actors playing vanquished demons actually died *either*.

Motors: Piper has a new car, a green Cherokee Classic.

Quote/Unquote: Piper: 'It's not like I'm some girly-girl who wants like a fairytale wedding, but I just thought there would be some things that would be givens.' Phoebe: 'Like fighting with the caterer and agonising over who makes the final cut on the guest list?'

Phoebe: 'If I had a dollar for every time an owl turned into a hot guy on our porch, I'd be rich ...'

Prue: 'Rules are meant to be broken.' Phoebe: 'Bodies weren't.' Piper: 'Neither are hearts.'

Prue, to Brooke: 'What love can't conquer, we will.'

Phoebe: 'If you wanted a supernatural low-jack, you came to the wrong witch.'

Notes: 'All this means nothing if I can't have what I want. I want *her*.' A *really* silly conceit, albeit nicely played by all concerned. The Brooke/Christopher subplot contrasts well with Piper's and Leo's on-going tribulations. It's just a shame that, whilst trying to settle both storylines by the end of the episode, there's such a load of faffing about in the middle 20 minutes.

Soundtrack: Beth Hart's 'Delicious Surprise' is used again. Also, Pachelbel's 'Canon in D'. Both Leo and Prue hum small snatches of 'The Wedding March' by Felix Mendelssohn (1809-47).

Did You Know?: The book-shop used in this episode was the Sherman Oaks branch of Borders.

47: ONCE UPON A TIME

19 October 2000

Writers: Krista Vernoff
Director: Joel J Feigenbaum

Cast: Boti Ann Bliss (Abbey), Nancy Everhard (Jana), Rachel David (Kate), Scout Taylor-Compton (Thistle), Tony Carreiro (Bill), Jake Dinwiddie (Fairie), Michael Bailey Smith (Belthazor)

> Phoebe meets Kate, a young girl being terrorised by trolls because she is protecting a fairy that they seek to harm. Although Prue and Phoebe believe Kate needs the help of the Charmed Ones, Piper goes on strike from helping innocents until the Elders allow her and Leo to be together again. Meanwhile, Cole attempts to gain access to *The Book of Shadows*.

Dreaming (As Blondie Once Said) is Free: The episode opens with Piper being visited by Leo in P^3. He tells her that he's returned to say goodbye. Then it all gets weirdly angular and the special effects take over and it turns out to be a dream. Or does it? Subsequent dialogue suggests that Leo's presence in Piper's head, at least, was real.

It's Witchcraft: Fairy dust can give adults who truly believe in fairies the ability to see them. However, it also has the somewhat unwanted side-effect of making them act like children. Prue hopes to be able to see the fairy princess, Thistle, by mixing together a spell to see what can't be seen combined with one to cultivate innocence and 'The Power of Three' spell. This begins: 'In this 'tween time, this darkest hour, we call upon the sacred power,' and goes on and on for ages, with some pretty terrible couplets involved. 'You've really gotta lay off the rhyming, Prue,' notes Phoebe.

A Little Learning is a Dangerous Thing: Fairies, elves and trolls are mystical creatures that live in an Enchanted Realm parallel to our own, but separated by a thin veil, the 'tween places. Phoebe gives several examples of 'tween places – doorways, windows, shadows and, the biggest 'tween place of all, midnight. It is said that, in the hour between night and day, the world itself becomes a 'tween place. According to Kate, fairies are the nominal rulers of the Enchanted Realm, but the trolls have recently kidnapped Thistle from the king and queen of the fairies.

SEASON 3: ONCE UPON A TIME

The Conspiracy Starts at the Witching Hour: *The Book of Shadows* moves whenever Cole tries to touch it. In this episode we see Cole's true form – as the demon Belthazor – for the first time.

References: Piper refers to the Elders as 'The Powers That Be', the name used in *Angel* for the forces of good. The make-up design for the demon Belthazor was based on the style used for the character Darth Maul in *Star Wars: Episode I – The Phantom Menace*. Kate has a Garfield clock. There are allusions to Tinkerbell (see 'Love Hurts').

'You May Remember Me ...': Boti Bliss played Valera in *CSI: Miami* and appeared in *Panic*. Nancy Everhard was Sharon Hart in *Everwood*. Her CV also includes *Another 48 Hours*, *The Punisher* and *Airwolf*. Rachel David played Moonglow Hardin in *Movie Stars*. Scout Taylor-Compton was Perry in *Chicken Night* and appeared in *Gilmore Girls*. Tony Carreiro appeared in *Lethal Weapon 2* and *Home Improvement*. Jake Dinwiddie played Alex Caldwell in *Au Pair*. Michael Bailey Smith's CV includes *Love Her Madly*, *Buffy the Vampire Slayer* and *Roswell*.

Behind the Camera: Krista Vernoff also worked on *Law & Order* and *Wonderfalls*.

Logic, Let Me Introduce You To This Window: When Piper is attacked by trolls in the P3 car park, she falls and her handbag is thrown outside the protective circle she has drawn. In the following shot, the bag is in the circle with Piper. Where are Kate's parents at midnight? In 'Pardon My Past', Piper's birthday was given as 7 March. Here, Phoebe notes that Piper is a Gemini, which should mean she was born in May or June. If the previously-given birthdate is correct, she'd be a Pisces.

Continuity: Phoebe notes that she's a Scorpio (consistent with the date of birth glimpsed in 'Pardon My Past'). Cole has compiled an extensive background file on Phoebe, which includes headings such as 'Fears', 'Vulnerability' and 'Known Love Interests'. (There are at least eight names listed in the latter section, including Rex Buckland – see 'Wicca Envy'.) Her favourite movie is, of course, *Kill It Before It Dies* (1958), and Cole mentions the character Billy Appleby (see 'Chick Flick'). The file also notes that Phoebe's favourite song is the Verve's 'Bittersweet Symphony' (see 'Wicca Envy'), her favourite book is Jane Austen's 'Sense and Sensibility' and her favourite work of art is Sandro Botticelli's *The Birth of Venus* (1485). Phoebe's hobbies are said to include arts and crafts and surfing the Internet. Piper finds the Valentine card that Leo bought for her in 'Animal Pragmatism'. At the end of the episode, Leo returns; he notes that he'd been forbidden from seeing Piper again but, thanks to

Piper's stroppy rant toward the Elders, they believe she has great courage, enough to make them reconsider. Piper and Leo are given the chance to prove that they can make their relationship work and that it won't disturb their duties.

Quote/Unquote: Piper, to her suddenly childish sisters: 'Okay, what ass-backward spell did you guys cast?' And, to the Elders: 'I bet you guys think this is real funny, dontcha? You have to send trolls to kick me when I'm down?'

Kate: 'The trolls are gonna kill her unless her parents hand over the kingdom.' Phoebe: 'It's a miniature *coup d'état*.'

Notes: 'It's time to stop believing in things like that.' That old acting maxim 'Never work with animals and children' took a real battering from both the previous week's episode and this one. Actually, to be fair, the owl came out of 'Magic Hour' far better than Rachel David does here. However, not wanting to be seen to pick on a child unnecessarily, most of the adults aren't exactly on top form either, and the whole episode meanders along to a signposted climax. Some interesting dialogue about the nature of sacrifice aside, it's a pretty dull and lifeless tale.

Soundtrack: Paul Van Dyke's 'Tell Me Why'.

48: ALL HALLIWELL'S EVE

26 October 2000

Writer: Sheryl J Anderson
Director: Anson Williams

Cast: Judy Geeson (Ruth Cobb), Clare Carey (Eva), Michael Bailey Smith (Janor), Dave Chisum (Micah/Mitch), Danielle Weeks (Sally), Sadie Stratton (Charlotte Warren), Tommy Perna (Kava), James Tumminia (Astrologer), Bobby Pyle (Youngster), Snake River Conspiracy (Themselves)

> On Halloween, the Grimlocks return to seek vengeance on the Halliwells. However, the sisters are sent by the Elders through a time vortex to Virginia in 1670, leaving Leo and Darryl to battle the Grimlocks. In the past, Prue, Piper and Phoebe learn that a coven of witches has summoned them to rescue Charlotte, a woman who is destined to give birth to their own ancestor, Melinda Warren. But Charlotte is being held by an evil witch, Ruth Cobb, whom a time-travelling Cole is secretly helping.

It's Witchcraft: To protect the sisters from Ruth Cobb's talisman, Eva gives Prue, Piper and Phoebe corn-dolly totems, which signify the wisdom and power of women. The witch's journey, she notes, is a walk of wisdom collected over the years. The black conical hat is a spiritual point that helps to channel their magicks. An apple holds a pentacle in its heart; add a laurel leaf and a witch can block the path of evil. Demons are said to walk freely on All Hallow's Eve, so a mask allows a witch to hide her identity and walk amongst them. A broom's traditional purpose is to sweep evil from one's path, from east to west – the same path as the sun travels.

A Little Learning is a Dangerous Thing: Eva tells the Charmed Ones that they have been brought to this time to save a magical baby who is prophesied to be born on that night. Ruth Cobb, a dark practitioner, has kidnapped the baby's mother in hopes of raising the child as evil. If that happens, good magic will never flourish in the new world. The sisters' task, therefore, is to rescue Charlotte so that the baby can be delivered within the coven's protective circle. Eva also notes that although the coven cast spells to prepare the way for the Charmed Ones, it was the power of All Hallow's Eve that brought them. She continues that this is a witch's

SEASON 3: ALL HALLIWELL'S EVE

most sacred day, when the source of all magic can be tapped into.

The Conspiracy Starts at the Witching Hour: The Grimlocks recognise Cole as the demon Belthazor (which is the first use of the name in *Charmed*). Cole notes that his plan has been approved by the Triad (see 'The Honeymoon's Over').

It's a Designer Label!: Pay particular attention to Cole's angel costume and his self-consciousness towards it. Phoebe's costume is that of Elvira, the Mistress of the Dark, whilst Piper is dressed as Glenda, the good witch of the North from *The Wizard of Oz*.

References: There are allusions to *The Wizard of Oz* ('We're not in Kansas anymore'); Shakespeare's *Romeo and Juliet*: *The Lone Ranger* ('Who was that masked man?'); the Rolling Stones' 'Time Is On My Side'. Also, a visual reference to the title sequence of *Bewitched* so blatant that you're impressed they actually had the nerve to do it.

'You May Remember Me …': Judy Geeson was born in Arundel in 1948. Her CV includes *Man in a Suitcase, Space: 1999, Spanish Fly, Danger UXB, Carry On England* (as Tilly Willing), *The Eagle Has Landed, Poldark, Brannigan, Fear in the Night, Goodbye Gemini, Prudence and the Pill, Here We Go Round the Mulberry Bush, 10 Rillington Place, Doomwatch, To Sir, with Love* and *The Newcomers*. She moved the US in the 1990s and subsequently appeared in *Touched By an Angel, Gilmore Girls, Mad About You* and *Star Trek: Voyager*. Clare Carey played Kelly Fox in *Coach* and also appeared in *Ally McBeal* and *Echo*. David Chisum was Bret in *Sunset Beach*. Danielle Weeks played Cousin Corky in *The Weird Al Show*. Tommy Perna was in *Crime + Punishment in Suburbia* and *Changes of Distance*, the latter of which he also directed.

Logic, Let Me Introduce You To This Window: When Phoebe goes to answer the door, she is carrying a plate of caramel apples. When she reaches the door, she puts down the plate and another plate that she has mysteriously acquired somewhere between the kitchen and the hall. When Darryl and Leo are in the attic, the Grimlocks have to wait until they are very close before they can attack. In 'Blind Sided', they could kill a businessman from the other side of the street. Leo has to heal Darryl before the latter recovers his sight. In 'Blind Sided', as soon as the Grimlocks were vanquished, all the people whom they had blinded regained their sight without any outside help. When the sisters first meet the witches from the past, Prue is wearing lots more glitter than she did when they arrived in 1670. During one sequence, Piper begins to put snacks on a plate. In a subsequent shot, the plate is empty. When Phoebe holds the picture of the witch it is facing right, but it later switches to face left. Prue's hair changes between scenes. Piper looks at her watch to get the time, but there's a three hour time difference between Virginia and California. When the sisters are sucked into the portal, three wigs fall to the floor. However, Prue wasn't wearing a wig – she had ribbons and butterflies in her hair. When the girls were first in the cave, Phoebe had her hair down. When Ava subsequently gives Phoebe a hat, her hair is in pigtails. Just before the sisters return to the present, Leo drops the vanquishing potion. When they emerge out of the vortex and Prue asks, 'Haven't I vanquished you somewhere before?', she uses her powers to send the potion to the Grimlock, killing it. But how could she possibly know that the potion was on the floor? Eva recovers from the agony of being shot in the arm remarkably quickly. And, come on, how could Phoebe fail to recognise the masked Cole?

Continuity: Melinda was born shortly before midnight on All Hallow's Eve, in a protective circle of magick. This perhaps explains why she was the first of the line that will culminate with Prue, Piper and Phoebe. Piper says she hates time travelling – thoughseemingly not as much as Phoebe, who reminds her sister that the last time it happened, she was burned at the stake (see 'Mortality Bites'). The Grimlocks are the first demons that Darryl has actually seen – apart from 'that blonde with the funky-snake-tongue-thingy' (see 'She's a Man, Baby, a Man'). He tells Leo that he regards the Halliwells as his own sisters. Grimlocks have green blood.

Quote/Unquote: Prue, on Piper's costume: 'You picked a role model that wears lots and lots of pink?' And, to Phoebe: 'I'm *so* impressed that you can make a protest statement and show cleavage all at the same time.'

Phoebe: 'Hooked-nosed hags riding broomsticks, that's what we're celebrating. Personally, I'm offended by the representation of witches in popular culture.'

Prue: 'From what they're wearing it looks to be, what, 16-1700s?' Phoebe: 'Where the life-expectancy of the average witch is, what, 15 minutes?'

Piper, on discovering that they were sent back in time by the Elders without any warning: 'Leave it to them to zap first and give instructions *never*!'

Leo: 'We need more thyme.' Darryl, looking at his watch: 'Can't help you there, buddy, it's almost nightfall.'

Notes: 'I come from the future. To change it.' Fabulous. There's something about time travel episodes that brings the best out of *Charmed*. A colourful and imaginative recreation of colonial Virginia becomes even more

SEASON 3: ALL HALLIWELL'S EVE

attractive with Julian McMahon striding around the place like somebody who's got lost on his way to the nearest Hammer movie. Throw in some Wiccan lore to explain away Halloween clichés (when Phoebe embraces this and goes riding on a broomstick, the smirk on Piper's face as she says *'There's* something you don't see every day' alone justifies the episode's existence) and you have a ready-made *Charmed* classic. Full of outstanding dialogue ('There's magic all around you') and clever plot-twists, this is one of the series' finest moments.

Soundtrack: Three songs by Snake River Conspiracy: 'You and Your Friend', 'Somebody Hates You' and 'Breed'.

Did You Know?: The WB used the promotional title *A Charmed Halloween* for this episode.

49: SIGHT UNSEEN

2 November 2000

Writer: William Schmidt
Director: Perry Lang

Cast: Boti Ann Bliss (Abbey), Eddie Cahill (Sean), Rick Hearst (Troxa), Nick Meaney (Snakehunter), Rick Overton (Evil Triad Member #2), Amir Aboulela (Evil Triad Member #1), Karen Stapleton (Rachel), Michael Bailey Smith (Belthazor), Shaun Taub (Evil Triad Member #3)

> When the Manor is broken into, Prue believes that something supernatural, sent by the Triad, is responsible. Her sisters think there could a more human perpetrator, and Darryl agrees with them. Cole is upset to learn that the Triad have sent another agent, Troxa, an old nemesis of Belthazor's, to destroy the Halliwells. Meanwhile, Piper feels that her inability to sleep with Leo is the result of interference from the Elders. Again.

It's Witchcraft: Prue casts a spell over some cydarite crystals, which creates a power grid with *The Book Of Shadows* as bait. When a demon steps into the grid, he'll be 'zapped'.

A Little Learning is a Dangerous Thing: Troxa is an invisible demon. He has an Achilles heel, however; his ectoplasmic biochemistry is sensitive to cold, and he becomes partially visible in low temperatures. As Cole notes, because Troxa cannot feel when it's cold, he doesn't know when he has been affected by this.

The Conspiracy Starts at the Witching Hour: Prue suggests that mirrors are the portals through which evil enters. Piper, however, suggests that the only demon they know of who used mirrors was Kali, and they've already 'vanquished her sorry ass' (see 'The Fourth Sister').

Leo describes Belthazor as an infamous demonic soldier of fortune, one of the most evil and vile creatures that exists.

It's a Designer Label!: The girls wear some fabulous dresses to P³, although the sneakers that Prue has provided in case of demon-attack go remarkably badly with all of them. Among the items stolen from the Manor by Abbey were Grams' necklace and Prue's 'good luck' fuchsia paisley blouse.

References: The scenes of a partially-blinded Prue being stalked around the Manor are highly reminiscent of *Wait Until Dark*. Also, allusions to Mickey Mouse; *The Big Chill*; and *Ace Ventura, Pet Detective* ('All-righty, then'). Posters glimpsed in P³ include one for REM's 'Up', plus one for The Goo Goo Dolls and another for Disturbed.

'You May Remember Me ...': Eddie Cahill played Mike Dolan in *Glory Days* and Tag Jones in *Friends* and appeared in *Haunted*. Rick Hearst was Ric Lansing in *General Hospital*. Nick Meaney's movies include *Gone in Sixty Seconds*. Karen Stapleton was in *Mr Murder*.

Cigarettes and Alcohol: When Prue rings Piper at P³ and is reminded that Sean, her date, is waiting, she tells Piper to give him a drink. Piper relies 'If we give him any more we're gonna have to send him to an AA meeting.'

Sex and Drugs and Rock n Roll: Piper complains that on the last two occasions when she and Leo have been about to do 'it', he's been suddenly called away by the Elders. This, she believes, proves that they are watching everything Piper and Leo do. At the end of the episode, the couple finally get to have uninterrupted sex, and Piper says that she hopes the Elders enjoyed the show.

Meanwhile, when Prue has a lengthy rant about the Triad, Phoebe suggests to Piper, 'We *really* need to get her laid, huh?'

Logic, Let Me Introduce You to This Window: Isn't Sean rather young to be going out with Prue, a woman on the cusp of 30? When Prue comes home to find all the mirrors smashed, a camera can be glimpsed in one of the splinters. If Prue's eyes were open when her head was pushed into the chemicals, wouldn't she be permanently blinded? How could Abbey be in the club at more or less the same time as she's attacking Prue at the Manor?

Continuity: Prue asks her sisters if they remember Micah, the man who helped them to rescue Charlotte in 'All Halliwell's Eve'. She has traced his ancestors and found an entire history of the village that the sisters visited, believing that this may give them a clue as to the identity of the demon that the Triad sent to kill them. Piper and Phoebe worry that Prue is becoming paranoid. Cole's dialogue with the Triad suggests that the period of time covered by the season so far is approximately one month. Cole also alludes to having made a bargain with the Triad – the lives of the Charmed Ones in exchange for Belthazor being given back some aspect of his demon life. By the end of the episode, it's clear that Prue no longer trusts Cole. Phoebe's list of potential stalkers runs to three pages, although, she notes, they are mostly guys she knew in New York. Prue says that she doesn't bother to lock the front door. Piper does, and so does Phoebe. Usually. However, since a demon tried to steal *The Book of Shadows* a couple of weeks earlier (see 'Once Upon a Time'), Prue *has* been locking the attic door.

Cruelty to Animals: There's a brief discussion about whether or not Prue's spell could injure Kit. Prue had thought of that and shut the attic door, keeping the cat out of harm's way. When Prue goes to photograph an amusingly stereotypical Australian snake-handler, she's told about how snakes eat mice and frogs.

Quote/Unquote: Darryl: 'I need you guys to put together a grudge list of any enemies you have, past or present.' Prue: 'Already done.' Darryl, reading from the list: 'Abraxas, Barbas, Yama ... What did you do? Date the United Nations?'

Prue: 'When I woke up there was a pillow hovering above my face about to smother me.' Phoebe: 'That must be the infamous pillow-smothering-demon.'

Piper: 'There are other evils in the world. Some of them are even human.' And, when freezing Abbey as she is about to shoot Prue: 'Everything's gonna be great as soon as I *fire her*.'

Leo, on the Elders: 'As far as the Triad's concerned, they don't know much.' Prue: 'Wow, 6,000 years of conflict and that's it? These guys are *serious* underachievers.'

Notes: 'Could be a stalker.' An episode that shows, with some success, that occasionally there are more scary things than demons and warlocks out there in the real world. There are a few, with hindsight very obvious, visual clues as to the identity of Prue's stalker, but the direction is tight and effective, and the dense, paranoid script works along similar claustrophobic lines.

Soundtrack: Marvelous 3 perform 'Beautiful', 'Cold as Hell' and 'Sugarbuzz '.

50: PRIMROSE EMPATH

9 November 2000

Writer: Daniel Cerone
Director: Mel Damski

Cast: Harry Groener (Father Thomas), Morgan Weisser (Vince), Ty Upshaw (Foreman), Sharon Madden (Secretary), Larry Weissman (Patient #1), Michael Fetters (Patient #2), Colin McClean (Dentist), Brittany Sabaski (Receptionist), Marianne Muellerleile (Receptionist #2), Randy Thompson (Deputy), Wendy Worthington (Nurse), Jill Brennan (Mrs Traister), Marcy Goldman (Woman), Cesar Lopapa (Salvador), Barna Moricz (Joey)

> After Prue casts a spell to save an empath, Vince, from feeling the emotions of the entire city, the man reveals himself to be a powerful demon, Vinceres, who four years earlier was cursed with the power of total empathy as a punishment. Meanwhile, Cole tells Phoebe that he doesn't want to see her anymore.

It's Witchcraft: Prue's spell aimed at curing Vince begins: 'Free the empath, release his gift, let his pain be cast adrift.'

A Little Learning is a Dangerous Thing: *The Book of Shadows* notes that Belthazor is as sinister as he is intelligent and that he is not to be trusted. The demon's abilities include throwing energy balls and 'shimmering from place to place.'
Leo notes that empaths are mortals who can feel what other people feel. It's a rare gift. When they die, they often return to earth as immortal empaths, blend into society as counsellors, elders or teachers and use their sensitivity to guide mortals.

The Conspiracy Starts at the Witching Hour: Vinceres is a demonic assassin – timeless and unstoppable. When he attempted to kill the immortal empath Father Thomas, the priest – much to his surprise – passed his empathic ability onto Vinceres.

It's a Designer Label!: It's a tight top fest, with Prue's purple number and Phoebe's red wraparound shirt taking the plaudits here. Having said that, the dreadful suede thing that Phoebe wears in the opening scene does, indeed, justify her comment that she is 'a fashion blunder'.

SEASON 3: PRIMROSE EMPATH

References: The title alludes to a classic 1940 Hollywood melodrama, *Primrose Path*, starring Ginger Rogers and Joel McCrea. Prue gains superpowers to fight Vinceres – their subsequent fight in the Manor is very similar to the scene in *The Matrix* in which Neo battles Agent Smith in the railway station. Also, allusions to Roger Corman's *Not of This Earth*; and Badfinger's 'Come And Get It.' A briefly glimpsed headline states: SHUT-IN REFUSES TO LEAVE DESPITE DEMOLITION. A plot concerning one of the heroines gaining unbearable empathic powers had been used recently by both *Buffy the Vampire Slayer* ('Earshot') and *Angel* ('To Shanshu in LA', 'That Vision Thing').

'You May Remember Me ...': Three-times Tony nominated, Harry Groener played Tam Elburn *Star Trek: The Next Generation*, Brockwell in *Mad About You* and Ralph Dang in the US version of *Dear John*, and also appeared in *Amistad*, *Dance With Me*, *The West Wing*, *About Schmidt* and *The Day the World Ended*. He'll be familiar to many readers as Mayor Wilkins in *Buffy the Vampire Slayer*. Morgan Weisser was Nathan West in *Space: Above and Beyond*. His CV also includes *Quantum Leap*. Ty Upshaw was in *24* and *CSI*. Sharon Madden appeared in *Turner & Hooch*, *Jagged Edge* and *The X-Files*. Larry Weissman was in *Vice Academy 5*. Michael Fetters appeared in *Without Evidence*. Marcy Goldman's CV includes *Airplane!*, *Star Trek: Generations* and *Friends*. Colin McClean appeared in *Clockstoppers*. Brittany Sabaski was in *November*. Marianne Muellerleile played Lucy in *3rd Rock from the Sun* and appeared in *The Terminator* and *Passions*. Randy Thompson was Dr Kriegalin in *Buffy the Vampire Slayer*. His CV also includes *Singles* and *The Montana Run*, the latter of which he also directed. Wendy Worthington appeared in *Teacher's Pet*, *Good Burger* and *Ally McBeal*.

Behind the Camera: Daniel Cerone also worked on *First Wave* and *Clubhouse*.

The Drugs Don't Work: After Prue finally has her dental work done, she says that she cannot wait for the Novocaine to wear off.

Sex and Drugs and Rock n Roll: Phoebe and Cole sleep together for the first time and, subsequently, spend a post-coital moment describing, in some detail, how orgasmically 'magical' the experience was.

When Prue first gets her empathic ability, she suggests that Leo and Piper have a 'couple of issues.' Resentment in his case, denial in hers. She then tells them to be nice to each other and goes upstairs. Leo and Piper have a discussion, seem to sort out their differences quite nicely and are getting comfortable on the sofa with much kissing-with-tongues when

SEASON 3: PRIMROSE EMPATH

Prue calls out from the attic, 'Not now, I have a headache.'

Prue also experiences the sensation that a young woman in the dentists feels when her boyfriend grabs her bottom. And she seems not overtly distressed by this.

Logic, Let Me Introduce You to This Window: After Phoebe has her premonition in the empath demon's apartment, her hair changes position – to tucked behind her ears – on at least two occasions. When the policeman knocks on the door before Prue casts the spell, the door chain is locked. When he subsequently tries to open it, Prue has to hold the door shut. When Prue gets the empathic power, she has curly hair. When she defeats Vinceres, her hair is straight.

Continuity: Prue is currently reading a book on telekinesis. Prue's dentist is Dr Timmons. Cole's telephone number is 415-555-0167 and his pager is 415-555-0166. Father Thomas suffered a nervous breakdown approximately three years earlier.

Quote/Unquote: Prue: 'What's your last name?' Vince: 'Misery.' Prue: 'In that case, would you like some company?'

Phoebe: 'How did the demon formerly known as Vince become empathic anyway?'

Piper, on Vinceres: 'Unstoppable hitman. Just keeps going until he gets his target.' Phoebe: 'Great, the Energizer demon.'

Father Thomas: 'From what I've seen, your sister is too far gone. She won't live to see the night.' Piper: 'No, I'm sorry, but this man has experienced the entire rainbow of human emotions and the best he has to give us is self-pity?'

Notes: 'An empath? And me without my dictionary.' Harry Groener always gets to play such sympathetic and 3-D characters. He's at it again here in a terrific story about unwanted gifts and lost missions. Shannen Doherty's best performance of the season is also a key part of the reason for the success of 'Primrose Empath'. Best bit, undoubtedly, is the awkward lunch date.

Soundtrack: The band at P^3 are Idol, performing 'Shameless'.

SEASON 3: POWER OUTAGE

51: POWER OUTAGE

16 November 2000

Writers: Monica Breen, Alison Schapker
Director: Craig Zisk

Cast: Jason Carter (Andras), Pamela Dunlap (Janice), Ron Marasco (Allen), Michael Bailey Smith (Belthazor), Amir Aboulela (Evil Triad Member #1), Rick Overton (Evil Triad Member #2), Shaun Toub (Evil Triad Member #3), Selma Archerd (Mrs Snyder), Desiree Walter (Claire)

> The Triad remind Cole that his job is to destroy the Charmed Ones and not to romance Phoebe. Cole decides to use the sisters' arguments against them and enlists the help of the demon Andras, who causes their everyday disagreements to spiral out of control. Once the sisters begin using their magic against each other, the Power of Three disappears, leaving the Halliwells defenceless against attack.

Dreaming (As Blondie Once Said) is Free: Cole suffers from what appears to be a Triad-induced nightmare of turning into Belthazor and killing Phoebe whilst the couple are in bed together.

It's Witchcraft: Andras is described as 'the spirit of rage' who uses anger as a portal to enrage his victims until they commit a great act of violence.

A Little Learning is a Dangerous Thing: The sisters are able to lose their powers. When this happens, *The Book of Shadows*' triquetra separates into three ovals. Cole claims that he lost his family a long time ago, which is technically true.

The Conspiracy Starts at the Witching Hour: At the episode's climax, Cole kills the Triad before they can destroy him.

Work is a Four-Letter Word: When Phoebe was 15, she had a job that entailed wearing a penguin costume and handing out balloons to kids. She can still do the walk.

It's a Designer Label!: Is it physically possible to show any more cleavage than Phoebe's low-cut black corset-type top does? Also, check out the girl

SEASON 3: POWER OUTAGE

in the pink lycra trousers dancing to the latino band when Phoebe and Cole have dinner.

References: There are allusions to actor Brad Pitt (*Kalifornia, Se7en, Interview With the Vampire, Twelve Monkeys, Fight Club*); *Survivor*; *The Seven Year Itch*; and *The Oprah Winfrey Show*. Also, a very obvious visual homage to *The West Wing* (with the camera circling the arguing sisters).

'You May Remember Me ...': Jason Carter played Marcus Cole in *Babylon 5* and appeared in *She-Wolf of London* and *Beverly Hills 90210*. Pamela Dunlap's movies include *I Am Sam* and *Nick of Time*. Ron Marasco was in *Freaks and Geeks*. Selma Archard's CV includes *Die Hard, The Brady Bunch, The Big Bus, Mommie Dearest* and *Indecent Proposal*.

Behind the Camera: The writing team of Monica Breen and Alison Schapker would subsequently work on *Alias*.

The Drugs Don't Work: When Piper is in mid-rant, Prue suggests that someone obviously needs some Midol, a reference to a popular over-the-counter medicine used in America primarily as a treatment for PMS.

Sex and Drugs and Rock n Roll: Phoebe feels that whenever she gets close to Cole, he pulls away from her.

Logic, Let Me Introduce You to This Window: When Cole is in bed talking to the Triad member, the face of one of the production team can be glimpsed in a mirror on the counter in Cole's bathroom. Andras is said to be the spirit of rage. Isn't his *raison d'être* pretty much the same as that of Strife from the Four Horsemen (see 'Apocalypse, Not?')? When Phoebe leaves Cole's apartment, the make-up used to cover one of Alyssa Milano's tattoos leaves a very obvious dark patch on her right shoulder.

Continuity: Leo suggests that the Charmed Ones' powers are rooted in their bond as sisters. Using those powers against each other must have severed the bond. When the sisters argue, Piper suggests that Grams always said Phoebe would never amount to much. Piper later confesses that this wasn't true and that Grams was always every bit as proud of Phoebe as she was of Prue and Piper. The Halliwells' squabbling neighbours include a couple named Allen and Claire and the opinionated Mrs Snyder.

Motors: Cole drives a tasteful silver BMW convertible (4QAP168).

SEASON 3: POWER OUTAGE

Quote/Unquote: Piper: 'You forget about our homeowners meeting tomorrow afternoon?' Prue: '... Will you cover for me?' Phoebe: 'No way. At the last one, it took them two and a half hours to decide where to put the garden gnomes.'

Piper: 'I already rescheduled my doctor's appointment twice.' Phoebe: 'Well, Leo was a doctor before he died.' Piper: 'That's *really* not the point.'

Leo: 'Maybe you need to tell your sisters how you feel. Better yet, next time, just say no.' Piper: 'You obviously don't have sisters. One minute you're arguing about something, and then suddenly you're arguing about who stole whose Malibu Barbie in 1979.'

Leo: 'Let's start with your little tiff.' Piper: 'That's a bit of an understatement. It was big.' Leo: 'How big?' Prue: 'Do you remember Pearl Harbor?'

Notes: 'Tell the Triad I've figured out how to destroy the Charmed Ones.' A morally simplistic and one-track story, as a consequence it's less interesting than many plotlines of this era. The Cole/Phoebe scenes continue to sparkle, and the sequences in which Prue, Piper and Phoebe turn on each other carry some real emotional impact. It would have helped, somewhat, if Jason Carter hadn't been given such licence to overact, as Andras is potentially a fascinating creation.

Soundtrack: Fastball perform 'You're An Ocean' and 'This Is Not My Life'.

52: SLEUTHING WITH THE ENEMY

14 December 2000

Writer: Peter Hume
Director: Noel Nosseck

Cast: Scott MacDonald (Krell), Keith Diamond (Reece Davidson), Mike Rad (Homeless Man), Charles Walker (Pastor), Michael Bailey Smith (Belthazor), Lynn Tufeld (Mourner)

> After being injured in Belthazor's form by the Charmed Ones, Cole disappears. As the sisters prepare a potion to destroy Belthazor, they encounter Krell, a demon bounty hunter sent by the Source for the same purpose. Piper reluctantly agrees with Prue to join forces with Krell, whilst Phoebe searches for information as to the current whereabouts of her lover.

It's Witchcraft: Prue intends to adapt the spell the sisters used to summon Melinda from the past (see 'The Witch is Back') to find Belthazor. In reality, the revised spell ('Magic forces black and white, reaching out through space and light, be he far or be he near, bring us the demon Belthazor here') is nothing like the spell used in 'The Witch is Back.' And it doesn't scan, either. The spell to create the vanquishing potion for Belthazor, 'Spirits of air, forests and sea, set us of this demon free; beasts of hoof and beasts of shell, drive this evil back to hell', is a little more poetic.

The Conspiracy Starts at the Witching Hour: Belthazor is half-human (as his father was a mortal).

It's a Designer Label!: Highlights include Prue's leopardskin top and, especially, Cole's *With the Beatles*-style black poloneck.

References: The title alludes to Joseph Ruben's 1991 suspense-thriller *Sleeping With the Enemy*. The episode includes a lengthy quotation from *The Psalm of David* (Psalm 37: 1-3).

'You May Remember Me ...': Scott MacDonald appeared in *Jack Frost*, *Fire in the Sky* and *Stargate SG-1*. Keith Diamond's CV includes *Dr Giggles*, *Two*

SEASON 3: SLEUTHING WITH THE ENEMY

Guys, a Girl and a Pizza Place and *The Drew Carey Show*. Mike Rad was in *Sunset Strip* and *Special Unit 2*. Charles Walker's movies include *Almost Famous*, *Say Anything* and *Splash*. Lynn Tufeld appeared in *Disclosure*, *California Girls* and *Parker Lewis Can't Lose*.

Behind the Camera: Noel Nosseck's movies include *Dreamer* and *King of the Mountain*.

Logic, Let Me Introduce You to This Window: When Krell is talking to Prue and Piper, Prue's hair is loose in one shot, but tucked behind her ears in the next. Phoebe's hairstyle (and, indeed, colour) has changed since the previous episode. It's been over a week since the events of 'Power Outage', but surely she's had more important things on her mind than a trip to the hairdressers?

Continuity: The episode ends with Phoebe creating an elaborate deception to convince her sisters that she has vanquished Cole when, actually, she hasn't. And you can just bet *that* is going to come back and bite her in the ass sometime.
    Leo cannot heal demons, only mortals. He also notes that the Elders' rules prevent him from healing mortals in any case – unless they've been injured by evil. Krell has more than one stomach.

Quote/Unquote: Prue: 'You can slice off a chunk of demon flesh, but you can't touch a pig's foot? Piper: 'I'm a vegetarian.' Prue: 'Since when?' Piper: 'Since *now*.'
    Krell: 'I am Krell, a Xotar.' Prue: 'I'm Prue, a Scorpio.'
    Davidson: 'And you are?' Phoebe: 'Phoebe.' Reese: 'Is that like Cher or Madonna, or do you *have* a last name?'
    Prue: 'Belthazor killed the Triad, now the Source wants him dead. Krell is trying to suck up to the Source, so he wants to kill Belthazor.' Piper: 'Belthazor wants to kill us so the Source won't kill him.' Leo: 'If you work with Krell you can vanquish Belthazor before he kills you.' Phoebe: 'Works for me.'

Notes: 'Vanquish Phoebe's boyfriend? That's gonna cause some problems.' A definite turning point for *Charmed* as a hint of moral ambiguity enters into the mix again. In many ways, this episode is like a new pilot for the series, moving it off in a completely different direction as Phoebe takes her first tentative steps on a bridal path that will lead to the apocalyptic events of season four.

53: COYOTE PIPER

11 January 2001

Writer: Krista Vernoff
Director: Chris Long

Cast: Rainn Wilson (Kierkan), Paige Rowland (Terra), Chad Willett (Justin Harper), Phillip Boyd (Drunk Guy), Debra Mayer (Mother), Sabine Singh (Missy), Andrew Bowen (Businessman), Jessica Randle (Concerned Woman), Adrianna Alvarez (File Clerk), Rick Warren (Hot Guy)

> An alchemist, Kierkan, creates Terra, a life-essence from his own blood, who can possess humans. Terra searches for the Charmed Ones, whom she plans to use to destroy her creator. Piper subsequently falls victim to Terra's possession, at the very moment when she is about to attend a high school reunion. Meanwhile, Phoebe researches Cole's family history.

It's Witchcraft: According to *The Book of Shadows*, alchemists can transform anything into anything else – water into gold and energy into matter are two examples given. They even have the ability to bring the dead back to life. A life-essence is comparable to a human soul, but made in a mixing lab by an alchemist. A well-made essence can possess any living being, but would prove toxic and eventually lethal to the being's pre-existing soul. Such life-essences are usually kept in a small bottle called an essence bearer. To vanquish Kierkan, the sisters use a spell that begins: 'Let flesh be flesh and bone be bone, the alchemist shall transform none, cruel scientist of evil born, with these words face the fire's scorn.' To attempt to remove Terra's soul from Piper's body, Prue and Phoebe chant: 'Host soul, reject the poison's essence. Let love's light end this cruel possession.' Unfortunately, it doesn't work.

A Little Learning is a Dangerous Thing: When Piper ran for freshman class secretary, she got so nervous that Prue had to go up on stage and finish her speech for her.

The Conspiracy Starts at the Witching Hour: Phoebe almost confesses to Leo that Cole is still alive. Cole's father was, as mentioned in the last episode, human. Benjamin Coleridge Turner (1859-88) was a California state assemblyman. Phoebe has a vision of Turner being killed by his

SEASON 3: COYOTE PIPER

demon wife when Cole (born in 1885) was just three years old.

It's a Designer Label!: Not much else to say, really, other than Piper's red leather top and black leather trousers.

References: The title is an allusion to David McNally's chick-flick *Coyote Ugly* (2000). Also, *The Brady Bunch*; *All of Me*; *Poltergeist*; *Death Wish*; fashion designer Betsy Johnson; and the Hari Krishna foundation. Posters glimpsed in P³ include those for Candlebox, Soul Coughing and Red Hot Chilli Peppers.

'You May Remember Me …': Rainn Wilson played Arthur Martin in *Six Feet Under*. His movies include *Almost Famous* and *Galaxy Quest*. Paige Rowland appeared in *Days of our Lives* and *Pitstop*. Chad Willett was in *The Chronicle*, *Madison* and *The Cape*. Phillip Boyd appeared in *Felicity*. Debra Mayer was in *Voodoo Academy*. Sabine Singh's CV includes *The Anarchist Cookbook* and *The Sopranos*. Andrew Bowen appeared in *Evolution* and *John Doe*. Jessica Randle was in *Triangle Square*.

Behind the Camera: Chris Long's CV includes *Glory Days*, *Gilmore Girls*, *Roswell* and *Lois & Clark*.

Cigarettes and Alcohol: Lots and lots of booze is drunk at the reunion. In the final scene, Piper and Prue share bottles of Miller's Lite.

Sex and Drugs and Rock n Roll: Prue's latest date had halitosis and got only two out of ten on her scoring criteria. Old flame Justin Harper spends most of the episode getting closer to at least six.

Logic, Let Me Introduce You To This Window: How did Terra know how to use Piper's power? Justin says he was Prue's love-slave in school and that she knew it. In 'Be Careful What You Witch For', Prue's 17-year-old self didn't seem the sort of girl who could inspire such affections. Piper is said to have graduated in 1992, but the sign at the beginning of the episode reads: 'Baker High, Class of '90.' Additionally, 'Pardon My Past' revealed Piper's birthdate to be March 1973, actually making her a member of the Class of 1991. And, of course, the Piper seen in 1975 in 'That 70s Episode' is clearly much older than two. Why did Terra have to wait to exit Piper's body until Leo removed the knife? When exiting the businessman, she simply left his body through his mouth. After Phoebe has her premonition in the mausoleum, she wipes away the dust from the crypt to reveal the name of Cole's father. However, the letters can be clearly seen in a previous shot. When Leo heals Piper's wound he also apparently repairs her clothes.

SEASON 3: COYOTE PIPER

Continuity: The Halliwells seem to have a troubled history with dentistry, judging by the high school photo of a braces-wearing Piper (see also 'Be Careful What You Witch For'). Prue notes that high school was really hard for Piper. She was like Jan Brady, the middle sister, not quite sure where she fitted in. Leo, inevtiably, doesn't understand the pop culture reference. Prue was both a cheerleader and class president. Missy suggests that, in school, Piper used to sit at the back of class and draw pictures on her jeans. Piper tells Prue that being around the people she went to school with makes her feel exactly as she did when she was 16 – invisible and inferior. Prue suggests that she helped Phoebe go blonde.

Motors: Justin drives a gorgeous vintage red MG.

Quote/Unquote: Missy: 'Wow, Piper, your face really cleared up. What'd you use? Acutane?'
Terra: 'What kind of witch can't kill a demon without her sisters?' Piper: 'What the hell kind of demon has a panic attack when her boyfriend comes to visit?'
    Phoebe, to Prue: 'I'm not saying you're wrong, I'm saying I *hope* you're wrong.' (She sees Piper table dancing.) 'Oh! Hope dashed.'
    Drunk guy: 'Catfight, dude!'
    Prue: 'You have ten seconds to leave on your own.' Terra: 'What are you going to do, hit me with another rhyming couplet?'

Notes: 'I'm going to my 10-year reunion and win "Most likely to scare people away at the door."' 'Coyote Piper' wears its source material cleverly, whilst exposing some universal truths about the effect of the passage of time on self-confidence. Many people, no matter how successful their lives have become, dread the thought of school reunions. For some, memories of school are as Muriel Spark describes them in *The Prime of Miss Jean Brodie*: 'The happiest days of their lives.' For most, however, schooldays were a time of intense pressure and loneliness when, cruelly, we were nowhere near mature enough to deal with many of these emotions. That's the central paradox of the teenage years that, for example, *Buffy the Vampire Slayer* managed to articulate so well. Here, *Charmed* gets in on the act with a very funny take on the principle of being yourself, no matter how great the temptation is to be someone else.

Soundtrack: EMF's 'Unbelievable', 'New Sensation' by INXS and '10 Yrs Later' by Collective Soul.

Did You Know?: Shannen Doherty choreographed Holly Marie Combs's erotic dance routine in the bar.

54: WE ALL SCREAM FOR ICE CREAM

18 January 2001

Writers: Chris Levinson, Zack Estrin
Director: Allan Kroeker

Cast: Erica Mer (Freckles), Robert Clendenin (Ice Cream Man), James Read (Victor Bennett), Paul Wittenberg (Caleb), Bobby Edner (Ari), Emmalee Thompson (Young Prue Halliwell), Jim Jenkins (Man in Lobby), Burnadean Jones (Receptionist), Dylan Kasch (Child), Soren Fulton (Jersey), Alexa Nikolas (Little Girl)

> Piper searches for her father, after hearing that he's in San Francisco. Prue tries to name a song the melody of which she's fixating on. She discovers that the source is an ice cream truck, the driver of which appears to have been abducting children. Prue and Phoebe, in attempting to stop a kidnapping, find themselves sucked into a wintry world on another plane of existence. But, as so often in the world of the Charmed Ones, all is not as it may first appear.

Dreaming (As Blondie Once Said) is Free: Prue's nightmare of the white-out landscape of the interior of the ice cream van is, as she subsequently discovers, actually a memory of her own experiences as a six year old.

A Little Learning is a Dangerous Thing: This episode includes what is probably *Charmed*'s first reference to e-mail. Cara, seemingly a schoolmate of Piper's and a friend of all the sisters, despite last seeing Victor when Piper was in first grade, spotted him in the city's Bay Tech Building. In fact, Victor has been back in San Francisco for three months and has been in secret (e-mail) contact with Phoebe during this time. Subsequently, Victor reveals that he has recently acquired a new job that, whilst it involves a lot of travelling, is based in San Francisco, meaning that he will – hopefully – see a lot more of his daughters from now on.

The Conspiracy Starts at the Witching Hour: A whole page of *The Book of Shadows* is dedicated to the Ice Cream Man. The Ice Cream Man plays 'The Devil's Chord' - a series of notes that, when sounded together, specifically attract demon children like moths to a flame. Inside the truck is a pan-dimensional force, the Nothing, the only entity that can vanquish such demon children. However, the Nothing is non-discriminatory and will destroy anything it can, including the Charmed Ones themselves. It appears that the Ice Cream Man works for pretty much the same people that Leo and sisters do. Each Ice Cream Man is mortal (and, sadly, expendable). After the present occupant of the van dies, his replacement, Caleb, is called. With Leo's help, he is able to assume his duties.

Work is a Four-Letter Word: Prue is working in the park in Nob Hill doing a photo shoot.

References: Piper quotes from George and Ira Gershwin's 'Let's Call The Whole Thing Off'. When Prue complains of having an anonymous song stuck in her head, Phoebe notes that she had the same problem, for three years, with the theme song from *The Facts of Life*. Also, allusions to *Hair* ('Morning, sunshine'); illustrator Norman Rockwell (1894-1978); *Yellow Submarine*; *The Lion, the Witch and the Wardrobe*; and *The Snow Queen*. Prue owns a Sony radio-alarm.

'You May Remember Me ...': Erica Mer played Kayla Jones in *The City*. Robert Clendenin's CV includes *8mm*, *LA Confidential*, *Scrubs* and *Popular*. James Read was Elle's Father in *Legally Blonde* and appeared in *Beaches*, *North and South* and *Remington Steele*. Paul Wittenberg played Joey in *Touched By An Angel* and was also in *Blossom*. Bobby Edner appeared in *The Penny Promise*. Jim Jenkins was in *ER*, *The Limey* and *CSI*. Burnadean Jones's movies include *Daughter of Sin*. Alexa Nikolas appeared in *Ted Bundy*.

Sex and Drugs and Rock n Roll: Justin (see 'Coyote Piper') has invited the sisters to his big annual family barbecue. Prue, however, notes that she and Justin are still in the 'flirtatious banter' stage of a relationship, and she believes that hanging out with his family might be counterproductive.

In trying to discover if Piper is one of the Charmed Ones, Caleb asks a few seemingly impertinent questions. Piper says that she doesn't know what kind of kinky stuff Caleb is into, but that there's a club down the street from P³ that might, perhaps, cater to his tastes. They have cages, rubber floors and a three-for-two special on Friday nights.

Logic, Let Me Introduce You to This Window: Piper says that the sisters last saw their father a year earlier. Actually, it was over *two* years earlier. Victor now has the last name Bennett instead of Halliwell as seen in the opening credits of 'Thank You For Not Morphing' (see, also, 'Pardon My Past', where it was Jones). Prue states that she cannot use her powers in the

SEASON 3: WE ALL SCREAM FOR ICE CREAM

other plane, however Phoebe touches the swings and gets a premonition. The Ice Cream Man tells Prue that *he* can be replaced, but *she* cannot. 'Charmed Again' proves the inaccuracy of that statement.

Continuity: Prue admits that she has some parental issues. Phoebe agrees that seeing complete connected families is hard on all the sisters, but adds that they cannot spend their lives avoiding what bothers them. When asked what he knows about the Playground, Victor reveals that when Prue was six, she was sick with a cold. Patty had some errands to run, so she took Piper and Phoebe with her, leaving Victor to look after Prue. Awakened from a feverish sleep by the haunting melody of an ice cream van, Prue watched from a window as a little boy – in reality, a demon child – was pulled into the truck. Prue ran out to help him and was also captured. Victor notes that, in a panic, he entered the netherworld and rescued Prue but, as a consequence, it was the last thing he ever did as the sisters' father. He left, as previously noted, because Grams wanted the girls to use their powers, something he violently disagreed with.

Phoebe has drawn up a document containing everything she knows about Cole. Most of it is information previously known, although his demon mother (see 'Coyote Piper') was apparently named Elizabeth and is possibly still alive. Under the heading 'Evil Allies', Phoebe has the Triad (although, of course, Cole himself ended that particular alliance in 'Sleuthing With the Enemy'). The other three entries – Andras, Troxa and Vinceres – were all killed by the sisters (in 'Power Outage', 'Sight Unseen' and 'Primrose Empath' respectively). Victor implies that he was married to Patty Halliwell for eight years. Piper refers to Leo's Whitelighter ability to find someone's location as 'supernatural radar'.

Quote/Unquote: When Prue hums the tune that she's trying to identify, Phoebe notes: 'I'm thinking if you try it again with a little bit more oomph, maybe some choreography, and Piper could back you up with some old-school beatbox?'

Prue: 'I've come to terms with our lack of parental involvement. Some people just weren't meant to have the Rockwellian portrait, the house, the two-car-garage, the picket fence, the golden retriever, and the doting mum and dad.'

Phoebe: 'Why couldn't you get a boy-band song in your head like everybody else?'

Piper: 'He's a demonic dog-catcher and he uses ice cream as bait? Great news for the lactose intolerant demon.'

Phoebe: 'We thought the good guys were bad guys, and in trying to vanquish them, we helped the real bad guys, which were dead ringers for good guys.' Leo: 'Was that English?'

SEASON 3: WE ALL SCREAM FOR ICE CREAM

Notes: 'Do you have a hankering for a snow cone?' A combination of sinister fairy-tale and over-the-top *Batman*-style supervillain parody, 'We All Scream For Ice Cream' continues the terrific run of episodes from this period, with a culmination to the subtle Prue character-arc and the reasons behind her rejection of her father as alluded to in many previous episodes. James Read's excellent performance helps to rehabilitate Victor back into the show's aesthetic. It's also, perhaps surprisingly, a story about not jumping to obvious conclusions, and works very well as a cunning morality tale whilst still getting its share of decent one-liners.

Soundtrack: Collective Soul's 'Skin' and 'Tonight' and 'The Rest Of My Life' by Nina Gordon.

Did You Know?: James Read replaces Tony Denison as the sisters' father for this and all subsequent appearances.

55: BLINDED BY THE WHITELIGHTER

25 January 2001

Writer: Nell Scovell
Director: David Straiton

Cast: Audrey Wasilewski (Natalie), Steve Valentine (Eames), Keith Diamond (Reece Davidson), Camille Langfield (Vivian), Graham Shiels (Victim), La'shan Anderson (Witch)

> The sisters encounter Natalie, a Whitelighter who recently lost her most powerful charge to a warlock named Eames. Natalie notes that Eames now has the power of deflection, which can be used to negate the Halliwells' own powers, leaving them vulnerable to attack.

It's Witchcraft: At the beginning of the episode, Piper and Prue are concocting a potion the ingredients of which include a teaspoon of baking powder and a teaspoon of bat guano. The potion is then given to Phoebe prior to her meeting with the DA investigator. A drop in Reece's coffee will out any demon. Reaction causes the throat to constrict. As it happens, Reece is not a demon, although he does have some allergies.

The spell – approved by Natalie – that the sisters use to vanquish Eames, begins: 'Time for amends and a victim's revenge. Cloning power, turn sour. Power to change, turn to strange. I'm rejectin' your deflection.'

A Little Learning is a Dangerous Thing: Scrying for warlocks doesn't work.

The Conspiracy Starts at the Witching Hour: Reece Davidson tells Phoebe that Cole was a fraud, a man who existed only on paper. He wormed his way into the DA's office for reasons unknown and, apparently, had a very dark side. Bloodstains were found on his carpet and a hidden cabinet full of occult paraphernalia was discovered in his apartment. Phoebe finally confides to Leo that Cole is still alive.

Eames is a warlock who, 10 years previously, murdered a witch in Glasgow and stole her power of cloning. He also possesses, via his latest kill, the power of deflection. They are not his only tricks, however. *The Book of Shadows* notes that Eames also killed a witch in Kenya in 1989 and

SEASON 3: BLINDED BY THE WHITELIGHTER

took the power of transmogrification – the ability to change shape or form. (He uses this to disguise himself as a Darklighter's crossbow.) His masterplan involves killing a Whitelighter to gain the power to orb to the Whitelighter domain. Once there, he would be able to destroy all Whitelighters, leaving their charges unprotected. He would then be able to wipe out all witches.

Work is a Four-Letter Word: Piper has lunch with a reporter from the *Chronicle* who wants to do a story on P^3. Then, she has a meeting with some dot com start-up guys who want to do 'an Internet thingy'.

It's a Designer Label!: Natalie notes that the sisters must prepare themselves for battle – mentally, physically and sartorially. They need outfits that are loose and move, which means no more braless, strapless, fearless attire. 'I have nothing to wear,' notes Prue sadly.

References: The title alludes to 'Blinded By the Light' (see 'Which Prue Is It, Anyway?'). Also, references to Shakespeare's *Julius Caesar*; and *A Few Good Men*. A copy of the book *The Rhyming Dictionary* is glimpsed in P^3.

'You May Remember Me ...': Audrey Wasilewski's CV includes *Catch That Kid*, *Carolina*, *She's All That* and *Monk*. Steve Valentine appeared in *Nikki* and *Mars Attacks!* Camille Langfield was in *Ophelia Learns to Swim*. Graham Shiels appeared in *The West Wing*.

Behind the Camera: Nell Scovell's CV also includes *Sabrina, the Teenage Witch*, *The Critic*, *The Simpsons* and *Coach*. David Straiton also worked on *Dead Like Me*, *Cold Case*, *Angel* and *La Femme Nikita*.

Logic, Let Me Introduce You To This Window: How does Prue suddenly have the ability to scan *The Book of Shadows* for cross references with her hands? Leo mentions that Piper likes to freeze him in bed for her own personal pleasure. Isn't that somewhat dangerous? Additionally, those whom Piper freezes, usually unfreeze when she touches them, so freezing Leo during a contact sport like sex would seem to be somewhat pointless. When Natalie throws energy balls at Piper during training, Piper freezes them, but they continue to move.

Continuity: Leo tells the sisters that Natalie and he were rookie Whitelighters together and, before that, as humans both fought in World War II. Natalie is considered one of the top Whitelighters. Leo notes that Whitelighters aren't supposed to eat on the job. Whitelighters communicate with each other in a language composed of clicking noises.

SEASON 3: BLINDED BY THE WHITELIGHTER

They also have staff meetings each morning, with mandatory attendance, unless a charge is in need. There doesn't appear to be a word for Piper in Whitelighterese. Every witch has a version of *The Book of Shadows*, which they must keep in a sacred and protected spot, usually an altar room. At the episode's end, taking into account the sisters' triumphant coup in destroying Eames, the Elders lift the probation on Leo and Piper.

Quote/Unquote: Leo: 'I was late, okay. It's not like I was out carousing with the boys. I was out being a force of good in the universe.' Piper: 'A *true* force of good would have called. Or, at least, orbed.'

Eames: 'Did I miss all the fun? No, wait, I *am* the fun.'

Phoebe: 'Who's Natalie?' Piper: 'She's a ...' Leo: 'Fellow Whitelighter. See, I finished your sentence.' Piper: 'That's *not* what I was gonna say.'

Notes: 'The only reason Eames would have killed a Darklighter is so that he can use the crossbow to kill a Whitelighter.' So, we finally get a glimpse of the Whitelighters domain – very much a *Bill and Ted / Heaven Can Wait* version of paradise, full of mist and white robed figures. The episode itself is quietly effective, with some nice internal Whitelighter politics mixed with Piper's green-eyed (and, after a while, tiresome) jealousy. Best bit: The training montage.

Soundtrack: 'It Takes Two' by Rob & DJ E-Z Rock Base rocks da shack at P^3.

SEASON 3: WRESTLING WITH DEMONS

56: WRESTLING WITH DEMONS

1 February 2001

Writer: Sheryl J Anderson
Director: Joel J Feigenbaum

Cast: Ron Perlman (Mr Kellman), Marco Sanchez (Tom Peters), Buff Bagwell (Slammer), Booker T Huffman (Thunder), Scott Steiner (Mega-Man), Shirley Prestia (Fran Peters), Dennis Dun (Chang), Marcus Dean Fuller (Client)

The sisters attempt to protect an innocent from a possible demon attack after Phoebe has a premonition. Prue is available to prevent the killing but lets the demon, Tom, escape when she realises that she has previously dated him. Research leads to the discovery that a human can become a demon through a recruitment and training programme that strips the mortal of his or her humanity. Before the process is completed, the individual must kill an innocent. Prue sees an opportunity to restore Tom's humanity.

It's Witchcraft: Phoebe mentions a spell to find a lost love in *The Book of Shadows*. She and Piper use an adaptation of the 'Lost and Found' spell that Phoebe recently wrote to find Cole: 'Guiding spirits I ask your charity, lend me your focus and clarity. Lead me to the one I cannot find, restore that and my peace of mind.' This produces a few awkward side-effects. A variant on this – 'Show me the past that I cannot find, to save Tom and restore Prue's peace of mind' – is used to find Tom. Having eventually vanquished Kellman, Phoebe chants, 'I return what I didn't want to find, let it be out of sight, out of mind,' to end the spell and banish the lost souls who are endangering the sisters.

A Little Learning is a Dangerous Thing: Prue asks Leo if it's possible to turn a human into a demon. Leo notes that there are rumours about demons who recruit humans in need and strike a Faustian bargain with them. The humans are then forced into a training academy, a programme that destroys their humanity and, it is alleged, turns them into demons. When the recruits graduate, they have to kill an innocent to seal the demonic conversion permanently. Indeed, *The Book of Shadows* has details about the academy, describing the process that renders the subject demonic and noting that those who have achieved demon status have a brand with six chevrons on their arm. It appears that Kellman has a contract with the Source to deliver five newly converted demons. The Elders believe that the key to destroying Kellman is to turn one of his recruits against him.

The Conspiracy Starts at the Witching Hour: There have been four vicious murders in the last week, the only common denominator of which is that the victim's picture was in the Metro section of the *San Francisco Herald* on the day of the murder.

It's a Designer Label!: Prue's tan suede jacket puts in another appearance.

References: Leo alludes to Goethe's *Faust* (see 'The Wedding From Hell'). Also, Wonder Woman; *Angel Heart*; *Earthquake*; and possibly Haircut 100's 'Love Plus One'. Kellman's office is littered with sporting memorabilia, including what appears to be a large statue of a Newcastle United footballer. There's also a photo of AC Milan's Paolo Maldini on Kellman's wall.

'You May Remember Me ...': Ron Perlman is best known as Vincent in *Beauty and the Beast*. His movies include *Romeo is Bleeding* and *Alien: Resurrection*. Marco Sanchez appeared in *seaQuest DSV* and *The Rookie*. Shirley Prestia was in *Rent Control*, *What Women Want* and *Suddenly Susan*. Dennis Dun played Billy Po in *Midnight Caller* and also appeared in *Big Trouble in Little China*. Marcus Dean Fuller was in *General Hospital*.

Don't Give Up The Day Job: Marcus Buff Bagwell, Booker T Huffman and Scott Steiner are all WCW wrestlers.

Logic, Let Me Introduce You to This Window: When Tom is frozen by Piper, he is looking straight ahead. However, one subsequent shot of him, still frozen, shows him with his head turned to one side. After Phoebe gets her brown hair back, it stays that way for the rest of the episode – except for the sequences in the Underworld when it's blonde in some shots. When they emerge from the lift to the Underworld, the sisters have swapped positions from when they entered it.

Continuity: According to Phoebe, Piper waters flowers when she's nervous. She also babbles a lot. Phoebe finally admits, first to Piper and then to a furious Prue, that she did not, in fact, vanquish Cole (see 'Sleuthing With the Enemy'). Prue reminds her sisters that they have saved bad boys before, mentioning the case of the priest with the warlock brothers (see 'When Bad Warlocks Turn Good'). Tom Peters dated Prue when the pair were at Gold State University. Tom was the captain of the football team and had one particularly outstanding season (seemingly as a Wide Receiver) with 96 receptions and 1255 yards. He turned pro after leaving school but, three weeks into his rookie year, a knee injury wrecked his career. He went missing soon afterwards, with rumours of gambling debts.

Cruelty to Animals: Grams's dog, Rasputin, went missing approximately seven years earlier. When Phoebe casts the 'lost and found' spell, it turns up again. However, at the end of the episode, Leo is able to find the family the dog has been living with and return it.

Quote/Unquote: Prue: 'Innocents and alleys. Don't they *ever* learn?'
Phoebe: 'I didn't know you dated the captain of the college football team. How suburban.'
Phoebe, to Leo: 'You lost mom's ring? It's a good thing you're dead already.'
Darryl: 'You were blonde when you answered the door. How'd it change?' Phoebe: 'It must be because I coloured my hair in that sink. So, technically, I lost it there ... I hope this doesn't affect my virginity.'
Prue, to Phoebe: 'I am going to win this fight and save your ass. That way I can kick it myself later.'

Notes: 'I dated that demon.' The idea of combining telefantasy elements with vainglorious wrestler *braggadocio* is not new (both *Star Trek* and *The X-Files* experimented with it) and, on past experience, it's usually only partially successful. That's also true of this episode, which is both amusing and yet frustratingly lightweight. Playing fights for laughs isn't the worst crime in the world, but if there isn't much drama on offer elsewhere to back up the slapstick then the whole thing comes over as shallow posturing.

57: BRIDE AND GLOOM

8 February 2001

Writer: William Schmidt
Director: Chris Long

Cast: Chad Willett (Justin Harper), Una Damon (Dantalian), Bobby Edner (Ari), Tom O'Brien (Zile), Michael Bailey Smith (Belthazor), Tracey Costello (Marie), Jason Tomlins (Waiter), DC Douglas (Craig)

> As a hyperactive Piper and Leo make plans for their wedding, Prue is kidnapped by a shape-shifting warlock named Zile. With no other way to find Prue, Phoebe turns to a returned Cole for help, even though he must risk his life to do so. Meanwhile, Prue is to be married to the warlock as part of high level priestess Dantalian's plan to obtain *The Book of Shadows*.

It's Witchcraft: When *The Book of Shadows* begins to revert to its dark side, amongst the evil spells that Piper reads are a 'Hemlock Killing Spell' and one 'To Call a Female Warrior.' Dantalian's ceremony begins: 'In the beginning we were damned. Through damnation, we found freedom, power and purpose. As I unite you today, I remind you of those gifts. And in your union, may these gifts increase your powers, may grow in the service of evil. So be it.'

The sisters' spell to vanquish Dantalian and Zile is: 'Powers of light, magic of right, cast this blight into forever's night.' Leo suggests that vanquishing Zile broke the bond and reversed all the evil that Piper and Phoebe had done.

A Little Learning is a Dangerous Thing: Cole says that he has been in hiding since the events of 'Sleuthing With the Enemy', shimmering from realm to realm to keep his survival from the Source. Phoebe is the only one who knows he is still alive. Except for her sisters. And Leo. 'Why didn't you just put an ad in the paper [and] tell the whole damn world' snarls Cole.

Leo notes that the Elders can detect when a witch dies.

The Conspiracy Starts at the Witching Hour: Once married, it is believed, Prue will turn to evil, and, because her magic is interconnected with that of her sisters and *The Book of Shadows*, this will allow an evil nature finally to possess the magical tome.

Phoebe reveals to Cole that a shape-shifter has abducted Prue, but the weird thing is, no-one from the side of good can get a read on where he's hiding her. Cole notes that warlocks don't have that kind of power and the shape-shifter must be working with somebody who does. Certain dignitaries in the evil underworld have the power to shield their activities – demonic judges, dark priests, anyone who needs privacy for rituals.

References: There are allusions to the Disney Corporation; *The Wedding Planner*; *Cinderella*; the Dave Clark Five's 'Catch Us If You Can'; and *Star Wars*.

'You May Remember Me ...': Uma Damon's movies include *The Truman Show* and *Deep Rising*. Tom O'Brien played Roger Nixon in *Smallville* and appeared in *The Astronaut's Wife* and *LA Law*. Tracey Costello was in *Ghosts of Mississippi*. Jason Tomlins appeared in *Postcards from the Edge* and *Matlock*. DC Douglas's CV includes *Emma's Wish*, *Grace* and *Boston Common*.

Sex and Drugs and Rock n Roll: Prue is still dating Justin (see 'Coyote Piper'). Although she considers him to be a sweet guy, he's also predictable – there's no mystery or *savoir-faire*.

Cigarettes and Alcohol: At the restaurant, Zile (disguised as Justin) orders a bottle of Berringer Private Reserve. Prue doesn't want to drink much, noting that she has to work that afternoon. So your photographs are a little fuzzy, says Zile, dismissively, 'call it *avant garde*.'

Logic, Let Me Introduce You to This Window: The priestess's plan to make the sisters evil is somewhat contrived. Additionally, viewers never really see Prue become evil, at least not in the way that Piper and Phoebe do. For over half this episode, Prue is merely unconscious on a slab. Why, in any case, do Piper and Phoebe turn evil just because Prue has? There are plenty of other episodes both before and after this in which one sister has flirted with the Dark Side and this hasn't affected the others. Cole says that evil can't love. However, as we've seen on several occasions, evil clearly *can* love – though not necessarily well, wisely or sanely (see, for instance, 'Heartbreak City', 'Pardon My Past' and 'Magic Hour'). When Dantalian is knocked down by Phoebe, she's wearing boots. In the next shot, they've changed into high-heeled shoes.

Continuity: Prue, as the oldest sister, feels that she is supposed to do everything first – get braces (see 'Be Careful What You Witch For'), get a boyfriend *and* find a husband. With regard to the latter, *technically* she is. At the beginning of the episode, Phoebe is watching *Kill It Before It Dies* (see 'Chick Flick') when Cole suddenly appears in the movie using a trick he learned from the Demon of Illusion. Piper is asked if she would like a flower girl for her wedding and suggests Kate (see 'Once Upon a Time'). Leo notes that it's a pity the sisters killed the demon bounty hunter Krell (see 'Sleuthing With the Enemy') since his information on the demon underworld could have been useful. Piper wants to have something in the region of 60 guests at her wedding – these, she notes, will include all the people from P3, various friends, Darryl, her father and her mother (despite the latter being, you know, dead).

Cruelty to Animals: Dantalian puts a scorpion in water as part of her enchantment potion to place on Zile's lips.

When the male wedding planner asks if Piper and Leo have thought of what kind of *hors d'eouvres* they'd like, Leo sarcastically suggests pigs in a blanket. Later, evil-Piper takes that suggestion under advisement and turns the wedding planner into a pig wearing a blanket.

Quote/Unquote: Prue: 'I've been dreaming of this day my entire life.' Leo: 'Piper's wedding?' Prue: 'No, *mine*.'

Phoebe, hitting Cole: 'That's for ruining my favourite movie. And, oh yeah, *my life too*.'

Phoebe: 'Welcome to Planet Narcissus.'

Notes: 'What do *you* get out of making Prue Halliwell my wife?' Some of the greatest episodes of series television have involved stories in which regular, and much-loved, characters have played dark variations of their standard persona. Sadly, some of the very worst episodes of series TV have hinged on similar conceits. It's not just about the performance, it also involves the subversion of an established character. 'Bride and Gloom' is nowhere near to being the worst example of its kind, but it's a long way short of the best, too. It's possible that the episode fails so spectacularly because everything is wrapped up too neatly. The explanations are too shallow, the redemptions for horrible sins too easy, the resurrection of Leo too straightforward. And despite Prue's impassioned speech about evil needing something to work with and the coda with Phoebe telling Cole that she can't see him again, the episode feels predictable. Worse, it feels like an exercise in subversion for subversion's own sake.

58: THE GOOD, THE BAD AND THE CURSED

15 February 2001

Writers: Monica Breen, Alison Schapker
Director: Shannen Doherty

Cast: J Hunter Ackerman (Man in the Crowd), Michael Greyeyes (Beau Lightfeather), James Read (Victor Bennett), Kimberly Norris (Isabel Lightfeather), Ed Lauter (Sutter), Scott Beehner (Cal), Alan Davidson (Buck), Blake Gibbons (Gil), Steve Larson (Slade), James Lashly (Bartender)

> During a trip to a ghost town with Victor, Phoebe becomes magically linked to Beau Lightfeather – who was murdered during the town's past – and begins to experience the effects of his injuries. When Beau suffers from a gunshot wound, Phoebe also falls victim. The sisters discover that the town is cursed and stuck in a time loop, doomed to repeat the same day over and over. Prue finds herself having to work with Cole on a parallel plane of existence to attempt to break the curse.

Dreaming (As Blondie Once Said) is Free: Phoebe is injured when she experiences psychic echoes of the things inflicted on Beau in the past. Beau also has prophetic dreams of the future, a gift he seemingly inherited from his father.

It's Witchcraft: *The Book of Shadows* contains a page on time loops. This notes: 'Certain spiritual traditions believe that a great evil or great injustice can be cursed into a time loop until righted.'

A Little Learning is a Dangerous Thing: Leo notes that ghosts don't bleed – then, realising that Victor is listening, he quickly adds, 'Or so I've read in books; obviously it's not my area of expertise.'

The Conspiracy Starts at the Witching Hour: Isabel tells Prue and Cole that Sutter is in tight with the railroads. He came to the town a couple of months earlier, promising to bring the tracks through and make it more than just an old mining town. This, however, was in exchange for a piece of everything profitable in the town – mines, the bank and the newspaper.

SEASON 3: THE GOOD, THE BAD AND THE CURSED

When the people resisted, his boys took over. At first, everyone stood up to them, but after they killed the sheriff, this stopped.

It's a Designer Label!: To make themselves inconspicuous in the 1870s, Cole and Prue steal some cowboy clothes. Cole thinks that Prue, instead of becoming the littlest cowgirl in history, should have taken a pretty red dress that was drying on a washing line. Prue notes it was a prostitute's dress – not exactly the kind of impression that she wanted to make. At least, she adds, she's not wearing some dead guy's clothes.

References: The title refers to Sergio Leone's legendary 1966 spaghetti-western *The Good, the Bad and the Ugly*. Amid numerous Western genre clichés, there are direct allusions to *High Noon*; *The Man Who Shot Liberty Valance*; *The Searchers*; *Rio Bravo*; *She Wore a Yellow Ribbon*; *Once Upon a Time in the West*; *Wild Wild West*; and *The Godfather*. Prue hums a short snatch of 'The Wedding March.' The *Star Gazette*'s headline for 25 April 1873 is: HALF-BREED TO DIE AT SUNDOWN.

'You May Remember Me …': Michael Greyeyes appeared in *ZigZag*, *Rude* and *Dr Quinn Medicine Woman*. Kimberly Norris was in *Folly Island*. Ed Lauter's movies include *Cujo*, *Family Plot*, *Coyote Summer*, *SeaBiscuit* and *Mulholland Falls*. Scott Beehner was in *Tomcats*. Alan Davidson appeared in *Hollywood Homicide* and *Arresting Gena*. Blake Gibbons was in *Very Bad Things*. Steve Larson's CV includes *Gia* and *Grounded for Life*. James Lashley appeared in *Wild Wild West* and *Howard the Duck*.

Cigarettes and Alcohol: In the saloon, Prue orders a Moonshine from the bemused barman. Cole translates this into whisky for those who haven't watched too many old movies. 'You're confusing me with Phoebe,' notes Prue. 'Not a chance,' he replies.

Logic, Let Me Introduce You to This Window: When Cole first enters the Manor, he has a chin-full of designer stubble. However, when he and Prue go back in time, he's clean-shaven. The stubble then reappears in the saloon, only to disappear again on several further occasions before making a triumphant return during the final scenes … Leo orbs out of a crowded diner in the middle of his lunch with Victor. Alyssa Milano mispronounces 'feng shui'. Twice.

Continuity: Phoebe claims that she inherited all Victor's traits, especially his abilities in the fine art of fibbing. Victor didn't know that Patty was a witch before he married her. Both Prue and Victor mention Patty's affair with her Whitelighter (see 'P^3 H^{2}0'). Leo points out that this happened after

SEASON 3: THE GOOD, THE BAD AND THE CURSED

Patty and Victor separated, though Victor suggests that Sam was 'putting the moves' on Patty long before they actually split up and that he and Patty never had a chance to get back together because of Sam.

Motors: Victor drives a champagne-coloured Audi Quatro (4OAP 168).

Quote/Unquote: Leo: 'As long as no demons come bursting through that door, I'm fine.' Piper: 'You *had* to jinx it.'
Cole, on shimmering to another dimension: 'Gotta hold my hand.' Prue: 'This *already* sucks.'
Phoebe: 'I got into a bar brawl. Well, actually, I didn't, two cowboys did. Beau and some other guy. I didn't catch his name, but I think he was the bad guy, coz he was wearing a black hat.' And, to Victor: 'Don't get mad at me, I've been shot!'
Buck: 'I'm gonna enjoy this. See you in hell.' Cole: 'Been there, done that.'

Notes: 'Are you seriously telling me you're willing to sacrifice your sister's life for a town full of cowards?' There are some genres that you wouldn't expert *Charmed* to work in, and the Western is one of them. Drag away some of the more obvious dramatic clichés that the episode is built around, however, and what we've got here is actually a really fun story about right-versus-might. And one that is full of clever characterisation and some startling imagery (the doves, the raven etc.) as a bonus. Some deliberately ambiguous elements don't work – what, exactly, *is* the deal with the appearance of the MacGuffin-style raven in the final shot? Is that supposed to be Beau's spirit? This, and a few other questions, remain unanswered. The direction is occasionally flat, too, particularly during the sequence that juxtaposes Sutter whipping Beau with Phoebe, in the future, feeling the effects of this scourging. However, aesthetics aside, this is another clever and witty episode, with the pairing of Prue and Cole producing the unexpected bonus of some sharp comedy into the bargain.

SEASON 3: JUST HARRIED

59: JUST HARRIED

22 February 2001

Writer: Daniel Cerone
Director: Mel Damski

Cast: Dana Ashbrook (T J), James Read (Victor Bennett), Michael Bailey Smith (Belthazor), Finola Hughes (Patty Halliwell), Whip Hubley (Inspector Krutchen), Douglas Bennett (Ray), Jennifer Rhodes (Penny Halliwell), Lauralei Combs (Girl in Bar), Franc Ross (Jack), Tom Yi (Uniform Officer), Ward Shrake (Biker)[44]

> As the day of Leo's and Piper's wedding arrives, Piper seeks reassurance from her sisters that nothing will ruin her special day. Prue finds herself disturbed by some recent dreams and fails to realise that she has been astral projecting in her sleep, to a local bar, where she has been seeing one of the regulars. On the night before the wedding, astral-Prue gets into a fight with a patron who is later found dead, leaving Prue as the main suspect in a murder enquiry.

Dreaming (As Blondie Once Said) is Free: Prue describes the recurring dream she's been having to Phoebe. It involves a 'biker guy and he's kinda cute and kinda dangerous.' Prue remembers little about what happens in her dreams except that she seems to wish to avoid waking up – as though her dreams are overpowering her. Phoebe notes that her premonitions feel similar, in so much as they pull her against her will. Prue speculates that, perhaps, someone is trying to pull her into a parallel world or a dream dimension.

It subsequently turns out that when Prue sleeps, her personality is divided into two classical Freudian stereotype – the ego and the id. The former is the control factor, while the sacrifices that Prue has made for her over the years, Phoebe believes, have made Prue suppress her id's inner desires. She suggests that Prue has to stop devoting her entire self to the Charmed Ones, otherwise it will, literally, tear her apart.

It's Witchcraft: Patty notes that after all the Elders put Piper and Leo through, they wanted to give her something back, so they allowed Patty to become mortal for her daughter's wedding day. The wedding ceremony

---
[44] Uncredited.

ends with Leo and Piper saying: 'Heart to thee, body to thee, always and forever, so mote it be.'

A Little Learning is a Dangerous Thing: Cole suggests that very few humans have the heart of a true killer – one who kills without prejudice. He, however, can always sense those who do. At least, he could before he suppressed his demonic-self for Phoebe.

It's a Designer Label!: Definite low-lights include Phoebe's orange trousers and Darryl's scarlet shirt. Also, a very large-chested lady wearing the tightest black top imaginable is seen on several occasions drinking and playing pool in Will's bar.

References: Phoebe suggests that a stressed-out Piper might like to watch her Celine Dion *Behind The Music* video cassette. Piper, by way of reply, asks Phoebe if *she* would like to get slapped. There's a prominent Cher poster in Will's bar. There are allusions to *American Beauty*; *The Addams Family* ('Showtime!'); *The Graduate*; *Friends*; Sigmund Freud (see 'Wicca Envy'); and *Apocalypse Now* ('This place must be like victory').

'You May Remember Me ...': Dana Ashbrook played Bobby Briggs in *Twin Peaks* and also appeared in *21 Jump Street* and *Dawson's Creek*. Whip Hubley's CV includes *Fangs*, *Flipper*, *Daddy's Girl* and *Murder She Wrote*. Douglas Bennett appeared in *Hungry*, which he also directed. Lauralei Combs – Holly Marie's mother – was in *Forces of Nature*. Franc Ross appeared in *The Guilt*, *Firefly* and *Buffy the Vampire Slayer*. Ward Shrake was in *American Girl* and was Philip Seymour-Hoffman's photo double on *Red Dragon*.

Cigarettes and Alcohol: Numerous champagne bottles are seen in the Halliwell kitchen. When Leo, Darryl and Cole investigate activities at Will's bar, Cole appears to be drinking Scotch.

Sex and Drugs and Rock n Roll: Prue's id, in astral form, seeks out danger in the form of bad boy biker T J, a Harley Davidson-driving, leather-jacket-wearing punk from the wrong side of the tracks.

Logic, Let Me Introduce You to This Window: When the girls point out that Piper is about to become Mrs Wyatt, Grams says that the women in their family keep their maiden name even after marriage. This is seemingly something that began only with the sisters' mother, since Grams herself used her first husband's name. If this really was a generational family thing going back to the dawn of the powers, then all the descendants of

Melinda Warren – including several that we've seen who have completely different surnames – should be called Warren. When Patty shows up, Piper notes that ghosts glow and asks why Patty isn't glowing. We've previously seen several ghosts in the series – Mark in 'Dead Man Dating' and Charlene in 'Ex Libris', for example – who don't glow. Melinda's blessing cup changes position on the table during the conversation between Prue and Phoebe. Aside from providing one of the best lines of the episode (see **Quote/Unquote**), Victor shows remarkably little surprise when Patty, dead for 20 odd years, suddenly turns up at their daughter's wedding. General question applicable not only to this episode, but many others: why is a close family friend like Darryl constantly referred to amongst his circle of friends by his surname rather than his forename? It's a television cliché, but it's not very realistic.

Continuity: At the beginning of the episode, there remains some lingering animosity between Leo and Victor (see 'The Good, the Bad and the Cursed'), but it subsequently thaws. Phoebe mentions the Dream Sorcerer (see 'The Dream Sorcerer'). Cole arrives at the wedding having had a recent run-in with a Zotar demon. Patty tells Phoebe that her road has been the longest travelled, but that Patty never worried about her or, indeed, any of the sisters. This was because she had a premonition the day that Phoebe was born in which she saw this future event; her three daughters standing before her as beautiful young women. Piper says that she kept her mother's wedding album after she died and looked at the pictures every night like a bedtime story. Patty suggests that Victor always had a way of saying the wrong thing when the sisters were young. Victor disagrees, saying that Patty was never open to what he had to say, because she wanted to raise Prue, Piper and Phoebe as little witches instead of little girls. Phoebe tells Prue that she and Piper have both passion and purpose in their lives and that Prue gave them those qualities.

Quote/Unquote: Grams: 'Is this the biggest arch you could get?' Prue: 'Without opening a fast food franchise, yeah.'

Piper: 'It's bad luck to see the bride's dress before the wedding.' Leo: 'You're not even wearing the dress.' Piper: 'The same rule applies to the bride's curlers. Go away.'

Piper: 'What's wrong?' Phoebe: 'Boy-bands. There's just too many of them, don't you think?'

Victor: 'I could probably get used to having a Whitelighter for a son-in-law.' Cole, entering the basement: 'Everybody having fun down here?' Leo, to Victor: 'How do you stand on demons?'

Victor: 'All right, who brought my ex-wife back from the dead?'

Piper: 'Look at the track record. The Halliwells – we're blessed as witches and we are cursed as women. Sometimes I think we're all destined to end up alone.'

Notes: 'Interesting place to dream about.' For some viewers, Piper's ceaseless fatalism can prove somewhat tiring after 50-odd episodes of moaning, whinging and grumbling about the general unfairness of life. It's a tribute to Holly Marie Combs that this fine actress can produce any sort of reaction – perhaps, especially, a negative one – from viewers in today's 'attention-span-of-seven-seconds' TV world. That said, Piper's frequent outbursts of misery are seldom as downright *amusing* as they are here. 'Just Harried' is a beautiful episode, full of wit and passion; it contains, in the initial scene between Finola Hughes and the three sisters, some of the finest and most touching moments in *Charmed*.

Soundtrack: 'Heaven and Hot Rods' by Stone Temple Pilots is heard in the bar. The wedding music is 'Canon in D' by Johann Pachelbel (1653-1706) – see 'Magic Hour'.

60: DEATH TAKES A HALLIWELL

15 March 2001

Writer: Krista Vernoff
Director: Jon Paré

Cast: Keith Diamond (Reece Davidson), Simon Templeton (Angel of Death), Christopher Shea (Uno), Wade Andrew Williams (Dos), Annie Abbott (Mrs Owens), Jeffrey Dean (Inspector), Roger Marks (Rabbi), Micheala Watkins (Andrea)

> Whilst at the beach with Phoebe, Prue notices a woman, Andrea, apparently spying on them. Andrea has a mysterious shadow lurking behind her. The sisters learn that Andrea is involved in Inspector Davidson's investigation of Cole. Prue follows Andrea and discovers that the shadow is actually the Angel of Death. Prue becomes obsessed with preventing Death from taking the life of another innocent – Davidson. Meanwhile, a pair of demons, Seekers, are responsible for various untimely deaths in an effort to locate Cole.

It's Witchcraft: To call Death, Prue uses the spell: 'Spirits of air, sand and sea, converge to set the Angel free, in the wind I send this rhyme, bring Death before me, before my time.' The spell to vanquish the Seekers begins: 'Knowledge gained by murderous means is wisdom's bitter enemy. The mind that burns with stolen fire, will now become your funeral pyre.'

A Little Learning is a Dangerous Thing: According to Leo and, indeed, the man himself, the Angel of Death is neither good nor evil, he simply exists to take mortals when their time is due. He is also non-corporeal, especially when being kicked by a girl.

The Conspiracy Starts at the Witching Hour: The Seekers extract information from their victims by feeding – vampire-like – on their brain-stems.

'West Hollywood': Cole's former landlady, Mrs Owens, tells the two Seekers that she has no problem with the whole alternative lifestyle thing, she just don't like loud tenants. Mr Turner, for instance, was a little strange and just disappeared without a trace. But he was nice and quiet, so Mrs Owens liked him.

References: The title alludes to Alberto Casella's play *Death Takes a Holiday* (filmed in 1934, starring Fredric March). Also, references to *A Christmas Carol*; *The Fly*; *The Terminator*; and *Bill and Ted's Bogus Journey*. The plot bears a vague similarity to elements within Neil Gaiman's *Sandman* story 'The Sound of Her Wings'. The Seekers' floating movements may have been inspired by the Gentlemen in *Buffy the Vampire Slayer*. The funeral service includes a lengthy quotation from the 23rd Psalm ('Yea, though I walk through the valley of the shadow of death …')

'You May Remember Me …': Simon Templeman's CV includes *Just Shoot Me*, *Live Nude Girls*, *The Professionals*, *Angel* and *Northern Exposure*. Wade Williams appeared in *Buffy the Vampire Slayer*, *CSI*, *24* and *Ali*. Christopher Shea was in *The Specials* and *Enterprise*. Roger Marks appeared in *Malcolm in the Middle*. Michaela Watkins's movies include *Inconceivable*. Annie Abbott appeared in *LA Law* and *Diaries of Darkness*. Jeffrey Dean was in *Nash Bridges*.

Sex and Drugs and Rock n Roll: Prue and Phoebe spend a day at the beach to give Leo and Piper some 'alone-married-people-time.'

Logic, Let Me Introduce You to This Window: Considering how many people die on any given day, the Angel of Death spends an awful lot of time hanging around San Francsico on this particular one. Aren't people dying elsewhere? A piece of stock footage shows what appears to be the sun rising above San Francisco from what looks like a vantage point to the West of the city. However, we've seen this particular bit of film before and it's always been used to depict night-fall, which suggest that the film is actually being shown in reverse. In the subsequent scene, Prue is on the beach (again, facing the West). This should take place shortly after dawn, for the establishing shot to mean anything, but all the shadows visible indicate that it's after noon. The next scene occurs in late afternoon – note that Phoebe mentions she's been in the car for 16 hours. Thus, apparently, for one day only we have the sun both rising and setting in the West. When Prue is in the mausoleum as the demons kill Inspector Davidson, her arms keep changing from covering her face to being at her sides from shot-to-shot. Cole and one of the Seekers crash into a concrete pillar in the mausoleum with such force that it shatters. Why doesn't this bring the roof down? And, indeed, turn at least one of their spines to dust with the trauma? If *The Book of Shadows* has pictures of individual Seekers *and* includes a vanquish, shouldn't that imply that all those Seekers featured

SEASON 3: DEATH TAKES A HALLIWELL

have already been vanquished?

Continuity: This episode takes place approximately four months after the events of 'Sleuthing With the Enemy'. The beach is where Grams brought Prue, Piper and Phoebe immediately after Patty's funeral to try to cheer them up. Prue was upset anyway, because she didn't cry at the funeral. Thus, sand and the ocean always make Prue angry. When Prue notes that Andrea had a shadow next to her, Phoebe asks if she means a Woogy (see 'Is There A Woogy in the House?'). Leo and Piper attend a Whitelighter reception at which they are given a rather ghastly (and apparently eternal) ornamental lamp. Piper subsequently breaks it. Accidentally, of course.

Quote/Unquote: Leo: 'I promise we'll be in calling distance if any demon-looking-shadowy-thingy attacks.'

Cole: 'If the demons get to you, they'll find out the way to get to me is to kill Phoebe, and I can't let that happen.' Reese: 'When you say demon ...?' Cole: 'I *don't* mean as a metaphor.'

Death: 'I've seen it so many times before. The anger, the pain. You lock up your tears and angrily steel yourself against me as if I was the ultimate evil.' Prue: 'You *are* the ultimate evil.' Death: 'I'm not good or evil, I just *am*.'

Cole: 'Inspector, you're in a room with three witches and a demon, do you really think that gun's gonna help?'

Phoebe: 'You tell a guy that Death is after him and he goes to a cemetery. How smart is that?'

Notes: 'Looks like there's a new demon in town.' A tremendously effective meditation on the Big Picture, taking in real 'eternal question' concepts. Making Death (a great performance by Simon Templeman) into a wise, if slightly haughty, civil servant with an 'It's a dirty job but someone's got to do it' attitude is quite inspired (see also 'Styx Feet Under'). So, too, is Shannen Doherty's brilliantly angry delivery. Overall, 'Death Takes a Halliwell' displays all the best qualities of *Charmed* when it's at its edgiest and most fractious.

61: PREWITCHED

22 March 2001

Writers: Chris Levinson, Zack Estrin
Director: David Straiton

Cast: Finola Hughes (Patty Halliwell), Sherri Saum (Ariel), James Sie (Shoe Salesman), Jennifer Rhodes (Penny Halliwell), W Earl Brown (Warlock), Marc Bossley (Officer)

> When a witch's familiar turns evil, the warlock that it turns into tries to have the Halliwell sisters kill it nine times. Should it succeed, it will become an immortal.

It's Witchcraft: Grams gives the sisters a helping hand, opening *The Book of Shadows* to a page entitled *How to perform a séance*. A ceremony to contact the dead. For this, they need six white and purple candles, cinnamon, frankincense and sandalwood.

The spell to vanquish Shadow begins: 'Nine times this evil's cheated death, felt no pain and kept his breath, this warlock standing in our midst, let him feel what he has missed.'

A Little Learning is a Dangerous Thing: Kit is seen hanging around the Manor long before the events of 'Something Wicca This Way Comes'. Presumably neither Piper nor Prue subsequently remembered their, admittedly brief, interaction with the cat, which they believed to be a stray when it landed on their doorstep more permanently some months later. In the meantime, it became attached to another witch – the one whom Jeremy killed in 'Something Wicca This Way Comes'.

On a similar lack-of-observation note, Piper bumps into her future husband some time prior to meeting him in 'Thank You For Not Morphing'. This suggests that the Elders were aware of the Charmed Ones' potential long before the sisters actually gained their powers.

Work is a Four-Letter Word: Prior to Grams' death, Piper worked in a bank, so the family was covered by health insurance.

It's a Designer Label: Phoebe's fetish for Prada shoes is witnessed. Also, check out Prue's miniskirt and kinky boots.

SEASON 3: PREWITCHED

References: The title refers to the 1960s US sitcom *Bewitched*. The Halliwells get the *San Francisco Chronicle* delivered. At breakfast, Phoebe is reading the business pages, Prue the sports pull-out and Leo the Metro section. Also, the traditional ballad 'I've Been Working on the Railroad'; Macey's department store; *The Avengers* (Phoebe using an umbrella as a lethal weapon); and, yet again, *Apocalypse Now* ('I love the smell of defeated witch in the evening').

'You May Remember Me ...': Sherri Saum appeared in *One Life to Live*. James Sie's movies include *Ghost World* and *Strawberry Fields*. Marc Bossley was in *Telling You*. W Earl Brown appeared in *Vanilla Sky*, *There's Something About Mary*, *Scream* and *Backdraft*.

Sex and Drugs and Rock n Roll: Leo and Piper are indulging in some naughty-shower-love when interrupted by Phoebe looking for her lip-gloss (see 'Cat House').

Logic, Let Me Introduce You to This Window: Phoebe is said to have moved to New York immediately after Grams died. Yet in 'Something Wicca This Way Comes,' she moved back to San Francisco *because* Grams died. 'PreWitched' also suggests that the events of 'Something Wicca This Way Comes' happened at least six months – and possibly longer – after Penny's death, contradicting the impression given in the first episode that it was a much more recent event. This sudden lengthening of the timescale between Grams dying and the sisters becoming witches throws up a question about Nicholas. In 'That's 70s episode,' he was said to have visited the Halliwells on the same day each year. This episode would seem to suggest that he missed a year. Kit is referred to as male by Phoebe, as it has been on previous occasions. By 'Cat House', however, he will have become a she. According to Ariel, if a familiar who has turned into a warlock fails in its attempt to become immortal, it will return to animal form forever. But when the sisters defeat him, Shadow explodes. Why didn't he turn back into a cat? Almost every time that another witch is seen on *Charmed*, they're doing various kind of wicca-y ritual stuff. Why is it that the Halliwells seem to be the only witches who lead relatively normal lives and don't spend every hour of the day chanting mantras and levitating candles? Grams makes a potion, after which Piper puts in some additional ingredients. After Piper leaves, Grams removes the potion from the pot and corks it. Wouldn't Piper's additions have automatically ruined the potion, particularly since (as Piper discovers three years later) it's a potion with such significance?

Continuity: Phoebe's criminal past is revealed – shoplifting. Tame.

SEASON 3: PREWITCHED

Sometime before Grams died, Prue and Piper shared an amazing apartment in North Beach. They subsequently moved back to the Manor when Grams first became ill, and gave up the apartment to friends with whom Piper has kept in touch. They are now moving out and will give Piper and Leo first refusal at taking over the lease. Piper bemoans the fact that she and her husband are living in a bedroom with wallpaper that she picked out when she was nine. There are several references to Slimy Roger, Prue's ex-fiancé (see 'Something Wicca This Way Comes'). There's also a reference to the time that Piper went to Hawaii (see 'The Power of Two'). Both Grams and Piper always had a fondness for double chocolate decadence cake. Indeed, who doesn't?

A Sinister Animal: A familiar that betrays its witch becomes a warlock, as Shadow does after killing Ariel.

Quote/Unquote: Phoebe: 'Life-altering plans cannot be squeezed between "Pass the newspaper" and "Who ate the Special K?"'

Cop: 'Mrs Halliwell?' Grams, looking at Phoebe: 'Can I hear what she did first before I answer that?'

Phoebe: 'I don't think I'm ever gonna be able to look at Kit in quite the same way. Or get undressed in front of him, for that matter.'

Piper: 'What's our level of confidence in this plan?' Phoebe: 'On a scale from one-to-ten, ten being we whip ass, one being he laughs at us while we're on fire and naked ...' Piper: 'Maybe you should lie to me.'

Demon: 'You've got something up your sleeve ...' Phoebe: 'Hello? Sleeveless!'

Notes: 'What's the matter, cat got your tongue?' The care and attention lavished on the *look* of the flashback sequences (if not, necessarily, the actual continuity) is the first thing to talk about here. All three sisters get haircuts and – Phoebe's sudden transformation into a *Wild Ones* style riot grrl, aside – characteristics in the style of the early episodes of season one. The story's enjoyable and effective, too, using some clever dramatic tricks to propel itself forward without resorting to any of the traditional devices to draw the audience's attention to what is a flashback and what isn't. On the minus side, the ending is somewhat weak and far too *easy* considering everything that has gone before.

62: SIN FRANCISCO

19 April 2001

Writer: Nell Scovell
Director: Joel J Fiegenbaum

Cast: Kevin Weisman (Lukas), Roark Critchlow (Robert Pike), J F Pryor (Cour), Michael Rodrick (Officer Dean), Julio Herzer (Pastor), Jim Jansen (Professor Kass), Beverly Sotelo (Female Reporter), Kimberly Wallis (News Anchor)

> The sisters encounter Lukas, a demon who attacks his victims by infecting them with one of the seven deadly sins. When the girls and Leo all become infected, they must struggle not only to vanquish the demon, but to prevent themselves from succumbing to their own secret desires.

It's Witchcraft: For once, there is no magical solution – it's the selfless acts displayed by Phoebe, Piper and Leo that cleanse them of their sins. Unfortunately for Prue, there appears to be no such thing as a selfless act when suffering from pride, so it's a combination of Leo's orbing skills and her sisters vanquishing Lukas that saves her from the bottomless pit of everlasting torment.

A Little Learning is a Dangerous Thing: When Phoebe accompanies Prue on a demon hunt, she notes that she should be at home procrastinating over her delinquent ethics paper and not chasing some wild goose. Subsequently, a lustful Phoebe attends a meeting with her ethics professor and ends up begin kicked out of class for a combination of a late paper and 'unzipping his pants with my teeth.' She turns this to her advantage, however, as she hands in a paper on sexual politics and claims that her indiscretion was an ethical experiment. She gets a B- for it and is, therefore, able to graduate.

The Conspiracy Starts at the Witching Hour: According to *The Book of Shadows*, Lukas's box contains balls of sin used to corrupt paragons of good – seven balls for seven sins and seven souls. They are able to do this because no-one – no matter how virtuous – is completely immune to sin. Infectors were once human, but were consumed by sin and are damned to spend eternity infecting others. When infected, Phoebe gets lust, Piper gluttony, Leo sloth and Prue pride.

Work is a Four-Letter Word: Prue shot a magazine cover the previous day, had a date the previous night, and this morning is searching for evil. It's difficult to have a more balanced lifestyle than that, she believes.

It's a Designer Label!: In her efforts to 'de-flannel' Leo, Piper orders him two Armani suits (size 42) and, for herself, adds a Donna Karan dress, three pairs of Stuart Weitzman shoes, a Gucci jacket and a Prada bag from Bloomingdales.

References: The movie that Leo watches whilst channel surfing is John Ford's *Fort Apache* (1948, starring John Wayne and Henry Fonda). There are references to *Cosmopolitan* (see 'She's a Man, Baby, a Man' and 'Heartbreak City'); the myth of Pandora's Box; the *Men's Fall* catalogue; MTV and presenter Carson Daily; the Biblical parable of the Good Samaritan (Luke 10); the bottomless pit (Revelation 9); 'Seek and ye shall find' (Matthew 7); and 'Pride goes before a fall' (Proverbs 16). Among the numerous items that Piper purchases is a bronze bust of William Shakespeare. The TV station carrying the breaking news of the hostage situation is KCSF Channel 8.

'You May Remember Me ...': Kevin Weisman played Marshall Finkman in *Alias* and appeared in *Roswell*, *Buffy the Vampire Slayer* and *Gone in Sixty Seconds*. Roark Critchlow was Dr Ackland in *Passions*. His CV also includes *Friends*. J F Pryor appeared in *24* and *Blown!*, the latter of which he also directed. Michael Rodrick was in *Astoria Fix* and *Another World*. Julio Herzer's movies include *Rocky IV*. Jim Jansen appeared in *Artificial Intelligence: AI*, *That's My Bush!* and *The X-Files*. Beverly Sotelo was in *Co-Incidence*. Kimberley Wallis's CV includes *Beat Boys Beat Girls*.

Cigarettes and Alcohol: Glutton-Piper has a glass of champagne along with her chocolates. Subsequently, Prue offers Piper a glass at the end of the episode. She's going to refuse, but Prue notes that it's okay to indulge, occasionally, and in moderation.

Sex and Drugs and Rock n Roll: Phoebe notes that Cole has been dodging demonic bounty hunters. He still manages to shimmer into her bedroom when he has a chance. 'Pops in and then pops right back out, if you know what I'm talking about,' she adds. Prue notes that she vaguely remembers what it's like. Phoebe says that even though she's happy to see him, the situation is starting to raise old issues. Like, does Cole really love her or is he just interested in her charms? Prue suggests that Phoebe knows for a magical fact that Cole loves her. She doesn't believe it's just about the sex. 'What if it was *really great sex?*' asks Phoebe. Prue, significantly, changes the subject. This is the first *Charmed* episode to feature condoms on-screen.

Logic, Let Me Introduce You to This Window: Watch closely the man getting hit by the bus. It appears that a cardboard figure was used. When Officer Dean is suspended by Darryl, he's told to go back to his station and turn in his weapon. Yet, when Lukas approaches Dean as he's leaving the station, Lukas removes a gun from Dean's trousers. In the Manor, Prue throws Dean into the wall and he then vanishes from the action. When Leo gets up from the bed to heal Piper, he has stubble. But when he's healing Phoebe a moment later, he's clean-shaven. (It would appear that removing his slothfulness includes giving him a free shave.) Amongst the things that Piper buys is the mannequin that Phoebe previously used when developing her martial arts skills in 'Which Prue Is It, Anyway?'. Prue receives a gunshot injury when she saves the hostage from the priest. It isn't treated, yet she seems fine for the rest of the episode. Phoebe is attacked by Dean, and Piper immediately rushes downstairs to help. Prue, who was with Piper, takes far longer to join them, giving Dean the chance to trash much of the Manor and seriously injure both sisters. The episode's timescale is rather confused – it appears to take place all in one day, or at most two. Phoebe notes that after her disastrous meeting with Professor Kass, she had time to reflect on events, write a paper about sexual politics and hand it in – all whilst still lusting after everything male that moved? To add to the confusion, the final scene appears to take place on the same day that Lukas was vanquished, judging by Prue's and Piper's conversation.

Continuity: Robert Pike, the businessman whom Lukas infected with greed, was married with two kids and worked for Briksen Investments as a – very successful – stockbroker. He was also something of a philanthropist, having hosted a fundraiser for the American Cancer Society.

Motors: When the Pastor is infected with envy, he creates a hostage situation at a local car dealership. His demand to release his prisoner is for a Jaguar. Specifically an XK convertible in British Racing Green.

Quote/Unquote: Professor: 'I'll have to give you an incomplete ... Do you have anything else to say to me?' Phoebe: 'I'm not wearing any underwear.'
    Prue, to Phoebe: 'My sin's not nearly as much fun as yours.'

Notes: 'Do you have any idea how important that box is?' A riotous amalgamation of disparate elements that somehow works against type and actually becomes a very sincere and heartfelt essay on indulgence and pride. There no such thing as original sin (except, possibly, poking a badger with a spoon), and one wouldn't have believed there could be an original story *about* sin, but that is proved wrong here. 'Sin Francisco' is joy to watch, because it treats the subject matter with humour and with emotion simultaneously.

Soundtrack: Orgy ('Interesting band,' according to Prue) perform 'Opticon' at P^3.

63: THE DEMON WHO CAME IN FROM THE COLD

6 April 2001

Writer: Sheryl J Anderson
Director: Anson Williams

Cast: Jennifer Tung (Klea), Ian Buchanan (Raynor), Gregory Scott Cummins (Vornac), Joseph Reitman (Tarkin), Barry Cutler (Prophet), Rocky McMurray (Chauffeur), Rob Steinberg (Pirelli)

> When Phoebe kills a prophet-murdering demon she learns that the creature was one of Cole's colleagues. Cole explains that he was hand picked by the Source to be in an elite demonic cabal called the Brotherhood of the Thorn. Cole poses as Belthazor in order to infiltrate an Internet company run by his old friends.

It's Witchcraft: Prue fashions the potion that ultimately destroys several of the Brotherhood from the piece of Belthazor flesh cut from him in 'Power Outage' (see also 'Sleuthing With The Enemy'), which she has kept in the Halliwells' freezer (much to Piper's disgust) for just such a situation.

A Little Learning is a Dangerous Thing: Piper wonders why demons would want to kill a crazy old street preacher. Cole notes that not all street people *are* crazy, or even human. Some of them are magical seers. However, they're frequently loud, dirty and smelly, so most people ignore them.

The Conspiracy Starts at the Witching Hour: The Brotherhood of the Thorn's members include the often-mentioned-but-little-seen Raynor; Vornac (who once saved Cole's life); the sinister Klea; the more likeable Tarkin; and Trigs, whom Phoebe kills in the pre-title sequence.

Merger talks between two multimedia giants, Lokseron and Meta-Satellite, have recently faltered after Frank Pirelli, the owner of Lokseron, came out against such a deal. The Brotherhood, however, are keen for the merger to happen, and, Cole believes, this explains why they have taken over an investment banking firm. The best way for evil to get a foothold in the human world is to take over their businesses.

SEASON 3: THE DEMON WHO CAME IN FROM THE COLD

References: The title alludes to John LeCarré's seminal Cold War spy novel *The Spy Who Came In From The Cold* (filmed in 1965, starring Richard Burton and Claire Bloom). KCSF Channel 8 (see 'Sin Francisco') seems to be the station of choice when it comes to news in the Halliwell house. There's a fabulous watercolour by Joseph Mallord Turner (1775-1851) visible on Pirelli's office wall. Cole alludes to the Biblical verse I Timothy 6:12 ('Fight the good fight'). The girls had planned to see Liv Ullmann's *Faithless* at the Avalon Theatre. However, Leo seems to have an intellectual block when it comes to foreign language films and, with Piper sycophantically voting with him and Phoebe opting for an evening of passion with Cole instead, Prue is forced to see a (nameless) thriller. Also referred to is Ben and Jerry's ice cream.

'You May Remember Me ...': Jennifer Tung's CV includes *What Lies Beneath*, *Star Trek: Insurrection* and *Alias*. Ian Buchanan was in *Panic Room*, *Double Exposure* and *Twin Peaks*. Gregory Scott Cummins appeared in *The Italian Job*, *Cahoots*, *Cliffhanger* and *Caged Fury*. Joseph Reitman's movies include *Clueless* and *Jay and Silent Bob Strike Back*. Barry Cutler was in *Deuce Bigalow: Male Gigolo* and *Superboy*. Rocky McMurray appeared in *The West Wing*. Rob Steinberg was in *Die Hard 2*, *Pacific Blue* and *Bikini Squad*.

Quote/Unquote: Phoebe: 'The prophet that I was trying to save was talking about Lokseron.' Piper: 'The Internet provider? What, demons want their own website now?'

Notes: 'You just vanquished my brother.' A very odd episode – structurally, it's all over the place. There are two main plot-strands: The Cole undercover stuff, focusing on the complex world of internal demon politics, is terrific and adds cunning layers to the series' lore. Unfortunately, the Charmed Ones themselves have a real off-week here, with Piper at her most disagreeable and annoying (her constant bitching about Cole, to whom she's always been more ambivalent than hostile, is massively out-of-character), Phoebe being as wet as the Atlantic and Prue having hardly anything to do. That's a shame as, visually and conceptually, this is a worthy attempt at doing something with a bit more depth than usual.

Soundtrack: 'Planets of the Universe' by Stevie Nicks, and Poe's 'Hey Pretty'.

64: EXIT STRATEGY

3 May 2001

Teleplay: Peter Hume, Daniel Cerone
Story: Peter Hume
Director: Joel J Feigenbaum

Cast: Michael Bailey Smith (Belthazor), Rachel Luttrell (Janna), Amy Moon (Leeza), Ian Buchanan (Raynor), Joseph Reitman (Tarkin)

> After learning of Cole's deception, Raynor decides to set him up to lose the one thing keeping him from realising his evil potential – Phoebe's love. Cole is instructed to steal a pair of protection amulets from two different witches. Even though Cole informs Phoebe of Raynor's plan and his belief that Raynor has learned of Cole's betrayal to the Brotherhood, Cole still finds himself tempted to revert to his demonic side.

It's Witchcraft: Janna helps the sisters create the potion to remove Cole's powers. She notes that Piper should shake the water vigorously for 200 heartbeats and then add a pinch of dandelion and a dash of chickweed. Prue observes that Piper is using bottled water. Piper suggests that, for Cole, the purer the better.

The amulet that Raynor sends Cole to recover is, in fact, one half of an ancient charm. Whoever connects the two amulets together become invincible. The amulets were divided between two local covens for safe keeping, but the bearers have always been kept secret.

A Little Learning is a Dangerous Thing: Cole says that he doesn't trust anyone. Tarkin notes that he never did, and adds that this is what made Belthazor so great – no allegiances, no conscience and no hesitation.

Not many demons are strong enough to survive being hit by an energy ball (but Belthazor, when at full power, would appear to be one of them).

The Conspiracy Starts at the Witching Hour: Raynor notes that during his dalliance with Phoebe, Cole has acquired the knowledge of how to kill the Charmed Ones, something that no other demon has been able to accomplish. That, along with his power, makes Belthazor a very precious commodity within the demon community, and one that is definitely worthy of saving.

Raynor has an orb that contains Cole's father's soul, which he uses as leverage to get Cole to steal the amulets. At the episode's end, Cole regains this, and kills Raynor, thus – much to Cole's distress – completing his mentor's over-complicated (if seemingly effective) plan to turn Belthazor back to the dark-side.

References: There are allusions to Aimee Mann's 'Save Me'; the Ten Commandments; and *Carrie*.

'You May Remember Me ...': Rachel Luttrell subsequently played Teyla in *Stargate: Atlantis* and appeared in *Joe's So Mean To Josephine* and *Forever Knight*. Amy Moon played Vervea in *Undressed* and was in *The Shield*.

Sex and Drugs and Rock n Roll: Several Phoebe/Cole scenes feature much kissing-with-tongues.

Logic, Let Me Introduce You to This Window: As Leo and Piper plan to go to France, Leo is learning French. In 'Siren Song', when he and Piper have their powers switched, Leo notes that Whitelighters can speak whatever language their charges speak. And, as we subsequently discover, one of his charges is a French witch who lives in Paris. He also mispronounces *Les Champs Elysée* (although that is possibly a deliberately scripted error). Leo's birth certificate shows he was born in 1924. As he died in 1942 (see 'Saving Private Leo'), that would mean he was 18 at the time of his death. Presuming that he hasn't aged since, he looks much older than 18. In 'Love Hurts', Leo noted that he left medical school to go to war. That should have meant he spent a few years in college before qualifying for medical school. Despite Piper faking the date on his birth certificate, he gets a passport immediately. It usually takes weeks. After Piper blows up the watermelon in the kitchen, keep your eye on Phoebe. The towel that she's holding moves position several times. Demon blood is said to be black (or sometimes green – see 'All Halliwell's Eve'), so unless Raynor is half-human like Cole, he should have bled black when Cole stabbed him. Prue falls on her side with her back facing Piper when Piper blows up a cabinet. In the next shot, she's lying on her stomach.

Continuity: It is 'over a week' since the events of the previous episode occurred. Dan is mentioned – along with the dossier of incriminating information he gave Piper concerning Leo. Leo 'vaguely' remembers Dan as the guy with perfect hair and a cleft chin who tried to steal Piper away from him. Enraged by – frankly – the gosh-awful stress of not being able to get her own way all the time, Piper suddenly develops a new (and uncontrollable) power; the ability to blow things up with her hands. Leo, after consulting with the Elders, notes that far from being 'wonky', her powers are, in fact, advancing. Piper's powers work, he adds, by slowing down molecules. Apparently now she can speed them up as well. Raynor is the head of the Brotherhood of the Thorn (see 'The Demon Who Came in From the Cold'), was Cole's mentor and taught the young Belthazor everything he knew. He has the power to read thoughts.

Quote/Unquote: Phoebe, to Piper: 'Honey, why did you vanquish watermelon?' And: 'Slowly put your hands down and no-one will get hurt.'

Piper: 'Phoebe, it's a huge deal. Cole tried to kill you.' Prue, to Janna: 'He's the demon.' Piper: '… And her boyfriend.' Phoebe: 'We have *very* complicated lives.'

Prue: 'You look like hell.' Cole: 'You have *no* idea.'

Notes: 'Cole knows what he's doing. You don't make demon of the century without having a few tricks up your sleeve.' The opening shot of a spider's web gives the viewer an idea of the forthcoming episode's intricate structure. 'Exit Strategy' features plenty of clever moments. Unfortunately a combination of Raynor's extremely convoluted plan to make Phoebe stop trusting Cole (which meanders all over the place before some resolution) and Piper's - by now, downright unpleasant - characterisation conspire to keep the episode from greatness. Did the producers really think that introducing a 'Piper's Moan of the Week' into every single episode around this period was such a good idea? It's an incredible tribute to Holly Marie Combs that she survives being turned into such a shrewish and scolding cipher and emerges, in season four, as one of *Charmed*'s biggest assets. Because you genuinely wouldn't believe that from the evidence of this episode.

Did You Know?: This was the lowest-rated first run episode of the series, probably due to CBS airing the two hour finale of *Survivor: The Australian Outback* against *Charmed*.

65: LOOK WHO'S BARKING

10 May 2001

Teleplay: Curtis Kheel, Monica Breen, Alison Schapker
Story: Curtis Kheel
Director: John Behring

Cast: Matt Battaglia (Journalist), Michael Bailey Smith (Belthazor), Joe E Tata (Inspector), Newell Alexander (Widower), Eric Castro (Man), Dianna Miranda (Woman), Jack Orend (Alchemist Demon), Ashley Tisdale (Runaway Teen), Dorenda Moore (Banshee)

> When Phoebe has a vision of an innocent being killed, she believes that Cole is the one responsible. Meanwhile, as Cole seeks the help of an alchemist to make himself immune to the potion the Charmed Ones have created to destroy him, Piper continues to struggle with her new power. The girls soon learn that a Banshee is actually responsible for the murder. But when they cast a spell to track the creature, it has an unwanted side-effect – turning Prue into a dog.

It's Witchcraft: Phoebe refers to using the 'magic to magic spell' to summon Cole and vanquish him but, as she subsequently discovers, there is a specific spell to summon Belthazor in *The Book of Shadows* ('Magic forces black and white, reaching out through space and light, be he far or be he near, bring us the demon Belthazor here'). The spell to track the Banshee begins, 'The piercing cry that feeds on pain, and leaves more sorrow than a gain, shall now be heard by one who seeks, to stop the havoc that it wreaks.'

Denial, Thy Name is Phoebe: Piper suggests that her sister is not the first Halliwell to fall in love with a demon and get burned (see, for example, 'Something Wicca This Way Comes'). Piper says that she knows how much it hurts but, she believes, Phoebe is in denial.

Denial, Thy Name is Piper: When Leo tells Piper that she will find a way to help her sisters, Piper doesn't believe she can. Prue and Phoebe are the super-witches, she notes. Piper herself just tags along and freezes things. And now she can't even do *that* right.

A Little Learning is a Dangerous Thing: A Banshee is a demon who feeds on souls in great pain. They hunt for victims using a high pitched call, something beyond the human hearing range, and find them by hearing an inner cry and zeroing in on the waves of pain that emanate from the stricken. Their call turns into a scream that kills. There is no spell to vanquish Banshees, but there is one to track them. The Elders subsequently inform Leo that Banshees are actually former witches, and that their scream doesn't kill witches, it turns them into Banshees.

The Conspiracy Starts at the Witching Hour: Cole explains to Phoebe that Raynor cast a spell to make Cole kill Janna against his will (see 'Exit Strategy'). He did this, Cole continues, because he wanted to turn Cole, and he knew that the only way to do that was to destroy the one thing that was keeping Cole good – he knew that Cole killing a witch would destroy Phoebe's faith in him.

References: The title alludes to Amy Heckerling's popular, if appallingly twee, movie *Look Who's Talking*. Two newspaper headlines on prominent display are: RESIDENTS HOWL OVER DOGS BARKING and MAN'S MURDER BAFFLES POLICE. Also, references to *Cujo*; *Lethal Weapon*; Baha Men's 'Who Let The Dogs Out?'; and controversial radio talkshow host Dr Laura Schlessinger. Phoebe paraphrases Tennyson's *In Memorium* (see 'Heartbreak City').

'You May Remember Me ...': Matt Battaglia appeared in *Raven*, *Joshua Tree* and *Showgirls*. Joe E Tata's CV includes *Beverly Hills 90210*, *Hollywood Wives* and *The Rockford Files*. Newell Alexander appeared in *Sordid Lives*, *Fire Down Below* and *Wonder Woman*. Eric Castro was in *Classified Love*. Dianna Miranda's movies include *Kiss the Girls* and *Truuco's Daughter*. Jack Orend appeared in *Casino*, *Big Shots* and *Knot's Landing*. Ashley Tisdale was in *Donnie Darko*. Dorenda Moore's CV includes *The Covent* and *Enterprise*.

Cigarettes and Alcohol: Canine-Prue likes imported beer.

Logic, Let Me Introduce You to This Window: One of the dogs used for canine-Prue is very definitely male. Massively so. Why are the 'Banshee' and the 'Track a Banshee' pages separated by the 'Summon Belthazor' spell in *The Book of Shadows*? Surely they should be together as they relate to the same demon? Why is Piper so worried about blowing up Leo? He is, after all, already dead, a point she subsequently makes herself. If Piper's freezing power doesn't affect her sisters then why should her new one? After Piper blows up her tape deck, the machine appears in a subsequent shot to be undamaged. When Phoebe is writing about Cole's demon side, she is moving the pen, but it's clearly not making contact with the book.

SEASON 3: LOOK WHO'S BARKING

Continuity: On the blank page of *The Book of Shadows* opposite the information about Belthazor, Phoebe sticks in some photographs of Cole and writes a lengthy pen picture about his human side, including the information that 'Cole likes walks in the park, jazz and fine wine,' and that he is ticklish. Prue believed that Piper was getting a handle on her new powers (see 'Exit Strategy'). Phoebe notes that this was before her new powers got a handle on her. In the attic, Piper accidentally blows up Grams' sewing machine.

Cruelty to Animals: Canine-Prue chases after Kit in the Manor. The dog is subsequently hit by a car but rescued by a hunky, dog-loving journalist.

Quote/Unquote: Prue, to Phoebe: 'I'd forget about my love life if I were you. Lately, mine's been rated PG.'
Piper: 'Why did the spell backfire?' Leo: 'I don't think it did.' Piper: '… Prue is walking around on all fours and barking. If that's not a backfire, what *is*?'
Phoebe: 'She's a pretty dog.' Piper: 'What else did you expect?' Leo: 'A Doberman?'
Piper, to Leo: 'Could you give me all the bad news at once? Do you have to keep doling it out for dramatic effect?'
Leo: 'Are you okay?' Piper: 'Prue is a dog and Phoebe is a Banshee. I am not even in the *vicinity* of okay.'

Notes: 'I think you're barking up the wrong demon.' Beginning with a genuinely disturbing pre-title sequence, 'Look Who's Barking' straddles two very different dramatic avenues with a confidence that spills over into the tone and structure of the episode itself. In short, parts of it are really shocking and scary, parts are wee-your-pants funny – and, often, there's little stop-over between the two. Despite the brilliant comedy moments surrounding Prue's life as a dog, the key element in the episode is, as the song says, 'Everybody Hurts'. Stories of back-stage tension during filming merely add to the episode's aura of greatness.

Soundtrack: The Corrs' 'Give Me a Reason' and 'Breathless'.

Did You Know?: Numerous media sources, including an official WB press release, claimed that Fleetwood Mac singer Stevie Nicks was to guest star in this episode. She didn't.

66: ALL HELL BREAKS LOOSE

17 May 2001

Writer: Brad Kern
Director: Shannen Doherty

Cast: Michael Bailey Smith (Shax/The Source), Rebekah Louise Smith (Female Classmate), Margaret Easley (News Director), Matt Malloy (Dr Griffiths), Mercedes Colón (Elana Dominguez), Marianna Elliot (Alice), Tommy Hicks (Captain), Joe O'Connor (News Editor), Mark Bennington (Cameraman), Lee Spencer (Lawyer), Joe Torrenueva (Reporter #1), John Torbett (Reporter #2), Gary Lane (Bystander at Hospital)[45], Larry Lane (Bystander at Hospital)[46]

> Whilst trying to protect a surgeon from Shax, a demonic assassin, Prue and Piper are filmed by television news using their powers. Meanwhile, Phoebe travels to the underworld in attempting to reverse the spell that turned Cole back to the Dark Side. With their powers secret no longer, Leo argues that Prue, Piper and Phoebe must convince Tempus to turn back time. And, as a consequence, Phoebe must make a deal with the Source to save her sisters' lives.

It's Witchcraft: Shax is the Source's assassin. He can be vanquished with a spell that begins: 'Evil wind that blows, that which forms below, no longer may you dwell, death takes you with this spell.'
Phoebe is still looking for a way to reverse the effects of the spell that Raynor cast on Cole (see 'Exit Strategy'). To this end she has prepared a potion that is, at least partially, successful (in so much as it stops Cole from choking her and makes him kiss her instead).

A Little Learning is a Dangerous Thing: When Leo suggests getting Tempus to reverse time, Prue notes that they vanquished him (see 'Déjà Vu All Over Again'). Leo replies: 'No, you defeated him, you didn't vanquish him.'

The Conspiracy Starts at the Witching Hour: Cole argues that he couldn't summon Tempus even if he wanted to, as he simply doesn't have that kind

---

[45] Uncredited.
[46] Uncredited.

of power. But you know somebody who does, notes Phoebe. Cole is incredulous at the suggestion that he ask the Source to help witches. However, Leo adds that such an intervention doesn't just help witches – the demonic world has been exposed too. Resetting time solves everybody's problem.

The Source tells Cole that Tempus's powers are still weakened from when he last turned back time. Doing so again will destroy him. Nevertheless, he offers Cole a deal to put to Phoebe: if she joins the Dark Side, the Source will have Tempus do as requested. Cole notes that she is unlikely to accept such a deal. 'Not even to save one of her sisters' lives?' asks the Source.

Phoebe accepts the offer, with a single condition – that Cole warn Prue and Piper before the Shax attacks them. Cole is seemingly unable to do this. The Source tells one of his henchmen that, once he has reset time, Cole should be detained and Phoebe killed. Seemingly, however, this doesn't happen (see 'Charmed Again' Part 1).

References: Allusions to NASA and to talk-show hosts Oprah Winfrey and Barbara Walters. And, once again, it's KCSF Channel 8, seemingly the *only* TV station that the Halliwells are allowed to watch.

'You May Remember Me ...': Rebekah Louise Smith appeared in *Straight Right* and *Early Edition*. Margaret Easley was in *Slackers* and *Gilmore Girls*. Matt Mallory's CV includes *Drop Dead Gorgeous*, *Elephant*, *Armageddon* and *Law & Order*. Mercedes Colon was in *JAG*. Marianna Elliott appeared in *Chicago Hope*. Tommy Hick's movies include *The Glass Shield* and *She's Got To Have It*. Joe O'Connor played Marshall Darling in *Clarissa Explains it All*. Lee Spencer was in *Notto* and *Matlock*. Joe Torrenueva appeared in *Melrose Place*. Mark Bennington played Kevin in *And Then Came Summer*.

Logic, Let Me Introduce You to This Window: How did the police – and Darryl especially – fail to notice Alice standing with the rifle on the roof of her minivan? Aren't the Special Forces team a tad slow in making any move when Prue seals the room with a stick between the door handles? When the Special Forces team are lining up their shoot at Prue, she is standing towards them. However, when the camera switches angle to inside the room, she is facing the side wall. Prue initially says that they're not sure who the demon is. Yet later in the same scene, she's confidently stating that it's Shax. When Piper was shot, the bullet should also have hit Prue (probably in the thigh) if Dr Griffiths' comments about an exit wound in her abdomen are accurate. When Piper is shot, look carefully at Shannen Doherty's hands – they're already tinged red. Clearly, this was a second take of the scene and they hadn't had time to wash all the fake blood off from the first. Prue still has blood on her hands when she tends to Piper's wound. When she gets into the car, however, there in no blood visible.

Continuity: It's possible that the Cleaners (see 'Forget Me ... Not') were created in direct response to Prue's, Piper's and Phoebe's exposure in this episode, in order to prevent something like this from happening again. When the Halliwells are outed, one television network interviews Suzie Johnson, who was in Prue's class in 10th Grade. She alleges that the sisters were always a little strange and that Prue once cast a spell to make Suzie's boyfriend break up with her. Piper jokingly notes that she'd had her suspicions about this for some time. In the initial timeline, Piper is shot and killed by a jealous wiccan wannabe, Alice. In the revised timeline, both Prue and Piper are seriously injured (and Dr Griffiths is killed) when Shax attacks them.

Quote/Unquote: Piper, to Prue: 'I think you're being paranoid. We kicked Shax's ass. We bad.'

Piper: 'Look at all these interview requests we're getting. Ted Koppel, *Time* Magazine, Jerry Springer ... *Sports Illustrated*?' Darryl: 'They probably want you for the swimsuit edition.'

Prue: 'If Leo doesn't succeed, we're gonna have to figure out what we're gonna do.' Piper: 'We're gonna do talk-shows and book signings and movie deals. And then get taken by the CIA and dissected.'

Dr Griffiths: 'What are you?' Shax: 'The end.'

Notes: 'Your secret is safe with me.' A truly apocalyptic end to the season, with one of television's finest ever cliff-hangers. Early in the episode, Prue notes that this whole year has been a series of tests for the sisters and that these events are, merely, the latest. That's an interesting textual acknowledgement of the changes and advances made during the season. *Charmed*, more than ever before, had the confidence to do outrageous conceits such as this and get away with them. The presentation of the media circus surrounding the revelation of the Halliwells' powers, and the blood-soaked carnage of Piper's shooting, are the kind of things that, even a year earlier, would have been unthinkable. Full of glorious moments (the reverse-time-effects; Prue losing her patience with the media to devastating effect; the Source telling his henchman to kill Phoebe), 'All Hell Breaks Loose' is a fittingly grave and funereal piece to mark the end of a significant chapter in the life of this series. The future, it seemed, would be in another direction entirely.

This was Shannen Doherty's final episode of *Charmed*, and she left the production during the summer. Several reasons have since been mooted for her departure. Readers are invited to watch the last seven or so episodes of this season and notice how astonishingly few scenes feature Doherty and Alyssa Milano in the same shot. Just an observation.

Soundtrack: Depeche Mode's 'Dream On'.

Did You Know?: In June 2001, Aaron Spelling announced, after several auditions had been carried out and many actresses considered (including Jennifer Love Hewitt, Sarah Brown, Tiffani Thiessen, Soleil Moon Frye, Susan Ward and Eliza Dushku), that Rose McGowan had won the role of Paige Matthews, a long-lost, never-previously-mentioned half-sister and replacement for Prue.

CHARMED SEASON 4 (2001-2002)

Consulting Producers: James L Conway, Jonathan Levin
Co-Executive Producer: Nell Scovell
Producer: Jon Paré
Executive Producers: Brad Kern, Aaron Spelling, E Duke Vincent
Co-Producers: Peter Chomsky, Daniel Cerone
Executive Consultant: Constance M Burge
Executive Story Editor: Krista Veraoff

Regular Cast:
Holly Marie Combs (Piper Halliwell)
Alyssa Milano (Phoebe Halliwell)
Rose McGowan (Paige Matthews)
Dorian Gregory (Darryl Morris, 67-68, 74, 76, 79, 81, 87-88)
Brian Krause (Leo Wyatt)
Julian McMahon (Cole Turner, 67-70, 73-76, 78-88)[47]

---

[47] Julian McMahon appeared in 'Womb Raider' only in voice-over.

67: CHARMED AGAIN PART 1

4 October 2001[48]

Writer: Brad Kern
Director: Michael Schultz

Cast: James Read (Victor Bennett), Jennifer Rhodes (Penny Halliwell), Jordan Bridges (Shane), Krista Allen (The Oracle), Finola Hughes (Patty Halliwell), Michael Bailey Smith (Shax), Yancey Arias (Inspector Cortez), Andi Carnick (Priestess), Ben Guillory (The Source), David Reivers (Bob Cowan)

> Mourning the death of Prue, Piper and Phoebe must also come to terms with the loss of the Power of Three. However, the Source discovers an unknown sister – the daughter of Patty and her Whitelighter, Sam. Paige – the youngest Halliwell (who has the ability to teleport herself and other objects at will) – can reunite the sisters' strength as witches, if she lives long enough to meet them.

It's Witchcraft: Phoebe says that she and Piper have tried every magical way to bring Prue back but that none have worked. Leo, apparently, arrived back from the underworld seconds after the previous episode ended. He was able to heal Piper, but not Prue, something that Piper feels deeply guilty – and not a little angry – about.

The spell to call a lost witch begins, 'Hear now the words of the witches, the secrets we hid in the night. The oldest of Gods are invoked here, the great magic is sought.' It concludes, 'Blood to blood, I summon thee. Blood to blood, return to me.'

When Piper tries to summon Prue across the Great Divide, she gets Grams instead (complete with a new haircut). Piper asks why Grams didn't come sooner – she did, after all, call for her when Prue died. Grams says that she was busy. She and Patty have been helping Prue through the trauma of her death and transfer to the afterlife. Piper asks if Prue is okay. Grams, however, isn't allowed to tell Piper this, just as Piper isn't allowed to see Prue – at least, not for a while. Seeing Prue's ghost and speaking to her would keep Prue alive for Piper which, as a consequence, would stop

---

[48] This episode was originally scheduled for broadcast on 27 September 2001. It was postponed as part of numerous network changes that resulted from the terrorist attacks on the New York World Trade Centre and the Pentagon on 11 September.

SEASON 4: CHARMED AGAIN PART 1

Piper from being able to move on with her life and continue with her destiny.

A Little Learning is a Dangerous Thing: Piper notes that Grams was a lousy liar when she was alive and, since she died, she's got worse.

The Conspiracy Starts at the Witching Hour: The Source has got every demonic bounty hunter looking for Cole. Saving Phoebe, he suggests, makes him a traitor. The Source can see into the future via the beautiful, but deadly, Oracle.

It's a Designer Label!: Paige's denim miniskirt and, later, her red dress and brown boots.

References: There are allusions to Shakespeare's *Macbeth* and to the Book of Genesis ('Apples don't fall far from the forbidden tree, I see'). Paige has a Garfield the Cat toy at her work station.

'You May Remember Me ...': Jordan Bridges was in *Dawson's Creek*. Krista Allen played Jenna Avid in *Baywatch* and appeared in *CSI* and *Anger Management*. Yancey Arias's CV includes *Dead Men Can't Dance* and *The Sopranos*. Andi Carrick was in *Fight Club*. Ben Guillory appeared in *Star Trek: Deep Space Nine*, *The Color Purple* and *Midnight Blue*. David Reivers was in *Malcolm X* and *Roswell*.

Behind the Camera: Rose McGowan's stunt double, Melissa Barker, also doubled for Sarah Michelle Gellar on *Buffy the Vampire Slayer* and *Scooby-Doo* and worked on *24* and *Alias*. She actually went to school with Shannen Doherty.

Cigarettes and Alcohol: In P^3, Shane orders two bottles of beer. Paige asks the waitress to make hers a mineral water. She says that she doesn't drink. She used to have lot of problems including heavy drinking, but that is all behind her now.

Sex and Drugs and Rock n Roll: Seemingly in reference to her sexual activities, Paige tells her rather wet boyfriend, Shane, that she likes an element of danger. They have been dating for a month.

Logic, Let Me Introduce You to This Window: Prue's – Wiccan – funeral appears to be taking place in a mausoleum full of Christian iconography. Didn't any of her daughters – particularly Prue, who would have been around seven at the time – notice that Patty was pregnant with Paige? In the attic, Cole has a sticking plaster on his left middle finger, but in the next shot, it's vanished. Why, anyway, would an upper-level demon such as Cole be bothered by a cut finger? In 'All Hell Breaks Loose', the Source had a red outfit. Here, he's swapped that for a – more demonstrably evil – black robe. Shane dances like someone with two broken legs trying to walk in a straight line. It remains unexplained exactly why the Source wanted Dr Griffiths dead so badly that he sent Shax after him. Do they have hairdressers in heaven?

Continuity: Prue's newspaper obituary that Paige reads says: 'Funeral Service will be held today at Memorial Cemetery, 11:00 am. Prue Halliwell, born October 28 1970 in San Francisco, died Thursday. She is preceded in death by her mother Patricia and her grandmother Penelope Halliwell. And survived by her two younger sisters, Piper and Phoebe Halliwell, and her father Victor Bennett. Prue graduated with honours from Gold State University. After working as an antiques appraiser at Buckland's Auction House, her love of photography ...' Piper reminds Phoebe that they have all cheated death before. Phoebe usually hates cleaning. Paige tells Shane that she was adopted as a baby and her adoptive parents are dead (see 'A Paige from the Past'). She has been unable to discover the identity of her birth-mother, who left her at a church. She believed that she might be related to the Halliwell sisters but, upon discovering that their mother died a long time previously, she discounted that theory. In reality, after Victor's and Patty's divorce, Patty became pregnant by her Whitelighter, Sam (see 'P^3 H^{2}0'), which explains Paige's ability, as a half-Whitelighter, to orb.

Quote/Unquote: Phoebe: 'We'd better get some rest. Prue will never forgive us if we look bad at her funeral.'

Grams: 'How are you?' Piper: 'Are you kidding? Do you guys not get the news up there?'

Grams, to Cortez: 'Well done, you found us out. Now what are you gonna do – shoot us?'

Cole: '... And I thought *my* family was screwed up.'

Paige: 'My name is Paige.' Phoebe: 'Another P, imagine that!'

Notes: 'Our destiny is to die.' Oh, Rose McGowan! Okay, this is the point at which this book turns into a slobbering fanboy rant. Sorry in advance, but it's a necessary qualification. When Paige says 'I like an element of danger', you can sense the writers making a deliberate policy statement within the series' format. *Charmed* had been a lot of things before Rose's arrival, and many of them were excellent. One thing it had *never* been, however, not even remotely, was dangerous. With one casting move, that situation changed forever. What we have here is a pilot episode for

SEASON 4: CHARMED AGAIN PART 1

Charmed Mark II, a show about a *really* dysfunctional family.

Soundtrack: 'I Miss You' by Stevie Nicks, 'Bell, Book and Candle' by Eddie Reader and 'Breakdown' by Tantric.

Did You Know?: The traditional *Charmed* title sequence did not appear when this episode first aired, as a two-hour special along with part two. Instead, the main cast was included as part of the secondary credits. Before the episode began, an overview of the series was presented in which Prue was, effectively, airbrushed from history. A clip from 'Just Harried' showed a brief shot of the back of Shannen Doherty's head, whilst Cole's first meeting with Phoebe (from 'The Honeymoon's Over') featured Doherty's face (seen over Phoebe's shoulder) digitally blurred.

68: CHARMED AGAIN PART 2

4 October 2001

Writer: Brad Kern
Director: Mel Damski

Cast: Jordan Bridges (Shane), Finola Hughes (Patty Halliwell), Krista Allen (The Oracle), Wendy Phillips (Sister Agnes), Yancey Arias (Inspector Cortez), Ben Guillory (The Source), Kim Little (Carol), Ben Parrillo (Jake), David Reivers (Bob Cowan), Michael Bailey Smith (Belthazor), Tish Daniels (Receptionist), Bobby Preston (Little Boy), Joe Goddard (Kind Man)

> With the Power of Three restored, the Source decides to use an ancient agreement that leaves 48 hours for a new witch to decide, of her own free will, whether to use her powers for good or for evil. The Source possesses Paige's boyfriend, Shane, in an attempt to trick her into using her power for evil and thus prevent the Halliwells from becoming the Charmed Ones again.

It's Witchcraft: Piper and Phoebe use an Enchantment spell to make a pair of Phoebe's shades into demon detectors. This begins: 'Magic forces far and wide, enchant these so those can't hide, allow this witch to use therein, so she can reveal the evil within.'

A Little Learning is a Dangerous Thing: When Cole found Inspector Cortez in Timbuktu he took him to a place where Cortez cannot tell a soul what he saw. This turns out to be a very narrow ledge over what appears to be a bottomless pit. Leo subsequently rescues the ungrateful policeman, who still places the Halliwells under surveillance. Cortez finally sees the light when Leo saves him from a nasty wound caused by the Source.

The Oracle tells the Source that seeing into the future is not always an exact science, especially when magical forces are involved.

Cole notes that Gargoyles are statues only in their resting state. They come alive to ward off evil.

The Conspiracy Starts at the Witching Hour: Cole suggests that demons can sense the Source's aura. The Source tells the Oracle that the Power of Three is strong and that Paige will be almost untouchable when she is united with her new sisters. The Oracle notes that this will be so once the bond is formed, but that has yet to happen, which means she's vulnerable and easily swayed. She refers to the window of opportunity, agreed to aeons ago by both sides to protect free will, and describes it as 'the great flaw in the grand design.'

Leo subsequently realises that the Source is trying to lure Paige to his side rather than kill her. There is, he notes, 48 hours during which a nascent witch who hasn't chosen to use her powers for good or evil yet can be swayed either way. Cole explains it has to be the witch's choice, but that the Source can tempt her. If the Source gets the witch to use her powers for evil, she becomes evil forever. 'Who makes up these cockamamie rules?' asks an anguished Piper.

The source has the ability to disguise itself as anyone it chooses – for instance, here it assumes the form of Paige's boyfriend, Shane, and the (incorrectly) suspected abusive father Jake Gristani.

Work is a Four-Letter Word: Paige works at South Bay Social Services as an assistant. She wants to be a social worker.

References: There are oblique allusions to *Live and Let Die* (the Source's conversation with the Oracle over the complexities of seeing the future); *The Last Temptation of Christ*; and *The Exorcist*.

'You May Remember Me …': Tish Daniels played Angie in *Ticker*. Wendy Phillips was Lisa Hull in *The Stand* and appeared in *Bugsy*, *Falcon Crest* and *CHiPs*. Kim Little's CV includes *The Hit*, *Wildflower*, *Rock and Roll Fantasy* and *Diagnosis Murder*. Ben Parrillo appeared in *Dragonfly* and *Captain Jack*. Bobby Preston was in *The Hunted*.

Cigarettes and Alcohol: In P^3, Cole has a cocktail (possibly a Martini), whilst Leo drinks a bottle of beer.

Logic, Let Me Introduce You To This Window: The South Bay Social Services building looks a lot like the dating service building from 'She's a Man, Baby, a Man.' When Piper freezes Cole in order to stop his wound worsening, in different shots – despite being frozen – his hand changes position; one moment it's on Phoebe's arm, then it's on the ground. Seemingly Piper has conquered her fear of blood (see 'The Witch is Back'). The Oracle claims there's a 48 hour-window after a witch discovers her powers. Why wasn't this pointed out to Prue, Piper and Phoebe in 'Something Wicca This Way Comes'? In that episode, for example, Prue used her powers to pull a series of naughty tricks on her ex-boyfriend, Roger, including tightening his tie to the point of choking him. That's not a terribly good deed, even if he *was* a complete slimeball. If the 48-hour rule applied then, shouldn't Prue have become an evil – or, at least, amoral – witch? There's also a question that Phoebe asks within the episode itself; how's it possible for Leo to be knocked unconscious? He's dead, after all. And Patty's sudden change from a non-corporeal ghost to a corporeal one remains unexplained. (In 'Just Harried,' it was suggested that this can happen *only* courtesy of the Elders.)

Continuity: Paige can't cook very well. She has an Uncle Dave, and an Aunt Julie who has a bad hip. Her adoptive family appear to have raised her as a Catholic. Patty and Sam delivered her to Sister Agnes on 2 August 1977, shortly after her birth. Phoebe once borrowed Prue's leather jacket and her boyfriend's cat peed on it. Prue got so mad, Phoebe thought she was going to have a stroke. However, she took out her anger on an completely innocent Piper, who never told Prue the truth, much to Phoebe's distress. Whitelighters can combine their healing powers by holding hands, and in that way have enough power to heal even demons (at least, half-human ones).

Cruelty to Animals: Paige has a pet budgie named Oscar, which the Source destroys.

Motors: Phoebe's new Royal Blue Cherokee Grand (4TZE 631) is briefly glimpsed.

Quote/Unquote: Piper: 'I think the more important question is how does a Whitelighter knock someone up?'
 Phoebe, on Cortez: 'I sort-of sent him to ...' Piper: 'Timbuktu. It rhymes with "undo".'
 Paige: 'When I said I wanted to find out who I was, I *didn't* want to find out I was a freak.' And, to Piper: 'Trust you? You just froze a nun?'
 Phoebe: 'Maybe the Whitelighter in her makes it work differently?' Piper: 'Half-breed.'
 Piper, to the Source: 'I guess blood's a little thicker than evil.'

Notes: 'No matter what we think, she's our sister. Sisters protect each other.' A thoroughly sharp meditation on desire and temptation, the second half of 'Charmed Again' works more or less along similar lines to the first – reformatting the show with each new revelation.

Soundtrack: 'I Feel Loved' by Depeche Mode.

69: HELL HATH NO FURY

11 October 2001

Writer: Krista Veraoff
Director: Chris Long

Cast: Becky Wahlstrom (Lila), David Reivers (Bob Cowan), Ben Tolpin (Billy), Ken Feinberg (Demon in Black), Scott Mosenson (Donnie)

> Paige takes *The Book of Shadows* to her work to cast spells that will help her colleagues. However, she's unaware of the potential consequences of such actions. Meanwhile Piper is possessed by a member of a supernatural band of vigilantes known as the Furies.

It's Witchcraft: *The Book of Shadows* seemingly has magical powers that prevent it from being photocopied. The 'Promote Compromise' spell that Paige casts begins: 'These words will travel through the minds, of stubborn parties and unbind, the thoughts too rigid to be kind, a compromise they'll disentwine.' This is reversed by her sisters with the chant: 'Guided spirits hear our plea, annul this magic, let it be.' The 'Vanishing Spell' starts: 'Let the object of objection become but a dream, as I cause the seen to be unseen.' The 'Karma Spell' can be used on mortals by swapping 'demon' to 'dirt-bag,' but has somewhat adverse effects, and ends: 'Reverse the torment he creates, to turn on him a crueller fate.' Piper summons the Furies with a spell that requires blood to be dropped into a candle flame and with the same chant that she tried to summon Prue in 'Charmed Again' (see also, 'How To Make a Quilt Out of Americans').

A Little Learning is a Dangerous Thing: Scrying for random evil, Phoebe, Piper and Cole have vanquished two demons already this week.

The book that Paige is reading notes that throughout history, witches have been misunderstood, persecuted and destroyed. The public hanging, drowning and burning of women suspected of witchcraft is a far more recent chapter of our history then most people realise.

Denial, Thy Name is Piper: Enraged by Prue's death and by her own perceived abandonment, Piper is covering this anger by an aggressively pro-active series of attacks on demons – much to Phoebe's concern and Cole's downright annoyance. Leo believes that she is doing this to avoid facing her true feelings. Paige tells Piper that it's okay to feel anger towards the dead – she, herself, hated her adoptive parents for leaving her alone when they died. There were some days when she thought she would never survive the sadness, but eventually it got better.

The Conspiracy Starts at the Witching Hour: Cole tells Piper and Phoebe that the Furies are similar to those in mythology – 'The dog-faced women from Hell – they're actually modern knockoffs, through their MO is still the same.' Piper notes that they punish evil-doers, and Phoebe wonders if that doesn't make them good. Cole adds that these Furies have no temptress, they'll go after a shoplifter as quickly as they would a murderer and they take great pleasure in the kill. When they focus their thoughts on someone, they force that person to hear the cries of all his or her former victims. Fury-smoke kills bad people but, in good people, it looks for a portal of unexpressed fury – it builds until it consumes their humanity and turns them into a Fury.

Work is a Four-Letter Word: Paige uses magic in the workplace to clear up Billy's acne and make the loathsome office stud Donnie's toupée fly off at inappropriate moments. She also sees her own boobs enlarge. ('You are so busted,' Piper says, with little obvious irony.) They subsequently interfere with her driving and she has to get Phoebe to change gear for her.

References: The much-used title comes from *The Mourning Bride* by William Congreve (1670-1729) – 'Heav'n hath no rage, like love to hatred turn'd, nor Hell a fury, like a woman, scorn'd.' Also, John Lennon's 'Instant Karma'; Betty Boop; Charles Bronson; and the Beatles' 'Let It Be' (see 'Awakened').

'You May Remember Me …': Becky Wahlstrom played Grace Polk in *Joan of Arcadia*. Ben Toplin was Gordo in *The Mullets*. Ken Feinberg's CV includes *The District*, *Alias* and *Buffy the Vampire Slayer*. Scott Mosenson appeared in *Friends*.

Sex and Drugs and Rock n Roll: When Paige mentions her student loan sharks, Donnie says that, as a lawyer, he could get the creditors off her back. And, if Paige can't afford to pay, he could always 'Take it out in trade.' 'Or, I could just sue your ass for sexual harassment and pay you with my big fat punitive settlement,' suggests Paige. The way Paige dresses, Donnie notes caustically, the judge would admire his restraint.

Logic, Let Me Introduce You to This Window: The red-haired Fury kicks open the Manor's front doors but, after Phoebe levitates and kicks her, the doors are closed. Between the scene in which Phoebe and Piper find Paige in the parking lot and the next one, Phoebe's hair changes style. When Piper grabs Paige at the end (just before Leo orbs them to the mausoleum), Piper has her hand on Paige's throat. As Leo starts to orb them, her hand is on Paige's face. Phoebe doesn't seem to know who Charles Bronson is, despite seeing him in *The Dirty Dozen* in 'Heartbreak City'.

Continuity: Phoebe is still struggling to control her new powers – she is, she notes, still freezing and exploding things at random. Piper suggests that Whitelighters are meant to guide, not judge. Phoebe tells Paige that Piper has been turned into a demon before (see 'The Wendigo'). And that she, herself, became a Banshee (see 'Look Who's Barking'). Cole claims to be good at lots of things, but not at waiting.

Quote/Unquote: Cole: 'The Source is coming after you.' Phoebe: 'And we won't be ready for him, because instead of teaching Paige how to be a witch, we're out hunting for every Tom, Dick and Beelzebub in San Francisco.'

Piper: 'This one could incinerate human flesh with his eyes. That must sting.'

Piper: 'I'm going to take out those chain-smoking bitches if it's the last thing I do.' Cole: 'It might be.'

Phoebe: 'Are you coming?' Cole: 'To vanquish your sister? I think I'll sit this one out.'

Paige: 'You *can't* say demons followed by, "Oh, my God." I'm new at this, I'm likely to panic.'

Cole: 'Woogy?' Paige: 'Don't ask!'

Notes: 'She has no regard for her life or anyone else's. She's Charles Bronson cubed.' A very funny episode that, nevertheless, take time to explore the loss felt by Piper in particular at Prue's death. Paige's early, fumbling steps as a witch (and the amusing consequences of her dabbling) all add up to an enjoyable, if rather lightweight, episode.

Soundtrack: Lily Frost's 'Who Am I?'

70: ENTER THE DEMON

18 October 2001

Writer: Daniel Cerone
Director: Joel Feigenbaum

Cast: Daniel Dae Kim (Yen-Lo), James Hong (Zen Master), Jeanne Chinn (An-Ling), Jacobi Wynne (Mason), Jamison Yang (Shopkeeper)

> When making a potion, Paige wishes to have a life more like Phoebe's, and inadvertently switches bodies with her. While the pair cover the accident from Piper, their older sister becomes involved with a Chinese Zen Master. His student, Yen-Lo, was seemingly killed by the Master's daughter, but remains alive by hiding in limbo to take his revenge. Paige and Phoebe deal with each other's romantic entanglements, then use a potion to switch Piper's soul with the Master's to defeat Yen-Lo and send him to his next karmic life.

It's Witchcraft: Any surface of water can be used as a portal between limbo and earth. Metaphysical and magical laws are amplified in limbo, Leo notes. As long as Yen-Lo stays there, his wound will never advance. He can, literally, cheat death forever.

At the end of the episode, a thoroughly chastened Paige has learned that Aloe plant has medical uses, Toro herbs are magical, St John's Wort is a medicinal herb, Ragged Robin is a magical herb, Cupid's Dart is strictly aromatic and Angelica is used, mostly, to flavour fish.

A Little Learning is a Dangerous Thing: The soul is apparently a bright glowy-type thing.

The Conspiracy Starts at the Witching Hour: Cole has recently been undercover for a week on what he describes as 'a fact-finding mission' concerning the Source. He has learned that the Source doesn't just want the Charmed Ones dead, he *needs* them to die. Ever since they escaped from his domain (see 'All Hell Breaks Loose'), factions have been forming to challenge the Source.

Work is a Four-Letter Word: Paige notes that her boss's son, Mason, is in town for the weekend and she thinks that going on a date will improve her career standing. Mason says that his father believes if he doesn't make Paige a social worker soon, she will quit and start her own agency. Either that, or end up in jail.

References: The title is an allusion to that of *Enter The Dragon* (1973), the film that made an icon of Bruce Lee. Much of the action derives from the contemporary hit movie *Crouching Tiger, Hidden Dragon* (Ang Lee, 2000). There are allusions to the Wicked Witch of the West from *The Wizard of Oz*; *Star Wars*; and Barbie.

'You May Remember Me …': Daniel Dae Kim played Gavin Park in *Angel* and Agent Tom Baker in *24*. He also appeared in *Crusade*, *Lost*, *CSI* and *ER*. James Hong's impressive CV includes *Bonanza*, *Hawaii 5-0*, *I Dream of Jeannie*, *Kung Fu*, *Charlie's Angels*, *Dynasty*, *MacGyver*, *The West Wing* and *Wayne's World 2*. Jeanne Chinn was in *The Ghost* and *Bastards*. Jacobi Wynne played Milo Reynolds in *Push*.

Sex and Drugs and Rock n Roll: Phoebe's and Cole's sweaty work-out is full of both unresolved sexual tension and perfectly filthy innuendo. Even a watching Paige fancies 'going a couple of rounds with the demon.'

When buying powdered toadstool for use in changing their souls back, Phoebe (in Paige's body) tells Mason that it's an aphrodisiac. She is guilty that she isn't showing him a very good time. Mason sarcastically notes that they're in Chinatown shopping for a sexual stimulant – he hasn't had this much fun in a long time.

Logic, Let Me Introduce You to This Window: Where did Paige's pink hat come from? She certainly didn't have it when she left the Manor with Mason. When the souls of the Zen Master and Piper switch back at the end of the show, keep your eyes on Piper. A soul neither enters nor leaves her body as the surroundings are changing. How did Yen-Lo know that the Zen Master had switched souls with Piper? When An-Ling steals the Dragonblade and Piper freezes the store, why doesn't An-Ling freeze? Is this due to the blade itself? There's a noticeable lack of blood spurting from the wound when An-Ling impales Yen-Lo with her sword. Once again, the *Charmed* universe's take on the afterlife throws up the possibility of reincarnation (see also 'Pardon My Past'), which doesn't explain how a bunch of non-reincarnated ghosts can come and go in the Halliwells' lives with such alarming regularity. An-Ling says that her father could use water as a looking glass into other worlds, and that when she was young, he reached into a bowl of water and picked her a plum from the Garden of Eden. Would a Buddhist accept this wholly Christian origin story as factual? Yen-Lo's vision of limbo appears to resemble an alien planet set

SEASON 4: ENTER THE DEMON

from *Star Trek*, complete with polystyrene rocks.

Continuity: Paige is being, essentially, fast-tracked through the various stages of witchcraft in anticipation of an attack by the Source. Piper thinks that Prue was pretty good at everything she did. Leo suggests that because Paige is half-Whitelighter, she is also half-pacifist. She may never develop the power to fight that Phoebe has. After they have swapped bodies, the biggest threat that Phoebe can make to Paige regarding the situation is that if her sister doesn't fix it soon, Phoebe will perm Paige's hair.

Quote/Unquote: Phoebe: 'Piper takes her witchcraft quizzes very seriously. You better be prepared. What's the subject?' Paige: 'Potion basics.' Phoebe: 'Well, you gotta start somewhere.'

Piper: 'After mixing your potion, what's the best method to preserve unused sea-slugs for future use? A) Pickle them? B) Sugar them? C) Smoke them? D) Freeze-dry them?' Paige: 'If I had extra sea-slugs, I'd let those little suckers go right on back to the ocean.' Piper: 'Freeze-dry them is the correct answer.' Paige: 'I was going to *guess* that.'

Piper, to Paige: 'Trust me, be patient and study hard and one day you'll get a big, sweaty demon of your own.'

An-Ling, on how Piper coped with Prue's death: 'Where did you find the strength?' Piper: 'I haven't yet. I'll let you know when I do.'

Notes: 'You took everything you've learned from here and used it for your own gain.' Predictable, frivolous and conceptually shaky. Yes, 'Enter the Demon' is, all these things. It's also *very* entertaining. Body-swap stories often are (admittedly, sometimes for the wrong reasons). This one rattles along at a furious pace, stomping on the occasional logic flaws with hobnail boots. Alyssa Milano makes a very good Paige and Daniel Dae Kim's 'evil' facial hair is an episode highlight. There are, sadly, a few unconsciously racist moments – Buddhist concepts sit somewhat uncomfortably within the essentially Judaeo-Christian *Charmed* world aesthetic. But ultimately, despite a lack of ambition, the episode works.

71: SIZE MATTERS

25 October 2001

Writer: Nell Scovell
Director: Noel Nosseck

Cast: Richard McGregor (Finn), Robert Englund (Gammill), Reynaldo Rosales (Treat Taylor), Heather Marie Marsden (Claudia), Kari Coleman (Interviewer), Aaron Brumfield (Bouncer), Dave Navarro (Himself), Alicia Keys (Herself)[49]

> Piper hires a manager to reinvent P³. Meanwhile, Paige senses something evil about a house and asks her sisters to investigate. Phoebe visits the house and is shrunk by a demon, Gammill, as part of a dastardly plan to make the Charmed Ones into highly collectable figurines.

It's Witchcraft: Having spent most of the day encased in clay and waiting to be baked, Phoebe has had plenty of time to think up a spell to vanquish Gammill: 'Small of mind, big of woe, the pain you caused, you now will know.' Paige is less than impressed, although Phoebe does point out that it worked.

A Little Learning is a Dangerous Thing: Phoebe thinks that she should be able to get a job easily enough – she is, after all, a college graduate. Her first attempt, however, proves that her lifestyle isn't necessarily compatible with a nine-to-five job.

The Conspiracy Starts at the Witching Hour: Gammill, also known as the Collector, has a passion for one-of-a-kind figurines. Leo wonders what he gets out of that. Piper reminds Leo about her great-aunt Sylvia, who collects Hummels; when people have a hard time dealing with others, figurines can be their best friends. Leo points out that being socially awkward doesn't usually land someone in *The Book of Shadows*. Gammill, he continues, went up against a witch sometime in the 1970s. (Given that *The Book of Shadows* is predominantly written by the sisters' ancestors, this would suggest that the witch Gammill faced was either Grams or Patty.) A spell was cast to make him as hideous on the outside as he was on the

---

[49] Uncredited.

inside. Gammill created the handsome young Finn to be his lure to obtain girls for his passion.

Work is a Four-Letter Word: Piper hires a new manager for P³, jive-talkin' dude Treat, the self-considered 'number one club promoter in all of San Francisco.' He makes massive changes, including a name-change (to the Spot). Leo is more impressed with the go-go waitress dancers than Piper ('Can you do *that* in public?').

It's a Designer Label!: Best item on display – Paige's tight purple top. Worst – Phoebe's trampy grunge look in the opening scene.

References: Aspects of the plot are very similar to that of an obscure 1970s British horror movie *Crucible of Terror*, which involved an artist creating sculptures from real women. There is a visual reference to *The People Under the Stairs*. Also, allusions to *Goodfellas* ('Made me? Is that like a Mafia thing?'); and *Land of the Giants*. There's a Lou Reed poster outside the rear entrance to Piper's club. Gammill's nickname comes from a John Fowles novel about a serial kidnapper, filmed in 1965 by William Wyler and starring Terrance Stamp.

'You May Remember Me ...': Robert Englund is best known as Freddy Krueger in *A Nightmare on Elm Street* and its numerous sequels. Richard McGregor appeared in *I'm Gonna Git You Sucka* and *21 Jump Street*. Reynaldo Rosales was in *Smallville*. Heather Marie Marsden played Cheryl in *Shark Hunter* and appeared in *The Army Show*. Kari Coleman was in *Seinfeld* and *Multiplicity*. Dave Navarro appeared in *Uptown Girls*. Aaron Brumfield's movies include *Bowfinger*.

Classic *Double Entendre*: Paige, to Finn: 'Remember me? The girl with the melons?'

Logic, Let Me Introduce You to This Window: Phoebe is said to have graduated from college the previous spring at the age of 27. If she was born in November 1975 (see 'Pardon My Past') and this episode takes place contemporaneously with the broadcast date, then she should be 25 now – a month away from her 26th birthday. If Leo can 'heal' broken objects, why has he never done this before? Or perhaps he has and we've just never seen it – certainly the Manor seems to get trashed with alarming regularity but, apart from a few occasions when one of the sisters has been seen doing a bit of sweeping up, the clear-up process has always remained a mystery. When Leo and Piper orb into Finn's – apparently empty – house after Paige has left with him, why do they whisper? How did Gammill

SEASON 4: SIZE MATTERS

know where the Charmed Ones lived? Why didn't Piper freeze Gammill before he shrank her? Why did Leo believe that Paige was at the club? Even if that's where Paige was supposed to be, wouldn't Leo have been able to sense that she was at her apartment? P³ can afford to hire some famous musical acts and has always seemed packed whenever we've seen it, so why does Piper suggest that it's been 'struggling' recently? It's hardly surprisingly the house gives Paige the shivers: it's like the Munsters' second home.

Continuity: Paige says that she loves being able to move stuff with her mind. She does, however, have some problems with orbing (although, ironically, it's this ability that saves her and her sisters at the episode's climax).

Quote/Unquote: Phoebe: 'You shouldn't have to carry the financial burden.' Piper: 'I'll worry about the source of our income if you worry about the Source of All Evil.'

Phoebe: 'Do you know anything about the house?' Paige: 'Just that this cute guy named Finn lives there. We bumped into each other at the grocery store, flirted a little, did the "Are these melons ripe" thing ...'

Phoebe: 'It all started with an interview, where a lady made me feel this big ... Now I *really am* this big.' And: 'The real world better start showing me some respect. Otherwise, I am going to stop saving it every week.'

Bouncer: 'You can't go in there. It's a VIP area.' Piper: 'You're assuming because I'm not tall, tattooed or big-breasted that I'm *not* important?'

Notes: 'You little witch. We'll see how long you last.' Yet another episode that, on the surface, seems mere eye-candy, with some decent set-pieces and a bunch of funny one-liners. However, again, there's a bit more going on here beneath the 'old creepy house' clichés. 'Size Matters' has, at its core, the still fractious relationship between Piper (who hates having to assume Prue's role of leader) and Paige (still unsure of her place in the group dynamic).

Soundtrack: Fuzz Townshend's 'At Auntie Tom's', The Crystal Method's 'Name of the Game' and Dave Navarro's 'Hungry'.

72: A KNIGHT TO REMEMBER

1 November 2001

Writers: Alison Schapker, Monica Breen
Director: David Straiton

Cast: Charlie Weber (Prince), Joie Lenz (Lady Julia), Jesse Woodrow (Glenn), David Reivers (Bob Cowan), Frank Crim (Driver)

> Paige tries to find the missing piece of a fairy tale that she believes she invented and that has haunted her since childhood. When she inadvertently casts what turns out to be a forgotten spell, a medieval Prince is summoned, who believes that Paige is his true love. The sisters learn that the tale was really a past life of Paige's, in which she was an evil enchantress. Meanwhile, Phoebe and Piper are unable to banish a Shocker demon without the Power of Three, and suggest that Paige moves into the Manor.

It's Witchcraft: Once upon a time, there lived a handsome Prince who was about to marry a beautiful maiden, the Lady Julia. But an evil enchantress with dark powers wanted the Prince for herself so that she could become Queen, bear him an heir and rule the kingdom. (Paige says that she always kind-of related to the enchantress.) The enchantress waited for a sign that her powers were at their darkest – a configuration of stars – and then cast her spell, bore an heir, killed the Prince, and ruled the kingdom forever (presumably, cackling at various points for dramatic effect). In reality, this is all part of Paige's wicked past. The spell she used, which Paige could never remember the end of, was: 'Bring together my Prince and me, let him fall on bended knee, I summon him to my side, that he may take me to be his destined bride.' The shocker demon lives in electricity. It requires the Power of Three to vanquish it with the following spell: 'Vanquish we three witches cry, one final shock and then you die.' Shocking.

A Little Learning is a Dangerous Thing: For non-US readers, a renaissance faire is something of a tradition in certain parts of America. It's just like the real middle ages, only without the Black Death and slavery and with craft stalls and much drinking of mead instead.

The Conspiracy Starts at the Witching Hour: Defiant, clever, and independent, the evil enchantress was a powerful witch who came to the

SEASON 4: A KNIGHT TO REMEMBER

'craft late but learned to use it quickly. Just like Paige, in fact.

It's a Designer Label!: Paige's fluffy pink top, tartan miniskirt and red leather boots. Also, Phoebe's stars-and-stripes top and Paige's appealing cap.

References: There have been two movies called *A Night to Remember* – an almost-forgotten 1943 whodunnit starring Loretta Young and, more famously, Roy Ward Baker's 1958 epic about the Titanic, featuring Kenneth More. There are allusions to *Prince Charming*; King Arthur and Sir Lancelot; *Someone to Watch Over Me*; and Futureworld at Disneyland. The book in Paige's apartment is called *Collected Fairy Tales – Fables, Tales and Nursery Rhymes*.

'You May Remember Me ...': Charlie Weber played Ben in *Buffy the Vampire Slayer* and also appeared in *Everwood*. Joie Lenz was in *The Guiding Light*. Jesse Woodrow's movies include *Deep Cover* and *LA Knights*. Frank Crim appeared in *Adventures in Home Schooling*.

Sex and Drugs and Rock n Roll: Leo has been secretly watching Paige throughout the previous week in case of demon attacks. This has included those moments when she and her boyfriend, Glenn, were engaged in sexual activity. Paige, upon discovering this, is less than impressed. (I didn't see anything, insists Leo. 'At least, nothing very interesting,' adds Phoebe).

When the Prince ('Sir Lust-a-lot' as Piper wittily dubs him) begins kissing Paige's hand, under the misapprehension that she is the evil enchantress, Paige asks Piper to freeze him. Piper is reluctant, not wanting to blow him up. 'Risk it,' says Paige, 'he's using his tongue.'

The Prince insists that he will not leave until Paige is with child. Paige thinks this is unlikely as she *always* uses protection.

Logic, Let Me Introduce You to This Window: In the *Charmed* universe, somewhere in medieval Europe, there was a small kingdom where everyone spoke with American accents. And, certainly in Lady Julia's case, had *very* 1980s hair. Paige's month of birth, given just a few episodes earlier, was August 1977, making her 24 – yet according to Glenn, she's 25. Paige's alarm clock goes off at 9 am, and she is upset because she's going to be late. Why did she set the alarm for that time if she wanted to be up earlier? It's also strange that Paige was so concerned about being late yet still took the time to drive to the Manor to research her half-forgotten fairy tale. When the evil enchantress goes to Paige's office and finds the photo of Paige on the wall, the person in the photo with her is Elise, Phoebe's future

SEASON 4: A KNIGHT TO REMEMBER

boss at the *Bay Mirror*.

Continuity: Phoebe hates camping and Piper hates instant coffee. Phoebe reminds Piper that her past life came back to bite her on the butt (see 'Pardon My Past'). Paige's boyfriend, Glenn, is a handsome and adventurous type who has climbed the world's second tallest mountain, K2, and swum the Great Barrier Reef. He's going to Australia and wants Paige to accompany him. She ultimately refuses and decides to move in with her sisters after her own apartment is trashed during the fight with the evil enchantress.

Motors: Our first look at Paige's car, a nifty little light green VW (4TYT 185).

Quote/Unquote: Paige: 'I told you I was a weird kid.'
Paige: 'How should I know?' Piper: 'Because it's your damn fairy tale and it's alive and frozen in our kitchen.'
Phoebe: 'He's just wandering around in chain-mail?' Piper: 'It's San Francisco. Nobody will notice.'
Paige, discovering that she was the evil enchantress in a past life: 'Does this mean I'm evil?' Piper: 'Yeah.' Phoebe: '*No!*' Piper: '... No.'

Notes: 'It's my story. I have to end it once and for all.' A definite case of the sum of all parts, here. 'A Knight to Remember' is silly to the point of being stupid, but it's also – in quite a decent number of places – laugh-out-loud funny. And it's got Leo's Errol Flynn moment. ('Very sexy,' considers a smirking Piper.) Ignore Piper's continuing angst over Prue, which is starting to get really boring by this stage, and concentrate on the amusing stuff and you'll be rewarded with 40 undemanding minutes of your life.

Soundtrack: Mazzy Star's epic 'Into Dust'. Some of the source music is based on the 16th Century madrigal 'Greensleeves'.[50]

---

[50] Often said to have been written by King Henry VIII for his second wife, Anne Boleyn, this is almost certainly apocryphal. Recent research suggests that it's actually a plagiarised version of a traditional French folk melody.

73: BRAIN DRAIN

8 November 2001

Writer: Curtis Kneel
Director: John Behring

Cast: Rachel Wilson (Becca), Ben Guillory (The Source), Alastair Duncan (Alastair), Krista Allen (The Oracle), Whitney Dylan (Wendy), Tom Billett (Bounty Hunter #1), Eric Ware (Orderly #1), Sheila J Cavanaugh (Patient #2), Angela Oh (Patient #3)

> Cole learns that the Source has sent a chameleon demon to the Manor to spy on the Charmed Ones. When the demon's cover is blown, the Source kidnaps Piper, using dark magic to put her in an illusory world in which she's a mental patient at Halliwell Hospital. The Source wishes to manipulate Piper into relinquishing her powers.

Dreaming (As Blondie Once Said) is Free: Phoebe has a terrifying premonition in which the Source steals *The Book of Shadows* and kills Phoebe and Paige using their own powers against them.

It's Witchcraft: Phoebe and Paige use the 'Find a lost witch' spell in an unsuccessful attempt to discover where Piper has been taken (see 'Charmed Again' Part 1). They eventually find a way to enter Piper's illusory world using a spell that begins: 'Life to life and mind to mind, our spirits now will intertwine, we mould our souls and journey to, the one whose thoughts we wish we knew.' They intend to use the reversal spell to get out again.

The chameleon demon is destroyed with: 'Evil hiding in plain sight, I use this spell with all my might, to stop you changing form and shape, this vanquish seals your fate.'

In a cleverly self-aware moment, when Piper begins to chant the relinquishing spell (see 'Wicca Envy'), one of the hospital orderlies notes that it doesn't even rhyme. (One of the most frequent complaints from dedicated *Charmed*-haters on the Internet is the usually appalling standard of the poetry used to cast the various spells in the show.)

The Conspiracy Starts at the Witching Hour: Chameleon demons can transform themselves into anyone, or seemingly any inanimate object. The

Source believes that Piper's yearning for a normal life is her greatest weakness.

Obsession, Thy Name is Piper: Phoebe reminds her sisters that Piper has told her to tell Piper when she is obsessing.

It's a Designer Label!: Paige's denim skirt is, surely, the most hideously inappropriate thing imaginable in which to go demon-chasing.

References: Allusions to *The Wizard of Oz*; *Mary Poppins*; and Loony Tunes cartoons.

'You May Remember Me ...': Rachel Wilson appeared in *Sheer Bliss*, *Breaker High* and *Gideon's Crossing*. Alastair Duncan played Collins in *Buffy the Vampire Slayer* and *Angel* and appeared in *A Difficult Woman*. Eric Ware's CV includes *Hulk*, *The Real McCoy* and *7th Heaven*. Tom Billett was in *Asylum* and *Babylon 5*. Whitney Dylan appeared in *Coyote Ugly* and *Jumbo Girl*. Sheila Cavanaugh's movies include *Student Affairs*. Angela Oh was in *Boys and Girls*.

The Drugs Don't Work: When Leo injects Piper, she giggles and says that she can see white lights all around him. That's the pain killers talking, he notes.

Subsequently, Piper's drug-induced fantasy garden features butterflies that look like they've escaped from the hallucinogenic depths of *Yellow Submarine*. Or, as Paige notes, either her and Phoebe's plan has worked, or they're stuck inside Mary Poppins' head.

Sex and Drugs and Rock n Roll: The final scenes feature much canoodling between Phoebe and Cole and Piper and Leo. Paige makes an excuse and leaves them to it.

Logic, Let Me Introduce You to This Window: General query: How many times has that grandfather clock been destroyed by a demon fireball or been crashed into by a flying Halliwell sister? There must be a 24-hour 'We repair any clock, even if it's been incinerated by the Source of All Evil' service in San Francisco, with which the sisters have a bill equivalent to the national debt of a small third-world country. When Piper's hit by the car, she's injured on the left side of the face. When shown in the underworld, the injury is to the right. In Piper's illusory world, she's a patient and, also, Leo's secret girlfriend, seemingly. Also, a conundrum – if Piper couldn't use her powers in her fantasy world, then why does saying the relinquishing spell work? The same back alley set is used in this episode as in the previous one (note that same Lou Reed poster in the background as the Source captures Piper).

Continuity: Phoebe tells Paige, annoyed by the destruction of her chair, that one can't, usually, claim on the household insurance for act of demon. There are a couple of references to the daughter that Piper will have in the future (see 'Mortality Bites'). Piper attends the baby shower of a pregnant friend named Wendy. This is held at P³ (which has, it would seem, reverted to its original name).

Quote/Unquote: Paige: 'What the hell happened?' Piper: 'The freaking furniture just attacked.'

Paige: 'Are we sure we wanna do this?' Phoebe: 'This was your idea, remember?' Paige: 'In the abstract, yeah. But, I have enough trouble being in *my* head, let alone someone else's.'

Notes: 'You have the power to give you the life you've always wanted. All you have to do is stop putting the illusion of being a witch in front of it.' A character in a fantasy TV show having his or her world revealed to be a series of elaborate delusions, the apparent result of mental illness, is not an original concept. *Deep Space Nine* did it years earlier with 'Far Beyond the Stars'. It's interesting that, at almost exactly the same moment that *Charmed* was broadcasting this episode, the producers of *Buffy the Vampire Slayer* were planning something very similar ('Normal Again', filmed in October 2001 and broadcast in February 2002). Of the three examples, 'Brain Drain' is probably the least dramatically clever, but – conversely – the most emotionally interesting. Downside: it's another 'Piper-doesn't-want-to-be-a-witch-any-more-or-does-she?' episode. Haven't had one of those in, oh, at *least* two weeks.

74: BLACK AS COLE

15 November 2001

Teleplay: Brad Kern, Nell Scovell
Story: Abbey Campbell
Director: Les Landau

Cast: Vincent Angell (Sykes), Heather Dawn (Emma), Bonnie Root (Susan Coleman), Michael Bailey Smith (Belthazor), Aaron Brumfield (Demon Sykes), Sara Lynn Moneymaker (Marika), Matthew Heron (Annoying Man), Kaycee Shank (Lam)

> While the sisters are tracking a demon believed responsible for killing witches, Cole proposes to Phoebe. The sisters learn that their quest was unsuccessful when another witch dies. Then they meet Emma, who is seeking to avenge the death of her fiancé. Emma reveals that Belthazor was responsible.

It's Witchcraft: Searching *The Book of Shadows* for an upper-level demon who likes to kill witches using an athame, sometimes with energy balls, Paige finds one. Unfortunately, it's Belthazor.

A Little Learning is a Dangerous Thing: The demon who attacks Phoebe and Cole is a scavenger. These feed on the remains of other demons' victims.

The Conspiracy Starts at the Witching Hour: A member of the Brotherhood, the new Assistant DA, Sykes, is really the demon that has been killing the witches, basing his *modus operandi* on that of Belthazor. He has the same detachable shadow that Cole once used.

References: The title is a probable allusion to lyrics from the Rolling Stones' 'Paint It Black'. There are allusions to *Casablanca* and to *Robocop*. Leo reads a copy of *Wheels* magazine. Phoebe's premonition is of Susan being attacked by a Belthazor-like demon in a park that Susan identifies as being in Stanley Arboreta.

'You May Remember Me ...': Vincent Angell appeared in *We Were Soldiers* and *24*. Heather Dawn played Nora in *Bull*. Bonnie Root was Amanda McCallister in *Trinity*. Kaycee Shank appeared in *Little Sister*.

SEASON 4: BLACK AS COLE

Logic, Let Me Introduce You to This Window: Cole mentions that only upper-level demons bleed red not green, directly contradicting 'Sleuthing with the Enemy', where he told Phoebe that he bleeds red only because he is half-human. In the previous episode, the Source bled black, and they don't come much more upper-level than he. After Cole explains that he may be unable to regain control after embracing his demonic half, he tells Phoebe she should have the Belthazor-vanquishing potion ready just in case. But in 'Look Who's Barking', Piper tried using that on Cole and it didn't work. Additionally, in 'Exit Strategy', the power-stripping potion for Cole was in a cup, indicating that he had to drink it. Now it's in a vial, and it works by being broken on him. What happened to the page Phoebe wrote in *The Book of Shadows* next to the Belthazor page (complete with photographs).

Continuity: Piper believes that having a baby at this time would be too risky. It would be in constant danger. Paige asks what Leo thinks and is told there's enough magic around to protect it. Paige suggests that maybe he's right. Paige subsequently gets Piper and Leo a mechanical baby to look after – which gets destroyed when Sykes attacks the Manor. The power-stripping potion that Phoebe creates is used by Emma and destroys Belthazor, leaving Cole as a (powerless) human.

Quote/Unquote: Piper, on Cole: 'You knew he was half-demon.' Paige: 'Yeah, but I didn't know he could turn into *that*.'
   Paige: 'You were a demon and a lawyer? Insert joke here.'
   Emma: 'Vengeance empowers me.' Cole: 'But it won't save you.'
   Cole: 'I've been a demon for over 100 years … What am I supposed to do now? Who am I?' Phoebe: 'You're still the good man I fell in love with.'

Notes: 'How can you live with yourself?' A long-overdue dramatic conceit, as one of Cole's old victims comes back to haunt him in a suitably morally-ambiguous way. The key themes of redemption and sin are handled without much of *Charmed*'s usually black and white worldview; and, for once, doing something a bit more serious actually suits the show (though the subplot about Piper's and Leo's mechanical baby is pretty funny). A great performance from Julian McMahon, and one of the best episodes of the season.

Soundtrack: Heather Nova's 'Like Lovers Do'.

75: MUSE TO MY EARS

13 December 2001

Writer: Krista Vernoff
Director: Joel J Feigenbaum

Cast: Anthony Starke (Devlin), Siobhàn Flynn (Melody), Cindy Ambuehl (Bev), John Prosky (Congressman), Chad Kukahiko (Jackson), Jorge-Luis Pallo (Hector), Graham Shiels (Homeless Man/Demon), Harley Zumbrum (Jake), Siena Goines (Inspirational Muse)

> Cole worries that other evil forces may target the sisters to prove themselves worthy of succeeding the Source. Those fears seem justified when Devlin, a powerful warlock, uses the Ring of Inspiration to capture muses. He hopes they will inspire his faction of warlocks to aid him in an attempt to kill the Charmed Ones.

It's Witchcraft: Muses are beings of pure light whose purpose is to inspire passion, talent and creativity. Like angels, they guide mortals with an unseen hand of inspiration. After Phoebe casts a spell ('Being of creativity, show yourself now to me, your light that shines upon our face, let our vision now embrace'), the sisters meet their own muse, Melody, who says that she has been inspiring them their entire lives. She is also an old friend of Leo's. Melody notes that she is not meant to stay in one place for too long, as the inspiration can get a little intense – which is what subsequently happens. Cole tells Leo that evil never experiences muses' inspiration and that he, personally, has never felt anything like it in his life.

Under Melody's influence, Phoebe's first attempt at a vanquishing spell for Devlin is: 'A warlock is a funny thing, he blinks from place to place. And when we say these words to him, his face they will erase.' Paige considers this to be more a limerick than a spell. Her next attempt is: 'Evil is a faithful foe, but good does battle best. We witches will, with these words, waste the warlock's evil zest.' Piper considers this witty, but rather wordy.

A Little Learning is a Dangerous Thing: Cole used to be able to hold fire in the palm of his hand. Now he can't even pick up a hot casserole dish.

Piper suggests that P³'s strobe lights will keep the warlocks from blinking. She intends to freeze the innocents – anyone that her sisters see still moving after this point, they should feel free to vanquish.

SEASON 4: MUSE TO MY EARS

The Conspiracy Starts at the Witching Hour: Demons regard warlocks as scum. There are laws to prevent demons being killed by warlocks to gain their powers – such eventualities are punishable by death. Demons convene to discuss such acts of treason in High Council meetings. Cole notes that without a strong leader, there's anarchy in the underworld. The Ring of Inspiration enables the wearer to see and capture muses – it was originally created by good magic, to channel inspiration in times of great need.

It's a Designer Label!: Anyone else of the opinion that Phoebe's frilly pantaloons are, possibly, *Charmed*'s worst fashion crime ever?

References: There are allusions to *The Cat in the Hat* author Dr Suess (who, like the inspired Phoebe, wrote rhyming prose); Bill Haley's 'See You Later, Alligator'; actress Veronica Lake; Martha Stewart (see 'Animal Pragmatism'); and the Biblical verse I Timothy 6:12 (see 'The Demon Who Came In From the Cold'). The posters outside P³ include one for the band Curiosity.

'You May Remember Me ...': Anthony Starke appeared in *Licence To Kill* and *Suddenly Susan*. Siobhàn Flynn played Lisa in *Jack of Hearts*. Cindy Ambuehl was Rene Peterson in *JAG* and also appeared in *Ellen*. John Prosky's movies include *Hulk*, *Lost Souls* and *The Nutty Professor*. Chad Kukahiko was in *Mid-Century*. Jorge-Luis Pallo appeared in *Minority Report*. Harley Zumbrum's CV includes *Tequila*, *Body Shots* and *Con Air*. Siena Goines played Tommy in *The Sweetest Thing* and was also in *Judging Amy*.

Cigarettes and Alcohol: Phoebe's and Cole's celebratory night includes glasses of white wine. At P³, Devlin drinks a Martini.

Sex and Drugs and Rock n Roll: Phoebe becomes frustrated with Cole's constant wish to talk about demon politics. She asks if he understands that, sometimes, a girl needs a night off. Then she wonders, whilst kissing him on the neck, if there is anything she can do to help him relax. A distracted Cole replies that the kissing certainly helps, and maybe she should keep doing that.

Logic, Let Me Introduce You to This Window: Phoebe's spell that Paige describes as a limerick, in fact isn't. It's only four lines long, whereas limericks have five. When Phoebe, Cole and Paige ascend the stairs, it appears the Rose McGowan's leg is caught by Julian McMahon. Piper freezes all of the innocents in P³, but seemingly she doesn't notice that

Melody is not frozen – it has previously been established that only upper-level demons and good witches cannot be frozen. In the same scene, when Phoebe kicks a warlock, a supposedly frozen woman in the background clearly moves. After a cutaway to Piper blowing up the warlock, the woman has disappeared.

Continuity: Phoebe devised the theme for her prom night – 'Almost paradise'. Paige describes herself as a perfectionist when it comes to her artistic aspirations.

Quote/Unquote: Phoebe: 'Us theme, you potion.' Piper: 'Me peeved, you annoying.'

Piper: 'The only good Source is a dead Source.'

Paige, to Phoebe and Piper: 'I'd rather do battle with warlocks than with the two of you.'

Leo: 'What exactly are you doing?' Phoebe: 'Basking in the brilliance of our failure.'

Notes: 'That, ladies and gentlemen, is what you call a faction.' On paper, this one had the potential to be shockingly bad. But, actually, it's a rather fun (if very lightweight) run-around with some nice character pairings and a genuinely lovely final scene.

Soundtrack: An appealing – if unidentified – acoustic ballad plays over the post-title sequence. At P³'s 1940s night, a trio sing Andrews Sisters-style versions of Don Raye's and Hughie Prince's 'Boogie Woogie Bugle Boy' and 'Don't Sit Under the Apple Tree (With Anyone Else But Me)' by Lew Brown, Charles Tobias and Sam H Stept. The final montage features an instrumental version of Hoagy Carmichael's 'Stardust'.

76: A PAIGE FROM THE PAST

17 January 2002

Writers: Daniel Cerone
Director: James L Conway

Cast: Sherman Howard (Clyde), M Scott Wilkinson (Paige's Father), Lisa Darr (Paige's Mother), Larry Brandenburg (Mr Martin), Alex Breckenridge (Michelle Miglis), Bradley James (Security Guard), Dwayne Macopson (Uniform Cop), Rhonda Stubbins (Principal Harris), Time Winters (Chaplin), Tommy Redmond Hicks (Captain)

> Piper and Phoebe learn that Paige still blames herself for the deaths of her parents. Leo suggests that Paige travel back in time to learn why her parents really died. In doing so, Paige attempts to change the past. Meanwhile, two ghosts possess Phoebe and Cole in order to complete some unfinished business.

Denial, Thy Name is Paige: Paige says that she wasn't the ideal high school student. She skipped classes and partied all night with her friends. Piper thinks that this sounds remarkably like Phoebe's teenage years, but Paige continues that she was also cruel, especially to her adoptive mother and father.

Denial, Thy Name is Phoebe: Piper believes that Phoebe is afraid of Cole's humanity. He was actually a much safer boyfriend, she suggests, when he was a demon. Leo adds that, on some level, Phoebe knew their relationship couldn't last. But now that Cole is a human, that safety net has gone, and for the first time, their future really does lie in Phoebe's hands.

A Little Learning is a Dangerous Thing: Leo suggests that Dickens didn't make the 'Ghost of Christmas Past' stuff up. Rather, he was visited by a malevolent spirit. Clyde is not the friendliest ghost that Leo knows, but he *is* the only one who helps the living visit their past. Clyde ignores summoning spells and can be called only by being cursed at until he gets angry. He doesn't do charity work but, fortunately, owes Leo a favour after Leo healed a client of Clyde's whom he carelessly returned from the past on the edge of a cliff. There were 32 broken bones.

The Conspiracy Starts at the Witching Hour: Cole and Phoebe are

SEASON 4: A PAIGE FROM THE PAST

possessed by a pair of ghosts named Frankie and Lulu. Jewel robbers from the 1950s, they killed three people before they were gunned down. Their ghosts used Clyde's time portal to seek out suitable bodies with which to complete their doomed (and rather tacky) love story.

It's a Designer Label!: Significantly, the first thing that Frankie and Lulu do before robbing the jewellery store is to buy some shades. Stylish ones, too. Also, Paige's red tights.

References: Allusions to Woodstock; Jimi Hendrix; John Lennon; *Natural Born Killers*; the Magna Carta (1215); Charles Dickens and his novel *A Christmas Carol* and its movie adaptation *Scrooged*; *Almost Famous* ('Ask me again'); and Blanche Dubois, the neurotic heroine of Tennessee Williams' *A Streetcar Named Desire*. There are Rolling Stones and Slayer posters in Paige's 1994 bedroom. Also, a visual reference to *Trading Places* (Cole at the police station).

'You May Remember Me ...': Sherman Howard's CV includes *Dexter*, *Ricochet* and *Mad About You*. M Scott Wilkinson appeared in *A Loss of Innocence* and *Touched By An Angel*. Lisa Darr played Susan Jackson in *Strong Medicine* and was also in *Popular*, *Ellen*, *Profit* and *CSI*. Larry Brandenburg appeared in *Fargo*, *Field of Dreams* and *The Shawshank Redemption*. Alex Breckenridge's movies include *Orange County*, *Vampire Clan* and *Opposite Sex*. Bradley James was in *The West Wing*. Dwayne Macopson appeared in *Chill Factor* and *Everybody Loves Raymond*. Rhonda Stubbins White was in *Sunset Park*. Time Winters' movies include *True Vinyl*, *Poison Ivy* and *LA Story*.

Cigarettes and Alcohol: Paige spent her high school years drinking, smoking and passing out at parties.

Sex and Drugs and Rock n Roll: When Cole says that he needs action, Phoebe gives him a flirty look and says that she believed they were doing okay in that department.

Logic, Let Me Introduce You to This Window: In Paige's room in 1994, there are two Metallica posters, one of which is from 1996 and the other from 1998. In addition, there is a Tiffany doll from *Child's Play 4: Bride of Chucky* – a movie that also wasn't released until 1998. Paige tells her sisters that the day her parents died, she told them they weren't her real parents. However, in the past, we discover that this conversation actually took place the night before. Phoebe suggests that Cole vanquished his demon half for her. He did no such thing, as he certainly wasn't a willing

SEASON 4: A PAIGE FROM THE PAST

participant in Belthazor's vanquishing (see 'Black as Cole').

Continuity: At the end of the episode, Phoebe finally accepts Cole's marriage proposal (see 'Black as Cole'). Having survived the car crash that killed her parents by (unconsciously) orbing, because it was her destiny not to die, Paige got into Berkeley University thanks to high test scores and a powerful essay on the death of her parents. She subsequently received a degree in social work. Paige's adoptive father was a fireman. Her first love was called Philip Lewicky. Paige tells her friend Michelle that she does not want the object of her affections, Donny. He winds up bagging groceries for a living and driving a Camero.

Quote/Unquote: Phoebe: 'You want to summon the Ghost of the Past? From where, the fiction shelf?'
  Leo: 'You're meant to relive the experience, not observe it.' Paige: 'I just wanted to come back, sit on the sidelines and make sarcastic comments about my lack of style.'
  Michelle: 'I got grounded for two weeks. My mum pulled this whole oestrogen-fest thing. I swear to God, she is *so* damaged.'
  Piper: 'Frankie and Lulu's unfinished business isn't criminal, it's matrimonial.' Darryl: 'Do you people have any *normal* weddings in your family?'

Notes: 'You can't change history, Paige, only learn from it.' Up until a disappointingly slushy final scene (which, admittedly, reinforces the themes of the episode), this had been one of the best *Charmed* stories in a long time. An essay on guilt and obsession and a brilliant reconstruction of the old time-travel conceit that dictates that time looks after itself to foil any efforts to amend so much as a single life, 'A Paige from the Past' delivers on just about every level. Well-acted, and with a funny and quietly effective second plot concerning Phoebe and Cole, it's just the slightly too obvious nature of the *denouement* that spoils – if only a little bit – the overall effect.

Did You Know?: On it's first syndication broadcast, TNT listed the title of this episode as 'A Paige To Remember.' A number of other media sources have the title as 'Paige From My Past'.

77: TRIAL BY MAGIC

24 January 2002

Writer: Michael Gleason
Director: Chip Scott Laughlin

Cast: Jesse Woodrow (Glenn Belland), Peter Siragusa (Stan Provazolli), Patrick Fischler (Foreman), Cleo King (Tanya), Käthe Mazur (Prosecutor), Lou Giovanetti (Juror), John Thaddeus (Andrew Wike), Shannon O'Hurley (Angela Provazolli), Scott Zeller (Mitch), Charles Walker (Judge), Bart McCarthy (Rat Demon), Ray Proscia (Demon in Charge), Andre Mayers (Bailiff), Jillian Johns (Susan)[51]

> Whilst serving on a jury in the case of a magician accused of murdering his wife, Phoebe has a premonition that the defendant isn't the real killer. Unable to convince her fellow jurors that the man was framed, she must prove that magic exists in order to win them over. Piper becomes irritated when Paige invites her boyfriend, Glenn, to stay.

Dreaming (As Blondie Once Said) is Free: The episode's central theme is the reality of premonitions (both Phoebe's and Stan Provazolli's).

It's Witchcraft: Paige casts a 'stretching the imagination' spell on Glenn ('Let mind and body soar, to heights not reached before, let limits stretch, that you may catch, a new truth to explore'), which gives them both more than they bargained for. The sisters use the 'Spirits of the other side' spell (see 'Charmed Again' Part 1) to summon Angela so that she can convince the jury of her ex-husband's innocence. To do this, Phoebe asks the bailiff for a sage stick, five white candles and some incense.

A Little Learning is a Dangerous Thing: Leo has 'memory dust,' which can be used to prevent mortals from retaining their memories of witchcraft. However, its use is strictly forbidden except in the most dire emergencies. Phoebe suggests erasing the jury's short term memories after they vote not guilty. Paige asks why Leo doesn't use this all the time. Leo replies that such an option is dangerous; one doesn't know what one may be erasing – doctor's appointments, children's birthdays, etc. Ultimately,

---

[51] Uncredited.

SEASON 4: TRIAL BY MAGIC

he *does* use the dust on the jury, although Glenn is allowed to retain his knowledge of Paige's powers, because she trusts him.

The Conspiracy Starts at the Witching Hour: Angela was really murdered by Andrew Wike, the owner of the magic club where her husband was a performer. She was killed in order to silence her when she threatened to expose Wike's money laundering operation. It subsequently transpires that Wike is merely a front for demons who, Phoebe notes, need money to insinuate themselves into the world – to buy clothes, rent apartments and fit in with society. It's probably the same method that was used to make Cole legitimate when he was a demon – they did, after all, put him through law school.

References: The episode is *Charmed*'s version of the classic movie *Twelve Angry Men*. Also, fictional detective Nancy Drew; Las Vegas illusionists Siegfried and Roy; and cosmetics company Avon. Piper wears a San Diego sweatshirt.

'You May Remember Me …': Patrick Fischler's CV includes *Mulholland Drive*, *Speed* and *Nash Bridges*. Cleo King played Helene Parks in *Boston Public* and appeared in *Magnolia* and *Six Degrees of Separation*. Käthe Mazur's movies include *Breast Man* and *Misery Loves Company*. John Thaddeus was in *Sea of Love* and *Ally McBeal*. Shannon O'Hurley appeared in *Minority Report* and *Copycat*. Scott Zeller was in *American Sweethearts*. Bart McCarthy's CV includes *Malcolm in the Middle*. Ray Proscia appeared in *Catch Me If You Can* and *Vanilla Sky*. Andre Mayers was in *Counterstrike* and *Relic Hunter*. Peter Siragusa's movies include *Home Alone*, *The Big Lebowski* and *Auggie Rose*. Jillian Johns was a voice artist on *Eek! The Cat*.

Logic, Let Me Introduce You to This Window: Paige suggests the spell she casts on Glenn 'always works' even though she's never been seen to use it previously. Two weeks is a very short duration for a murder trial – even one with as shaky a defence case as this. At one point Paige holds a glass, but when Phoebe subsequently takes it from her, it's turned into a coffee mug. When Piper tries to help Phoebe with her summoning spell, she says she would not like to relive the hell they went through with Prue, referring to their exposure as witches in 'All Hell Breaks Loose'. However, she shouldn't remember that – time reset itself toward the end of that episode and, effectively, those events never happened.

Continuity: Piper is afraid of rats. She tells Paige that they don't usually encourage houseguests at the Manor, for all the obvious reasons. Piper considers that she can be a little harsh, but notes that this is part of her charm. Glenn refers to Paige by her nickname, 'Noogie.' He has been a friend of Paige's since kindergarten. Having returned from Australia (see 'A Knight To Remember'), Glenn is heading, next, to Tibet. He's also travelled in Africa. Cole has temporarily left, saying that he needed some time to find himself. When giving her sceptical fellow jury members a brief history of magic, Phoebe notes that the origin of magic dates back to prehistoric times, when people from all cultures believed in it. There are angels, she notes, and fairies (see 'Once Upon a Time'). Cupid is also real (see 'Heartbreak City').

Cruelty to Animals: After the Rat Demon turns Wike into a rat, he is eaten by the other Rat Demons.

Quote/Unquote: Paige: 'I pay rent here too.' Piper: 'No, you don't.' Paige: 'It's a figure of speech.' Piper: 'No, it's not.' Paige: 'It *should be*.'
Paige: 'Do we hunt killers that aren't demons?'
Piper: 'I told you to lock all the doors before you go.' Paige: 'I thought you meant the front door. Maybe you should've been more specific.'

Notes: 'Since when do demons give a rat's ass – no pun intended – about laundering money?' A really queer fish, this one. Some of it is very funny, though the plot is virtually non-existent (and what there is seems highly derivative). Odd things happen for no adequately explained reason and huge emphasis is given to, frankly, inconsequential parts of the story. And yet, despite that, there are still a lot of good things on offer.

78: LOST AND BOUND

31 January 2002

Writers: Nell Scovell
Director: Noel Nosseck

Cast: Ray Wise (Ludlow), Alex Black (Tyler), Dwier Brown (Foster Father), Ashley Gardner (Foster Mother), David Reivers (Bob Cowan), Lori Alan (Cynthia), Angelo Tiffe (Security Guard), Kirk Ward (Head Guard), Rick Cramer (Guard #2), Nils Allen Stewart (Demon Bounty Hunter)

> Paige brings Tyler, a runaway, to the Manor after finding him starting a fire with his mind. Piper learns that Tyler's foster parents intend to send him to a demon academy that trains bodyguards for the Source. Elsewhere, Cole starts a new job and Phoebe is given Grams' wedding ring. But, the ring has been hexed to transform the wearer into a stereotypical 1950s housewife.

It's Witchcraft: Phoebe's short and unsuccessful spell to open the academy gates is: 'Door lock, no magic block.' Not one of her finer efforts. Paige, given the job of writing a Power of Three spell for the chief demon, Ludlow, comes up with: 'The brutal winter gives way to flowers of spring, Ludlow is vanquished.' This works, to Phoebe's and Piper's surprise. It's haiku, notes Paige, who couldn't do the rhyming thing.

A Little Learning is a Dangerous Thing: Grams put a curse on her ring with the legend: 'To gain another, to lose oneself.' Although, as Cole points out, she must have felt marriage had *some* good points, otherwise she wouldn't have done it so often.

The Conspiracy Starts at the Witching Hour: Demonic bounty hunters are driven by greed and, according to *The Book of Shadows*, are heartless low-level demons who will stop at nothing to collect their bounty. Firestarters are extremely rare and coveted magical creatures. Their power is linked to their emotions and first manifests itself in adolescence. They're often trained to be the bodyguards of the Source.

Work is a Four-Letter Word: Paige suggests Cole get a job with her at Social Services as a legal aid lawyer. His first case is that of slum landlord Alan Yates, who cut off the heat to his tenants the previous week. A furious Cole beats Yates and then resigns before he can be fired.

It's a Designer Label!: Two outstanding items worth mentioning – Paige's ginger miniskirt and Piper's leather trousers. Cole wears white boxer shorts, seemingly.

References: Phoebe refers to Samantha Stevens in *Bewitched*, saying it was her favourite TV show when she was growing up. Stephen King's *Firestarter* is an apparent influence on the plot.

'You May Remember Me ...': Ray Wise played Leland Palmer in *Twin Peaks* and also appeared in *Resurrection Blvd*, *Bob Roberts*, *Cat People* and *T J Hooker*. Alex Black was in *Spider-Man*. Dwier Brown's movies include *Red Dragon*, *Galaxies Are Colliding* and *To Live And Die in LA*. Ashley Gardner played Ellen in *Johnny Suede* and appeared in *He Said She Said*. Lori Alan was the voice of Pearl Krabs in *SpongeBob Squarepants* and Diane in *Family Guy*. Angelo Tiffe appeared in *Doogie Howser MD*, *Vital Signs* and *3 Ninjas Kick Back*. Kirk Ward's movies include *Camera Obscura* and *Forrest Gump*. Nils Allen Stewart was in *Barb Wire*, *Space Cowboys* and *Undisputed*.

Cigarettes and Alcohol: Phoebe says she'll have a Martini waiting for Cole when he gets in from work.

Logic, Let Me Introduce You to This Window: Why is Piper, the sister normally most interested in having a normal life, so opposed to Leo's suggestion that their children should have their powers bound? When Piper talks about Grams binding the girls' powers, she says Penny did it so they could have a normal childhood. 'That 70s Episode' suggested, on the contrary, that it was done solely to prevent Nicholas from stealing the Charmed Ones' powers. Phoebe, twice, says that Grams was married six times. In 'Magic Hour', and all subsequent episodes, it was four times.

Continuity: Paige has a belly-button ring.

Quote/Unquote: Cole: 'We're hardly typical. I proposed to you under a hail of demon goo and you accepted while I was bleeding to death.'
Phoebe: 'Notice anything different about me?' Piper: 'Engagement ring. Notice it or wear coffee.'
Leo, on potential children: 'Ours will be doubly magical. Half-Whitelighter, half-witch.' Paige: 'Hey, that's like me. Oh. You might have some trouble.'
Paige: 'This is your office. A desk, a chair, a lamp, what more do you need?' Cole: 'Oxygen?'

SEASON 4: LOST AND BOUND

Paige: 'Full frontal Phoebe.' Cole: 'She just flashed.' Paige: 'Yeah, I got that.' Cole: 'No, she just flashed black and white.'

Notes: 'I'm only human, you know.' Phoebe in a bubble bath. Twice. Yes, I know it's a shallow and probably sexist reason for recommending any episode but, to be honest, apart from some nice, experimental ideas surrounding the *Bewitched* simile, there's not much else of any quality going on here. 'Lost and Bound' relies, again, too heavily on schmaltz as a replacement for drama, and wastes its chief bonus – the excellent Ray Wise – by giving him only two scenes. Add Leo's and Piper's pointless (and far too easily resolved) argument about power-binding and you've got a major disappointment on your hands. So ... Phoebe in a bubble bath. Let's leave it at that.

Soundtrack: Phoebe sings a song based on 'Jingle Bells' concerning cooking Cole's dinner. Some of the source music is reminiscent of the *Bewitched* theme tune.

79: CHARMED AND DANGEROUS

7 February 2002

Writers: Monica Breen, Alison Schapker
Director: Jon Paré

Cast: Peter Woodward (The Source), Camilla Rantson (Carolyn), Caprice Benedetti (Angel Guardian), Debbi Morgan (The Seer), Lawrence Smilgys (Demon Guard), Robert Madrid (Darklighter)

> The Source learns from his Seer that his future plans to kill the Charmed Ones will lead to his destruction. The Source then breaks an ancient agreement between Good and Evil and steals the Hollow, a box that can absorb magics. With the Hollow under his control, the Source sends a series of assassins who, in being destroyed by the Charmed Ones, will take the sisters' powers. The Seer, believing that the Source's actions will destroy the future, summons Cole to the Underworld.

It's Witchcraft: Paige uses on her friend Carolyn the 'seen/unseen' spell that she previously used in 'Hell Hath No Fury'. The spell to call a witch's power (see 'How to Make a Quilt Out Of Americans') is also used. Cole and Phoebe believe that they can produce a spell to vanquish the Source by drawing the magic from their ancestors in the Halliwell line.

Five magic crystals, orientated East to West, are required for a magic circle. The spell to vanquish the Source begins: 'Prudence, Patricia, Penelope, Melinda, Astrid, Helena, Laura and Grace, Halliwell witches stand strong beside us, vanquish this evil from time and space.'

A Little Learning is a Dangerous Thing: The Source's face was disfigured in the battle that brought him to power. Only upper-level demons have ever seen it.

The Conspiracy Starts at the Witching Hour: The Seer serves a similar purpose to the Oracle, except that her visions are more powerful and more accurate. She suggests that the Charmed Ones' power is simply greater than that of the Source.

The Hollow is something that consumes all magic, good or evil, and that both sides agreed to guard. The last time it was unleashed, aeons ago, Good and Evil had to combine forces and use their strongest magics, and even then all they could do was contain it.

Work is a Four-Letter Word: Paige is currently involved in the case of Carolyn, a woman who was previously a drug user in an abusive relationship. She has been out of rehab for two years and is currently working at the police station. Paige and Darryl are committed to helping her get a court order for the return of her son.

Oooo, Didn't Expect *That*: At the Seer's suggestion, Cole takes in the Hollow so that he can absorb the Source's power when he attacks the sisters. The Seer says that she has had a vision in which she and Cole will do great things together. After Cole absorbs the Source's power and the Source is vanquished, the Hollow is closed, returning the Charmed Ones' powers to them. Paige wonders where the Source's power went, and the Seer suggests 'Into the void.' However, the episode's final shot, and the (literal) fire in Cole's eyes, would indicate otherwise.

References: The title may be an allusion to Mark Lester's laboured 1986 comedy *Armed and Dangerous*. The Guardians of the Hollow play chess in possible homage to Ingmar Bergman's *The Seventh Seal*.

'You May Remember Me ...': Camilla Rantsen appeared in *Last Exit To Earth*. Peter Woodward is the son of Edward Woodward. His CV includes *The Patriot* and *Bergerac*, on the latter of which he was the fight arranger. Caprice Benedetti's movies include *Shaft* and *The Devil's Advocate*. Debbi Morgan was in *Taxi Driver*, *Roots: The Next Generation*, *Trapper John MD* and *She's All That*.

Sex and Drugs and Rock n Roll: During a celebratory meal at P³, Leo suggests that he and Piper return home and 'get started on [their] future.' Piper has a counter-proposal; going home and sleeping, then working on their future the next night.

Logic, Let Me Introduce You to This Window: If the Elders know about demons attacking the Charmed Ones, then why don't they subsequently realise that Cole is the Source? Cole shows a basic misunderstanding of the legend of Pandora's Box. She wasn't the one in the box, as he suggests, she was the one who opened it, letting out all the evil inside. When the Source opens the Hollow for the first time, some black wires can be seen. In 'All Hell Breaks Loose', the Source had red hands. In 'Brain Drain', they were black. Now, they're white. On virtually every occasion that Piper has wanted to test her powers or to demonstrate that she's lost them, she always seems to throw breakable objects in the air. Couldn't she use something bounceable, like a tennis ball? It's a good job that the girls have an ancestor whose name rhymes with 'space' and that they weren't depending on, for example, finding something that rhymed with Muriel for a successful vanquishing.

Continuity: Piper is in the process of making a will leaving everything to Leo in the event of her death. When Leo is shot with a Darklighter's poisoned arrow, Piper suggests swapping his powers with Phoebe's, something she and Leo had previously done in 'Love Hurts'.

Quote/Unquote: Phoebe: 'Are you still on that will and testament kick?' Piper: 'It's very responsible. Prue did it, and thank God she did, coz if she didn't, we'd still be dealing with lawyers. No offence.' Cole: 'None taken. I've come to terms with my evil past.'

Phoebe: 'One fabulously written Source vanquishing spell.' Cole: 'Don't get cocky.' Phoebe: 'Not cocky, confident.' Piper: 'We are talking about the Source of All Evil. Maybe measured optimism is best.'

Notes: 'Damn the repercussions. I won't stop until I have all three of their powers coursing through my veins.' One of the most important *Charmed* episodes, right up to the – shocking – final shot. From this point onwards, effectively, it's a different show (and in many ways a better one). 'Charmed and Dangerous' takes a while delivering its set-pieces but, when they arrive, they're beautifully formed.

Soundtrack: Natalie Imbruglia's 'Goodbye'.

80: THE THREE FACES OF PHOEBE

14 February 2002

Writer: Curtis Kheel
Director: Joel J Feigenbaum

Cast: Harry Van Gorkum (Kurzon) Frances Bay (Old-Phoebe) Samantha Goldstein (Young-Phoebe) Debbi Morgan (The Seer) Andrew Abelson (Jax) David Reivers (Bob Cowan) Christian Keiber (Scott) Jason Matthew Smith (Demon #1)

> Phoebe develops cold feet over marrying Cole and casts a spell that brings a young, innocent Phoebe and an aged, cynical Phoebe to the Manor to help her make a decision. Meanwhile, Cole finds himself being slowly taken over by the Source. Paige learns that a recent spell has given her the edge over a colleague for a promotion.

Dreaming (As Blondie Once Said) is Free: Cole dreams of, literally, fighting himself as the Source.

It's Witchcraft: Phoebe, with Piper's blessing, casts a spell to hear her heart's desire. This begins: 'Where love is strong, my spirit weak, it is an answer that I seek, the question burns within this fire, so I may hear my heart's desire.'
   To vanquish Kurzon, the spell is: 'Hell threw you from its inner core, but earth won't hold you anymore, since heaven cannot be your place, your flesh and blood we now erase.'

The Conspiracy Starts at the Witching Hour: Vanquishing the Source set evil back by decades, Leo notes. But that doesn't make the Charmed Ones any less of a target. Meanwhile, the Underworld is in chaos, with the Source presumed dead. Kurzon – an enemy of the Source who was banished from the Underworld for inciting a failed coup – is attempting to fill the void.

Work is a Four-Letter Word: Thanks to her success in handling the Carolyn Seldon case (see 'Charmed and Dangerous'), Paige is rewarded with a promotion to social worker, which comes with a flexible work schedule. However, because she used magic to help Carolyn, Paige feels that this is personal gain, and intends to turn down the promotion in favour of her colleague, Scott.

It's a Designer Label!: Paige wears an excellent Siouxsie Sioux sweatshirt. Old-Phoebe suggests that no-one is going to take her seriously until Phoebe stops dressing like a tramp. Phoebe seems delighted by such a description, noting that look is '*so* in right now.'

References: The title refers to Nunnally Johnson's Oscar-winning evocation of multiple personality disorder, *The Three Faces of Eve* (1957). Phoebe notes that *Cinderella* was her favourite story as a child. Young-Phoebe sings a short snatch of the traditional campfire song, 'Row, Row, Row Your Boat'.

'You May Remember Me ...': Harry Van Gorkum appeared in *Under Pressure*, *Brush Strokes* and *The Nanny*. Frances Bay's CV includes *Arachnophobia*, *The Dukes of Hazzard*, *Fane*, *Happy Days*, *The Commish* and *The Wedding Planner*. Samantha Goldstein appeared in *Anywhere But Here*. Andrew Abelson is the son of singer Frankie Vaughan and was in *Gypsy Boys*. Christian Keiber's movies include *My Favourite Martian*. Jason Matthew Smith appeared in *Six Feet Under*.

Logic, Let Me Introduce You to This Window: It's surprising that Piper doesn't recognise Young-Phoebe. They did, after all, grow up together. Young-Phoebe also seems less than concerned about Prue's lack of presence in her future. Piper refers to the events of 'Charmed and Dangerous' as having taken place the night before. However, Paige says that she cast the spell on Carolyn – which happened on the same day that the Source was vanquished – 'last week.' How doesn't Cole waking, screaming, from his nightmare, also wake Phoebe lying next to him? The page in *The Book of Shadows* opposite the Belthazor page, which used to contain Phoebe's photographs of Cole and lots of handwritten annotations, now bears the 'Summon Belthazor' spell, which used to be a few pages later.

Continuity: Paige's orbing powers have improved somewhat and continue to improve as the episode progresses, to such an extent that by the climax she can get halfway across town with both her sisters as passengers. Paige says that she is starving. Leo notes that this is a side-effect of the orbing – it burns a lot of calories. This, he notes, is one of the main reasons why he married a chef. Cole has seemingly told the sisters a little about the Seer's operations (at least enough so that Phoebe recognises the name). The Seer says that good witches are overly cautious by nature. Old-Phoebe, despite knowing that Cole is the Source (and, presumably, what happens to him subsequently), nevertheless still feels enough of the love that she always had for him to save his life and to use her dying breath to give her younger self the advice that seemingly she needed to hear.

Quote/Unquote: Paige: 'I hate it when you're right.' Piper: 'Really? See I usually like it.'

Young-Phoebe: 'Are we going on a plane?' Leo: 'No, but you might see some clouds.'

Piper: 'This demon didn't even seem to know who we were. Which, by the way, I find insulting.'

Old-Phoebe: 'You can't kill me, Cole. You never could.'

Notes: 'You cannot change your fate.' A neat and well-constructed look at the complexities of time as an abstract concept; it contains some terrific performances (Frances Bay is particularly impressive in what could have been a silly conceit) and a rather moving final act. Apart from a somewhat rushed feeling to the climax, this is a terrific example of *Charmed*'s ability to surprise.

81: MARRY-GO-ROUND

14 March 2002

Writer: Daniel Cerone
Director: Chris Long

Cast: Coolio (Lazarus Demon), Debbi Morgan (The Seer), James Read (Victor Bennett), Tony Amendola (Dark Priest), David Doty (Minister)

> The Seer informs Cole that his unborn son will become the most powerful force the magical world has ever seen. However, he will side with good unless certain steps are taken. Cole plans to sabotage his planned wedding, in order to trick Phoebe into entering a dark union.

It's Witchcraft: After Paige's face-cream seems to cause Phoebe to break out in a rash, Paige tries to use the 'Seen/unseen' spell (see 'Hell Hath No Fury'). This goes disastrously wrong when attempts to reverse this make Phoebe become invisible.

A Little Learning is a Dangerous Thing: The Seer notes that Cole's love of Phoebe still exists within the Source.

The Conspiracy Starts at the Witching Hour: Lazarus demons are rare, high-level demons, with telekinetic powers. They are also mean and unreliable and get stronger the longer they are out of cemetery ground. The only way to keep them from resurrecting is to bury them.

A dark wedding ceremony is performed by a dark priest at night and in a cemetery. During this, the groom must drink the bride's blood.

References: Allusions to *Cinderella* and *The Hand that Rocks the Cradle*.

'You May Remember Me ...': Tony Amendola played Bra'tac in *Stargate SG-1*, Sorrel in *Kindred: The Embraced*, Carl Jasper in *Cradle Will Rock* and Sanchez in *Blow*. He also appeared in *Seinfeld*, *Alias*, *Angel*, *24* and *She-Wolf of London*. Most famous as the rapper behind 1995's 'Gangsta's Paradise', Coolio's acting CV includes *Stealing Candy*, *Submerged* and *Batman & Robin*. David Doty appeared in *Never Been Kissed*, *Johnny Skidmarks* and *Daredevil*.

Cigarettes and Alcohol: Leo doesn't smoke cigars. Victor does. Darryl,

SEASON 4: MARRY-GO-ROUND

Victor and Leo throw Cole an unexpected bachelor party with beer, poker, corn chips and (possibly) pornographic videos. Classy.

Logic, Let Me Introduce You to This Window: When Phoebe is invisible, in one scene, Milano can be clearly seen in the mirror. Doesn't Leo recognise a dark wedding when he's an active participant in one?

Continuity: The address of Sophie's Bridal Gowns is 17245 34th Avenue, San Francisco. The (seemingly rather large) lady whose dress – thanks to Cole's intervention – Phoebe ends up with is called Millie Platt. Paige is an aromatherapy practitioner. When Paige shows Piper the death card in her tarot pack, Piper says that death looks nothing like that – Prue met him (see 'Death Takes a Halliwell'). Prue's memorable departure from Piper's wedding on a Harley Davidson (see 'Just Harried') is also mentioned. Phoebe buys Piper and Paige a bonsai tree each for balance and harmony and a dreamcatcher so that all their dreams will come true. Plus some tarot cards.

Cruelty to Animals: Phoebe objects to the throwing of rice at her wedding. Birds can't digest it, she notes. Neither can the guests release balloons as an alternative, as these float to the ocean and whales mistake them for squid.

Quote/Unquote: Piper: 'Phoebe, let's not blow this out of proportion.' Phoebe: 'My wedding dress could double as a circus tent.'
    Cole: 'Are you questioning my leadership?' Seer: 'No. You inherited the world's evil, I'll follow that anywhere.'
    Paige: 'I have been nothing but supportive of that demon.' Phoebe: 'Ex-demon.' Paige: 'Is that like ex-convict?'
    Paige: 'We kick evil's ass every day.' Piper: 'Sometimes twice a day.'
    Cole: 'It's bad luck for the bride to see the groom before the wedding.' Leo: 'I don't think that that's going to be a problem.'

Notes: 'Don't worry, honey. It took Leo and me three times to get married.' The main difference between *Charmed* and other series that coves ostensibly similar dramatic areas is highlighted here. *Charmed*, when it puts it's mind to it, can be downright ludicrously silly. And that can be a *good thing*. The entire third act of this episode (the whole wedding ceremony/fight sequence) is a case in point. Elsewhere, 'Marry-Go-Round' is full of cunning twists and a really clever ending.

82: THE FIFTH HALLIWHEEL

21 March 2002

Writer: Krista Vernoff
Director: David Straiton

Cast: Debbi Morgan (The Seer), Molly Hagan (Karen Young), Mario Schugel (Power Broker), Becky Wahlstrom (Lila), Rebecca Balding (Elise Rothman), Rebekah Ryan (Herself), Chris Butler (Male Law Clerk), Rob Luke (Lingerie Guy), Anne Girard (Lingerie Girl), Dominic Kurtyan (Reporter)

> Paige feels like the fifth wheel around Piper and Leo (celebrating their first anniversary) and the newlywed Cole and Phoebe. Cole learns that he must impregnate Phoebe within the next 24 hours in order to have the prophesised child. Meanwhile, the sisters encounter an innocent advice columnist who was used by a demonic power broker to store a power that may soon kill her.

A Little Learning is a Dangerous Thing: Cole buys Leo and Piper reservations for the finest hotel in Hawaii (along with a couple of nice dinners) as an anniversary gift and because he feels it's not right that they never got a honeymoon. He didn't buy them plane tickets, however, and notes they'll have to orb there.

The Conspiracy Starts at the Witching Hour: The Seer's fertility ritual takes place on the harvest moon, and it will be Cole's one chance to impregnate Phoebe. The power of the moon combined with a specifically-created tonic (mixed into some expensive chocolates that Cole gives her) will make her fertile to a demon's seed and override any preventative measures she may have taken. 'You must feed it to her in the morning and then finish the job when the moon is high in the night's sky,' Cole is told. If he succeeds, the evil spawn growing inside Phoebe will influence her so that when she finally discovers the truth, she will bend to Cole's will.

Power brokers use mortals to store powers until they find a buyer, so that thieves can't get to them. A human possessed of a demonic power will become confused, paranoid, violent and finally demonic, and will ultimately die if the power isn't withdrawn.

Work is a Four-Letter Word: Karen is the advice columnist at the *Bay*

SEASON 4: THE FIFTH HALLIWHEEL

Mirror, where her column has something of a following. She has a very awkward relationship with her editor, Elise Rothman. Whilst Karen is under the power broker's influence, Phoebe has to write her latest column, which she does successfully (it makes Elise laugh). Karen considers that Phoebe's advice to a lonely girl to get a dog is proactive and non-judgmental and that the whole column had a freshness and a passion that it hasn't had for a long time. Karen intends to tell Elise that Phoebe wrote it and then resign to spend more time with her family, but not before recommending that Phoebe takes over.

It's a Designer Label!: Phoebe and Piper go shopping for sexy nightwear at a shop called Intimates.

References: There are oblique allusions to Neil Young's 'Harvest Moon' and to 'Let's Call the Whole Thing Off' (see 'We All Scream for Ice Cream'). Karen has a KEEP SAN FRANCISCO BEAUTIFUL! poster in her office.

'You May Remember Me ...': Molly Hagan's CV includes *Herman's Head*, *Knots Landing* and *Election*. Rebekah Ryan played Heather in *Just Can't Get Enough*. Mario Schugel appeared in *The Division*. Chris Butler was in *Roswell*.

Cigarettes and Alcohol: Only Cole is drinking beer in the opening scene; everybody else seems to be on the Perrier water.

Sex and Drugs and Rock n Roll: Phoebe notes that it's weird how sex can replace sleep and wonders if scientists have done any studies on that. Paige begins to relate a story about her ex-boyfriend, Dave, but Phoebe says that it's different with boyfriends and that sex is better when you're married. Piper suggests that husbands are incredibly sexy.

After Piper eats one of Cole's erotically-enhanced chocolates, she and Leo get down to some serious lovin' in P^3 (thankfully, during a period when there are no customers present).

Logic, Let Me Introduce You to This Window: When Cole gives Phoebe the chocolate, he has it held in his hand for some time. Then the camera angle changes when he talks to Karen, and the chocolate has now disappeared. The doll house that Paige destroys in the attic with her lightning bolt appears to be the same one that was burned by the Evil Enchantress in 'A Knight To Remember'. There doesn't seem to be much of a crowd in P^3 to see Rebekah Ryan. All the girls' hair styles change at least twice during the episode – this is particularly noticeable in Phoebe who starts the episode with long, straight hair, has a shorter, more spiky, style for most of the episode, then ends with it looking more or less how it did at the beginning.

Continuity: Piper tells Paige that you're not a Halliwell until you've gone all demon on your sisters at least twice.

Motors: Cole's new (fake) job – with the law firm Jackson, Carter and Klein – entitles him to a company car, a silver Porsche (which Leo takes an immediate shine to).

Quote/Unquote: Cole, to the Seer: 'I'm trying to be the perfect husband. The perfect brother-in-law. It would help if I didn't have demons waving at me from the dance floor.'
Phoebe: 'What would you tell a 28 year old woman who's still living in her parents' house because she's afraid of living alone.' Piper: 'I'd tell her to get a life.'
Phoebe: 'How do you spell oblique?' Piper: 'With spell-check.'

Notes: 'Spying on the husband. Now that's a sure fire way to reconnect with your sister.' A nicely constructed house of cards, with Julian McMahon at his most deliciously two-faced and Rose McGowan acting her cotton socks off in the scenes where Paige succumbs to paranoia. It's not wholly successful (the Phoebe subplot is a bit weak) but it's got a number of laugh-out-loud moments (Leo and Piper orbing in from Hawaii when Paige attacks Phoebe, and Cole's and Piper's annoyed 'This had better be important!' for example). Watch – with some pleasure – Leo's giddy-schoolboy act when given the chance to drive Cole's Porsche, or that great moment in the shop when Phoebe emerges wearing a sexy night-dress, asks Piper what she thinks, and a guy in the background, shopping with his wife, says 'Wow!'

Soundtrack: Groove Armada's ambient-trance classic 'Join Hands', Kylie Minogue's 'Can't Get You Out Of My Head', 'Let's Get It On' by Marvin Gaye and Rebekah Ryan's 'Big Trouble (Lots of Fun)'.

83: SAVING PRIVATE LEO

28 March 2002

Teleplay: Daniel Cerone
Story: Doug E Jones
Director: John Behring

Cast: Evie Peck (Maria), Costas Mandylor (Rick Lang), Louis Mandylor (Nathan Lang), Rene Heger (Greg), Deborah Kellner (Julie), James Greene (Old Man), Lauri Johnson (Secretary), Obie Sims (Security Guard), Colin McClean (Lawyer), Joel Anderson (Billy), Tom Finnegan (Franklin), Cheryl Anderson (Curious Woman), Charles C Stevenson Jr (Surdez)

> The girls encounter the ghosts of two of Leo's war comrades who are seeking revenge because they believe that he left them to die. Confronted by the memory of letting down his friends, Leo loses his powers when the ghosts kill one of his charges. Cole enlists the help of a demon to make Phoebe's life unhappy at the Manor in order to get her to move away from her sisters.

It's Witchcraft: Leo can self-heal so long as the injury is non-fatal. It is suggested that Leo's powers are, just like the sisters' powers, tied to his emotions.

There is a potion to vanquish ghosts. This must be poured over their bones. (Piper notes that they used it a couple of years ago – see 'The Power of Two'). There also exists a vanquishing spell for ghosts – 'Ashes to ashes, spirit to spirit, take their souls, banish this evil' – but it works only if it's said *by* another ghost (see also 'Necromancing the Stone'). Fortunately (in a roundabout way) Piper is, briefly, killed by Rick and Nathan and can thus vanquish them.

A Little Learning is a Dangerous Thing: Paige notes that Rick and Nathan are the first ghosts she's met that she wasn't related to (see 'Charmed Again', 'A Paige from the Past').

The Conspiracy Starts at the Witching Hour: Cole interviews Julie for the job as his new PA. She has previously worked as a paralegal, drafting various kinds of legal documents including administrative, pre-trial, trial, motions and pleadings. Her dictation speed is 120 words per minute. She's also a demon and can shimmer across town at a rate of 30 miles in two seconds. Her powers include using fireballs and shape-shifting. Her last kill was two years earlier, though she considers that killing is messy. Her services, she notes, are usually a little more discreet. Cole initially gives her a trial period, but she impresses by impersonating Cole when Phoebe rings, so then she's given the job permanently.

Work is a Four-Letter Word: As suggested at the end of the previous episode, Phoebe has, indeed, replaced Karen as the advice columnist on the *Bay Mirror*.

It's a Designer Label!: Phoebe's white drawstring trousers.

References: The title alludes to Steven Spielberg's World War II drama *Saving Private Ryan*. Also references to *Ghostbusters*; *The Terminator*; and *Cinderella*. There's a very obvious visual allusion to *Basic Instinct*.

'You May Remember Me …': Evie Peck appeared in *Gilmore Girls*. Costas Mandylor's movies include *Cover Story* and *Mobsters*. Rene Hegar played Stefan in *September Song*. Louis Mandylor was Nick in *My Big Fat Greek Wedding* and appeared in *Martial Law* and *Relic Hunter*. Deborah Kellner was in *Blast From the Past* and *Unhappily Ever After*. Lauri Johnson was a voice artist on *The Jetsons* and appeared in *Laurel Canyon*. Tom Finngean's movies include *Hoffa*, *Die Hard 2*, *Dick Tracy* and *Repo Man*. Joel Anderson was in *The West Wing* and *Cold Case*. Cheryl Anderson's CV includes *Two Idiots in Hollywood* and *Mirrors*.

Cigarettes and Alcohol: Many cocktails are being drunk at the swanky drinks party that Cole takes Phoebe to.

Logic, Let Me Introduce You to This Window: The title is erroneous – Leo was a corporal. When Leo meets the ghosts, one of the brothers has his hands crossed in front of him. From a different camera angle, however, they're behind his back. Paige's lipstick changes colour between two consecutive scenes. Piper tells Paige that Leo posthumously won the Medal of Honour. In 'Ex Libris' it was a Purple Heart.

Paige's research indicates that Nathan and Rick died on the same day as Leo, but she later finds out that they were buried on 22 November 1942 and Leo, very definitely, died two days later. Usually when Piper freezes a projectile, it will continue on its path once unfrozen. In this episode, she unfreezes the knife thrown at her and it drops to the floor. Leo's guilt over the death of his friends doesn't really make sense (he could have done nothing to prevent the explosion and he died just a few days later himself). Then again, guilt is frequently based on illogicality. On one occasion,

SEASON 4: SAVING PRIVATE LEO

Phoebe switches off her laptop by unplugging it from the wall without powering it down first, which is a recipe for losing unsaved documents. When subsequently the power cuts out, the machine dies on her, something it shouldn't don if its battery is charged. The headline of the article that Phoebe is working on, briefly glimpsed on her computer, is VAN LEWEN FAMILY ESTATE CHOSEN AS TREASURE HOUSE FOR SAN FRANCISCO. This may be a reference to 'Reckless Abandon', but it wouldn't seem to have an awful lot to do with the job that the *Bay Mirror* hired Phoebe for.

Continuity: Passing himself off as his own grandson, Leo attends a 60th Anniversary Reunion for local veterans of the Battle of Guadalcanal.[52] Corporal Leo Wyatt was born on 6 May 1924 and died, having saved the life of at least three of the elderly men who attend the reunion, on 24 November 1942 (see 'Exit Strategy'). Leo, Rick and Nathan grew up together in Burlingame, andLeo and Nathan went to school together. When the war came, they made a deal with their recruitment officer that they would enlist as long as they could join the same unit. For some odd reason, Piper's wheatgerm pancakes prove to be very unpopular. Cole's deposition papers are in the folder with the jelly stain and not, as he believed, the folder covered with cream cheese spread.

Quote/Unquote: Leo: 'The only courage that matters is the kind that gets you from one moment to the next.'
    Rick: 'Payback's a witch.'
    Phoebe: 'Leo lost his powers and then Piper died and it got really dicey when she turned into a ghost but everything worked out.' Cole: 'Glad it was nothing serious.'

Notes: 'Some say hatred can harden the heart.' Scratch the revenge-saga scenario of 'Saving Private Leo' and you'll find some disappointments; it's a frequently illogical episode, in which things happen for no real reason, explanations often make little sense and the *denouement* is pretty tame. That's a shame, because much of the acting is really good.

---

[52] One of the most bloody and difficult battles of World War II, in which the island of Guadalcanal in the Solomon Islands was invaded by US forces in early November 1942. What was expected to be a short contest against a small Japanese garrison ended up as a campaign that lasted over six months – the first of a series of intense, savage battles across the Pacific.

84: BITE ME

18 April 2002

Writer: Curtis Kheel
Director: John Kretchmer

Cast: Elizabeth Gracen (Vampire Queen), Samuel Ball (Rowan), Deborah Kellner (Julie), Jay Acovone (Keats), Shishir Kurup (Doctor), Michael DeVorzon (Vampire), Michael Bailey Smith (Grimlock), Betty K Bynum (Harpy Leader), April Mills (Orlin)

> Cole conspires to bring a number of evil factions together in an alliance. An old enemy of the Source, the Vampire Queen, plots to turn Paige into a vampire and use her power to defeat Cole. Once Paige is bitten, her sisters rush to stop her before she drinks the blood of an innocent, which will complete her transformation. Piper, meanwhile, begins to share Paige's suspicions that Cole may be evil again, and Phoebe learns that she is pregnant.

It's Witchcraft: To vanquish the Harpy that attacks them, the sisters' spell is: 'Cause of pain we have dissevered, demon you are gone forever.'

A Little Learning is a Dangerous Thing: Vampires have excellent hearing.

The Conspiracy Starts at the Witching Hour: Vampires have been ostracised from the Underworld for centuries after the Vampire Queen tried to exterminate the previous Source.
Amongst those Underworld figures attending the Source's gathering of the clans are the leaders of the Grimlocks (see 'Blind-Sided', 'All Halliwell's Eve') and the Furies.
Piper, Phoebe and Leo search *The Book of Shadows* for the potential attackers of Paige. They discuss the Manticore (fights but doesn't fly), the Phoenix (flies but doesn't fight), *el Chupacabra*[53] (flies and bites but attacks only livestock) and shapeshifters.

References: There's a very amusing visual gag referring to *The Evil Dead II*, and an allusion to Hammer's classic *Kiss of the Vampire*. Also, *Highlander*;

---

[53] The mythical Mexican vampiric 'goat-sucker', as used in *The X-Files* episode 'El Mundo Gira'.

novelist Anne Rice; and the Dave Clark Five's 'Catch Me if You Can'. Posters glimpsed in P3 include those for the Kenny Wayne Shepherd Band, Rage Against the Machine and U2. Manticore was the name of the sinister group in *Dark Angel*.

Oooo, Bitchy!: When Leo comments that vampires are 'part of a whole different network now,' this is a thinly-veiled reference to the extremely acrimonious move of *Buffy the Vampire Slayer* from the WB to UPN a year earlier.

'You May Remember Me …': Elizabeth Gracen played Amanda Darieux in *Highlander* and appeared in *The Flash*. Samuel Ball's movies include *Kingpin* and *Chasing the Dragon*. Jay Acovone appeared in *Crocodile Dundee in Los Angeles*, *Snitch*, *Studio City*, *Stargate SG-1*, *Foxfire*, *Times Square*, *Stepfather III* and *Cold Steel*. Shishir Kurup was in *Friends*, *Chicago Hope*, *The Prime Gig* and *Anywhere But Here*. April Mills played Ren in *Shasta McNasty* and Celeste in *Boy Meets World*. Michael DeVorzon was in *Sons of the Beach*. Betty K Byrum appeared in *ER*.

Cigarettes and Alcohol: Phoebe checks that she still gets free drinks at P3. (As she's co-owner, is there any reason why she *shouldn't*?)

Sex and Drugs and Rock n Roll: There's the expected 'vampirism-as-a-euphemism-for-sex' angle to Rowan's and Paige's conversation in the Underworld.

Leo and Piper have been trying for a baby for approximately four months now. So far, they've been unsuccessful, despite their hopes being briefly raised by Piper's late period this month.

Logic, Let Me Introduce You to This Window: Phoebe's shoulder injury disappears between the Manor and her apartment but reappears the next morning. When Cole tells his minions to exterminate the vampires, his hairstyle is gelled down, different from how it was either prior or subsequent to this scene. When Phoebe discovers that she's pregnant, she faints. She falls to the right, so she should be lying on her left side. However, when we see her on the floor, she's lying on her right. When Paige leaves P3, the ground appears wet. However, in a close up of her on the ground when she's attacked by bats, it's completely dry. Surely, despite keeping her own surname, Phoebe should be *Mrs* Halliwell now, not Miss as the doctor calls her?

Continuity: Phoebe's usual breakfast is a vegetarian egg-white omelette. 'I've turned into so many things, I can't keep track,' notes Piper wearily

SEASON 4: BITE ME

(see 'The Wendigo', 'Coyote Piper', 'Hell Hath No Fury' etc).

Cruelty to Animals: No vampire bats were injured during the filming of this episode, apparently.

Quote/Unquote: Julie: 'Pretty little witch. If you're into that sort of thing.' Cole: 'I am.'

Piper: 'You got attacked by bats outside of my club? That can't be natural.'

Piper: 'According to the book, if you kill a vampire queen then all her little vampires die with her.' Cole: 'Really? Interesting. They certainly don't like to spread *that* around.'

Queen: 'We are offering immortal life. An eternity together as sisters. Isn't that preferable to death?' Piper: 'Are those our only two choices? Because I prefer the scenario where you die and we get to stay human.'

Notes: 'It's a demon-eat-demon world out there.' They'd done *so* well, they'd steered clear of vampires for *so* long ... Finally, the lure proved irresistible, and *Charmed* risked ridicule by entering the territory of its biggest rival. And, remarkably, it just about gets away with it too. 'Bite Me' is, of course, a completely different take on the vampire genre than Joss Whedon's (more *Dark Shadows* than Terence Fisher, more *Dracula AD 1972* than Tod Browning), but it's got a lot of fun ideas and, perhaps as importantly, it takes the subject just as seriously as it needs to be taken, without going all Anne Rice on us (which, ironically, puts it and *Buffy the Vampire Slayer*, for once, in *exactly* the same corner). Nevertheless, the best bits of the episode involve Cole's dealing with his Underworld minions and avoid much in the way of genre-stretching conceits. Perhaps that's just as well.

Soundtrack: Dropline's 'Graduation Day', and 'Welcome To My Party' by Rusted Root.

85: WE'RE OFF TO SEE THE WIZARD

25 April 2002

Writers: Alison Schapker, Monica Breen
Director: Timothy Lonsdale

Cast: Armin Shimerman (Wizard), Michael Des Barres (Dark Priest), Deborah Kellner (Julie), Debbi Morgan (The Seer), Dayo Ade (Bodyguard #3), Jeff Henry (New Bodyguard), Osman Soykut (Dark Priest #2)

> Cole's coronation cannot take place if a wizard steals *The Grimoire* (an evil counterpart of *The Book of Shadows*). To achieve this, the wizard seeks the help of the Charmed Ones. While Piper works on a plan to steal *The Grimoire*, Paige tells Phoebe that both she and Piper believe Cole to be a demon again. Phoebe subsequently learns the truth when she has a premonition. However, Phoebe's pregnancy, and her love for Cole, cause her to become conflicted between good and evil.

It's Witchcraft: Fire-throwing is said to be an upper-level demonic power.

Wizards are supposed to have been extinct for many centuries – they were all wiped out by a previous Source. According to the Elders, some wizards are evil, and this, it would seem, includes the final representative of the race. He wants *The Grimoire* for himself as it contains a spell that can consecrate a weapon and make the wizard strong enough to kill (and replace) the Source. He will then have enough magic to resurrect his people.

A Little Learning is a Dangerous Thing: Like *The Book of Shadows*, *The Grimoire* protects itself – although in this case, it cannot be handled by good.

Julie describes Phoebe as just a means to an end, a way to sire a magical child. Phoebe then, very satisfyingly, vanquishes the demon.

The Conspiracy Starts at the Witching Hour: It's been 500 years, give or take a decade, since the previous Source's coronation.

References: The title comes from *The Wizard of Oz*. There are dialogue

SEASON 4: WE'RE OFF TO SEE THE WIZARD

allusions to *The Lord of the Rings*, to the Harry Potter novels and to Merlin the Magician from the Arthurian legends.

'You May Remember Me ...': The great Armin Shimerman played Pascalion *Beauty and the Beast*, Quark in *Star Trek: Deep Space 9* and Principal Snyder in *Buffy the Vampire Slayer*. He also appeared in *Stargate SG-1*, *The West Wing*, *Ally McBeal*, *The Lazarus Man*, *Blind Date*, *Girls Club*, *The Hitcher* and *Stardust Memories*. Michael Des Barres was the singer with 70s rock-band Detective. His acting CV includes *Mulholland Drive*, *Melrose Place*, *WKRP in Cincinnati* and *To Sir, With Love*. Dayo Ade was in *Degrassi Junior High* and *The Shield*. Jeff Henry appeared in *Boxing's Been Good To Me*. Osman Soykut's movies include *The Killing Machine*.

Sex and Drugs and Rock n Roll: Julie tells Cole that she is worried about him and about Phoebe's influence on him; specifically, that their forthcoming baby will make the pull of love even greater. She believes that Cole's humanity will weaken him, unless he allows the Seer to perform her dark magic and let Julie herself carry the baby. He then won't need the witch anymore, and Julie can be his queen. The Underworld, she continues, will not tolerate a leader who's conflicted with any signs of weakness.

Subsequently, the Seer adds that the Source's biggest problem is suppressing Cole. The human streak within him is growing stronger, and at the worst possible time. Cole cannot believe that the Seer tricked him into hiring a seductress. The Seer says that she was concerned about the baby's influence on Cole. 'Then what?' asks Cole. 'You hoped if I'd gotten laid ...'

Logic, Let Me Introduce You to This Window: When Cole beheads the guard, the middle of the blade severs the head. But when we see the weapon, the blood stain is near the handle. When Phoebe tells her sisters that she's pregnant, she is wearing high-heeled shoes. Later, when she abruptly leaves for work, these have changed to black boots. The Seer tells Cole that it's the Source that protects him against the Charmed Ones' powers and Phoebe's premonitions. But in 'Charmed and Dangerous', Phoebe received a premonition about the Source.

Continuity: The episode takes place 'a couple of days' after the events of 'Bite Me'. Phoebe gets a bunch of new powers – teleportation and pyrokinesis, for example – though these seem to be the powers of her son. She subsequently loses them in 'Womb Raider'. Paige doesn't have wisdom teeth. There's an allusion to Phoebe's evil former life in 'Pardon My Past'.

SEASON 4: WE'RE OFF TO SEE THE WIZARD

Quote/Unquote: Paige: 'If it looks like a demon and walks like a demon …' Piper: 'That's ducks, not Phoebe's husband.'

Phoebe: 'What makes you think I'm lying?' Cole: 'Coz every time you lie, I can see your wisdom teeth.'

Piper: 'What an idiot. Doesn't every demon know by now whose house this is?'

Piper: 'You need to stand still or you're gonna go poof like your friend in there.' Wizard: 'You're the touchy one, aren't you? I've heard about you. Peeper?' Piper: 'Piper.' Wizard: 'Whatever.'

Wizard: 'Merlin was an overrated hack. Tell me he's not the only wizard you've heard about.' Paige: 'Does Harry Potter count?'

Notes: 'Screw the Power of Three.' The beginning of the 'Dark-Phoebe'-arc, during which *Charmed* told some of its most ambiguous and interesting stories. Gone, for the moment, were the clear-cut monochrome issues that the series had previously (mostly) dealt in, to be replaced by shades of grey. 'We're Off to See the Wizard' is an unusual start to thi,s, in so much as it is first and foremost a comedy episode. Yet in the extraordinary final moments, we have *Charmed* becoming dangerous and subversive out of left-field, with Phoebe embracing her 'new destiny.'

86: LONG LIVE THE QUEEN

2 May 2002

Writer: Krista Vernoff
Director: Jon Paré

Cast: Jaime P Gomez (Greg Conroy), Jeffrey Meek (Dane), Michael Burgess (Demon), Rebecca Balding (Elise), Debbi Morgan (The Seer), Joel West (Malek), Aldis Hodge (Trey), Susan Balboni (Secretary), David Heckel (Seedy Demon), Jeff Henry (Demonic Bodyguard), Matthew Grant (Demon), James Leo Ryan (Raum)

> Phoebe find herself the Queen of the Underworld and is given a tonic by the Seer that will suppress the remnants of her good side. However, after having a premonition that one of Cole's demons will kill an innocent, she surprises her sisters by requesting their help.

It's Witchcraft: The sisters use the Source-vanquishing spell (see 'Charmed and Dangerous') to destroy Cole. Amongst the potions that Piper is seen preparing is one that duplicates her freezing power, plus it scalds the flesh. She suggests that they should use that one only in a dire emergency.

The Conspiracy Starts at the Witching Hour: The Seer suggests that there's nothing regular about Phoebe's pregnancy, and that the new power Phoebe is experiencing is a mere shadow of what's to come.

Work is a Four-Letter Word: Phoebe tells the Seer that, despite her new status as Queen of the Underworld, she wants to carry on with her day job as an advice columnist.

It's a Designer Label!: Phoebe's leatherette/dominatrix look.

References: Phoebe is reading a copy of *Playing Straight* magazine.

'You May Remember Me ...': Jaime P Gomez appeared in *Nash Bridges*, *Crimson Tide* and *LA Story*. Jeffrey Meek was in *She's No Angel*, *Mortal Kombat: Conquest* and *Raven*. Aldis Hodge's movies include *Big Momma's House*. David Heckel played Ned in *Orson Welles Sells His Soul to the Devil*. Matthew Grant was the writer/producer of the movie *Down the Barrel*. James Leo Ryan appeared in *Psycho Beach Party*. Joel West was in *Elite* and

SEASON 4: LONG LIVE THE QUEEN

Firefly.

Cigarettes and Alcohol: A depressed Piper gets wasted on Jack Daniels.

Logic, Let Me Introduce You to This Window: When orbing in, Piper calls to Phoebe in the bathroom, with its door closed. How does Piper know Phoebe's in there? Leo clearly moves whilst frozen in P³.

Continuity: Leo cannot heal self-inflicted wounds.

Quote/Unquote: Phoebe: 'Can you do anything about this thunder, because it is making me nuts.' The Seer: 'I have no sway over the weather. I do have a friend who works with wind, but she's out of town.'
  Malek: 'The Charmed Ones interfered with my kill.' Cole: 'I have no control over my in-laws. If you want them out of the way, I suggest you take backup.'
  Elise, reading Phoebe's latest column: '"Dear Betrayed, I suggest you beat your cheating husband with his secretary's stapler. Then he'll think twice before bending her over her desk again."'
  Cole, on the Underworld: 'If they think we're working both sides, they will revolt. If they do that, if they unite against us, I promise we will pray for death.'

Notes: 'This is not a game, Phoebe. You walked through a one way door. You try to turn around now, they will destroy us.' A magnificent conclusion. All the regulars are given plenty to do, with the barbed interplay between Piper and Phoebe sandwiched between some surprising and welcome wisdom from Paige. 'Long Live the Queen' also includes one of *the* great moments in *Charmed*'s history, as Phoebe suddenly morphs into Cole and the innocent the sisters have been protecting is killed.

Soundtrack: Sarah Polley's 'Courage' plays at the end, as her sisters comfort a heartbroken Phoebe.

87: WOMB RAIDER

9 May 2002

Writer: Daniel Cerone
Director: Mel Damski

Cast: Debbi Morgan (The Seer), Jeffrey Meek (Dane), Tony Amendola (Dark Priest), Carel Struycken (Giant Demon), Aaron Lustig (Dr Harris), Mike Pavone (Doctor), Nicholas Cascone (Inspector Miles), Cynthia Yoshikawa (Nurse), Matthew Kaminsky (EMT)

> Phoebe dreams that the Seer intends to steal her unborn child. Meanwhile, the baby begins to use magic – mainly to harm Paige. The Seer offers an imprisoned demon his freedom in return for capturing Phoebe.

Dreaming (As Blondie Once Said) is Free: A recurring nightmare sees Phoebe trapped in the 'devil baby' genre (see *Rosemary's Baby, I Don't Want to Be Born, To the Devil a Daughter* etc).

It's Witchcraft: Paige uses the 'Seen/unseen' spell to clear up the carnage at Cole's and Phoebe's penthouse apartment. The sisters use the Power of Three spell (see 'Something Wicca This Way Comes') to hold off the Seer.

A Little Learning is a Dangerous Thing: Through some sort of – unexplained – energy inversion, the Power of Three added to the power of the Source within her causes the Seer to self destruct and take the entire Underworld council with her. As Piper notes, the balance of power has been significantly tilted in favour of good. Subsequently, Leo tells Piper that *The Grimoire* now has a new home in a mountain of rock in the West Andes.

The Conspiracy Starts at the Witching Hour: Darryl helps the sisters cover up Cole's death, making it seem as though Cole and Phoebe have had an argument and Cole has left.
Dane (see 'Long Live The Queen') is due to be the new Source until the Seer intervenes. The succession of Sources is, unless otherwise unavoidable due to extermination, decided by direct lineage through blood, or by magic. *The Book of Shadows* notes that the Seer has served multiple Sources and has been around for thousands of years. She is immune to spells and

SEASON 4: WOMB RAIDER

charms, but *The Book of Shadows* classifies her as an upper-level demon.

Oral tradition tells of a giant demon whose body served as a portal to other dimensions. Because he was imprisoned centuries ago, no-one knows the demon's name, or if he even exists. There is no known vanquish for him, and the Source was so threatened that he condemned the giant to spend eternity in a cage designed by the Seer. Phoebe – with a little help from her evil baby – vanquishes the giant.

References: The title comes from the *Tomb Raider* series of computer games. Also, allusions to *Poltergeist* (the vortex in the closet); Wolfgang Amadeus Mozart (1756-91); Ozzy Osbourne; and the character Chucky from the *Child's Play* movies. The Seer paraphrases the Biblical verse Mark 10:14.

'You May Remember Me ...': Carel Struyckun played Lurch in *The Addams Family* and appeared in *Twin Peaks* and *Star Trek: The Next Generation*. Aaron Lustig's movies include *Edward Scissorhands*, *Bedazzled* and *Clear and Present Danger*. Nicholas Cascone was in *The West Wing*, *18 Again!* and *Locust Valley*. Matthew Kaminsky is best known as the announcer of T-Mobile's TV adverts. He also appeared in *The Sky is Falling*.

Sex and Drugs and Rock n Roll: Paige's most recent date was so quiet during dinner that she believed she could hear his stomach digesting. Piper says she prefers quiet men – they make good listeners.

Logic, Let Me Introduce You to This Window: When Piper knocks the raw steak from Phoebe's hand, watch the fruit bowl move positions between this and the following scene. Haven't the sisters bothered to look up the Seer in *The Book of Shadows* before now?

Continuity: Piper learns that – due to various bits of blunt force trauma on her body – she may have problems bearing a child. Phoebe's pregnancy ends when the Seer absorbs the baby.

Quote/Unquote: Paige: 'I guess that's what you get when you breed with the Source of All Evil.' Phoebe: 'Can we not say breed? I'm not a horse.'

Phoebe: 'My head was on fire like a tiki-torch a few seconds ago.' Piper: 'Do not change the subject. Did your baby just electrocute the nice doctor man?'

Giant: 'Nobody comes down to the Source's dungeon. Unless they are dead, damned or desperate. Which are you?'

Paige, awaking to find herself in the Seer's cage: 'So, what are you, into some kind of dominatrix thing now?'

SEASON 4: WOMB RAIDER

Piper: 'You summoned me here just in time to be sacrificed?' Paige: 'The plan *does* have a few flaws, admittedly.'

Notes: 'How can I go to the doctor when I have a demonically-challenged baby?' A strange, stilted, almost lifeless end to the lengthy, season-spanning arc. Admittedly it is enlivened by the pyrotechnic overload of the last act, but that still can't quite mask the weak and disappointing aspects of the episode.

Soundtrack: 'Stealing Babies' by Our Lady Peace.

88: WITCH WAY NOW?

16 May 2002

Writer: Brad Kern
Director: Brad Kern

Cast: Dakin Matthews (Angel of Destiny), Bruce Campbell (Agent Jackman), Leslie Grossman (Phoebe's Assistant), Samantha Shelton (Selena), Gwen Stewart (TV Psychic)

> The Charmed Ones are visited by the Angel of Destiny, who offers them non-magical lives again as a reward for vanquishing the Source. While Paige wants to keep her powers, Piper and Phoebe seriously consider the offer. Phoebe discovers that Cole is still alive on another plane of existence, the Wasteland. The girls are blackmailed by an FBI agent, who claims to be after a woman he believes to be a serial killer of witches.

It's Witchcraft: The spell that Phoebe uses to find a lost love begins: 'Wither my love, wherever you be, through time and space, take my heart near to thee.'

Jackman has an amulet that makes him immune to Piper's freezing powers.

The Angel of Destiny tells the girls that, should they take his offer, *The Book of Shadows* will pass to some future descendent.

The Conspiracy Starts at the Witching Hour: The Wasteland is where all vanquished demons end up. The Angel of Destiny notes that Cole (and, presumably, everyone else there) is outside destiny's reach. Through a series of random events that frankly defy logic, Cole survives, kills the Beast (the creature within the Wasteland) and returns to this plane of existence to save Phoebe from the insane Jackman. He tells her that he has a whole bunch of new powers.

A Little Learning is a Dangerous Thing: Cole suggests that Phoebe can save him using the same resurrection spell from *The Grimoire* that the Wizard was attempting to acquire (see 'We're Off to See the Wizard').

Work is a Four-Letter Word: One of Cole's desperate attempts to contact Phoebe from the Wasteland seems him using a TV psychic, Tasmin.

SEASON 4: WITCH WAY NOW?

It's a Designer Label!: Highlight – Paige's bodice.

References: The Angels of Destiny (there are several) normally don't intervene in the specific destinies of mortals – except in extraordinary cases. These include Mozart at the age of seven (see 'Womb Raider'), Michelangelo (1475-1564), Albert Einstein (1880-1952) and Britney Spears. Also, *Bewitched* (Piper uses Samantha's trademark nose-twitch as a signal to Phoebe that the coast is clear).

Bruce Campbell: A legend in his own lifetime, Bruce Campbell played the title characters in *Jack of All Trades* and *The Adventures of Brisco County Jr*, William Roberts in *Timequest*, Ed Billik in *Ellen*, Autolycus in *Hercules: The Legendary Journeys* and *Xena: Warrior Princess* and, most famously, Ash in *The Evil Dead* and its several sequels. His movies include *Spider-Man*, *Intolerable Cruelty*, *The Majestic*, *From Dusk Till Dawn 2: Texas Blood Money*, *Escape from LA*, *Fargo*, *The Hudsucker Proxy*, *Mindwarp*, *Darkman*, *Maniac Cop*, *Crimewave* and *Oedipus Rex*.

'You May Remember Me ...': Dakin Matthews appeared in *Thirteen Days*, *Flubber*, *Gilmore Girls* and *Eve of Destruction*. Leslie Grossman enjoyed an enormous cult following playing Mary Cherry on *Popular*. She was also in *CSI*, *Can't Hardly Wait* and *Nip/Tuck*. Samantha Shelton's movies include *Sorority Boys* and *Hairshirt*. Gwen Stewart appeared in *24*.

Sex and Drugs and Rock n Roll: Piper refers to Paige's sexual allure as her 'God-given magic.'

Logic, Let Me Introduce You to This Window: Jackman buries amulets around the area where he intends to burn Selena. The effect of these is to nullify magic. Therefore, how do the sisters orb into this area? Piper is suspicious of Jackman because, she says, there are no cones around his van. However, at least one is clearly visible. Cole's facial hair continues to grow even in the Wasteland. Paige's outrageous hairstyle in the final scene makes her look like Mickey Mouse.

Continuity: At the end of the episode, we learn that Piper is pregnant. Paige refers to the events of 'Bite Me', 'Size Matters' and 'Enter the Demon'. Leo, somewhat against the rules, orbs Agent Jackman's files on the Charmed Ones into a volcano.

Quote/Unquote: Piper, to Paige: 'Did you not have the sense to sense if anybody else was in the room before you orbed us in here?'
Angel of Destiny: 'Frankly, I thought you were being a bit premature.'

SEASON 4: WITCH WAY NOW?

Piper: 'Then, why didn't you say something?' **Angel of Destiny:** 'Can't. Free will and all. Let me know when you're ready.'

Notes: 'I'm the Angel of Destiny and I'm here to change yours.' Another pilot episode for another new *Charmed* – and a really good one. 'Witch Way Now?' deliberately provides a blind alley for the girls to be trapped in and then gives them a new purpose and a new destiny in a truly thrilling chunk of unadulterated 'Be careful what you wish for' plotting. Excellent performances all round (Bruce Campbell and Julian McMahon battle it out for who can acheive the best evil snarl) and great set-pieces add to the fun (Paige serving the workmen lemonade as a distraction is brilliant). A fine episode, albeit one with a somewhat signposted conclusion.

Soundtrack: Ozzy Osbourne's 'Gets Me Through'.

Did You Know?: 'I like the opportunity to play characters who have these dark sides but make the audience empathise with them,' Julian McMahon has noted. 'I consider playing what was, essentially, the devil in *Charmed* and have the audience rooting for me quite an honour. The Source wanted to kill the sisters, and seemingly so did most of the audience.'

CHARMED SEASON 5
(2002-2003)

Consulting Producer: Jonathan Levin
Co-Producers: Mark Wilding (88-100), Laurie Parres (88-100), Krista Vernoff (88-100), Peter Chomsky, Alison Schapker (101-110), Monica Breen (101-110)
Producers: Daniel Cerone (880-100), Holly Marie Combs, Alyssa Milano, Jon Paré, Krista Vernoff (101-110)
Supervising Producer: Daniel Cerone (101-110)
Co-Executive Producer: James L Conway
Executive Producers: Brad Kern, Aaron Spelling, E Duke Vincent
Executive Story Editors: Alison Schapker (88-100), Monica Breen (88-100), Curtis Kheel (103-110)
Story Editors: Curtis Kheel (88-102), Henry Alonso Myers

Regular Cast:
Holly Marie Combs (Piper Halliwell)
Alyssa Milano (Phoebe Halliwell)
Rose McGowan (Paige Matthews)
Dorian Gregory (Darryl Morris, 89-90, 98-100, 106,[54] 109-111)
Brian Krause (Leo Wyatt)
Julian McMahon (Cole Turner, 89-93, 95-100, 106[55])

---

[54] Dorian Gregory's appearance in 'Cat House' is archive footage from 'Just Harried'.
[55] Julian McMahon's appearance in 'Cat House' is archive footage from 'Just Harried'.

89: A WITCH'S TAIL PART 1

22 September 2002

Writer: Daniel Cerone
Director: James L Conway

Cast: Jaime Pressly (Mylie), Dan Gauthier (Craig), Diane Salinger (Sea Hag), Charles Walker (Judge), David Reivers (Bob Cowan), Judson Scott (Necron), Fred Koehler (Necron's Lackey), Sybil Azur (Assistant), Ellen Bradley (Ticket Agent)

> Piper, Phoebe and Paige help Mylie, a Mermaid, who has made a pact with an evil Sea Hag. If Mylie can find a true love, she can become human. If not, she must give her life-force to the Hag. Meanwhile, Phoebe unsuccessfully attempts to divorce Cole.

It's Witchcraft: Paige's Eastern-influenced spell to find the Sea Hag begins: 'Powers of the witches rise, find the Hag who speaks in lies, balance chakra, focus chi, lead us through the cruel sea.' This unexpectedly turns Phoebe into a mermaid.

A Little Learning is a Dangerous Thing: Skeletal beings aren't known for their patience.

Paige disproves a theory that Borneo demons (like the one that attacks the Charmed Ones at the episode's beginning) are impervious to magical powers. She can't wait to tell the local witch doctors about this. Leo suggests that Paige is getting too caught up with her magical kick. Her hair, for instance, has turned red from a potion that blew up the previous night. Paige asks if Leo has any idea how much that look would cost in a salon.

Denial, Thy Name is Piper: Piper must protect her unborn baby and face her fear of water (stemming from her mother's death – see 'P³ H²O') when she suffers a series of panic attacks in the face of danger. Leo notes that Patty believed she was indestructible, a trait that, he believes, Piper shares with her mother.

Denial, Thy Name is Phoebe: Depressed by Cole's sudden reappearance, Phoebe seeks an escape from the complexities of her life. The opportunity presents itself when she becomes a mermaid and is exposed to the call of the sea.

The Conspiracy Starts at the Witching Hour: Cole's new powers include being able to slow down time and the ability to turn people (in this case Darryl) into water-coolers. In an effort to prove to Phoebe that he's good, Cole helps Darryl arrest a gunman in a diner.

The Book of Shadows states that the Sea Hag has power over her natural environment, including rainstorms, hurricanes and tidal waves.

Work is a Four-Letter Word: Leo is busy transforming Piper's closet (which used to be full of shoes) into a nursery.

References: The title is a probable allusion to the contemporary movie *A Knight's Tale* – supposedly a comedy but actually about as funny as an afternoon at the torturers. Also, allusions to the Discovery Channel; *The Cruel Sea*; and the *Buffy the Vampire Slayer* episode 'Go Fish' ('Get in touch with your inner fish'). Phoebe has an interview with the Skip and Peter radio show, and has also been contacted by TV chat show host Nancy O'Dell (see 'A Witch's Tail' Part 2).

'You May Remember Me ...': Jaime Pressly's films include *Not Another Teen Movie* and *Poor White Trash*. Dan Gauthier appeared in *Groom Lake*, *Ellen*, *Tour of Duty* and *Friends*. Diane Salinger played Apollonia in *Carnivàle* and was also in *Batman Returns* and *Pee Wee's Big Adventure*. Fred Koehler was Leo in *Taken* and appeared in *Pearl Harbor*. Judson Scott's CV includes *The X-Files*, *The Colbys* and *Blade*. Sybil Azur was in *Monkeybone* and *The Others*. Ellen Bradley played Claudia in *Goodbye, Casanova*.

Logic, Let Me Introduce You to This Window: When Mylie stabs the Sea Hag, it bleeds. But on each subsequent occasion that the Hag is injured, it appears to be composed of water. Leo says that he's been watching the girls since birth. How, therefore, did he miss Patty's pregnancy with Paige (see 'Charmed Again')? Paige gets soaked in the storm. When she returns home, however, her hair is perfectly styled. The letter opener that Phoebe uses to stab Cole must be the sharpest on record. Leo is seen putting a window into what will eventually become the baby's room. Exterior shots in every future episode never feature this window.

Continuity: Phoebe is now something of a celebrity in San Francisco as a result of her advice column (which, judging from the billboard that Mylie sees, seems to be called 'Ask Phoebe ...'). Phoebe is a better swimmer than her sisters and is allergic to shell fish. Paige has read about the Water Demon but was unaware that it killed her mother (and, indeed, her father

SEASON 5: A WITCH'S TAIL PART 1

– see 'P³ H²O'). Darryl is now sporting a beard. The Charmed Ones are said to be very famous where Mylie comes from. Mermaids are immortal (due to their cold hearts). The Sea Hag's lair is, according to Phoebe, somewhere in the North Atlantic.

Motors: Phoebe's new car is a silver Mini (3DML 545).

Quote/Unquote: Phoebe: 'Nothing perks up a girl's career like sending her husband straight to hell.'
Leo: 'Can we refrain from blowing up demons in the nursery?' Piper: 'Oh, honey, it was just one.'
Mylie: 'You must be Paige. You have a very big underwater fanbase.'
Phoebe, to Cole: 'Good people don't turn other people into water-coolers.'
Paige: 'That's, actually, the most fun I've seen Phoebe have since Cole died.' Leo: 'Which time?'
Craig: 'Who are you people?' Paige: 'Witch.' Leo: 'Angel.' Phoebe: 'Mermaid.'

Notes: 'You may be half-fish, but you're still a woman, and women generally know when a man's in love even before he does.' An exceptionally silly episode, packed with great dialogue, amusing conceits and daring ideas. The effects aren't perfect, but that's a very minor complaint in what is, essentially, a twisted, iconoclastic fairy-tale.

Soundtrack: 'Blame it on the Weather Man' by B*Witched.

Did You Know?: This isn't the first occasion that Alyssa Milano has been turned into a mermaid. As a teenager, she was the inspiration behind the look of Ariel from Disney's *The Little Mermaid*.

90: A WITCH'S TAIL PART 2

22 September 2002

Writers: Monica Breen, Alison Schapker
Director: Mel Damski
Cast: Finola Hughes (Patty Halliwell), Judson Scott (Necron), Nancy O'Dell (Herself), Tom McCleister (Sailor), David Reivers (Bob Cowan), Patrick Gallo (Fisherman #1), Amanda Sickler (Intern)

> Piper, Paige and Leo struggle to convince Phoebe, now a mermaid, to return to her life as a Charmed One. Meanwhile, Piper casts a spell to stop her panic attacks. Instead of allowing her to face her fear, this merely suppresses it. In order to help Phoebe, Paige takes drastic measures and enlists the aid of Cole and his new demonic powers.

It's Witchcraft: Paige chastises Piper for dangerously attempting to make a vanquishing potion with a mixture of burdock root and eye of newt.

Paige casts a spell to let Cole see what is in Phoebe's heart ('Open Phoebe's heart to Cole, reveal the secret that it holds, spring forth the passion of love's fire, that he may feel her true desire'). Her Power of Three spell to vanquish Necron begins: 'Tide of evil wash the shore, bring it darkness evermore, with all our strength we fight this fate, make this evil obliterate.'

A Little Learning is a Dangerous Thing: Leo tried following Phoebe underwater, but she was too fast for him and he lost her somewhere in the gulf of Mexico.

The Conspiracy Starts at the Witching Hour: Necron is a skeletal being who hovers between life and death and has the power to incinerate. *The Book of Shadows* suggests that Necron is a serious threat, as the only two witches ever to vanquish such a being died in the process.

Denial, Thy Name is Piper: Challenged by Leo to remove her fear, Piper casts a spell ('Locked in, boxed in, full of fear, my panic grows manic till I can't hear, in need of reprieve so that I can breathe, remove my fear, please make it leave'). This suppresses her fear and makes her act with reckless courage.

SEASON 5: A WITCH'S TAIL PART 2

Denial, Thy Name is Phoebe: Mylie said that mermaids are cold hearted. Paige speculates that's why her spell turned Phoebe into a mermaid in the first place (see 'A Witch's Tail' Part 1). However, she subsequently reasons that, far from seeking an escape from her hatred of Cole, Phoebe is actually seeking to escape from the remnants of her love. Nancy O'Dell observes that Phoebe's advice to lovers in her column has become particularly heartfelt lately. Ultimately, having been convinced by Darryl to leave town if he really loves Phoebe, Cole is persuaded to stay by Paige. He and Phoebe meet on the beach. Phoebe believed she could escape into the ocean and that the waves would wash away her pain, Cole notes. But they won't – at least, until Phoebe admits what's in her heart. Cole says that Phoebe mustn't spend eternity alone just to avoid the truth. Phoebe's humanity is then restored. She admits that she does love Cole and probably always will, but that doesn't change anything. It's still over between them.

Work is a Four-Letter Word: As alluded to in the previous episode, Cole has returned to work for Jackson, Carter and Klein.

Paige quits her job, ironically just one day after she received a promotion (see 'A Witch's Tail' Part 1), to focus on her saving innocents.

References: Allusions to *Die Hard*; *The X-Files*; *Goldfinger* ('Shocking!'); and *Dead Poets Society*. Piper quotes a famous maxim often attributed to General George Patton ('A good plan violently executed this week is better than a perfect plan executed next week').

'You May Remember Me ...': Tom McCleister played Red Wood in *Midnight Run*, Ike in *Married ... with Children* and Lorne's Mother in *Angel*. He also appeared in *Fletch Lives*, *Twins*, *Cheers*, *Nowhere Man*, *Blossom*, *Roswell* and *Grosse Pointe*. Amanda Sickler was Maria in *The Fig Tree*. Patrick Gallo appeared in *American Wedding*.

Logic, Let Me Introduce You to This Window: Phoebe misspells her own name ('Pheobe') when signing her divorce papers. Alyssa Milano's underwater body double looks remarkably little like her.

Continuity: Piper's and Leo's unborn baby appears to have inherited its father's ability to heal.

Cruelty to Animals: Phoebe uses her interview on *At Home with Nancy O'Dell* to prove how passionate she has become concerning depleted fish stocks.

SEASON 5: A WITCH'S TAIL PART 2

Quote/Unquote: Paige: 'It's official. Phoebe's on the run.' Leo: 'On the *swim*, technically.'

Piper: 'We've established, I was a spineless coward in the face of evil.' And: 'What about this demon? Where is it? I'd like to thank it and then kill it.'

Piper: 'You wanted fame – go ahead and grab it. *Carpe diem*.' Phoebe: 'Don't mention carp around me, please.'

Piper, on Phoebe: 'She's doing a TV interview.' Paige: 'In the bathtub?' Piper: 'Don't worry, she's not showing any tail.'

Notes: 'You didn't mean to do a lot of things, but they happened. You're a one man death-squad. Bodies, blood and pain follow you wherever you go.' A reasonably competent conclusion to the set-up from Part 1. There are some terrific moments (particularly Darryl's and Paige's heart-to-hearts with Cole). However, the whole thing would have worked an awful lot better if the episode's climax hadn't been quite such a blatant remake of 'From Fear to Eternity' – even down to exactly the same *deux ex machina* being used (a sister saved from drowning by the intervention of her dead mother). That unoriginality condemns an otherwise impressive episode to faint praise.

Did You Know?: These two episodes – broadcast together opposite the Emmy ceremony – received a 5.2 million rating, one of *Charmed*'s worst to date.

91: HAPPILY EVER AFTER

29 September 2002

Writer: Curtis Kheel
Director: John Kretchmer

Cast: Charlie Shanian (Apprentice), Sean Patrick Flanery (Adam), Jennifer Rhodes (Penny Halliwell), Natalija Nogulich (Evil Witch), Danny Woodburn (Head Dwarf), Kay E Kuter (Keeper), Tinsley Grimes (Phoebe's Assistant), Arturo Gil (Dwarf #1), Clay Rivers (Dwarf #2), Carl Ciarfalio (Huntsman)

> In a realm where fairy tales are reality, an evil witch escapes from a magic mirror, killing the realm's caretaker and imprisoning his handsome young apprentice. The witch then learns from the mirror who is the most powerful witch of all – and it's *not* her. In a fury, the witch tries to destroy the Charmed Ones using elements from her world. Meanwhile, Piper summons her grandmother when she doubts her abilities to protect her unborn child. Phoebe learns that her newspaper has been purchased by a businessman who is a client of Cole's.

Dreaming (As Blondie Once Said) is Free: Phoebe notes that she had a nightmare in which Cole took her back to the Underworld as his queen. Piper suggests that she's had that dream before. Phoebe insists that she has *lived* it.

It's Witchcraft: When Paige eats the poisoned apple and dies, Piper finds a spell in *The Book of Shadows* that begins: 'Hear our call, for those who fall, urge her to awaken, from this toxic taken.' This doesn't revive Paige, but it is followed by seven dwarves turning up at the Manor.

Paige is having a miserable time attempting to create a protection potion. Piper suggests that possibly it can't be done. Paige notes that Grams was working on the entry, which suggests she was close to discovering an answer.

A Little Learning is a Dangerous Thing: Grams tells Paige that not all fairy tales are fables. Some are race memories or subconscious recollections of ancient battles between Good and Evil. They are as much part of Wiccan heritage as anything in *The Book of Shadows*.

SEASON 5: HAPPILY EVER AFTER

The Conspiracy Starts at the Witching Hour: Paige asks how the evil witch can rewrite or corrupt fairy tales, since they're already in print. Leo notes that every copy is a manifestation of an original – one that was entrusted to the Keeper long ago for protection.

Denial, Thy Name is Phoebe: Having proved that he had nothing to do with the fairy tale-related malarkey that has plagued the Charmed Ones, and having saved Phoebe from life as a pumpkin, Cole takes time to convince Phoebe that Adam was unwillingly duped by the evil witch to do her bidding. Phoebe asks why Cole is doing this. Cole replies that it's because unless Phoebe can learn to trust herself again, she'll never learn to trust him.

References: Whilst Phoebe attends a ball as Cinderella and meets Prince Charming, Paige has a taste of Snow White's poisoned apple and Piper, as Little Red Riding Hood, encounters a big, bad wolf. Amongst the other fairy tales alluded to are 'Sleeping Beauty'; 'Jack and the Beanstalk'; and 'Hansel and Gretel'. Also, Jacob Ludwig Grimm (1785-1863) and Wilhelm Carl Grimm (1786-1859), authors of many fairy tales; *The Incredible Shrinking Man*; and Nancy Sinatra's 'These Boots Were Made for Walking'.

'You May Remember Me ...': Sean Patrick Flannery played the title role in *The Young Indiana Jones Chronicles* and Greg Stillson in *The Dead Zone*. He also appeared in *Kiss the Bride, Powder, Simply Irresistible, Stargate SG-1* and *Suicide Kiss*. Natalija Nogulich was in *The Lazarus Man, Star Trek: The Next Generation, Murder One, The Practice* and *Dazzle*. Danny Woodburn played Carl the Gnome in *Special Unit 2* and appeared in *Jingle All The Way, Sticks* and *CSI*. Kay E Kuter was Newt Kiley in *The Virginian*. Her CV also includes *Green Acres, Petticoat Junction* and *The Hollywood Sign*. Arturo Gil appeared in *Passions, Glam* and *Bill & Ted's Bogus Journey*. Clay Rivers' movies include *She's All That*. Carl Ciarfalio appeared in *Traffic, Fight Club, Natural Born Killers* and *Magnum PI*. Tinsley Grimes was in *Never Been Kissed*.

Sex and Drugs and Rock n Roll: Grams tells Paige that she occasionally spies on events concerning her granddaughters, though never, she is keen to stress, during 'any private moments.'

Logic, Let Me Introduce You to This Window: One of the fairy-tales-come-to-life involves the ruby slippers from L Frank Baum's *The Wizard of Oz*. However, in the novel, the slippers were silver – MGM changed the colour for the Judy Garland movie version because red looked better in Technicolor. Phoebe bumps into Adam and spills coffee down her blouse.

SEASON 5: HAPPILLY EVER AFTER

The stain, however, does not appear until after she has entered her office. Paige's off-the-shoulder top is on-the-shoulder in some shots, but not others. Grams has got yet another new hairstyle (and, indeed, *colour*) from heaven's hairdresser (see 'Charmed Again' Part 1). Phoebe's glass slippers are clearly plastic. Why doesn't Piper freeze the wolf when it attacks her?

Continuity: The baby seems to have even greater powers than previously suspected. Piper and Leo conclude that it was the baby who summoned Grams. Paige, according to Grams, has her mother's eyes. Piper tells Grams that she needs her advice on how to get ready for this baby. Grams asks if Piper has been exercising her powers daily to keep them under control. Piper is also told to perform a ritual to promote growth, and cast a spell to ward off demonic parasites.

Quote/Unquote: Adam: 'I read your column. You seem surprised?' Phoebe: 'You're not exactly my target audience. Unless you're a closet housewife pining for love?'

Cole: 'Don't you think you're being a little paranoid?' Phoebe: 'With my *demon ex-husband from Hell*? No.'

Cole, to Adam: 'Keep your hands off my pumpkin.'

Head Dwarf: 'Someone here eat a poison apple?'

Paige: 'Can someone please tell me how I got in a coffin?' Grams: 'You were dead, dear. But, bright side, at least now we have something in common.'

Notes: 'Aren't you dead yet?' A very funny episode that, when you scratch the surface, reveals some surprising levels of depth and creativity. There's a pointed dismissal of rank PC attitudes towards things like fairy tales (Leo noting that, these days, the dwarves prefer to be called 'little people'). It also includes one of *Charmed*'s most genuinely shocking moments – the shadow of the wolf on Piper's face as she turns, screaming, towards the camera.

Soundtrack: At the charity ball, the waltz that Adam and Phoebe dance to is 'The Blue Danube' by Johann Strauss (1825-99).

92: SIREN SONG

6 October 2002

Writer: Krista Vernoff
Director: Joel J Feigenbaum

Cast: Melinda Clarke (The Siren), Amy Laughlin (Melissa), Michael Burgess (Mur-Man), Rebecca Balding (Elsie Rothman), Hawthorne James (Healer Demon), Branton Boxer (David), Greg Provance (Darklighter), Robert Merrill (Married Man), Tisha Gonsalves (Nurse), Tera Hendrickson (Simone), Daniel Betanles (TV Reporter)

> The Charmed Ones discover that the Siren is seducing and murdering married couples. Cole's good-deed-of-the-week is to save Melissa after her husband falls victim to the Siren. The sisters learn that Melissa is a future Whitelighter and must be protected, but they are hindered when Leo's and Piper's powers become switched.

Dreaming (As Blondie Once Said) is Free: Phoebe's Cole-related nightmare is an excuse for the production team to fling open the archives for numerous flashback clips.

Piper dreamed an (off-screen) animated musical the previous night, and asks Leo if this sounds normal.

A Little Learning is a Dangerous Thing: Piper becomes frustrated at Leo's inability to understand her pregnancy. Leo, by contrast, has problems making Piper appreciate *his* responsibilities. So their unborn-child, who has clear potential as a stand-up comedian, switches their powers. Piper had already noted that the baby was trying to turn her into a pacifist (shooting fireworks and flowers instead of demon-vanquishing bolts, for example).

With Leo's Whitelighter powers, Piper is called to Paris, where she becomes involved in the attempted murder of a (presumably magic) rooster that she brings back to the Manor for protection. Subsequently, Piper has several off-screen adventures (evading assassins, preventing two crimes of passion – in Portuguese, no less – and delivering a baby).

It's Witchcraft: Leo's first attempt at creating a vanquishing spell begins promisingly ('Oh singing lady of the dusk, who preys on men, turns love to lust'). However, the third line ('We harken ye …') causes Phoebe to ask if he's trying to summon a leprechaun.

The Conspiracy Starts at the Witching Hour: Although Darryl isn't seen, he is mentioned – Paige noting that he's suggested there were three previous male victims of the Siren in San Francisco (and, presumably, three female victims too) prior to Melissa's husband David.

As a mortal, the Siren fell in love with a married man. When they were caught, the man was held blameless ('Typical', notes Piper) whilst the Siren was condemned for her sin. The village women subsequently burned the Siren to death. Her rage turned her into a vengeful demon who has spent eternity seducing married men with her song, then destroying both the men and their wives with the flames that once consumed her.

Cole asks Phoebe if he's proven that he isn't evil anymore. Phoebe replies that his blood is acidic and everything he is, he stole from the demonic wasteland (see 'Witch Way Now?'). Cole argues that, this morning, his firm agreed to do *pro bono* work, and that he also used his powers to vanquish three demons this week. But none of this impresses Phoebe.

Work is a Four-Letter Word: Elise asks Phoebe to interview Cole as a human interest story after he dramatically saves Melissa on national television. She'd like a reluctant Phoebe to do this as a personal favour to her. And, by favour, she means *order*.

It's a Designer Label!: Melinda Clarke – a vision in leather.

References: Allusions to *Superman*; Depeche Mode's 'Blasphemous Rumour' ('Magic has a sick sense of humour'); and Labelle's 'Lady Marmalade' ('Voulez vous couchez avec moi?').

'You May Remember Me ...': Melinda Clarke played Julie Cooper in *The OC* and Lady Heather in *CSI*. She also appeared in *Spawn*, *Enterprise* and *Xena: Warrior Princess*. Amy Laughlin was in *The Curse*. Hawthorne James's movies include *Amistad*, *Se7en*, *Speed*, *The Doors* and *I'm Gonna Git You Sucka*. Branton Boxer appeared in *New Suit*. Greg Provance was in *Teach Me*. Robert Merrill's CV includes *Tail Sting*. Tera Hendrickson appeared in *Murphy Brown* and *Gunshy*. Daniel Betanles was in *CSI: Miami*.

Cigarettes and Alcohol: The Siren drinks a Martini whilst seducing a victim.

Sex and Drugs and Rock n Roll: Having finally got their respective powers back, Piper flirtily asks Leo (in French) if he'd like to go to bed with her. Leo wears aftershave (a particularly potent brand is the implication). Which, of course, raises the question whether or not angels need to shave.

Logic, Let Me Introduce You to This Window: When the Siren is being healed, she is clearly holding the pole next to her, when it's supposed to have been impaled through her. When Piper and Paige fall out of the hospital window and land in the dumpster, in a wide shot the garbage bags are white, but in close-up, they're blue. There's a new TV network in the *Charmed* universe – KQSF, Channel 3.

Continuity: Phoebe suggests that Cole borrow a horse from 'one of those apocalypse guys' (see 'Apocalypse Not'). Whitelighters can speak whatever language their charges speak – for example, one of Leo's charges is French, so he can speak French (however, see 'Exit Strategy'). Piper tells Paige that it's the Charmed Ones' compassion, not their powers, that separates them from the bad guys.

Quote/Unquote: Piper: 'I'm trying to get a little attention ... Which these days seems to require a small explosion.'

Paige: 'You two are only gonna get your powers back once you've learned your lessons.' Piper: 'I hate that. It's just *so* after-school-special.'

Cole, to Piper: 'You're pregnant?' Piper: 'I was. Now, I think Leo is.'

Cole: 'Did you get my flowers?' Phoebe: '"Sorry I tried to strangle you." Probably not a card that the florist gets to write every day.'

Notes: 'They may be powerful, but they are no different than any other woman when it comes to love.' An episode with some serious points to make but which, almost from the first moment, decides to go for laughs, with devastating effect. The dialogue is dripping with pithy humour and most of the situations are, similarly, given amusing twists. For the girls, there's Julian McMahon shirtless; for the guys, Melinda Clarke literally bursting out of her leather top. A terrific episode during a period when *Charmed* was beginning to hit a consistent run of good form that would last for most of the season.

Soundtrack: Edie Carey's 'Come Close'.

SEASON 5: WITCHES IN TIGHTS

93: WITCHES IN TIGHTS

13 October 2002

Writer: Mark Wilding
Director: David Straiton

Cast: Andrew James Allen (Kevin), Craig Young (Dave), Gerry Becker (Ramus), Mark A Sheppard (Arnon), David Pressman (Ed Miller), Tinsley Grimes (Phoebe's Assistant), Ernie Reyes Jr. (Kaz), Kasim Saul (Security Guard), Todd Tucker (The Aggressor), Jeannie Epper (Elderly Woman)

> A demon, Arnon, takes advantage of a young witch, Kevin, tricking him into using his powers of thought projection to create an unstoppable superhero, the Aggressor. Arnon wants to destroy an Elder, Ramus, and steal his powers. Kevin turns to the Charmed Ones into costumed super-heroines in order to fight his creation. Meanwhile, Piper tries to return P³ to its former glory, Paige has problems controlling her orbing while sleeping with her new boyfriend, and Phoebe confronts a landlord who is evicting innocent families.

The Conspiracy Starts at the Witching Hour: Kevin, a bullied 13 year old boy with great artistic gifts, possesses the power to see his drawings come to life. Arnon – who has the ability to sense great power (even if he doesn't, actually, have any himself) uses Kevin to gain the retiring Elder Ramus's powers, which must be transferred during an equinox. After the death of Arnon, Ramus's powers pass to Kevin.

A Little Learning is a Dangerous Thing: Leo suggests that Elders are like kings, in that they can be of any age.

Work is a Four-Letter Word: Leo suggests that P³ is still doing great. 'Not as great as it used to be, thanks to me,' argues Piper. However, hiring a bangin' new DJ by the episode's climax seems to have revived the club's reputation as the hottest spot in town.

Denial, Thy Name is Phoebe: Cole tries to interest Phoebe in the case of Edward Miller, a really despicable slum landlord. Miller subsequently discovers Phoebe's masked identity, videotapes her activities and threatens to expose the sisters if his blackmail demands are not met. Cole dismissively sends Miller to Hell to protect Phoebe, much to Phoebe's disgust when she finds out what Cole has done.

It's a Designer Label!: The little red something that Phoebe is almost wearing in the opening scene and Paige's sexy negligée are both worthy of mention. But then, when Kevin's drawings take over, there's little competition to the superheroine Charmed Ones' lycra-and-spandex costumes ('Nice outfit, sis!' notes Paige eagerly when Phoebe turns up at the Manor).

References: The title probably alludes to Mel Brooks' spoof *Robin Hood: Men in Tights*. Also, *The Invisible Man*; *Wonder Woman*; *The Critic*; and *The Lone Ranger*. And to just about every superhero cliché imaginable.

'You May Remember Me ...': Andrew James Allen appeared in *Run of the House*. Craig Young was a former GMTV presenter and is best known as Alex Williamson in *Dream Team*. Gerry Becker played Nathan Reed in *Angel* and Myron Stone in *Ally McBeal* and appeared in *Spider-Man*, *Donnie Brasco*, *Man on the Moon* and *Stonewall*. Mark Sheppard was Paddy Armstrong in *In the Name of the Father*, Badger in *Firefly* and Cecil L'Iverly in *The X-Files*. Ernie Reyes Jr's movies include *Pool Hall Junkies*, *Surf Ninjas* and *Red Sonja*. Kasim Saul was in *Judging Amy*. Todd Tucker appeared in *Nine Months*. Prior to that he was a make-up technician on *A Beautiful Mind*. Jeannie Epper's CV includes *Die Hard With a Vengeance*, *Switchblade Sisters*, *Foxy Brown* and *Laverne & Shirley*. David Pressman appeared in *Lip Service*, *Godzilla*, *Stargate* and *The Golden Girls*.

Behind the Camera: Mark Wilding's CV also includes *Becker* and *Jake 2.0*.

Cigarettes and Alcohol: Dave drinks a beer at the club.

Sex and Drugs and Rock n Roll: English Dave is Paige's new boyfriend. They've been going out for three weeks and he is the only man (apart from Glenn – see 'A Knight to Remember', 'Trial By Magic') with whom she's had sex since she became a witch. Or, at least, he would be if she wasn't having such trouble reaching orgasm for fear of orbing out during climax. Despite her reservations about discussing this with Piper (and the absolute horror they both have at the thought of discussing it with *Leo*), by the end of the episode, Paige seems to have overcome her problems in that area. It must have been the pink leather, suggests Piper. Paige agrees that leaping over tall buildings in a single bound is the kind of thing that will 'free any girl up.'

SEASON 5: WITCHES IN TIGHTS

Logic, Let Me Introduce You To This Window: Who owns the car that's seen in the background of two lengthy scenes featuring Kevin? The lights are on, the motor's running and it's given huge visual prominence, but the identity of its owner is never revealed. Paige apparently disappears in the middle of an intimate act with Dave, and he doesn't notice? Not very likely, is it? In the scene where Phoebe dangles the landlord from the roof, the TransAmerica Pyramid can be seen behind Phoebe and Cole. A subsequent shot, from an opposite angle, still shows the building in the background. The external shot of Dave's apartment is the same one previously used in episodes like 'Dream Sorcerer' and 'The Witch Is Back'. How could the landlord find Phoebe going into the airport hangar? She and her sisters have been super-speeding around town, so it's impossible for him to have been trailing her, and neither he nor the guard he tells to check up on her would have been able to find her location so quickly. Arnon says that the equinox comes around 'once in a lifetime.' No it doesn't, there are two every year. Overseas prints of this episode feature Dorian Gregory on the title sequence, even though Darryl isn't in the episode.

Continuity: Her sisters consider Piper a very confusing woman. Her pregnancy has caused her to acquire a sudden taste for pickle, hot fudge and mustard sandwiches. There's a reference to the Demon of Illusion (see 'Chick Flick'). With her newly acquired super-hearing, Paige describes the noises that she's picking up in the warehouse – rats, dripping water, cockroaches. She suggests it may as well be her old apartment (see 'Charmed Again' Part 1). Ramus tells Leo that his and Piper's unborn baby with not only be healthy, it will be more powerful than Leo can imagine.

Cruelty to Animals: Kevin draws a tiger, which comes to life. Arnon notes that destroying Kevin's creations is easy and, to prove it, rips up the drawing. The tiger promptly disappears.

Quote/Unquote: Leo: 'You're having a baby, your priorities have changed.' Piper: 'Haven't you heard, women can have careers and babies now? It's been in all the papers.'
    Paige: 'He could still be a demon.' Phoebe: 'He was in *tights*.'
    Paige, to Arnon: 'Fortunately, since you have Ramus's powers, you should be able to foresee what's gonna happen next.' Piper: 'It's gonna hurt, isn't it?'

Notes: 'Who was that masked man?' Completely brilliant, mindless, trashy entertainment that will have any fan who grew up on superhero comics falling around on the floor laughing at the sheer cheek of it all. 'Witches in

SEASON 5: WITCHES IN TIGHTS

Tights' is, possibly, the finest example of *Charmed*'s sometimes uneasy relationship with the pulpier end of telefantasy. It's as if a script for *The Avengers* turned up in the production office and, when they came to film it, nobody noticed. Having said all that, it must be noted that in the middle of all the outrageous conceits, fantasy-costumes and riotous hilarity is a marvellous little commentary on the power of authorial intent bursting to make itself heard. Whatever, this is a great example of the series to show to any non-fans to get them interested. Has there ever been a finer *Charmed* moment than the one – much used in trailers – in which Piper and Paige emerges in their striking costumes from a misty alley with dramatic music playing?

Soundtrack: 'Love Me' by MD Says is the techno-track playing at the episode's beginning.

Did You Know?: The WB used the promotional title 'Magic Wears A Mask' for this episode.

94 : THE EYES HAVE IT

20 October 2002

Writer: Laurie Parres
Director: James Marshall

Cast: Rebecca Balding (Elise), Emmanuelle Vaugier (Eva), Tobin Bell (Oren), Shareen Mitchell (Lydia), Channon Roe (Cree), Lorna Raver (Madame Theresa), Ivan Shaw (Attendant), Joe Camareno (Male Nurse), Heather McPhaul (OR Nurse), Mary Kara (Gypsy)[56]

> Phoebe asks a fortune teller to explain why she hasn't been getting premonitions. She learns this is because her life is out of balance. The sisters also discover that the son of a gypsy hunter is stalking the last of a tribe in order to restore the sight that the gypsies took from his father.

The Conspiracy Starts at the Witching Hour: Oren, the blinded gypsy hunter, is searching for the one who has 'Waffediyok, the evil eye,' the symbol of which is Eva's family emblem. It is, however, evil only to those who wish it to do harm. Many feared the evil eye, but the family was protected by the talisman. Folklore said that the Keeper of the eye could use it to magnify or channel her powers. Eva's aunt, Lydia – the Shivane or high priestess – possesses the magical eyes that Oren seeks.

Work is a Four-Letter Word: Phoebe is somewhat overwhelmed with work. Besides her column and some personal appearances, Elise has got her a slot giving advice on a radio show – *Hotline*.

References: Some of the episode's concepts seem drawn from Irvin Kershner's *Eyes of Laura Mars* (1978). The subplot concerning a gypsy curse – if not the actual curse itself – may have been inspired by Angel's story in *Buffy the Vampire Slayer*. The book and video *The Joys of Home Birthing* feature heavily. There's also an allusion to Neil Diamond's 'I'm a Believer'.

'You May Remember Me ...': Emmanuelle Vaugier was Susie in *40 Days and 40 Nights* and also appeared in *Hysteria* and *Smallville*. Tobin Bell played David Ferrie in *Ruby* and appeared in *Stargate SG-1*, *The West Wing*,

---

[56] Uncredited.

SEASON 5: THE EYES HAVE IT

24, *Alias, Goodfellas, Serial Killer* and *Malice*. Shareen Mitchell was Lucy in *Hudson Street*. She was also in *The Lone Gunmen*. Channon Roe's CV includes *Buffy the Vampire Slayer, Boogie Nights* and *Can't Hardly Wait*. Lorna Raver appeared in *Freeway*. Ivan Shaw was in *All My Children*. Joe Camareno was the writer/director on *Ambition* and also appeared in *Roswell*. Mary Kara is one of *Charmed*'s technical consultants and also the co-founder of the popular Psychic Eye bookchain.

Sex and Drugs and Rock n Roll: There's a wonderfully gratuitous shot of Alyssa Milano's – not inconsiderable – chest close to bursting out of a very tight orange vest in the final scene.

Logic, Let Me Introduce You to This Window: Lydia has green eyes, but when Oren extracts them in the morgue, the eyes he puts into his head are blue. Phoebe's vision shows her that Piper's explosion power doesn't work on Orin. So why does Piper subsequently try to blow him up anyway? That's a trifle stubborn. Then again, this *is* Piper we're talking about ... At Teresa's funeral, the box of crackers is on top of the bananas, then it disappears in the next shot. When the gypsy is helping Phoebe to find her balance, the reflection of a member of the production crew can be seen. In the scenes in Phoebe's office, her laptop's Apple logo (seen in many previous episodes) is missing. Then it reappears. Paige's hair is tucked behind her ears for some shots, but not others, during the sequence in which Piper and Leo watch the birthing video. Paige shows Eva the 'All upon your ancestors' spell in *The Book of Shadows*. It, like most of the other spells in the book, is written in beautiful, archaic gothic script, suggesting it's been there since at least Grams' death and possibly much longer. (Note the similarity of this writing, for example, to that on the regularly-seen Belthazor page.) However, it cannot have been in the book for more than a few months, as not only did we see Phoebe actually composing the spell in 'Charmed and Dangerous', but Prudence is one of the names written in the book to be invoked. The major premonition that Phoebe gets also includes a gentle wind that ruffles her hair whilst she's having it. Darryl is mentioned but not seen, although again he is featured in the title sequence on overseas copies of the episode. The same is true, in this instance, of Cole as well.

Continuity: Phoebe says that Cole is soul searching ... or, possibly, searching *for* a soul.

Quote/Unquote: Elise (reading): '"Dear Phoebe, my career is on the fast-track, I'm wildly popular and the money is pretty damn good. What should I do?"' Phoebe: 'Stop whining?' Elise: 'Damn, you *are* good.'

SEASON 5: THE EYES HAVE IT

Piper, to Paige: 'Pre-natal yoga this morning, and now you want to crash a stranger's funeral? You really *do* need friends.'

Piper, to Phoebe: 'So, your new and improved premonitions are just a more vivid way of telling us that we're screwed?'

Notes: 'You cannot change what you were born to be.' A simplistic tale in contrast to some of the complex narrative conceits of late, but no less worthy for all that. 'The Eyes Have It' includes some clever observations on the various problems in the sisters' life – Piper's pregnancy, Paige's lack of self-worth without a vocation, and the pressure of Phoebe's job – and then gives them something *real* to worry about in the shape of Tobin Bell's dryly sinister Oren.

95: SYMPATHY FOR THE DEMON

3 November 2002

Writer: Henry Alonso Myers
Director: Stuart Gillard

Cast: Billy Drago (Barbas), James Read (Victor Bennett), Jennifer Rhodes (Penny Halliwell), Ken Marino (Miles), Troy Blendell (Barbas's demon), Todd Eckert (Lawyer), David Grant Wright (Suit #1), Kim Delgado (Businessman), Steve Heinze (Heavyset Demon), Hunter Ansley Wryn (Little Piper)

> Cole seeks the help of the Charmed Ones when he believes that he's being manipulated into hurting someone. Phoebe and Piper, influenced by the Demon of Fear, won't help him. Paige, however, creates a potion to remove Cole's powers. Barbas takes advantage of this and steals Cole's powers to free himself from his eternal prison. Consumed with the thirst for revenge, Barbas traps the Halliwells in the Manor.

It's Witchcraft: The 'Astral Projection Spell' was previously seen in 'Which Way Now?' when Phoebe used it to find Cole and was transported to the demonic wastelands.
   The Charmed Ones attempt to use the crystal cage and the spell created to destroy the Source (see 'Black As Cole') to vanquish Barbas. Neither works.

The Conspiracy Starts at the Witching Hour: Barbas has been working on the Charmed Ones (and, presumably, Cole) for weeks, having been taught by his demon friend how to project from the rocky ledge above Hell where they are trapped.

A Little Learning is a Dangerous Thing: Piper suffers from arachnophobia whilst Paige is claustrophobic. Phoebe's fears include one that every guy she dates is evil (and that, in fact, she is herself.)

References: The title is an allusion to the Rolling Stones' 'Sympathy for the Devil'. Also, *Dr Jekyll and Mr Hyde*; and *Hamlet* ('Aye, there's the rub').

'You May Remember Me ...': Ken Marino appeared in *Dawson's Creek,*

SEASON 5: SYMPATHY FOR THE DEMON

Men Behaving Badly and *Gattaca*. Troy Blendell played Jinx in *Buffy the Vampire Slayer* and was also in *Love & Sex*. Todd Eckert's CV includes *The Rowdy Girls* and *Will & Grace*. David Grant Wright appeared in *Silk Stalkings*. Kim Delgado's movies include *Terminal Error*, *Loved* and *Kindergarten Cop*. Steve Heinze appeared in *Double Deception*.

Behind the Camera: Henry Alonso Myers also wrote for *The Chronicle*.

Cigarettes and Alcohol: Phoebe's new friend, Miles (they're up to four dates by the episode's end), drinks red wine in P^3.

Logic, Let Me Introduce You to This Window: There are references to Phoebe using a power-stripping potion on Cole. However, it wasn't Phoebe who used the potion in 'Black As Cole' – it was Emma. Paige says that the power-stripping potion is the same as Pheobe's from 'Black as Cole' 'with some adjustments.' These include giving it a different colour (the previous one was pink, this is blue) and a different way for it to be administered (Emma threw it at Belthazor, here Cole drinks it). Cole says that Barbas can use his power to become the Source. However, 'Womb Raider' established that an aspiring Source also needs *The Grimoire*, which Leo hid in a secure location. We've also got the old question of how Barbas keeps returning. In 'From Fear To Eternity', it was established that Barbas appears once every 1300 years. Since then, he's been back twice for a go at the Halliwells. (A vague reason was given in 'Ms Hellfire' for *that* reappearance, but this one's a total mystery). When Phoebe hugs Paige after Leo brings her back to life, in some shots Paige's head is on Phoebe's left shoulder, in others it's on her right. Victor is shown walking out of the sisters' lives after Piper was endangered by a demon attacking Grams. This broadly fits with information given in various episodes, but the little girl who plays the young Piper is too old for the time-scale established in 'The 70s Episode' and 'Charmed Again'. (Patty was pregnant with Paige in 1977 and Victor was long gone. Piper would have been four then. Here, she appears to be about 9 or 10.)

Continuity: Phoebe considers Barbas is the worst demon the sisters have ever faced.

Cruelty to Animals: Paige is attempting to conjure some doves using a spell that Prue created. She eventually gets it right.

Quote/Unquote: Miles: 'How long were you married?' Phoebe: 'We were together for two years. The beginning was great ... the end was Hell.'
Barbas: 'You will be rewarded for your service.' Demon: 'That's good.

'Coz this whole eternal banishment thing is really starting to get me down.'

Phoebe: 'Time to get over your fears right now.' Piper: 'Easy for you to say, you're not facing killer spiders.'

Notes: 'I think I'm going crazy ... or someone is messing with my mind.' Rose McGowan and Julian McMahon are *Charmed*'s two finest acting assets, so giving them several scenes together is inspired. It's also great to have Billy Drago back with his most over-the-top performance to date. Stuart Gillard's direction is superb, with much use of wide-angle lenses and zooms.

Soundtrack: Barbas's demon friend plays a few chords from Beethoven's Fifth Symphony on the piano.

96: A WITCH IN TIME

10 November 2002

Writer: Daniel Cerone
Director: John Behring

Cast: Ken Marino (Miles), Jason Brooks (Bacarra), Joseph Paneno (Max), Maurice Smith (Driver), L Sidney (Police Officer), Tosh Ayers (Youth), Butch Klein (Bacarra Twin)[57]

> Phoebe has a vision of Miles being shot, an event that she subsequently prevents. However, it transpires that this was Miles's time to die, and saving him has caused a time-ripple that Bacarra, a warlock from the future, uses to travel into his own past on a mission. Bacarra reveals that unless Miles dies, it will eventually lead to Phoebe's death.

It's Witchcraft: Deprived of *The Book of Shadows*, the sisters still conjure an 'obscuring fog' spell. Their (unsuccessful) spell to vanquish the two Bacarras begins: 'We call upon Medusa's bones, turn their flesh into stone.'

A Little Learning is a Dangerous Thing: There are numerous allusions to the Angel of Death and how he can't be escaped ('Death Takes a Halliwell'). Despite knowing this, Phoebe is unable to resist spending the episode trying.

The Conspiracy Starts at the Witching Hour: Bacarra tells Cole that Phoebe saved the life of a man destined to die. The Angel of Death, however, never gives up a claim, and keep coming for Miles. For the next six months, Phoebe averts Miles's death over and over until she finally loses her own life in the process. Cole himself sent Bacarra back in time to prevent this from happening. (Bacarra brings proof in the form of Cole's wedding ring.) Cole says that he would never send a warlock with a message this important. Bacarra replies that Cole had no choice. In the future (and sooner than Cole may think), he will unite demons and warlocks and lift the Underworld to its greatest power in history.

Leo notes that whenever something stops a pre-destined event from occurring, it sends a ripple through time. A powerful warlock like Bacarra

---

[57] Uncredited.

can use such an anomaly.

References: Allusions to *Star Wars* ('You could've told us he was a Jedi Master warlock'); Agatha Christie's *And Then There Were None*; and *The Terminator*.

'You May Remember Me ...': Jason Brooks appeared in *Baywatch*, *The Pretender* and *Friends*. Butch Klein played Darren Richards in *24*.

Cigarettes and Alcohol: Phoebe and Miles share a bottle of red wine in Miles's apartment.

Sex and Drugs and Rock n Roll: According to Phoebe, great dates never end on the front porch. And, indeed, her date with Miles doesn't. Meanwhile, downstairs, Paige and her 'couch buddy', Max, have lots of fun too.

Logic, Let Me Introduce You to This Window: When Bacarra steals *The Book of Shadows*, he finds a spell to disempower a witch – previously seen in Tuatha's evil spell book in 'That Old Black Magic'. Why is it in *The Book of Shadows*, particularly as the spell requires a human heart to complete it? All the flowers around the Manor's porch at the beginning of the episode are surprisingly alive, considering this is San Francisco in November. The gun-toting youth's hand moves noticeably when he is supposedly frozen. Technically, Paige's orbing is not a witch power and, therefore, shouldn't have been stripped. A dozen dozen is a gross – Piper (as a part of the retail industry) should know that. When Phoebe runs into the building to see if Miles is there, she's wearing black high-heeled shoes. When she comes out, these have changed to brown moccasin boots. Didn't the sisters burn the power-relinquishing spell in 'Wicca Envy' after Rex was vanquished? Piper suggests that the Charmed Ones are not supposed to fall in love with the innocents they're assigned to save. Since when? There are *at least* half a dozen example of *exactly* that happening over the previous five years. Paige alludes to 'a century's worth of magic' in *The Book of Shadows*. If, as implied elsewhere, the book is the sum of all knowledge of the entire Melinda Warren line, then it surely should be *several* centuries.

Continuity: The latest issue of the *Ask Phoebe* column features the headline *Rebounding in Rockport*. Miles is a computer programmer. Like Phoebe, he's recently become divorced. He owns a cabin in Tahoe. Paige's friend Max is 'wickedly smart, perversely funny and has just the right touch of weird style' for her.

SEASON 5: A WITCH IN TIME

Quote/Unquote: Miles: 'You saved my life.' Phoebe: 'Oh, it was nothing.' Miles: 'It was *my life*.'
Phoebe: 'Death isn't after Miles, Bacarra is.'

Notes: 'I'm having a really bad day.' One of the finest *Charmed* episodes ever, 'A Witch in Time' takes an age-old science fiction concept (interfering with fate is damned dangerous and, usually, impossible to get away with) and samples it beautifully into the series' aesthetic. A charming, challenging, superbly written episode, complete with brilliant passage-of-time effects and a heart-rending climax, 'A Witch in Time' is an example of just how deep *Charmed* can be.

Soundtrack: 'Sympathy' by the Goo Goo Dolls.

97: SAM I AM

17 November 2002

Writers: Alison Schapker, Monica Breen
Director: Joel J Feigenbaum

Cast: Scott Jaeck (Sam Wilder), Tony Todd (Avatar of Force), F J Rio (Ronan), Joel Swetow (Avatar of Power), Eric Winter (Trevor), Niki Botelho (Elf Woman), Bruce Comtois (Thug #1), Sharon Turner (Tina)

> Paige meets her first Whitelighter charge, Sam Wilder – her own father. Meanwhile, Cole tries to get himself vanquished by the Charmed Ones. Piper and Leo have problems in finding a magical nanny.

It's Witchcraft: When last seen ('P^3 H^{2}O'), Sam was, as Phoebe notes, 'riding into the afterlife with our mother.' Sam notes that the Elders made him a Whitelighter again and he screwed up again. Hence his current half-mortal status.

A Little Learning is a Dangerous Thing: There is a Whitelighter manual, although, inevitably, Paige hasn't yet seen it.

The Conspiracy Starts at the Witching Hour: The Elders aren't known for their sense of humour.
Trackers are stronger and more powerful than the average Darklighter. They traditionally search for fallen Whitelighters, especially those who are a step away from losing their wings.
The Avatars are few in number. They don't have to limit themselves to choosing between Good and Evil and wish Cole to join their morally ambiguous ranks.

References: The title is from a Dr Seuss book. Allusions to Neil Sedaka's 'Breaking Up Is Hard To Do'; chat-show host Jenny Jones; *Mary Poppins*; and the Biblical book of Samuel.

'You May Remember Me ...': Tony Todd played the title role in *Candyman* and also appeared in *The Rock*, *Stir*, *Platoon* and *Silence*. F J Rio was in *Star Trek: Deep Space Nine*. Joel Swetow's CV includes *Alias*, *Stargate SG-1* and *Parker Lewis Can't Lose*. Eric Winter played Rex DiMera in *Days of our Lives*.

SEASON 5: SAM I AM

Niki Botelho appeared in *Batman Returns*. Bruce Comtois is a stuntman who worked on *Buffy the Vampire Slayer* and *24*. Sharon Turner was the co-host of *The Gong Show*.

Cigarettes and Alcohol: Cole is busy getting plastered on Jack Daniels in a biker bar when he finds himself in the middle of a violent robbery.

Logic, Let Me Introduce You to This Window: When the Charmed Ones try to vanquish Cole, Paige says that their newest potions are 'at least as strong as the ones [we] used on the Source.' But they didn't use any potions on the Source – at least, none that had any effect. They trapped him in the crystal cage and used the 'ancestor' spell. Paige's bra-strap disappears and reappears at regular intervals between shots. In P^3, when Piper and Phoebe talk about nannies and the camera is on Piper, several people in the background disappear, only to reappear in the next shot. When Leo and Piper orb in the kitchen while Cole is impersonating Sam, Leo has his hand on Piper's arm. When the camera is behind them and we see Phoebe mixing a potion, the couple are standing much further apart. If Sam's healing powers are currently idle and he is off the Elders' radar, then how can he still orb? Phoebe says that the Flaming Lips are her favourite band. What happened to her love affair with the Verve (see 'Wicca Envy')? Paige tells Sam that she used to think that if she never met her father, her life would be 'perfectly fine.' That's a completely different story to the one she told in 'Charmed Again' – that she was keen to meet her birth parents.

Continuity: Paige has recently dumped three – seemingly eligible – guys, including likeable-but-sulky Trevor. Both Phoebe and Piper feel that Paige has commitment issues. Phoebe also suggests that Paige has a fault of being quick to judge. By the end of the episode, Cole appears to be unvanquishable.

Quote/Unquote: Phoebe: 'The vigilante is tall, dark and handsome and can send people flying with the wave of a hand.' Piper: 'That doesn't mean it's Cole.' Phoebe: 'Did I forget to mention the scorch marks?' Piper: '*That* means it's Cole.'
Sam: 'Everything I touch, I hurt.'
Phoebe: 'Having an invincible ex-husband is making me really nervous.'

Notes: 'Sooner or later you will join us.' Somewhat awkward in construction, 'Sam I Am' has one fundamental flaw that destroys most of the good stuff surrounding it. Cole's hugely complex plan comes close to succeeding until Phoebe figures it all out in a dramatically unsatisfying instant. That apart, the episode also has the disadvantage of being a bit mawkish and obvious in places. Well acted, though. (Scott Jaeck is particularly good.) The 'Piper and Leo searching for a magical nanny' subplot is pretty funny but far too inconsequential – either build an episode around it, or don't bother with it at all.

Soundtrack: 'Do You Realise?' by the Flaming Lips.

98: Y TU MUMMY TAMBIEN

5 January 2003

Writer: Curtis Kheel
Director: Chris Long

Cast: Adrian Paul (Jeric), Shannon Engemann (Sandra), Amy Leland (Saleswoman), Dwight Bacquie (Coroner), Greg Benson (Officer Worley), Doug Sinclair (Officer #1), Brian David Cohen (Officer #2)

> An ancient demon, Jeric, desperately in need of a witch's body to contain the spirit of his dead lover, Isis, kidnaps Phoebe. When Cole discovers this, he offers Paige in exchange for his mummified ex-wife.

It's Witchcraft: To discover the location that Isis recently used, Paige uses the spell: 'Scrying secrets come to me, drop again so I might see'. It turns out to be the corner of Fifth and Hyde, Phoebe's office

The Insanity Starts at a Dramatically Appointed Moment: Thanks to his recently-discovered indestructibility (see 'A Witch in Time'), Cole has begun to exhibit genuine mental instability – complete with an occasional manic snigger, deranged and over-complicated schemes and pointless attempts to commit suicide. Plus, of course, 'evil' facial hair.

The Conspiracy Starts at the Witching Hour: Cole notes that Jeric is a legend in demonic circles. In ancient Egypt, no-one had the power to vanquish him, so they mummified him instead. An evil witch, Isis, cast a spell that released him. They promptly fell in love, but Isis was flayed alive by Jeric's enemies. Jeric has been murdering witches ever since – most of his previous killings were isolated to areas of the Middle East like Cairo, Istanbul and Tripoli. Leo says that Jeric is trying to find the perfect body to host the spirit of his lover. Unfortunately two spirits cannot occupy the same body. Jeric mummifies the corpse to trap Isis's spirit and keep her from moving on until he can find the next host body.

Work is a Four-Letter Word: Darryl notes that it has taken him a long time to lose 'the freaky deaky' reputation on the force, and he's particularly keen to avoid it recurring at this particular moment, as he's

SEASON 5: Y TU MUMMY TAMBIEN

up for promotion. With a little help from Leo, he ends the episode as a lieutenant.

It's a Designer Label!: Dissatisfied with the frilliness of most maternity clothes, Piper asks the sales assistant if the shop has: '... anything that will go with combat boots? Something for the mum-to-be who kicks some ass upon occasion ... in black or grey?' Piper also suggests that felon-orange really isn't Leo's colour.

References: The title alludes to Alfonso Cuarón's *Y Tu Mamá También*. The plot is a cunning variant on *Sophie's Choice*. Isis, whilst occupying Phoebe's body, performs the Dance of the Seven Veils.

'You May Remember Me ...': Adrian Paul is best known as Duncan MacLeod in *Highlander*. He also appeared in *The Masque of the Red Death* and *The Colbys*. Shannon Engemann was in *Brigham Hill*. Amy Leland appeared in *My So-Called Life*. Dwight Bacquie's CV includes *Open Season* and *Forever Knight*. Greg Benson was in *Random Shooting in LA*. Doug Sinclair appeared in *Up Michigan!*. Brian David Cohen's movies include *Avoiding the Hollywood Hooker*.

Logic, Let Me Introduce You to This Window: Police officers usually aren't allowed to touch evidence without gloves. Shouldn't Piper know a bit more about possession? She has, after all, been possessed herself – in 'Coyote Piper' and 'The Wendigo'. A spot of rain can be seen on the camera lens in one establishing shot. Brian Krause appears to have had his hair cut mid-episode. Leo and Piper were converting their closet into a nursery earlier this season. Now, it's a closet again.

Continuity: Leo has previously used his Whitelighter power to assume another identity (in 'Power Outage', when he appeared as Belthazor). He notes that to do so requires some rule-breaking on his part.

Quote/Unquote: Piper, to Paige: 'Explain to me the touching thing. Why is my stomach suddenly public property?' And, to Darryl when he moves to touch her stomach: 'Do it and you pull back a bloody stub.'

Cole, when Piper and Paige interrupt his latest suicide attempt: 'Can't you at least let me *not* die in peace?'

Paige, on Jeric's history: 'That'd almost be romantic if he hadn't killed so many witches.' Cole: 'He's just a guy trying to get his love back. There's nothing wrong with that.'

Notes: 'She's going to evict someone from their own body? That's rude.' Only *Charmed* could do a story about insanity and lost love and make it a thigh-slapping comedy. There's a great sexual chemistry between Adrian Paul and both Milano and McGowan, whilst Julian McMahon gives his most deliberately over-the-top performance to date – the sequence in which Cole and Piper try to destroy each other in the attic is especially amusing.

Soundtrack: Nichole Nordeman's 'This Mystery'.

SEASON 5: THE IMPORTANCE OF BEING PHOBE

99: THE IMPORTANCE OF BEING PHOEBE

12 January 2003

Writer: Krista Vernoff
Director: Derek Johansen

Cast: Christopher Darga (Dex), Erik King (Bail Bondsman), Angela Little (Kaia), Rebecca Balding (Elise Rothman), Armando Valdes (Officer Garcia), Garry G (Guard), Steven M Porter (Health Inspector), Natasha Aiello (Driver), Joe Sabatino (Demon Guard), Dawn Lewis (Demon Dancer), David Figlioli (Brute Demon), David Neckel (Seedy Demon), Alex Paez (Cop #1), Casey Smith (Rat Demon #1)

> Phoebe, and her newspaper, are sued by a woman who claims that Phoebe destroyed her marriage as a result of her own bitter divorce. Meanwhile, Paige is framed in a hit and run incident, and Piper has health inspectors visit P³.

It's Witchcraft: Piper's spell to temporarily remove Phoebe's powers begins: 'This witch's power can not fight, the lure of evil's magic might, before misuse lands her in Hell, remove the powers of Phoebe Halliwell.'

Denial, Thy Name is Phoebe: Piper says that Phoebe seemed cheerful considering the prospective state of her career. That's denial, adds Paige. 'The Phoebe I know would never roll over for lawyers like that.'

Work is a Four-Letter Word: Both Piper and Phoebe have problems in their respective employment.

It's a Designer Label!: Whilst searching through Phoebe's panty drawer, Kaia finds a ceremonial athema and notes that Phoebe is her kind of girl.

References: The title alludes to Oscar Wilde's Victorian comedy of manners, *The Importance of Being Earnest*. Posters glimpsed in P³ include those for Green Day, Orgy and Faith Hill. Paige alludes to *Macbeth*. Kaia reads a copy of *Tempo* magazine, whilst Elise mentions the *National Enquirer*.

SEASON 5: THE IMPORTANCE OF BEING PHOEBE

'You May Remember Me ...': Christopher Darga's movies include *Dude, Where's My Car?* and *The Mask*. David Figlioli was in *Dating Rosie*. Erik King appeared in *Oz* and *Kindred: The Embraced*. Angela Little's CV includes *Speedway Junkies*. Armando Valdes appeared in *Six Feet Under*. Steven M Porter was in *Sabrina, the Teenage Witch* and *Jake's Women*. Joe Sabatino appeared in *The Ring*, *NYPD Blue* and *Rocky V*. Dawn Lewis featured in *Hard Ball*. Alex Paez was in *The West Wing*.

Behind the Camera: Derek Johansen was a second assistant director on *Blade*.

Sex and Drugs and Rock n Roll: Cole has taken to frequenting a demonic lap-dancing club where Kaia (a shape-shifting Kieran demon) assumes the form of Phoebe and satisfies his needs. According to Dex, Kierans are manipulative vixens, and this particular one has an agenda that goes way beyond a crush.

Logic, Let Me Introduce You to This Window: If Cole's apartment is protected by magic, how can he and Kaia get in and out – as, indeed, could Piper and Paige in the previous episode – yet Leo can't? Piper says that she has to save the sole source of their income. Doesn't Phoebe get paid (and pretty well paid, at that) in her job, too? When Phoebe kicks Kaia, she clearly misses. An unconscious Phoebe is seemingly able to wrap her arms around Cole's neck when he carries her. Cole's claim on the Manor cannot be based solely on having the deeds to it. A valid claim over property needs to be signed over and recorded with the jurisdiction – Cole's a lawyer, though, so he's probably just bluffing on the assumption that the girls don't know the minutiae of the law. The Shadow Demon in this episode looks nothing like it did in its previous appearance. Also, in both 'Is There a Woogy in the House?' and 'Witch Trial', the vanquishing spell concluded: '... you *cannot* have this Halliwell.' Here, Phoebe says: '... you *can't* have this Halliwell.' The basement set used in 'Is There a Woogy in the House?' looked radically different from the set used for several episodes in seasons three and four. Here, however, they seem to have reverted to the original. How does Phoebe get the Manor's deeds back from Cole?

Continuity: Cole mentions that the Halliwell Manor is the doorway to the spiritual nexus (see 'Is There a Woogy in the House?'). Paige has obviously read of these events in *The Book of Shadows*, asking Phoebe if the nexus was what 'made you evil before.'

Cruelty to Animals: An annoyed Piper, having just had her club closed down by the health inspectors, narrowly fails to vanquish a rat (which is, actually, a demon in disguise).

Quote/Unquote: Cole, on the nexus: 'When we tap into it, evil spreads.' Dex: 'How far?' Cole: 'The police, the politicians, and Phoebe. She will be consumed by evil and she will finally give into our love. Then I'll torture and kill her sisters and we'll live happily ever after.'

Darryl: 'You just disappeared from jail?' Paige: 'No. I put pillows in the bed first. It always worked at my parents house.'

Paige, after having apparently found Phoebe kissing Cole: 'We need a plan.' Piper: '... We go home, we vomit.' Paige: 'And?' Piper: 'That's all I got so far.'

Kaia: 'I'm more of a looker than a talker.' Phoebe: 'You're blonde, I should've known.'

Notes: 'Using the law to bring down the Charmed Ones was genius.' There's a slight feeling of treading water in this episode, especially as the series' publicity was definitely aimed during this period at the forthcoming 100th episode. There's nothing much actually wrong with 'The Importance of Being Phoebe' (indeed, it's something of a *tour de force* for Alyssa Milano), but the various elements used never quite coalesce for the intended pathos to work as effectively as they should.

SEASON 5: CENTENNIAL CHARMED

100: CENTENNIAL CHARMED

19 January 2003

Writer: Brad Kern
Director: James L Conway

Cast: Joel Swetow (Avatar of Power), Steven Daniel (Lazarus Demon), Debbi Morgan (The Seer), Deanna Russo (Eve), Kristin Richardson (Darla), Sandra Prosper (Sheila Morris), Ricki Lopez (Homeless Man), Sean Morgan (Designer), Greg Provance (Demon Guard), Michael Bergin (Handsome Demon), Michelle Branch (Herself)

> In his twisted attempt to win back Phoebe's heart, Cole casts a spell that alters reality, eliminating Paige as a Halliwell and destroying the Power of Three. Paige finds that her sisters have no knowledge of her existence just as past villains come back to haunt them all.

It's Witchcraft: Paige notes that what makes Cole indestructible is his protection shield. She has therefore created a potion that makes her invisible long enough so she can get past the shield, say a spell and blow him up from the inside. Nice idea (and, as Leo notes, cool potion). But it doesn't work.

The Charmed Ones have agreed to take a vanquishing hiatus during Piper's last trimester.

A Little Learning is a Dangerous Thing: Paige discovers than whilst an attempted vanquishing doesn't kill Leo, it still hurts.

Paige notes that she has been feeling a little suppressed recently.

The Conspiracy Starts at the Witching Hour: Cole now wants to join the Avatars (see 'Y Tu Mummy Tambien') to get enough power to change reality. He is repeatedly warned that the Avatars' powers are not supposed to be used to settle personal vendettas. He refuses to listen and, ultimately, it costs him his life.

It's a Designer Label!: Piper's silver dress is quite effective. Phoebe's white T-shirt and braces combination isn't.

References: There are allusions to *Superman* (Bizarroworld); *La Femme*

SEASON 5: CENTENNIAL CHARMED

Nikita; and *The Long Goodbye*.

'You May Remember Me ...': Steven Daniel appeared in *The Other Sister*. Deanna Russo was in *Virgins*. Kristin Richardson's CV includes *Man on the Moon* and *Angel*. Sandra Prosper played Kayla Turner in *First Mondays*. Ricki Lopez appeared in *King Rikki*. Sean Morgan was in *True Crime*, *Grease* and *The West Wing*. Michael Bergin played Jack Davis in *Baywatch*. Michelle Branch also appeared in *The Hot Chick* and *Buffy the Vampire Slayer*.

Cigarettes and Alcohol: Cole smokes a celebratory cigar whilst playing pool in the Manor. Back in the normal reality, Leo brings bottle of champagne (and several glasses) to the table of Darryl and his wife Sheila at P^3.

Logic, Let Me Introduce You to This Window: In 'Charmed Again' Part 2, Paige instinctively orbed to avoid an attack by Shax. In 'A Paige from the Past', Paige discovered that she's alive only because she orbed during the car accident that killed her adoptive parents. Since orbing is seemingly such a natural part of Paige – having nothing whatsoever to do with the Power of Three – then why couldn't she orb in the alternate reality? Paige's tombstone reads 'Born 1975. Died 2001', directly contradicting 'Charmed Again', in which the year of her birth was given as 1977. When Paige appears in the alternate reality in the back room of P^3, the room looks almost exactly like it does in the real world. But when Paige opens the door, which falls off its hinges, the club itself is a mess. So why was the back room so tidy? In the alternate reality, if Paige had never joined Phoebe and Piper, then surely the Source should still be alive? Why, therefore, is the Seer serving Cole? When Cole comes home at the beginning of the episode, the photograph of himself and Phoebe is on the left side of the table and the box is on the right. Subsequently, they switch places. It's Cole's 100th birthday. In 'Coyote Piper', however, it was established that he was born in 1885. (Or, as implied by the demon, is Cole lying about his age?) The actress portraying Eva is different from the one in 'The Eyes Have It', and the character name changes from Eva to Eve.

Alternate Continuity: Cole regards the events of 'Charmed Again' and Phoebe meeting Paige for the first time as the point at which their relationship began to unravel. In the changed reality, Piper walked away from P^3 shortly after Prue's death and became obsessed with vanquishing Shax (see 'All Hell Breaks Loose'). She and Leo are divorced. Phoebe is trapped in a loveless marriage with Cole (they both openly have affairs), which she tolerates, having extracted a promise that, if she stays with him, Piper will not be harmed. Darryl works as a bodyguard to Phoebe. Cole is the Source, and the Seer is alive and working her nefarious skulduggery. Paige is dead – killed in 2001 by the Source.

Quote/Unquote: Phoebe: 'What about water birth? Can we do that at home?' Eve: 'Sure, we can rent a tub.' Piper: '... I'm not giving birth to fish.'

Cole: 'Our love's so strong, nothing can destroy it, not even this. We're meant to be together.' Phoebe: 'I don't think so.'

Paige, on Cole: 'I'm telling you, he's gone for good.' Phoebe: 'That's what we thought last time.' Piper: 'And the time before that.'

Notes: 'Happy birthday, Cole.' Julian McMahon's last episode is a suitable critical summation of the many positive points that this brilliant actor brought to *Charmed* over 50-odd episodes. A cunning variant on *It's a Wonderful Life*, the key phrase of 'Centennial Charmed' is 'Maybe it just wasn't meant to be,' spoken twice by Phoebe in two different realities. The climax is a little unsatisfying, in so much as (as Piper herself notes) vanquishing the series' biggest baddie almost seemed too easy. But there's plenty to admire elsewhere – particularly a great performance by Rose McGowan.

Soundtrack: Michelle Branch performs the classic 'Goodbye To You' at P^3.

101: HOUSE CALL

2 February 2003

Writer: Henry Alonso Myers
Director: Jon Paré

Cast: Jesse Woodrow (Glen Belland), Richard Gant (Elder Witch Doctor), Googy Gress (Spencer Ricks), Wolfgang Bodison (Witch Doctor), Rebecca Balding (Elise Rothman), Erinn Bartlett (Jessica), Todd Sherry (Photographer), Keith Sellon-Wright (Minister)

> Glen returns to Paige's life with a big surprise – he is getting married to a girl called Jessica. Meanwhile, the sisters summon a witch doctor whom they want to dispatch all the evil remnants that surround the Manor.

It's Witchcraft: The spell to call the witch doctor begins: 'Free us from the ties that bind, of evil magic intertwined, we call upon the one who cures, he who's to the dark, inured.'

Having made the house (and Phoebe) disappear, Piper uses a variation of the 'seen/unseen' spell ('Let the object of objection return, so its existence may be reaffirmed') to bring it back.

A Little Learning is a Dangerous Thing: The Manor experiences several ghostly manifestations. Leo notes that the activity is, mostly, residual energy left over from all the demons vanquished there. The Elders say they will dissipate over time. But they're not going quickly enough for the sisters, who summon a witch doctor to help.

The Conspiracy Starts at the Witching Hour: Phoebe notes that witch doctors expel evil spirits. Leo, however, adds that this doesn't make them good. Witch doctors are something of a wild card, which is why the Elders don't want the Charmed Ones working with them. Having expelled the spirits, the witch doctor – alarmed by the haphazard way in which the sisters are living their lives – casts a hex upon them to destroy them through their secret obsessions.

Work is a Four-Letter Word: The final scene shows Leo doing a stint behind the bar at P^3.

SEASON 5: HOUSE CALL

It's a Designer Label!: Huge highlight – Phoebe's pink shorts.

References: Allusions to *When Harry Met Sally*; *Playboy*; *The Osbournes*; and the anonymous Cornish prayer 'Things that Go Bump in the Night'. The Paige subplot is, in part, inspired by the movie *Basic Instinct*.

'You May Remember Me ...': Richard Gant's CV includes *Special Unit 2*, *Godzilla*, *Bean* and *Friends*. Googy Gress appeared in *Big Girls Don't Cry ... They Get Even*, *Stuck on You*, *Jack Frost*, *Apollo 13*, *Kingpin* and *G Vs E* (as Decker Benbow). Wolfgang Bodison was in *Most Wanted*, *Freeway* and *A Few Good Men*. Erinn Bartlett's movies include *Shallow Hal* and *Deep Blue Sea*. Todd Sherry was in *Tail Sting*. Keith Sellon-Wright appeared in *Almost Heroes*.

Logic, Let Me Introduce You to This Window: When the piece of ceiling falls on Piper, in close-ups she's covered in debris with a big piece of plaster sitting on top of her head, but in the long-shot there is little dust and no plaster. A legal wedding usually requires the couple, an official and a witness. When Leo takes Jessica back to the church and leaves with Paige, it is still day. When they get back to the Manor, it's night.

Continuity: Paige's obsession is with Glen's marriage to Jessica. By contrast, Piper becomes obsessed with cleanliness, and Phoebe with killing her advice column opposition – stereotypical sexist pig Spencer Ricks of the *Daily*. The photospread that Phoebe does is for *415* magazine, for whom Prue used to work. Piper notes that Paige loses her keys daily. Glen has been climbing the Matterhorn, which is where he met Jessica.

Quote/Unquote: Witch doctor: 'Ever vanquished a demon in this house by any chance?' Phoebe: 'Only about a hundred.' Piper: 'Give or take ...' Phoebe: '... Another hundred.'
Piper: 'There will be no fleeing the country until you clean up after yourself.' Phoebe: 'I'm sorry, I can't. I'm possessed.'
Piper: 'Is that a wedding dress?' Paige: 'You *just* noticed?'

Notes: 'In my defence, I *was* under a spell.' The worst episode in some considerable time, 'House Call' starts off on a bad foot with the over-the-top poltergeist malarkey, then it gets sillier and progressively more nasty (the Paige subplot, in particular, is needlessly offensive), before all being wrapped up with a mixture of bluff, evasion and off-screen action. A disappointingly banal effort after such a run of quality.

Soundtrack: Kylie Minogue's 'Come Into My World'.

102: SAND FRANCISCO DREAMIN'

9 February 2003

Writers: Monica Breen, Alison Schapker
Director: John T Kretchmer

Cast: Henry Gibson (Sandman), Austin Peck (Ryder), Rebecca Balding (Elise Rothman), Darin Heames (Demon), Tim Kelleher (Axel), Allison Munn (Wendy), Clarissa Romano (Becca), Beth Orton (Herself), Troy Blendell (Slappy the Clown), Shauna Sand (Sienna), Shari Shaw (Soccer Mom), Chris Ufland (Bill), Jossie Thacker (Reporter #2), Christian Keiber (Reporter #3), Amanda Sickler (Assistant)

A demon attacks the Charmed Ones with dream dust, causing their nightmares to come to life. Paige is harassed by a clown at a baby shower, Piper has an affair and Phoebe is chased by a maniac with a chainsaw. The sisters must put themselves to sleep to re-enter their nightmares and unmask their dreams' symbolic meanings.

Dreaming (As Blondie Once Said) is Free: This episode focuses on the recurring dreams of the sisters and Leo. Paige is attending a baby shower in P³, but each time she tries to give her toy clown, Slappy, to the baby, everyone abandons her. Subtext: Paige's own insecurity at being abandoned as a baby. Piper finds herself in a lustful and, frankly, *wrong* affair with a hunky guy from a TV soap. Subtext: Piper's femininity is threatened by her pregnancy. Phoebe has a black and white dream in which she is menaced by a masked, chainsaw-wielding maniac in the basement. Subsequently, the masked assassin is revealed to be Phoebe herself. Subtext: as Phoebe herself notes, this is something of an old issue – self-sabotage. She constantly beat herself up over the whole Cole affair, not thinking that she deserved to move on after it. Leo dreams that he becomes pregnant. Subtext: classic anxiety issues related to his inability to feel close to his soon-to-be-born child. Apparently, demons don't dream.

It's Witchcraft: The spell the Charmed Ones cast to enter a dream-state is: 'Let we who waken from our sleep, return at once to slumber deep.'

A Little Learning is a Dangerous Thing: *Vir-du-somnio* is, Leo notes, the original Latin term for a Sandman. There isn't just one Sandman, there are many – like angels and cupids. They visit mortals during their sleep and sprinkle them with dream dust so they can dream. They exist on a different plane.

The Conspiracy Starts at the Witching Hour: Tracer demons are lower-level mercenaries, able to track magical beings through different dimensions.

It's a Designer Label!: Have a look at the state of Beth Orton's bongo-player's hair and clothes. Wow, it's 1967 all over again.

References: The title alludes to the Mamas and the Papas' 'California Dreamin''. Also, *Rosemary's Baby* ('This is not a dream ...'); Sigmund Freud; and *Mr Mom*. Much of the imagery of Phoebe's dream comes from horror movies – particularly *Halloween* and *The Shining*.

'You May Remember Me ...': A television legend, Henry Gibson played Thuston Howell in *Magnolia* and also appeared in *The Blues Brothers*, *Bewitched*, *Rowan & Martin's Laugh-In*, *Stargate SG-1*, *Wonder Woman*, *McCloud*, *F Troop* and *Sunset Beach*. Austin Peck was in *Breaking Down*. Darin Heames appeared in *The Fear*, *Dr Giggles* and *24*. Tim Kelleher's CV includes *Thirteen Days*, *Dark Skies* and *Malcolm X*. Allison Munn played Tina in *What I Like About You*. Clarissa Romano's movies include *Bringing Rain*. Shauna Sand was in *Air America*. Shari Shaw appeared in *The Disappearing Girl Trick*. Chris Ufland featured in *The X-Files* and *Rules of Engagement*. Jossie Thacker appeared in *The West Wing* and was one of the Fly Girls in *In Living Color*.

Cigarettes and Alcohol: The Tracer demon smokes a cigar.

Logic, Let Me Introduce You to This Window: In Phoebe's dream, when the murderers multiply, three murderers appear in reality. So when Piper's lover changes into Leo and when Phoebe unmasks the murderers in her dream, why don't their real counterparts also change? When Piper's lover disappears, it should leave Leo in the cage. When the sisters created the spell to induce sleep, why is Leo also dreaming? While Paige is holding Slappy and talking to Leo, her hand position on the doll changes several times between the shots

Continuity: Piper is allergic to bees. Phoebe has given Leo a book entitled *1000 Unexpected Dangers for Babies*. In it, easy-opening cabinets are number 32.

SEASON 5: SAND FRANCISCO DREAMIN'

Quote/Unquote: Phoebe: 'I vanquish demons every day. Real ones. Some guy from my dreams should be a piece of cake ... even *with* power tools.'

Elise: 'Some of you guys are gonna have to double up. Angry man ploughs into Farmer's Market in his car. Angry woman attacks school principal with a knife. And, in sports, angry coach knocks out umpire with a baseball bat.'

Piper: 'This isn't right. I'm married.' Ryder: 'Not in your dreams you're not.'

Piper: 'The killer was you?' Phoebe: 'Yeah. How narcissistic is that?'

Notes: 'Why would a demon be interested in killing people's dreams? They're just harmless, erotic fun.' A *Charmed* episode full of Freudian symbolism. Not exactly a first (and an episode dealing largely with the meaning of dreams isn't the most original idea either), but done with a stylish flourish that makes the unoriginality acceptable. Excellent direction too in a story that required a lot of visual impact (far more than in a standard episode).

Soundtrack: The episode opens with The Chordettes' 1954 version of Pat Ballard's 'Mr Sandman'. Beth Orton performs 'Thinking About Tomorrow' at P^3.

103: THE DAY THE MAGIC DIED

16 February 2003

Writer: Daniel Cerone
Director: Stuart Gillard

Cast: Cheryl Ladd (Doris), James Read (Victor Bennett), J P Manoux (Stanley), Maggie Baird (Doctor), Richard Lynch (Cronyn), W Morgan Sheppard (Merrill), Yan Birch (Warlock)

>Phoebe and Paige go to a summit meeting with the leaders of evil and discover that all magic has disappeared, enabling the leaders to steal Piper's about-to-be-born baby and welcome the child into the kingdom of evil. Meanwhile, the sisters meet their new stepmother.

It's Witchcraft: Phoebe attempts to get rid of the unicorn with a truly awful spell ('Take this beast, before I end her. Ship her back, return to sender'). Thankfully, this occurs just after she has lost her powers. Later, she's grateful to still have the creature around, as it plays a vital part in vanquishing Cronyn: 'Beast of legend, myth and lore, give my words the power to soar, and kill this evil evermore.'

A Little Learning is a Dangerous Thing: 'It's like magic and science and fairy tales all rolled up into one,' notes Phoebe as the sisters watch the Northern Lights. Actually, Paige adds, it's ions speeding into the Earth's magnetic field and then colliding with air molecules. Paige asks if her sisters think it's weird that the Aurora Borealis is happening the night before the Wiccan Festival of Lights.

According to Cronyn, gnomes and garden nymphs are real. Mortals don't know that magic exists, but it infuses all their hopes and dreams.

Piper is suffering from toxaemia, a form of high blood pressure in pregnant women. Toxaemia is often caused by stress. It restricts blood flow, food and oxygen to the placenta. It can result in a small baby or a premature delivery.

Cronyn's suggestion for the venue of the summit is one of his dark chambers. Paige insisted, instead, on Manny's Pizzeria. Of course, it's all a trap.

The Conspiracy Starts at the Witching Hour: Merrill, whom Cronyn describes as a high-ranking wizard and Cronyn's own personal mentor, says that centuries ago, he unearthed a quatrain from the tomb of a wise apothecary. This stated that when three planets burn as one over a sky of dancing light, magic will rest for a holy day to welcome a twice-blessed child. Paige realises that the prophecy refers to the various signs – the Aurora Borealis, the planetary alignment of Jupiter, Mars and Saturn in Gemini (something that happens only once every 300 years) and the Wiccan Sabbat. Magic won't return to the world until Piper's baby is born.

Love is a Four-Letter Word: Victor arrives at the Manor with a new wife, Doris, whom he recently met on a singles' cruise in Mexico. Perky and somewhat pushy, Doris states that her previous husband died a couple of years ago from a heart attack. (She has recently put Victor on a low-fat, high-fibre diet, with a monthly colonic.) In reality, she's an associate of the sorcerer Cronyn. (Piper suggests that she's a demon, although that remains unconfirmed.)

References: The title alludes to lyrics in Don McLean's 'American Pie'. Also, the character of Darren Stevens from *Bewitched*; and film director Frank Capra (*It Happened One Night*, *It's a Wonderful Life*).

'You May Remember Me …': A genuine TV icon as Kris Munroe in *Charlie's Angels*, Cheryl Ladd's CV also includes *The Haunting of Lisa*, *Poison Ivy*, *When She Was Bad*, *Satan's School for Girls*, *Chrome and Hot Leather*, *The Muppet Show*, *Las Vegas*, *The Fantastic Journey*, *Happy Days*, *The Partridge Family* and *Ironside*. Richard Lynch appeared in *Starsky & Hutch*, *Hunter*, *Battlestar Galactica*, *Scanner Cop*, *The Garbage Man* and *First Watch*. Irish-born W Morgan Sheppard was a TV regular on both sides of the Atlantic with credits in *Z Cars*, *The Sweeney*, *Hammer House of Horror*, *Shogun*, *MacGyver*, *The Flame Trees of Thika*, *seaQuest DSV* and *Max Headroom*. J P Manoux appeared in *Angel*, *Will & Grace*, *The District*, *Meet the Fockers*, *Galaxy Quest* and *Ocean's Eleven*. He also did voice-work on *Scooby Doo* and *Monsters Inc*. Maggie Baird was in *Picket Fences*, *Manic* and *Rode vs Wade*. Yan Birch appeared in *Essence of Echoes* (which he also produced) and *The People Under the Stairs*.

Sex and Drugs and Rock n Roll: Before Paige and Phoebe go to the summit, Paige gives Phoebe some protection – a chainmail top from her club days; steel-toed boots from her mosh pit days; and handcuffs – from the previous Friday.

Logic, Let Me Introduce You to This Window: In 'Awakened', Piper stated that she hates hospitals, so why is she so is intent on having the baby in hospital when everyone else wants the birth to occur at the Manor?

SEASON 5: THE DAY THE MAGIC DIED

Why doesn't Leo orb after the goose instead of jumping around after it? When Paige orbs into Piper's and Leo's bedroom, the ruffles of her shirt are on the right side, but when she and Phoebe go downstairs, they are on the left. As recently as 'House Call', there were trees behind the Manor. Here, the same view is a clear shot of the city. The baby's magical powers have been healing Piper (and, indeed, itself) for some time – why, therefore, do they suddenly stop even before all the magic goes away? In the scene where Piper is lying on the stairs, she knows that all magic is gone, so why does she keep telling Phoebe to vanquish the demon. Since Paige is the daughter of Patty Halliwell and Sam, she should have no connection to Phoebe's and Piper's father, and Doris would most definitely not be her stepmother. Stanley says that the Aurora Borealis is a rare sight. It's not *that* rare. It depends where you live – most of the northern half of the Northern Hemisphere can see a display about once a year. Wasn't the wizard in 'We're Off to See the Wizard' supposed to be the last of his kind? The baby used is clearly not newborn.

Continuity: Piper gives birth to a baby boy, rather than the daughter everyone believed she was having. Paige notes that she was very good at chemistry in high school – a talent she puts to excellent use in making a series of magically-enhanced bombs for her and Phoebe's summit with the representatives of evil.

Cruelty to Animals: Amongst the gifts that Piper has recently been sent are golden egg-laying geese and, from the Elders, a unicorn. She suggests that one would think the magical community could find something more original to give the baby, and asks Leo about the policy on returning magical gifts. After all, they don't want a curse put on the family. Ultimately, the unicorn comes in useful – as the Elders intended. Its horn is made from the pure essence of magic and is unaffected by the general loss of magical powers. The sisters use it to vanquish Cronyn and Doris and to heal Victor's stab wound.

Quote/Unquote: Cronyn, persuading Stanley to attack the Halliwells: 'This is a kind of mission that turns demons into legends. Your name will go down in infamy.' Stanley: 'Really?' Cronyn: 'Yes. What *is* your name again?'

Phoebe, after Cronyn gives her his card: 'Since when do sorcerers have cellphones?' Cronyn: 'You think that's bad? I've got a taxi waiting out front.'

Piper: 'Dad?' Victor: 'Yeah, honey?' Piper: 'I'm sorry about your demon wife.'

SEASON 5: THE DAY THE MAGIC DIED

Notes: 'It's like someone's taken the magic and erased it from our entire family.' *Charmed* back to doing what it does best – a mixture of serious family drama, including some pretty accurate (i.e. *painful*) child-birth scenes, and slapstick comedy. The latter includes one of the best bar-room-style brawls the series has ever attempted. There are some super performances from the guest cast (particularly Richard Lynch) and loads of great one-liners.

104: BABY'S FIRST DEMON

30 March 2003

Writer: Krista Vernoff
Director: John Kretchmer

Cast: Grace Zabriskie (The Crone), Eric Dane (Jason Dean), Rebecca Balding (Elise Rothman), Andy Mackenzie (Suck), Jack McGee (Hawker Demon), Nicholas Sadler (Leech), Damian Foster (Demon Guard #2), Jonathan Joss (Brutish Demon), Taira Soo (Power Broker), Kate Anthony (Reporter Kate), Amanda Sickler (Phoebe's Assistant), Tim Sitarz (Demon Guard #1), Doug Budin (Nerdy Demon), Bob Cicherillo (The Strong Man)[58]

> The Charmed Ones must protect Piper's new-born son from two demons. But the baby has a few surprises of his own. Meanwhile, Paige goes undercover as a bounty hunter, and Phoebe's future with the *Bay Mirror* is threatened by a handsome new owner.

Naming Wyatt: Suggested names for the new baby include Peter, Patrick and Potter. Piper is chided for not having thought of any boy names, but she defends herself by noting that when she went to the future, she had a daughter (see 'Mortality Bites'). Her intended name for the child – Prudence Melinda – is, sadly, no longer applicable. Peter is rejected because Phoebe once dated a Peter who wasn't nice. And, as Paige notes, it's a euphemism for a penis. From the family tree, Hubert, Clarence and Milton are also rejected (as is Jason). Eventually, Piper comes up with Wyatt Matthew Halliwell, which seems to satisfy everyone.

It's Witchcraft: The Crone's wisdom is, according to the Hawker, ancient and renowned.

A Little Learning is a Dangerous Thing: Paige created the baby alarm system by enchanting a few cowry shells. She later places a protection spell around the Manor using apples and sage. She suggests that all the neighbours who didn't already think the sisters were crazy now, officially, do.

The Conspiracy Starts at the Witching Hour: Hawkers are a breed of demon known for hawking magical goods at the demonic market. The

---

[58] Uncredited.

Parasites were once powerful demons but were cursed by a witch and lost most – though not all – of their power. They are seeking a self-sustaining, never-ending source of magic, which, they feel, Wyatt will provide.

Work is a Four-Letter Word: Piper notes that the club is not raking in the dough these days and, as Paige remains unemployed, what with the cost of diapers, they need Phoebe to keep her job. At that very moment, the *Bay Mirror* has been bought by hunky Jason Dean ('New money, some kind of dot-com millionaire,' according to Elise). Dean is really taken with Phoebe and considers her the paper's biggest asset (although he thinks some of her recent columns have been rather baby-centric). Indeed, he wants ideas to expand her column. He suggests a series of features road-testing her advice, or a series on the best singles' spots in San Francisco based on her undercover experience. Phoebe and Elise come up with further concepts, beginning with Phoebe trying out some of the pick-up lines that she suggests in her column, then reporting back on how they work off the page and in the world. Jason thinks this is 'sexy as hell.'

It's a Designer Label!: Paige's undercover figure-hugging, blue-leather ... thing. I dunno what it's called, but I like it a lot.

References: Allusions to the Harry Potter novels; *Superman* (the *Daily Planet*); the 'Dear Abby' column; and the Pulitzer Prize.

'You May Remember Me ...': Grace Zabriskie's extraordinary CV includes *Tales of the Gold Monkey, Moonlighting, The Executioner's Song, Seinfeld, Falcon Crest, Norma Rae, Even Cowgirls Get the Blues, John Doe, The Grudge* and *Twin Peaks*. Andy Mackenzie appeared in *CSI, The Shield* and *Rock Star*. Nicholas Sadler's movies include *Mobsters, Stop! Or My Mom Will Shoot* and *Twister*. Jack McGee was in *The Huntress, Sunset Beat, Besame Mucho* and *Carnivàle*. Eric Dane appeared in *Las Vegas* and *Gideon's Crossing*. Damian Foster's movies include *Blue Streak*. Jonathan Joss was in *Walker, Texas Ranger*. Doug Budin featured in *Friends*. Taira Soo appeared in *Rendezvous*. Kate Anthony's CV includes *The Sopranos*. Tim Sitarz was in *Longshot* and *VIP*. Bob Cicherillo appeared in *Demons at the Door*.

Sex and Drugs and Rock n Roll: Piper notes that Phoebe is something of an expert on breasts.

Logic, Let Me Introduce You to This Window: Victor is listed on the family tree as Victor Jones (see 'Pardon My Past') instead of Bennett. His date of birth is given as 16 February 1929, making him 21 years older than his ex-wife and, frankly, the best looking 74 year old currently on the planet. The tree seems to be the one previously seen in 'Pardon My Past', so all the same continuity errors noted there also apply here (i.e. Grams' date of death being in 1963). Note also that Prue is recorded as Prue rather than Prudence. The baby is clearly a doll when the hawker first attacks. When Leo tries to stop the parasites from attacking the baby, he hits one on the head with a lamp. What happened to the other parasite to make him stop the attack? Why is Paige risking entering the demonic market wearing just a cheap wig instead of morphing, as in, for example, 'House Call'? Although they'd been expecting a girl for the last nine months, Piper and Leo had still kept their options open by obtaining a blue blanket (complete with the triquetra symbol) for the baby.

Continuity: The episode takes place approximately three weeks after the events of 'The Day the Magic Died'. Wyatt, who weighed 6lbs 8oz at birth, can generate force fields to protect himself from demons, which is seemingly what made Piper invincible during her pregnancy. Also, Wyatt quickly realises that when the baby alarm goes off, his family will come running. The Crone notes that the child is powerful beyond comprehension. Asked to elaborate, she simply adds, 'He is our end.' Piper notes that the sisters have gone up against invisible demons ('Sight Unseen'), demons that morph into lamps ('Brain Drain') and demons in the walls (a probable allusion to 'House Call').

Quote/Unquote: Piper: 'It just pisses me off. I can't believe they would come in the house and try to steal the baby.' Paige: 'Demons aren't exactly known for their moral compass.'

Paige: 'We vanquish them, everyone they've ever met, and proceed with our original demon-killing, message-sending plan.' Piper: 'It's a very wordy, very good plan.'

Leo, on the baby: 'Look on the bright side, growing up with your sisters, he was bound to be neurotic anyway.'

Notes: 'I suggest you rest well and preserve your energies. From what I've foreseen, you're going to need them.' Probably the best overall episode of the season, 'Baby's First Demon' leaves most of its cutesy-pie nonsense in the opening scene and then develops into a really clever essay on maternal love and family bonding, in which each of the sisters learns a few lessons about the changing world that they are suddenly a part of. Much great dialogue peppers the episode, and there are some terrific special effects on offer too. All in all, a bit of a classic, and a positive sign of an emerging new direction post-Julian McMahon.

Soundtrack: 'Count On Me (Somebody)' by Tonic.

105: LUCKY CHARMED

6 April 2003

Writer: Curtis Kheel
Director: Roxann Dawson

Cast: Dominic Fumusa (Saleel), Mark Povinelli (Shamus), Monika Schnarre (Jenna), Phina Oruche (Jayda), Cork Hubbert (Head Councilman), Michael Gilden (Finnegan), Drew Wood (Erik), Eric Dane (Jason Dean), Pat Benatar (Herself), Neil Giraldo (Himself), Jake Alston (Street Performer), Kevin Thompson (Connor), Amanda Sickler (Sophie), Eugene Pidgeon (Liam), James Wellington (Croupier), Jack Kyle (Chet), Frank Cohen (Leprechaun)[59]

The Charmed Ones face a demon, Saleel, who has been killing Leprechauns and stealing their magic. The Leprechaun Shamus blesses the sisters with good luck, which enables Paige to gain material wealth, Phoebe to meet a man and Piper to book Pat Benatar to play P^3. But not all luck is good.

It's Witchcraft: To repair her damaged top, Paige uses the spell: 'Personal loss should not be mine, restore this sweater and make it fine.' In an attempt to improve her credit rating, she creates another spell: 'To find good luck, finances have run a-muck, creditors I soon must duck. I cast this spell to find good luck and hope my life will cease to suck.' That one brings her to the attention of the Leprechauns.

The Luck of the Irish, Begorrah: Leprechauns are like bees, notes Paige. They pollinate the world with luck. Sometimes the seeds don't stick, but on other occasions they grow into full-blown hot streaks. Phoebe argues that not all luck is good, and Shamus agrees, noting that a nugget can go either way depending on a Leprechaun's intention. Piper suggests that, since they hand out bad luck as well as good, Leprechauns could be considered evil. Leprechauns might be tricksters, notes Leo, but they're definitely not evil. The world needs bad luck as much as it needs good, to keep the natural order in balance. Bad luck helps people just as much as good luck, maybe even more so. Because of adversity, people learn, they grow. Rainbows enable Leprechauns to travel between dimensions. The

---

[59] Uncredited.

SEASON 5: LUCKY CHARMED

Leprechauns locate rainbows with their shillelaghs.

A Little Learning is a Dangerous Thing: According to Leo, the Elders believe that good has been going through a curious string of bad luck lately and that demons are getting the upper hand.

The Conspiracy Starts at the Witching Hour: Saleel is a lower-level reptile demon and is considered very elusive. He has been stealing the Leprechauns' gold nuggets and giving them to other demons in a power bid in the Underworld.

Work is a Four-Letter Word: Piper is impressed that Phoebe can say Jason's name without swearing. Sadly, Phoebe notes that her new boss is still driving her crazy, even if he did recently give her a raise. But that, she suggests, was just a bribe so she wouldn't quit.

It's a Designer Label!: From whence did Phoebe obtain her Rubettes-style white cap? 1974?

References: Holland, Dozier and Holland's 'Where Did Our Love Go?'; *The Wizard of Oz*; *The Tonight Show*'s and *Star Search*'s Ed McMahon; George Clooney; and Alyssa Milano's then-boyfriend Justin Timberlake. There's a not-even-remotely-subtle allusion to Pat Benatar's 'Hit Me With Your Best Shot'.

'You May Remember Me ...': Dominic Fumusa appeared in *The Guru* and *Law & Order: Special Victims Unit*. Mark Povinelli was in *Polar Express*. Monika Schnarre's CV includes *Beverley Hills 90210*, *Andromeda* and *Sanctuary*. Phina Oruche played Olivia in *Buffy the Vampire Slayer* and also appeared in *How Stella Got Her Groove Back*, *Nip/Tuck* and *The Forsaken*. Cork Hubbert was in *ER*, *Legend* and *Knee High PI*. Michael Gilden appeared in *Pulp Fiction* and *CSI*. Drew Wood played Jason in *Hitch*. Pat Benatar featured in *Union City*. Jake Alston was in *The Last Castle*. Kevin Thompson's CV includes *The Tick*, *Blade Runner* and *Weird Science*. Eugene Pidgeon appeared in *Inhabited*. James Wellington was in *Las Vegas*. Jack Kyle appeared in *Without a Trace*, *Killing Time* and *Intolerable Cruelty*. Frank Cohen's movies include *Tiptoes*.

Cigarettes and Alcohol: Phoebe tells Jason that she drinks Martinis.

Internet Sex and Drugs and Rock n Roll: Instructed by Jason to write an article concerning online dating, Phoebe sets up several dates (including one with a demon at P^3) using her Internet identity Cinderella29. One of her most persistent pursuers is Cyrano73, who turns out to be Jason himself. Jason confesses that he is often stubborn, a control freak and pretty arrogant. But he seems to like Phoebe.

Logic, Let Me Introduce You to This Window: Only good witches are supposed to be immune to Piper's freezing power (although that rule *has* been stretched on occasions). Why, therefore, doesn't Phoebe's demon date freeze when Piper freezes the whole club? The TransAmerica Pyramid is seen from the attic window of the Manor for the first time in over 100 episodes. Phoebe's ability to talk during her premonitions is also a previously unseen skill.

Continuity: Whilst debating the negatives of personal gain spells, Piper asks Paige if she's forgotten the 'big-boobs fiasco' (see 'Hell Hath No Fury'). Paige hasn't, and confesses that her back still hurts. To enable Piper not to have to sell the club, Leo is granted some paternity leave by the Elders.

Cruelty to Animals: Piper has a fear of snakes.

Quote/Unquote: Shamus, landing on top of Paige after evading Saleel: 'Ever date a little person?'
Phoebe: 'I know what women like ... We like eye contact. And conversations where you can actually see the other person's lips moving, and long, late night walks and candles and roses.' Jason: 'And you don't think you can get that over the Internet?' Phoebe: 'I think you can get CDs over the Internet, books, a purse maybe. But not a date.'
Paige, rolling the dice: 'Baby needs a new pair of shoes. And, by baby, I *do* mean me.'

Notes: 'Tough break, Paddy.' Oh dear. On general principle – particularly regarding the highly dubious and horrible *Oirish begorrah* accents – it's tempting to write 'Lucky Charmed' off with a simple 'Worst! Episode! Ever!' declaration. And, ultimately, that's exactly what it deserves. This is banal, quasi-racist rubbish unredeemed by any sort of saving irony or much intelligence. An episode that panders to ignorant stereotypes and flatly unfunny comedy characters. Just pretend this one never happened and move along quickly.

Soundtrack: The episode opens with Israel Kamikawino'ole's cover of 'Somewhere Over the Rainbow'. Pat Benatar and Neil Giraldo perform 'Heartbreaker' at P^3. Jake Alston plays an interesting rearrangement of 'Greensleeves' (see 'A Knight to Remember').

106: CAT HOUSE

13 April 2003$

Writer: Brad Kern
Director: Mel Damski

Cast: Marita Geraghty (Katrina), John Rubinstein (Dr Berenson), Zachary Quinto (Warlock)[60], Jennifer Rhodes (Grams)[61], James Read (Victor Bennett)[62], Finola Hughes (Patty Halliwell)[63], Una Damon (Dantalian)[64]

> When Piper and Leo have marital difficulties, Piper casts a spell to allow them to literally see the past together. However, the spell traps Phoebe and Paige in time, reliving Piper's memories. A warlock, bent on destroying the Charmed Ones, hitches a ride.

Pussy, Galore: The family cat, Kit (last seen in 'Look Who's Barking'), ran away from the Manor around the time of Prue's death (certainly prior to Paige coming into contact with Piper and Phoebe). As seen in 'Something Wicca This Way Comes' and 'PreWitched', Kit was, in fact, the sisters' familiar (even if they didn't know it). Familiars are enchanted creatures who follow and guide new witches to protect them while they learn the craft. Seemingly Kit performed a similar task for Paige prior to her becoming a witch – Paige notes that the cat reminds her of a stray that used to hang around her old apartment. Once the Charmed Ones were reconstituted, after Paige's appearance, it was time for Kit to move on and become Katrina. Only special familiars, like Katrina, are rewarded for their service by becoming human to guide future familiars.

It's Witchcraft: Piper casts a memory spell, 'Let the truth be told, let our lives unfold, so we can relive our memories, and stop being enemies.' It helps her and Leo to overcome their marital problems, but has decidedly unexpected side-effects for Phoebe and Paige.

A Little Learning is a Dangerous Thing: Dr Berenson is a marriage counsellor who has previously helped Phoebe with her column. She called

---

[60] Uncredited.
[61] Appears only in archive footage from 'Just Harried.'
[62] Appears only in archive footage from 'Just Harried.'
[63] Appears only in archive footage from 'Just Harried.'
[64] Appears only in archive footage from 'Bride and Gloom.'

SEASON 5: CAT HOUSE

in a favour for Piper and Leo to attend one of his sessions.

It's a Designer Label!: Piper's beige boots. Paige is a riot of colour this week: blue velvet shirt, bright yellow T-shirt and (very tight) red trousers.

References: The shots of cats attacking the warlock include visual allusions to *The Uncanny*.

'You May Remember Me ...': Marita Geraghty's movies include *Broadcast News* and *Groundhog Day*. John Rubinstein played Harrison Fox Jr in *Crazy Like a Fox* and Linwood Murrow in *Angel*. He appeared in *The Boys from Brazil*, *Enterprise*, *The West Wing*, *Cannon*, *Red Dragon*, *Roots: The Next Generation* and *The Car*. The son of piano virtuoso Arthur Rubinstein, John was a composer on series like *China Beach* and *Harry O*. He also won a Tony in 1980 for his performance in *Children Of A Lesser God*, and was the original lead in the Broadway production of Bob Fosse's *Pippin*. Zachary Quinto played Adam Kaufman in 24.

Logic, Let Me Introduce You to This Window: Kit, previously described as a male cat, has had a sex change on becoming human. When Paige is talking to Katrina, the necklace that she was wearing isn't around her neck, but when she orbs to help Phoebe, the necklace is back. When the warlock slashes Katrina, the wound appears a distance above where the knife touched her neck. Paige seemingly knows the innocent's name is Katrina before it's been mentioned. In the material drawn from 'Coyote Piper', a different song is playing when Piper is dancing. The American Flag fridge-magnet seen regularly in the kitchen is present on the newly-shot sequences of Paige and Phoebe hiding during Piper's wedding. However, it wasn't on the fridge at the time of 'Just Harried'.

Continuity: The episode features clips from – in order – 'The Fourth Sister', 'Bride and Gloom', 'Just Harried', 'Love Hurts', 'The Witch is Back', Once Upon a Time', 'Look Who's Barking', 'A Knight to Remember', 'PreWitched', 'Coyote Piper' and 'The Honeymoon's Over'. Although he's only briefly seen in one of the flashbacks, Darryl is mentioned – it's his day off and Paige has arranged for him to look after Wyatt whilst Leo and Piper attend their meeting with the counsellor. Phoebe gives Paige a potted history of Piper's previous boyfriends, including Dan, a warlock (Jeremy, see 'Something Wicca This Way Comes'), two bankers (Rob in 'Witch Trial', Jack Manford in 'Dream Sorcerer'), a rock-climber (Lucas in 'From Fear to Eternity') and a ghost (Mark in 'Dead Man Dating'). And, notes Phoebe, the ghost was the best of the bunch. Paige says that she's already been to one alternate reality, and doesn't wish to go to another (see

'Centennial Charmed'). She also mentions the muses and the potion that Piper made to blind the warlock and keep him from blinking (see 'Muse to My Ears').

Cruelty to Animals: The warlock brutally stabs Kit, makes a lame pun about curiosity killing the cat, then leaves.

Quote/Unquote: Dr Berenson: 'The fact that you seem to be able to relive your wife's experience to such a degree is very telling.' Leo: 'It is?' Dr Berenson: 'I think you might have some co-dependency issues.'
Leo: 'You want to talk co-dependent? Ask her about her damn sisters. They're frickin' inseparable.'
Phoebe: 'You just said something.' Paige: 'I did? Was it smart?'

Notes: 'It's uncanny how well you both seem to remember exactly what happened. Especially after five years.' It's a rare thing to be able to do a clip show and make it inventive, funny and brilliantly scripted. *The Simpsons* manages it once a season, but most other series that resort to clip shows do so for simple cost-cutting reasons. Therefore *Charmed*'s first foray into the archives is a major triumph on any level, full of complex story ideas, and not an inconsiderable amount of self-referential humour. ('Finally, one *I* remember' says Paige as she and Phoebe become part of a clip from an episode after she joined the show.) 'Cat House' is a smart and thoroughly sussed little gem.

Soundtrack: 'But I Do Love You' by LeAnn Rimes.

Did You Know?: All we see of Prue during the flashbacks are a brief glimpse of her back, leaving Piper's wedding on a motorbike from 'Just Harried', and a more lengthy clip from her as a dog in 'Look Who's Barking'.

107: NYMPHS JUST WANNA HAVE FUN

20 April 2003

Writers: Andrea Stevens, Doug E Jones
Director: Stewart Schill

Cast: Katherine Cunningham-Eves (Daisy), Eric Dane (Jason Dean), Ruth Powell (Lily), Susan May Pratt (Miranda), Jaimz Woolvett (Tull), Pat Healy (Xavier), Todd Duffey (Satyr), Jim O'Brien (Reporter), D J Lockhart (Officer #1), Jason Lasater (Band Manager), Jossie Thacker (Female Reporter), Loudermilk (Themselves)

> When a demon attacks and kills one of three nymphs who protect the eternal spring, the Charmed Ones try to help. However, once the demon is destroyed, the nymphs decide that Paige should replace the fallen nymph.

It's Witchcraft: The spell that Paige and Piper cast to turn Tull into a tree begins: 'Changing seasons changes all, life renews as creation calls. Nothing is immune, everything transmutes, so take this demon and give him roots.'

A Little Learning is a Dangerous Thing: Paige, with plenty of time on her hands, has recently colour-coded *The Book of Shadows*, much to Piper's chagrin.

The Conspiracy Starts at the Witching Hour: Wood nymphs are frolicking tree-sprites. Together with their Satyr, they are protectors of the forest. They are considered to be the personification of nature and wear a droplet from the eternal spring around their necks to remind them of what they are protecting. Only certain types of magical creatures can be turned into a nymph, and these include witches.

Work is a Four-Letter Word: Phoebe has just won a Columnist of the Year award.

It's a Designer Label!: Check out Phoebe's slinky (and bosom-revealing) black dress in the opening few scenes. Paige's little green nymph number is also recommended to the discerning viewer as, indeed, is the Union Jack T-shirt and beige miniskirt worn by the girl in the front row when Loudermilk are rockin' P³.

References: The title alludes to Cyndi Lauper's hit 'Girls Just Wanna Have Fun'. Also, Steppenwolf's 'Born To Be Wild'; and the Biblical verse Matthew 7 ('Ask and ye shall receive').

'You May Remember Me ...': Katherine Cunningham-Eves appeared in *Out of Courage 2*. Susan May Pratt played Mandella in *10 Things I Hate About You* and was in *CSI* and *Drive Me Crazy*. Jaimz Woolvett was Mark Snow in *White Fang*. His CV also includes *JAG*, *Dead Presidents* and *Helter Skelter*. Pat Healy appeared in *Six Feet Under*, *Magnolia*, *Ghost World* and *Mullitt* (which he also wrote and directed). Todd Duffey played Murk in *Buffy* and was in *Office Space*. Jim O'Brien appeared in *Bar Flies*. D J Lockhart was Doc Reese in *As the World Turns*. Jason Lasater's movies include *Carnal Passion*.

Cigarettes and Alcohol: At the party Jason has organised in Phoebe's honour, much Möet champagne appears to have been drunk ...

Sex and Drugs and Rock n Roll: ... after which, a tired-and-emotional Jason and Phoebe get attracted to each other. Literally. It must have been a jolly cold day in the park when they were filming the scenes with Tull and the nymphs, judging from the prominence of Rose McGowan's nipples.

Logic, Let Me Introduce You to This Window: It must be a *really* slow news day if Jason is so insistent on getting the nymphs on the front page. Three scantily-clad women dancing around a fountain in downtown San Francisco doesn't seem a particularly newsworthy story. And why call them 'the Godiva Girls'; they're not even close to being naked (Phoebe, in that dress, was closer)! Tull can demon-teleport himself wherever he wants, so why does he casually stroll down the hill shouting dire threats about what he intends to do to the nymphs and the witches when he gets to the bottom. Paige's footware changes, mid-episode, from beige- to dark-coloured sandals.

Continuity: Piper, when looking through *The Book of Shadows*, refers to the Bunyip (see 'Chick Flick').

Quote/Unquote: Piper, on Phoebe and Jason getting horizontal: 'How did this happen?' Phoebe: 'It was very fast.' Paige: 'Oh, downer.' Phoebe: 'No, *that* part wasn't fast ...'

SEASON 5: NYMPHS JUST WANNA HAVE FUN

Paige: 'Vanquishing demons is not a sport.' Piper: 'It is if you're good at it.'

Notes: 'Somebody's doing the walk of shame.' An episode that has a reputation slightly lower than rattlesnake urine among fans and critics alike. Well, looking for positives, it's certainly no worse than 'Lucky Charmed' … and, that's about it, really. This is a godawful, lousy episode, full of crass ideas and stupid dialogue. It makes you wonder how the actors managed to get through the thing with a straight face.

Soundtrack: Loudermilk perform 'Rock 'n' Roll and The Teenage Desperation' and 'Elekt' at P^3, accompanied by Rose McGowan's almost pornographic dancing. Nice. Also, the excellent 'Take It Off' by the Donnas.

108: SENSE AND SENSE ABILITY

27 April 2003

Teleplay: Daniel Cerone, Krista Vernoff
Story: Brian Krause, Ed Bokinskie
Directors: Joel J Feigenbaum, Stewart Schill

Cast: Norman Reedus (Nate), Grace Zabriskie (The Crone), Jerome Butler (Kazi King), Nynno Ahli (Kazi Demon), Rebecca Balding (Elise Rothman), Daniel R Escobar (Richard Jean), Sean Sweeney (Emcee), Colleen McDermott (Laura)

> To get closer to baby Wyatt, the Crone steals one sense from each of the Charmed Ones. With hilarious consequences.

A Little Learning is a Dangerous Thing: Centuries ago, a sorcerer created a monkey to steal his enemies' senses. The sorcerer, however, mistreated the monkey, which – in revenge – stole his master's voice, and was turned into a wooden totem as punishment. Piper notes that the whole monkey business about speak no evil, hear no evil, see no evil is seemingly based on this event.

The Conspiracy Starts at the Witching Hour: The Kazi demon king creates his minions out of his own body.

Work is a Four-Letter Word: Jason wants to syndicate Phoebe's column nationally. Phoebe believes that she may be working on Saturdays from now on.

It's a Designer Label!: Highlight: Paige's black, slinky dress.

References: The title comes from Jane Austen's *Sense and Sensibility*. Also, an allusion to james's 'Laid'.

'You May Remember Me ...': Norman Reedus's movies include *8MM*, *Bent* and *Octane*. Jerome Butler appeared in *Seven Days*. Nynno Ahli was in *Brother*. Daniel Escobar's CV includes *Lizzie McGuire* and *Blow*. Sean Sweeney appeared in *Boys Don't Cry* and *Once and Again*. Colleen McDermott played Sandra in *Dementia*.

SEASON 5: SENSE AND SENSE ABILITY

Cigarettes and Alcohol: Paige and her new boyfriend, piano bar owner Nate Parks, share a glass of red wine.

Logic, Let Me Introduce You to This Window: When the Crone throws Leo backwards into the door, he falls forward onto his face. However, when the Crone kidnaps him, Leo is lying on his side and in a different position in relation to the door. Why didn't Phoebe recognise the Crone (given that they had previously met in 'Baby's First Demon')? At the office meeting, Phoebe has her hand at her ear when she asks if anyone hears the buzzing. A cut to a different angle shows her hand on the table. *The Book of Shadows* isn't colour-coded as it was in the previous episode. Piper has a serious car accident and seemingly requires no hospital treatment. And what happens to the car once the sisters get their senses back? Paige speaks at least twice when she is supposed to have lost her voice.

Continuity: Wyatt uses his orbing power for the first time. The sisters had an Aunt Pearl whose old couch they have in their attic. Piper notes that, when he walks, Leo shuffles his feet. Paige doesn't like monkeys, whilst Piper thinks that clowns are scary (see 'San Francisco Dreaming'). Phoebe desperately doesn't want to be one of those annoying cellphone people that mime artists make fun of. At her eighth grade graduation ceremony, Paige was supposed to sing the school song. Eight hundred people were watching, the band began to play, but Paige froze, ran out and missed her own graduation. Paige considered it the worst day of her life; all her friends laughed at her; and her boyfriend, Bobby Maynard, dumped her. All the sisters seem to have a sixth sense that manifests itself when they are deprived of one of the other five; Leo speculates that this is in part what makes the Power of Three so strong. The baby carrier in which Leo carries Wyatt at the street fair is the same one in which he carried the mechanical baby in 'Black As Cole'.

Motors: Piper's Royal Blue Cherokee Jeep (4IZE 631) ends up wrapped around a lamppost.

Quote/Unquote: Phoebe, to Paige: 'Did you ever think that maybe your Kazi buddy here can't read?' Kazi Demon: 'I tried to tell her that.' Paige (writing on her pad): 'Demons lie.' Phoebe: 'Not about literacy.'

Kazi King: 'You dare mock me?' Crone: 'On occasion. But not at the moment.'

Phoebe: 'Paige is proposing violence against the monkey.'

SEASON 5: SENSE AND SENSE ABILITY

Notes: 'I had a vision. A mere taste of the future, of the child, of power like we've never known.' Amusing, if somewhat embarrassingly overdone in places, 'Sense and Sense Ability' has an intriguing central premise. It's not a wholly successful piece (Alyssa Milano somewhat hams-up the acting deaf routine), but it's certainly an improvement on some recent episodes.

Soundtrack: Rose McGowan sings a variation of the traditional lullaby 'Mockingbird' to Wyatt. Subsequently, at the piano bar, she begins to sing Steven Sondheim's 'Send in the Clowns'. However, after two words, the monkey's curse strikes and her voice disappears. At the end of the episode, she sings a very sultry version of 'Fever'.

109: NECROMANCING THE STONE

4 May 2003

Writers: Henry Alonso Myers, Alison Schapker, Monica Breen
Director: Jon Paré

Cast: Eric Dane (Jason Dean), Jennifer Rhodes (Penny Halliwell), Norman Reedus (Nate Harper), Chris Sarandon (Armand), Sam Pancake (Lacky Demon), Lisa Reneé Pitts (Co-Pilot), Scout Taylor-Compton (Fairy), Todd Tucker (Creeper Demon)[65]

> When Grams comes to the Manor for Wyatt's birthing ceremony, the sisters discover that she has brought with her a former lover, Armand. Phoebe contemplates Jason's invitation to go with him to Hong Kong, even though it will take her away from her family. Paige casts a truth spell to ascertain if Nate can accept her being a witch, and gets more than she bargained for.

It's Witchcraft: The truth spell was first used in 'The Truth Is Out There ... And It Hurts'. Paige uses it and discovers that Nate doesn't really have a problem with her witch abilities. But he has a wife and two children. The summoning spell for the creeper demon begins: 'Demons who dwell in slivers of night, uncloak your shadows to witches' sight.' Only a ghost can read the ghost vanquishing spell, as established in 'Saving Private Leo'.

A Little Learning is a Dangerous Thing: Paige recognises Nate's tattoo as the Celtic wheel of being, in which all four elements are balanced and connected to each other.

The Conspiracy Starts at the Witching Hour: Piper notes that the Charmed Ones have destroyed every demon that could harm spirits during Wyatt's Wiccaning, including zombies, rigors and creeper demons. However, Grams mentions Armand, the Necromancer, who attacked during Patty's Wiccaning ceremony.

The Necromancer is actually the ghost of a demon who has dominion over the dead. A former lover of Penny Halliwell's before she banished

---

[65] Uncredited.

him back to the spirit realm, he is searching for magical spirits with enough power to resurrect him.

Work is a Four-Letter Word: Jason has his own private jet. He's been in Hong Kong for some weeks and is about to return there for up to six months to set up an Asian media conglomerate. He wants Phoebe to accompany him. She would like to but, for a variety of reasons, elects to stay in San Francisco for the time being.

It's a Designer Label: Phoebe gets – quite fashionable – advice on which lipstick to use from her baby nephew.

References: The title alludes to Robert Zameckis's 1984 film *Romancing the Stone*. Phoebe mentions *GQ* magazine. There's an oblique reference to *A Few Good Men*. The Necromancer is said to enjoy Clark Gable movies, and his favourite dinner is lamb chops with mint jelly. Also, William Congrave's *The Mourning Bride* (see 'Hell Hath No Fury').

'You May Remember Me ...': Chris Sarandon's CV includes *Felicity*, *ER*, *Dog Day Afternoon*, *The Princess Bride* and *Perfume*. Sam Pancake appeared in *Girls & Boys*, *Friends*, *The Thin Pink Line* and *The West Wing*. Lisa Reneé Pitts was in *Showtime*.

Sex and Drugs and Rock n Roll: The episode begins with Paige and Nate in bed together in clear post-coital glee.

Logic, Let Me Introduce You to This Window: Why didn't Grams know that Piper's baby was a boy? Hasn't she been peeking recently (see 'Happily Ever After')? Piper notes that Grams vanquished the Necromancer 60 years earlier. If Penelope was born in 1937 (see 'Pardon My Past'), she would have been six. That's a bit young to be having an affair with a demon.

Continuity: Leo mentions that Penny has been married four times (see 'Magic Hour'). The future events of 'Mortality Bites' are discussed when Gram notes that Wyatt is not the baby that Piper was destined to have. Grams suggests that there has not been a male born in the Halliwell line for over 300 years.

Quote/Unquote: Paige, after Piper's phone-call interrupts her and Nate's intimate moment: 'Timing bad. What part of that don't you understand?'
   Grams, on Phoebe's and Paige's men: 'They'd be better off with a dog. More loyal and they die sooner.'

SEASON 5: NECROMANCING THE STONE

Piper: 'Paige, there will be no talk of testicle orbing in front of the child.'
Leo: 'And not around his daddy, either.'
Phoebe: 'How do you guys feel about intercontinental orbing?'

Notes: 'I will be resurrected.' A quietly effective comedy episode. It has a strangely all-over-the-place plot (what, exactly, is Armand's plan?; it seems to change about three times) but some nice characterisation. Phoebe not wanting to end up bitter and twisted like her grandmother when it comes to men is a very interesting touch.

Soundtrack: Chantal Kreviazuk's 'Weight Of The World'.

Did You Know?: Wyatt is played by not one child actor but two – twin brothers Jason and Kristopher Simmons.

# 110: OH MY GODDESS! PART 1

11 May 2003[66]

Writers: Krista Vernoff, Curtis Kheel, Daniel Cerone
Director: Jonathan West

Cast: Brian Thompson (Cronus), Sandra Prosper (Sheila Morris), Drew Fuller (Chris Perry), John Cothran Jr (Cecil), Will Kempe (Demetrius), Niki Botelho (Elf Nanny), Michael Gilden (Finnegan), Danny Woodburn (Head Dwarf), Eyal Podell (Roland), Lisa Thornhill (Meta), Lee Arenberg (Mordock), Rebecca Balding (Elise Rothman), Nick Kiriazis (Evan), Damani Roberts (Michael Morris), Trey Alexander (Rick), Scout Taylor-Compton (Fairy), Channing Pourchet (Sara), Frank Cohen (Leprechaun)[67]

> When the Titans kill many of the Elders, Leo is forced to assume their duties. Meanwhile Chris, a mysterious Whitelighter who claims to be from the future, guides the Charmed Ones. Leo gives the sisters ultimate power to vanquish the Titans, by turning Piper, Phoebe and Paige into gods. However, can the girls avoid being seduced by their vast new powers?

Dreaming (As Blondie Once Said) is Free: Paige has been having strange, disturbing fire-and-brimstone dreams about ancient wars and doomsday-type scenarios.

It's Witchcraft: Paige has studied the *I-Ching*, tarot cards, runes and tea leaves, and they're all telling her that something big is going on in the supernatural world. The potions that Phoebe and Paige use in a wholly unsuccessful attempt to vanquish Meta are said to be stronger than those used on the Source.

A Little Learning is a Dangerous Thing: Leo is told that even the Elders cannot change what's meant to be – one of many ominous moments of foreshadowing in this and the next episode.

Chris notes that most statues seen in museums, universities and town centres are not really statues, they're people who have been turned into stone by demons.

---

[66] This episode and the next were originally shown as one in the US.
[67] Uncredited.

SEASON 5: OH MY GODDESS! PART 1

The Conspiracy Starts at the Witching Hour: Three thousand years ago, the Titans – ancient Greek gods – began a reign of terror. The only way the Elders could stop them was by infusing some mortals – including Zeus, Athena and Aphrodite – with the power of gods. Even then, they were still unable to vanquish the Titans, but they did entomb them. Meanwhile, power went to the mortals' heads. They declared themselves gods and forced the world to worship them. The Elders swore that they would never allow such a thing to happen again.

Work is a Four-Letter Word: The *Bay Mirror* sponsors only one charity event each year. This particular one is for the Children's Foundation.

References: There are several allusions to *Buffy the Vampire Slayer* (a homage that *Buffy* repaid, using this episode's title as a line of dialogue for Willow in the episode 'Chosen'). Also, *Hair*; *Mary Poppins*; *Back to the Future*; and *Quantum Leap* ('future boy').

'You May Remember Me ...': John Cothan Jr appeared in *The Cell*, *Spawn*, *Ricochet* and *The West Wing*. Will Kempe played Legs Diamond in both *Mad Dog Coll* and *Hit the Dutchman*. Israeli-born Eyal Podell appeared in *The Chaos Factor*, *Behind Enemy Lines*, *Ally McBeal*, *Angel* and *Deep Blue Sea*. Lisa Thornhill was in *Becoming Marty*, *Veronica Mars* and *Meet Wally Sparks*. Lee Arenberg played Pintel in *Pirates of the Caribbean: The Curse of the Black Pearl* and appeared in *Cradle Will Rock*, *Waterworld*, *CSI* and *Action*. Trey Alexander was Greg Johnson in *Deuces*. Channing Pourchet appeared in *One World*. Nick Kiriazis's movies include *Laurel Canyon*. Damini Roberts was in *The King of Queens*.

Sex and Drugs and Rock n Roll: With Jason still in Hong Kong, Phoebe confesses that she is really missing sex.

Logic, Let Me Introduce You to This Window: Why is Phoebe paying for phonecalls to Hong Kong? Surely a millionaire like Jason should be ringing her? Piper and Phoebe talk about getting air conditioning installed in the Manor, something the house already had in 'Sight Unseen'. 'Happily Ever After' established that dwarves prefer to be called 'little people.'

Continuity: Sheila Morris appears to know about the sisters' secret. (Presumably Darryl told her.) There are several references to indicate that Piper and Leo are still attending Dr Berenson's counselling sessions (see 'Cat House'). The nymphs (see 'Nymphs Just Wanna Have Fun') are back to a full complement of three.

SEASON 5: OH MY GODDESS! PART 1

Future Continuity (Allegedly): Chris says that he is from 20 years into the future, a future only some aspects of which he can discuss with the sisters. He prevents Paige's death, an event that, he says, will shape much of what follows – allowing Titans to rule and create a world that, he indicates, the sisters do not want to see. He also suggests that Piper update *The Book of Shadows* to include more information on goblins. This will come in handy some day, because it's going to get ugly.

Quote/Unquote: Paige: 'I have work to do.' Piper: 'What're you gonna do? Scry for mother nature and have a Wiccan word with her?'

Paige: 'Witch's advocate. There are evil gods running around on the loose that we should eliminate before Wyatt gets home.'

Phoebe tells Piper that Paige is no longer a statue: 'Look who's not stoned.'

Paige: 'What are we?' Chris: 'You're gods.'

Notes: 'I love it when you smite so unexpectedly.' A terrific set-up for the season finale, featuring fine performances (from Drew Fuller, Brian Thompson, Danny Woodburn, Sandra Prosper) and lots of funny lines. With the benefit of hindsight, the introduction of Chris (and his sly manipulation of many events in this, and many subsequent, episodes) was a conceptual masterstroke that moved *Charmed* in yet another new direction. It's got to be said, however, that Michael Gilden's Irish accent hasn't improved since 'Lucky Charmed'.

Soundtrack: 'Extraordinary' by Liz Phair.

111: OH MY GODDESS! PART 2

11 May 2003

Writers: Krista Vernoff, Curtis Kheel, Daniel Cerone
Director: Joel J Feigenbaum

Cast: Brian Thompson (Cronus), Sandra Prosper (Sheila Morris), Drew Fuller (Chris Perry), Will Kempe (Demetrius), Eyal Podell (Roland), Michael Gilden (Finnegan), Rebecca Balding (Elise Rothman), Nick Kiriazis (Evan), Niki Botelho (Elf Nanny), Dina Sherman (Hot Woman), Kelly Cole (Demon)

> Now goddesses, the Charmed Ones try not to be seduced by their powers and remain focused on vanquishing the Titans. Leo, meanwhile, must decide whether to become an Elder or stay with Piper and Wyatt.

The Godlike Ones: Paige becomes the goddess of war (complete with a magical trident), Phoebe is the goddess of love and Piper is the Earth goddess, given dominion over the planet and all its natural elements.

A Little Learning is a Dangerous Thing: An excellent variant on a traditional joke: what does a Whitelighter wear under his robes? Answer: more robes. This is the first time the Elders' domain is described (by Leo) as 'the heavens.'

References: Chris's entire backstory – someone sent back in time to assure the birth of a child who will change the future for the better – is a straight combination of *The Terminator*, *The Outer Limits* episode 'Soldier' and the British SF play *The Flipside of Dominick Hyde*. Also, allusions to *Logan's Run* ('sanctuary'); George and Ira Gershwin's 'Someone to Watch Over Me'; *Xena: Warrior Princess*; the Captain and Tennille's 'Love Will Keep Us Together'; J D Miller's 'I'm a Lover Not a Fighter'; and Pat Benatar's 'Hit Me With Your Best Shot' (see 'Lucky Charmed'). Phoebe's 'Don't give us that creepy pod-people smile,' refers to *Invasion of the Body-Snatchers*. Paige quotes from Archimedes ('Give me one firm spot on which to stand and I will move the Earth') and from Roman historian Tacitus (c. 55-120) ('Reason and judgment are the qualities of a leader.')

'You May Remember Me ...': Dina Sherman was a voice actress on

SEASON 5: OH MY GODDESS! PART 2

Digimon: Digital Monsters. Kelly Cole appeared in *Sucker Shram* and *Raw Nerve*.

Logic, Let Me Introduce You to This Window: Wyatt's hair changes colour between episodes. Phoebe's conversation with Elise at the end of the episode indicates that mortals will retain their memories of the period during which the Charmed Ones were goddesses. Does this also include Evan and the rest of Phoebe's Love Cult? 'The Honeymoon's Over' established that time in the domain of the Elders runs differently from on Earth. Here, however, there's no obvious indication that any significant length of time has passed when everyone returns to San Francisco. After Roland is attacked by Cronus, he stands up and his hood is on his back. The shot switches to Cronus, then back to Roland, whose hood is now on his left shoulder. Paige describes Archimedes (c. 287-212 BC) as 'a great warrior.' He was actually a mathematician. He *did* construct the seige engines the Greeks used against the Romans, but did little or no fighting himself.

Continuity: Elves called the Elders 'Wise Ones.' Among Leo's previously unknown skills are the power to become invisible. After Piper, Phoebe and Paige have confessed how much they take Leo for granted and how helpless they are without his influence and motivation, Leo notes that Phoebe lost herself to the darkest love that existed and came back from it (see 'Long Live the Queen'). In an inspiring speech, he notes that he's always believed the sisters' power comes from their emotions. Leo ultimately decides to remain as an Elder, but he does remove a heartbroken Piper's pain (leaving Phoebe highly suspicious at the episode's end).

Future Continuity (Allegedly): Note that when Phoebe asks if Chris has a girlfriend in the future and comes very close to seducing him, Chris seems as freaked out by this as one would be if the female involved was one's auntie. Also, the very significant moment when he is left alone with Wyatt. Chris looks at his brother, who raises a force-field. 'Don't worry,' says Chris, sinisterly. 'You'll come to trust me in time. They *all* will.'

Quote/Unquote: Cronus: 'Who are you?' Paige: 'The Supremes!'
Piper: 'I need to talk to my husband. I appreciate him becoming a magical folk-hero for the masses, but enough is enough.' And: 'It's not nice to piss off Mother Nature.'
Paige: 'On your knees. Kiss the hand of the Paige.'

That Final Scene, in Full: Leo notes that Chris has been the subject of heated discussion – he cannot return to the future as the timelines have changed. Ultimately the Elders have decided to make him the Charmed Ones' new Whitelighter as a reward for his help in defeating the Titans. However, Leo believes that Chris may have known this was going to happen. As Piper suggested earlier, he wonders if this wasn't part of Chris's plan all along. He adds that he will be watching over Chris closely. As Leo orbs away, Chris waves his hand, and the white light explodes and vanishes. Has Leo been destroyed? Banished? Given a helping hand back up to the heavens? We'd have to wait for the new season to find out. Meanwhile, Chris looks around furtively, then walks into the Manor, closing the door with another wave of the hand.

Notes: 'I'm watching history repeat itself and nobody's willing to do a damn thing about it.' The second half of season five contained some bitter disappointments and, for a while, it looked as though the second half of the season finale was to follow this trend. However, a triumphant final four scenes (the last one, especially) strip away all the silly conceits and stretched out plotting to effectively reformat *Charmed* once again. That this series can continue to keep pulling off bold, audacious strokes like this is one of the best reasons there is to keep watching it.

CHARMED SEASON 6
(2003-2004)

Consulting Producers: Jonathan Levin, David Simkins
Co-Producer: Peter Chomsky
Producers: Holly Marie Combs, Alyssa Milano, Jon Paré
Co-Executive Producers: Curtis Kheel, Daniel Cerone, James L Conway
Executive Producers: Brad Kern, Aaron Spelling, E Duke Vincent
Executive Story Editors: Henry Alonso Myers, Jeannine Renshaw
Story Editor: Julie Hess

Regular Cast:
Holly Marie Combs (Piper Halliwell)
Alyssa Milano (Phoebe Halliwell)
Rose McGowan (Paige Matthews)
Dorian Gregory (Darryl Morris, 112-113, 120, 122-123, 130-131, 133-134)
Brian Krause (Leo Wyatt, 112-127, 129-134)
Drew Fuller (Chris Perry, 112-118, 120-123, 125-134)

112: VALHALLEY OF THE DOLLS PART 1

28 September 2003

Writer: Brad Kern
Director: James L Conway

Cast: Ivana Milicevic (Mist), Melissa George (Freyja), Colleen Porch (Kara), Stephen Snedden (Hangin' Chad), Sandra Prosper (Sheila Morris), Smash Mouth (Themselves), Tracey Aileen Leigh (Leysa), Damion Poitier (Magi Warrior), Nicole Bassanda (Valkyrie Trainer), Teddy Chen Culver (Asian Perp), Arnold Chon (Samarai Warrior), Lee Coleman (Braveheart Warrior), Dan Lemieux (Soldier), Aria Wallace (Crying Little Girl)

> Chris tells the Charmed Ones that his future knowledge suggests a demon is going to come after Wyatt. Phoebe and Paige search for Leo after Paige accidentally causes Piper to get amnesia. The sisters learn that Leo is being held on the mythical Island of Valhalla, home of the Valkyrie. Meanwhile, Phoebe discovers she is now an empath.

It's Witchcraft: Among the demons that Chris reads about in *The Book of Shadows* are the Tracer Demons (see 'Sand Francisco Dreamin''). Trok Demons are two-headed – at least until Piper uses her power on one. To kill the (by now single-headed) creature, Phoebe creates the spell: 'From other worlds far and near, let's get him the Trok out of here.'.
  Paige's memory spell – 'Powers and emotions tide, a witch's heart is where it hides, help her through her agony, bless her with her memory' – succeeds only in giving Piper amnesia.

A Little Learning is a Dangerous Thing: Needing a warrior's soul to get into Valhalla, Phoebe and Paige ask – nicely – if they can borrow Darryl's for a couple of hours. It's perfectly safe, they note; Darryl's body will merely slip into a coma, and as long as they get his soul back in time, he'll be fine.

The Conspiracy Starts at the Witching Hour: Mist is sent by Freyja to express the Valkyries' concern at having to keep an Elder imprisoned. Chris is incredulous: Leo was banished to an island filled with beautiful women and he's *complaining*? Chris apologises, but states that he hasn't

SEASON 6: VALHALLEY OF THE DOLLS PART 1

finished what he came from the future to do. And, he continues, he needs Leo out of the way until these tasks are completed. More importantly, the sisters can't find Leo before Chris is ready. In the best scene of the episode, Chris subsequently shows himself to be perfectly prepared to kill an ally (the Valkyrie Leysa) to further his agenda, even if he does apologise to her as he does so. Then, just as the audience think they have him figured out as an obvious, manipulative villain, he saves a dying police officer's life by radioing in his position to the man's colleagues.

There's actually a *huge* (retrospective) clue as to Chris's identity when it's revealed that he doesn't possess the power to heal. Chris notes, defensively, that Paige can't heal people either. 'That's because I'm only half-Whitelighter,' adds Paige. The obvious *next* question, concerning exactly who Chris's parents are, is *never* asked.

The Valkyrie Island is in the middle of the Indian Ocean. Valkyries are a powerful race of demigoddesses who scout the battlegrounds of the world for dying warriors and then take their souls to Valhalla, where they are preparing an army for the final world battle between Good and Evil.

Work is a Four-Letter Word: Phoebe is the featured guest on Hangin' Chad's radio show. Her column has sky-rocketed in popularity, with all the critics raving about how amazingly insightful her advice is.

A disturbingly cheerful Piper has begun to run a play-group in P^3 during the day. Paige, meanwhile, has signed up with a temp agency and gets a job as a dog-walker. Which is going fantastically badly.

It's a Designer Label!: Both Phoebe and Paige have stunning new haircuts. There are a couple of references to Leo's love of plaid shirts.

References: The title alludes to Mark Robson's infamously awful 1967 movie *Valley of the Dolls*. Also, *A Hard Day's Night*; Toys R Us; and Sally Fields' embarrassing 1980 Oscar acceptance speech ('He liked me. He *really* liked me').

'You May Remember Me ...': Ivana Milicevic's CV includes *Buffy the Vampire Slayer*, *Vanilla Sky* and *Love, Actually*. A former Australian rollerskating champion, Melissa George played Angel Brooks in *Home and Away* and Lauren Rech in *Alias* and appeared in *Mulholland Drive* and *Dark City*. Colleen Porch was in *Carnal Knowledge*. Stephen Snedden played Jimmy Bond in *The Lone Gunmen* and appeared in *Coyote Ugly*. Tracey Aileen Leigh featured in *Law & Order*. Damion Poitier appeared in *World's Finest*. Nicole Bassanda's movies include *D.E.B.S.* Teddy Chen Culver was in *Fresh Like Strawberries*. Arnold Chon appeared in *Guardian*. Lee Coleman's movies include *Advising Michael*. Dan Lemieux was in *Tasteless*.

SEASON 6: VALHALLEY OF THE DOLLS PART 1

Aria Wallace appeared in *That 70s Show*.

Logic, Let Me Introduce You to This Window: Chris seemingly can't heal. Didn't the Elders bother to check this before making him the Charmed Ones' Whitelighter, a position that healing powers would surely be a minimum requirement for? In one of the final scenes, Piper's dialogue doesn't match the movement of her lips. From where did Chris get the two Valkyrie amulets he gave to Phoebe and Paige? Chris's surname should, as we subsequently discover, be Halliwell. Or, at a pinch, Wyatt. So where does the alias Perry come from? Dialogue in this episode suggests approximately one month has gone by since the events of 'Oh My Goddess' Part 2. In the next episode, Leo suggests it's five weeks.

Continuity: It would appear that Darryl and Sheila Morris have a second son, Darryl Jnr, in addition to Michael (see 'Oh My Goddess' Part 1). Piper, rightly as it happens, thinks that Leo did something to her before he left. Leo remembers that Piper's anger almost destroyed a city and her pain almost destroyed Piper herself. He says that he was going to reverse the pain removal spell he cast in 'Oh My Goddess' Part 2 slowly so that Piper could feel a little more each day, but then somebody banished him to Valhalla.

Cruelty to Animals: One of the dogs that Paige is looking after seems determined to hump her leg at every given opportunity (see the next episode for an explanation as to why).

Quote/Unquote: Chris: 'I don't see Piper complaining.' Phoebe: 'No, because Piper doesn't complain about anything anymore. Ever since Leo left to become an Elder, all she does is walk around the house all chipper.'

Phoebe finding Paige scrying on three maps; San Francisco, the world and the solar system: 'Where exactly are you trying to find Leo? Jupiter?'

Chris, when Wyatt puts up a force-field around himself: 'If anyone should be protecting themselves, it's me from you.'

Notes: 'If Piper ever gets her memory back, she's gonna kill you. She hates wearing those costumes as much as we do.' An epic opening to the new season, full of excellent in-jokes and self-deprecating comments. Phoebe's discussion with Hangin' Chad on the problems that many men have with successful women could almost be this series' mission statement. It's nice that both Brian Krause and Dorian Gregory get more meaty roles than normal, and Drew Fuller is an inspired addition to the cast – his exasperation at his new charges' inability to do what they're told is worth the price of admission alone.

SEASON 6: VALHALLEY OF THE DOLLS PART 1

Soundtrack: 'You Are My Number One' by Smash Mouth is the highlight of the KQSF Beach Bash. Also, 'New Favourite Thing' by Balligomingo featuring Lucy Woodward. The score, which is excellent, features one section seemingly inspired by Massive Attack's epic torch-song 'Unfinished Sympathy'.

Did You Know?: Drew Fuller told *SCI-FI Wire*: 'Because the show is established, I've been given this gift of not having to worry about "Is it going to get picked up? Are we going to get an audience?" This show is getting better every year.' Fuller, who had previously appeared in the WB's martial-arts drama *Black Sash*, added, 'I love going into new situations where I can meet new people and form strong bonds.' As for his character, Fuller remained coy. 'I'm very mysterious,' he said. 'They're keeping me shrouded in secrecy the entire time.'

113: VALHALLEY OF THE DOLLS PART 2

28 September 2003

Writer: Brad Kern
Director: James L Conway

Cast: Ivana Milicevic (Mist), Melissa George (Freyja), Colleen Porch (Kara), Evan Marriott (Oscar), Eric Dane (Jason Dean), Damion Poitier (Magi Warrior), Teddy Chen Culver (Asian Perp), Arnold Chon (Samarai Warrior), Lee Coleman (Braveheart Warrior)

> Fuelled by her recently-recovered pain, Piper has remained on the Valkyrie Island. Back in San Francisco, her sisters have further problems when a trio of warriors follow them through the portal.

It's Witchcraft: Paige's spell to free Oscar begins: 'I call upon the Halliwells, I call our powers to undo this spell, make right again that we must, reverse the curse that made this mutt.' Remarkably, it works. Her hastily-written reversal spell to bring Piper back to the fold – 'Spell was cast, now make it pass, remove it now, don't ask me how' – proves less successful. Paige subsequently uses a variant on the spell she cast on Cole to reveal Phoebe's true feelings to him (see 'A Witch's Tail' Part 2).

A Little Learning is a Dangerous Thing: Witches have become Valkyries before.

The Conspiracy Starts at the Witching Hour: The Elders' leading theory, much to Chris's obvious relief, is that a demon stuck Leo in Valhalla. Nevertheless, the other Elders want Leo to stick around until he finds out exactly who was behind this deed, to make sure that no-one is targeting the Charmed Ones or Wyatt again. But Piper has other ideas.

Work is a Four-Letter Word: Paige tells Leo that she is determined, more than ever, to have a life separate from being a witch.

It's a Designer Label!: Paige's purple miniskirt for her date with Oscar.

References: Allusions to *Gladiator*; Attila the Hun; and *Xena: Warrior*

SEASON 6: VALHALLEY OF THE DOLLS PART 2

Princess.

'You May Remember Me ...': Best known as an early contestant on *Joe Millionaire*, Evan Marriott played Mongo in *Motocross Kid* and also appeared in *The Simpsons* and *See Jane Date*.

Sex and Drugs and Rock n Roll: Overwhelmed by Jason's feelings of lust towards her, Phoebe shares a passionate few moments with him behind the desk in his office.

Logic, Let Me Introduce You to This Window: Why does a super-warrioress like Kara lie still when someone is about to stab her? In order to scry, Piper needs both a map and an enchanted crystal – neither of which she seems to have. Holly Marie Combs's stunt double is clearly visible in one scene. Brian Krause mispronounes Freyja as 'Frasier.'

Continuity: Phoebe alludes to Prue's problems with handling the power of empathy in 'Primrose Empath'. An SWA Properties sign can be glimpsed in the alley in which Piper, Freyja, Mist and Kara emerge from the portal (see 'From Fear to Eternity', 'Witch Trial', 'How To Make a Quilt Out of Americans' and 'Be Careful What You Witch For').

Cruelty to Animals: Oscar, the dog whom Paige is looking afte,r is in reality a handsome man who was cursed by an evil witch. He notes that he's been trying to get Paige's attention for two days but, until she accepted there may be a reason why she got this particular job, she wasn't going to be open to helping him.

Quote/Unquote: Piper: 'This isn't Valhalla. You don't have dominion over men here.' Freyja: 'Then how do ... they take orders?' Piper: 'They don't, they do what they want.'

Paige: 'As long as you don't hump my leg anymore we'll be cool.' Oscar: 'Sorry, it's just what dogs do when they like someone.' Paige: 'That's *very* sweet.'

Phoebe, to Piper: 'I know why you'd rather be one of them. It's because you don't wanna feel pain. But you have to, because if you can't feel the pain, then you can't feel the good stuff either.'

Notes: 'This day couldn't get much suckier.' More action-packed than Part 1 (particularly the 'lesbian biker chicks' fight-sequence, which is well done but goes on far too long). There also doesn't really seem to be enough plot for an entire episode here, with a completely needless diversion back to Valhalla for a few scenes before an effective, and emotionally unexpected, wrap-up.

Soundtrack: The score uses an obvious, if amusing, snatch of Richard Wagner's 'Ride of the Valkyries'.

Did You Know?: The WB used the promotional title 'Valkyrie Vixens' for this feature-length episode.

114: FORGET ME ... NOT

5 October 2003

Writer: Henry Alonso Myers
Director: John T Kretchmer

Cast: Scott Klace (Mr Stewick), Melissa Greenspan (Flo), Shaun Robinson (Kinesha), Sarah Aldrich (Natalie), Rick Hall (Man with Baby), Michael Manuel (Weatherman), Rebecca Balding (Elise Rothman), Andrew Reville (Co-Worker), Kirk B R Woller (Cleaner One), Darin Cooper (Cleaner Two), Christian Kelber (Frank), Amanda Sickler (Sophie)

> The Cleaners take Wyatt and erase his existence after he accidentally brings a dragon to life. When Piper, Phoebe and Paige regain their memories, they must relive the day all over again and prevent what has happened from reoccurring. Meanwhile, Phoebe continues to struggle with her new-found empathy, and Leo gives Chris a new assignment.

It's Witchcraft: 'Moments lost make witches wonder, warlocks plot or demons plunder. If this is not a prank, help us to fill in the blanks,' is the spell used to rewind the day. Subsequently, Piper uses the 'seen/unseen' spell (see 'Hell Hath No Fury') to make the Golden Gate Bridge disappear.

A Little Learning is a Dangerous Thing: Dragons pre-date *The Book of Shadows*.

The Conspiracy Starts at the Witching Hour: The Cleaners are white-suited entities who live outside time. They are empowered by both Good and Evil to prevent knowledge of magic from reaching the masses. They have the power to rewrite history.

Work is a Four-Letter Word: Having left a career in dog-walking behind her, Paige has another temporary job, as a telephonist at Ritz, Teukolsky and Ruben. Piper, however, notes that the pay is lousy and Paige's boss, Mr Stewick, is a sexist pig, and wonders why she doesn't quit. Paige says that it's because she wants a life outside magic.

References: The Halliwells' telly has, suddenly, acquired a new station, KLMV. (Are they boycotting KCSF for some reason?) The dragon stages one of its attacks within the Presido Tunnel. Piper makes an allusion to *Godzilla*.

'You May Remember Me ...': Melissa Greenspan played Krystal in *Diamond Man* and Kim in *Providence*. Scott Klace appeared in *When Billie Beat Bobby*, *The District* and *Sliders*. Shaun Robinson is a former Miami WSVN-TV news reporter. His movies include *Bruce Almighty*. Sarah Aldrich was in *General Hospital*. Rick Hall played Artie Popowski in *Stand By Your Man* and also appeared in 3rd *Rock from the Sun*. Michael Manuel was in *Broken*. Andrew Reville's CV includes *Malcolm in the Middle* and *Grounded for Life*. Kirk B R Woller appeared in *Hulk*, *Minority Report*, *Swordfish* and *The X-Files*. Darin Cooper was in *24*, *Angel* and *Roomies*.

Cigarettes and Alcohol: Chris appears to be living in P^3 at present. When we first see him, he's drinking a bottle of Corona ...

Sex and Drugs and Rock n Roll: ... and getting *very* friendly with his new charge, Natalie. (When Leo notes that Chris is supposed to protect her, Natalie adds, helpfully, that he *was* using protection.)

Logic, Let Me Introduce You to This Window: Do they ever change the posters at P^3? That Red Hot Chilli Peppers one has been there since the middle of season three, for instance. When the sisters relive the previous day, in all the scenes in the Manor, it's raining heavily outside, but whenever they go outside, it's suspiciously dry. Having just been, effectively, blackmailed into putting right what once went wrong, why do the Cleaners do Phoebe a further favour by erasing the *Bay Mirror* riot from history. It's got to be said, that must be one tense office to work in, if Phoebe punching Elise can spark a full-scale, bar-room-style brawl. There's also a huge logic flaw in the episode. The reason why the Cleaners were called is that Wyatt created the dragon. This happened because he was watching television on his own. The only reason he was doing *that* is that Piper, Paige and Phoebe are busy trying to work out what the Cleaners did in the past to stop it happening again in the future. In other words, there is no reason why Wyatt would have been left alone watching the TV without the Cleaners having initiated these events. In 'The Power of Three Blondes', Leo says that, as an Elder, he watches over Leo every moment of the day and night. Seemingly, he wasn't watching very closely when Wyatt created the dragon.

Continuity: Wyatt reveals another magical ability: he can change TV channels by blinking his eyes. This is the second occasion that Wyatt is seen to orb – this time to play with his new friend, the dragon. Later, Piper finds a way to get rid of the dragon – she runs in front of it, thus posing a threat to her own life. Wyatt quickly makes it disappear. Phoebe is currently spending much of her time in the basement (having apparently conquered her fear of the Woogyman.) Piper notes that she intends to stay there long enough to be sure she doesn't shove her tongue down the throat of the next delivery guy. Phoebe, hearing this, points out that they are lucky that guy didn't sue her for sexual harassment. The Cleaners drop a very heavy hint about events later in the season, wishing Piper good luck with her son and telling her that she's going to need it.

Quote/Unquote: Phoebe: 'Why are you blaming yourself? It's not your fault.' Piper: 'I haven't actually verbalised guilt yet, so in the future let me confess before you analyse.'

Piper: 'You're asking me to remember what I've apparently forgotten?'

Notes: 'I feel like I'm forgetting something.' A mechanics-of-time episode that, like previous forays into this area ('All Hell Breaks Loose', 'A Paige from the Past', 'Cat House'), confirms that time ultimately looks after itself, even if it sometimes needs a little outside help. The Cleaners are a great idea – although you have to wonder why they've never interfered in the Charmed Ones' lives previously. The slapstick fight at Phoebe's office goes on a bit too long to be as effective as it could have been, and Paige's subplot, concerning a loathsome office stalker, is a bit weak. But this is compensated for by the amusing Leo/Chris scenes.

Did You Know?: *Charmed*'s average audience in the US at the time of the sixth season was around 5.3 million per episode.

115: THE POWER OF THREE BLONDES

12 October 2003

Writer: Daniel Cerone
Director: John Behring

Cast: Jennifer Sky (Mabel Stillman), Melody Perkins (Margo Stillman), Jenny McCarthy (Mitzy Stillman), Eric Dane (Jason Dean), Michael Patrick McGill (Ray), Kip Martin (Jack), Rebecca Balding (Elise Rothman), Robert Alan Beuth (Salesman), Niki Botelho (Elf Nanny), Jernard Burks (Security Guard), Joanna Sanchez (Lupita), Bill Smillie (Husband), Glenn Taranto (Foreman), Todd Tucker (Gremlin), Gwen Van Dam (Wife)

> When three evil sisters magically steal the Halliwells' identities and powers, Piper, Phoebe and Paige must convince Chris that they are the *real* Charmed Ones in order to get their lives back. Meanwhile, Piper realises that Wyatt needs time with Leo, who continues on his quest to find out who put him on Valhalla.

It's Witchcraft: The Stillmans' spell to take the Charmed Ones' powers begins: 'Blinking faces blank and ho-hum, we are they and they are no-one, grant to us the Power of Three, and turn them into nobody.'

The Conspiracy Starts at the Witching Hour: The Stillman sisters – Mabel, Mitzy, Margo – are common witches, known for their small time activities, who merit a mere single paragraph in *The Book of Shadows*. This advises that they're not worth vanquishing and, if they become a nuisance, the Charmed Ones should cast a spell to bind their magic. After their skulduggery is uncovered, Piper, Paige and Phoebe do bind the Stillmans' magic and hand them over to Darryl. There was evidence in the house across the street on which to charge them with murder. If that doesn't stick, they are also, apparently, wanted in eight other states.

Work is a Four-Letter Word: Paige's latest temp job is working on the production line at North Shore Citrus, a fruit packing plant infested by pan-dimensional gremlins.

It's a Designer Label!: The opening scene appears to show Phoebe in

SEASON 6: THE POWER OF THREE BLONDES

fishnet stockings and a leather miniskirt, Paige in an outrageous pink boob-tube and Piper in a black dominatrix bodice. Of course, all is not what it seems. Also, Mabel's red miniskirt and matching boots.

References: Includes allusions to *The Sound of Music* and, visually, to *Charlie's Angels*. Having previously noted the lack of new posters in P^3, check out the new(ish) looking Four Star Mary and Speed of Evolution ones visible here.

'You May Remember Me ...': Jennifer Sky played Amarie in *Xena: Warrior Princess* and appeared in *Shallow Hal*, *CSI* and *Buffy the Vampire Slayer*. Melody Perkins' movies include *Planet of the Apes*. Jenny McCarthy starred in the title role in *Jenny* and was also in *Scream 3*. Michael Patrick McGill's CV includes *Angel* and *Passions*. Kip Martin appeared in *The Deep End*. Robert Alan Beuth was in *Heartbreakers*, *When Harry Met Sally* and *Ghostbusters II*. Jernard Burks appeared in *Random Hearts*, *The Shield* and *Léon*. Joanna Sanchez featured in *Boston Public* and *Conspiracy Theory*. Bill Smillie's CV includes *The Waltons*, *The Philadelphia Experiment* and *Die Hard 2*. Glenn Taranto was in *8 Heads in a Duffel Bag*. Gwen Van Dam appeared in *Take My Daughter, Please*, *Dark Shadows*, *Stir Crazy* and *Mannix*.

Sex and Drugs and Rock n Roll: Phoebe mentions the empathic lust she picked up from Jason last time he was in town (see 'Oh My Goddess' Part 2).

Logic, Let Me Introduce You to This Window: The triquetra does not split into three separate ovals in this episode as it did in 'Power Outage'. Rather, it disappears from the book altogether. How can Phoebe plant a vision in Mitzy's mind when she no longer has her powers? Mabel asks her sisters if they want to remain 'Chiselers' all their lives, suggesting that they're demons. However, as we subsequently discover, they're actually just (bad) witches. And not even particularly powerful ones, either. How do Mabel, Mitzy and Margo get back to the Manor so quickly – and have a lengthy flirtation with Chris – before the Charmed Ones arrive, given that they were all in different locations moments previously (especially as none of them has the power to orb)? The spell to call for a witch's power requires the victims to drink a potion (as seen in 'How to Make a Quilt Out of Americans'). Who put the Stillman sisters in *The Book of Shadows*? Piper, Phoebe and Paige obviously had no knowledge of them and, presumably, neither did Prue. They don't seem old enough to have been a factor when Grams was still alive. What happened to Piper's leg? Apparently she was injured so badly that she could hardly walk. However, after the motel sequence, the injury is never mentioned again.

SEASON 6: THE POWER OF THREE BLONDES

Continuity: Chris tells the sisters that he's known them all his life, which confuses them considerably. Piper has now hired the Elf Nanny to look after Wyatt (see 'Sam I Am', 'Oh My Goddess'). Leo seems fully aware that it was Chris who sent him to Valhalla, but lacks proof.

Quote/Unquote: Phoebe, as both she and Paige come off simultaneous cellphone calls: 'Emergency at work?' Paige: 'Yeah.' Phoebe: 'Unfortunate coincidence?' Paige: 'Not likely.'

Mabel: 'We're standing in the home of the Charmed Ones, we've got their powers, we got their book, and we got blonde multi-tonal hair. Who's the nuisance now?'

Phoebe, as Piper goads Mabel: 'Piper, death bad, life good.' Paige: 'Don't worry, this bimbo couldn't hit the broadside of a beauty parlour. Check out that dye-job.'

Notes: 'Everyone thinks we're these trashy blondes. I do have to hand it to them, though, they've taken identity theft to a whole new level.' Ignoring one, very badly-staged fight sequence, 'The Power of Three Blondes' is a great deal of fun. Particularly impressive is the sequence of Jason and 'Phoebe' at the restaurant. The Stillmans are great – pouty, bitchy and very stupid. It's a shame that they couldn't have been given a shade more power (really there's no way they should have manoeuvred Piper, Phoebe and Paige into the position that they do) and a decent exit, as they could have made potentially fascinating returning characters.

SEASON 6: LOVE'S A WITCH

116: LOVE'S A WITCH

19 October 2003

Writer: Jeannine Renshaw
Director: Stuart Gillard

Cast: Balthazar Getty (Richard Montana), Rachelle LeFevre (Olivia Callaway), James Sutorius (James Callaway), Michael Muhney (Seth), Daniel Hagen (Carl), Marjorie Lovett (Rosaline Montana), Christine Healy (Grandma Callaway), Mako (Asian Alchemist), J Michael Flynn (Benjamin Montana), David Greene (Steve Montana), Carl Anthony Nespoli (Burt Callaway)[68]

> When Paige falls for Richard Montana, the Charmed Ones become involved in a dangerous feud between two magical families – not to mention Richard's deceased lover, who possesses Paige's body. Meanwhile, Leo is suspicious when Chris travels to the Underworld in search of a potion.

It's Witchcraft: *The Book of Shadows* includes details of a potion to banish ghosts who are stuck in limbo. Presumably this is a less deadly version of the 'vanquishing a ghost' spell (see 'The Power of Two', 'Saving Private Leo'). The 'blood-calling-blood' spell (see 'The Witch is Back') is used. One of Phoebe's unsuccessful attempts to obscure Piper's and Paige's emotions begins: 'In the name of the Halliwell line, bind my sisters from this power of mine.'

A Little Learning is a Dangerous Thing: Plasma, according to Piper, occurs only on the spiritual plane.

The Conspiracy Starts at the Witching Hour: Leo follows Chris to an alchemist's, where Chris asks for a potion to hide a secret. When confronted by Leo, Chris claims that he needs the potion to give to Piper and Paige to protect Phoebe from their emotions. Significantly, however, Chris has the alchemist prepare another batch, which he takes himself when no-one is looking.

The Montana and Callaway families have been feuding for generations. The previous year, Olivia Callaway, who was dating Richard Montana,

---

[68] Uncredited.

was killed in the crossfire. Desperate for revenge, Olivia's ghost tried manoeuvring the families into all-out war. When that didn't work, she possessed Paige.

Work is a Four-Letter Word: Among the temp jobs that Carl at the agency offers Paige are mail clerk at Dutton and Houser, greeter at Yarn Mart, pre-school assistant, bagger at Grocery Plus and cashier at Lucy's Landscaping. He begins to ask about computer programming, then changes his mind. When Paige asks for something normal, she is given a job as a home help to Mrs Callaway.

It's a Designer Label!: Major highlight: Paige's extremely short yellow skirt.

References: Allusions to *Sleeping with the Enemy* and to *The Matrix* ('Spare me the Morpheus speech').

'You May Remember Me ...': Balthazar Getty appeared in *Corsairs*, *Lost Highway*, *December* and *Young Guns II*. James Sutorius was in *Space*, *The Practice*, *Kojak* and *St Elsewhere*. Michael Muhney plays Don Lamb in *Veronica Mars*. Rachelle LeFevre's CV includes *See Jane Date* and *The Legend of Sleepy Hollow*. Marjorie Lovett appeared in *Ophelia Learns to Swim*, *Apt Pupil*, *Quantum Leap* and *The Fan*. Christine Healy's CV includes *ER*, *Don't Touch My Daughter*, *Sledge Hammer!*, *Buffy the Vampire Slayer* and *Star Trek: Deep Space Nine*. Mako provided the voice for Akii on *Samuri Jack*. He has also appeared in *The Time Tunnel*, *Kung Fu*, *77 Sunset Strip*, *Rising Sun*, *M*A*S*H*, *Pacific Heights* and *Conan the Destroyer*. Daniel Hagen was in *Roswell* and *CSI*. Carl Anthony Nespoli was a stuntman who worked on *Alias* and *Charlie's Angels*. J Michael Flynn was in *Fall From Grace*. David Greene's movies include *Summerland*.

Behind the Camera: Jeannine Renshaw was initially an actor playing the teacher in *Hook* and appearing in *Home Improvements* before co-creating the series *VR.5*. She also worked on *Angel* and *Tracker*.

Sex and Drugs and Rock n Roll: Piper's first date with fellow divorcee, Seth, is interrupted on account of Whitelighter intrusion.

Logic, Let Me Introduce You to This Window: Phoebe mentions that Piper dated a demon, a warlock and a ghost. The last two refer to 'Something Wicca This Way Comes' and 'Dead Man Dating', but when did Piper ever date a demon? Chris's hair changes during the time it takes him and Piper to orb from the restaurant to the Manor. Paige asks Richard why he doesn't have any scars, completely ignoring the very prominent scar on his eyebrow. If a mere ghost can possess a powerful witch, why has it been so hard for demons and warlocks to do the same? The amount of mud on Chris's clothes changes from scene to scene. Since when do witches have the demonic power to throw energy balls? When Phoebe is meditating, she's sitting on a pillow. Is the pillow itself magic? And, if not, how is it floating? Richard says that one can't magically curse someone who doesn't practice magic. However, there have been many occasions when an innocent has been cursed.

Continuity: Paige doesn't believe in co-incidences. Phoebe has begun meditating in an effort to block out the empathic feelings of her sisters.

Quote/Unquote: Phoebe: 'This empath power is driving me crazy.' Piper: 'You?' Phoebe: '*You* try having PMS for three sisters every month. It's a good thing no-one in this family is having sex, I'd be feeling that too.'

Piper, to Phoebe: 'Let's look at the bright side. We settled a family feud, we set free a tortured soul, maybe your new power and Paige's new solo path away from the Sisterhood, is some kind of synergy, that it's all working together in some kind of divine way.' Phoebe: 'Nah.' Paige: 'Nah.'

Notes: 'This feud's been going back for generations. I don't even think *they* know how it started.' A strange mixture of *Romeo and Juliet* and *The Premature Burial*, featuring a sultry performance from Rose McGowan. The episode, unfortunately, has to pack in so much that many issues are dealt with off screen and, for once, a fast pace actually works against the story. This one might have been better as a two-parter and given room to breathe.

Soundtrack: 'Tears From the Moon' by Conjure One.

SEASON 6: MY THREE WITCHES

117: MY THREE WITCHES

26 October 2003

Writers: Scott Lipsey, Whip Lipsey
Director: Joel J Feigenbaum

Cast: Desmond Askew (Gith), Eric Dane (Jason Dean), Gina Ravera (Mary), Kathryn Fiore (Elizabeth), Annabelle Gurwitch (Nina Halter), Kathryn Joosten (Wife), Sam Vance (Blake), Art Frankel (Old Magician), Lynn Turfeld (Nurse), Susan Allison (Bored Woman), Marty Papazian (Assistant Director), David Backus (Deranged Fan), Ken Weiler (Fan #1), Jessica Friedman (Fan #2), Alex Estornel (Male Model), Catherine Reitman (Excited Fan)

> The Charmed Ones attempt to escape magical realities where their secret desires come true, after Chris – aided by the unwitting demon Gith – try to teach them a lesson. Meanwhile, Leo demands that the Elders strip Chris of his Whitelighter status.

A Little Learning is a Dangerous Thing: Piper's secret desire isfor a normal life without magic and demons (not so secret, that one), and Paige's is being part of a world where everyone knows about her magic and accepts it. Phoebe, due to her empathic abilities, gets stuck in Jason's desire, in which she is a celebrity with her own talk-show and numerous stalker fans.

Leo believes that he has enough evidence that Chris killed Leysa in order to steal her amulet (see 'Valhalla of the Dolls' Part 1) to initiate an Elders' Council. However, he abandons plans to do so at the episode's end, after Chris almost dies saving the Charmed Ones from Gith.

The Conspiracy Starts at the Witching Hour: Demon-created vortices suck their victims into pocket-realms of alternate-realities. Gith creates worlds out of people's desires, but he doesn't control them.

Work is a Four-Letter Word: Phoebe is filling in as a guest host on the afternoon TV show *Chit Chat This & That*. Paige's latest job, meanwhile, is as an assistant to a geriatric magician.

References: The title alludes to the ABC sitcom *My Three Sons* (1960-72). Also, references to *Sex and the City*; *The Twilight Zone*; The Beatles' 'Fixing a

Hole'; Indian politician and spiritual leader Mahatma Gandhi (1869-1948); and Matthew 7 (see 'Nymphs Just Wanna Have Fun').

'You May Remember Me ...': British actor Desmond Askew made his TV debut aged eight in a Cadbury's commercial. He's a veteran of *Grange Hill*, played Simon Baines in *Go* and Brody Davis in *Roswell* and appeared in *Give My Regards to Broad Street* and *Repli-Kate*. Gina Ravera was Sara Gerard in *The Fugitive* and also featured in *Show Girls* and *Illegal in Blue*. Kathryn Fiore is a regular on *Mad TV*. Annabelle Gurwitch appeared in *Ladies Room LA*, *The Cable Guy* and *Red Shoe Diaries*. The great Kathryn Joosten is best known as President Bartlet's late secretary Dolores Landingham in *The West Wing*. Her CV also includes *Code Blue*, *Joan of Arcadia*, *Phoenix*, *Murphy Brown* and *Buffy the Vampire Slayer*. Sam Vance was in *NYPD Blue* and *Cold Case*. Art Frankel's movies include *The Ring*, *Magnolia* and *Critters*. Susan Allison appeared in *Angel's Don't Sleep Here*. Marty Papazian was in *VIP* and *All You Need*. David Backus appeared in *The Shield*. Ken Weiler was in *Surviving Eden* and *Friends*. Jessica Friedman played Stacy in *Undressed*. Catherine Reitman's movies include *Space Jam*, *Dave* and *Twins*.

Sex and Drugs and Rock n Roll: Phoebe interviews Nina Halter, the author of a provocative new book, *The Five-Minute Orgasm*.

Logic, Let Me Introduce You to This Window: When the sisters were pulled into their fantasy worlds, what was going on in the real world? Chris states that he will know Gith in the future. How, if Gith is killed at the end of this episode? Why does it take Paige so long to cast the vanishing spell – especially given that she's cast it on several occasions previously ('Siren Song', 'Womb Raider')? The warehouse in which Paige saves the girl is patently obviously the redressed Manor basement set. Why does Gith stand there like a big drip when the car is about to explode? Stains from the blood used on Jason are clearly visible on Alyssa Milano's hand *before* Jason is shot. Shouldn't Paige using real magic in her job as a magician's assistant count as doing so for personal gain? Phoebe can sense Piper's distress when they're both in separate fantasy pocket realms, despite the fact that in the previous episode Piper and Paige took a potion specifically so that Phoebe wouldn't be able to pick up their emotions empathically.

Phoebe's bodyguard, Blake, has to be the most incompetent in the history of bodyguarding. He spots someone with a gun and, instead of trying to tackle the potential assassin, he shouts 'Gun!' Thanks, man, that really helped. How, exactly, does Paige's power enable her to split herself in half?

SEASON 6: MY THREE WITCHES

Continuity: Phoebe tells Jason that she doesn't like surprises (although his announcement of his desire to fly Phoebe in a helicopter to Carmel for dinner wins some cautious approval from her). Another of his wooing stunts was a private concert by the San Francisco Philharmonic. When Chris goes to initiate contact with Gith, he gives Wyatt a vicious look and says that it's the baby's fault he has to do this.

Quote/Unquote: Phoebe: 'Are you offering me the world, Jason Dean?' Jason: 'All except Kazakhstan. I don't have stations there.'
Piper: 'So you guys do this a lot?' Mary: 'Stare at half-naked men under a socially-accepted pretence?' Elizabeth: 'Every chance we get.' Mary: 'Our lives used to be very *Sex and the City*. Then we got married, had kids and now it's celibacy in the suburbs.'

Notes: 'Do you know how much energy is contained in an unfulfilled desire? People spend their whole lives wanting something, usually never getting it.' A very interesting, if logically flawed, story about desire, 'My Three Witches' benefits from a terrific, eye-bulging performance from Desmond Askew. It's also got a lot of funny little detours down avenues of characterisation and character motivation. (Paige, especially, has got a quasi-Messianic complex brewing, whilst Piper is, clearly, a frustrated housewife in rather desperate need of some quality man-action.) There's also more complexity in Chris's backstory, with him, on this occasion, quite clearly aiding the Charmed Ones, even when he is ostensibly working against them. It does kind of reduce your faith in Leo somewhat that he hasn't by this stage put together three or four very big clues as to Chris's identity.

Soundtrack: 'Maybe Tomorrow' by Stereophonics.

Did You Know?: In one of the hospital scenes, note that a Dr Kern is paged to 'Demonology.'

SEASON 6: SOUL SURVIVOR

118: SOUL SURVIVOR

2 November 2003

Writer: Curtis Kheel
Director: Mel Damski

Cast: Balthazar Getty (Richard Montana), Keith Szarabajka (Zahn), Johnny Sneed (Larry Henderson), Googy Gress (Spencer Ricks), Alla Korot (Mrs Henderson), Rob Farrior (Ryan), Brian Wedlake (Brett), Steadman (Themselves), Craig Gellis (Gray), Simon Brooke (Grimlock), Jean St James (Female Lawyer), Justine A Moore (Female Demon), John Bisom (Confederate Soldier), Gwendolyn Osborne (Demon Bidder #1), Patrick Stinson (Demon Bidder #2), Chris Gann (Navy Stunts)[69]

> Paige is forced to make a bargain with a demon to recover the soul of her boss; Piper learns that Wyatt has been sabotaging her dates; Phoebe gets a writing partner; and Chris and Leo travel back in time.

It's Witchcraft: 'We call upon the ancient powers, to summon one to save a soul,' is the spell used to call Zahn. Richard suggests that Piper and Phoebe use the 'call a lost sister' spell to find Paige's Underworld location.

A Little Learning is a Dangerous Thing: Chris attempts to use a time portal and return to the future to see whether the timelines have now changed *vis-à-vis* Wyatt. A mistrusting Leo follows and the pair get stuck, first in the Cretaceous period and then during the American Civil War.

The Conspiracy Starts at the Witching Hour: Zahn was formerly a low-level demon until he began trading souls for powers. His auctions, which attract soul collectors, eaters and traders, have made him vastly powerful.

Work is a Four-Letter Word: Having seen the loathsome Spencer Ricks hired to work with her at the *Bay Mirror*, Phoebe repeats what she did in 'House Call' and turns him into a turkey. Then she turns him into a pig.

Paige's latest job – which she's actually very good at – is as a PA to lawyer Larry Henderson, who, unfortunately for her and, indeed, him, sold his soul to the demon Zahn five years earlier.

---

[69] Uncredited.

SEASON 6: SOUL SURVIVOR

References: The title alludes to Paul Stanley's classic 1969 TV movie *Sole Survivor*. Also, *Back to the Future*; *Jurassic Park*; *The Godfather* ('I'm gonna make him an offer he can't refuse'); John Hancock (1737-93); and Faust (see 'The Wedding from Hell').

'You May Remember Me ...': Keith Szarabajka played Charles Gracen in *Profit*, Daniel Holtz in *Angel* and Mickey Kostmayer in *The Equalizer*. His CV also includes *We Were Soldiers*, *Spy Game*, *Golden Years*, *Unnatural Pursuits*, *Walker*, *Missing*, *Roswell*, *Law & Order* and *Babylon 5*. Johnny Sneed was in *Pale Blue Moon*, *Bar Flies* and *The Guardian*. Rob Farrior appeared in *Callback* and *Space: Above and Beyond*. Brian Wedlake featured in *Fake Stacy* and *Cold Case*. Craig Gellis's movies include *Reno 911!* Simon Brooke appeared in *CSI*, *Mementos* and *Firefly*. Justine A Moore was in *Las Vegas*. John Bisom was one of the voice artists on *Shrek*. Gwendolyn Osborne played Jade Dominquez in *Ocean Avenue*. Alla Korot was Erin in *The District* and also appeared in *The Arsonist*. Patrick Stinson's movies include *Catch That Kid* and *The Perfect Storm*. Jean St James was in *Eight Days a Week*, *Ice*, *Cocktail* and *Friends*. Chris Gann appeared in *Swatters* and *xXx*.

Cigarettes and Alcohol: After their bonding trip through time, Chris and Leo share a couple of cold beers at P^3.

Logic, Let Me Introduce You to This Window: Paige says that Faustian bargains have been around for more than 100 years but aren't mentioned in *The Book of Shadows*. Since the character first appeared in Christopher Marlowe's *The Tragical History of Dr Faustus*, published c.1600, such deals with evil are considerably older than a mere century. The clock moves from 11:58 to 12:00 in far less than 61 seconds! Given that Leo's Elder duties were said to require him to be away for much of the time, he seems to be on Earth (and near the Charmed Ones) with great regularity. Makes one wonder why Piper created such a fuss in the first place. When Paige is reading *The Book of Shadows*, she flips past the entry for Vampires and stops at the Monkey Totem page. The camera then switches to Piper and Phoebe. When it returns to Paige, the book is open to the entry for Kurzon (see 'The Three Faces of Phoebe'). The whole point of Paige's plan was to destroy the contracts *before* vanquishing Zahn, otherwise, those who signed the contracts would burn in Hell for eternity. Many of the contracts clearly *aren't* destroyed when Zahn is vanquished. How is Phoebe able to push an energy ball back at the demon that threw it at her? That's a good trick she could have certainly done with on many occasions over the previous five years. Does nobody go into Phoebe's office whilst she's not there? If they do, why do they think she's got a pig in there?

SEASON 6: SOUL SURVIVOR

The Big Question: A vastly important concept in the *Charmed* universe is that of free will. All of the souls sold to Zahn were those of people who made their own choice to complete the deal (and there's no suggestion at any stage that Zahn tricked people into signing away their soul – it was a simple financial arrangement). The concept of free will has been something that even the Elders, the Source and the Angel of Destiny (see 'Witch Way Now?') couldn't interfere with. So how do the Charmed Ones conspire to interfere with it here so massively without anyone doing anything to stop them?

Continuity: Wyatt does something supernaturally spooky with his eyes in front of each of Piper's dates – Ryan and Brett – to scare them off. This is discovered only when Richard spots him and tells Piper. Piper alludes to the time Wyatt conjured a dragon ('Forget Me ... Not'). Since the events of 'Love's a Witch', the surviving members of Richard's family have moved East.

Quote/Unquote: Phoebe: 'I have half a mind to call Jason and complain about it, but I don't want to use our relationship for leverage.' Piper: 'What's the use of sleeping with your boss then?' Phoebe: 'Because I actually enjoy sleeping with my boss.' Piper: 'Yeah, don't brag.'

Notes: 'I know a good soul when I see one.' A rather fine, well-paced episode concerning some big issues (actions and consequences) but kept nicely grounded by a terrific performance from Keith Szarabajka. The Chris/Leo subplot had the potential to be awful but, actually (thanks to subtle characterisation) works well. The only real drawbacks are some really tacky special effects.

Soundtrack: Steadman's 'The Bitter End' opens the show, and the band perform 'No Big Deal' later at P³.

Did You Know?: The location of the dinosaur's lair where Leo and Chris are trapped is Vasquez Rocks in Santa Clarita. A perennial favourite of Western series like *Bonanza*, the site may be familiar to many readers from its use in the *Star Trek* episode 'Arena', and also in *Bill and Ted's Bogus Journey* and *Roswell*.

119: SWORD AND THE CITY

9 November 2003

Writer: David Simkins
Director: Derek Johansen

Cast: Balthazar Getty (Richard Montana), Mark Aiken (Dark Knight), Danny Woodburn (Head Dwarf), Brian Leckner (Head Executioner), Edward Atterton (Mordaunt), Danielle Bisutti (The Lady of the Lake), Simon Brooke (Grimlock), Bjorn Johnson (Cranky Satyr), Lamont Johnson (Soul Blaster Demon), Matthew McGrory (Ogre), Amanda Sickler (Sophie), Scout Taylor-Compton (Fairy)

> The Charmed Ones help the Lady of the Lake to protect Excalibur. Numerous magical creatures arrive at the Manor, each intending to pull the sword from the stone and achieve overwhelming power.

It's Witchcraft: Piper says that the Charmed Ones have a vanquishing potion ready and waiting if the Dark Knight turns up again. Mordaunt asks what's in it. When told it's a mandrake variation with a little bit of griffin's blood, Mordaunt says this is good ... if the sisters are intending going up against a pusteous knave, which they're not. The spell includes ingredients like Wearboar tusk, a lock of Nymph hair (Phoebe hopes it isn't from someone they know – see 'Nymphs Just Wanna Have Fun'), wraith essence and black poppy. Richard notes that the last two should never be mixed, and the sisters realise that they have been duped.

A Little Learning is a Dangerous Thing: The Dark Knight is described as 'a power-mad paladin of destruction.' Executioner Demons are said to be low-level bad-asses for hire.

The Conspiracy Starts at the Witching Hour: When Piper removes Excalibur from the stone, Mordaunt appears and tells her that she is: '... the new saviour. The champion of good.' However, according to the Elders, Piper was meant to pass the weapon on only to whoever it was really meant for. Which would seem to be Wyatt. Mordaunt subsequently absorbs the powers of the four creatures that Piper recruits as members of her Round Table – a Grimlock, a Creeper, a Banshee and the soul-releasing demon.

SEASON 6: SWORD AND THE CITY

Work is a Four-Letter Word: Paige's new job is as Phoebe's assistant (or desk manager, her own preferred title). By the end of the day, she has initiated a system that tracks Phoebe's column ideas, columns written and columns considered, plus a separate file for questions, comments and fan-mail. Then, gleefully, she quits before she can be fired.

References: The title alludes to the series *Sex and the City*. Also, *The Sword in the Stone*, *Excalibur* and various other Hollywood variations on the Arthurian legends; Grumpy from *Snow White and the Seven Dwarves*; *Elvis: That's The Way It Is* (see 'The Devil's Music'); and, obliquely, *Monty Python and the Holy Grail*.

'You May Remember Me ...': Edward Atterton appeared in *Carolina*, *Sharpe's Honour*, *Medics* and *Alias*. Mark Aiken's CV includes *The Hello Girls*, *Soldier Soldier*, *Waking the Dead*, *Mersey Beat*, *Jonathan Creek* and *Black Books*. Brian Leckner was in *Joyride*, *Fire Down Below* and *Quantum Leap*. Danielle Bisutti appeared in *Seeing Iris* and *The OC*. Bjorn Johnson's movies include *Birth of a Vampire*. Lamont Johnson appeared in *American Virgin* and *Jerry Maguire*. The official record holder for having the world's biggest feet (size 29 ½), Matthew McGrory was also in *Big Fish*.

Sex and Drugs and Rock n Roll: Paige and Richard spent the night together prior to this episode.

Logic, Let Me Introduce You to This Window: Why has Paige suddenly started addressing people as 'my dear'? Would the sisters really leave Wyatt home alone? And, even if they did, would they cover him up with a blanket over his face? Richard seems remarkably powerful for a common witch – he can throw energy balls *and* he's telekinetic. That's nearly as much power as the Charmed Ones have *put together*. Given that Arthur Pendragon was probably based on a real person (most likely a Romano-British – or possibly Welsh – tribal leader from the Fifth Century) the sword used for Excalibur here is anachronistic by about six or seven hundred years. (It seems to have come directly from John Boorman's *Excalibur* rather than any other version of the legend.) In Sir Thomas Malory's *Morte D'Arthur* (1470) Excalibur was *not* the sword in the stone. That nameless sword, to test the worthiness of the young Arthur, was discarded after he removed it from the stone. Excalibur was given to him later and ended up in Avalon after his death. It's only relatively recent versions of the Arthurian myths (starting with Tennyson's *The Lady of Shallott* and T H White's *The Once and Future King*) that have confused the two. It's stated that Merlin never existed, contradicting the Wizard's observation in 'We're Off to See the Wizard' that Merlin was a hack.

SEASON 6: SWORD AND THE CITY

From whence did Piper acquire the black leather outfit? She was wearing jeans and a T-shirt when she left the Manor. Doesn't a potion to vanquish an upper-level demon require a piece of its flesh – as with Cole and the Source? If so, then how does Piper vanquish the Dark Knight? The Charmed Ones have defeated the Source three times ('Charmed and Dangerous', 'Long Live the Queen', 'Womb Raider'), not twice as stated here. Piper and Paige vanquished the king of the Creepers in 'Necromancing the Stone', an action that was said would destroy all of them. So where did Mordaunt and Piper find one? A muse can be seen trying to pull the sword from the stone. How can everyone see her? According to 'Muse to My Ears', muses can be seen only by angelic creatures such as Whitelighters or those who are wearing the ring of inspriration.

Continuity: Wyatt, like his aunts Prue and Paige, has the power of telekinesis. He uses the power to lift the sword and send it across the room to score his debut demon-kill. This is the second occasion on which we see Paige using her telekinetic power without calling for an object – she orbs Excalibur to the attic simply by waving her hand. Contrary to what he told Paige in 'Love's a Witch', Richard *does* still – occasionally – use magic; at least, for little things like fixing the garbage disposal unit. Phoebe is highly suspicious of this.

Quote/Unquote: Piper, when Phoebe informs her that she had a date with Jason even though he's still in Hong Kong: 'Is Chris orbing you?' Phoebe: 'No, we're video conferencing. We just open our laptops and there we are. In colour.' Piper: '... In each other's laps.'

Phoebe, on Paige being her assistant: 'I can't tell you what to do. I mean, how weird is that?' Paige: 'Well, it's no weirder than usual.'

Leo: 'Only the ultimate power on Earth can handle Excalibur. That's why the Lady stayed in the lake, to insulate herself from the power of the sword.' Paige: 'Okay, so we should find Piper and then drown her?'

Notes: 'Bet you didn't expect this when you got up this morning?' Taking all the best bits from a variety of Arthurian legends, 'Sword and the City' is – like many a good *Charmed* episode – almost fatally flawed by the 'Hey ma! Look at me!' nature of wearing such source material so blatantly on its sleeve. Conversely, because *Charmed* absolutely refuses to take such sacred cows seriously, therein lies the show's chief source of entertainment.

Soundtrack: 'I'm Ready' by Cherie.

120: LITTLE MONSTERS

16 November 2003

Writer: Julie Hess
Director: James L Conway

Cast: Eric Dane (Jason Dean), Seth Peterson (Derek), Caleb Pinkett (Virgil), Alec Ledd (Tristan), Armando Pucci (Wine Captain), Brady Smith (SWAT Commander)

> After vanquishing a female Manticore demon, Piper, Phoebe and Paige become foster parents to its orphaned, reptilian-tongued infant. Chris urges the sisters to vanquish the child, but they believe that if they raise the baby with love, they can change its destiny. Phoebe surprises Jason when she reveals her true feelings; and Paige gives Darryl a super-power.

It's Witchcraft: Paige's spell to give Darryl super-strength begins: 'Blessed with powers from my destiny, I bless this hero with invincibility.'

A Little Learning is a Dangerous Thing: Piper says that she doesn't see herself having more children anytime soon. Oh, really? (See 'The Courtship of Wyatt's Father'.)

The Conspiracy Starts at the Witching Hour: Manticores (previously mentioned in 'Bite Me') are vicious, reptilian, fleshing-eating demons with supernatural strength and venomous claws. They communicate with high-pitched cries and tend to travel in packs. They mate with humans to create hybrids, so that they can blend into society. They kill their mates after conception. There is no known potion to vanquish a Manticore.

Leo notes that not everyone is born morally neutral. This is specifically true of demon infants. Some are simply genetically predisposed toward evil.

Work is a Four-Letter Word: Leo apparently communes with the other Elders whilst on top of the Golden Gate Bridge.

References: The episode is a basic variant on the *Beauty and the Beast* story.

'You May Remember Me ...': Seth Peterson appeared in *Providence*. Caleb

Pinkett's movies include *In Your Eyes*. Alan Ledd was in *Can't Hardly Wait*. Armando Pucci appeared in *Ancient Warriors* and *The West Wing*. Brady Smith was in *Getting Rachel Back*.

Cigarettes and Alcohol: The waiter interrupts Phoebe's and Jason's canoodling (with tongues) to offer them a bottle of '95 *Brunelo di Montacino*. Jason has recently purchased an Italian vineyard that once belonged to his grandfather.

Logic, Let Me Introduce You to This Window: Wouldn't officers working with Darryl find it surprising that he's now impervious to bullets and has suddenly developed super-strength? The glass door to the building where the hostages are being held is obviously closed, but when Tristan shoots at Darryl, who's outside, the glass remains intact. In the previous episode, Leo told Piper that he had taken Chris off the Halliwells' account. Now, he's back without further explanation. Why doesn't Piper escape from Derek's house when she has the chance to? Why, exactly, does Paige's spell not only make Darryl invincible but also require him to do a really bad Eddie Murphy impression? Derek said that the only way he could become human again was if he died. This clearly isn't true.

Quote/Unquote: Phoebe: 'Was that Jason?' Paige: 'No, that was my *raison d'être*.' Phoebe: '*Pardon!*'
　Phoebe: 'I've heard of guys running when they hear the L word. But, running all the way to Italy? That's gotta be some kind of new record.'
　Phoebe: 'Since when did you become an expert on hostage situations?' Paige: 'About an hour ago.'
　Piper: 'Come on, show a little spine. What kind of demon are you?'

Notes: 'There's a demon in the play-pen.' The age-old environment-versus-biology debate occupies much of this episode. It's somewhat mawkish and sentimentally played, but eventually resolves itself in a reasonably satisfying way. Unusually, the episode's comedy subplot (Paige giving Darryl invincibility), which had a lot of potential on paper, seems leaden-footed and disappointing after a promising first scene.

Soundtrack: Shanti's 'The Beauty'.

121: CHRIS-CROSSED

23 November 2003

Writer: Cameron Litvack
Director: Joel J Feigenbaum

Cast: Marisol Nichols (Bianca), Balthazar Getty (Richard Montana), Rebecca McFarland (Lynn), Rebecca Balding (Elise Rothman), Lisa Kushell (Tour Guide), Wes Ramsey (Adult Wyatt), Jason Shaw (Greg), Ashlyn Sanchez (Little Bianca)

> Bianca, a witch from the future, arrives to steal Chris's powers. Meanwhile, Paige decides to move in with Richard, whilst Phoebe again ponders joining Jason in Hong Kong.

It's Witchcraft: The spell that Chris and Bianca used to send Chris back in time begins: 'I call upon the ancient power, to help us in this darkest hour, let the book return to this place, claim refuge in its rightful space.'

The Conspiracy Starts at the Witching Hour: *The Book of Shadows* contains a page concerning a tattooed fire-throwing demon called Jodzoman. The Phoenix (previously mentioned in 'Bite Me') are a family of assassin witches who are very elite and powerful and who were born with a distinct birthmark symbolising their rise from Salem's ashes.

Work is a Four-Letter Word: Elise tells Phoebe that there's a whole generation of women who followed the dream and built successful careers, but at the expense of everything else. Some of them are very happy, but some (including Elise herself) woke up one day and realised that all they had was their career. So seemingly in the *Charmed* universe, successful career women are also bitter, lonely, 'Eleanor Rigby'-style spinsters who would give up all their achievements if only a dashing young man would come along and sweep them off their feet. This week's statement in lipstick feminism, ladies and gentlemen, was brought to you by a man: Cameron Litvack. Thank you, and goodnight …

It's a Designer Label!: Bianca's figure-hugging leather outfit.

References: Allusions include FatBoy Slim's 'Praise You'; *Julius Caesar*; and the Audubon society. Observe the prominent Ziggy Marley poster in P^3.

SEASON 6: CHRIS-CROSSED

'You May Remember Me ...': Jason Shaw appeared in *Liars Club* and *LA Knights*. Marisol Nichols was is *Resurrection Blvd*, *Bowfinger*, *Cold Case* and *Can't Hardly Wait*. Wesley Ramsey appeared in *Latter Days*. Lisa Kushell's movies include *Legally Blonde*, *Mission Hill* and *The X-Files*. Rebecca McFarland appeared in *Elvis Took a Bullet*.

Behind the Camera: Cameron Litvack also worked on *Smallville*.

Sex and Drugs and Rock n Roll: Phoebe makes a saucy S&M allusion concerning Paige being 'tied up' with Richard. Piper is currently seeing Greg, a fireman. They've been going out for three weeks and have reached the hand-holding stage. Until a spell intervenes.

Logic, Let Me Introduce You to This Window: Seemingly, 20 years into the future, there will be airborne surveillance probes. And miniskirts. How did Leo discover that Bianca cast a lowering-inhibition spell? And how was he able to find an antidote to it so quickly? Presumably, Piper made up some explanation to Greg as to why she had to leave in the middle of their naked romp on the fire truck. (The implication of the scene whilst he's frozen is that she simply intends to get dressed and go.) The clothes that Chris wears when he leaves the future are different from those that he had on when he arrived in 'Oh My Goddess' Part 1. He also had shorter hair and was wearing sunglasses in the earlier episode. Piper wonders how the sisters travelled last time if it's such a difficult process (see 'Mortality Bites'). Leo says that the Elders made that happen. However, on the contrary, the Elders told Leo to turn *The Book of Shadows* to the time-travel page, the spell on which the girls then used. Phoebe can speak a little Mandarin (which, she notes, she learned from Berlitz's pocket travel guides). Unfortunately, this won't be much use to her in Hong Kong, where the main language is Cantonese.

Future-Continuity: Chris reveals that he's part-Whitelighter, part-witch. Amongst the things he won't reveal to the sisters are that Wyatt will turn evil in the future (with his own cadre of demons) and that the Charmed Ones will, themselves, be vanquished after destroying over 1000 demons. The Manor will be turned into the Halliwell Memorial Museum, where a hologram containing a clip from 'Charmed Again' Part 1 is used to scare the customers. Chris will fall in love with assassin witch Bianca and she will help him to return to the past to save the Charmed Ones.

Continuity: Phoebe says that she can never sense what Chris is feeling (see 'Love's a Witch').

SEASON 6: CHRIS-CROSSED

Quote/Unquote: Leo: 'Paige, when I said I needed you, I meant a fully-clothed you.'

Lynn: 'Can't I help?' Bianca: 'Yeah. Someday when I ask you what it feels like to kill, don't lie to me. Don't tell me you don't feel a thing.'

Chris, to the baby Wyatt: 'If I can't save you, I swear to God I'll stop you.'

Notes: 'There's nothing left in the future.' One of the most beautifully-structured and unusual *Charmed* episodes, 'Chris-Crossed' is another of the series' regular mini-pilots, establishing a whole bushel of new lore and a backstory for the way in which events will unfold in the immediate future. It's a beautiful love story, with elements of betrayal (future-Bianca's conversation with her mother) and the fate-versus-free will debate (Chris telling Bianca that there's nothing left for him in the future once Wyatt has indoctrinated her back to the dark side). There's also a cunning critique on commercialism – note that, in the Halliwell Memorial Museum, many of the sisters' classic potions are available for purchase in the gift shop on the way out. Even the heavy-handed attempt to marry *Charmed*'s shaky feminist credentials with some positive comment (see **Work is a Four-Letter Word**), despite coming over as little more than tokenism, has an element of accuracy to it. One of the best *Charmed* episodes, with Drew Fuller at his finest and a really powerful and nasty look at what lies in store for Wyatt.

122: WITCHSTOCK

11 January 2004

Writer: Daniel Cerone
Director: James A Contner

Cast: Jennifer Rhodes (Penny Halliwell), Kara Zediker (Young Penny Halliwell), Jake Busey (Nigel), Patrick Cassidy (Allen Halliwell), Kam Heskin (Robyn), Peter Pergelides (Guard), Michael Storer (Sawmill Worker), Gabe Vanderwalker (Stoner), Tim Elwell (Officer), Jill Small (Celene)

> Paige finds herself transported back in time to 1967. There she meets a younger Grams, who is on a crusade to rid the world of evil through the power of love. Never trust a hippie.

It's Witchcraft: For a time in the 1960s, Penny used to cast spells on items of her clothing so that, if she ever lost then, they would return to her. (Here, the items in question are a pair of stylish, red leather kinky-boots that Paige wears.) The spell that Piper uses to convince the policeman of Phoebe's charms begins: 'Come to me and be seduced, I have a girl to introduce, fall for her, you can't resist her, trust me mister, she's my sister.' Penny casts a spell to vanquish Nigel. This begins: 'Snuff this warlock, his days are done, but make him good for the ecosystem.'

It's a Designer Label: Phoebe's outstanding crimson kimono ... before it gets covered in demon goo, of course.

References: The title refers to 'Woodstock', the legendary rock and free love gathering of the '60s. There's a specific dialogue allusion to Timothy Leary's *The Psychedelic Experience* ('Turn on, tune in, drop out'). Also, *Macbeth*; folk-singer Joan Baez; *Hair*; *Alice Doesn't Live Here Anymore*; and a possible oblique reference to Richard Alpert's *Be Here Now*. There are visual allusions to, amongst otheres, *Crouching Tiger, Hidden Dragon*; *Tremors*; *The Doors*; and *Zabriskie Point*. Allen's and Penny's 'Rainbow Bus' clearly takes its inspiration from Tom Wolfe's book *The Electric Kool-Aid Acid Test* concerning the 1966 cross-America tour by Ken Kesey's Merry Pranksters in their dayglo-painted Magic Bus.

'You May Remember Me ...': Kara Zediker's CV includes *24*, *Enterprise*

SEASON 6: WITCHSTOCK

and *Rock Star*. Kam Heskin appeared in *This Girl's Life*, *Catch Me if You Can* and *Angel*. Patrick Cassidy was in *Hitler's Daughter* and *Smallville*. Jake Busey played Dennis in *Shasta McNasty* and also appeared in *Identity*, *Tomcats* and *Starship Troopers*. Peter Pergelides was in *JAG*. Gabe Vanderwalker was previously a second unit director on *Pranksters*. Tim Elwell's movies include *Born Bad*. Jill Small played Dorothy in *DysEnchanted*.

Sex and Drugs and Rock n Roll: Penny notes that they do not allow acid to be dropped in the Manor.

Logic, Let Me Introduce You to This Window: Most of the clothes in the 1967 sequences are anachronistic – far fewer flares than there should be, for instance – as is Penny's clear allusion to John Lennon's 'Give Peace a Chance' (which wasn't even *written* until 1969). It has been previously well established by the Halliwell family tree (see 'Pardon My Past' and others) that the sisters' grandfather was named Jack Halliwell and that he died in 1964. Here, Allen is described as Penny's 'first and only' husband and, very definitely, as the sisters' grandfather. Given that her first *granddaughter* was born a mere three years after the events of this episode, Penny looks *awfully* young in the 1967 sequences – remember, according to references elsewhere in the series, she should be approximately 40 at that time. (A popular fan rumour is that the episode was originally written with the intention of having *Patty* rather than Penny involved but Finola Hughes was unavailable, leading to the substitution and all manner of continuity errors into the bargain.) If the sisters' powers don't work in the past (as established in 'That 70s Episode'), how can Piper cast a spell on the guard? Piper said that Grams taught her never to try to negotiate with warlocks. When exactly did Grams tell Piper that? Piper wasn't even a witch when Grams died (see 'Something Wicca This Way Comes'). Origami is a Japanese artform, not Chinese. Phoebe says Paige was born in the Year of the Ox, which would have been 1973. As previously established, Paige was born in 1977, a Year of the Snake. 'The summer of love', in the *Charmed* universe, seems to have begun in *January* 1967.

Continuity: The events of this episode take place 'a few weeks' after those of the previous episode. Both Phoebe and Paige have now moved out of the Manor. Phoebe is living in Hong Kong with Jason, studying numerology, the Chinese zodiac and origami and quoting lots of really obscure Chinese proverbs. Paige, meanwhile, has moved in with Richard, but the couple do not practice magic around the house, and because of this she's missed the last five vanquishings that Chris has set up. In the Manor, Phoebe's room had been turned into a gym, whilst Paige's is being used as

SEASON 6: WITCHSTOCK

Wyatt's nursery and playroom. Paige arrives on 13 January 1967 (the day before the Golden Gate Park 'Human Be-In'). Penny notes that Allen was a sweet man who lead her 'straight down the hippie-dippy trail.' He was killed by Robyn, and this event, Penny notes, ended her peacenik days fast. Darryl's father, Luther Morris, was a bad-ass mother constantly stickin' it to the Man and with a seriously huge Afro. Right on, brother. The Halliwell 8-Track machine (see 'That 70s Episode') is glimpsed (brilliantly described by a nonplussed Paige as a 'big-fat-tape-thingy'). Allen Halliwell had a sister, Janice, whom he notes looks exactly like Paige.

Future-Continuity: Chris suggests that, in the future, everyone tried to control the demon with no name, but it couldn't be done. Grams argues that this is hardly a winning attitude, and asks why the people of the future couldn't find a name for the slime demon.

Quote/Unquote: Paige: 'I'm not on drugs. Just having a bad trip.'
Grams: 'You have Paige stuck in the past and a demonic blob roaming the Manor. Exactly how are you "handling things"?' Piper: 'We're still in an adjustment period.'
Phoebe: 'I don't wanna be raised by that flower-child-loose-in-the-park. We'd never make it to puberty.'

Notes: 'The '60s was, like, the worst fashion era.' Not so much far out as, like, *really untogether*, 'Witchstock' features some hilarious conceits. It plays these for all they're worth and provides plenty of laughs in all the right places. Whether or not it's a historically accurate summation of a very important part of recent US history is another question altogether, but taken purely as entertainment, it works on most levels. There's actually a really clever – and very postmodern – piece of social comment at the episode's core, which notes that for all the marvellous intentions of the late-'60s peace movement, it was pretty much still-born, because, in real life, pacifists always get trampled to death by bullies. That's where 'make-love-not-war' scenarios as part of any drama format *always* have problems (as *South Park* has been keen to point out – 'What a load of tree-hugging hippie *crap!*'). Even Gandhi knew that, ultimately, you sometimes have to fight for what you believe in. Check out, for instance, the wholly obvious 'the kids getting hassled by the pigs' sequence in Golden Gate Park. Mind you, Allen's outrageously bad Jim Morrison-style poetry is reason enough for the raid in and of itself. More power to the voices of the establishment, I say – use your night-sticks, officers, and not unharshly either. Elsewhere, depicting the 1967 Leo as a spaced-out, blond, astrology-quoting lurv machine with some of the worst chat-up lines in recorded history (in best Haight-Ashbury tradition) is a *really* nice touch of characterisation. As, indeed, is Dorian Gregory's *wonderful* cameo as Darryl's Shaft-like dad. George Harrison, incidentally, visited real-life San Francisco roughly during the period in which this episode is set, and described it as 'full of horrible spotty drop-out kids on drugs.' It might've been nicer if it had been inhabited by groovy witches and Whitelighters chanting 'Hell no, we won't go' and turning guns into flowers. Sadly, in its own way, this episode conforms to all the reactionary, conservative and contemptible prejudices that then-California governor Ronald Reagan advocated in relation to youth culture. Having said that, Luther's Afro keeps the viewer *just* the right side of taking it all too seriously.

Soundtrack: A cheesy instrumental version of Smokey Robinson's 'Get Ready' is playing whilst Leo is performing his light-show. Jennifer Rhodes sings a brief snatch of the traditional protest anthem 'We Shall Not Be Moved'. J Peter Robinson's score is very '60s influenced, including a section apparently based on Procol Harum's 'A Whiter Shade of Pale'.

123: PRINCE CHARMED

18 January 2004

Writer: Henry Alonso Myers
Director: David Jackson

Cast: Eduardo Verástegui (David), Sandra Prosper (Sheila Morris), Bruce Payne (Order Leader), Joseph Hodge (Acolyte #1), Luke Massy (Acolyte #2), Joe Cappelletti (Acolyte #3), Jason-Shane Scott (Dream Guy), Ryan Culver (Dream Guy #2)

> After Piper vanquishes a demon, she has an epiphany concerning Wyatt's future. Unable to deal with Piper's revelation, Paige and Phoebe decide to remind Piper of the importance of love by conjuring her a perfect date as a birthday present. Chris, meanwhile, convinces the sisters to bind Wyatt's powers – but demonic cult members kidnap the baby.

Dreaming (As Blondie Once Said) is Free: Piper is still having variants on those erotic dreams (see 'Sand Francisco Dreamin'').

It's Witchcraft: The spell that Phoebe and Paige cast to produce Piper's special birthday gift begins: 'A perfect man we summon now, another way we don't know how, to make our sister see the light, somewhere out there is Mr Right.'

A Little Learning is a Dangerous Thing: Phoebe notes that Jason is currently in Zimbabwe. 'Or somewhere.' (He actually appears to be in New York when he speaks to Phoebe on the phone later in the episode.)

The Conspiracy Starts at the Witching Hour: A demonic cult, the Order, were the most powerful force in evil until their leader was vanquished. They now believe that he's been reincarnated as Wyatt.

It's a Designer Label!: Phoebe's green miniskirt and furry suede booties.

References: The title comes from *Cinderella*. There's an allusion to *The Dating Game*.

'You May Remember Me ...': Eduardo Verástegui appeared in *CSI: Miami*.

SEASON 6: PRINCE CHARMED

Jason-Shane Scott was in *One Life to Live*. Bruce Payne's movies include *Newton's Law* and *Britannic*. Joseph Hodge appeared in *24*. Luke Massy was in *Charlie's Angel: Full Throttle*. Joe Cappelletti featured in *Slings & Arrows*. Ryan Culver appeared in *Spin City*.

Logic, Let Me Introduce You to This Window: Why, when thinking that Wyatt is being attacked, does Leo run up the Manor's stairs instead of orbing? During the food fight, Piper freezes the birthday cake and then throws it at Paige, who promptly redirects it toward Phoebe. When the action cuts back to Piper, she has something orange and squishy in her hands. It's also worth noting that the Charmed Ones had a very similar fight in 'Power Outage' and lost their powers as a consequence. When the sisters battle the Order, Alyssa Milano's stunt double is clearly identifiable in several shots.

Continuity: Chris reveals to the disbelieving sisters (and Leo) that, in his future, Wyatt will turn to the dark side, although he flatly refuses to give any further details. Wyatt's first word – 'Mama' – alerts Piper to the Order member in his room. Piper once owned a charm-bracelet given to her by her mother. Prue subsequently lost it, and Phoebe has been unable to find it, despite using the 'lost and found' spell. Leo, however, has had more luck, and returns the bracelet to Piper as a birthday gift. Piper is said to like long walks on the beach, shopping at the Embarcadero, lunching at Zuni's, and having deep-tissue massages. Chris has begun to arrange his conferences with Leo on top of the Golden Gate Bridge (see 'Little Monsters').

Quote/Unquote: Piper, on Wyatt's would-be kidnapper: 'It's no big deal, I blew him up, he's gone.' Paige: 'Every time you say that, they come back with a vengeance.'

Phoebe, when Piper suggests that she intends to devote her life to protecting and raising Wyatt: 'What about sex?' Piper: 'I'm the mother of one of the most magical creatures ever. Sex rather pales in comparison.'

Notes: 'She doesn't need a party, she needs an intervention.' An episode in which the highlight is a food fight. No, really, it's true. There's very little good to say about 'Prince Charmed', frankly. It's top-heavy with crude characterisation, unfunny conceits (some lines of dialogue aside) and a very unsatisfying subplot concerning Chris's 'need-to-know' policy towards his charges.

Soundtrack: 'Rinse' by Vanessa Carlton. David sings 'If You're Happy and You Know It' to Wyatt. There are some lovely flourishes of Spanish guitar that decorate the score.

124: USED KARMA

25 January 2004

Writer: Jeannine Renshaw
Director: John T Kretchmer

Cast: Balthazar Getty (Richard Montana), James Black (Swarm King), Eric Dane (Jason Dean), David Greene (Steve Montana), Tom Schanley (Swarm General #1), Derek Anthony (Swarm General #2), Jean-Christophe Febbrari (French Army Sgt), Lisa Canning (Reporter #1), Joe Torrenueva (Reporter #2), Rock Reiser (Reporter #3)

> Jason breaks up with Phoebe when he learns of the sisters' magical abilities. Richard attempts to free himself of his family's bad karma. Piper and Paige try to vanquish a group of Swarm Demons.

It's Witchcraft: Richard amends an aura-cleansing spell that he finds in *The Book of Shadows* in an attempt to cleanse his karma: 'I call to thee, pure witch's fire, through vortex flow the heavenly mire, cleanse brackish karma of debris, from dark to light sweep history.'

A Little Learning is a Dangerous Thing: Paige tells Richard that there's an aura cleanse and a chakra cleanse but no karma cleanse.

The Conspiracy Starts at the Witching Hour: Swarm Demons are distant relatives of Kazis (see 'Sense and Sense Ability') and Vampires (see 'Bite Me'), which means they come from a hive. A witch must kill the king to vanquish the hive.

It's a Designer Label!: Highlight: Phoebe's (very) little red number.

References: Allusions to *Les Miserables*; *To Die For*; James Bond; Napoleon Bonaparte (1822-91); Queen Marie Antoinette (1755-93); Queen Isabella (1292-1358); and 'the She-wolf of France' (an almost certain reference to Guy Endore's *The Werewolf of Paris*). Mata Hari (Gertrude Zelle, 1876-1917) was a Dutch-born exotic dancer in Paris who was a double-agent for Germany during World War I. She was convicted by the French and executed by firing squad.

'You May Remember Me ...': James Black's movies include *Unshackled* and *Soldier*. Tom Schanley was in *Conspiracy Theory* and *Dynasty*. Derek Anthony appeared in *Angel*. Jean-Christophe Febbrari featured in *Dream of the Lizard*. Lisa Canning is best known as the former presenter of *Entertainment Tonight*. Joe Torrenueva appeared in *Dillinger and Capone*. Rock Reiser's CV includes *Never Been Kissed*.

Cigarettes and Alcohol: When Phoebe curses Jason's merger, all the champagne bottles in the room explode, whilst the food turns into snails, frogs and pigeons.

Logic, Let Me Introduce You to This Window: Those champagne bottles discharge a disproportionate amount of liquid. When Paige and Piper receive injuries from the demon fireballs, both have their blouses ripped. However, in the final sequence, both are wearing the same clothes, and they're apparently undamaged. Phoebe says '*mi amore*' (Spanish rather than French) at one point. Jason says he and Phoebe have been in a relationship for 15 months. However, Jason first met Phoebe shortly after Wyatt's birth (see 'Baby's First Demon'). In 'The Legend of Sleepy Halliwell', Piper says that Wyatt isn't yet a year old.

Continuity: Jason and Phoebe have recently been in Rome and are scheduled to fly to Paris shortly. Jason is about to initiate the second biggest French media merger of the decade. Having discovered Phoebe's secret, Jason mentions some previous unusual occurrences that Phoebe refused to explain – 'the Godiva girls' (see 'Nymphs Just Wanna Have Fun') and her 'cousin' Shamus ('Lucky Charmed'). Paige believes that Phoebe has a big problem with avoiding conflict. In an effort to make sure that Wyatt doesn't end up as the ultimate evil (see 'Prince Charmed'), Piper is trying to bathe Wyatt in goodness and nurture peace and serenity by playing him Mozart CDs and giving him a powder blue blanket to keep him calm. Richard's brother Steve (see 'Love's a Witch') is a lawyer.

Quote/Unquote: Paige: 'Famous female spies … Mata Hari.' Piper: 'Wasn't she one of the Bond girls?'
   Piper, on Phoebe's public display of magic: 'We fix Phoebe first, and then we take care of the Swarm King. And, if we're still alive after that, we'll worry about it then.'
   Jason: 'Please, I'm begging you.' Phoebe: 'Don't *beg*. I stared my killer right in the eye. So much more dignified a way to die.'

Notes: 'Karma is the DNA of the universe. It's what balances everything out. You start screwing with that, you could mess up the entire cosmic order of things.' In his final appearance, Eric Dane gives a smashing little performance in a story about the difficulties of maintaining a relationship without complete trust on both sides. Almost half the episode is taken up with a very uninvolving subplot about the Swarm Demons, but it's the soap opera-like trials and tribulations of Phoebe and Paige that provide the most interest.

Soundtrack: Sarah McLachlan's 'Fallen'.

125: THE LEGEND OF SLEEPY HALLIWELL

8 February 2004

Writer: Cameron Litvack
Director: Jon Paré

Cast: Dean Shelton (Zachery), Christopher Neiman (Sigmund), Betsy Randle (Mrs Winterbourne), Elena Finney (Enola), Sarah Rafferty (Carol), Ziggy Marley (Himself), Gildart Jackson (Gideon), J Anthony Woods (Herman), Adam Hendershott (Slick), Mitchah Williams (Quentin), Cate Cohen (Teacher's Aid), Maximillian Orion Kesmodel (Younger Boy)

> The sisters help Leo's mentor, Gideon, when he wants to discover who cast a spell of darkness over the magic school that he runs and conjured the headless horseman who has been beheading all the teachers. Meanwhile, Phoebe goes on a vision quest.

Dreaming (As Blondie Once Said) is Free: Following a spirit-guide (a wolf), Phoebe enters into a shamanistic vision quest and finds herself being given insight into a future in which Piper will have two sons; she herself will be pregnant; Paige will have become a magic school teacher; and there appear to be no demons.

It's Witchcraft: The spell used to vanquish the headless horseman and restore Piper, Phoebe and Paige to their bodies begins: 'Power of Three unite to end this grisly fright, reverse the roles and make us whole.'

References: The title, and the character of the headless horseman, come from Washington Irving's classic folk tale *The Legend of Sleepy Hollow*. One of the opening stock footage shots of San Francisco is of Lombard Street, reputed to be the twistiest street in the world. There's a poster for Sonic Jesus visible in P³. Also, allusions to Chinese philosopher Confucius (551-479 BC); Obi Wan Kenobi; *The Usual Suspects*; David Bowie's *Hunky Dory*; and the Osmonds' 'One Bad Apple'. There are visual allusions to *Harry Potter and the Philosopher's Stone*;, *Yellow Submarine*;, *The Doors*; and *The Devil Rides Out*; and conceptual ones to the *Buffy the Vampire Slayer* episode 'Intervention'.

SEASON 6: THE LEGEND OF SLEEPY HALLIWELL

'You May Remember Me ...': Dean Shelton appeared in *ER*. Christopher Neiman's CV includes appearances in *The Shield*, *The West Wing* and *Ally McBeal*. Betsy Randle was in *Boy Meets World* and *Home Improvement*. Sarah Rafferty played Casey Matthews in *Tremors*. Gildart Jackson played Jack Palmer in *Providence*. J Anthony Woods' movies include *Little Black Boot*. Adam Hendershott appeared in *CSI*. Mitchah Williams was in *Lizzie McGuire*. Cate Cohen featured in *Firefly*. Maximillian Orion Kesmodel played Young David in *Six Feet Under*.

Logic, Let Me Introduce You to This Window: Why has Piper, at the beginning of the episode, suddenly stopped trusting Chris again? There was no hint of that previously. When Leo places Piper's decapitated head on the table, her hair changes position between shots. Phoebe's vision would seem to take place several years into the future. Yet she still has exactly the same haircut as in this episode. And she's wearing the same clothes. In 'Charmed Again', it was established that Penny and Patty hid Paige from the Elders. Here, Gideon suggests that he saw Paige when she was young. After Paige and Gideon fail to stop the horseman in the alleyway, they seemingly walk back to the Manor rather than orb. How did Zachary have the time to freeze an entire room, collect Piper's head, get back to the School and astrally project himself back to the Manor, all without anyone realising that he was gone?

Continuity: From a clue in her vision, Phoebe (correctly) guesses that Chris is actually Leo's and Piper's yet-to-be-born second son. Gideon is an Elder, and Leo's old mentor. They first met when Leo became a Whitelighter, and Gideon took Leo under his wing. Gideon fought for Leo and Piper to get married. He has also met the sisters when they were much younger (although none of them remembers him) and knows their grandmother well.

Quote/Unquote: Piper: 'Okay, neurotic people, can we get back to my neurosis right now, please?'
Piper, when Leo sees Sigmund's head on the living room table: 'Just so you know, *this* is what's keeping your son from developing social skills.
Gideon: 'It all started innocently enough, actually. Pranks, really. Setting rats loose from the Pied Piper, turning the North dawn into a gingerbread house. Kids.' Leo: 'And then ...' Gideon: 'Someone cast a spell that brought forth the darkness. And days became nights, nights became terror, and the headless horseman has roamed the campus ever since, targeting teachers.'
Phoebe: 'Are you Wyatt's little brother?' Chris: 'Only if I can get Piper and Leo back together in time.'

SEASON 6: THE LEGEND OF SLEEPY HALLIWELL

Notes: 'All you people with legs, follow me.' A really important episode – this is another one of those reformatting scripts that take the show in a new direction. The big revelation is, of course, Chris's true identity (although anyone who'd been putting the clues together would have had a vague idea half-a-dozen episodes before now). There's also a significant new character in Gideon (a great performance by Gildart Jackson).

Soundtrack: Third Eye Blind's 'Danger', and 'Fall Into You' by Soulstice. Ziggy Marley performs 'Rainbow in the Sky' at P³.

126: I DREAM OF PHOEBE

15 February 2004

Writer: Curtis Kheel
Director: John T Kretchmer

Cast: Saba Homayoon (Jinny), Balthazar Getty (Richard Montana), Mark Deklin (Bosk), Joey Naber (Head Thief), Jason Shaw (Greg), Amanda Sickler (Sophie) J Michael Flynn (Benjamin Montana), David Greene (Steve Montana), Marco Kahn (Thief #1)

> When Phoebe frees Jinny the genie from a bottle, she discovers that she must take Jinny's place. Meanwhile, anxious to get Leo and Piper back together so that he can be conceived, Chris uses Phoebe to make his wish come true. But she takes his instructions rather too literally.

It's Witchcraft: An ancient artefact called the Eye of Akhbar is said to protect against witches' magic.

A Little Learning is a Dangerous Thing: When Phoebe asks why Chris split his parents up, Chris replies that Leo had to become an Elder to make room for Chris himself as the Charmed Ones' Whitelighter. It was the only way he could protect Wyatt from turning evil.

The Conspiracy Starts at the Witching Hour: Jinny's last master was Bosk, a low-level demon – cruel, even for a demon. She says that her bottle has been passed around from demon to demon for centuries. The truth subsequently emerges that Jinny is, herself, a demon: an ancient sorcerer condemned her into the bottle for not marrying him. Whoever tries to free her – in this case, Phoebe – has to switch places with her.

References: The title (and much of the imagery), together with an allusion to the character of Major Nelson (as played by Larry Hagman), comes from the 1960s sitcom *I Dream of Jeannie*. Also, David Crosby's 'Everybody's Been Burned'; the Cliff Notes series; and several references to *The History of Ali Baba and the 40 Thieves*.

'You May Remember Me ...': Saba Homayoon appeared in *Without a Trace*. Mark Deklin was in *Frasier*. Joey Naber's movies include *Three Kings*.

SEASON 6: I DREAM OF PHOEBE

Marco Khan appeared in *Crossfire*.

Sex and Drugs and Rock n Roll: When Phoebe arrives at work and asks Sophie if she's had any calls, the reply is: 'Take your pick. We've got adulterers, cross-dressers, 34-year-old virgins …' Piper is still dating Greg the Fireman (see 'Chris-Crossed'), though that relationship bites the dust during the course of this episode, thanks to Chris.

Logic, Let Me Introduce You to This Window: How did Leo heal Piper if she was already dead? The Charmed Ones technically died the second that genie-Richard granted Jinny's wish. Seemingly Elders have greater power than Whitelighters. If that's the case, then why is Chris (half-Elder/half-witch) *less* powerful than Wyatt (half-Whitelighter/half-witch)? In 'Be Careful What You Witch For', it was established that a genie cannot grant a wish to kill someone, yet here, Richard does exactly that. When Phoebe and Chris are in Phoebe's office talking, her scarf moves position several times between shots.

Continuity: Paige discovers Chris's true identity in this episode. Chris can, it seems, put Phoebe's calls to him on mute. Chris suggests that, when he was growing up, he got lots of letters from his father, who was seldom around.

Quote/Unquote: Chris: 'Oracles, fortune tellers, soothsayers. They all say the same thing. If Mum and Dad don't screw this month, *I'm* screwed.'
Phoebe: 'You're unbelievable. Most kids who're the cause of their parents' divorce actually feel guilty. You're sitting here like it's part of your masterplan.'
Phoebe: 'I feel so bad.' Chris: 'As well you should. If we don't do something soon, I'll end up half-fireman instead of half-Whitelighter.'
Jinny: 'When I form my empire, the first thing I'm gonna do is rid the world of witches.' Paige: 'When you're back in your bottle, the first thing *I'm* gonna do is put you in the *microwave*.'

Notes: 'No wishes. I know all about Genies.' An oddly moving tale of fate and redemption, which, despite its overly comic conceits (Phoebe, in full Barbara Eden get-up asking Piper 'Why do I always get stuck with the wig?'), actually has some quite serious things to say. Paige's and Richard's break-up is handled with considerable integrity, and Chris's agenda becomes more focused than previously. Bits of the plot stretch credulity, and the special effects (flying carpets, a magical city rising from the desert sands *et al*) aren't special in the least, but this is still another fine episode.

SEASON 6: THE COURTSHIP OF WYATT'S FATHER

127: THE COURTSHIP OF WYATT'S FATHER

22 February 2004

Writer: Brad Kern
Director: Joel J Feigenbaum

Cast: Gildart Jackson (Gideon), Edoardo Ballerini (Damien), Lou Beatty Jr (Darklighter #1), Bruno Gioiello (Darklighter #2), Derrick McMillon (Darklighter #3), Jon Erik (Darklighter #4), Linda Tran (Sara), Ellis E Williams (Bus Driver), Wayne Mitchell (Frank), Jenny Pulos (Mom #1), Sian Heder (Mom #2)

> Gideon makes a deal with the Darklighters to get rid of Leo, but they accidentally send Leo and Piper to the ghostly plane, leaving Phoebe and Paige to believe that they are both dead. Meanwhile, Chris begins to disappear, and reveals that he must be conceived before the night is over or he will vanish forever.

It's Witchcraft: Phoebe and Paige cast a spell to see Piper: 'Sister's spirit, I call to thee, cross on over so we may see.'

A Little Learning is a Dangerous Thing: The ghostly plane (also known as the spirit realm) is a kind of way-station between reality and the afterlife. Wondering how to access the spirit realm, the sisters ask Gideon. He produces an ancient volume that contains 'Everything you wanted to know about portals but were afraid to ask.' ('Handy,' notes Paige, with little obvious irony.)

The Conspiracy Starts at the Witching Hour: The final scene reveals that it was Gideon who made the deal with the Darklighters to kill Leo. Gideon notes that a mistake was made in allowing Wyatt to be born. But now, with Leo gone and the Charmed Ones unsuspecting, Gideon says that he is one step closer to being able to correct that mistake. For good.

References: Gideon's 'The ties that bind' alludes to the work of John Fawcett (1740-1817). Clarence, the Angel of Death who comes for Chris, is a probable nod in the direction of *It's a Wonderful Life*. Also, Jerry Springer; and Oprah Winfrey.

SEASON 6: THE COURTSHIP OF WYATT'S FATHER

'You May Remember Me ...': Edoardo Ballerini's CV includes *Romeo Must Die*, *The Last Days of Disco* and *24*. Lou Beatty Jr was in *The Kid*. Sian Heder played Ellie in *Dorian Blues*. Bruno Gioiello appeared in *Jumbo Girl* and *The West Wing*. Derrick McMillon was in *Buffy the Vampire Slayer*. John Erik featured in *JAG*. Jenny Pulos's movies include *Hairshirt*. Wayne Mitchell appeared in *Angel*. Linda Tran's CV includes *Scrubs*. Ellis Williams was in *Ali* and *The Hughleys*.

Cigarettes and Alcohol: In an effort to get Leo and Piper back together, Phoebe and Paige, using the cover of Wyatt's party, have prepared various aphrodisiacs. These include champagne, chocolate-covered strawberries and oysters. Unfortunately, as Leo notes, Elders aren't allowed to drink.

Sex and Drugs and Rock n Roll: It would appear that Chris was actually conceived in an alley. Paige notes that she can't believe how hard it is to get two people laid.

Logic, Let Me Introduce You to This Window: The Charmed Ones have all died on several previous occassions, so why did they never end up in the spirit realm? This particular limbo seems very different from the place seen in 'Enter the Demon'. Why is Piper suddenly not allowed to the domain of the Elders? She's gone there previously to collect Wyatt. When Phoebe and Paige are in the hospital, the same blonde woman in a wheelchair approaches them twice. Leo claims that Elders aren't allowed to drink. Wasn't that a beer he had in P^3 in 'Soul Survivor'? (Perhaps it was a non-alcoholic one.) This episode, in which Wyatt's first birthday is celebrated, confirms that Jason was wrong when he said in 'Used Karma' that he and Phoebe had dated for 15 months. During the sequence at the magic school, in one shot Sarah has nothing in her hands, but in the next she is holding a number of books.

Continuity: Wyatt's first birthday is celebrated. (Piper thinks he behaved impeccably at his party – she had to freeze the room only once.) Piper finally learns Chris's true identity and discovers that she is pregnant. Paige, according to Piper, has been weird since she recently changed her hair colour. (Let's be fair, she was pretty weird before that.) The house directly opposite the Manor had a weather vane featuring a cat motif.

Quote/Unquote: Leo, to Piper: 'Look at everything we've overcome. This is just one more thing. This isn't where it ends. I promise.'
Phoebe: 'What, now you're a pessimist?' Paige: 'A girl's allowed to vacillate. It's not like this is an exact science.'
Leo: 'What are you doing here?' Chris: 'Ceasing to exist, I think.'

SEASON 6: THE COURTSHIP OF WYATT'S FATHER

Notes: 'If I'm not conceived by midnight tonight, that's it. I won't be born.' A stunning episode about causality and destiny, 'The Courtship of Wyatt's Father' moves along the future-imperfect concepts of Chris's existence in leaps and bounds, culminating in his delighted 'Yes!' when he discovers that he has (or, rather, his aunts have) succeeded in making sure he will be born.

Soundtrack: 'Strict Machine' by Goldfrapp.

128: HYDE SCHOOL REUNION

14 March 2004

Writer: David Simkins
Director: Jonathan West

Cast: James Read (Victor Bennett), Jeffrey Pierce (Todd Marks), Lesli Margherita (Ramona Shaw), Rodney Rowland (Rick Gittridge), Claire Rankin (Paula Marks), Mary-Pat Green (Ms Hickock), Sheila Levell (Stacy), David May (French Waiter), Lou Richards (Lawyer), Kevin Burke (Male Sheriff), Jeanie Hackett (Female Lawyer), David Hugghins (Armoured Car Driver), Chris Gann (Sheriff)[70]

> Phoebe casts a spell on herself that allows her wild teenage personality to emerge. Meanwhile, Piper asks her father to find out why Chris is avoiding her.

It's Witchcraft: Something written in Phoebe's school yearbook ('Those who mock who I am, let them always remember when') seemingly has a magical effect on Phoebe when she reads it aloud.

A Little Learning is a Dangerous Thing: In the Baker High yearbook, there is a page dedicated to 'a panorama of our favourite pariahs and pantheons.' Next to Phoebe's photo is the legend 'Most likely to serve ... time!' At school, Phoebe was in a bad boy gang with Todd Marks (her 'first lust'), the psychotic Rick Gittridge and dumpy fat girl Ramona Shaw. Ramona remembers a night when Phoebe snuck her into the country club in the trunk of her car and then left her so Phoebe could make out with Todd on the golf course. Todd, now a personal injury lawyer, suggests that Phoebe once broke into the principal's office just to make out with some guy on the desk. (Phoebe recalls that it was, actually, Todd himself who did that, and Phoebe just tagged along out of curiosity.)

The Conspiracy Starts at the Witching Hour: Scaber Demons are Underworld assassins who, as Paige graphically notes, vomit 'icky stuff' that kills their targets.

It's a Designer Label!: Phoebe's unavoidably hot leather look.

---

[70] Uncredited.

SEASON 6: HYDE SCHOOL REUNION

References: The title combines Robert Louis Stevenson's *The Strange Case of Dr Jekyll and Mr Hyde* and the contemporary reality TV show *High School Reunion*. Paige refers to the film version of Stephen King's *Carrie* (Brian De Palma, 1976) and to its sequel, *The Rage: Carrie 2*. Also, *Freaky Friday*; and the 'Get Out of Jail Free' card in Monopoly (see 'The Power of Two').

'You May Remember Me ...': Jeffrey Pierce played Brent Masse in *Astronauts*. Lesli Margherita appeared in *The District*. Rodney Rowland's CV includes *Space: Above and Beyond*, *Angel* and *The Sixth Day*. Claire Rankin was in *Emily of New Moon*. Mary-Pat Green played Odessa in *Any Day Now*. Sheila Levell's movies include *The Last Run*. Lou Richards appeared in *Hulk* and *The X-Files*. Jeanie Hackett was in *The West Wing*. David Hugghins was in *Last Lives*.

Cigarettes and Alcohol: Victor and Chris share a couple of Cuban cigars, though the latter suggests that the former may consider giving them up. (There's an implication that he may develop lung cancer in the future.)

Sex and Drugs and Rock n Roll: Paula Marks refers to Phoebe as 'Freebie', her less-than-flattering school nickname previously revealed in 'Love Hurts'.

Logic, Let Me Introduce You to This Window: Phoebe is a celebrity, as most of her ex-classmates obviously know. However, her old gym teacher (Ms Hickock) seemingly doesn't read the *Bay Mirror*, as she's surprised that Phoebe isn't in jail. What happened to the 'protect the innocent, not punish the guilty' idea (see 'Mortality Bites')? Rick is undoubtedly a total scumbag, but that's still not a death sentence, surely? It's very convenient that the Scaber Demons come after Chris only at the exact time when Phoebe and Paige want them to. Chris was, after all, in a public restaurant for some time with Victor when they could have easily attacked. Chris stated in 'Oh My Goddess' Part 1 that he came back in time to change the future by saving Paige, which he was happy to discuss with her. Yet here, he suggests that telling Piper when she is going to die will, in some way, irrevocably change the future. Well, he's done *that* already. Not only that but it's been well established in *Charmed* that, when it's your time, it's your time (see 'Death Takes a Halliwell', 'A Witch in Time'), and that no amount of forewarning can change that. In the scenes where Phoebe is driving the car, Alyssa Milano's stunt double can be clearly seen.

Continuity: Four months have passed since the events of the previous episode. Chris has been avoiding Piper for the last few weeks, and we subsequently learn that this is because, in Chris's time, Piper died when he was 14 and he was mostly raised by Victor. There's an allusion to Phoebe's shoplifting past (see 'Pre-Witched').

Cruelty to Animals: Phoebe describes Todd's wife, Paula, as a bitch. And that's what she turns into. Literally.

Quote/Unquote: Piper: 'Give me the good.' Paige: 'I think I know what Phoebe was like as a teenager. That's *also* the bad news.'

Paige, on Phoebe: 'She's under the influence.' Chris: 'Of alcohol?' Paige: 'No, adolescence.'

Notes: 'Those were the best times of my life.' The full ghastly horror of late-'80s/early-'90s America – in all its break-dancing and big-haired glory – is covered in this moderately amusing tale of teenage rebellion. There are a few logic flaws (most notably Phoebe and Paige, basically, surrendering Rick to be killed by the Scabers, which seems to go against all of the morality that the series stands for) and some of the scenes played for laughs really aren't funny at all. One of the less successful episodes of the season, although it's always nice to see James Read back.

Soundtrack: 'Sex Type Thing' by Stone Temple Pilots.

129: SPIN CITY

18 April 2004

Writers: Doug E Jones, Andy Reaser
Director: Mel Damski

Cast: Jodi Lyn O'Keefe (Spider Demon), Gildart Jackson (Gideon), Kieren Hutchison (Mitch), Scout Taylor-Compton (Fairy), Christopher Neiman (Sigmund), Hamilton von Watts (Denis), Scott Adsit (Man in Dress), Andy Stochansky (Himself), Danielle Aubry (Old Woman Fairy), Sonje Fortas (Ugly Witch), Katie Everard (Wood Nymph), Matthew McGrory (Ogre), Billy Beck (Rathmere), David Joseph Steinberg (Riley), Nathaniel Lamar (Jeremy), Jeff Asch (Wimpy Guy)

When Piper is kidnapped and cocooned by the Spider Demon, Chris is infected with the Demon's venom, causing him to mutate into a spider. Leo, meanwhile, finally learns exactly why Chris resents him.

It's Witchcraft: Riley, the brother of Shamus, seeks out Paige to inform her that the Wicked Witch from the Enchanted Forest is causing havoc in the Magic Kingdom. Paige creates a quick improved spell to help: 'You who found me in this bar, turn back to who you really are.'

A Little Learning is a Dangerous Thing: Leo has become very meditative during his six months in the Elders' domain. That all lasts a few moments until he's told that Chris is his son. At which point he becomes considerably more befuddled. Elders apparently aren't allowed to swear.

The Conspiracy Starts at the Witching Hour: The Spider Demon is an evil creature that emerges from its hidden lair every hundred years to capture and feed off the most powerful and magical creature it can detect. Her last victim was the wizard Rathmere. He created over 500 spells and potions before mysteriously disappearing in 1904.

Gideon tells Sigmund that, when the time is right, Wyatt will be sacrificed and the greater good will be served.

References: The title is taken from a popular US sitcom starring Michael J Fox. Also, Arthur Hamilton's 'Cry Me a River'; *Eight Legged Freaks*; *Shane* ('You have to do what you have to do'); and the *Austin Powers* movies ('mini-me').

SEASON 6: SPIN CITY

'You May Remember Me ...': Jodi Lyn O'Keefe played Debbie Strong in *Teacher's Pet* and also appeared in *Nash Bridges* and *She's All That*. Kieren Hutchinson was Andy Hargrove in *One Tree Hill*. Hamilton von Watts appeared in *Girls Will be Girls*. Scott Adsit was in *The Italian Job*. Danielle Aubry featured in *Dynasty*. Sonje Fortag's CV includes *Cheers*. Billy Beck appeared in *The Monkees*, *Stir Crazy* and *Near Dark*. David Joseph Steinberg was in *The Hebrew Hammer*. Nathaniel Lamar was in *CSI: Miami*. Jeff Asch featured in *Friends*.

Sex and Drugs and Rock n Roll: Phoebe is involved in a desperate quest to discover the father of the child that she saw herself pregnant with in her vision in 'The Legend of Sleepy Halliwell'. She seems to be working her way through every man in San Francisco alphabetically.

Logic, Let Me Introduce You to This Window: How exactly does the Spider Demon know that Chris is Piper's child? Leo bleeds after Chris punches his nose. Since when has Leo ever bled previously, except when shot with a Darklighter's arrow? At the end of the episode, a Nymph, a Leprechaun, and an Ogre are sitting having a casual drink in a crowded San Francisco club, and no-one notices. Phoebe channels Chris's emotions when he escapes as a spider. However, Chris took the empath-proof potion at the same time as Paige and Piper (see 'Love's a Witch'). The colour of the vanquishing potion changes from blue to orange several times. What exactly is the point of locking Chris in the basement? After all, he has retained his orbing power.

Continuity: Piper and Wyatt are now staying at the magic school until Piper gives birth. Piper discovers that, with this pregnancy, Chris does not have any magical powers from the womb, unlike Wyatt. Six months have passed since the events in 'The Courtship of Wyatt's Father'. Chris is said to be 22. He notes that, in the future, Paige is the one he usually goes to for money. Paige asks if this means she will become rich, but Chris won't tell her.

Quote/Unquote: Paige, on Piper's general state of anxiety: 'No wonder Chris grows up to be such a neurotic little freak.'
Chris, discovering that Wyatt had supernatural powers whilst still in his mother's womb but that he, himself, doesn't: 'It's not like I don't have an inferiority complex with him *already*. Thank you.'
Spider Demon: 'Dammit, can't a demon eat in peace?'

Notes: 'What did I do to become such a bad dad?' Very much a story of three thirds. The Spider Demon stuff is really good, with Jodi Lyn O'Keefe putting in a deliciously vampish performance and Drew Fuller at his best as a possessed Chris. The subplot about Gideon's and Sigmund's masterplan is, similarly, very effective (although it occupies only a few moments). However, put Paige and a Leprechaun together and you're usually guaranteed lousy accents, dreadful acting and desperately twee plot conceits (see 'Lucky Charmed'). To be fair, at least the Wicked-Witch-of-the-Emerald–Forest plot isn't dragged out for all it's worth (there's a lovely *Raiders of the Lost Ark* feel to the witch being vanquished in her only appearance in the episode), but it's undeniably true that *Charmed* is often at its worst when there are fairies and Leprechauns about. We should, therefore, be thankful that so little of the episode is devoted to them.

Soundtrack: Andy Stochansky's 'Shine', and 'Life is Short' by Butterfly Boucher.

130: CRIMES AND WITCH DEMEANORS

25 April 2004

Writer: Henry Alonso Myers
Director: John T Kretchmer

Cast: Gildart Jackson (Gideon), Billy Drago (Barbas), Kirk B R Woller (Cleaner One), Ian Abercrombie (Aramis), Darin Cooper (Cleaner Two), Sandra Prosper (Sheila Morris), Esteban Powell (Phinxs), Ken Page (Adair), Christopher Cazenove (Thrask), James Horan (Crill), Jenya Lano (Detective Sheridan), Keith Mackechnie (PD Clayton), Dennis Keffer (Killer in Alley)[71]

> Phoebe and Paige are caught on video using their powers. The Cleaners cover up this situation by implicating Darryl in a murder. When the Charmed Ones try to help, *they* end up on trial in front of a celestial tribunal. Meanwhile, Leo and Chris search for a way to help the sisters *and* Darryl.

It's Witchcraft: To attract the Cleaners' attention, Phoebe and Paige cause magical havoc in a San Francisco street, including casting a spell ('Flowers that bring desire, make them turn into fire') that engulfs a defenceless coffee cart in a raging inferno.

A Little Learning is a Dangerous Thing: The tribunal consist of two demons and two Elders and is said to be a power not to be trifled with. It is part of the grand design to allow magic to influence but not to take over free will, this being the one thing that Good and Evil could agree upon. The tribunal created the Cleaners to prevent magical exposure and gave them the power to erase events and memories or change them. When the tribunal is convened, the holographic Circle of Truth becomes enchanted, reads thoughts and shows what needs to be seen.

The Conspiracy Starts at the Witching Hour: Barbas is described as the Charmed Ones' worst enemy. Having been sent to the fires of Hell after his

---

[71] Various archive clips are also used featuring Julian McMahon, Bruce Campell, Ted King, David Pressman, Nicholas Cascone, Keith Diamond, Tracey Costello, D C Douglas, Christopher Shea, Wade Andrew Williams and Bruce Comtois.

last escapade (see 'Sympathy for the Demon'), he has made a deal with two Phantasms – spirit creatures that can travel back and forth between dimensions. One of these Phantasms has inhabited Darryl's colleague, Inspector Sheridan.

After the collapse of the trial, Barbas tells Gideon that he knows the Elders' greatest fear is that, somehow, the Charmed Ones will discover that Gideon intends to harm Piper's son.

It's a Designer Label!: What on earth is Phoebe wearing? Whatever it is, it's got sleeves but no shoulders.

References: The title alludes to Woody Allen's *Crimes and Misdemeanors* (1989). The tribunal owes a visual debt to *Superman: The Movie*. Also, references to the Yellow Pages; and *The Fugitive*.

'You May Remember Me …': Ian Abercrombie's CV includes *Santa Barbara* and *Army of Darkness*. Ken Page was in *South Central*. Esteban Powell featured in *Random Acts of Violence*. Christopher Cazenove appeared in *The Duchess of Duke Street*, *Royal Flash*, *Zulu Dawn* and *A Fine Romance*. James Horan was in *Enterprise*. Jeyna Lano's movies include *Stealing Candy* and *Blade*. Keith Mackechnie appeared in *Deep Zone*, *Big Girls Don't Cry … They Get Even* and *Buffy the Vampire Slayer*. Dennis Keiffer was in *Carnival of Wolves* and *Alias*.

Sex and Drugs and Rock n Roll: Paige asks about Phoebe's date. Her sister replies that she could see nothing in the future for them besides sex, and she isn't interested in that. 'Sex?' asks Paige, incredulously.

Logic, Let Me Introduce You to This Window: Leo tells Chris that the tribunal won't acknowledge anything a demon had to say – as there are two demons *on* the tribunal, that seems a trifle unlikely. During the exchange concerning Piper not being present at the tribunal, the word 'abstentia' is used; it should be 'absentia.' The entire subplot concerning the Cleaners accelerating time with regard to Darryl's execution is incredibly convoluted and illogical. (Most convicted killers under sentence of death spend *years* on death row whilst every avenue of appeal is explored.) There are also a number of procedural errors (such as a policeman listening in on a private lawyer/client discussion; that in itself would probably be grounds for a retrial).

Continuity: Facing the tribunal, Gideon argues that the Charmed Ones have never once failed in their duty to keep the big secret. As a consequence of the events of this episode, Phoebe loses her active powers

SEASON 6: CRIMES AND WITCH DEMEANORS

of premonition, levitation and empathy, although she can still cast spells and make potions. She will get her powers back only if she and her sisters are more careful in the future with regard to magical exposure. This episode features clips from 'From Fear to Eternity', 'Womb Raider', 'Bride and Gloom', 'House Call', 'Witches in Tights', 'Sam I Am', 'Déjà vu All Over Again', 'Death Takes a Halliwell' and 'Witch Way Now?' Yet again, all pre-season four clips pointedly fail to feature so much as a glimpse of Shannen Doherty (see 'Cat House').

Quote/Unquote: Phoebe: 'If all the good we've done in the last six years isn't good enough, then nothing is.'

Barbas: 'I'm surrounded by idiots!' And, when asked to explain his duplicitous actions by the tribunal: 'I'm a demon, what do you expect?'

Piper: 'Guess there's some cleaning up to do there.'

Notes: 'Have we ever let you down?' Oh fantastic, it's another clip-show – must be getting close to the end of the season, then. Actually, that's a little unfair as, despite that dreadfully clichéd plot (how many series have done a trial-like scenario as an excuse to throw open the video archives?), 'Crimes and Witch Demeanors' does, at least, have a few things going for it. Chief amongst them is Billy Drago in his most nostril-flaring performance to date.

Did You Know?: The WB used the promotional title 'Charmed on Trial' for this episode.

131: A WRONG DAY'S JOURNEY INTO RIGHT

2 May 2004

Writer: Cameron Litvack
Director: Derek Johnson

Cast: Gabriel Olds (Vincent), Chad Gabriel (Blake), Christopher Neiman (Sigmund), Jennifer O'Dell (Elisa), Amy Bernhardt (Demonatrix One), Annie Wersching (Demonatrix Two), Sy Richardson (Father Wilkins)

> With Piper at the magic school and Phoebe without her powers, an overworked Paige conjures herself a Mr Right for some light stress relief. Unknown to her, Mr Right has an evil twin, Mr Wrong.

It's Witchcraft: Paige's spell to create Vincent begins: 'A perfect man I summon now, another way I don't know how.'

A Little Learning is a Dangerous Thing: Whilst searching for a clue as to Wyatt's future, Piper asks Sigmund to check Lazardo's *Book of Prophecies*.

The Conspiracy Starts at the Witching Hour: For the past three weeks (co-incidentally, ever since Paige secretly created a perfect man for herself) a demon has been going around San Francisco doing the Charmed Ones' job for them. Recent victims of this inter-demon culling have included a Succubus and a Vortex Minion. Given that Mercury is currently in retrograde, Paige speculates that the next likely targets will be Smoker Demons, who traditionally surface during such a confluence. Chris discovers that the assassins are a group of leather-wearing female demons known as the Demonatrix.

Denial, Thy Name is Paige: When Paige notes that she still has responsibilities, Vincent suggests that her greater responsibilities are to herself and her *raison d'être*. If she keeps ignoring them, he believes that she will be useless to her sisters. She made Vincent to understand her, to pamper her and to fill her every neglected need.

Later, Vincent tells Leo and Phoebe that Paige has a dark side just like everyone else, and that evil-Vincent is appealing to what Paige secretly wants – to be independent and able to use her magic without fear of

SEASON 6: A WRONG DAY'S JOURNEY INTO RIGHT

consequence. These are extremely seductive ideas to her.

Work is a Four-Letter Word: Phoebe is having problems with her current column, which she blames on losing her empathic powers. Her proposed advice to 'Sad of San Jose,' whose husband is impotent, is to try either a cold shower or Viagra.

References: The title alludes to Eugene O'Neill's 1940 play *Long Day's Journey Into Night*. Also, *Last Man Standing*; Limmie and the Family Cookin's 'You Can Do Magic'; *Pinocchio*; and *I'm No Angel* ('Shouldn't you be off peeling Paige a grape or something?').

'You May Remember Me ...': Gabriel Olds was in *DC* and *Animal Room*. Chad Gabriel played Danny Mellon in *Hang Time*. Jennifer O'Dell's CV includes *The Lost World*. Sy Richardson appeared in *Beat*, *Evil Obsession* and *They Live*. Amy Bernhardt's movies include *Totally Blonde*. Annie Wersching appeared in *Bruce Almighty*.

Cigarettes and Alcohol: To stay awake whilst writing her column, Phoebe drinks Red Bull.

Sex and Drugs and Rock n Roll: Phoebe tells Leo that Paige was 'tossing and turning all night,' which is brilliantly intercut with Paige waking up next to Vincent.

Logic, Let Me Introduce You to This Window: Chris describes the Demonatrix as 'deadly assassins.' Is there any other sort of assassin? (Unless they're not very good at their job, of course.) When Chris is arrested, Leo worries that 'they' (presumably meaning the police) will work out who Chris is. Oh yes, *that*'s likely – the San Francisco PD will discover Chris's lack of a birth certificate and immediately assume that he's positive proof of the existence of time travel. Or possibly not. Vincent ends the episode as a mortal, and seemingly will have Leo looking after him. This suggests that he's still got his magical powers. When evil-Vincent casts the 'shall soon be gone, with no haste' ageing spell, the target of his wrath actually ages and dies *very* quickly. Why does Phoebe think a demon driving a Porsche is 'something different'? Cole had one (see 'The Fifth Halliwell').

Continuity: Chris call Leo 'Dad' for the first time in this episode. It appears that Darryl has retained his memories of the horrors that he went through in the previous episode and, for that reason at least, has decided he no longer intends to help the Charmed Ones. Vincent tells Phoebe that Paige

SEASON 6: A WRONG DAY'S JOURNEY INTO RIGHT

looks up to her more than Phoebe realises. Paige alludes to the occasion when she and Phoebe created a perfect man as a birthday gift for Piper (see 'Prince Charmed'). Evil-Vincent reminds Paige that the reason she chose his name was that her first love – a boy who promised her the world – was called Vincent. What Paige desires more than anything, according to Evil-Vincent, is freedom, independence and power.

Motors: One of *Charmed*'s few car chases – and it's a good one. Evil-Vincent steals a magnificent royal blue Porsche Carrera S-4 Turbo (*nice*). Chris chases after him in an equally stolen Alfa Romeo.

Quote/Unquote: Chris: 'You talking about me?' Phoebe: 'No, your foetus. Did you find something?' Chris: 'Not something, someone. Demonatrix.' Phoebe: 'Chris, what you do in your spare time …'

Paige: 'What I really need is …' Vincent: 'A vacation. Driving through Tuscany, topless.' Paige: 'Topless?' Vincent: 'Not you, the Porsche.'

Phoebe: 'I thought you knew him.' Vincent: 'I said I knew Paige. There's a difference.' Phoebe: 'What? Testicles?'

Piper: 'I can't stay here when all hell is breaking loose.' Leo: 'You save one son and I'll go save the other.'

Notes: 'Could this day get any worse?' Fundamentally, a remake of 'Prince Charmed' with a novel Janusian twist that keeps it vaguely interesting. There is, however, an unfortunate sense of tiredness that permeates 'Wrong Day's Journey'. We are getting towards the end of a long season and, whether by accident or design, this episode very much feels like a holding exercise. Still, the dialogue is terrific, at least.

Soundtrack: Series favourite Kylie Minogue's 'You Make Me Feel'.

SEASON 6: WITCH WARS

132: WITCH WARS

9 May 2004

Writer: Krista Vernoff
Director: David Jackson

Cast: Gildart Jackson (Gideon), Christopher Neiman (Sigmund), Jim Pirri (Corr), Elaine Hendrix (Clea), Bodhi Elfman (Kyle Donny), Vicki Davis (Tali), David Ramsey (Upper Level Demon), Betsy Randle (Mrs Winterbourne), Steve Cell (Apprentice Demon), Kevin Grevioux (Brute Demon), Steve Gibbons (Shapeshifter), Paul Vinson (Bald Demon in Bar), James Joseph O'Neill (Darklighter), Daniel Blinkoff (Thur)

> Believing it's only a matter of time before the sisters discover his plot, Gideon conspires with two demons to make Piper, Phoebe and Paige part of *Witch Wars*, a demonic reality TV show where demon contestants compete to hunt down the Charmed Ones.

It's Witchcraft: Paige has bought a new scrying crystal to replace the one destroyed in the previous episode. The 'return to sender' spell is mentioned (see 'The Day the Magic Died'). Worried about Phoebe's lack of powers, Paige gives her sister three potions – an explosive, an acid and a smoke bomb – in case of demon attack.

A Little Learning is a Dangerous Thing: The 'crystal thingies' that the demons use as their 'cameras' are, according to Gideon, an ancient form of magical voyeurism – the Ronyx crystal – that predates even the crystal ball.

The Conspiracy Starts at the Witching Hour: Sigmund has one of those sudden changes of character motivation that seem to happen quite a lot in *Charmed*, and is about to tell Leo and the sisters the truth regarding Gideon's plan. Gideon promptly kills him.
Brute Demons are upper-level creatures with overwhelming physical strength. They work alone, generally crushing the skulls of their victims.

It's a Designer Label!: Paige's green miniskirt.

References: There's a reference to Donald Trump and his reality TV show *The Apprentice*. Parts of the plot resemble *The Truman Show*. The idea of a bar that caters exclusively to demons was first popularised in *Buffy the*

SEASON 6: WITCH WARS

Vampire Slayer and then taken to its logical extreme in *Angel*. Also, *Pulp Fiction*; and *Survivor*.

'You May Remember Me ...': Bodhi Elfman's movies include *Almost Famous* and *Gone in Sixty Seconds*. Vicki Davis played Mia in *Maybe it's Me* and also appeared in *Cherry Falls*. Jim Pirri was Jack Pappas in *Union Square*. Steve Cell was in *CSI* and *The Shield*. David Ramsey's movies include *Con Air* and *The Nutty Professor*. Elaine Hendrix appeared in *Bad Boy*, *The Parent Trap* and *Superstar*. James Joseph O'Neill was in *Sex and the City*. Daniel Blinkoff featured in *With Honors*. Steve Gibbons's CV includes *Nudity Required*. Kevin Grevioux appeared in *Planet of the Apes* and *Bowfinger*.

Cigarettes and Alcohol: Chris, Leo and the sisters are drinking champagne at the episode's climax, having, they believed, vanquished those behind the plot to turn Wyatt evil.

Logic, Let Me Introduce You to This Window: Let's get this straight. There's a TV show made by demons that is broadcast exclusively to at least one demon bar? So, not much disbelief to suspend *this* week, then? Chris says that whatever turned Wyatt evil, did so before Chris was born. In 'The Legend of Sleepy Halliwell', when Phoebe has a premonition about the future, Wyatt seems reasonably unevil as a child. It's twice stated that the most recently killed witch had the ability to shoot fire from her hands, directly contradicting what was stated in 'We're Off to See the Wizard' (that throwing fire is an upper-level demonic power). It has previously been established that no-one can die within magic school, so how does Gideon kill Sigmund?

Quote/Unquote: Upper-Level Demon: 'How did you come up with the idea anyway?' Clea: 'We can't take all the credit. You'd think demons would've invented reality television but, somehow, humans beat us to it.'

Chris reveals that he heard a rumour concerning a demonic game-show. Paige: 'And you didn't tell us this *why*?' Chris: 'Because I didn't think it was relevant.' Paige: 'That's your theme song for today, did you notice?'

A, suddenly re-empowered, Phoebe: 'God, that was great. I wanna kill somebody else. Who can I kill? Chris, find me another demon to kill.'

Notes: 'It'll be winner takes all, and we will take all: their lives, their powers, and last but not least, their progeny.' A pointed and rather foot-stamping critique on the horrors of reality TV – how frightfully arch. 'Witch Wars', on a basic 'lots of cool TV-industry parodies and excellent one-liners' level, works extremely well (it's probably the funniest *Charmed* episode in months). It's got to be said, however, that an allegory as unsubtle as this needs far more in the way of additional bonuses than some good jokes. There also something really quite tacky about a TV show saying, in effect, 'Anyone who watches reality TV is a moron,' when half its audience will have sat through *High School Reunion* immediately prior to this episode.

133: IT'S A BAD BAD BAD BAD WORLD: PART 1

16 May 2004

Writer: Jeannine Renshaw
Director: Jon Paré

Cast: Billy Drago (Barbas), Gildart Jackson (Gideon), Jenya Lano (Inspector Sheridan), Sandra Prosper (Sheila Morris), Betsy Randle (Mrs Winterbourne), Blake Robbins (Patrol Officer), Lorna Scott (Mrs Nobles)

>Gideon gets the sisters to create a portal that sends Chris and Leo into a parallel world where evil prevails and a dark version of the Charmed Ones exists. In their place, Darklighter versions of Chris and Leo travel the other way. Phoebe and Paige journey to the other dimension on a rescue mission. Piper, meanwhile, goes into labour.

It's Witchcraft: The spell that Gideon creates for the sisters to use to send Chris back to the future begins: 'In this place and in this hour, we call upon the ancient power, open the door through time and space, create a path to another place.' Of course, that's not where the portal sends Chris and Leo at all.

A Little Learning is a Dangerous Thing: Gideon reminds Leo that, when it comes to time travel, there are no guarantees.

The Conspiracy Starts at the Witching Hour: Gideon has made contact with his counterpart in a parallel world in which evil is predominant (and in which Barbas is the Demon of Hope). They both realise that they are tinkering with the grand design and risking its tenuous stability by creating an imbalance of power on one side. However, both consider that it's a far greater risk to allow Wyatt to grow up and threaten *both* worlds – Good and Evil.

Gideon tells Paige that the grand design maintains a balance in the universe. For good to prevail in *this* world, then an equally evil world must also exist, on another plane of existence. Balance is everything, he continues. Without it, the cosmos doesn't spin.

References: The title alludes to Stanley Kramer's 1963 comedy *It's a Mad*

SEASON 6: IT'S A BAD BAD BAD BAD WORLD : PART 1

Mad Mad Mad World. The alternate-reality Leo's 'evil' facial hair may be a reference to Spock's beard in *Star Trek*'s 'Mirror, Mirror', or to famous doppelgänger episodes of *Knight Rider* and *South Park*. For more 'evil twin' stories, see John Wyndham's *Random Quest*; DC's *Crisis of Infinite Earths*; *Stargate SG-1*'s 'Point of View'; *Red Dwarf*'s 'Dimension Jump'; *Doctor Who*'s 'Inferno'; and *Buffy the Vampire Slayer*'s 'The Wish'. Also, *Pollyanna of Sunnybrooke Farm*; *Back to the Future*; Tiffany's jewellery chain; and the Google Internet search engine.

'You May Remember Me ...': Blake Robbins played David Brass in *Oz*. Lorna Scott's movies include *Bad Santa*, *Seconds to Die* and *Ghost World*.

Cigarettes and Alcohol: Phoebe threatens evil-Darryl with a broken Jack Daniels bottle. Darklighter-Chris drinks a bottle of beer on top of the Golden Gate Bridge before dropping the empty bottle onto the traffic below.

Sex and Drugs and Rock n Roll: In the alternate reality, P^3 is a rather seedy lap-dancing club.

Logic, Let Me Introduce You to This Window: Paige uses just four crystals to trap Darklighter-Chris and Darklighter-Leo. In most previous episodes, the crystal cage has needed five crystals to form a pentagram. Who redrew the triquetra in the attic when Paige and Phoebe were stuck in the alternate reality with their evil counterparts and Piper was in hospital? Sheila mentions that she and Darryl never fight. However, in 'Cat House', Darryl admitted to Piper and Leo that they, too, have been to see a marriage counsellor. Gideon says that Piper should relax as she may go into labour prematurely – but as she is apparently only two days away from her expected date, there's surely little to worry about in this regard.

Continuity: The Halliwells' neighbour (living in Dan's old house) is the rather frumpy and annoying Mrs Noble. Leo reminds Chris that the last time they went through a time portal, Chris almost ended up as dinosaur food (see 'Soul Survivor'). Wyatt's powers are growing with every episode. Here, he puts up his force field when left alone with Gideon. Subsequently, after Gideon breaches that force field and tries to stab Wyatt with the athema, Wyatt blinks and the weapon orbs out of Gideon's hand. Wyatt redirects it to stab Gideon in the chest. At the episode's climax, when Paige, Phoebe, Chris and Leo return, the world has been subtly altered and Phoebe is shot. (Note that the ice cream van from 'We All Scream for Ice Cream' briefly appears.)

SEASON 6: IT'S A BAD BAD BAD BAD WORLD : PART 1

Motors: Briefly glimpsed in the driveway is Paige's new green VW (40YW 682).

Quote/Unquote: Darklighter-Leo: 'First we gotta get back to our world, though. We're gonna need the Power of Three to do that.' Darklighter-Chris: 'We can't trust those Pollyanna witches, they're too good. Who do I have to kill so we can get out of here?'

Phoebe: 'We need to find his Piper.' Evil-Gideon: 'If you do, she'll probably kill you. She's evil, remember and she's got a terrible temper. Worse when she's pregnant.' Phoebe: 'Yeah, that's not much different in our world.'

Notes: 'For every second that they're in our world, they risk throwing off the balance by doing something evil.' A suitably rich and varied first part of a quite wonderful season closer. The parallel universe stuff is especially good – most telefantasy series have a bit of fun with this kind of *doppelgängland* conceit at some stage, and *Charmed* has occasionally flirted with it before. Evil-Phoebe and evil-Paige are really good fun, and the episode's shocking ending comes as a complete surprise to the audience as much as to the characters.

Soundtrack: 'Take A Look' by Liz Phair.

134: IT'S A BAD BAD BAD BAD WORLD: PART 2

16 May 2004

Writer: Jeannine Renshaw
Director: Jon Paré

Cast: Gildart Jackson (Gideon), Billy Drago (Barbas), Betsy Randle (Mrs Winterbourne), Wesley A Ramsey (Adult Wyatt), John Todd (Elder), Jenya Lano (Inspector Sheridan), Jim Abele (Dr Roberts), Kerry O'Malley (Nurse Ann), J Lamont Poper (Mike), Deyna Devon (Female Vulture Demon), Kristopher Logan (Male Vulture Demon), Samantha Miller (Cindy)

> Gideon allies himself with Barbas in a final desperate hope of gaining access to Wyatt. Meanwhile, in the 'too happy' world that Paige, Phoebe, Leo and Chris have returned to, danger lurks in the most unexpected of places.

A Little Learning is a Dangerous Thing: Chris wonders about Gideon. If he has always viewed Wyatt as a threat, why does he turn him evil in Chris's future? Leo speculates that Gideon probably didn't intentionally do this. Gideon will try to kill Wyatt but will discover that Wyatt can protect himself. So, he will kidnap the child. Leo asks Chris to imagine being taken away from Piper and Leo for weeks, maybe even months, constantly fending off Gideon's attacks – it's no wonder the poor little chap turned to the dark side.

The Conspiracy Starts at the Witching Hour: Gideon suggests that any shift between Good and Evil is supposed to happen naturally over time. By intervening, he has allowed too much good to corrupt the mirror world, and the only way to get the balance back is for a great evil to corrupt his (and the Charmed Ones') own world.

References: Allusions to *Pleasantville*; *To Die For*; and *The Prez* (with the smiley face in the sky above the Manor).

'You May Remember Me ...': Jim Abele's CV includes *24* and *Angel*. Deyna Devon appeared in *Antitrust* and *The West Wing*. Kristopher Logan was in *Parker Lewis Can't Lose* and *Star Trek: Generations*. Kerry O'Malley's

SEASON 6: IT'S A BAD BAD BAD BAD WORLD: PART 2

movies include *Rounders*. J Lamont Pope appeared in *The Crow* and *Road Dogs*.

Logic, Let Me Introduce You to This Window: Why is the sun continually shining in the world that Phoebe, Paige, Leo and Chris return to? Day and night are cosmic phenomena that aren't in any way influenced by whether a world is good or evil. The hospital elevator appears to be the same one that was used in Cole's penthouse. After Chris dies, Leo is overcome with uncontrollable grief and rage and begins a wrecking spree. However, he does so in the attic, not in the bedroom where Chris actually died. When Paige calls for Leo, he mentions that he was in the Underworld. In 'All Hell Breaks Loose', Leo orbed to the Underworld to get Phoebe, and Piper died precisely *because* he was unable to hear Prue's calls. Gideon says he was unsure if Wyatt could orb. Yet he knows that Paige, the daughter of a Whitelighter and witch, can orb.

Continuity: Phoebe and Paige work with their evil counterparts in the mirror world. Subsequently, Leo also co-operates with *his* Darklighter doppelgänger in a successful bid to vanquish Gideon and to save both their sons. Chris was named after Leo's father. His date of birth is 16 November 2004. When Leo kills Gideon, it is the act of 'great evil' that restores the balance to the grand design. (Although it's never specified, it's probable that, in the mirror world, Darklighter-Leo killed Evil-Gideon, which, given that world's nature, could be regarded as an act of 'great good', thus also helping to restore balance.) When Barbas plays on Leo's greatest fear – being unable to prevent Wyatt from turning evil – Leo imagines a grown-up version of his son (see 'Chris-Crossed') who uses Excalibur (see 'Sword and the City') to stab Leo. Wyatt can now, it appears, vanquish demons with a mere blink of his eye. After Chris dies, his body disappears for reasons no one took the trouble to explain.

Quote/Unquote: Leo: 'By getting us all to the evil world, Gideon screwed up the balance, messed up with the grand design.' Paige: 'Well, if you ask me, the grand design is pretty messed up in the first place.'
Barbas: 'This particular day couldn't get much worse.' Gideon: 'Actually, it could. You could die.'
Gideon: 'Family means everything to Piper. In *any* world.' And his final words to Leo: 'You have *no* idea what you've done.'

Notes: 'You can still save his future and you can still save Wyatt.' A well-constructed and suitably intense finale that wraps up many of the themes of the season and, via a noble death, reconfirms *Charmed*'s occasional use of progression-through-redemption. Chris was a character whom the fans initially had some problems with but came ultimately to admire, and his death – valiantly trying to protect the brother he travelled through time to save – was, frankly, the only way in which he could have exited. Great performances all round (with a special word here for Brian Krause, who goes from calmly understated to ragingly insane and back again within the space of two acts). The villains are great, too; a cool, chilling (yet, in a kind-of pathetic way, almost sympathetic) performance from Gildart Jackson, which is magnificently balanced by Billy Drago going for the Scenery Chewer of the Year Award yet again. And winning. It almost makes you forget the fact that a hugely pregnant Holly Marie Combs appears in this episode for all of three scenes.

Did You Know?: With a flood of popular TV shows on DVD proving so successful over recent years, many media commentators were bemused by the long delay in the release of any *Charmed* episodes. For some time, the rumour in fan circles was that this was largely due to the amount of pop music used in the show, which would need additional clearances and royalty payments before the episodes could be sold in a new format. 'I share the fans' frustration,' Brad Kern told *TV Zone* magazine in 2004. 'My understanding is that because we're owned by Paramount, they have a vast and paranoid legal department and must dot every 'I' and cross every clearance 'T', and that's a long process.' Eventually these issues appear to have been resolved: season box sets of episodes are now being released albeit with – disappointingly – no extra features whatsoever.

CHARMED SEASON 7
(2004-2005)

Consulting Producer: Jonathan Levin.
Co-Producers: Debra J Fisher, Erica Messer, Jeannine Renshaw.
Producers: Rob Wright, Henry Alonso Myers, Curtis Kheel, Peter Chomsky, Holly Marie Combs, Alyssa Milano, Jon Paré.
Supervising Producer: Mark Wilding.
Co-Executive Producer: James L Conway.
Executive Producers: Brad Kern, Aaron Spelling, E Duke Vincent.
Story Editor: Cameron Litvack.

Regular Cast:
Holly Marie Combs (Piper Halliwell)
Alyssa Milano (Phoebe Halliwell)
Rose McGowan (Paige Matthews)
Dorian Gregory (Darryl Morris, 135, 138-139, 143-144, 148)
Brian Krause (Leo Wyatt)

135: A CALL TO ARMS

12 September 2004

Writer: Brad Kern
Director: James L Conway

Cast: Nick Lachey (Leslie St Claire), Billy Drago (Barbas), James Avery (Zola), Betsy Randle (Mrs Winterbourne), Jenya Lano (Inspector Sheridan), Rebecca Balding (Elise Rothman), Hawthorne James (Demonic Healer), Branscombe Richmond (Fierce Demon), Eddie Matos (Paramedic Garcia), Kiran Rao (Priest), Reggie Rolle (Attendant), Amanda Sickler (Sophie), Todd Tucker (Creature Head Demon)

> Still mourning for Chris, Piper and Leo attend a wedding, where they are inadvertently possessed by a pair of Hindu love gods. It's therefore down to Phoebe and Paige to keep them from consummating their love in order to save the universe. Or something.

It's Witchcraft: Paige casts the spell that removes the Hindi influence from Piper and Leo: 'We call upon the mortal ways and Gods who guide but may not stay, we seek those of divinity to separate from and set them free.'

A Little Learning is a Dangerous Thing: Paige uses magic to change Chris's nappies. When Piper complains about a potential 'personal gain' clause, Paige rejects the idea and suggests that Piper wait till she sees how Paige intends to apply the ointment to Chris's skin.

As we've seen on several occasions, the only way to defeat one's greatest fear is with one's greatest desire.

The Conspiracy Starts at the Witching Hour: Leo has become obsessed with tracking and vanquishing Barbas. However, he is subsequently manipulated by both the demon and a mysterious disembodied spirit into killing another Elder, the kindly Zola.

Inspector Sheridan is still investigating the Halliwells and has requested Darryl Morris to be her partner. She confronts Phoebe regarding Chris – noting that he mysteriously broke out of jail but doesn't seem to appear in any database. She wonders why the Halliwells didn't have a funeral for him and what happened to his body. When Phoebe fails to keep an appointment at the station, Sheridan comes to the Manor and forces her way in, only to be attacked by an outraged Leo when she pulls a gun on him. Subsequently, a concussed Sheridan cannot remember the exact circumstances of her becoming injured. (Phoebe and Darryl suggest that she slipped.)

Work is a Four-Letter Word: Phoebe is feeling in a rut. Paige agrees, noting that Phoebe recently gave some advice to 'Lost in Los Altos' about finding new love, but, unfortunately, it was the same advice she gave to 'Dumped in Daly' the previious year. Phoebe is horrified to think that she is plagiarising herself. So, whilst advertising posters may suggests that *Ask Phoebe* has 'all the answers', she confesses to Elise that she needs a break. Elise is surprised, feeling that Phoebe is producing some of her most brilliant work and that she makes the newspaper look classy when her advice is provocative and insightful. She tells Phoebe not to worry about reusing material – columnists recycle stuff all the time. However, she does add that if Phoebe really feels she need to recharge her batteries, it's no big deal, they can hire a ghost-writer to cover for her. The readers, she notes, will never know. The writer that Elise eventually hires is, to Phoebe's horror, a man – Leslie St Clair. He had his own advice column in Philadelphia, which was similar to Phoebe's, 'hip and hot.' He's relocating to LA in a couple of months. Leslie is a doctor of psychology – he wrote his doctorate on women's intuition. Phoebe, despite herself, is attracted to him and also, subsequently, admires his work.

References: Allusions to *Rugrats* (see 'Reckless Abandon'); and advice show host Dr Phil McGraw.

'You May Remember Me ...': James Avery played Philip Banks in *The Fresh Prince of Bel-Air*. Branscombe Richmond's movies includes *The Scorpion King* and *Curly Sue*. Mary Castro was in *Cellular*. Eddie Matos appeared in *General Hospital*. Kiran Rao's CV includes *The Shield* and *Scrubs*. Reggie Rolle was in *The Bold and the Beautiful*.

Sex and Drugs and Rock n Roll: 'Is this a wedding or an orgy?' asks Piper when she, Leo and Phoebe arrive at the Hindu ceremony of their friend Christy Peters and Javeed Armand. During the ceremony, as the circle is the symbol of the earth and the sun and the universe, the priest calls upon the goddess and god that created all things ... and, for some unexplained reason, Piper and Leo become possessed by Shakti the Goddess of Creation and Shiva the God of Destruction. They are commonly invoked at weddings because they're considered to be the Ultimate Lovers. Shakti, also called the Ultimate Mother, and Shiva together created all things, and if they consummate their love again, all things will be obliterated and the

Universe will be reborn. ('I'm thinking it's meant to be symbolic' says Phoebe, hopefully.) As a consequence of this, Piper grows six extra arms, whilst Leo confesses he hasn't felt this potent in years. ('Oversharing' adds Phoebe.) Paige notes this isn't the first time that members of the Halliwell family have been hijacked by Gods (see 'Oh My Goddess'). Meanwhile, Phoebe (much to her own surprise) gets a touch of the 'divine horniness' with her ghost-writer, Leslie.

Logic, Let Me Introduce You to This Window: This episode marks the fourth time that Barbas has been 'finally' vanquished. What's the betting he'll be back? It seems odd that Zola doesn't have any way of protecting himself from Leo's attack. He's an Elder, so he and Leo should be evenly matched. When Phoebe discovers that her ghost-writer is to be a man, she asks if anyone knows of an advice column written by a man. Not only are there *dozens* of male writers of such columns in reality, but even *Charmed* previously featured one – Spencer Ricks. Whitelighters are able to sense evil, so shouldn't Elders also have this power? After Leo has killed Zola and wonders what he has become, Piper says that nobody else has to know. Surely the Elders will be aware that one of their own has killed another? In the first scene in the kitchen when Piper comes in, she's wearing slippers; these subsequently turn into flip-flops. On at least two occasions when he's being held by first Paige, then Piper, baby Chris is, clearly, a doll. The building used for the exterior of the *Bay Mirror* office is different from the one used previously. No judge would give Sheridan a search warrant for the Manor two months after an alleged crime has been committed.

Continuity: This episode takes place approximately two months after the events of 'It's a Bad Bad Bad Bad World'. Piper mentions the fact that she and Leo have already 'seen a shrink' (presumably an allusion to 'Cat House'). Zola tells Paige and Phoebe that a powerful threat is looming on the horizon – unlike anything that the Elders have sensed before. They will need everyone back into the fold to defeat this menace. Zola notes that Leo hadn't really wanted to kill him, but if he had, there would have been no redeeming him; he would have had to be 'recycled' – sent back and reborn, to start the cycle of life over again. The Elders don't want to punish Leo for killing Gideon, but they will not stand by whilst he harms innocents in the name of revenge.

Paige, meanwhile, is told by Ms Winterbourne that the magic school is being closed down. Gideon started the school and, without him, there's no-one left to fight for it anymore. Gideon was the only one who could convince the other Elders that he could keep the school safe from demons discovering them. Paige is outraged, asking where the next generation will be able to learn what needs to be learned. Ultimately she decides to fight to keep the school open herself. (Phoebe appears not to have told her that it's her destiny to do so – see 'The Legend of Sleepy Halliwell'.)

Quote/Unquote: Piper, on Chris: 'How's his rash? Does he need ointment?' Paige: 'I've been kind of procrastinating on that one. It's not my favourite thing to check.' Piper: 'You don't have a problem checking Wyatt.' Paige: 'That's coz I don't flash forward to Wyatt being 22 like I do with Chris.' Piper: 'Oh. Yeah. Eww.'

Paige: 'Tell me what it's like out there in the world where men don't poop or spit on you.' Phoebe: 'You really do need to get out.' Paige: 'Maybe we can just swap jobs for the day. I'll pay you.'

Phoebe: 'You're gonna have to choose a side, Darryl. It's just the way it works.' And when Barbas is vanquished: 'I never get tired of seeing that.'

Phoebe: 'If they consummate their love, all things will be obliterated and the universe reborn.' Paige: 'Talk about your big bang theory.'

Notes: 'If you want to stop the Elder, go after the baby.' Another pilot episode for another new beginning. *Charmed*, post Chris and Gideon, is a strange, slightly darker place than before, with an undercurrent of hidden menace (manifested by the skull demon spirit that manipulates both Barbas and Leo here). 'A Call to Arms' has some interesting ideas but, even at this stage, Sheridan's targeting of the Halliwells has absolutely no sense to it.

Soundtrack: The score includes a terrific Indian/Arabesque elements – sitar, tambura, tabla, sarod.

Did You Know?: 'I thought the broadest section of fans would be 11-year-olds,' Rose McGowan told the *Sun* newspaper in 2004. 'It's not that at all. People come up to me all the time – 60-year-old cab drivers, 50-year-old women. A lot of great queeny gay guys are into it. Female African-Americans love *Charmed*. It's so broad, and that's what I love about it.'

SEASON 7: THE BARE WITCH PROJECT

136: THE BARE WITCH PROJECT

19 September 2004

Writer: Jeannine Renshaw
Director: John T Kretchner

Cast: Nick Lachey (Leslie St Claire), Kristen Miller (Lady Godiva), Maury Sterling (Lord Dyson), Blake Bashoff (Duncan), John de Lancie (Odin), Elizabeth Dennehy (Sandra), Kenneth Schmidt (Simon), Bru Muller (Policeman), Baajda-Lyne Odums (Female Elder), Chris Breslin (Customer), Trey Ellett (Ray), Todd Tucker (Creature Head Demon), Dennis W Hall (Editor)[72], Vladimir Rajcic (Reporter)[73]

> Thanks to a bored magic school student, the Charmed Ones must keep Bad Lord Dyson from killing Lady Godiva before she can complete her infamous naked ride through Coventry. Phoebe, meanwhile, continues to have reservations about Leslie being able to write an advice column for women.

It's Witchcraft: The spell that Duncan uses to send Lady Godiva back was previously used by Patty and Penny in 'That 70s Episode' when they returned Prue, Piper and Phoebe to their own time.

Denial, Thy Name is Piper: Lord Dyson uses Piper's repressed anger at Leo over his alleged 'moping.'

The Conspiracy Starts at the Witching Hour: Lord Dyson was an evil 11th Century land baron who fed on the pain of peasants and oppressed them. He was the weasel who convinced Lady Godiva's husband to tax the people harshly.

Work is a Four-Letter Word: The ghost-written *Ask Phoebe* column that gets Phoebe so riled is entitled *Glass Ceiling in Sausalito*.
   Having successfully argued her case that the magic school is worth keeping open, Paige is told by Odin that as long as she is the one to keep running it, then she can. Paige hadn't bargained on that.
References: It's suggested – spuriously – that Lady Godiva was an

---

[72] Uncredited.
[73] Uncredited.

inspiration to many other strong and capable women throughout history, including Queen Elizabeth, Joan of Arc and Catherine the Great. The alternate world, in which women are subjugated and those who talk in public are flogged, bears a strong resemblance to that in Margaret Atwood's *The Handmaid's Tale*. There's a San Francisco '49ers banner on the wall of Phoebe's office (see 'Secrets and Guys', 'She's a Man, Baby, a Man'). Leslie alludes to *Tarzan*.

'You May Remember Me ...': Kristen Miller appeared in *She Spies, That's My Bush!* and *Malibu Shores*. Maury Sterling was in *Behind Enemy Lines*. Blake Bashoff's movies include *Minority Report*. John de Lancie was Q in *Star Trek: The Next Generation* and several spin-offs, Colonel Simmons in *Stargate SG-1* and Al Kiefer in *The West Wing*. He was also in *Good Advice, Legend, Andromeda, The Onion Field, Multiplicity* and *The Fisher King*. Elizabeth Dennehy appeared in *Gattaca*. Kenneth Schmidt was in *7th Heaven*. Bru Muller appeared in *Framed* and *Maxwell*, the latter of which he also wrote and produced. Baajda-Lyne Odums was in *The Ladykillers, Flatliners* and *The Shield*. Chris Breslin appeared in *Law & Order: Special Victims Unit*. Vladimir Rajcic's CV includes *24* and *The West Wing*. Dennis W Hall was in *First Watch*.

Logic, Let Me Introduce You to This Window: In California, it's wholly legal for mothers to breastfeed in public places, including stores and restaurants. Managers of establishments do not have any right to refuse service to anyone unless they are breaking the law, and if they try, they're laying themselves wide open to significant legal action. After Lady Godiva is sent back, a sequence shows night and day passing, yet when Paige returns to comfort the student at magic school, she's still wearing the same green dress she wore the previously day. When Leslie decides to answer Phoebe's letter, he appears to be looking for it in his post tray. It's *clearly* on top of the pile – it's very pink, he can hardly miss it. This is an episode written by someone who knows Britain and the British not even *slightly*. Lady Godiva, from 1040, who should be speaking some form of Chaucer-like Middle-English, instead has a dreadfully *faux-naif* finishing school accent, as though the only English person the actress has ever heard speak is Diana Spencer. The episode, of course, relies heavily on the romanticised legend of Godiva, written by the 13th Century chronicler Roger of Wendover, instead of historical fact. Godgyfu – the widow of Leofric, Earl of Chester – owned the land around Coventry herself, and could have lowered the taxes if she'd wished. Quite why she rode naked through the town (if, indeed, she ever did) is unknown. Piper claims P^3 is the sisters' only source of income. This presumably means that Phoebe is taking unpaid leave.

SEASON 7: THE BARE WITCH PROJECT

Continuity: The Elf Nanny (see 'Sam I Am') is mentioned. Paige alludes to a demon who feeds off anger, but says that her sisters 'already got him' (see 'Power Outage').

Quote/Unquote: Piper: 'How much history could a naked lady on horseback really affect?'
Piper: 'We have bigger naked breasts to worry about.'
Piper: 'How am I supposed to know I was so repressed?' Paige: 'You couldn't tell?' Piper: 'I'm a working single mother of two kids. I barely have time to brush my teeth, let alone self-reflection.'

Notes: 'Woman, keep your clothes on. This is a family show.' This is rubbish of the highest order. It's got some good intentions, admittedly, but it's done so heavy-handedly, and with such crassly ignorant characterisation and downright sloppy research, that these are completely undermined. What, exactly, is Jeannine Renshaw (a fine writer, on past evidence) trying to say here? That the way to challenge sexist attitudes is for ladies to ride naked through the streets? Excellent – let's have some then ... We'll ignore the stupid *non-history* elements and an alternate world created by changing a 'historical' event that probably never happened in the first place. Let's just call 'The Bare Witch Project' an over-ambitious attempt to shoehorn *Charmed*'s extremely circumstantial feminist credentials, through acts of defiance in a male-dominated world, into a wholly inappropriate place in the Sisterhood's heart. It's never gonna happen, kids, just accept that and move along. Cool pyrotechnics, however.

137: CHEAPER BY THE COVEN

26 September 2004

Writer: Mark Wilding
Director: Derek Johansen

Cast: Charisma Carpenter (The Seer), Nick Lachey (Leslie St Claire), James Read (Victor Bennett), Jennifer Rhodes (Grams), Finola Hughes (Patty Halliwell), Tac Fitzgerald (Ben), Peter Breitmayer (Emcee), Mandy Freund (Female Fan), Mark Wilson (Rex)

> When Paige and Phoebe summon Grams for Chris's Wiccaning, Grams puts a spell on Wyatt and Chris in an attempt to end their sibling rivalry. Instead, it reverts the sisters to bickering teenagers. Phoebe attends an awards ceremony with Les, whilst Leo consults a Seer to determine who is behind the recent attacks on Wyatt.

Dreaming (As Blondie Once Said) is Free: Wyatt's dreams are manifesting themselves, and it is he who created Dark-Leo. Patty and Victor tell Piper than when she was a little girl, around the time that her parents split up, she started having a lot of bad dreams – the doctors described them as 'night terrors.' It was her subconscious way of blaming herself for the break-up (not, both her mother and father stress, that she *was* to blame – there were many other factors). Something similar is happening to Wyatt – he blames himself for Piper's and Leo's strained relationship and, as a consequence, his dreams are becoming reality.

It's Witchcraft: Grams reveals that she used spells on the girls to stop them misbehaving, much to Victor's annoyance. She casts a spell to end sibling rivalry between Wyatt and Chris. ('Cast your petty jealousies to darkest night. Let these feuding siblings no longer fight.') The spell works but, unfortunately, their lost rivalry immediately goes into the nearest set of siblings – Piper, Phoebe and Paige. It eventually requires Patty to cast a reversal spell – 'Reverse the spell from the book and please restore what was took' – which she admits she made up when she was nine.

A Little Learning is a Dangerous Thing: Grams considers Leo 'a lost soul.'

The Conspiracy Starts at the Witching Hour: The Seer suggests to Leo that no demon is likely to attack Wyatt now – they know better. She asks what makes Leo so sure that it's not an Elder, someone who thinks that, maybe, Gideon was right. Leo says that no more Elders will die by his hands, but that he can't say the same for demons. The Seer asks if he can even tell the difference anymore.

The Charisma Show: She's in only three scenes but, yes, it pretty much is. A former cheerleader with the San Diego Chargers, the great Charisma Carpenter began her acting career in *Baywatch*, playing Hobie's girlfriend Wendie. Aaron Spelling personally auditioned her for the über-vixen-bitch Ashley Green in NBC's *Malibu Shores*. She also played Beth Sullivan in the *Josh Kirby: Time Warrior* TV movies and appeared in a legendary advert for Spree sweets ('It's a kick in the mouth!'). Subsequent to the seven years she spent playing the much-loved Cordelia Chase in *Buffy the Vampire Slayer* and *Angel*, she starred as the eponymous Jane Grant in *See Jane Date*.

Work is a Four-Letter Word: Phoebe's column has won a Readers' Choice award. However, it's for one of the issues that Leslie wrote. (Must have been a recent one – he's only been there a couple of weeks.)

'You May Remember Me …': Tac Fitzgerald's movies include *Blackhawk Down*. Peter Breitmayer appeared in *Jingle All the Way*. Mandy Freund played May Tuna on *Popular* and was also in *The West Wing*. Mark Wilson appeared in *Forget Paris*.

Cigarettes and Alcohol: Phoebe shares a glass of red wine with Les at the awards ceremony and later blames her bizarre behaviour on the alcohol.

Sex and Drugs and Rock n Roll: Paige, with her hormones raging, and Ben, the personable 21 year old grad student at magic school, get to know each other's tonsils quite well.

Logic, Let Me Introduce You to This Window: The summoning spell that Paige uses is different from that spoken in most previous episodes. It one shot, the fact that the set had no ceiling is clearly apparent. The sign at the awards ceremony says, *San Francisco Bay Area Reader's Choice Awards*. Note the grammatical error! Leo heard Victor calling him when he was in the Underworld – something he's not supposed to be able to do. Grams didn't know that Piper was pregnant, let alone the fact that Chris has been born – yet she is up to date on Leo killing Gideon. Grams asks Piper if she remembers the first time she was this age (i.e. a teenager), 'when I sat you and your sisters down and we had "the Witch Talk"'? This is completely inconsistent with what was established in 'Something Wicca This Way Comes' and several subsequent episodes, when it was said that Prue, Piper and Phoebe had no idea they were witches until after Grams died.

Continuity: Phoebe chewed gum as a teenager. Wyatt, who is now two, uses his powers to orb Chris's dummy and blanket away from him and, later, to orb Chris himself from the magic school to Victor's arms outside the Manor. Wyatt's Wiccaning ceremony was held when he was six months old and, as Piper points out, it didn't really protect him from evil (see 'Necromancing the Stone'). Amongst the demons who wear masks are Aztec demons and Chinese false-face demons.

Quote/Unquote: Grams, on being summoned: 'Not a good time, girls. I'm busy.' Paige: 'You're dead.' Grams: 'It doesn't mean I can't have a life.'

Seer, to Leo: 'I have a problem. You kind of have a temper. If I don't tell you, then, well, you'll probably choke me to death. And if I do tell you and you don't like the answer, well, then you'll probably choke me to death.'

Victor, to Penny, after Grams has stormed off in a huff: 'She always was a bad loser.'

Notes: 'We've got a demon to kill and a child to save.' *Charmed* episodes can often resemble Easter eggs – nice to look at but, once you take a bite, rather hollow inside. However, the series is frequently saved from embarrassing tweeness by its cunning take on dysfunctional family values (and, as an aside, the interplay between the sisters – which, in this episode, is at its most brilliant). This variant on the old 'adults-acting-like-children' concept looks truly dreadful on paper but, somehow, it works. It's got one of the great *Charmed* moments as the demon appears in the attic and the three, suddenly-teenage, witches see it, scream and run away. (Paige throws her shoes at the creature, rather ineffectually.) A smashing episode, full of clever ideas and some interesting depth. Oh yes, and Charisma Carpenter's in it.

Did You Know?: Baby Chris is usually played by Holly Marie Combs's son Finley Donoho.

SEASON 7: CHARRRMED

138: CHARRRMED!

3 October 2004

Writer: Cameron Litvack
Director: Mel Damski

Cast: Nick Lachey (Leslie St Claire), Jenya Lano (Inspector Sheridan), Kerr Smith (Agent Brody), Harve Presnell (Black Jack Cutting), Shelby Fenner (Carly), John Todd (Elder), Michael E Rodgers (First Mate Reznor), Sam Rubin (Movie Critic), James Patric Moran (Young Black Jack), Bre Blair (Brenda), Donna Hardy (Old Paige), Gloria LeRoy (Old Brenda), Todd Tucker (Creature Head Demon)

> The Charmed Ones discover that a 300 year old cursed pirate, Captain Black Jack Cutting, is kidnapping witches. Paige attempts to rescue an innocent and is cut by a cursed dagger that ages her dramatically. Phoebe and Piper must steal a golden chalice in order to activate the mythical Fountain of Youth to save Paige. Meanwhile, Inspector Sheridan gets some unexpected assistance from the mysterious FBI Agent Brody.

It's Witchcraft: The spell that Piper reads to open the fountain of youth begins: 'With these offerings, I call on thee, Goddess of Fertility, rise now show us the truth, give us the gift of eternal youth.'

A Little Learning is a Dangerous Thing: Leo admits that he has been seeing things and hearing voices. This, he thinks, might be the consequence of a guilty conscience over his killing of Zola (see 'A Call to Arms'). Piper feels it's more likely to represent self-doubt. In actual fact, the hallucinations are very real, and related to the 'Gathering Storm' that both the Elder and Captain Cutting mention.

Cutting tricked a witch into falling for him in the 18th Century so that she could give him the gift of immortality. He cut out her heart with the same athame that she used to curse him.

The Conspiracy Starts at the Witching Hour: Darryl has the unwelcome task of staking out the Charmed Ones with the annoyingly persistent Inspector Sheridan. Just as it seems that officialdom is about to abort Sheridan's campaign of blatant harassment on the sisters, Agent Brody from the 'Classified' section of the Department of Homeland Security arrives.

Brody is *incredibly* well-informed about the sisters – knows that they're witches and is aware of Darryl's relationship with them. He says that he's been working 'a long time' to prove his theories. Brody notes that the recent rash of missing women that Darryl has been ignoring matches a pattern that goes back for decades in Barbados, Panama, Newfoundland and New Orleans. He is also up to date enough to know that the Charmed Ones will need a golden chalice to save Paige's life but he isn't interested in catching them involved in 'minor' crimes like breaking and entering. As Sheridan pulls a gun on Phoebe and Piper at the pirates' cave, he shoots the police officer with a tranquilliser dart, telling the sisters that they 'owe' him.

In relation to the blood that Sheridan said she found in Piper's bedroom, Brody notes that it's not human – the DNA showed a triple helix, and there are significant differences in plasma, platelets and Rh factors.

Work is a Four-Letter Word: Leslie organises a 'win a date with Phoebe' competition in the *Bay Mirror* and fixes it so that he wins. Ultimately his plan is foiled, though the couple still end the episode with their lips locked together.

References: Hugely influenced by Gore Verbinski's *Pirates of the Caribbean: The Curse of the Black Pearl* – its star, Johnny Deep, is specifically mentioned. The movie critic at Phoebe's paper suggests that the Charles Laughton/Clark Gable version of *Mutiny on the Bounty* (1935) is the best pirate movie ever made. Leslie argues it isn't a pirate movie, it's a swashbuckler, and there's a big difference. Phoebe wonders if Leslie has a doctorate in pirates as well (see 'A Call to Arms'). He suggests that he grew up watching pirate movies with his father, and names *Captain Blood* (1935), *Blackbeard's Ghost* (1968) and the risibly awful Geena Davis vehicle *Cutthroat Island* (1995) amongst his favourites. He also describes Graham Chapman's and Peter Cook's *Yellowbeard* (1983) as 'a great spoof.' (The film was directed by Mel Damski ... who, completely co-incidentally, also directed this episode.) Also, *Treasure Island*; and Spanish explorer and privateer Juan Ponce de Leon (1460-1521). Visual allusions to *The Fog*; *Entrapment*; and *Moonlighting* (with the Phoebe/Leslie sequence at the end).

'You May Remember Me ...': Kerr Smith played Jack McPhee in *Dawson's Creek* and also appeared in *Lucid Day in Hell*. Harve Presnell's movies include *Saving Private Ryan*, *Fargo* and *Paint Your Wagon*. Shelby Fenner was in *Swatters* and *CSI*. Michael E Rodgers appeared in *The Patriot* and

SEASON 7: CHARRRMED

American Dreams. Sam Rubin is an entertainment reporter on *KTLA Morning News*. James Patric Moran was in *Officer Down*. Bre Blair played Stacey Twelfthmann in *Cherry Falls*. Donna Hardy's CV includes *The Truman Show* and *When Harry Met Sally*. Gloria LeRoy appeared in *Sordid Lives*, *Sid and Nancy* and *Passions*.

Logic, Let Me Introduce You to This Window: Piper suggests the Fountain of Youth it's a myth. No it isn't, as the Charmed Ones already know – see 'Nymphs Just Wanna Have Fun'. Old Paige's shoes change when the rest of her clothing doesn't. How did Agent Brody, Darryl and Sheridan get to the pirate's cave? Paige, Piper and Phoebe got there only by scrying for its location and then orbing. In previous episodes when the sisters are in the attic, whenever an exterior is shown through the attic window, it's usually a neighbourhood of Victorian houses somewhat similar to the Manor. Here, we see lots of white houses. How did Sheridan recover blood from Piper's bedroom? When she walked in, Leo knocked her unconscious immediately (see 'A Call to Arms'). She then woke up on the couch in the living room. Both demons and witches have been shown to breed with mortals and have children. So they can't have triple-helix DNA, and altered plasma and platelets. But if the blood in Piper's bedroom wasn't from a human or a demon or a witch, then ... from whom did it come? If the parrot was a ghost and could travel only at night and by fog, then how did it get to the Manor in daylight? Before Piper freezes Sheridan, the Inspector says, 'Look, if you think that this is going to get me off ...' When she is unfrozen, she continues, '... get me off your tail.' During the break-in at the museum, Phoebe clearly steps through one of the frozen lasers. And wouldn't it have been so much simpler to have got Leo to orb the chalice to Piper and Phoebe rather than for the girls to go cat-burgling? When we see the sleeping Leo, the book on his chest appears and disappears between shots.

Cruelty to Animals: Piper wants to blow up Captain Cutting's parrot but is prevented from doing so by Phoebe.

Quote/Unquote: Leo: 'The fog rolled in just before they disappeared.' Piper: 'Well, of course the fog rolled in. It's San Francisco. What?' Leo: 'Nothing. It's just I miss this.' Piper: 'Sleepless nights and endless exposition? Not me.'

Phoebe, on Sheridan: 'We're experiencing a bit of a pest problem.'

Phoebe: 'Yo-ho, hello.' Piper: 'Did you just call me a ho?'

Piper, on the Fountain of Youth: 'That's a myth.' Cutting: 'So are 300 year-old pirates who sail the high seas searching for revenge.'

SEASON 7: CHARRRMED

Notes: 'Don't you just love clichés?' *Charmed* at its silliest and most watchable. You can just imagine the writers sitting around pitching ideas for this one: '*Pirates of the Caribbean*'s really popular, so let's do an episode with pirates.' 'Only if we can have Phoebe doing the "Catherine Zeta Jones in *Entrapment*" bit as well.' 'Charrrmed!' is a fabulous example of how genuinely funny this series can be when it puts its mind to it. How they got away with Cap'n Cutting's parrot squawking 'Shiver me bitches!' is beyond belief. Great dialogue and performances. (Harve Presnell is especially good.) You can keep yer Keira Knightley, *this* is what the kids want.

139: STYX FEET UNDER

10 October 2004

Writer: Henry Alonso Myers
Director: Christopher Leitch

Cast: Nick Lachey (Leslie St Claire), Charisma Carpenter (The Seer), Kerr Smith (Agent Brody), Simon Templeman (Angel of Death), Zack Ward (Sirk), Michael Milhoan (Artie Casey), Ely Pouget (Harriet Casey), Eddie Velez (Detective), Katie Wagner (News Reporter), Tac Fitzgerald (Ben), Christopher Carroll (Older Man), Carrie CeCe Cline (Lexie), Eddie Lehler (Coroner), Beans Morocco (Elderly Man), Naveen (Doctor)

> In an effort to stop a demon on a rampage of violence against his human relatives, Paige casts a spell that inadvertently blocks all death. The Angel of Death is, needless to say, outraged, and gives the Charmed Ones an ultimatum to put things to right – whatever the consequences. Agent Brody reveals that he has been following the Halliwells for much longer than they thought, and Phoebe must deal with her feelings toward Leslie.

It's Witchcraft: Paige casts a protection spell on the innocent that she and Piper are trying to protect. With catastrophic (if vaguely amusing) consequences.

A Little Learning is a Dangerous Thing: Death alludes to the uniqueness of the present situation. People have to die in a particular order (according to the list that Death has in his possession – though this changes from time to time as events conspire to change future history). If one person doesn't die at his or her appointed time, a bottleneck is created and, if the situation is not quickly rectified, all death may cease. Which, as Death tells Piper, wouldn't be the wonderful situation she might imagine. After all, what meaning does life have without death at the end of it? For this reason, and needing to clear a large number of souls who should have already passed to the afterlife, the Angel of Death kills Piper and makes her help him. He promises that she will get her soul back once the task is complete.

The Conspiracy Starts at the Witching Hour: After Piper has been returned to her body in the morgue, she awakens to find Brody waiting for her. He tells her that he has arranged a cover story to explain her death.

SEASON 7: STYX FEET UNDER

(The story is that her death was faked as she was undercover helping him with an entrapment scenario.) In exchange for this, Brody will need the sisters' help with 'something even greater' (as previously alluded to in 'Charrrmed!').

It's a Designer Label!: Sartorial highlight of the season, if not *all* TV, ever: Paige's extremely short skirt.

References: The title alludes to the cult HBO comedy series *Six Feet Under*. There is also an allusion to *The Terminator*.

'You May Remember Me ...': Zack Ward played the Legendary Red Dog in *Almost Famous*. Michael Milhoan's CV includes *First Daughter*, *Anywhere But Here* and *3rd Rock from the Sun*. Ely Pouget was in *Curly Sue*. Eddie Velez appeared in *Traffic* and *The A-Team*. Katie Wagner's movies include *Scabber Cop II*. Christopher Carroll played Hitler in *Little Nicky*. Carrie CeCe Cline appeared in *Web Girl*. Beans Morocco was in *The American President*. Naveen appeared in *Million Dollar Baby*.

Cigarettes and Alcohol: The episode begins with Piper, on the phone, arguing about a missing shipment of beer for P^3.

Sex and Drugs and Rock n Roll: Since Phoebe slept with Leslie (see 'Charrrmed!'), she has avoided talking to him and has been discussing nothing with her sisters but demons and vanquishings.

Logic, Let Me Introduce You to This Window: How does Phoebe get from magic school to the Manor? Neither Leo or Paige could have orbed her, yet Piper and the others show no surprise when she casually walks in through the door. While Leo pulls away from Artie Casey after examining the hole in his stomach, his hand, which can be seen through the hole, should move with him; it doesn't, so it's obviously not Brian Krause's hand. Death is not supposed to be seen by mortals, but when the list that he gives to Piper appears in his hand, his shadow is cast on the man standing behind him on the sidewalk. Sirk says that he picked up a new power from everyone he killed. How did he pick up demonic powers from humans? There are no army bases in or reasonably near to San Francisco. When Death first arrives at the Manor and says people on his list have to die in order, a close-up is shown of the list, and Artie's name isn't on it in either the 'Dead' column or the 'To Die' column. Why, apart from plot contrivance, can't Leo heal Paige? He's previously been seen to have healed the sisters – and others – after they've been dead for several seconds.

SEASON 7: STYX FEET UNDER

Continuity: Death tells the sisters that he knew their sister (see 'Death Takes a Halliwell'), mother and grandmother. Phoebe has her first premonition since her active powers were removed in 'Crimes and Witch-Demeanors.' Inspector Sheridan has been transferred to another district. The Cleaners are mentioned. Leo thinks they will be reluctant to get involved in this particular adventure.

Quote/Unquote: Piper: 'We've given up a lot to make sure you have less work. I have two kids and a business, and I still find time to fight demons, too. It's not our fault you can't keep up.' Paige: 'Stop yelling at Death!'

Paige: 'Oh, no.' Piper: 'What can be more "Oh, no" than they're taking my body away for an autopsy?'

Piper: 'I'm not dead. I *am* Death. As if my life wasn't busy enough already.'

Phoebe: 'Relax, Piper's been dead before.' Leo: '*Not* on the midday news.'

Sirk: 'I'm so close to losing this foul human soul, but the Charmed Ones still thwart me.' The Seer: 'Well, they *are* the Charmed Ones, and they're pretty good with the thwarting.'

Notes: 'By messing with the grand design, they've created a bottleneck. One where death literally ceases.' Out of a morass of potentially ridiculous storylines comes a really rather classy and (s'cuse the pun) charming episode that deals with some important theoretical issues but in a moving and morally ambiguous way. Simon Templeman returns and puts in another great, world-weary performance as Death – this time taking Piper along for the ride, as he once did with Prue four years earlier. We also get further examples of Brody's opaque operating methods and some great scenes of Paige and Phoebe at their collective ditziest. Something of classic, then, continuing the upturn in quality after the early-season disaster of 'The Bare Witch Project'.

140: ONCE IN A BLUE MOON

17 October 2004

Writer: Erica Messer, Debra J Fisher
Director: John T Kretchmer

Cast: Nick Lachey (Leslie St Claire), Kerr Smith (Agent Brody), John de Lancie (Odin), T J Thyne (Danny), Joel Swetow (Alpha), Patrice Fisher (Beta), Ian Anthony Dale (Gamma), John Ross Bowie (Marcus), Carrie CeCe Cline (Lexie), Christian Stokes (Possessor Demon), Todd Tucker (Creature Head Demon)

> A rare bi-annual blue moon causes an outbreak of strangeness in San Francisco just as the girls are assigned a new Whitelighter. Agent Brody tells Paige everything he knows concerning a powerful new threat, whilst Phoebe and Leslie confess their true feelings for each other. And then, Leslie leaves.

Dreaming (As Blondie Once Said) is Free: Phoebe describes the dreams that she's been having as 'violent and painful.' It's subsequently revealed that, in fact, these are not dreams at all but latent memories of what she and her sisters were up to the night before.

It's Witchcraft: Two blue moons in one year is an occurrence that happens only once every five decades. During such times, a mystical confluence of events, coupled with natural phenomena like pre-menstrual stress, can cause the Charmed Ones to become ... different.

The Conspiracy Starts at the Witching Hour: The Avatars (see 'Sam I Am') have designs on bringing Leo into their fold, just as they once did with Cole.
Brody tells Paige everything he knows about the coming cataclysmic events – which, frankly, isn't much. 'They' – whoever 'they' are – come from ancient times, when they were all powerful (see 'Charmageddon'). Something happened and then they went away, but now they're trying to come back. Brody also reveals that they killed his parents when he was five and that's why he became a cop (see 'Ordinary Witches').

Work is a Four-Letter Word: Phoebe returns to work at the *Bay Mirror* when Leslie's contract ends and he moves to Los Angeles (see 'A Call to

Arms').

References: There are references to Creedence Clearwater Revival's 'Bad Moon Rising', whilst the title alludes to Richard Rodgers' and Lorenz Hart's much-covered 'Blue Moon', written in 1934 for the movie *Manhattan Melodrama*. There are visual and dialogue references to numerous classic werewolf films including *The Wolf Man*, *Curse of the Werewolf*, *Dr Terror's House of Horror*, *The Beast Must Die*, *The Howling* and *An American Werewolf in London*. Plus, conceptual elements shared with the *Buffy the Vampire Slayer* episode 'Phases'. Agent Brody's backstory is a curious mixture of those of Bruce Wayne and Fox Mulder.

'You May Remember Me ...': T J Thyne's CV includes *What Women Want*, *Ghost World*, *Friends*, *Angel* and *Cold Case*. Patrice Fisher appeared in *CSI* and *How High*. John Ross Bowie's movies include *Road Trip*.

Cigarettes and Alcohol: Piper is drinking wine in the opening scene when talking to her sisters.

Logic, Let Me Introduce You to This Window: Brody knows a great deal about the sisters, as this episode and previous ones have documented, yet he seemingly wasn't aware of Paige's ability to orb. It's been revealed on several occasions previously that the Elders can listen in on conversations when they're not present – is it, therefore, really a good idea for the sisters to be discussing Leo's situation? Why, exactly, did the sisters turn into wolves? One would imagine that if something like this happens once every 50 years, something related to it would have appeared in *The Book of Shadows*. When Paige grabs the ice-cream carton, it still has the cover on and there's no spoon. Then Phoebe starts talking to Paige about personal gain and, in the next shot, a close-up reveals that the cover has been removed and Paige has a spoon filled with ice-cream in her hand. When the Charmed Ones are at the magic school, the blue moon rises over San Francisco outside. It's previously been established that, wherever the school is, it's *not* in San Francisco. It's presumably not even on *Earth*.

Continuity: Phoebe gets emotional during times of PMS. She claims that Paige tends to be mean, although evidence suggests she's more afflicted by nervous energy. Piper, on the other hand, manifests her discomfort through anger. Phoebe believes in horoscopes and often uses them to aid in the writing of her advice column.

Quote/Unquote: Phoebe: 'Would you stop finishing my sentences, please?'
Leslie: Why not? They all end the same way.'

SEASON 7: ONCE IN A BLUE MOON

Paige, as the sisters prepare to imprison themselves: 'Do you think we should put some snacks in the cage?' Phoebe: 'Like what, a wildebeest?'

Odin: 'What if you turn back?' Phoebe: 'Oh, that was just the blue moon. That won't happen for another 50 years or so.' Piper: 'And by that time, we'll just be a menace to a rest home.'

Notes: 'We turn into monsters.' Very much a game of two halves. Parts of 'Once Upon a Blue Moon' are terrific. Take a bunch of old changeling clichés and having some real fun with them, add in some (possibly *Buffy*-inspired) nods to the werewolf/PMS juxtaposition and a lot of really funny dialogue, and you're three quarters of the way to a classic – particularly with John de Lancie throwing in a few acid-bombs of wit from the sidelines. Unfortunately, the Phoebe/Leslie 'will they/won't they' nonsense reaches breaking point here with a tissue-paper-thin subplot that spends the whole episode doing and saying nothing even remotely interesting. (To be fair, though, Alyssa Milano spends half the episode dutifully trying to stop her chest from falling out of an incredibly low-cut, vest-type T-shirt, so we'll be charitable and say the poor girl had her mind on other things.) Worse, Brody's introduction, which had promised great things in the previous two episodes, takes one step forward and about six sideways here as his backstory reveals nothing but evasion and empty rhetoric. Given that he is so clued up on the Charmed Ones, his rationale for becoming involved in their lives is, ultimately, disappointing.

Soundtrack: 'Taste You' by Auf Der Maur.

141: SOMEONE TO WITCH OVER ME

31 October 2004

Writer: Rob Wright
Director: Jon Paré

Cast: Drew Fuller (Chris Perry), Kerr Smith (Kyle Brody), Neil Hopkins (Sarpedon), Peter Woodward (Aku), Joel Swetow (Alpha), Ian Anthony Dale (Gamma), The Donnas (Themselves), Tommy Smeltzer (Quincy's Guardian), Deji LaRay (Firefighter), Mark Chadwick (Quincy)

> Brody and Paige discover that the demon Sarpedon is capturing innocents' Guardian Angels and using them to protect himself. Piper and Phoebe, meanwhile, encourage Leo to go on a vision quest to face his inner demons.

Dreaming (As Blondie Once Said) is Free: Leo's vision quest begins in his own past (via a clip from 'Saving Private Leo'). With Chris as his spirit guide – Chris's death represents Leo's root-pain – Leo relives the joyous moments of his recent past: Chris's conception (see 'The Courtship of Wyatt's Father'), Wyatt's birth ('The Day the Magic Died') and Chris's birth (see 'It's a Bad Bad Bad Bad World' Part 2).

However, just as Leo is at peace and ready to emerge, he's hijacked by the Avatar Alpha (see 'Sam I Am'). Alpha reveals the inevitable future for the entire Halliwell family – death. The Creature Heads, Alpha suggests, were necessary to guide Leo to the truth that lies beyond traditional notions of Good and Evil. The Avatars offer a solution. The future-Chris failed in his mission, Alpha claims. The deaths of all the people that Leo loves are pre-destined; sometimes peaceful, sometimes painful, but always inevitable, and *all* well before their time. Leo suggests that death is a merely part of life. Alpha agrees – with regard to *natural* death, at least. But not in relation to deaths caused by the pointless, eternal battle between Good and Evil. Duality is self-perpetuating, he concludes. That's why the battle has been raging since the dawn of time. There will never be a winner. With Good, there is always Evil, and visa versa, until there's nothing left. This is the real future – mutual destruction and an eternal void. There is, however, another way: utopia, a world where Good and Evil no longer exist. That is what the Avatars represent, but they will need

SEASON 7: SOMEONE TO WITCH OVER ME

Leo's help to implement it; and the help of the Charmed Ones, when they're ready. 'What's the catch?' asks Leo. Only the courage to change, replies the Avatar. Ultimately, Leo does accept Alpha's help to enable him to save both Piper's and Phoebe's lives.

It's Witchcraft: The spell Paige uses to reveal her Guardian begins: 'Show me what the evil sees, even if at lightning speeds.'

A Little Learning is a Dangerous Thing: Four people have recently miraculously escaped from fires only to die subsequently in more mundane incidents like traffic accidents. It is revealed that all mortals (even witches) are watched over by Guardian Angels, who are, for the most part, invisible to their charges. Sarpedon, having been told of the coming of a powerful force – the Avatars – that demons fear, has been stealing such Guardians for his protection. In the course of her investigation of Sarpedon, Paige's own Guardian is taken. (Without the Guardian, Paige becomes very accident-prone.)

Celerity Demons are powerful beings who can move at the speed of light and feed off lesser demons.

The Conspiracy Starts at the Witching Hour: It appears that the Avatars have been responsible for Leo's visions of the Creature Head Demon-type thing. This brings up a very important question: if the Avatars are, indeed, 'the gathering storm' that the Elders, Brody and various demons have been prophesieing, they seem far less powerful, as threats go, than, for instance, the Source.

References: The title alludes to George and Ira Gershwin's much-covered 'Someone To Watch Over Me.' The latter was also the title of a 1987 Ridley Scott movie. There are oblique references to T S Eliot's *The Hollow Men*; 'I'm a Believer' (see 'The Eyes Have It'); *Charlie's Angels*; and the Doors' 'The End'.

'You May Remember Me ...': Neil Hopkins, played Charlie's brother, Liam, in *Lost*. Mark Chadwick appeared in *Batman & Robin*. Tommy Smeltzer was in *Chill Factor*. Deji LaRay's CV includes *American Dreams* and *The Shield*.

Logic, Let Me Introduce You to This Window: In 'Styx Feet Under', it was revealed that the moment a person dies, the Angel of Death appears to escort him or her to the afterlife. However, in this episode, Piper and Phoebe are dead for a considerable amount of time before Leo revives them. The burning building at the beginning is supposed to be on the corner of Polk and Gough. These are, indeed, streets in San Francisco, but they run parallel to each other and do not meet at any point. Quincy's body, after he's been hit by the speeding truck, is remarkably unscathed. Why do the Charmed Ones need a banishing potion for the Celerity Demon, if Piper can simply blow it up as she does later on? Paige and Brody are still preparing the ingredients for the potion immediately before the attack upstairs. However, when they hear the crash and Paige orbs up, she takes a finished bottle of potion with her.

Continuity: With his new Avatar powers, Leo heals both Piper and Phoebe at the same time, and when they're dead. Enola is mentioned (see 'The Legend of Sleepy Halliwell'). Since she took Phoebe on her vision quest, Enola has graduated from magic school.

Quote/Unquote: Phoebe, to Paige: 'We don't *do* fires. Firemen do fires. We do *fireballs*.'

Phoebe, on Leo: 'Hopefully his Guardian Angels are taking care of him.' Piper: 'I don't think Angels *have* Angels, Phoebe. It's redundant.'

Phoebe: 'I guess I get a little testy when someone kills me.'

Leo: 'You can save them?' Alpha: 'We can save everyone, Leo, with your help.'

Notes: 'What do you have to lose? Your mind? Your family? Your life? You've already lost all those things, haven't you?' Hmmm. Lots of good bits in this – Brody and Paige make a very interesting team; and Leo's vision quest and his conversation with Alpha voice, pretty much, *Charmed*'s mission statement in just a handful of scenes. But ... there's something not quite right about this episode; it's almost as though, having moved all the pieces into position to reveal their overall plan for the year, the writers got nervous at the last moment and throttled back. With hindsight, many of the Avatars' actions earlier in the season make little sense now.

Soundtrack: The Donnas perform a fiery version of 'Fall Behind Me' at P^3.

Did You Know?: The opening street sequences were shot on the backlot at Paramount Studios.

142: CHARMED NOIR

14 November 2004

Writer: Curtis Kheel
Director: Michael Grossman

Cast: Kerr Smith (Kyle Brody), Bug Hall (Eddie Mullen), Joel Swetow (Alpha), Patrice Fisher (Beta), Ann Cusack (Miss Donovan), Al Sapienza (Johnny the Gent), Michael Lee Gogin (Gnome Professor), Beverly Sanders (Mrs Mullen), Chris Diamantopoulos (Inspector Davis), Sal Landi (Lieutenant Snyder), Rick Pasqualone (Lips), Dennis Flanagan (Flashback Dan), Brian David (Gangster)[74]

> Paige and Brody are accidentally drawn into an unfinished crime novel. They must elude both corrupt policeman and gangsters in pursuit of the famed Burmese Falcon. Phoebe, Piper and Leo attempt to re-write the novel to help.

A Little Learning is a Dangerous Thing: Gnomes have no natural enemies, although, as a species, they do have a tendency to piss people off.

The Conspiracy Starts at the Witching Hour: Approximately 20 years ago, Eddie and Dan Mullen, two teenage brothers who attended magic school, began writing a New York-based detective novel. Both were, unbeknown to everyone, drawn into the fiction of the novel. Dan was soon killed, but Eddie has remained trapped within the novel ever since.

Denial, Thy Name is Piper: When Leo asks Piper on a date, she's reluctant. She notes that she has spent months trying to keep Leo from falling into this psychotic abyss.

Work is a Four-Letter Word: Phoebe is currently writing a series on matchmaking for her column.

---

[74] Uncredited.

SEASON 7: CHARMED NOIR

References: A respectful parody of the *film noir* genre,[75] via similar conceits in the movie *Dead Men Don't Wear Plaid*, *Star Trek: The Next Generation*'s 'Dixon Hill' stories and the *Moonlighting* episode 'The Dream Sequence Always Rings Twice'. Also, Nancy Drew (see 'Something Wicca This Way Comes', 'Trial By Magic'); *CSI: Crime Scene Investigation*; actress Lana Turner; both versions of *The Postman Always Rings Twice* (Tay Garnett, 1946 and Bob Raefelson, 1981); *The Maltese Falcon* and its hero Sam Spade; Raymond Chandler's iconic detective Philip Marlowe; *Casablanca* ('Of all the books in all the libraries in all the world, you get sucked into this one?'); *The Burns and Allen Show* ('Say goodnight, Gracie'); *Who Framed Roger Rabbit?* ('We wrote 'em that way'); Mary-Chapin Carpenter's 'Shut Up and Kiss Me'; and Johnny Nash's 'I Can See Clearly Now' (see also 'Extreme Makeover: World Edition').

Among the books that the Gnome Professor wants to see banned from the magic school library are *The Lord of the Rings* ('Historically inaccurate'), the Harry Potter novels ('Filled with juvenile delinquents') and *The Wizard of Oz* ('Disparaging to little people. Munchkins being persecuted'). Johnny the Gent was the name of a jewel thief in *Adventures of the Junior Detection Club* by Captain W E Johns.

'You May Remember Me ...': Bug Hall's movies include *Arizona Summer*. Ann Cusack appeared in *Tank Girl*, *Stigmata* and *Grosse Point Blank*. Al Sapienza was in *The Hollywood Sign*, *Co-Ed Call Girl*, *CSI* and *The Sopranos*. Michael Lee Gogin appeared in *Fear and Loathing in Las Vegas* and *Runaway Train*. Beverly Sanders' CV includes *The Flintstones in Viva Rock Vegas*, *The Mary Tyler Moore Show* and *Kojak*. Chris Diamantopoulos appeared in *Drop Dead Roses*. Sal Landi featured in *24*, *The X-Files* and *Bulletproof*. Rick Pasqualone was in *Romy and Michele's High School Reunion* and *Friends*.

---

[75] *Film noir* (literally 'black cinema') was a term first used by French critics to describe the trend of many American crime and detective movies in the immediate post-war era, which seemed to exude an atmosphere of anxiety, pessimism and paranoia. These films, with their dark sexual politics, often cynical and world-weary male leads and *femme fatales* counter-balanced the fey optimism of much Hollywood product of the era. The violent, misogynistic, greedy perspectives of many characters in *film noir* were a metaphoric symptom of capitalist society's perceived evils, with a strong undercurrent of moral conflict. Most of the early *film noirs* were detective thrillers, often taken from adaptations of the hard-boiled pulp novels of authors like Raymond Chandler, James M Cain and Dashiell Hammett. Notable works of the genre include: *The Maltese Falcon*, *The Blue Dahlia*, *The Big Sleep*, *Double Indemnity*, *The Postman Always Rings Twice*, *The Killers*, *Build My Gallows High* (US: *Out of the Past*), *Touch of Evil*, *White Heat* and *The Naked City*. Some modern period dramas like Roman Polanski's *Chinatown* and Curtis Hanson's *LA Confidential* have attempted to capture the mood of *film noir*.

SEASON 7: CHARMED NOIR

Brian David's CV includes *Six Feet Under*.

Cigarettes and Alcohol: In the novel, Eddie smokes cigarettes, despite Paige's warning that 'Those things'll kill you.'

Logic, Let Me Introduce You to This Window: Why does the book say 'Written by the Mullen Brothers and the Halliwell Sisters?' Phoebe was the only Halliwell ever seen to write anything in it (although, to be fair, Piper did make some suggestions). Certainly, Paige did only what the plotlines created by others allowed her to. Lana Turner was, famously, a blonde – Paige looks *nothing* like her. Although no specific date is given for the events of *Crossed, Doublecrossed*, most of the novels and movies it resembles took place during the early-to-mid-1940s. However, *The Burns and Allen Show*, which is alluded to by Johnny the Gent, didn't begin until 1950. (Just to confuse matters, when the Gnome Professor expresses his expectation that the novel will be filled with violence, Paige notes that the '30s was a fabulous era.) Paige says that the Charmed Ones have never ended up in monochrome before. Well, she may not have, but Phoebe certainly has (see 'Lost and Bound').

Continuity: Miss Donovan is the magic school librarian. The Gnome Professor refers to the events of 'The Bare Witch Project.'

Quote/Unquote: Piper: 'Who would shoot a gnome? And why is the "G" silent?'

Kyle: 'Sucked into the book?' Paige: 'Don't worry, magical things happen to us all the time. But this is the first time in black and white.'

Paige, on discovering the Mullen Brothers have an investigation agency: 'They're dicks?'

Notes: 'This story can never end.' A conceptually-inspirational mixture of experimental tricks and some cunning social comment (specifically, the entire opening scene concerns attempts to stifle freedom of speech via the banning of books). 'Charmed Noir' includes enough genre clichés to satisfy any passing devotee of '40s Hollywood and *looks* incredible. The episode's many plus points far outweigh a few aesthetic drawbacks and a couple of huge logic flaws. One of the best episodes of the season.

Soundtrack: J Peter Robinson's stunning period-style score is one of the best in the series' history.

143: THERE'S SOMETHING ABOUT LEO

21 November 2004

Writer: Natalie Antoci, Scott Lipsey
Director: Derek Johansen

Cast: Kerr Smith (Kyle Brody), Joel Swetow (Avatar Alpha), Patrice Fisher (Avatar Beta), Kevin Alejandro (Malvoc), Brad Hawkins (Vassen), Elizabeth Dennehy (Sandra), Nicholas Davidoff (Sokol Leader), Jaren Ryan Shaw (Sokol Guard), David Leitch (Innocent)

> Leo confesses to Piper that he's an Avatar, despite the strong objections of the others of his kind, who all believe that Piper should find out on her own. Phoebe and Paige, meanwhile, ask Kyle for help, but his reaction proves disastrous.

Dreaming (As Blondie Once Said) is Free: Technically, three-quarters of the episode constitutes one entire dream sequence.

A Little Learning is a Dangerous Thing: According to Alpha, reversing time can be very dangerous.

The Conspiracy Starts at the Witching Hour: Subsequent to the events of 'Charrrmed!', Darryl notes that Inspector Sheridan has disappeared off the face of the Earth.

A group of invisible demons (of indeterminate origins) have been killing innocents as part of complex plot to gain control of a section of San Francisco. The Charmed Ones inadvertently aid them in this when they frame a rival demon collective (the Sokol) as the perpetrator. Leo eventually reverses time to put right the mistakes.

References: The title refers to the Farrelly Brothers' scatological comedy *There's Something About Mary* (1998). Also, allusions to *Twin Peaks*; and *A Few Good Men*.

'You May Remember Me ...': Brad Hawkins appeared in *American Dreams* and *VR Troopers*. Kevin Alejandro was in *24* and *Dr Vegas*. David Leitch's CV includes *The Savage* and *Martial Law*. Jared Ryan Shaw was the boxing

SEASON 7: THERE'S SOMETHING ABOUT LEO

consultant on *The Contender*.

Logic, Let Me Introduce You to This Window: Piper isn't in the least bit suspicious about Leo's suddenly-acquired knowledge of how to defeat the invisible demons, or of his ability to shoot lightning bolts from his hands. In 'Déjà Vu All Over Again', Phoebe could sense time-loops, but she seems oblivious to one here. While Piper is first frozen, her hand changes position at least once. When Leo tells Piper that he's an Avatar, Piper has her back to the camera and is putting an orange basket on the table. In a subsequent shot, from a different angle, she's still doing the same thing. When the invisible demons attack the Charmed Ones, they remain invisible until the dye is thrown, at which point they're revealed to be holding energy balls. Yet Piper previously noted that they had to become visible in order to attack.

Continuity: Piper suggests that Phoebe's 'I'm covering something' look hasn't worked since the sixth grade. The Source is mentioned in relation to how much power the Avatars possess. The Avatars, like witches, appear to have an equivalent of a 'personal gain' clause. One of the sisters' ancestors, Beatrice Warren, had only one leg. Kyle Brody reveals that his parents discovered a battle that happened 5000 years earlier over humanity's very future. They fought the Avatars and were killed by them.

Quote/Unquote: Phoebe: 'The good thing about getting up so early is how much you could get done. Already today, I've made demon dye, I've saved an innocent, I've e-mailed in my column ... If it wasn't for sleep deprivation, I'd be okay.'

Phoebe, after Leo drops his bombshell: 'Do you think he's telling the truth?' Piper: 'It would be a *really* stupid lie if he wasn't, don't you think?'

Notes: 'What aren't you telling me?' A fascinating idea, but one that only partially works, due to a needlessly complicated script. Who, exactly, are the demons? What is their purpose? How do they know so much about the Charmed Ones? Matters aren't helped by having yet more bluff and evasion over Brody's background. Brian Krause gives his best performance in a long while, however, and there are several key moments in the developing Leo story-arc. It's just a shame somebody couldn't have tightened a few loose ends.

Soundtrack: 'Lie to Me' by Stacy Wilde.

SEASON 7: WITCHNESS PROTECTION

144: WITCHNESS PROTECTION

28 November 2004

Writer: Jeannine Renshaw
Director: David Jackson

Cast: Kerr Smith (Kyle Brody), Charisma Carpenter (Kyra), Oded Fehr (Zankou), Joel Swetow (Alpha), John de Lancie (Odin), Patrice Fisher (Beta), Ian Anthony Dale (Gamma), Jeyna Lano (Sheridan), Corey Stoll (Photographer), Matt Winston (Manny), Sierra Parks (Young Girl), David Ury (Shapeshifter), Dex Elliot Sanders (Swarm King), Sierra Miller (Vulture Demon), Vince Lozano (Thrull Demon), Ryan Bradford Hanson (Young Wyatt), Billy Beck (Demonic Wizard)

> The Charmed Ones are asked to protect the Seer, Kyra, who wants to make a deal with the Elders to become human in exchange for what she knows about the Avatars. Darryl, with Kyra's and Phoebe's help, finds Inspector Sheridan at last.

A Little Learning is a Dangerous Thing: Kyra tells Leo that she has seen her own death and that there were no babes involved. Phoebe later shares this vision. It eventually comes true (albeit in a location different from the one that Phoebe saw.)

The Conspiracy Starts at the Witching Hour: Darryl notes that when he confronted Brody on the subject of Sheridan's disappearance (see 'Charrrmed!'), Brody claimed that the Inspector left to work for a top secret taskforce and that was why there was no official record of her transfer. Darryl, however, does not believe the agent, and tells Phoebe that Sheridan's apartment, records and files have all been cleaned out – it was, he concludes, a very professional job. Subsequently, Darryl finds Sheridan in a coma at the Hawbrooke Mental Hospital. Brody had apparently told Paige at some stage what he'd done to Sheridan, causing an instant schism to develop between Paige and her sisters.
Many years earlier, the Source banished the demon Zankou because he was too powerful.

It's a Designer Label!: It's the *complete* Charisma Show this week, with honours even between her revealing purple outfit and the pink, fluffy dress she wears when preparing for her humanity.

SEASON 7: WITCHNESS PROTECTION

References: Allusions to *The Simpsons*; *Rugrats*; and Don Henley's 'New York Minute'.

'You May Remember Me ...': Oded Fehr's movies include *The Mummy* and *Deuce Bigalow: Male Gigolo*. Vince Lozano appeared in *Pirates of the Caribbean: The Curse of the Black Pearl*, *Dark Wolf* and *Alvarez & Cruz*, the latter of which he also wrote and directed. Matt Winston's CV includes *The Cape*, *The Amati Girls*, *Enterprise* and *Fight Club*.

Sex and Drugs and Rock n Roll: Kyra claims that, after dinner, Kyle and Paige are going to have a 'really, *really* great' time. Judging from the evidence of Paige's bum going up and down in the background as Phoebe tries to ring her sister, that is indeed exactly what happens.

Logic, Let Me Introduce You to This Window: Kyra received a premonition of her own death. Why, therefore, doesn't she at least attempt to transport herself away during Zankou's attack? Leo previously mentioned that she could 'shimmer'. When Phoebe and Kyra are talking to Leo, he points at them with his right hand as he's leaving. Next, the camera switches angle, and Leo is seen orbing away, but it's now his left hand that he's pointing with.

Continuity: Piper and Phoebe discover that Leo is now an Avatar and, at the end of the episode, are introduced to Alpha, Beta and Gamma. They are both keen to talk to the Avatars after Phoebe's vision of an Avatar-created utopian future. Kyra observes that Sandra has been making Darryl sleep on the couch for the last week and that's why he's so crotchety. However, she believes that Sandra will come round as soon as Darryl buys her some of the marzipan she likes so much. Brody claims that he can't remember the last time he had a cooked meal. He's allergic to egg-plant. The Furies (see 'Hell Hath No Fury') and the Grimlocks (see 'Blind-Sided') are amongst the demons who have special reason to hate Kyra.

Future Continuity: In the utopian-future vision that Phoebe has, after the Avatars have destroyed all the demons, she will have a daughter.

Quote/Unquote: Darryl, on Sheridan: 'Someone does not want me to find her. And I think that someone just went upstairs with your sister.' Phoebe: 'Forget happy endings, we can't even have a happy beginning.'
Piper: 'Why in hell would a powerful demon want to be made human?' Kyra: '"Hell" being the operative word. As in, "I live there and it *sucks*."'
Phoebe: 'So, what I'm gathering is pretty much every demon in this book hates you?' Kyra: 'Pretty much. Which is sad, because they're my

family. Well, I mean, it *would* be sad if I had feelings.'

Zankou: 'Hello, sugar.' Kyra: 'Did I call you that ever? What I meant to say was "Hello, swirling particles of scum."'

Notes: 'I saw the most beautiful thing ever. And the most terrible.' One of the best *Charmed* episodes in *years*, 'Witchness Protection' clicks effortlessly into gear the moment that Charisma Carpenter – one of the finest deliverers of a pithy quip that American television has produced in the last two decades – describes Piper as 'the surly one!' From then, it just can't fail on any level. The episode is littered with astonishing one-liners, clever plot-twists and intricate shifts of character motivation (suddenly, the Avatars seem like the good guys and Brody, a very shady and untrustworthy character). This a genuinely *great* stuff, and an emphatic retort to those in the media and on the Internet who still fail to grasp the show's inherent comedy genius.

Did You Know?: The WB used the title 'Charmed, with Charisma' in trailers for this episode.

145: ORDINARY WITCHES

16 January 2005

Writer: Mark Wilding
Director: Jonathan West

Cast: Kerr Smith (Kyle Brody), Oded Fehr (Zankou), Max Perlich (Laygan), Joel Swetow (Avatar Alpha), Patrice Fisher (Avatar Beta), Jon Hamm (Jack Brody), Jessica Steen (Ruth Brody), Brian Howe (Ronnie), Anne Dudek (Denise), Bruce Gray (Elder), Elizabeth Dennehy (Sandra), T Lopez (Ronnie's Girlfriend), Peter Woodward (Aku), Ricky Kurtz (Young Kyle), Brian D Johnson (Customs Agent), James Wellington (Craps Dealer), Lorin McCraley (Kazi), Michael Malze (Zyke)

> Piper attempts to switch her powers with Phoebe's to allow her to see a vision of the utopian world that the Avatars promise. Zankou interferes and causes the two sisters' powers to be transferred into the bodies of a pair of innocent bystanders. Brody's pathological desires prompt Paige to take him on a journey into the past to learn the truth about his parents' deaths.

It's Witchcraft: Piper and Phoebe use the same 'switching powers' spell that Piper previously used in 'Love Hurts' to swap her own with Leo's.

A Little Learning is a Dangerous Thing: Leo uses memory dust to remove Ronnie's and Denise's memories of the events of this episode. This is the first time that the dust has been mentioned since 'Trial By Magic'.

The Conspiracy Starts at the Witching Hour: Zankou is mobilising the Underworld against the Avatars. He suggests that without the Charmed Ones, the Avatars do not have the combined power to remake the world.

References: The episode's title alludes to Robert Redford's *Ordinary People* (1980). Paige says that she's always wanted to see *Raiders of the Lost Ark*. Kyle's favourite story as a child was *The Mummy's Curse*. He also mentions King Tut. Headlines in the December 1981 *New York Monitor* include: PRESIDENT REAGAN ANNOUNCES SANCTIONS AGAINST USSR; AMNESTY BRINGS CHALLENGING OPPORTUNITY FOR SOLIDARITY; and BOYCOTT HAS LITTLE EFFECT.

SEASON 7: ORDINARY WITCHES

'You May Remember Me ...': Max Perlich played Angel's guru Whistler in *Buffy the Vampire Slayer* and appeared in *Ferris Bueller's Day Off*, *Drugstore Cowboys* and *Blow*. Jon Hamm was in *We Were Soldiers*. Jessica Steen's CV includes *Armageddon*, *Murder One* and *Stargate SG-1*. Brian Howe appeared in *Catch Me If You Can* and *Law & Order*. Anne Dudek played Sara in *The Naughty Lady* and Tiffany in *White Chicks*. Bruce Gray was the President in *Spy Hard*. Brian D Johnson appeared in *Cold Case* and *CSI*. Michael Maize was in *Angel*. Lorin McCraley's movies include *My Favourite Martian*. James Wellington appeared in *Las Vegas*.

Logic, Let Me Introduce You to This Window: A loose strand of Holly Marie Combs's hair appears and disappears between distance shots and close-ups in one scene. When, exactly, did Paige learn that Leo was an Avatar? This can only have occurred off-screen and between the last episode and this, which is a hell of a contrivance for the writers to pull. How can Piper and Phoebe get to Lake Tahoe so quickly without anybody to orb them there? (Paige is in the past, and Leo has orbed to see the Elders.) Those New York streets look *remarkably* like redressed San Francisco streets. When Phoebe tells Ronnie that she's a witch, she speaks so loudly that she can hardly fail to have been overheard by someone in the area. Denise freezes both Phoebe and Ronnie, but shouldn't be able to: either the freezing shouldn't work on Phoebe, because she's a good witch, or it shouldn't work on Ronnie, because he has Phoebe's powers. In 'Witchness Protection', Phoebe showed Odin all about the Avatars via her vision. Why, then, do the rest of the Elders have a problem with Leo being an Avatar? How did Ronnie and Denise manage to control their powers so quickly? It took the Charmed Ones at least a few episodes fully to grasp the nature and limits of their emerging powers. Phoebe still cannot call premonitions on command all the time (and it took her several years to be able to do so at all). The last time a mortal gained access to the sisters' powers, it sent him mad (see 'Astral Monkey').

Continuity: The Avatars' portal transports Kyle and Paige not only through time but also through space, to New York on 28 December 1981, the day of his parents' deaths. Jack and Ruth Brody were actually killed not by Avatars, as Kyle has always believed, but by demons attempting to obtain the vials of Avatar poison. This occurred at JFK Airport at 7:52 pm. The Elders, despite their considerable efforts, are unable to kill Leo now that he is an Avatar. Beta suggests that if even one of the Avatars were to die, it could weaken the collective to the point where they are unable to implement their planned changes.

Quote/Unquote: Phoebe: 'I was just trying to get you to see what I saw.'

Piper: 'Yes, and now I can see that we are going to die, and I don't need your powers for that.'

Phoebe, after Ronnie has been thrown out of his apartment by his unfaithful girlfriend: 'You don't know me, but I know you've been seeing certain things.' Ronnie: 'Don't tell me *you're* sleeping with her, too?'

Denise: 'You guys fight demons here all the time, don't you?' Piper: 'Pretty much. Why?' Denise: 'See, I always thought that you just threw a bunch of wild parties. You know, things breaking, people screaming. I had no idea.' Piper: 'Well, at least now you know why we never invited you.'

Phoebe: 'Without powers, I don't know how we're gonna convince them to give them back.' Piper: 'We'll jump off that bridge when we get to it.'

Notes: 'It's one thing to save the world from evil every week. It's another thing entirely to change the world just because we can.' The elegant opening sequence – burning toast as a metaphor for the changes that the Avatars may bring to the world – is one of the best things *Charmed* has ever attempted; a subtle and clever moment of depth a million miles removed from many casual viewers' perceptions of the show. Unfortunately, from there onwards, the episode falls apart. Not that it's bad, exactly, but the Phoebe and Piper subplot is given too little room to breathe, whilst the clunky grafting on of a more complete backstory for Kyle comes across as little more than pale window dressing – despite it being beautifully acted. Ultimately, 'Ordinary Witches' tries too hard to do too much.

Did You Know?: The original US broadcast of this episode was followed by a tsunami relief appeal by Alyssa Milano on behalf of UNICEF.

146: EXTREME MAKEOVER: WORLD EDITION

23 January 2005

Writer: Cameron Litvak
Director: LeVar Burton

Cast: Kerr Smith (Kyle Brody), Oded Fehr (Zankou), Max Perlich (Laygan), Joel Swetow (Avatar Alpha), Patrice Fisher (Avatar Beta), Ian Anthony Dale (Avatar Gamma), Rebecca Balding (Elise Rothman), Lorin McCraley (Kazi), Michael Malze (Zyke), John Hillard (Celebrity Demon #3), Gino Montesinos (Van Driver), Alex Avant (Car Driver), Jordan Murphy (Patron #1), Laura Kelly (Patron #2)

> As the Avatars plan to transform the world into their envisioned utopia. Zankou kidnaps Kyle Brody and seeks the agent's help to cast a paranoia spell on the Charmed Ones.

It's Witchcraft: The Charmed Ones are said to have already vanquished most of the high-level demons when Leo, Piper and Phoebe return to magic school after destroying Grimlock eggs.

A Little Learning is a Dangerous Thing: Alpha explains that the Avatars' spell will put the entire world to sleep long enough for them to erase the universal mind-set of duality and create their utopia. A planetary alignment must be in place before they can make the changes.
    Zankou claims to have the gift of prescience.

The Conspiracy Starts at the Witching Hour: Zankou gives Kyle a paranoia crystal to use on Paige. They both hope this will stop the sisters from helping the Avatars.

Work is a Four-Letter Word: Phoebe believes that she will be out of a job as soon as the Avatars make their changes. After all, she reasons, how much advice will a world without conflict actually require? Phoebe's *Bay Mirror* colleagues include Michelle, Donald and Greg (whom Phoebe has never really got along with, a situation she expects to change soon).

It's a Designer Label!: Paige's bosom-revealing red top.

SEASON 7: EXTREME MAKEOVER: WORLD EDITION

References: The title alludes to the reality TV show *Extreme Makeover: Home Edition*. There are dialogue allusions to Hammill on Trial's 'Bill Hicks'; Johnny Nash's 'I Can See Clearly Now' ('A bright new sunshiney day'); *Star Trek II: The Wrath of Khan*; and Shakespeare's *Troilus and Cressida* (with references to the Trojan Horse). Conceptually, the episode owes a debt to *Village of the Damned* (and its source novel, John Wyndham's *The Midwich Cuckoos*), plus *The X-Files* episode 'Je Souhaite'. Stock footage includes shots of famous landmarks in London (the Houses of Parliament), Moscow (the Kremlin and Red Square) and Tokyo. A poster for the – apparently fictitious – movie *She's Come Unplugged* is briefly glimpsed as Leo and Phoebe orb back to the Manor.

'You May Remember Me ...': Alex Avant's CV includes *Hair Show* and *First Daughter*.

Behind the Camera: LeVar Burton is a two-time TV legend, as Kunte Kinte in *Roots* and as Geordi La Forge in *Star Trek: The Next Generation* and several spin-offs and movies.

Logic, Let Me Introduce You to This Window: Piper suggests that if the sisters alter the tracking spell they used to locate the Source (see 'Charmed and Dangerous'), it should point to Zankou's location. Why would it do that? There's no obvious physical link between the Source and Zankou. More importantly, that particular spell worked on the previous occasion only because the Source had stolen the Charmed Ones' powers. There's a page in *The Book of Shadows* concerning the Elders. Why, exactly? When Paige is at magic school, she's wearing a jacket that mysteriously disappears between shots. Do all the demons in the *Charmed* universe live in San Francisco? That appears to be the only location that the sisters bother to look in for straggler demons to vanquish when the rest of the world is asleep. According to this episode, the Avatars' plan – at least, as far as the Charmed Ones are concerned – is to fashion a world where no demons exist, the sun always shines and everyone is really together and mellow and spouts hippie nonsense about love, peace and harmony. Man. That's *exactly* the alternate reality the girls saw for themselves in 'It's a Bad Bad Bad Bad World', and we know how horrific *that* ended up being. So why are they going along with this utopian malarkey? In the sequence during which the population of San Francisco fall asleep in the streets, the building used as New York's Columbia University in the previous episode is clearly visible. Despite Phoebe asking a very specific and pertinent question, it's never explained how all those people flying helicopters and aeroplanes around the world survive the Avatar-induced sleep.

SEASON 7: EXTREME MAKEOVER: WORLD EDITION

Classic *Double Entendre*: Zankou: 'When the Avatar turns up to give her one, that's when you release the potion.'

Continuity: After the Avatars effect their changes to the world, the sisters retain their memories of previous battles with demons. And Paige retains the knowledge that Kyle is dead – although she doesn't exactly seem devastated about it. Brody is killed by Beta when he attempts to release the last vial of potion. Beta, however, is too late to prevent its release, and the potion subsequently kills her as well. However, this does not overly affect the Avatars' plans, as Zankou and Brody hoped that it would.

Kyle tells Paige that he's spent 10 years learning who the Avatars really are. Zankou subsequently kills two of the demons – Kazi and Zyke – who were responsible for the death of Kyle's parents (see 'Ordinary Witches'). Zankou does this, he notes, as a favour, which he expects Kyle to repay. Elise's former husband was 'a schmuck' named James L Connors.

Quote/Unquote: Zankou: 'Remind me why I tolerate you.' Laygan: 'Because you're running low on demons?'

Piper, to Paige: 'I'm angsty, Phoebe's nostalgic, and you're scared. *That's* how we do things.' And: 'I'm tired of sleeping with one eye open, wondering which demon is finally gonna get me.'

Notes: 'Without evil, there can be no good.' A story about myopia in all its forms, 'Extreme Makeover: World Edition' manages to keep various plot-strands going when they threaten to unravel and, generally, does a magnificent job of setting up the most radical shift in the series' focus in 140-odd episodes. It's not without flaws, but it's beautifully shot (particularly that sequence of San Francisco coming to standstill as everyone goes to sleep in the streets). And, in Zankou, we've got the best returning villain since Julian McMahon left the show.

Soundtrack: 'Bring it On' by Seal.

147: CHARMAGEDDON

30 January 2005

Writer: Henry Alonso Myers
Director: John T Kretchmer

Cast: Oded Fehr (Zankou), Max Perlich (Laygan), Joel Swetow (Avatar Alpha), Ian Anthony Dale (Avatar Gamma), Rebecca Balding (Elise Rothman), Jeremy Kent Jackson (Minion), Tom Virtue (Angry Man), Kerr Smith (Kyle Brody), Jordan Murphy (Patron #1), Laura Kelly (Patron #2), Gino Montesinos (Van Driver), Reggie Jordan (Cop), Alex Avant (Car Driver), René Hamilton (Wife)

> Leo discovers that the Avatars' conflict-free world comes with one significant drawback – the complete loss of free will for the human race. He joins Zankou in a suicidal effort to reverse the changes that have already been set in motion. But they face a formidable obstacle in returning the world to a battle between Good and Evil: the Charmed Ones.

A Little Learning is a Dangerous Thing: Despite the apparent success of the Avatars' plan, Leo is conflicted, particularly over Paige's lack of obvious emotion at Kyle's death.

The Conspiracy Starts at the Witching Hour: As alluded to by Brody earlier in the season, the Avatars have tried to create a good-and-evil-free utopia before, several thousand years earlier in Egypt. They were, on that occasion, more or less successful, and remade the world. But the people weren't told the cost, and they ultimately rose up against the Avatars and stopped them. Alpha indicates that, one day, the world will be ready for what the Avatars have to offer.

Work is a Four-Letter Word: One of Phoebe's *Bay Mirror* colleagues, Oliver (a young man with a lot of anger), seems to have been an early victim of the Avatars' purge.

References: Allusions to *Hamlet*; *Macbeth*; and *The Prisoner*.

Cigarettes and Alcohol: There's plenty of red stuff being drunk at Piper's party.

SEASON 7: CHARMAGEDDON

'You May Remember Me …': Tom Virtue played the title role in *Even Stevens*. René Hamilton played Theresa in *Gilmore Girls*.

Sex and Drugs and Rock n Roll: Elise shows Phoebe the day's newspaper, which is, she notes, the thinnest copy they've ever produced. No crime, no corruption, no scandals – it's like everybody took a happy pill. She notes that it's a good job the obituaries are up, otherwise the paper would consist of one sheet.

Logic, Let Me Introduce You to This Window: For an Elder, Leo has a surprisingly poor grasp of Egyptology, having to be told that the 'dog-faced guy' is Anubis. It also proves he's never watched *Stargate SG-1*. Phoebe pours an entire bowlful of ingredients into a pie crust. Then, moments later, she picks up the, suddenly empty, crust and puts it in the oven. The opening shot shows cars taking turns at going through an intersection (traffic lights appear to be no longer necessary). Yet, later in the same scene, a man is being given a ticket for running a red light. Where, exactly, did the sisters mix the potion with which they threaten the Avatars? Possibly in the pyramid, but would all the necessary ingredients be there to hand? During the scene in the kitchen, Piper has a bowl of chocolate chips on her left. Subsequently this appears on her right. Then it turns up on her left again. Phoebe sees all the deaths that have impacted her life during her vision … except for her mother's.

Continuity: When Phoebe touches *The Book Of Shadows*, she sees the following flashbacks: Andy's demise in 'Déjà Vu All Over Again', Grams' fall downstairs in 'PreWitched', Miles's death in 'A Witch in Time', Piper's – temporary – death in 'All Hell Breaks Loose', Prue's funeral in 'Charmed Again' Part 1 (although Prue herself is, once again, absent from any of the flashbacks – she's represented by her gravestone), Chris's death in 'It's a Bad Bad Bad Bad World' Part 2 and Cole being vanquished in 'Long Live the Queen'. Piper isn't sure that she knows how to socialise with 'normal' people. Following his noble death in the previous episode, the Elders reward Brody with a new life as a Whitelighter. He tells Paige that they may meet again.

Quote/Unquote: Zankou: 'You know, deep down, that something's very wrong with the world, Leo, something you never foresaw in your myopic zeal to make it all better. People don't have free will anymore. The Avatars now dictate their destinies – and *you* let it happen.'

Paige: 'Why did they do this?' Phoebe: 'To give us what we wanted … or, what we *thought* we wanted.'

SEASON 7: CHARMAGEDDON

Notes: 'It was not our intention to deceive; we merely gave you the world you asked for.' One of the few occasions when *Charmed* really does bite off more than it can comfortably chew. 'Charmageddon' features some tremendous ideas and lovely acting, but it really has far too much crammed in to work effectively. Never mind a two-parter, this could have done with covering about five episodes. Good points abound, with the amusing opening and closing scenes being particular highlights; and Oded Fehr is terrific as Zankou. It's all just a bit too frantic for its own good. And the complete negation of Kyle Brody's selfless act in the previous episode is a bit of a let-down, too.

Soundtrack: 'This is Your Life' by Switchfoot.

148: CARPE DEMON

13 February 2005

Writer: Curtis Kheel
Director: Stuart Gillard

Cast: Billy Zane (Drake), Sebastian Roché (The Sorcerer), Ann Cusack (Ms Donovan), Jenya Lano (Inspector Sheridan), Kurt Fuller (John Norman), Elizabeth Dennehy (Sandra), Bruce Gray (Kheel), Tara Platt (Muse), Kevin Daniels (Rathbone), Scott Anthony Leet (Flynn), Erica Shaffer (Anna Woods), Jayden Lund (Tall Man/Little John), Denver Dow Ridge (Man #2), Anthony DeSando (Office Manager)

>Paige interviews potential new professors for the magic school. One of the candidates, Drake, is an ex-demon who has made a deal with a sorcerer to become human. Leo, meanwhile, faces the wrath of the Elders.

A Little Learning is a Dangerous Thing: Ms Donovan learned to astral project from her predecessor, Ms Winterbourne (who is said to be currently on sabbatical). Paige notes that they have satellite TV at magic school.

The Conspiracy Starts at the Witching Hour: The Avatars have 'put the world back', as Phoebe asked them to. Everyone seems slightly meaner than normal but, apart from that ...

One of Brody's first acts as a Whitelighter was to bring Inspector Sheridan out of her coma. However, he also performed some manipulation on her brain, so that she forgot about the events that led up to her incapacity. Darryl now has the unwelcome task of trying to keep Sheridan away from anything that might trigger the recovery of her hidden memories.

Work is a Four-Letter Word: The current manager of P^3, Rick, is about to get married.

References: Dancer Gene Kelly; *Cyrano de Bergerac*; *Pocahontas*; *Hair*; and *Macbeth*.

'You May Remember Me ...': Billy Zane's CV includes *Back to the Future,*

SEASON 7: CARPE DEMON

Dead Calm, *Titanic*, *Twin Peaks* and *Hendrix*. Sebastian Roché appeared in *Odyssey 5*, *Alias* and *CSI*. Erica Shaffer's movies include *The Socratic Method*.

Logic, Let Me Introduce You to This Window: Kevin Daniels provides the worst British screen accent heard since Keanu Reeves's in *Bram Stoker's Dracula*. When Piper puts Chris on the changing table, the baby is wearing a hat. When she picks him up, it's disappeared. However, it's back on his head in the next shot. What security officer would leave the door of an armoured truck, loaded with cash, open with people standing beside it? Why is Phoebe surprised that Drake knows she was married to a demon? Cole was the Source and she was Queen of the Underworld; it doesn't get much more famous than that in the demonic community. And, of course, we have yet another crap American take on *Robin Hood*. Still, it's only about the twelfth of those, so why be over-critical here? And a special word for Billy Zane, who had to say 'Stand and deliver' and managed to keep a straight face whilst he did so. Top man. The manacles used on Ms Donovan are clearly far too big for her, and she has to hold them on her wrists when she's talking to the Sorcerer.

Continuity: Drake was a demon who, through his love of literature, came to love humanity and, as a consequence, has never killed an innocent. (He is, though, mentioned in *The Book of Shadows* as a demon with the power to fire thermal blasts that melt people's skin in seconds – a Power of Three spell will vanquish him.) Almost a year ago, he made a deal with a Sorcerer to become human for twelve months. He also retained his powers, but if he uses them before the year is up, the Sorcerer will get them and he will spend eternity in Purgatory. He now has just a fortnight of the year left to go. He has studied at the Julliard, performed musical comedy on Broadway and penned a memoir, which he intends to complete on his deathbed.

Phoebe and Paige are immediately charmed by him. Piper, slightly less so.

Motors: Drake rides a rather bashed-about Triumph motorbike.

Quote/Unquote: Drake, to Piper: '[Paige] needs to trust her instincts and believe in herself again. [Phoebe] needs to remember what it feels like to do good, to love. And you, honey, you're just plain mean.'

Piper, to Phoebe: 'How many times have I told you not to play dress-up with demons?'

Drake: 'You had lots of experience with demons who were human. You married one, didn't you?' Phoebe: 'Yes. And divorced. How did you know that?' Drake: 'Gossip.'

SEASON 7: CARPE DEMON

Drake: 'Some of the world's greatest lovers were drawn to each other during an epic conflict. Admittedly, most of them were doomed, but they still found the romance in it. So why can't you?'

Notes: 'Tell me, what do you know about Robin Hood?' For God's sake, somebody keep *Charmed* and British mythical icons on separate continents. The Robin Hood stuff is so bad it's actually quite funny. For all the wrong reasons, of course. There's quite a bit wrong with 'Carpe Demon' elsewhere – particularly a dreadfully pointless two minute scene of pure exposition between Piper and Phoebe early on that manages to name-check about 20 characters and half-a-dozen major storylines. Listen, if people aren't watching the show by this stage, they're not gonna catch up now. It's a shame, actually, because, for the first time in a long time, Phoebe gets a relationship that actually has some spark of charisma to it.

149: SHOW GHOULS

20 February 2005

Writers: Erica Messer, Debra J Fisher, Rob Wright
Director: Mel Damski

Cast: Billy Zane (Drake Robin), David Anders (Count Roget), Rebecca Balding (Elise Rothman), Charles Robinson (Mike), Lisa Arturo (Michelle), Jim Cody Williams (Toulouse), Kristen Ariza (Marie), Todd Mason Covert (Father), Anna Bikales (April), Vanessa Vander Pluym (Inex/Gypsy Fortune Teller), Eric Cohen (Piano Player), Muttalib J Ibrahim (George), Kristin Bryant (Waitress), Andrew M Chuckerman (Drake's Pianist)[76]

> When Darryl's mentor, Mike, is possessed by the spirit of a man killed in a fire 106 years earlier, Phoebe and Drake use magic to transport themselves back in time to the cabaret club where this incident happened. Due to the machinations of the evil Count Roget, however, they find themselves stuck in the past.Piper, meanwhile, convinces Leo that they need to take a family vacation.

It's Witchcraft: The spell that Drake uses to get himself and Phoebe back to the past begins: 'Free our souls from their shells, see where the lost spirits dwell, long enough to find their pain, quick enough to return again.'

A Little Learning is a Dangerous Thing: Drake owns a very useful book called *Possessions, Confessions and Ghostly Obsessions: A Demon's Guide to Everything Magical*. He used to sell these, door-to-door, to other demons.

The Conspiracy Starts at the Witching Hour: Drake tells Phoebe and Paige that lost souls are spirits unable to move on because of spiritual confusion. This happens when souls die together in a sudden, violent manner (like, for instance, in the fires of Gomorrah or in the Great Flood). When several souls die at once, the good ones can't move on because the bad ones hold them back, and vice versa. They become lost, stuck in-between their respective afterlives, unaware of their tragic state.

In reality, the Club Fantome's owner, Count Roget, made a deal with a demon, Sargon, a trader of souls, to curse everyone in the club (including himself). Seemingly, Roget preferred the idea of spending eternity stuck in

---

[76] Uncredited.

a time-loop than the alternative of being damned to Hell. Although not mentioned in dialogue, the newspaper article that Paige and Phoebe reads suggests that Roget was bankrupt, thus explaining why he made a deal with Sargon. The Charmed Ones vanquished Sargon five years earlier (presumably in an off-screen adventure).

Work is a Four-Letter Word: *Cosmopolitan* magazine are doing an interview and a photo-shoot with Phoebe. In the end, Phoebe is too busy helping Drake investigate the Club Fantome, so she suggests that Paige use a glamour to impersonate her. This she does, and – apart from attributing much of Phoebe's success to her younger sister – she makes a pretty good job of it.

Drake is described by Paige as the magic school's 'visiting lecturer in Advanced Magical Compositions.'

References: The plot, concerning time-loops, is yet another to be influenced by *Groundhog Day* (see 'Déjà Vu All Over Again'). Also, allusions to Jules Verne's *Around the World in 80 Days*; *Ghost* (Roget being attacked by the shadow-demons); and the eruption of Vesuvius, which engulfed the town of Pompeii and the surrouonding area in 79 AD. The headline from the 1899 issue of the *Daily Clarion* is: DIABOLICAL DEATH AT CLUB FANTOME.

'You May Remember Me …': David Anders played Julian Stark in *Alias*. Charles Robinson was Mac in *Night Court*. Kristen Ariva appeared in *Friends*. Lisa Arturo played Amber in *American Pie 2*. Vanessa Vander Pluym appeared in *Grounded For Life*. Jim Cody Williams was in *Bill & Ted's Excellent Adventure*. Kristin Byrant appeared in *The West Wing*.

Cigarettes and Alcohol: When Count Roget spots Drake and Phoebe and realises that they are out of place in the Club, he tells Toulouse to make them comfortable – with champagne for the lady and a fine cigar from the man.

Logic, Let Me Introduce You to This Window: Drake mentions visiting the 1890s. However, he wasn't in the room when Phoebe discovered that Mike had been possessed by someone from that particular era, and she certainly doesn't mention the fact when he arrives. Given that the time-loop was supposed to dissolve when the person holding the other souls prisoner was no longer present, why doesn't it do so immediately when Roget first escapes and possesses Drake? Additionally, Mike doesn't recover from his possession by George when Roget escapes. During the final scene, even though the on-screen band consists of only a pianist and a trumpet player, the soundtrack features an obvious (and extensive) string-section. Seemingly, in the *Charmed* universe, the human soul is a bright-glowy-shimmering thing. The story that Paige is telling April and her father in the opening sequence appears to involve a wizard who taught at magic school. Weren't all wizards – bar one – supposed to have died out eons ago (see 'We're Off to See the Wizard')?

Continuity: Piper, Leo and the boys are due to go on holiday – an 'around the world in eighty orbs' affair that will include Italy and Hong Kong (where Piper suggests Leo can pick up some bootleg DVDs) amongst other destinations. They set off for the Leaning Tower of Pisa and appear to have got as far as Venice (they're about to take a gondola ride) when Paige calls them back. Mike brought Darryl into the police service. Mike has since retired and is currently working as a security guard in a San Francisco jewellery store. The Elders have still not yet made a decision on what to do with Leo (see 'Chamageddon', 'The Seven Year Witch').

Quote/Unquote: Leo, on Paige and Piper: 'They made us this big send-off dinner last night.' Piper: 'Oh, please. They ordered pizza!'

Piper: 'What's my middle name?' Phoebe: 'Surly?' Piper: '*That's* my girl.' And, Piper: 'What are we supposed to do?' Phoebe: 'What you always do. *Worry!*'

Drake: 'Paige, there's a lot more to life than work. There's adventure.' Paige: 'Really? I wouldn't know.'

Notes: 'If that's not possession, what is?' Another almost-decent episode that is sadly ruined by aesthetic elements and by a script that – whilst it has some nice ideas – is disappointingly short on anything resembling logic. However, once again Billy Zane and Alyssa Milano make a terrific partnership.

Soundtrack: Butterfly Boucher's 'I Can't Make Me' features during the opening sequence. At Club Fantome, the pianist performs songs like 'A Bicycle Made for Two' and 'When the Saints Go Marching In'. At the climax, Billy Zane sings Andrew Chuckerman's 'Everything's Kind Of Good' in P^3.

150: THE SEVEN YEAR WITCH

10 April 2005

Writer: Jeannine Renshaw
Director: Michael Grossman

Cast: Julian McMahon (Cole Turner), Billy Zane (Drake Robin), Kathleen Wilhoite (Nadine), John De Lancie (Odin), Elizabeth Dennehy (Sandra), David Wells (Car Driver), Brett Rice (Sheriff), Stacy Reed (Suzanne), Thomas Lumberg Jr (Uniform).

> Piper is attacked by a Thorn Demon and lapses into a coma. She hovers in a limbo between life and death, with an interesting companion – Cole. He wants to help restore Phoebe's seemingly lost faith in love, and (as a side issue) help Piper back to the real world so that she can be with Leo. Phoebe, Paige and Drake – who is having his final day as a human – attempt to locate Leo. But Leo's memory has been wiped by the Elders as part of a test in which he can choose his own true destiny; either to become a mortal with a wife and family, or to remain an Elder and forget ever knowing the Charmed Ones.

A Little Loving is a Dangerous Thing: Phoebe feels that the Halliwell women are predestined to be 'spinsters for the greater good.'

The Conspiracy Starts at the Witching Hour: Piper asks Cole what he actually *is* – a ghost, a demon or just a nightmare? Cole replies that he is none of the above. They are in the cosmic void between life and death.

References: The title alludes to Billy Wilder's 1955 comedy *The Seven Year Itch* starring Marilyn Monroe. Also, allusions to Scott MacKenzie's '(If You're Going to) San Francisco'; the Taj Mahal; Niagara Falls; Tim Rice and Andrew Lloyd Webber's 'Don't Cry For Me Argentina'; Tennyson's *In Memoriam* (see 'Heartbreak City', 'Exit Strategy'); and the Biblical parable of the Prodigal Son (as told by Jesus in Luke 15). Drake likens Leo's and Piper's epic love to those of Romeo and Juliet, Antony and Cleopatra and Brad Pitt and Jennifer Aniston. 'All tragedies, can I mention?' notes Piper. Among several Shakespeare allusions are *Romeo and Juliet* ('She doth teach the torches to burn bright', 'Parting is such sweet sorrow') and Sonnet 60 ('Like as the waves make towards the pebbled shore/so do our minutes

SEASON 7: THE SEVEN YEAR WITCH

hasten to their end').

'You May Remember Me ...': Kathleen Wilhoite played Betsy in *Private School*, Patricia in *Cop Rock*, Chloe in *ER* and Rosalie in *L.A. Law* and appeared in *Angel Heart*, *Nurse Betty*, *24* and *Pay it Forward*. She's also a singer/songwriter; her ballad 'Wish We Never Met' features prominently in an episode of *Buffy the Vampire Slayer*. David Wells's movies include *Society* and *Basic Instinct*, and he played the Cheese Man in *Buffy the Vampire Slayer*. Brett Rice appeared in *Kalifornia*.

Logic, Let Me Introduce You to This Window: When Piper asks Leo if he's upset at having lost his powers, Leo replies that this is what he's been hoping for since he first met her. He has seemingly forgotten that he previously *had* his wings clipped when he healed Piper without permission in 'Awakened'. He was then unhappy about this because he could no longer help the sisters, and asked the Elders to give him his powers back – which they did in 'Murphy's Luck'. Phoebe pulls off her gloves as she talks to her sisters. A moment later, they're back on.

When Drake puts Piper's unconscious body on the couch, her legs move several times during the scene. Piper tells Cole that she was partly responsible for his being vanquished. No, she wasn't; it was Phoebe (and an alternate-universe Phoebe at that) who threw the potion that killed Cole in 'Centennial Charmed'. Perhaps Piper is referring to Cole's *first* vanquishing (in 'Long Live the Queen'), since she makes several references to Cole being 'the Source of All Evil.' But, as we know, Cole ultimately survived this (see 'Witch Way Now?'.) In 'Carpe Demon', Drake told Phoebe he had just two weeks to live. Here, Phoebe describes having known him for three weeks. How does the diner waitress know that Leo left in a 'big rig'? She certainly wasn't outside the diner when Leo climbed on board – in fact, no-one was there to see him leave with Odin. Leo's 'fall from grace' involves him plummeting, face-first, hundreds of feet from the top of the Golden Gate Bridge to the road beneath. One would imagine this would result in some pretty serious injuries, if not instant death. Instead, he's left with just a rather nasty graze on his face.

Continuity: Cole is trapped for eternity in limbo as a punishment for his sins. (By whom? It's a question well worth asking.) Phoebe wonders how Drake walked into her life at exactly the right time. We subsequently discover that it was actually Cole who was responsible for Drake's mortality. (Cole introduced Drake to the Sorcerer seen in 'Carpe Demon', with whom he made his bargain.) And that Cole orchestrated Drake and Phoebe meeting as part of huge and very complex plan to save Phoebe from giving up on love altogether – Cole has come to terms with his fate,

SEASON 7: THE SEVEN YEAR WITCH

he tells Drake at the episode's climax, especially as he now knows that it won't be one that Phoebe will share. Cole reminds Piper that he has known her for a long time, referring to Prue and to his attendance at Piper's and Leo's wedding (see 'Just Harried'). As part of Drake's last day, he and Phoebe have visited the Alps.

This episode marks the final appearance of Drake, who dies and, as a reward for his various good deeds (including this one), appears to have secured a place in Heaven. Leo, with some sneaky intervention by Odin, initially chooses to become an Elder and forsake his human life, but later 'falls from grace' and returns to Piper and his family, without any powers as either a Whitelighter or an Elder. Wyatt is capable of healing people, as he demonstrates on his mother. Darryl mentions Inspector Sheridan.

Quote/Unquote: Piper: 'Oh, no. Am I dead *again*?'

Piper, to Cole: 'I don't know which is worse, the fact that I'm dying or that, apparently, I'm gonna be spending my last moments with *you*.' And: 'The last Halliwell that trusted you ended up bearing your demonic spawn!'

Cole: 'I'm the one who's here for all eternity.' Piper: 'Paying penance for your evil past?' Cole: 'You always were the smart one.' Piper: 'Cut the crap!' Cole: 'And *direct*. I miss that. Actually, no, I don't.'

Drake's last words to Phoebe: 'Think of me when you dance.'

Notes: 'Love never dies.' Celebration time again and, as with the 100th episode, this one works almost entirely because of Julian McMahon's presence. The story starts rather flat and dull, and for the first 10 minutes, there's genuinely very little on offer – aside from a couple of nicely self-aware lines of dialogue. Then it becomes 'the Cole and Piper show' and gets *much* more interesting. There's also another fine turn from Billy Zane – what a pity a way couldn't have been found to keep him on for a bit longer. The theme of redemption is something that *Charmed* has flirted with over the years, but this is by far the best example – with Cole finally coming to realise that the only thing he cares more about than himself is Phoebe and her ultimate happiness. Not perfect, then, but very entertaining – *Charmed*'s story in microcosm.

SEASON 7: SCRY HARD

151: SCRY HARD

17 April 2005

Writer: Andy Reaser, Doug E James
Director: Derek Johansen

Cast: Oded Fehr (Zankou), Rebecca Balding (Elise Rothman), Mailon Rivera (Craven), Peter Siragusa (Bauer), Patrick Bristow (Fashion Editor), Collective Soul (Themselves), David Goryl (Ad Exec), Julian Bailey (Copy Editor), Tom Schmid (Phil), Jim O'Brien (Waiter), Mark Kubr (Burly Demon)[77]

> In a somewhat overcomplicated plan to lure the Charmed Ones from the Manor so that he can open the Spiritual Nexus and release the Shadow, Zankou sends a demon to attack Leo. To protect his parents, Wyatt shrinks Leo and Piper and traps them inside a dolls' house in the attic. Phoebe, meanwhile, is left in charge of the evening edition of the *Bay Mirror*.

It's Witchcraft: The 'I am light' spell, previously used in 'Is There A Woogy in the House?', 'Witch Trial' and 'The Importance of Being Phoebe', is heard again. The 'calling a lost witch' spell is also mentioned (see 'Charmed Again Part 1').

The Conspiracy Starts at the Witching Hour: Zankou plans to open the Spiritual Nexus beneath the Manor and release the Shadow (see 'Is There a Woogy in the House?') whilst none of the sisters are present and the Manor is 'in evil's grasp.' He believes that he will then be able to harness ultimate power. Leo realises that if the Shadow is released whilst both good and evil elements are present it will seek 'neutral territory', in this case, the only human in the vicinity – Leo himself. With the power of the Shadow, Leo is able to overcome Zankou, although the demon escapes to return another day (see 'Something Wicca This Way Goes').

Work is a Four-Letter Word: Paige and Phoebe are both having a bad day at work. In Paige's case, the preparation of curriculum timetable schedules at magic school depresses her, and she is frankly relieved to have a family emergency as a distraction. (At the end of the episode, much to Paige's

---

[77] Uncredited.

further relief, Leo accepts an offer to take over the running of the magic school from her.) Elise, meanwhile, leaves an (at first, desperately) out-of-her-depth Phoebe in charge of the evening edition of the newspaper. In the event, Phoebe copes admirably with her new responsibilities and still finds time to sneak away quietly a couple of times to help save her sister.

It's a Designer Label!: Check out that little red nothing that Paige is almost wearing in the final scene. 'Hope you guys got a discount on all the leather,' Phoebe tells a couple of the uniformly-dressed demons.

References: The title alludes to John McTiernan's classic action movie *Die Hard*. The episode owes an obvious debt to both *Land of the Giants* and *The Borrowers*. A B-52's poster can be seen in P³.

'You May Remember Me ...': Patrick Bristow played Peter Barnes in *Ellen* and appeared in *Curb Your Enthusiasm*. Tom Schmid was in *The Bold and the Beautiful*. Julian Bailey's CV includes *For the People*. Dave Goryl appeared in *There's Something About Mary*. Mailon Rivera was in *The Shield* and *Issues*.

Cigarettes and Alcohol: As a potential solution to some oversold advertising space in the paper, Phoebe suggests that the advertising editor shrink the ads and, if the advertisers complain, simply send them a bottle of Cristal champagne. On Elise's tab.

Sex and Drugs and Rock n Roll: Having left Phoebe in the lurch at the newspaper, Elise is finally tracked down whilst sharing a cocktail with her (supposedly sick) assistant, Richard Dillard. The pair are subsequently spotted at P³, dancing like some uncle and auntie embarrassing themselves at a family wedding.

Logic, Let Me Introduce You to This Window: Would a small electronic device like Phoebe's cellphone really explode in sparks after being stomped upon? The dolls' house is said to be an 'almost perfect' replica of the Manor. However, the sides of it certainly don't match those of the real house. Piper and Leo mention on at least three occasions that Leo can no longer self-heal; but when could he *ever* heal himself? It was established as early as 'Love Hurts', and repeated on numerous occasions thereafter, that Whitelighters can't do this. (However, see 'Saving Private Leo' and 'Sam I Am' for some variations.)

Continuity: Leo is having problems adjusting to life without powers and, to keep his mind occupied, he has done lots of obsessive rearranging around the Manor. Piper describes Leo as 'practically a walking *Book of Shadows.*' Zankou finds what appears to be Piper's diary, and reads a description of her feelings of hopelessness and isolation when Prue died.

Quote/Unquote: Paige, when Phoebe's cellphone rings as they are hiding from Zankou: 'Will you shut that freakin' thing off?' Phoebe: 'I'm sorry, but you gotta admire the range, huh?'

Piper: 'You can't self-heal anymore. Hunting demons is too dangerous.' Leo: 'You can't self-heal either. It's never stopped you.' Piper: 'But I can *blow things up.*'

Leo, asking Piper to stitch his wound: 'You're the one who said improvise.' Piper: 'Since when does *anybody* listen to me?'

Leo, concerning Zankou tapping the Nexus: 'We're not going to let that happen.' Piper: 'How? We're three inches tall.'

Notes: 'I can't believe we've been miniature for two hours and demons have taken over the house.' Ultimately far too inconsequential to deliver fully on the many points in its favour, 'Scry Hard' is almost a casebook example of the average *Charmed* episode: it's got quite a clever little plot; the actors seem to be having a good time; there are several really funny lines of dialogue; and, logically, it holds together until you start to poke at it with a stick – at which point, it comes to pieces in your hands. There isn't enough depth, diversity and strangeness for it to acquire any more levels as such – there are no metaphors or allegories at work. Here, what you see is pretty much what you get. And what you get is, actually, really entertaining.

Soundtrack: The episode opens with Dido's 'Sand in My Shoe'. Later, Collective Soul perform 'Better Now' at P^3.

152: LITTLE BOX OF HORRORS

24 April 2005

Writer: Cameron Litvack
Director: Jon Paré

Cast: Brooke Nevin (Hope), Elizabeth Dennehy (Sandra), Michelle Hurd (Katya), Hayley DuMond (Nina), Shani Pride (Darcy), Don Swayze (Lucius), Steve Bean (Roger), Stacy Barnhisel (Linda), Greg Lindsay (Trey), Sammi Hanratty (Wendy), Kevin R Kelly (Father)

> The Charmed Ones attempt to recover Pandora's Box when this mythical item falls into the hands of a shapeshifting demon who intends to open it and fill the world with sorrow. Paige's Whitelighter powers require a focus, whilst Leo and Piper argue over how best to raise Wyatt.

It's Witchcraft: Nina confirms a long-held suspicion – everyone in the magical community is aware of the Charmed Ones. Piper adds that this is starting to become a problem.

A Little Learning is a Dangerous Thing: Sandra mentions the 'grand design' (see 'Charmed Again'), noting that if a human were to open Pandora's Box, then that is part of humanity's free will. However, the Elders *certainly* don't want a demon opening it. The Box itself is entrusted to the Guardians who, like the Charmed Ones, are chosen beings, and part of a magical lineage. The Box moves to its next Guardian only when the previous one dies.

The Conspiracy Starts at the Witching Hour: Kayta, a shapeshifter, used to work for a demonic Dark Lord, but has since gone rogue. She wishes to impress Zankou by opening Pandora's Box and unleashing its contents – plagues, famines, sorrow and misery – on an unsuspecting world.

Work is a Four-Letter Word: To help bring some clarity and focus to her life, the Elders give Paige the task of helping a Whitelighter-to-be, and she finds herself trapped in an elevator with several likely candidates. However, having saved at least one life, she is subsequently told by Sandra that, actually, the Whitelighter she was helping was herself.

SEASON 7: LITTLE BOX OF HORRORS

References: The title alludes to Roger Corman's celebrated 1960 trash-classic *The Little Shop of Horrors*. In Greek mythology, Pandora was the first woman, created by Zeus as part of a punishment on mankind for Prometheus giving them the gift of fire. Due to her curiosity concerning the contents of a mysterious box, she opened it, unleashing all of the horrors inside. However, one thing was left within the box – hope. The impressive opening fight sequence between Nina and Kayta is a blatant homage to *The Matrix*. When Nina describes the Guardians as a magical lineage into which in 'every generation a girl is born' she *very narrowly* avoids a direct quotation from *Buffy the Vampire Slayer*. Also, allusions to *The Good, the Bad and the Ugly*; *Mr Mom*; Bob Dylan's 'Only a Pawn in their Game'; and 'Mockingbird' (see 'Sense and Sense Ability').

'You May Remember Me ...': Brooke Nevin played Nikki Hudson in *The 4400*, Missy Carrow in *Guilty Hearts* and Claudia in *Seriously Weird*. Hayley DuMond's movies include *Raptor Island*, *Hello Girls* and *US Seals*. Michelle Hurd was Monique Jeffries in *Law & Order: Special Victims Unit* and Fire in *Justice League of America*. Don Swayze appeared in *Evasive Action*, *Sexual Malice* and *Carnivàle*. Shani Pride played Jasmine in *Love Don't Cost a Thing*. Sammi Hanratty was in *Passions*. Stacy Barnhisel's CV includes *The Shield* and *CSI*. Greg Lindsay appeared in *Hang Time*. Steve Bean was in *Blast from the Past*. Kevin R Kelly featured in *Boston Legal*.

Logic, Let Me Introduce You to This Window: The bruise and two cuts on Nina's face appear and disappear between shots with mind-numbing regularity during her conversation with Phoebe and Piper. What, exactly, is the deal with Phoebe's Minnie Mouse haircut? Did somebody *really* think it looked cool? The computers and monitors in Hope's dorm room are not connected to anything. Moreover, the one glimpsed behind her when she's on the telephone isn't even a computer, it's merely an unused ATX case. Note that Hope has exactly the same *She's Come Unplugged* poster on her bedroom wall as was previously seen on the bus shelter in 'Extreme Makeover ... World Edition'.

A close-up of Kayta's foot in the Underworld, supposedly walking on a stone floor, reveals that it's actually cunningly disguised carpet. When Paige is sitting on the couch with one hand on her head, Phoebe gives her a coffee mug and she starts to drink, whilst still holding her other hand to her head. The shot subsequently switches angle, and both her hands are now on the cup. Piper and Phoebe find a copy of *The Complete Encyclopedia Of Demons* at magic school, which proves to be very useful. What a pity that they haven't had *that* to supplement the occasionally unhelpful *The Book of Shadows* for the previous seven years. Piper notes that there is still a demon on the loose and that: '... as long as *he* is, the more we're all gonna

SEASON 7: LITTLE BOX OF HORRORS

be affected.' Surely Kayta's a *she*?

In Greek mythology, Pandora's Box was *not* given to Prometheus, as Nina suggests, it was actually given to Pandora's husband, Epimetheus, Prometheus's brother. Paige's demonstration of how to perform CPR includes a suggestion that her helper should put his hands together 'on the xyphoid process.' This should *never* be done, as it may cause serious liver or spleen damage. Guardians exist, it is stated, to protect the Box from being opened by demons, but both Katya and Lucius seemed unable to open the box anyway. When Hope reopens the box at the episode's climax and takes back all the sorrows released, shouldn't she also be taking all the sorrows that existed prior to the Box being opened in this episode? Indeed, shouldn't this mean that, temporarily at least, the world is without any misery at all?

'All the evils in the world' is visualised as a large black cloud of wriggly stuff.

Continuity: Piper notes that since Excalibur is real (see 'Sword and the City'), she's not really surprised that Pandora's Box is also. Wyatt is currently going through a magical equivalent of the 'terrible twos' syndrome. He has begun to orb himself and his toys around at will.

Quote/Unquote: Phoebe, on Paige's headache: 'Maybe it's psychosomatic.' Paige slaps Phoebe's face. Phoebe: 'What was that for?' Paige: 'Does *that* seem psychosomatic to you?'

Nina, to Hope: 'You've come into possession of something more powerful than you've ever known.' Piper: 'Okay, I was trying a less intimidating tack ...'

Hope: 'You're both calm, like this kind of stuff happens every day.' Piper: 'Actually, it does.'

Darcy: 'Will somebody please tell me what the hell is going on here?' Hope: 'That's her.'

Notes: 'This is not good *at all*,' notes an unusually surly Piper at one point, but – for once – she's dead wrong. 'Little Box of Horrors', despite some flaws (Michelle Hurd's character is too much of a cliché to be truly menacing and Brooke Nevin's performance is all over the place), is actually a cracking episode full of conceptual depth and some perceptive allegorical ideas. Katya's keynote speech to Hope about how the concept of a 'greater purpose' in the action and reaction of everyday life is fundamentally flawed, could almost be a direct challenge to one of *Charmed*'s central themes – that helping others is its own reward. While this is essentially a story about 'hope' in all its forms (note Phoebe's conversation with Piper on exactly that subject), there's also a pointed essay on 'freedom versus responsibility' that runs right through the subplots involving Hope, Leo and, most obviously, Paige. *Charmed* at its most philosophical and cautiously optimistic. Terrific stuff.

Soundtrack: The episode begins with the Swiss-American Federation Club Mix of Sarah Brightman's 'Free' played over stock-shots of San Francisco landmarks.

153: FREAKY PHOEBE

1 May 2005

Writer: Mark Wilding
Director: Michael Grossman

Cast: Jenya Lano (Inspector Sheridan), Seamus Dever (Mitchell Haines), Suzanne Krull (Imara), Eric Winzenried (Lantos), Alan Wilder (Dr Randall), Rebecca Balding (Elise Rothman), Frank Novak (Councilman Worker), Ralph Meyering Jr (Judge Hendricks), Will Collyer (Lawrence), Antonio D Charity (Minion Guard), Russell Edge (First Security Guard), Dean Cudworth (Cop), Scott Roth (Inspector Ryan), Cassandra McCormick (Woman in Wreck)[78]

> A wicked sorceress performs some body-swap trickery that leaves Phoebe caged in the Underworld. Paige, meanwhile, faces a problem when her new charge, Mitchell, refuses her help.

It's Witchcraft: Considered to be little more than a hag by most upper-level demons, Imara dreams of the power and beauty denied to her in the Underworld. She is a master of spells and incantations, and according to *The Book of Shadows* her ambitions make her dangerous.

The spell that Paige and Piper cast to bring Phoebe's soul back to her body begins: 'Lock of hair completes our goal, to help us reclaim our sister's soul. Banish this demon, spare no pain, bring Phoebe back from the ghostly plane.'

The Conspiracy Starts at the Witching Hour: A soul-swapping demon, the hideously ugly Imara has a plan to weaken Zankou by assassinating his lieutenants, many of whom have been strategically placed in powerful positions. These include Daleek (posing as a Councilman), Benzor (a judge) and Linson. For her plan to work, Imara needs the impersonate one of the Charmed Ones. She has been formulating this scheme for many months and stole all Zankou's intelligence materials on the sisters.

Work is a Four-Letter Word: Mitchell stopped using witchcraft some time earlier, after his fiancée, Jennifer, was killed by demons who were after him.

---

[78] Uncredited.

SEASON 7: FREAKY PHOEBE

It's a Designer Label!: Two staggering highlights – Phoebe's slinky boots of evil and Paige's delightful green dress in the coda. Phoebe notes that she recently spent $250 on a haircut.

References: The title (and aspects of the plot) allude to Gary Nelson's 1977 body-swap comedy *Freaky Friday* (remade in 2004). There are dialogue allusions to Google; *Little Red Riding Hood*; *The Flash*; and Carly Simon's 'You're So Vain'.

'You May Remember Me …': Suzanne Krull appeared in *Stripping for Jesus, Go, Buffy the Vampire Slayer* and *Sam and Mike*, the latter of which she also wrote. Seamus Dever was in *She's No Angel*. Ralph Meyering's CV includes *The West Wing*, *The American President* and *Born Bad*. Eric Winzenreid appeared in *Jay and Silent Bob Strike Back*. Alan Wilder's films include *Kiss the Girls*. Dean Cudworth was in *24*. Will Collyer appeared in *Jack & Bobby*. Ali Costello's movies include *Bottom's Up*. Antonio D Charity featured in *The Salon* and *Law & Order*. Cassandra McCormick is a stunt woman whose TV series include *24, Alias, Angel* (as Amy Acker's stunt-double) and *Buffy the Vampire Slayer* (as Emma Caulfield's double).

Logic, Let Me Introduce You to This Window: How does Leo know that Paige's charge is a man before she actually tells him? Since when do any demons have a soul? Possessing one was, surely, what made Drake so unique? At P^3, when the demon attacks, Piper instinctively raises both her hands. Their position subsequently changes when the camera angle does. Leo suggests that the sisters didn't want anything to do with their powers when he first met them (circa 'Thank You for Not Morphing'). That's a rather Stalinist rewriting of season one continuity – only Piper ever really had any problems with deciding if she wanted her powers or not. Phoebe, in particular, was always *very* keen on the idea. On a similar note, Paige repeatedly says that Mitchell is her first charge as a Whitelighter. She has forgotten that she's already had one other – her father, in 'Sam I Am'. And she gave almost the same speech that she gives to Mitchell when she helped Melissa, the future Whitelighter, in 'Siren Song'. Elise notes that Phoebe's column has never run into legal problems. Wasn't Phoebe being sued over advice she gave in 'The Importance of Being Phoebe'? At what point did *The Book of Shadows* stop being able to sense when one of the sisters is possessed by evil? Piper, apparently, fails to notice that Phoebe has become a staggering narcissist. Changing clothes three times in a couple of hours is extreme, even by Phoebe's standards.

Paige tells Mitchell that she used magic to go back in time and attempt to 'fix' her parents' death. That's not even a remotely accurate description of the events of 'A Paige From the Past'. After Piper freezes everyone in the

SEASON 7: FREAKY PHOEBE

Councilman's office, then vanquishes him, she and Phoebe leave instead of returning to their positions and unfreezing the room. To those who were frozen, it would surely seem as though Piper and Phoebe had suddenly vanished. How didn't the security camera reveal what had really happened? It's previously been well established that such devices are immune to the effects of Piper's time freezing (see 'Blind Sided', 'Witches in Tights'). The hair that Mitchell pulls from Phoebe's head is clearly fake. Piper notes that Imara won't let them close enough to cut her hair. Why doesn't Piper simply freeze her?

Phoebe has a Bachelors degree, which she says took her four years studying to acquire. However, as we know, she began her most recent stint in college in 'Awakened' and graduated in 'Sin Francisco' a little over a year later. There were references to her having previously attended – and then dropped out of – college before the series began, but her age in 'Something Wicca This Way Comes' (22) means it's unlikely that she'd spent three years in further education by that stage. 'PreWitched' certainly doesn't appear to show a Phoebe who is currently in college, despite taking place during a period when she should be.

When Phoebe asks if the demon who attacked Piper had 'a long coat and greasy hair,' Piper says nothing to suggest otherwise, despite the fact that Lantos, although he had a long coat, was bald. Sheridan is onto the case of the missing Councilman remarkably quickly. Piper and Phoebe have arrived back at the Manor within an hour of their visit to vanquish him (established by Phoebe's comments about needing to change her clothes). Sheridan arrives just a moment afterwards, having had time to be called to the scene, investigate it *and* obtain a still frame of Piper and Phoebe from the security cameras.

Continuity: Paige gets her first official charge as a Whitelighter and, with some guidance from Leo, persuades him not to give up using his powers. Phoebe decides to return to college (again) to obtain a graduate degree in psychology. The episode takes place 'a couple of weeks' after Sheridan met Phoebe during the events of 'Carpe Demon'. Paige mentions that memory dust (see 'Trial By Magic') was used on Sheridan after Brody put her in a coma (see 'Witchness Protection'). Darryl is said to be 'out of town taking some personal time.'

Cruelty to Demons: Among some rather questionable S&M allusions in the episode, there's the implication that the Imara deliberately scars her pretty handmaidens' faces for the sole reason that they are more beautiful than she.

Quote/Unquote: Leo: 'You're a Whitelighter.' Paige: 'I'm also a chick in her

SEASON 7: FREAKY PHOEBE

20s ... I don't have time for this.'

Phoebe: 'You want me to have a life, don't you?' Piper: 'If you *must*.'

Imara: 'Damn, that was my favourite minion!'

Piper: 'What happened to the woman who said her readers didn't care about credentials?' Phoebe: 'As a future psychologist, I can honestly say that I ...' Paige: '... was swimming in a big bag of denial?'

Notes: 'She took over Phoebe's body to kill demons. It's what Phoebe does!' A rather bland and inconsequential variant on a traditional telefantasy staple. Suzanne Krull is, frankly, the best thing about the episode – eye-rollingly over-the-top when playing Imara and managing to sound (if not look) just like Phoebe after the body swap. The rest of the episode feels like auto-pilot material, however, with some phoned-in performances and infuriatingly 'So what?' subplots (the Paige one, especially). A major disappointment.

Soundtrack: 'Be The Girl' by Aslyn and 'Me Against The World' by Simple Plan.

154: IMAGINARY FIENDS

8 May 2005

Writer: Henry Alonso Myers
Director: Jonathan West

Cast: Wesley A Ramsey (Adult Wyatt), Marcus Chait (Vicus), Billy Kay (Hugo), Susan Santiago (Ms Henderson), Christina Carlisi (Professor Slotkin), Kristopher and Jason Simmons (Wyatt Halliwell)

> Wyatt's new imaginary friend is, in reality, a demon – Vicus – who is trying to gain the boy's trust as part of a plan to turn him evil. Piper creates a spell in an attempt to understand her son's needs but, inadvertently, conjures a twentysomething Wyatt from the future.

It's Witchcraft: In an effort to discover the truth behind Wyatt's increasingly solitary nature (and unable to come up with a rhyme for the word 'communicate'), Piper casts a spell that begins: 'Help this mother understand, the thoughts inside her little man, even though his mouth be quiet, let us hear his inner-Wyatt.' This has the effect of bringing a rather boyish-looking 25-year-old Wyatt back from the future. Once he becomes evil, Piper and Leo try a series of spells to reverse the effect (including 'Evil taints what was once held dear, remove this curse away from here'), none of which works. Leo eventually manages to reverse the effects by regaining Young-Wyatt's trust. Then, another spell is used to return Adult-Wyatt to the future ('Son in the future, son in the past, seeing anew what once had passed, return him now from whence he came, right when he left, all now the same'.)

The Conspiracy Starts at the Witching Hour: A series of demon attacks take place in the Manor whenever the telephone rings. Paige, for one, believes that Wyatt may be subconsciously responsible. In actual fact, the demon behind the attacks is Vicus, who preys on magical children and turns them evil. He does so by gaining their trust and cursing an object in their possession. The curse works incrementally over a long period of time so that the children gradually travel to the dark side and add their powers to the Collective. As a consequence of being freed from a lifetime of repressed morality, Adult-Wyatt becomes the long-haired, bearded Evil-Adult-Wyatt previously glimpsed in 'Chris Crossed' and 'It's a Bad Bad Bad Bad World'.

SEASON 7: IMAGINARY FIENDS

A Little Learning is a Dangerous Thing: Phoebe asks her psychology professor about Wyatt's communication difficulties, and a lengthy discussion on the subject of imaginary friends follows. However, when Phoebe begins to write down some of Professor Slotkin's comments, the Professor notes that previous week they discussed Lorenz's theories of imprinting, and a few days later she read a simplified version in Phoebe's column. She therefore imagines that they're actually discussing the following week's content. In vain, Phoebe protests that, no, this really *does* concern her two year old nephew, and that the reason she's taking the class is that she wants to be a better columnist and to understand human behaviour. Slotkin notes that she's spent years studying psychology and that she will be damned if she's going to allow Phoebe to steal a few cheap soundbites for her column.

Subsequently, Phoebe delivers an impressive paper on imaginary friends, to which Slotkin gives due praise – it is not a shallow, pop-psych examination of the subject, as Slotkin expected, but something that, despite it's questionable use of Coburg's moral stages, is quite insightful.

References: Allusions to *Back to the Future*; *Hamlet*; and William Cowper's *Olney Hymns* ('Mysterious Ways'). There are several references to Sigmund Freud.

'You May Remember Me ...': Marcus Chait appeared in *Million Dollar Baby*. Billy Kay played Scott in *Halloween: Resurrection*. Susan Santiago's CV includes *The Milagro of Boyle Heights* and *CSI*. Christina Carlisi was in *The Division* and *Six Feet Under*. Juliette Tinelle appeared in *ER*.

Logic, Let Me Introduce You to This Window: Why does Adult-Wyatt have an English accent when he's evil, but an American one when he isn't? What kind of message are you sending out to your friends across the Atlantic, America?! Adult-Wyatt should not have been able to use his powers whilst in the past – as established in several previous stories starting with 'That 70s Episode'. When they are hugging each other during the final scene, Holly Marie Combs's and Wes Ramsey's hand positions change a couple of times along with the camera angle.

Continuity: Wyatt is currently attending the Robin Blake Pre-school. There are references to him having previously conjured a dragon (see 'Forget Me ... Not') and a demon who kidnapped him ('Cheaper By the Coven'). 'I tried to change the world for you,' Wyatt is told by Leo (see 'Charmageddon'). One of Paige's charges is a New Zealand Maori.

Future Continuity: There is nothing in Adult-Wyatt's actions or anything he says to suggest that anything particularly bad is going to happen to any of the Halliwells during the next 20 years – apart from an unfortunate incident of his brother swallowing a marble. All would appear to be still alive, although it's only Leo to whom Wyatt makes a specific comment about how he will look in the future. (He's going to get somewhat greyer and a touch more rotund.) However, Wyatt does drop a couple of heavy hints to his mother and aunts: Piper will become more of an optimist, Paige will teach Wyatt about being a Whitelighter, and Phoebe will have the child that she has dreamed about for so long. Wyatt – as one would perhaps expect from the son of a Whitelighter and a witch – seems to have grown up to be the most powerful Halliwell of all. When vanquishing demons, he channels enormous power through his hands. Evil-Adult-Wyatt notes that his parents were not the sort of people who hit their children. (Piper believes that spanking is barbaric.) He also claims to have always hated magic school.

Quote/Unquote: Paige: 'Right, I'm up to speed. Sorry, it's just hard, you know, juggling new charges and demon fighting. I'm a little scattered.' Piper: 'And that's different *how*, exactly?'

Phoebe, introduced to Adult-Wyatt: 'Spell backfire?' Paige: 'How'd you guess?'

Piper: 'Are you telling me our child is evil? *Again!*' And: 'I can't just sit here and let my son corrupt himself.'

Notes: 'This is gonna be *so* confusing.' The message of this episode is that some problems cannot be solved by magic and require more obviously human solutions. It's an interesting message for a series like *Charmed* to put out, particularly in a story that includes such obvious fantasy elements as time paradoxes and the like. 'Imaginary Fiends' doesn't quite work, for a number of, mostly aesthetic, reasons, although it must be said that the acting is particularly good. However, it's a brave and imaginative attempt at something different from a series that is often accused of a lack of both bravery and imagination by those who fail to get past its showy visuals.

Soundtrack: 'Fallen' by Sarah McLachlan (see 'Used Karma').

155: DEATH BECOMES THEM

15 May 2005

Writer: Curtis Kheel
Director: John D Kretchmer

Cast: Oded Fehr (Zankou), Jenya Lano (Inspector Sheridan), John Kassir (The Alchemist), Sandra Prosper (Sheila Morris), Keith Diamond (Inspector Reece Davidson), Colin Egglesfield (Tim Cross), Laura Regan (Joanna), Dax Griffin (Karl), Mercedes Connor (Kim)

> Phoebe's vulnerability after the death of an innocent creates an opportunity for Zankou to steal *The Book of Shadows*. Paige has a new – and also vulnerable – charge, whilst Piper and Leo plan Chris's first birthday party.

A Little Learning is a Dangerous Thing: Hunky student Tim Cross is attending college with Phoebe – he alludes to how dull Dr Rousseau's lecture on cognitive dissonance was. As the episode begins, he's fixing Phoebe's flat tyre and arranging a dinner date with her. Then he dies.

Paige's new charge is Joanna, a Whitelighter-to-be who as yet doesn't know about magic. Joanna has a scummy and seemingly violent boyfriend, Karl, who is in reality yet another Zankou creation. Joanna also dies as part of Zankou's plan.

The Conspiracy Starts at the Witching Hour: Zankou's ability to shapeshift is demonstrated again – he pretends to be Piper in order to gain Phoebe's trust. On this occasion, he is aided by an old friend, the Alchemist. Zankou notes that it has been an eternity since they worked together, and mentions the Crusades[79], the September massacres[80] and the

---

[79] The name given to the eight Christian military expeditions (1099-1291) to recapture the Holy Land from the Muslim Saracens.
[80] Also known as 'The Severe Justice of the People'. This occurred in Paris between 2 and 7 September 1792. Over a thousand French royalists were killed by mobs, whipped into revolutionary bloodlust by rumours that nobles were planning to slaughter the wives and children of patriots who had, two weeks earlier, forced the collapse of the monarchy.

Black Plague[81], adding, amusingly, 'Good times!' His plan is to use the raised corpses of various innocents whom all three sisters were unable to save, in order to undermine their confidence and increase their guilt ('Not as witches, but as women'). This will, he (correctly) believes, sever the link between them and *The Book of Shadows* and enable Zankou to steal the book at the episode's climax whilst the sisters are busy vanquishing the zombies.

Raptor Demons are hired assassins. According to *The Book of Shadows*, demonic Alchemists have the ability to control the dead, but not the power to actually bring people back. For that, they need an upper-level demon.

Denial, Thy Name is the Halliwells: The story concerns Zankou manipulating the sisters into questioning how much damage they've done. As zombie-Tim asks Phoebe (whilst attempting to choke her), have they done *any* good at all?

Work is a Four-Letter Word: Phoebe is so upset by the death of Tim that, on Paige's advice, she throws herself into her work, personally answering hundreds of letters, e-mails and faxes sent to her advice column at the *Bay Mirror*.

It's a Designer Label!: Paige's little red dress.

References: The necromancy of the entire zombie movie genre is central to the plot. Also, a paraphrase from *Frankenstein* ('He's *alive!*').

'You May Remember Me ...': John Kassir is best known as a voice artist on *Tales of the Cryptkeeper*, *Sonic the Hedgehog*, *Samurai Jack*, *Buzz Lightyear of Star Command* and *The Simpsons*. He also appeared in *Cold Case* and *CSI*. Colin Egglesfield's CV includes *Nip/Tuck* and *Gilmore Girls*. Laura Regan played the title role in *Saving Jessica Lynch*. Dax Griffin appeared in *Sunset Beach* and *Firefly*. Mercedes Connor was in *The Starlet*.

Sex and Drugs and Rock n Roll: When Phoebe asks Piper to prove that she really *is* her sister and not Zankou, Piper mentions an incident involving Jake Singer in 10th grade in the backseat of a car.

Logic, Let Me Introduce You to This Window: In 'Coyote Piper', an Alchemist Demon was able to reanimate the dead. Why, therefore, does

---

[81] Another name for the Black Death – a pandemic of bubonic plague, probably carried by rats, that swept mercilessly across Europe between 1347 and 1350, killing an estimated quarter of the population of the continent.

SEASON 7: DEATH BECOMES THEM

this Alchemist need Zankou to bring Tim and the others to life again? When Paige and Joanna are talking at P^3, a bald man passes behind Joanna. On each of the three subsequent occasions that the camera is focused on Joanna, the same bald man walks behind her, heading in the same direction. What on earth has happened to Piper's ability to freeze people? Couldn't she have frozen the zombies instead of simply blowing them up as a final solution? In 'The Wendigo', Phoebe seemingly knew how to change a tyre. Here, she doesn't even know what a tyre-iron looks like. The inability to get the actors involved aside, if Zankou were *really* looking for some zombies to make the sisters feel guilty, what about Prue or Chris? Or any of a number of others whose deaths they were either unable to prevent or were far more directly responsible for than those of Davidson, Tim and Joanna.

Continuity: Sheridan mentions the deaths of Andy Trudeau ('Déjà Vu All Over Again') and Inspector Rodriguez (same episode) to Darryl. To further Phoebe's mental anguish, the Alchemist raises Reece Davidson (who died in 'Death Takes a Halliwell'). In relation to the inevitability of his demise, Phoebe alludes to the Angel of Death. Darryl has semingly neglected to tell Sheila about Sheridan's amnesia – they met at a medals ceremony six months earlier, but Sheridan doesn't remember. Whilst Sheila assures Darryl that she has no intention of revealing the sisters' secret (to Sheridan or anyone else for that matter) she *does* give him an ultimatum – he must choose between the Halliwells and his own family. At the end of the episode, he tells Sheridan that he is taking a vacation with his family. Then he bluntly states that Sheridan will not be able to bring the sisters down, adding: 'They won't let you.' Sheridan asks if that is supposed to be a threat. Darryl replies that, on the contrary, it's a friendly warning. What Phoebe, Piper and Paige are doing is beyond reproach, and he advises Sheridan not to interfere in their lives (see 'Something Wicca This Way Goes').

Quote/Unquote: Piper, to Leo: '*Now* can we cancel Chris's party before any of the walking dead crash it?'
    Leo: 'Where's Phoebe going?' Paige: 'Probably to a mental institution.'
    Phoebe: 'Inspector Davidson?' Davidson: 'In the flesh ... Or, what's left of it.'
    Paige, scrying for Joanna: 'Found her. Cemetery.' Phoebe: 'Not good. Never good.'

Notes: 'With all the knowledge I've gained, I'm gonna shake them to there core. Make them more vulnerable than they've ever been.' Moral ambiguity – something that in the *Charmed* universe is usually dealt with in only a roundabout way – smacks Piper, Phoebe and Paige squarely in the face during this fine episode. By vanquishing the Alchemist, Zankou – in effect – does the sisters' job for them, and presumably that's how he is able to take *The Book of Shadows*. The lines between good and evil have blurred to such an extent that the artefact is no longer able to tell one from the other. In a story about ends not always justifying the means, 'Death Becomes Them' takes *Charmed* right to the edge in terms of style and content and sets up, in it's final 'To Be Continued' moment, what was intended, at the time, to be the series' final curtain.

Soundtrack: 'San Francisco' by Vanessa Carlton.

156: SOMETHING WICCA THIS WAY GOES

22 May 2005

Teleplay: Brad Kern
Story: Brad Kern, Rob Wright
Director: James L Conway

Cast: Oded Fehr (Zankou), Jenya Lano (Inspector Sheridan), Glenn Morshower (Agent Keyes), James Read (Victor Bennett), Sandra Prosper (Sheila Morris), Elizabeth Dennehy (Sandra), Jacqui Maxwell (Young Piper), Danneel Harris (Young Paige), Danielle Savre (Young Phoebe), Becki Newton (The Vampire Queen), Evan Parke (Kaan), Agim Kaba (Handsome Man), Justin Baldoni (Salko), Dean Cudworth (Officer Williams), Laura McLachlin (Female Demon #1), Stacy Soloman (Female Demon #2), Scout Taylor-Compton (Fairy #1), Jake Donahue (Fairy #2)

> Whilst the sisters try to divert Zankou's attention away from the Nexus, he steals Phoebe's powers. The Charmed Ones realise that the only way to stop Zankou may be for them to sacrifice themselves.Sheridan, meanwhile, finally learns the sisters' secret. Then she dies. Horribly. Hurrah!

It's Witchcraft: The sisters use an (unheard) spell to cast the Shadow out of Zankou. Subsequently, as part of a spell to turn Zankou - briefly - into a pig, they chant: 'Something wicked in our midst, in our house where he exists.' They also, crucially, co-opt Prue's ability to astral project (which all three sisters now seem to possess) to create a diversion and allow them to recover *The Book of Shadows*. And they use, for what they believe may be the final time, the Power of Three spell (see 'Something Wicca This Way Comes').

A spell in *The Book of Shadows* - 'How to Banish a Suxen' - will destroy the Nexus. It was seemingly placed in the book by the Elders many years earlier as a last resort in the event of a demon like Zankou gaining access to the Manor. This begins: 'From ancient time this power came, for all to have but none to reign. Take it now, show no mercy, for this power can no longer be.'

A Little Learning is a Dangerous Thing: Zankou notes that the Nexus itself is neither good nor evil, just sheer unadulterated power of the kind that shamans have possessed for 'far too long.'

The Conspiracy Starts at the Witching Hour: Sheridan meets Brody's boss, Agent Keyes from Homeland Security, who confesses that it was he who ordered Brody to put Sheridan in a coma, because her crusade against the Halliwells was endangering their operation (see 'Charrrrmed'). Sheridan enters the Manor with a hidden camera in the hope of getting proof of the supernatural goings-on that occur there; and, for her troubles, she is (highly satisfyingly) killed by Zankou in full view of the Homeland Security forces.

'You May Remember Me ...': Glenn Morshower is one of only three men who worked in the administrations of both Presidents Bartlet and Palmer – playing Defence Analyst Mike Chysler in *The West Wing* and Secret Service Agent Aaron Pierce in *24*. He was also Sheriff Mobley in *CSI*, and his CV includes appearances in *Black Hawk Down*, *Buffy the Vampire Slayer*, *The Core*, *Godzilla*, *Air Force One*, *Enterprise*, *Millennium*, *Under Siege*, *The Dukes of Hazzard*, *Drive-In* and *JAG*.

Jacqui Maxwell appeared in *Sadie's Dream* and played Janet York in *24*. Danneel Harris was Katie Harper in *Joey* and Kate in *What I Like About You*. Danielle Savre played Callie in *Summerland* and also featured in *The X-Files*. Becki Newton was in *The Guiding Light*. Evan Parke's movies include *Planet of the Apes* and *The Cider House Rules*. He also appeared in *Alias*. Agim Kaba played Aaron Snyder in *As the World Turns*. Justin Baldoni was in *Spring Break Shark Attack*. Laura McLaughlin played Rosa in *Vampires and Other Stereotypes*.

Logic, Let Me Introduce You to This Window: Wasn't that fairy princess killed in 'Once Upon a Time'? And let's not even get into the question of who this Vampire Queen is and where she came from. Zankou states he's the first demon to be in magic school. Not so; in 'Witchness Protection', a demon entered the school. The spell to separate a witch from her powers was torn from *The Book of Shadows* after the events of 'How to Make a Quilt Out of Americans'. Yet now, it's back in there for Zankou to use. Also, when it was previously used, it required that the victim swallow a potion in order for it to work, not merely have the potion thrown in her general direction. In the basement, Phoebe is clearly wearing high heels, but when Zankou throws the sisters into the debris, she's wearing tennis shoes. In 'Bite Me', it was revealed that vampires are immune to witches' magic. Here, Piper is able to casually blow up numerous bats to attract the Queen's attention. In 'That Old Black Magic', Tuatha and the Charmed Ones all confirmed that there was no such thing as a confidence spell. At the episode's climax, who has *The Book of Shadows*? It is presumably left in the attic for Keyes and his people to find and study at their will.

Continuity: Piper and Phoebe remember the confidence spell that Piper once used on a waiter at [quake] ('Dead Man Dating'). Piper suggests turning Phoebe into a Banshee again ('Look Who's Barking'). There are also allusions to body-swapping ('Freaky Phoebe'); love spells ('Witchstock'); spells to hear the thoughts of others ('They're Everywhere'); spells to stretch the imagination ('Trial By Magic'); and, for absolutely no reason whatsoever, that time the sisters turned the clientele of P³ into animals ('Animal Pragmatism'). Various Leprechauns, Fairies, Gnomes, Trolls and Valkyrie warrior maidens (not forgetting an Ogre) offer to help the sisters, fighting Zankou's forces to keep them occupied. (Many appear to be killed during these exchanges, though it's unclear if that was part of the plan.) Later, the Charmed Ones seek the help of the Vampire Queen (see 'Bite Me'), but Zankou, having gained access to Phoebe's innermost thoughts, second guesses them and makes the Queen a better offer. In the episode's best scene, assuming that she and her sisters will all be killed in their final battle with Zankou, Piper takes her sons to stay with Victor and gives him the deeds to the Manor and P³. (Note that in 'Hyde School Reunion', Chris did say he was raised by his grandfather.) Among the various files that Sheridan has collected is one marked 'Gordon,' which suggests that she has been speaking to Dan (see 'Be Careful What You Witch For'). Or possibly Jenny (see 'The Devil's Music').

That Final Scene, In Full: Zankou is destroyed by the elimination of the Nexus. Seemingly the sisters have also been blown to smithereens, despite the lack of any body parts discovered by Darryl and Keyes in the Manor's basement. Meanwhile, just round the corner, a distraught Leo is confronted by three stunningly beautiful young women who reveal that they are Piper, Phoebe and Paige. They tell a gobsmacked Leo that this was their plan all along: to use their astral projections to say the Suxen spell, and thus to convince everyone – human forces like Keyes *and* the demon community alike – that they are all dead. They can now live a normal life in peace and quiet and prepare the next generation to pick up where they left off. Then they change Leo's appearance to that of a handsome young stud.

As Darryl emerges from the Manor, heartbroken at the loss of his friends, he sees the quartet of young people walking away down the street. The new Phoebe looks at Darryl and gives him a sly, knowing grin. Seemingly, Darryl realises instantly what has happened (which suggests a sudden increase in his powers of perception entirely not in keeping with the character as thus established) and is, from his smile, very happy about it. Then, symbolically, the door to the Manor closes behind him (see 'Something Wicca This Way Goes', 'Déjà Vu All Over Again' *et al*).

Quote/Unquote: Phoebe: 'If [Zankou] succeeds, then everything we've done in the last seven years means nothing. I'm not willing to live with that.' Piper: 'You might not have to.'
Phoebe: 'These demons do have a way of keeping you warm at night.' Piper: 'That's only because they have fireballs.'
Sheridan, to Keyes: 'You can do whatever you want with them afterwards. You can expose them, hide them, dissect them, I don't care. I just want to be the one to bust them.'

Notes: 'Something tells me we're not getting out of this one, girls.' Intended as a series finale if the WB didn't renew the show (the effect was rather undercut by an announcement four days before the episode's broadcast that *Charmed had* been recommissioned), 'Something Wicca This Way Goes' falls somewhat short of covering all the bases. Kern's and Wright's story tries to do too much, frankly. There is necessary tying up of many lose threads (Sheridan, Brody's backstory, Zankou), but much of the good – and important – stuff gets submerged in a script that seems determined to provide continuity references to nearly every single previous episode. (That scene where Piper and Phoebe sit for three minutes asking each other, 'Why don't we try … like we did when …?' is painfully self-aware.) Nevertheless, for once the structure of the episode means that we know that there will be a conclusion. Quite how they write themselves out of the new reality in which the season ended is a question that will be answered in season eight.
Soundtrack: Billy Idol's 'Evil Eye'.

THE SEVEN YEAR WITCH.

In January 2005, Brad Kern told *SCI-FI Wire* that he had still not received word from WB as to whether or not the network intended to renew Charmed for an eigth season. He added that if he didn't hear by late-February, he would be writing a series finale. "They want the right to hold off as long as they can and they have that right,' Kern noted. 'I only keep appealing to them on behalf of the fans [who] deserve a series finale if this is going to be the last season.' Kern continued that he didn't want to hold a gun to the network's head and 'bug them so much that they finally say, "Listen if you want us to tell you now then you're gone." So, it's a balancing act. I'm trying to cajole them.'

On 19 April the cast and crew had their season wrap party after the completion of the final episode. Throwing a shadow over the event was the uncertainty over what the event actually was – a party or a wake. Alyssa Milano confirmed to *Zap2it.com* that no one had yet received a defintive answer from the network. 'Even at the wrap party, there's something very foreignabout [it] ... I get that the WB is in a transitional phase. Logically, I get it, but I don't get disrespecting the fans to not give them what they deserve for hanging in for seven years.'

'I'm not going to sugarcoat it, I am *not* pleased,' added Holly Marie Combs. 'After this amount of time on a network, we deserve better. I think they're torturing us on purpose. If this was our final season things would have been different. We would have been able to do a more spectacular series finale, as opposed to an ambiguous season finale. We're all like a gaggle of banditsin denial. We're just going to go about our business, pack up our trailors and leave them where they're parked, and hopefully we'll have something to come back to.'

'I find this an atrocious way to live, period,' added Rose McGowan. 'I feel like I'm stuck out in some hallway with all the doors closed and I'm just pacing up and down, waiting for the frickin' door to open.' At least Rose had something to keep her mind occupied during the hiatus, playing Ann-Margaret in a mini-series bio-pic of Elvis Presley.

THE SEVEN YEAR WITCH

The show had been, journalists noted, a steady performer for thew WB despite a constantly shifted time-slot. However, it had faced some signigicant competition during season seven – notably ABC's *Extreme Make-Over. Home Edition* and CBS's *Cold Case*. Brad Kern was reported as noting that 'the network loves *Charmed* creatively and have been especially happy with it this season, but whether we come back or not still all boils down to ratings – which means its up to the fans.'

There was some encouraging signs during April 2005, with the normally on-the-button *Aint It Cool* website confidently predicting that the show would be renewed, but it was still an agonising wait for fans until 18 May when, finally the WB announced their autumn schedule with, noted *Entertainment Tonight*, 'the seemingly unkillable *Charmed*' as part of it.

The eighth season – which began on 25th September 2005 was an episode entitled 'Charmed and Still Kicking' – remained in its 8pm Sunday slot and faced significant competition, particularly from NBC's acclaimed politial drama *The West Wing*. But, as so often in the past, to the fans' delight, The Charmed Ones lived to fight another day.

SELECTED BIBLIOGRAPHY

The following books, articles, interviews and reviews were consulted in the preparation of this text:

'… and finally', *Metro*, 12 July 2001.
Atherton, Tony, 'Fantasy TV: The New Reality', *Ottawa Citizen*, 27 January 2000.
Behring, John, 'Behring Up', interview by Steven Eramo, *TV Zone*, issue 151, May 2002.
Betts, Hannah, 'And now, ladies, just for yourselves … When Harry Met Garry, *The Times*, 7 July 2001.
Billings, Laura, '"Like , Duh," says Gen Y', *St Paul Pioneer Press*, 10 October 2000.
Britt, Donna, 'The Truth About Teen TV', *TV Guide*, 28 October 2000.
Campagna, Suze, 'TV Tid Bits', *Intergalactic Enquirer*, June 2001.
Carter, Bill, '*Dawson's Clones*: Tapping into the youth market for all it is, or isn't, worth', *New York Times* 19 September 1999.
Conway, James L, 'Spellbound', interview by Steven Eramo, *TV Zone*, issue 159, January 2003.
Conway, James L, 'Fighting Talk', interview by Steven Eramo, *Xposé*, issue 81, November 2004.
Cornell, Paul, Day, Martin, and Topping, Keith, *Guinness Book of Classic British TV*, 2nd edition, Guinness Publishing, 1996.
Cornell, Paul, Day, Martin, and Topping, Keith, *X-Treme Possibilities: A Comprehensively Expanded Rummage Through the X-Files*, Virgin Publishing, 1998.
Feigenbaum, Joel J, 'Wrestling with Wiccans', interview by Steven Eramo, *Cult Times*, issue 79, April 2002.
Ferguson, Everett, *Backgrounds of Early Christianity* [second edition], William B. Eerdmans Publishing, 1993.
Fuller, Drew, 'Timely Action', interview by Jenny Eden, *TV Zone*, Special 59, August 2004.
Gilbert, Matthew, 'Teenage Wasteland', *The Boston Globe*, 7 December 2001.
Giglione, Joan, 'Some Shows Aren't Big on TV', *Los Angeles Times*, 25 November 2000.
Greenman, Jennifer, 'Witch love spells death', *News Review*, 6 June 2002.
Gross, Ed, 'Happily Ever After', *SFX*, issue 98, December 2002.
Huff, Richard. 'WB Net Returns to Gender-Build on Initial Appeal Among Young Women', *New York Daily News* 14 September 1999.
Kern, Brad, 'The Wicca Man', interview by Steven Eramo, *TV Zone*, issue

159, January 2003.

Kern, Brad, 'Making Magic', interview by Joe Nazzaro, *TV Zone*, Special 59, August 2004.

Kern, Brad, 'Set for Seven', interview by Joe Nazzaro, *TV Zone*, Special 59, August 2004.

Kern, Brad, 'Seventh Heaven', interview by Steven Eramo, *TV Zone*, Special 61, January 2005.

Krause, Brian, 'Guardian Angel', interview by Steven Eramo, *Xposé*, issue 53, March 2001.

Krause, Brian, 'Heaven Sent', interview by Steven Eramo, *TV Zone*, issue 150, April 2002.

Krause, Brian, 'Someone To Watch Over Me', interview by Steven Eramo, *Xposé*, issue 79, July 2003.

Krause, Brian, 'Romantic Krause', interview by Jenny Eden, *TV Zone*, Special 59, August 2004.

Keveney, Bill, 'When it's quality vs. ratings, casualties abound', *Charlotte Observer*, 31 August 2000.

Lambert, Brian, 'The WB network contemplates life after *Buffy*', *St Paul Pioneer Press*, 17 July 2001.

Lowry, Brian, 'WB Covers A Trend Too Well', *Los Angeles Times*, 29 June 2000.

Malcolm, Shawna, 'The Witching Hour', *TV Guide*, 25 August 2001.

Mansfield, Sonia, 'Women on Top', *The San Francisco Examiner*, 27 December 2001.

May, Dominic, 'New Shorts', *TV Zone*, issue 158, December 2002.

McGowan, Rose, 'Fresh Paige', interview by Jenny Eden, *TV Zone*, Special 59, August 2004.

McIntee, David, *Delta Quadrant: The Unofficial Guide to Voyager*, Virgin Publishing, 2000.

McMahon, Julian, 'Cole Face', interview by Steven Eramo, *Xposé*, issue 52, January 2001.

McMahon, Julian, 'Quenching Cole's Fire', interview by Steven Eramo, *Xposé*, issue 76, January 2003.

McMahon, Julian, '60 Second Interview', *Metro*, 24 February 2004.

McMahon, Julian, 'Surgical Strike', interview by Paul Rigby, *TV Zone*, Special 59, August 2004.

Moore, Ronald D, 'Moore the Merrier', interview by Jim Swallow, *SFX*, issue 74, February 2001.

Morgan, Spencer, 'Shannen Doherty vs Tara Reid (Again)', *New York Metro*, 8 March 2004.

Mosby, John, 'UK-TV', *DreamWatch*, issue 71, August 2000.

Newman, Kim, *Nightmare Movies: A Critical History of the Horror Movie From 1968*, Bloomsbury Publishing, 1988.

SELECTED BIBLIOGRAPHY

O'Hare, Kate, 'Fist of fury – TV's high-flying on-screen battles', *St Paul Pioneer Press*, 14 April 2002.
Peary, Danny, *Guide For the Film Fanatic*, Simon & Schuster, 1986.
'Potty About Paganism', *Alternative Metro*, 24 August 2000.
Rayner, Jacqueline, 'Saving the world is important, but what's more important is saving the world with the right hair', *TV Zone*, Special #45, April 2002.
Rayner, Jacqueline, 'A Witch's Tail' to 'The Eyes Have It', *TV Zone*, issue 157, November 2002.
Rayner, Jacqueline, 'Sympathy for the Demon', to 'Sam I Am', *TV Zone*, issue 158, December 2002.
Ross, Louise, '*Charmed* Season-By-Season', *TV Zone*, Special 59, August 2004.
Roush, Matt, 'Shows of the Year '99', *TV Guide*, 25 December 1999.
Sangster, Jim and Bailey, David, *Friends Like Us: The Unofficial Guide to Friends* [revised edition], Virgin Publishing, 2000.
'Single Women: If The She Fits, Air It', *St Paul Pioneer Press*, 6 January 2000.
Smith, Kerr, 'The Kyle Files', interview by Steven Eramo, Xposé, Special 27, October 2004.
Spragg, Paul, '10 Things You Never Knew About Holly Marie Combs', *Xposé*, issue 58, August 2001.
Spragg, Paul, 'Bite Me' to 'Witch Way Now?', *TV Zone*, issue 152, June 2002.
Spragg, Paul, 'The Charm of *Charmed*', *TV Zone*, Special 59, August 2004.
Topping, Keith, *High Times: An Unofficial and Unauthorised Guide to Roswell*, Virgin Books, 2001.
Topping, Keith: *Inside Bartlet's White House: An Unofficial and Unauthorised Guide to The West Wing*, Virgin Books, 2002.
Topping, Keith, *Hollywood Vampire: A Revised and Updated Unofficial and Unauthorised Guide to Angel*, Virgin Books, 2004.
Topping, Keith, *The Complete Slayer*, Virgin Books, 2004.
Topping, Keith, *Beyond the Gate: The Unofficial and Unauthorised Guide to Stargate SG-1*, Telos Publishing, 2002.
Topping, Keith, *A Day in the Life: The Unofficial and Unauthorised Guide to 24*, Telos Publishing, 2003.
Topping, Keith, 'Changing Channels', *Intergalactic Enquirer*, August 2001.
Topping, Keith, 'Minority Report', *Intergalactic Enquirer*, February 2004.
Wurtzel, Elizabeth, *Bitch*, Quartet Books, 1998.

NEVER MIND THE WARLOCKS

Keith Topping's previous work includes co-editing two editions of *The Guinness Book of Classic British TV* and books on television series as diverse as *The X-Files*, *The Sweeney* and *Doctor Who*. He has also written four novels (including the award-winning *The Hollow Men*), and a novella (Telos's own *Ghost Ship*). His other books include Do You Want to Know a Secret?, Beyond the Gate, *A Day in the Life*, *Hollywood Vampire*, *Inside Bartlet's White House* and *Slayer*, his best-selling guide to *Buffy the Vampire Slayer*. He is a contributor to both *TV Zone* and *Shivers* magazines and a former contributing editor of *DreamWatch* magazine. Keith is considered something of an expert on the bewildering complexities of US network television. No, *he* doesn't know why either.

Keith was born in Newcastle in October 1963, and has remained cold and miserable ever since. He is the presenter of BBC Radio Newcastle's The Book Club and has a fortnightly TV/Media review section on The Julia Hankin Show and has contributed to the BBC television series *I Love the 70s*, the *Daily Telegraph* and *The Sunday Times Culture Supplement*. Keith's hobbies include socialising with friends, foreign travel, loud guitar-based pop music, trashy SF television, even trashier British horror movies of the '60s and '70s, football and cricket. *Triquetra* is his 39th book.

OTHER GUIDES FROM TELOS PUBLISHING

DOCTOR WHO

BACK TO THE VORTEX: THE UNOFFICIAL AND UNAUTHORISED GUIDE TO *DOCTOR WHO* 2005 by J SHAUN LYON
Complete guide to the 2005 series of *Doctor Who* starring Christopher Eccleston as the Doctor

SECOND FLIGHT: THE UNOFFICIAL AND UNAUTHORISED GUIDE TO *DOCTOR WHO* 2006 by J SHAUN LYON
Complete guide to the 2006 series of *Doctor Who*, starring David Tennant as the Doctor

THIRD DIMENSION: THE UNOFFICIAL AND UNAUTHORISED GUIDE TO *DOCTOR WHO* 2007 by STEPHEN JAMES WALKER
Complete guide to the 2007 series of *Doctor Who*, starring David Tennant as the Doctor

MONSTERS INSIDE: THE UNOFFICIAL AND UNAUTHORISED GUIDE TO *DOCTOR WHO* 2008 by STEPHEN JAMES WALKER
Complete guide to the 2008 series of *Doctor Who*, starring David Tennant as the Doctor.

END OF TEN: THE UNOFFICIAL AND UNAUTHORISED GUIDE TO *DOCTOR WHO* 2009 by STEPHEN JAMES WALKER
Complete guide to the 2009 specials of *Doctor Who*, starring David Tennant as the Doctor.

CRACKS IN TIME: THE UNOFFICIAL AND UNAUTHORISED GUIDE TO *DOCTOR WHO* 2010 by STEPHEN JAMES WALKER
Complete guide to the 2010 series of *Doctor Who*, starring Matt Smith as the Doctor.

RIVER'S RUN: THE UNOFFICIAL AND UNAUTHORISED GUIDE TO *DOCTOR WHO* 2011 by STEPHEN JAMES WALKER
Complete guide to the 2011 series of *Doctor Who*, starring Matt Smith as the Doctor.

THE TELEVISION COMPANION: THE UNOFFICIAL AND UNAUTHORISED GUIDE TO *DOCTOR WHO* 1963 – 1996 by DAVID J HOWE and STEPHEN JAMES WALKER
A two-volume guide to the classic series of *Doctor Who*.

TORCHWOOD

INSIDE THE HUB: THE UNOFFICIAL AND UNAUTHORISED GUIDE TO *TORCHWOOD* SERIES ONE by STEPHEN JAMES WALKER
Complete guide to the 2006 series of *Torchwood*, starring John Barrowman as Captain Jack Harkness.

SOMETHING IN THE DARKNESS: THE UNOFFICIAL AND UNAUTHORISED GUIDE TO *TORCHWOOD* SERIES TWO by STEPHEN JAMES WALKER
Complete guide to the 2008 series of *Torchwood*, starring John Barrowman as Captain Jack Harkness

24

A DAY IN THE LIFE: THE UNOFFICIAL AND UNAUTHORISED GUIDE TO *24* by KEITH TOPPING
Complete episode guide to the first season of the popular TV show.

TILL DEATH US DO PART

A FAMILY AT WAR: THE UNOFFICIAL AND UNAUTHORISED GUIDE TO *TILL DEATH US DO PART* by MARK WARD
Complete guide to the popular TV show.

SPACE: 1999

DESTINATION: MOONBASE ALPHA: THE UNOFFICIAL AND UNAUTHORISED GUIDE TO *SPACE: 1999* by ROBERT E WOOD
Complete guide to the popular TV show.

SAPPHIRE AND STEEL

ASSIGNED: THE UNOFFICIAL AND UNAUTHORISED GUIDE TO *SAPPHIRE AND STEEL* by RICHARD CALLAGHAN
Complete guide to the popular TV show.

THUNDERCATS

HEAR THE ROAR: THE UNOFFICIAL AND UNAUTHORISED GUIDE TO THE HIT 1980S SERIES *THUNDERCATS* by DAVID CRICHTON
Complete guide to the popular TV show.

SUPERNATURAL

HUNTED: THE UNOFFICIAL AND UNAUTHORISED GUIDE TO *SUPERNATURAL* SEASONS 1-3 by SAM FORD AND ANTONY FOGG
Complete guide to the popular TV show.

THE PRISONER

FALL OUT: THE UNOFFICIAL AND UNAUTHORISED GUIDE TO *THE PRISONER* by ALAN STEVENS and FIONA MOORE
Complete guide to the popular TV show.

BATTLESTAR GALACTICA

BY YOUR COMMAND: THE UNOFFICIAL AND UNAUTHORISED GUIDE TO *BATTLESTAR GALACTICA* by ALAN STEVENS and FIONA MOORE
A two volume guide to the popular TV show.

A SONG FOR EUROPE

SONGS FOR EUROPE: THE UNITED KINGDOM AT THE EUROVISION SONG CONTEST by GORDON ROXBURGH
A five volume guide to the popular singing contest.

FILMS

BEAUTIFUL MONSTERS: THE UNOFFICIAL AND UNAUTHORISED GUIDE TO THE *ALIEN* AND *PREDATOR* FILMS by DAVID McINTEE
A guide to the *Alien* and *Predator* Films.

ZOMBIEMANIA: 80 MOVIES TO DIE FOR by DR ARNOLD T BLUMBERG & ANDREW HERSHBERGER
A guide to 80 classic zombie films, along with an extensive filmography of over 500 additional titles

SILVER SCREAM: VOLUME 1: 40 CLASSIC HORROR MOVIES by STEVEN WARREN HILL
A guide to 40 classic horror films from 1920 to 1941.

SILVER SCREAM: VOLUME 2: 40 CLASSIC HORROR MOVIES by STEVEN WARREN HILL
A guide to 40 classic horror films from 1941 to 1951.

TABOO BREAKERS: 18 INDEPENDENT FILMS THAT COURTED CONTROVERSY AND CREATED A LEGEND by CALUM WADDELL
A guide to 18 films which pushed boundaries and broke taboos.

IT LIVES AGAIN! HORROR MOVIES IN THE NEW MILLENNIUM by AXELLE CAROLYN
A guide to modern horror films. Large format, full colour throughout.

TELOS MOVIE CLASSICS: *HULK* by TONY LEE
A critique and analysis of Ang Lee's 2003 film *Hulk*.

APE-MAN: THE UNOFFICIAL AND UNAUTHORISED GUIDE TO 100 YEARS OF *TARZAN* by SEAN EGAN
Guide to *Tarzan* in all the media.

STILL THE BEAST IS FEEDING: FORTY YEARS OF *ROCKY HORROR* by ROB BAGNALL and PHIL BARDEN
History and appreciation of Richard O'Brien's *Rocky Horror Show*.

TELOS PUBLISHING
Email: orders@telos.co.uk
Web: www.telos.co.uk

To order copies of any Telos books, please visit our website where there are full details of all titles and facilities for worldwide credit card online ordering, as well as occasional special offers.

www.ingramcontent.com/pod-product-compliance
Lightning Source LLC
LaVergne TN
LVHW021650060526
838200LV00050B/2284